Controversies in the Gospels

An Analysis of Controversies in the Gospels

Controversies in the Gospels

An Analysis of Biblical Controversies

David Criswell

FORTRESS

ADONAI
PRESS

North Charleston, S.C.

Controversies in the Gospels

An Analysis of Biblical Controversies

David Criswell

ISBN NUMBER 0-61573-271-2

Cover Design by David Criswell

FORTRESS

ADONAI
PRESS

Dallas, TX

Printed in the United States of America

Dedication

For my *bahin*.

"Be always ready to make a defense to everyone who asks you to give an account for the hope that is in you" (1 Peter 3:15).

Preface

A friend of mine once told me, "I don't care about controversies. I just want to learn from God's word," or something to that effect. My answer was essentially this, "Be always ready to make a defense to everyone who asks you to give an account for the hope that is in you" (1 Peter 3:15). I have always been a seeker. I do not object the notion of being critically minded, but I do object to the notion that being critically minded means being critical of one thing, but uncritical of another. Lest anyone believe that this is not the case with so-called Bible critics I will note that one of professors once scolded me for not being "critically minded" but when I told her that she was only mad because I *was* being critical ... of *her* beliefs, she became strangely silent.

Studying controversies is a way of strengthening our understanding of the Bible and of God's Word. It is way of getting closer to the Word of God; not further from it. If a war begins, you flee to the safety of the strongest bunker, and yet it is that bunker which the enemy most wants to eliminate. So it is with the Word of God. The Bible is attacked *because* of its strength. To be fearful of controversies is to be fearful that the Bible does not have all the answer we claim, and yet it does. It is our strength, because it is the Word of our Strength, the Lord God.

Sir Robert Anderson once said, "for the Christian to solve difficulties by repudiating the teaching of Christ, is like committing suicide to escape from danger."[1] Unfortunately, this is exactly what many Christians do. They hear that "science as disproven" X, Y, or Z, and instead of delving into the science and issues to debate and refute such attacks, they retreat, thinking to themselves that no harm will come to them if they just concede, "well, maybe it is just a story meant to tell a story." But of what inspiration can I draw from Cinderella if I know in my heart that I will always be a servant girl who can never be anything more than that. I can only draw inspiration from stories that are true because I know that it *can* be true. I draw inspiration from the story of Joseph in Genesis because I know *it is* a true story, and not a fairy tale. I have hope in eternal life because I know Jesus *was* resurrected from the dead!

David Criswell, November 2112

"Know this first of all, that no prophecy of Scripture is *a matter* of one's own interpretation, for no prophecy was ever made by an act of human will, but men moved by the Holy Spirit spoke from God" (2 Peter 1:20-21).

Table of Contents

✝   ✝   ✝

xiii

1

Introduction

The gospels are first and second hand accounts of the life and times of Jesus Christ. While they are not the only time sensitive sources which acknowledge the historical person of Jesus, his ministry, and his subsequent trial and execution (as sometimes claimed by skeptics[2]), they do contain the only extant eyewitness accounts of his life. As a result, the very existence of the gospels is controversial to those who seek to deny Jesus' claims to deity. Atheists attempt to discount the gospels as fabrications or lies while liberal theologians seeks to cast doubt on their accuracy (and honesty) by erroneously misdating the composition of the gospels while attempting place them side by side with known forgeries like the "gospel of Thomas"[3] as so unethically done in the infamous "five gospels" publication.[4]

Of course it should be no surprise that a man who has changed the history of the world should be so controversial. Those who do not hate him seek to conform His image to their own liking. To that endevor it is essential for them to alter the Bible's depiction of Him. Sir Robert Anderson, the former Chief Inspector of Scotland Yard, once said that "it is easy to convict an accused person if all his witnesses are put out of court and refused a hearing, and his own words and acts are misrepresented and distorted."[5] This is what Bible critics attempt to do with the Bible. They attack the Bible and its authors, hoping to discredit their testimony and then convict Jesus by default, having no evidence or witnesses of their own.

Like my other books in the *Controversies* series I will dwelve into a variety of controversies which revolve around the gospels and Jesus. My purpose is to allow the reader to have at his disposal evidence from all sides, in order that he might be better equipped to debate the critics and defend the Word of God.

Types of Controversies Addressed

Many of the controversies in the Gospels are different from the controversies found in the Old Testament. There are some similar issues, but there are also many different topics and debates. I will endeavor to discuss all the following issues wherever possible.

Historical Controversies
Among the most numerous, and often frivolous, of controversies are those revolving around allegations of historical errors. Once, before the rise of

"liberal scholarship" in the nineteenth century, no one doubted the general historicity of the Bible, *even if* they doubted the specifics (such as the miracles). Why would they? No one ever doubted that general historical life, ministry, and death of Jesus Christ until the modern era. Even the enemies of Christianity never denied the basic background of the life and times of Jesus. Now, however, a great deal of the Bible is treated as "historical myth." Even where there is not the slightest evidence to contradict the Bible, the "higher critic" dismisses the Bible.

The fad of revisionist historical criticism is of recent origin. It is not based on research, as some erroneously believe, but rather upon minimalist assumptions. In other words, the trend among modern historians is not to do historical research, but rather to act like a criminal defense lawyer who seeks to destroy the credibility of all witnesses whose testimony does not support his client and to dismiss all evidence contrary to his client's interest. He does not seek objective truth, for he believes there is no such thing. Having studied history in college and even in graduate school, I can testify that revisionist historians reject all forms of traditional scholarship and research for unfounded assumptions. They call themselves "critical thinkers" but they are only critical of what they choose to be critical.

Legitimate historical research must be consistent. It cannot employ different standards for the Bible than it employs in Egyptology or Assyriology. While it may be fair, from a historical standpoint, to say that Jesus walking on water cannot be confirmed by history, it is blatant hypocrisy to deny that Jesus sailed the sea of Galilee with his disciples.

The reader will see that such hypocrisy is not uncommon for the Bible critic. I will, therefore, examine the evidence, refute the assumptions of the "higher critic," and demonstrate what portions of the Bible are confirmed as historical in nature, and what portions must be taken on faith. Of course, even those portions that we must take on faith, we accept based upon the credibility of the witnesses. If the authors are proven to be historical and reliable and honest in other matters, why should be make them out to be madmen or liars when they speak of miracles?

Apostlic Authorship
Closely related to the historical criticism are the accusations of the "higher critics" in which the authors of the gospels are said to plagerize one another, to "borrow" their writings from an unknown source, to have "forgotten" what really happened so many years ago, and similar insinuations designed to belittle the eyewitness and second hand accounts of the life and times of Jesus. They are designed not to get closer to the "historical Jesus" but rather to make the reader suspect the accuracy of the eyewitness accounts. These criticisms will be debated wherever possible.

Chronological Issues
A famous historian once remarked, "chronology is the backbone of history."[6] Indeed, many of the allegations of historical error can be traced not to errors in Biblical history, but to the critics' errors in chronology. Now chronology involves math, and math is, in a word, boring. This is one reason that so many people ignore chronological difficulties, but ignoring an alleged problem only gives fuel to the enemy. Careful study, although tedious and even boring, will demonstrate that the Biblical chronology is perfectly consistent and is the key to resolving many historical and archaeological difficulties found in the Bible.

Alleged Contradictions
Perhaps the greatest of controversies in the gospels are those that involve alleged contradictions. This is particularly true of the synoptic gospels for they all record the same incidents, but each account appears to differ in some form. This is not unusual for any student of criminal justice knows that eyewitnesses will always appear to have differing accounts, but this does not mean that the accounts are inaccurate or false. As Chief Inspector Sir Robert Anderson once said, "when in my official life I have found a conflict of testimony between persons of known integrity, I have always sought some way of reconciling them."[7] To do so is not bias, as the critic suggests, but common sense. If two witnesses give two entirely different descriptions of a perpetrator then the police may begin to look into the question of whether or not there were more than one perpetrator. To *ignore* this possibility is bias, not to *explore* the possibility.

Continuing the criminal justice analogy, I again refer to Sir Anderson who noted that "when I set myself to investigate the case against Daniel [of the Bible], I did so in the same spirit in which I have not infrequently prosecuted criminal charges against persons, whom, though I greatly wished to save, I was determined to bring to justice if guilty."[8] His conclusion was that the Bible was historically accurate in every facet in which it is able to examined, and even commented somewhat sarcastically that, "I owe much to the Higher Critics for settling my faith in Scripture; and I confess that my full acceptance of the [Biblical books] dates from my study of their reasons for rejecting it."[9] So also a fair objective examination of the Gospels and their alleged "contradictions" will render the same conclusions in the New Testament.

Textual Errors
Another issue of importance to the inerrantist is that of textual errors. No one seems to deny that copyists occasionally made minor mistakes in transcribing manuscripts, but the extent of those errors and their impact upon the Biblical doctrine of inerrancy is in question, and remains, among conservatives, a major controversy. The liberal scholar seems content to argue that our manuscripts are but shadows of the original, while the conservative points to textual apparatii to demonstrate that we have faithful copies of the originals.

Having said this, there is no doubt that occasional questions arise as to what the original writing said and whether or not the original manuscript, if different from ours, would have had any real impact upon the meaning of the text. Because the evangelical seeks to truly understand the Word of God he must walk a careful line between seeking to understand the original meaning of the text and simply discarding one reading for another that he may like better. These controversies will not be neglected.

Theological and Exegetical Controversies
Of course the most numerous of all controversies are those that emerge from theological arguments. Many theologians (although they will never admit it) tend to read *into* the text what they want to be there. This has sometimes been called *eisogesis* as opposed to *exegesis*. Obviously, many of the controversies addressed will be of this nature. What do the Biblical authors seek to say versus what we want to hear.

A final word should be said as to what my own personal approach will be. Let me, therefore, state that while I am an evangelical who believes in the inerrancy and accuracy of the Bible in everything of which it speaks, including history, science, and all other matters which may be reflected in it, I was by no means raised to believe these things. I was raised in a liberal church with a pastor who not only denied the reality of hell, but upon his deathbed he conveyed to me a fear that there was no heaven. He did not teach me anything that I have come to learn. I was taught that the Bible was myth; that it was stories told to promote a "moral" but that had no real historical meaning. That also meant that it had no practical meaning. My belief in the inerrancy of the Scriptures, therefore, was not a belief I inherited or was taught, but one that I came to me by personal study. I believed only that the Bible should be treated with the same respect that all other works of antiquity receive, and that the authors were not liars or fools. Beyond that my personal bias was not to accept all things. This I have come to believe by faith; but that faith is grounded in the fact that the Biblical authors have *proven* themselves reliable, honest, inspired, and trustworthy. Fact and faith have always been brothers. It is a myth to present them as enemies for, as Sir Robert Anderson would have said, the testimony of the eyewitness is accepted on good faith provided he is proven honest in all other matters which can be verified. This is my approach to the Scriptures and their interpretations thereof. My conclusion is that there is no other work in human history as trustworthy as that of the Bible.

My final word is that I entrust this volume to the reader so that he might be better able to comply with the command of the apostle Peter:

Be always "ready to make a defense to everyone who asks you to give
an account for the hope that is in you" (1 Peter 3:15).

2
—
The Synoptic Gospels - Matthew

Matthew is one of two gospels written by an apostle of Christ. Matthew lived with and served under Jesus for the duration of his ministry. His gospel represents the first eyewitness account of the ministry, death, and resurrection of Jesus.

Matthew is unique from the other gospels in several ways. First, he is the only gospel writer to use the term "kingdom of heaven" as opposed to the "kingdom of God."[10] He is also the only gospel writer to mention the "church."[11] Despite the fact that no other gospel mentions the church by name, it is Matthew who speaks directly to Israel and the Jews more than any other gospel. He makes constant references to Old Testament prophesies and specifies which prophecies were fulfilled under Christ. His genealogy of Christ is also used to prove to the people of Israel that He is the rightful heir to King David, and the true Messiah. Consequently, his gospel is considered the most "Jewish" of the gospels, and most believe that it was originally written in Hebrew.

Additionally, Matthew's gospel is probably the first gospel to be written. This is disputed by many (and debated below), but it most likely true. As I attempt to prove in the following pages, Matthew almost certainly wrote his gospel in Hebrew to the Jews before he left for missionary work in Egypt and Ethiopia (probably around 40 to 50 A.D.). It is only after years in the mission field that he translated his own work, by his own hand, into the Greek language (around 60 A.D.). It is that translation, by Matthew's own hand, which we have today and it is that translation from which our modern translations come.

An Eyewitness Account?
The Authorship and Date of Matthew

The barrage of internet conspiracy and atheistic websites have served to promote erroneous, and laughable, conspiracy theories which suggest the gospels were the work of people who lived hundreds of years after the time of Jesus. Of course even the most die hard atheist, if he is sincere and educated, knows that we have manuscripts which predate this. Matthew is quoted by the earliest of apostolic fathers and tradition ascribes that he was the first to write a gospel, hence its position as the first book of the New Testament. One honest Bible critic admits that the gospel of Matthew was written by Matthew's hand about twenty to thirty years after Jesus' death on the cross, but then argues that the apostle must have "forgotten" what transpired all those many years ago.[12] This is the argument most used by educated Bible critics. Did the apostle "forget" what happened? Could they have accurately recounted what happened all those many years ago?

The mere fact that Bible critics suggest that the gospel of Matthew relied on earlier source material (see Appendix A for more on this theory) is an admission that Matthew could easily have taken notes during his time with Jesus. Why should not the apostles have written diaries or notes of what transpired? Nevertheless, even if we assumed that they had no notes or diaries, but only memory, how many of you readers can remember the first words your spouse said to you? How many of you can recount exactly what happened on your first date? Certainly the events of the life and times of Jesus are even more memorable than these. Can we expect that these events, which would change the course of human history, were really hazy fuzzy memories to the people who lived through those events?

There seems no serious doubt that the apostles knew what happened to them. All but one would die for his faith in Jesus, and most lived with rocks for pillows as they went out as missionaries around the world. They did not profit from Jesus, nor have any motive to lie; let alone die for a lie. What is written in Matthew is most certainly the account of an eyewitness. Whether Matthew relied on notes he took while serving Jesus is debated, but it seems logical. He was an educated tax collected who would have had to take notes and accounts for his job. Moreover, if the λογια mentioned by Papias (see Appendix A) is not Matthew's gospel, then it is most certainly the very notes that Matthew wrote when he was following Jesus! Nonetheless, questions as to the authorship, date, and circumstances of Matthew's gospel remain in an age of agnosticism. Let us, therefore, take a closer look at the facts.

The Authorship of Matthew

From the earliest of times "Matthaean authorship was undisputed."[13] All the apostolic and church fathers are in agreement that Matthew wrote the gospel which bears his name. "Since Matthew was a comparatively obscure member of the apostolic band, there seems to be no good reason for making him the author of a spurious work."[14] Some have also pointed out that circumstantial evidence also supports this. Why, for example, does the gospel of Matthew make numerous references to specific coins of the realm (17:24, 27; 18:24 etc.)?[15] It is argued that only a tax collector who was used to working with money would have been so specific as the denominations and types of money used.

Of course the Bible critic appeals to the "Q theory" (see Appendix A) which suggests that Matthew "borrowed" from other sources. This theory is addressed in the appendices in detail, so I will only say here that even if Matthew "borrowed" from other sources, it does not change the fact that Matthew wrote the gospel which bears his name; a fact undisputed until modern times, and still accepted by all but the most extreme Bible critic.

Date of Writing

As aforementioned, no sincere scholar, whether he is a Bible critic or not, denies that Matthew wrote the book in question. The question is then, how far removed from the time of Jesus was Matthew's writing?

Scholars have offered dates ranging from 37 A.D. to nearly 100 A.D. Of course, the later date can be rejected since Matthew died no later than 70 A.D.,[16] having been tortured and beheaded.[17] Since all but the most ardent conspiracy buff accept Matthew's authorship, we can therefore reject the late dates. Moreover, it seems unrealistic to say that the book was written after the fall of Jerusalem since the prophesies of Jerusalem's fall make no mention of it having been fulfilled,[18] and no Bible critic from the time of the apostolic fathers makes this assersion; something which they would not have neglected to do if it were so. Thus while Merrill Tenney places its authorship somewhere bewteen 50 and 70 A.D.,[19] it was almost certainly written before 60 A.D. at the latest.

"Church tradition has strongly advocated that the Gospel of Matthew was the first Gospel account written, perhaps a date somewhere around A.D. 50."[20] C.I. Scofield believed that tradition points to a date as early as 37 A.D., just a few years after the Crucifixion and resurrection.[21] Merrill Unger places it between 40 and 45 A.D.[22]

In favor of a later date of writing, say between 50 and 60 A.D. is the fact that Matthew uses the term "even to this very day" on several occasions. That gives the impression that some time has passed, thus nullifying the force of it having been written long before 40 A.D. Furthermore, some argue that because Matthew uses the word "Church" (twice) it "betrays a later period when the doctrine of the church was assuming more importance."[23] The problem with this argument is that not only was the "church" found in the epistles of Paul from the earliest of times but Matthew was certainly written to a predominantly Jewish community which would not have been the case had Matthew been written late after the split between Jew and Christian became wider. Another argument is based on the assumption Matthew's gospel must have followed Mark's gospel,[24] but this is assumption based largely on the "Q theory" (see Appendix A) and has no solid evidence to support it. Finally, tradition states, in Irenaeus, that Matthew was written "among the Hebrews in their own dialect, while Peter and Paul were preaching at Rome."[25] The preaching of Peter and Paul would then place the gospel after 50 A.D., or would it?

Evidence for an earlier date, before 50 A.D., includes the tradition that Matthew was the first gospel written.[26] This tradition is supported by the fact that it was originally written in either Hebrew or Aramaic. As Robert Gundry noted "if Matthew wrote for Jews, it seems less likely that he wrote late, after the breach between church and synagogue widened, than early, when Christian Jews still dominated the church."[27] According to historian and martyriologist van Braght, "before he left Judea, he, through the illumination of the Holy

Spirit, wrote his Gospel, in the Hebrew language."[28] Thus all evidence points to Matthew having written his gospel *before* leaving for the mission field in Egypt and Ethiopea where he died. Certainly, the emphasis on Jewish prophesies points to a time when Matthew was living in Judea.

If we examine all the evidence, it is unquestionale that the Matthew can be placed sometime between 37 A.D. and 60 A.D., but to further deliniate its writing is hard. Indications seem to favor an early date, but with enough time to allow of Paul to have preached in Rome and to accomodate Matthews phrase "even to this day." Thus Merrill Unger's assersion that it was written sometime between 40 and 45 A.D.[29] seems best, if we allow that it could have been written as late as 50 A.D.

Having said this there is no doubt that Matthew wrote his gospel not based on memory alone, but based on notes he took while he was a disciple of Christ. Matthew should rightly be considered the first of the gospels to be written, and was clearly addressed to the predominantly Jewish community of Judea. This leads to the next question; was it really written in Hebrew? If so, is our Greek version a mere copy?

The Original Language
All the oldest and most ancient copies of the New Testament are found in the Greek tongue which was the international language of Rome. Since Paul preached the gospel to the Greeks (or rather gentiles) it is logical that he wrote in the language they understood. However, in the earliest days of Christianity, the majority of Jesus' followers were Jews. It seems likely that the earliest books, with the exception of Paul's epistles which were written to gentile Churches, could have been penned in the language of the Jews. Matthew is believed to have been such a book.

Tradition from as early as the apostolic father Papias, who lived when the apostle John was still alive, says that "Matthew composed the oracles in the Hebrew language."[30] This tradition has been echoed and supported down through the ages. Not only Papias, but also Irenaeus, Origen, Eusebius, and Jerome all contend that Matthew wrote originally in either Hebrew or Aramaic.[31] Now some have questioned whether or not the "oracles" referred to by Papias is truly the gospel of Matthew or perhaps, as Louis Barbieri suggests, a collection of sayings by Matthew and not the gospel. Thus he argues that Matthew "was probably penned by Matthew in Greek and has survived until today. Matthew's *logia* did not survive."[32] This, however, is speculation. The term "gospel" was not universal until a later date and the "words" of Jesus almost certainly refers to the gospels, from which these authors quoted.

Now the reader may ask why such a question is relevant at all. He is justified in doing so, but the answer is more than just a technical one. First, if the original was written in Hebrew, where is it? Are we relying on a poor translation of the original? If so, this would be problematic for the devout

Christian. Second, the question of the original language does arise in regard to certain passages where the Greek seems problematic itself, as will be discussed in the pages to come. Consequently, this is more than mere academia, but it is also an inflated issue. As Merrill Tenney said, "the tradition that this Gospel was originally written in Aramaic does not preclude the possibility that the author may have published later a Greek edition that quickly superseded the older writing."[33] Linksi also believed that Matthew composed both a Hebrew and a Greek version of his gospel.[34] Support for this is in the fact that the famed Jewish historian Josephus, from the same time period, himself testifies that he wrote *The Jewish Wars* in both Aramaic and Greek, but only the Greek survives to this day.[35]

Because Matthew was writing to Jews in Judea and quotes repeatedly from the Hebrew scriptures as proof of Jesus' Messianic credentials, it seems only logical that Matthew would have written in Hebrew. Although Aramaic was the common tongue of the Jews at that time[36] (Aramaic is a sister language of Hebrew), the official language used in writings and synagogues remained Hebrew. Internal evidence also slightly favors Hebrew over Aramaic.

The only evidence which can be given against this is the question, "why would Matthew give the Semitic originals and Greek translations of just a few terms, such as 'Immanuel' (1:23), if his whole gospel were a translation from Hebrew or Aramaic?"[37] As the reader will see in the pages to come, there are questions regarding certain terms in Matthew's gospel which stir debate. Why, for example, do Matthew and Mark seem to differ on whether or not Jesus said "*Eloi, eloi, lama sabachthani*" (Mark 15:34) or "*Eli, eli, lama sabachtani*" (Matt. 27:46)? The one is Aramaic. The other a Hebrew and Aramaic mixture.

In short, the evidence strongly favors Hebrew, or possibly, but less likely, Aramaic as the original language of Matthew. The Greek translation in our hands was probably composed by Matthew himself at a later date to accomodate his disciples in Egypt and Ethiopia where it became widely distributed and accepted.

Conclusion

The evidence leads us to accept the tradition that Matthew was the first to write a gospel and that he originally composed it in Judea in the Hebrew language before leaving for the mission field in Egypt and Ethiopea, probably between 40 A.D. and 50 A.D. at the latest. He most likely composed a Greek translation of his own work for his disciples in Egypt and Ethiopea years later, no later than 55 or 60 A.D. There the Greek translation of his work, composed by himself, became a standard for the gentile church. Although both are equally inspired, the Greek is the version from whence all our modern Bibles are derived.

The notion that Matthew misremembered or forgot the events which transpired in the life and times of Jesus is untenable as the evidence, as well as common sense, leads us to believe that Matthew, and probably other apostles as well, took notes during the ministry of Jesus to which he referred when compiling the gospel. Matthew is, therefore, a first hand eyewitness account of the ministry of Jesus, and of His death and resurrection. There is no evidence to reject its credibility or accuracy other than the desire to justify the rejection of the gospel itself. If we cannot believe the words of a man who lived with Jesus, taught with Jesus, and died for Jesus then we cannot believe *anything* we read in history.

The Genealogy of Jesus
Matthew 1:2-17 – Luke 3:23-38

"To Abraham was born Isaac; and to Isaac, Jacob; and to Jacob, Judah and his brothers; ... to Matthan, Jacob; and to Jacob was born Joseph the husband of Mary, by whom was born Jesus."

"Jesus ... being supposedly *the* son of Joseph, the *son* of Eli, the *son* of Matthat, the *son* of Levi, ... the *son* of Enosh, the *son* of Seth, the *son* of Adam, the *son* of God."

The most obvious, and oft asked question, is why do the two genealogies differ? Should they not be the same? The short answer is "no." Contrary to popular opinions, genealogies differ greatly because *any* family can be traced from different roots and branches. That is why it is often termed a "family tree." There are countless tree branches and leaves which may sometimes converge and then depart again. My parents took up genealogy as a hobby in their retirement years. Composing a history of the Criswell family back only 400 years, they wrote a thousand page book outlining all the different family branches and people. Are we really surprised when we hear Barack Obama and George Bush are really "10th cousins once removed"?[38] After all, are we not all related to one another by Adam and Eve?

Nevertheless, this only answers the problem in a general way. Some specific question still arise as to the differences in genealogies. Before addressing those questions specifically, the reader should be aware that Jews were accute genealogists. They kept meticulous records so as to demonstrate to what tribe they properly belonged.[39] Since only Levites could serve as priests, this also served for government and religious purposes as well. A priest had to prove his lineage. These "public registers",[40] therefore, assisted the enforcement of the Law since only Levites were permitted to intermarry with other tribes. Consequently, it is not fair to argue that Matthew or Luke were engaging in embellishments, speculations, or half-truths for the public records were available to all. No wonder then that the Jewish Talmud supports the genealogies found in Matthew and Luke![41] How so? According to the Talmud, the genealogy of Luke is apparently that of Mary's anscestry.[42] It clearly records a Mary, daughter of Heli,[43] but is it the *same* Mary as the mother of Jesus? Even if it is,

as Christian scholars believe, "doesn't Luke say 'Joseph' rather than 'Mary'?",
asks the critic. Yes, it does, so let us examine the issue more closely.

The Genealogy of Joseph or Mary?

It is commonly believed by the majority of scholars that the genealogies of Matthew and Luke differ because Matthew traced the ancestry of Joseph through whom the legal rights were transferred whereas Luke traced the ancestry of Mary through whom Jesus was descended in the flesh.[44] In other words, Matthew used Joseph as the lawful heir through whom Jesus' legal heritage was established whereas Luke traced the direct lineage of Jesus.[45]

Now this view has the support of the Jewish Talmud,[46] a non-Christian source, and this is doubtless one of the reasons that it is so strongly supported, but there are critics of the view, and with reason. The most obvious reason is that Luke says "Joseph," *not* "Mary." As John Calvin retorted, those who believe Joseph is envisioned in Matthew, but not Luke "might be accused of folly or stupidity, for vainly relating the source of Joseph's line ... [since] the anscestry of Joseph had nothing to do with Christ."[47] Of course Calvin believes that both are the ancestry of Joseph,[48] so his criticism is a little bit of a double standard. Nevertheless, there are legitimate questions raised by this. Why is Joseph's name used instead of Mary's?

One answer is that "since Mary was a woman, her name, according to Jewish usage, could not come into the genealogy."[49] This arguments seems very reasonable (but see notes below). Since Luke says Jesus "was supposed the son of Jospeh," the phrase "'as was supposed' indicates that Jesus was not really the biological son of Joseph ... it further calls attention to the mother, Mary ... her genealogy is thereupon listed."[50] Further it is has been suggested that "the feminine gender of ἡς prepares for the virgin birth by shifting attention from Joseph to Mary."[51] If so then Joseph was the son-in-law of Heli;[52] a notion accepted by men like H.A. Ironside, John Darby, and John Wesley.[53]

Nevertheless, there are those, like John Calvin, who hold that *both* genealogies are the genealogies of Joseph, and not Mary. Frederic Farrar, the late Dean of Canterbury, once held to the notion that Luke's genealogy was of Mary, but came to recant it saying, "this view is untenable ... Joseph and Mary were cousins, so that the genealogy of *both* was deducible from David."[54] How then can the differences be explained? "If we merely assume that in two instances – that of Joseph's father, and that of Zerubbabel's father, there had been what the Jews call 'a Levirite marriage', i.e. the taking, by a brother, of a childless brother's widow,"[55] then all problems are resolved.

Allow me to briefly explain this law of Levirite marriage to those unfamiliar with it. According to ancient law, also practiced in Israel, if an eldest brother died without leaving a son and heir, the brother was to take the widow of his brother as his own wife. He would then bear a son who would carry the inheritance of his *older* brother. This was because of the importance placed in antiquity of leaving an inheritance for the elder brother. If an elder brother died without an heir, the family was considered disgraced and fear that the lineage might come to an end enveloped the family. The younger brother then took the wife of his brother for the purpose of producing an heir. In the context of this debate it is suggested that Jacob (Matthew 1:16) and Heli (Luke 3:23) were brothers and that one died without heir. The other then took his wife to produce an heir (Joseph). If this were true then Joseph could rightfully and legally be said to be the son of either Jacob *or* Heli. This idea, that of the Levirite marriage, was actually quite popular throughout history. It is promoted in *Barnes' Notes*[56] as well as many older commentaries, although in recent years its light has faded.

Still one other minority view should be addressed; the view that it is Matthew, rather than Luke, who traces the lineage of Mary. It is argued that while the Talmud says Luke's genealogy is of Mary, the Peshitta (an ancient Syriac translation) allegedly attributes Mary's genealogy to Matthew.[57] The problem is that this is a suspect interpretation of the Peshitta. For one thing the Peshitta manuscripts do not even agree with each other. Furthermore, the Syriac word used can refer to either a father or a husband as it is a word used for a male member of the immediate family. The original Greek manuscripts all explicitly say that it is "Joseph, the *husband* of Mary" (1:16).

Obviously, this debate can be rather technical. It is sufficient to say that while the Levirite marriage can explain the differences in the genealogies its greatest drawback is that it must be assumed. It cannot be proven as the genealogical records no longer exist. What does exist, however, is the Jewish Talmud which supports the notion that Luke's genealogy is that of Mary (Hagigah 2:4). Since ancient Jewish genealogies always listed the male heir, even if traced through the mother (father-in-laws were regarded the same as a natural father for genealogical purposes), this view is most likely. On these merits the popular view seems to be the strongest although the possibility of a Levirite marriage should not be ruled out.

The Women of Matthew's Genealogy

It has previously been illustrated that genealogies are traced through the male heir, even if it is on the woman's side of the family. In other words, if Jane marries John, John's name would appear in the traditional genealogy even if you were tracing Jane's line. This is why Luke mentions Joseph, even though it is Mary's lineage he is tracing. However, in Matthew, who all agree is tracing Joseph's lineage, there are four *women* named. Three of these women had shady sexual pasts, and two of them (technically three) were gentiles. Why does Matthew deviate from the traditional genealogy to specifically mention these four women?

12

First, let us glance at the four women mentioned. Tamar was the wife of Judah's first son, but he died without heir, so he wedded her to his other son Onan who also died young without heir. Judah then decided to keep Tamar a widow, but she decieved Judah into thinking she was a prostitute (her face covered with a solid veil) and conceived a child by Judah (Genesis 38). Technically she was a gentile (as there were only a dozen or so true Jews in the world at that time!) but was obviously the mother of many Jews to follow, having born the child of Judah! Rahab was a prostitute who helped the Jews conquer Jericho and became a Jewish bride (Joshua 2; 6). Ruth, of course, was yet another gentile who married into the Jewish family and was an ancenstor of King David. Finally is Bathsheba who betrayed her husband Uriah by having sex with King David and bearing his son. It is interesting that Bathsheba's name is not mentioned. She is only called "the former wife of Uriah."

So three of the four women had sexual sins in their past (some unfairly accuse Ruth of sexual indiscretions as well) and three were gentiles while the fourth, Bathsheba, had been married to a gentile (Uriah). Why the mention of these four women, in deviation from the standard genealogical practice of the day which Matthew seems to follow elsewhere? Several theories exist.

The first theory is that Matthew wanted to emphasize that gentiles were also a part of God's plan. One put it less charitably by saying that Matthew wanted "to put Jewish pride in its place."[58] A second theory says that these women were chosen because of their shady past in order to emphasize God's forgiveness and grace. Finally, some have suggested that this was all preparation for Mary who was the true mother Jesus, since Joseph was not truly his biological father.[59] While there is doubtless some grain of truth to each of these, they all have drawbacks. Bathsheba, for example, was not a gentile. Ruth, on the other hand, was a virtuous woman and only poor exegesis can attribute sexual sin to her. As for Mary, it is nearly blasphemous to suggest that the sexual sins of other women were somehow mentioned to lessen the gossip made about Mary, for Mary was a virgin at the time of Jesus' birth. One does not compare a virgin to a former prostitute in her defense! On the other hand, it is suggested that the emphasis on women simply prepares the reader for Mary's introduction to the story, but why compare the virgin Mary with three women of shady past? And why introduce Ruth?

The simple answer is the best. Matthew certainly wanted to emphasize God's grace to both gentile and sinner. The introduction of both gentile women and women of dark pasts emphasizes God's grace to both. One might object that there were other women who might have been named, but a careful examination of the Bible shows these women, who were in the lineage of Joseph, are the most recognizable and important. It cannot be proven, moreover, that any other women of importance in the Old Testament (either gentile or sinner) was in the lineage of Joseph. So this answer seems best.

Forty-Two Generations?

A strange curiousity of Matthew's genealogy is the apparent omission of certain names and the seeming division of his genealogy into three equal groups of fourteen generations. Notice that I said "apparent" and "seeming." Many scholars take this for granted, but there are questions regarding these statements which are too often neglected and deserve debate.

First, regarding what Clement of Alexandria called the "three mystic intervals" from Abraham to Christ[60] it is to be admitted that Matthew specifically states in Matthew 1:17 that "all the generations from Abraham to David are fourteen generations; and from David to the deportation to Babylon fourteen generations; and from the deportation to Babylon to *the time of* Christ fourteen generations." The problem is that "there appear to be only thirteen generations in each division."[61] In fact, there are actually fifteen names in the first division. However, if we do not count Abraham as a part of the divisions then we get fourteen in the first two division, but only thirteen in the third. Let us look at the breakdown carefully.

	First Division	Second Division	Third Division
	Abraham	*David (name repeated)*	*Jeconiah (repeated)*
1.	Isaac	Solomon	Shealtiel
2.	Jacob	Rehoboam	Zerubbabel
3.	Judah	Abijah	Abihud
4.	Perez	Asa	Eliakim
5.	Hezron	Jehoshaphat	Azor
6.	Ram	Joram	Zadok
7.	Admin	Uzziah	Achim
8.	Amminadab	Jotham	Eliud
9.	Nahshon	Ahaz	Eleazar
10.	Salmon	Hezekiah	Matthan
11.	Boaz	Manasseh	Jacob
12.	Obed	Amon	Joseph
13.	Jesse	Josiah	Jesus
14.	David	Jeconiah	

Now it is has been said that Jeconiah's name is repeated in the third division to equal fourteen, but that cannot be a valid argument for David's name is also repeated in the second division. That would make fifteen in the second division if the repetition of a name was supposed to count for two seperate generations. Moreover, it is not legitimate to count a single person as a part of multiple generations. It is true that there are forty-two names in the genealogy, counting Abraham but the divisions are clearly marked by Matthew.

To complicate matters is the fact that some names appear to be omitted from the genealogy. Jehoiakim, the father of Jeconiah, is the most obvious and his omission is debated debated below. Nevertheless, Leon Morris noted that "had Jehoiakim been included, we would have fourteen names in his third section."[62] Still others have claimed that the Second Coming of Christ rightly occupies the spot as the fourteenth generation![63] This argument, however, is beyond speculation since Matthew explicitly says it is fourteen generations unto Christ. How many generations have passed between the first and second comings? Finally, it has also been suggested that Joseph was not only the name of Mary's husband, but also her father. If true, this would make Mary the thirteenth generation and Jesus the fourteenth, resolving the problem of generations discussed below. Unfortunately, this conflicts with both Luke and Matthew for Luke 3:23 says Jesus was "supposedly the son of Joseph." Why "supposed" if the Joseph here mentioned is Mary's father? Matthew is even more explicit in calling Joseph "the husband of Mary" (Matthew 1:16). Obviously, this Joseph is the husband of Mary. We must look elsewhere for the answer to this "missing" generation.

If we allow for the doubling of names, counting Abraham as part of the first generation then we do get fourteen generations in the third division, but fifteen in the first! Obviously Abraham was not intended to be counted as part of the first division. The only problem is how Matthew can say there were fourteen generations from exile to Christ. The answer is probably more simple than we wish to admit. For the purposes of counting generations Matthew rightly recognized Jehoiakim, but he omitted Jehoiakim from the genealogy for reasons debated below. So there are truly fourteen generations, or are there?

Curious Omissions
Three other names are alleged to have been omitted by Matthew.[64] These are Ahaziah, Joash, and Amaziah (cf. 1 Chronicles 3:11) who should be between Joram and Uzziah (also called Azariah). Several explanations are offered for this. First, it has been suggested that these omissions are scribals errors not attributable to Matthew but a later scribe. The evidence is the fact that Ahaziah and Azariah could easily have been mistaken for one another, so the scribe inadvertently skipped from Ahaziah to Azariah, leaving out the three names. This is supported by a single ancient copy of the Codex *Bezae* and some Syriac manuscripts which date back to the fourth century. The problem is that we have far older manuscripts which support the current reading; not to mention Matthew's explicit remark about fourteen generations. It would be impossible for Matthew to say there were fourteen generations if all three names were introduced. Consequently, this cannot be a scribal error.

Another argument is that Matthew purposely left "gaps"[65] in his genealogy. This, they say, is acceptable since the word "sons" can refer to "descendants" and "father" to "forefathers."[66] Unfortunately, Matthew does not use either of these terms. Were he to have used the terms "son of" or "father of" the argument would be easily settled, but Matthew uses the much more restrictive genealogical term γεννάω (*gennao*) which is literally translated as "to beget."[67] It is a verb! The name "Genesis" comes from this root word, for it means to be born. Only a father or mother can beget a son. A grand-father is never properly said to *beget* a grandson, although he can be called a "father" of a grandson. This leads to the question of whether or not Matthew was originally written in Hebrew or Greek.

If Matthew was originally written in Hebrew, then it is possible that Matthew uses the idiom "father of" rather than "begot." Of course this only opens up more problems for most agree that Matthew translated his own gospel himself![68] Now I do not wish to engaged in a protracted debate here. It is sufficient to say that Matthew does omit these three names and does not intend to include those in the genealogy. The question is "why"?

One argument is that "the infamous character of some of the persons may explain their deletions."[69] Matthew Henry remarks "it is not through mistake or forgetfulness that these three were omitted."[70] The most common answer is that these names were "dropped because of their connection with Ahab and Jezebel, renowned for wickedness (2 Kings 8:27), and because of their connection with wicked Athaliah (2 Kings 8:26), the usurper (2 Kings 11:1-20). Two of the three were notoriously evil; all three died violently."[71] The response is that a number of those kings who Matthew did include are of suspect character as well. Nevertheless, anyone familiar with the Bible is accutely aware that Ahab and Jezebel were among the worst and most evil of all the characters of Israel. Therefore, the alliance of these kings of Judah to Ahab's dynasty is more than sufficient to warrant a sort of disinheritance from the genealogical records!

Why Fourteen Generations?

Having established that Matthew was well within Jewish tradition in omitting the names of four wicked and disinherited kings from the genealogy, we are left with the question of generations. Why use three divisions of fourteen generations?

The simple answer is that it is a "mnemonic device"[72] and that "a certain symmetry accrues to the genealogy for memorial purposes by omitting the less important names."[73] This "literary symetry"[74] makes sense, but there could be another reason as well. Some have argued that numberical symbolism and Jewish tradition combined with the Messianic hope of a Davidic king made the number fourteen an important Biblical number not unlike seven and three (seven days in a week, the Trinity, etc.). In this case the number fourteen is derived from "the numerical values of the Hebrew letters in the name David [which] add up to fourteen : ד (4) + ו (6) + ד (4)."[75]

16

Although this theory cannot be proven, there is nothing to contradict it. It is obvious that Matthew used three divisions of fourteen as a "mnemonic device."[76] Why he chose fourteen is irrelevant. It may have had symbolic value or it may simply have been the best way to divide the genealogy into three equal sections after omitting the dishonorable kings. Either answer is sufficient.

Summary

It is apparent that Matthew used the division of fourteen generations as an aid to memory. The omission of kings was probably because of their disinheritance and disobedience rather than in an arbitrary attempt to arrive at fourteen generations a piece, or he would surely have left Jeconiah's name in the list. This omission, more than that of Ahaziah, Joash, and Amaziah, deserves to be discussed, for it is actually an important one in regard to the prophecy of the coming Messiah.

<h3 style="text-align:center">Jeconiah's Descendants</h3>

Irenaeus pointed out that Jeremiah 22:24-28 records God's curse upon Jechoniah and his disinheritance.[77] There are two things to be considered here. First, if Jechoniah was disinherited, then why is it that Jehoiakim is the name omitted from the genealogy? Second, if Jechoniah (also called Jehoiachin) was disinherited then how could Christ be descended from Jechoniah and be the rightful heir to David?

The first answer is easy. If we read the prophecy carefully, we will remember that a curse was often carried out upon the first born son of the one cursed. First-born sons were revered so a curse was usually carried out on the son. For example, the curse of Ham was for Ham's sin and yet it is was Canaan, his first born son, to whom the prophecy was addressed (Genesis 9:18-27). This form of punishment was practiced throughout antiquity. When we read the curse of Jechoniah carefully, it is clear that Jechoniah (although evil himself) was cursed because of the sins of his father, Jehoiakim (cf. Jeremiah 22:18). Moreover, a careful reading of the prophecy does not say that no descendant of Jechoniah shall sit on the throne but that he would be handed over to Babylon and disinherited (Jeremiah 22:24-25). This is exactly what happened!

So it was Jehoiakim to whom God's wrath was initially directed, for "Pharaoh Neco made Eliakim, the son of Josiah, king in the place of Josiah his father, and changed his name to Jehoiakim ... So Jehoiakim gave the silver and gold to Pharaoh, but he taxed the land in order to give the money at the command of Pharaoh. He exacted the silver and gold from the people of the land, each according to his valuation, to give it to Pharaoh Neco ... he did evil in the sight of the LORD, according to all that his fathers had done" (2 Kings 23:34-37).

Jechoniah reigned for only three months before he was taken into captivity in Babylon (2 Kings 24:8-12). So the prophecy was fulfilled in the past. Nothing in the prophecy denies that a descendant of Jechoniah can sit on the throne. Moreover, "Jesus' legal descent from David, which was always traced through his father, came through Jeconiah to Joseph. But His blood descent, and *His human right to rule,* came through Mary', who was not in Jeconiah's lineage. Thus the curse of Jeconiah's offspring was circumvented, while still maintaining the royal privilege."[78]

Comparisons to Luke's Genealogy

The differences in Matthew and Luke's genealogy have already been addressed by simple virtue of the fact that the one is of Joseph and the other that of Mary, although by Jewish tradition only the male head of the family is named regardless of which side of the family (in this case Mary's) is traced. Nevertheless, some critics argue that there are too many similarities in the genealogies for this to be true! This is an ironic argument from those who say that there are too many differences, but the casual observer may well be confused, so it is important to address these similarities and differences more closely.

Shealtiel
In Matthew, Shealtiel is said to be the son of Jechoniah, but in Luke, he is the son of Neri. Some consider this a contradiction but when looking back through the Old Testament it is clear that Shealtiel was not an uncommon name and the genealogies of both Matthew and Luke accord perfectly with these two different Shealtiels who were, in fact, separated almost a hundred of years!

According to 1 Chronicles 3:17 Jechoniah's son was named Shealtiel. This is clearly the Shealtiel recorded in Matthew. Luke 3:27, however, list a Shealtiel as the son of Neri. Can we assume it is a contradiction? No for this Shealtiel is also found in the Bible and lived nearly a hundred years after the Shealtiel of 1 Chronicles 3:17. He is found in the genealogy of Nehemiah 12:1.

So Matthew was descended from the line of David through Jechoniah, but Mary was descended through the Levitic lineage found in Nehemiah's records. This, however, leads to another debate. Critics point out, however, that if Mary was not descended from David, then Jesus could not be the Messiah as prophesied. Moreover, based on Jewish law different tribes were not allowed to intermarry.

Now there is no doubt that Mary had Levitic blood. In addition to the evidence of Luke's genealogy we are told that Mary and Elizabeth were related and that Elizabeth was from the line of Aaron (Luke 1:5). Nevertheless, this is not a problem as critics imply for the law permitted Levites to marry into other tribes since they had no land inheritance of their own.[79] Consequently, Mary could have both Levitic blood and the blood of Judah in her heritage! This is exactly what Luke proves in his genealogy!

18

Zerubbabel

Although it has been established that the Shealtiels found in Matthew and Luke are not the same person, critics point out that both have sons named Zerubbabel. Although this was by no means an uncommon name in ancient Israel, it should be addressed.

From a strictly exegetical standpoint it is obvious that these Zerubbabels are different for they had different children and different grand-parents as well. The one recorded in Chronicles and Matthew is of the tribe of Judah. The one recorded in Nehemiah and Luke is of the tribe of Levi. Nevertheless, there is another question. Specifically, that of Matthew's Zerubbabel. *If* this Zerubbabel is the same as that of Chronicles then there *appears* to be a problem, for that Zerubbabel is said to be the son of Pedaiah, Shealtiel's *brother* (1 Chronicles 3:19). Zerubbabel would appear to be the nephew of Shealtiel, and not his son!

Although it has been suggested that both might have had sons by the same name there is another solution proposed which makes better since in light of ancient Israeli law. The practice of Levirite marraiges has already been mentioned. Although its application to the genealogy is suspect in some places, it appears from the text of 1 Chronicles that this was the case with Shealtiel.[80] Had Shealtiel died without heir, it would have been the legal obligation of Pedaiah to take Shealtiel's wife to produce an heir *in Shealtiel's name*. Thus Shealtiel, although not the biological father, is called the father of Zerubbabel, as well as Pedaiah. This was standard practice in antiquity, not only in Israel but throughout the Middle East.

In short, these Zerubbabels were different individuals. In Matthew the genealogy is traced through Abihud (Matthew 1:13), but in Luke 3:27 it is Rhesa. Now while Zerubbabel could have had more than one son, and hence more than one line, the anscestry of Shealtiel should be sufficient to prove that these were different Zerubbabels; one from the tribe of Judah, and the other (Mary's line) was from the tribe of Levi (cf. Luke 1:5) as well as Judah (Luke 3:33).

Cainan

The name Cainan found in Luke creates problems for the inerrantist. The problem is that Cainan's name is not found in the Hebrew Old Testament at all, but only in the Greek translation known as the *Septuagint*. So, they argue, either Genesis is wrong or Luke is wrong they argue; one *must* be wrong. Or do they?

A common argument, aforementioned, is that genealogies can omit names, thus the omission is acceptable. However, I reject this view here for the text of Genesis uses a specific verb יוֹלֶד (*yoled*) which can *only* refer to a father, and *not* a forefather. There is another possibility.

According to the doctrine of inerrancy only the original manuscripts need be free from error.[81] Minor scribal errors, which are of no significant, can

19

and do occur in various manuscripts but *none* effect any doctrine or major event of history. The question is, therefore, whether or not Luke's manuscript ever mentioned this Cainan. If not, it is likely that a Greek reader added the name, having seen it in the Greek *Septuagint* and assumed that Luke made "orthogrophical variations or simple confusion of names"![82] In fact, it was not Luke who made the mistake. Let us look at the evidence.

First, there is not a single manuscript outside the *Septuagint* before New Testament times that mentions this Cainan. Not one! Says John Gill:

> "This Cainan is not mentioned by Moses in Ge. 11:12 nor has he ever appeared in any Hebrew copy of the Old Testament, nor in the Samaritan version, nor in the Targum; nor is he mentioned by Josephus, nor in 1 Ch. 1:24 where the genealogy is repeated; nor is it in Beza's most ancient Greek copy of Luke: it indeed stands in the present copies of the *Septuagint*, but was not originally there, and therefore could not be taken by Luke from there."[83]

Indeed, no serious scholar doubts that the Old Testament passage never included the name of Cainan. Now some have suggested that Luke accidentally copied the error from the Greek *Septuagint*, as Gill alluded to, but this is also in doubt. The most ancient manuscript of Luke known to exist is $\mathfrak{P}^{75}$ and it does *not* include Cainan's name. Neither does the Codex *Bezae*, which ranks as one of the oldest complete manuscripts of the New Testament.

It is far more logical to assume that later copiest copied the *Septuagint* error than to assume that Luke made the error! Consider that by the time the Church was well established, most scribes were now gentiles who were incapable of reading the Hebrew. Since they relied on the *Septuagint* as their Old Testament the monks would have compared Luke's gospel to the text of Genesis found in the *Septuagint* and *assumed* that Luke had accidentally omitted the name, when the name was really *never there*.

Conclusion

John Wesley said of these genealogies "if there were any difficulties ... they would affect the Jewish table, rather than the credit of the Evangelists; for they act only as historians setting down these genealogies, as they stood in those public and allowed records. They were therefore to take them as they found them. Nor was it needful they should correct the mistakes, if there were any."[84] In fact, the only "difficulties" are in the minds of modern men unaquainted with the laws and traditions of ancient Israel. Genealogies were not only common in ancient Israel, but a part of their life. Paul even lamented the "endless genealogies" (1 Timothy 1:4) of many in the community. Too often it was a source of pride. Nevertheless, the genealogies are repeated here simply to prove that Jesus did have the rightful and lawful right to be heir to King David and the promised Messiah. Through Joseph, the legal right of kingship was bestowed upon Jesus even though Joseph was technically only his step-father. Through Mary Jesus' very blood was of the same royal blood, although from a different line. Thus the genealogies prove that Jesus could have been the Messiah. Had he not been descended from David he would automatically be nullified from any claim to the throne, but because he is from David's lineage, he had the right. This is what the gospel authors wanted to demonstrate.

Were Mary and Joseph Married?
Matthew 1:18-19

> "When His mother Mary had been betrothed to Joseph, before they came together she was found to be with child by the Holy Spirit. And Joseph her husband, being a righteous man, and not wanting to disgrace her, desired to put her away secretly."

There are several debates involved in this passage. Whether or not Joseph and Mary were married yet is but one. The greater debate actually revolves around the issue of divorce and is addressed more fully under Matthew 19:9. As for the question of their marriage itself, there is really no doubt that Joseph and Mary were technically engaged as it is called today, but the ceremonies and laws were different; hence the confusion. The Greek word is not γαμέω (*gameo*) meaning to "marry,"[85] but μνηστεύω (*mnesteuo*) meaning to "betroth."[86] A betrothal was similar to an engagement but with a greater degree of commitment than American engagements.

To this very day in India, an engagement is a formal ceremony in which partners are pledged to each other. The engagement ceremony is often as big a ceremony as the wedding itself. During the engagement period, however, sexual union is still forbidden. Only after the marriage ceremony are they allowed to consummate the marriage and move in together. This is very similar to ancient Israel.

This leads to the second debate which is concerning his desire to "divorce" her. How can he divorce her if they were not married? Unfortunately, both sides of the debate often get this one wrong. Some have argued that you could leave a woman for any reason during the engagement period,[87] but this is not so. As aforementioned, betrothals were not like American engagements. A separation needed to have cause. Those who argue against this wish to imply that there is no "adultery exception" in Jesus' condemnation of divorce.[88] Therefore, believing it would be a sin to divorce Mary even if she had been unfaithful, as Joseph doubtless assumed, they argue that divorce was only legal during the betrothal period, but this is incorrect. Mosaic law did indeed allow divorce for "indecency" (Deuteronomy 24:1-4).

On the issue of the "adultery exception" in Matthew 19:9 I will defer to that section. Only the last issue need be addressed here. Did Joseph believe that

Mary was still a virgin before the angel visited him? Curiously enough, a number of scholars believe that Joseph did believe Mary's story,[89] but if he did, then why did he resolve to divorce her?

It is argued that a "righteous man" (1:19) would not divorce the Virgin Mary, nor assume she was lying. Therefore, some argue that Joseph was writing out the divorce certificate because "he felt unworthy."[90] This, however, is an overeager attempt to make Joseph more than righteous, but saintly. It is not logical to assume that he believed Mary's seemingly wild story until the angel confirmed it (Matthew 1:20). In fact, it would doubtless require great faith to believe the story even after the angel had appeared to him in but a dream! But how can he said to be "righteous" if he was wrongly resolved to divorce her? The answer is simple. First, he would have been wrong to divorce her had he believed her story! That would have been the most cowardly of acts. Second, if she had commited adultery she could have been stoned to death even during the engagement period (Deuteronomy 22:23-24). Consequently, by resolving to divorce her quietly (1:19) Joseph was very righteous in sparing her life! We need not elevate Joseph to sainthood while he yet lived. His acts were righteous enough without attempting to make him superhuman.

In summary then Mary and Joseph had not yet had sexual intercourse because they were only betrothed and not yet married. Nonetheless, he would still have had to file a divorce certificate as betrothals were not private promises as today, but binding pledges witnessed by family and friends.

The Prophecy of Isaiah
Matthew 1:23

"Behold, a virgin will be with child and bear a son, and she will call His name Immanuel."

This prophecy is from Isaiah 7:14. Jews have objected to the passage's application to Jesus on several grounds; most notably that they claim it is not a prophecy of a virgin birth at all, but merely a "young woman" who will give birth (hardly a miraculous event). As I addressed this topic in *Controversies in the Prophets* I will repeat much of what I said there with a few omissions and additions.

The word "virgin" is found in every Christian translation and affirmed in the ancient Jewish translation, the Greek *Septuagint*, as well. However, medieval and modern Jewish translations, such as the Tanakh, translate the word as "young woman." Christians believe that this is the sign of the Messiah's birth, but Orthodox Jews usually see this as a prophecy of either King Hezekiah's birth or of the birth of Isaiah's son. More recently, Christian scholars have begun to argue for a double fulfillment, agreeing with most Jews that Isaiah's son is envisioned, but maintaining that it is also, more literally, a prophecy of the birth of Jesus, the Messiah.

The word translated "virgin" here is אַלְמָה (*alma*) in Hebrew, as opposed to בְּתוּלָה (*bethula*), the normal word for "virgin." Should the word be translated "virgin?" Is the "sign" that of a virgin birth or something else? Moreover, what of the other prophecies? Is this the Messiah, a great king, or merely the child of a prophet?

Historical Overview

The oldest clear reference to the interpretation of this passage is the Greek *Septuagint* which was written in the mid-third century before Christ. It translates אַלְמָה (*alma*) as παρθενος (*parthenos*) or "virgin." That this was the interpretation accepted by the Jews of antiquity is further supported by the fact that the apostle Matthew, in writing his gospel to Jews,[91] quotes this verse without any attempt to justify its usage. In other words, he assumed that its application to the birth of the Messiah was to be taken for granted, and not disputed. Indeed, one might assume that it would be more simple to deny the virgin birth than to deny that the passage speaks of a virgin, but for whatever reason (perhaps out of respect to Christians) the Jewish community at large soon began to refute the teaching that the Messiah should be born of a virgin, and argued that אַלְמָה (*alma*) should be translated as "young woman," as the Aramaic Targum does.[92]

It should not be a surprise that Christians have held fast to the teaching that the prophecy speaks of a virgin, and only a virgin. Tertullian suggests that "a daily occurrence – the pregnancy and parturition of a young female – cannot possibly seem anything of *a sign*."[93] He insist that the sign is that of a virgin birth. Ignatius too sees this as a prophecy of Mary,[94] as does Irenaeus who refutes the translation of אַלְמָה (*alma*) by Theodotian the Ephesian and Aquila of Pontus (both Jewish proselytes), who renders the verse "young women."[95]

Later Church Fathers like Saint Cyril of Jerusalem concur.[96] Saint Jerome maintains that אַלְמָה (*alma*) means "a hidden virgin, that is, not merely a virgin, but ... a virgin secluded, and guarded by her parents."[97]

Although Christians are united on this issue, Jews soon became divided. Some began to argue that this was a prophecy of Hezekiah but others argued that the prophecy referred to Isaiah's son, mentioned in 8:3. Some even argued that it was an allegorical prophecy referring to the kingdom of Judah![98]

Rashi, the famed medieval Jewish scholar, holds, with most Jews, that the prophecy refers to Isaiah's son. So popular did this view become that by the Middle Ages some Christians began to decipher Isaiah 7:14 as a dual prophecy. This view was supported by Martin Luther[99] who argues that there are actually two signs; "the first one does not apply to Ahaz, because he did not live to see it, but the second does."[100]

Despite Luther's support for the dual prophecy theory, it did not become a popular view among Christians until relatively recently in history.

Christian scholars such as John Lightfoot,[101] Matthew Poole,[102] John Wesley,[103] Charles Spurgeon[104] John Gill,[105] John Nelson Darby,[106] and C. I. Scofield[107] all continue to accept the prophecy as a sole reference to Christ. It is only recently that the position of Martin Luther has become dominant.

A Virgin?

The first question is most obviously, "is the woman a virgin?" Since the Christian era most Jewish scholars have insisted that the word עַלְמָה (*alma*) should be translated as "young woman." Even modern Christian translations have begun to translate the word that way in most other passages, but is this the correct translation?

The word עַלְמָה (*alma*) appears in the Bible only seven times (Gen. 24:43, Ex. 2:8, Ps. 68:25, Prov. 30:19, Song of Solomon 1:3, 6:8, and, of course, Isaiah 7:14). Its translation has varied from translation to translation depending on the time and culture of the translation. Matthew Poole insist that "this word constantly signifies a virgin in all other places of Scripture where it is used"[108] but Hebrew language scholar Gesenius denies this saying that it was often translated by Jews in the Greek *Septuagint* as νεανις (*neanis*)[109] or "young girl." However, this is misleading, for the Jews translated עַלְמָה (*alma*) as παρθενος (*parthenos*) or "virgin" in two of the seven passages, including Isaiah 7:14. The other passage is Genesis 24:43 where עַלְמָה (*alma*) is translated as παρθενος (*parthenos*) as is evident in verse sixteen where, as Matthew Poole points out, Rebekah is most definitely called a virgin or בְּתוּלָה (*bethula*).[110]

Of the remaining passages, it has been argued that not one of them clearly refers to a woman who is not a virgin and in at least three of the remaining five verses it is almost certain that the woman in question was a virgin. In Exodus 2:8, for example, it can be demonstrated that the girl in question was a virgin for this woman is accepted by Jewish tradition to be Miriam, Moses' own sister who would then still have been a child.[111] Psalms 68:25 is somewhat ambiguous although it should be pointed out that the women are spoken of as part of a religious ceremony, and were usually virgins. Also in Song of Solomon 6:8 one would certainly expect that a king might obtain virgins for himself, hence the term *virgin* is likely here as well.

The best argument against the idea that an עַלְמָה (*alma*) should be translated "young woman" is Jerome's objection that "a virgin [is] properly called *Bethulah*, but a young woman, or a girl, is not *Almah*, but *Naarah*!"[112] Indeed, if the passage merely spoke of a "young woman" one would expect to see נַעֲרָה (*na'arah*)[113] rather than עַלְמָה (*alma*).

So what then is an עַלְמָה (*alma*) and why does it differ from בְּתוּלָה (*bethula*)? The root of the word for עַלְמָה (*alma*) is עָלַם (*alam*) which means "hidden" or "concealed."[114] The connotation is obviously of hiding one's anatomy or sexuality. A virgin conceals herself from others. Saint Jerome defines עַלְמָה (*alma*) as "a hidden virgin, that is, not merely a virgin, but ... a virgin secluded, and guarded by her parents"[115]

Nevertheless, Rosenberg offers Proverbs 30:19 as proof that עַלְמָה (*alma*) is not a virgin,[116] but the passage is inconclusive. In fact, the context of the "way of a man with a woman [עַלְמָה (*alma*)]" seems to support the deflowering of a virgin rather than of an experienced woman.

One thing is clear. Even the Orthodox Jews admit that the עַלְמָה (*alma*) is a young woman of marriageable age, but in *no instance* can the word be found to refer to a married woman, thus עַלְמָה (*alma*) is usually translated as "maiden." Now, as H. A. Ironside has pointed out, if she is a maiden then "every maiden is presumably a virgin – if not, something is radically wrong."[117]

The strongest possible support for the translation "virgin" is not only the Jewish translators of the *Septuagint* but the fact that the apostles, themselves Jews, referred to this prophecy in a matter of fact manner. In Matthew's gospel he nowhere seeks to prove that "virgin" is the correct rendering of the passage, though he himself wrote in Hebrew,[118] but instead assumes that the Jews to whom he was writing already knew the prophecy (1:23)! Indeed, it is not until after Christianity became dominated by gentile converts that many Jews began to deny the prophecy referred to a virgin.

Perhaps it is out of respect for the Christian that the Orthodox Jew now denies that the prophecy speaks of a virgin birth, for they obviously do not truly believe that Mary was a virgin. Nevertheless, it seems apparent that the Jews of antiquity did believe she was to be a virgin, as the *Septuagint* reads. Moreover, the virtually unanimous opinion of the ancient Jew was that this was, indeed, a prophecy of the Messiah. If the promised son is the Messiah then the woman *must* be a virgin. *Could the Messiah be born of any other?*

The Sign

Of course, the question then follows, "is this son the promised Messiah?" What is the "sign" of which Isaiah spoke? For centuries the sign was held to be the virgin birth of the Messiah. However, as with the "virgin," some Orthodox Jews soon came to deny not only the virgin birth, but also whether or not the prophecy referred to the Messiah at all. So if the "sign" is not of a virgin birth of the Messiah, what is it?

How a "young woman" giving birth is said to be a sign bewilders the Christian. Surely the "sign" is related to the birth of this Immanuel? If not, what? The medieval Jewish scholar Ibn Ezra declared that "the sign was that the child was to eat butter and honey, for it is not usual that children eat these things immediately after birth,"[119] but such a "sign" would hardly be convincing since anyone familiar with the prophecy could feed their son butter and honey, thus making a "self fulfilling prophecy." As Cyril declared "the sign certainly must be something astonishing."[120] We cannot, therefore, assign to the sign an

25

ordinary event or something which any charlatan could emulate. To quote Tertullian, "a daily occurrence – the pregnancy and parturition of a young female – cannot possibly seem anything of *a sign*."[121] The question then remains, "what, if not a virgin birth, does the 'sign' refer to?"

John Darby believes that "Immanuel is the sign"[122] and John Gill confers, saying that the sign was nothing less than "the promised Messiah."[123] Such an argument is, perhaps a valid alternative except that many no longer believe the prophecy even refers to the birth of the Messiah at all! Five views have been put forth.

The first view is that it is the Messiah who is promised. The second view is that the prophecy refers to the birth of Hezekiah, the great king of Israel. This view, however, is not well accepted even among many Orthodox Jews. Rashi points out that Hezekiah "was born nine years before"[124] this prophecy was made, thus nullifying the idea that his birth could be what was referred to here, for, as Cyril remarks, "he said not, 'hath conceived,' but 'the virgin shall conceive,' speaking as with foreknowledge."[125] Ibn Ezra also rejects this view on the same grounds[126] as do most Christian commentators such as Martin Luther[127] and John Calvin.[128]

A third view holds that the child is allegorical for the whole kingdom of Judah![129] Even John Calvin hints that the child in verse sixteen might refer to "all children in general"[130] and others make the virgin out to represent the house of David,[131] but this view, and its variants, has few supporters. Ibn Ezra rejects it entirely, remarking that it completely ignores the "mother and father" of 8:4 (which he believes refers to the same child).[132]

The most dominant view aside from the first is the belief that Isaiah's son is envisioned. Rashi holds to this view,[133] as does Ibn Ezra.[134] They hold that Isaiah's wife is the "young woman" spoken of in verse fourteen[135] and that the fulfillment of the prophecy is itself recorded in 8:3-4, for in those verses the Lord declares to Isaiah concerning his son, "name him Maher-shalal-hash-baz; for before the boy knows how to cry out 'My father' or 'My mother,' the wealth of Damascus and the spoil of Samaria will be carried away before the king of Assyria." This is held to be parallel to verse 7:16. However, there are many problems with the view. First, as Charles Spurgeon says, "it does strike me that this Immanuel, who was to be born, could not be a mere simple man."[136] Furthermore, "here is a government ascribed to Immanuel, which could not be His if we were to suppose that the Immanuel here spoken of was either Shear-Jashub, or Mahar-Shalelhach-Baz, or any other of the sons of Isaiah."[137] Secondly, Franz Delitzsch points out "it is inconceivable that in a well-considered style, and one of religious earnestness, a woman who had been long married, like the prophet's own wife, could be called *ha almah* without any reserve."[138] John Calvin, in his usual uncharitable manner maintains that it would be "absurd to hold out this is a sign or a miracle."[139]

A fifth view holds that both the fourth and first views are correct. With Albert Barnes, many choose to believe that this is a dual prophecy[140] or, as Calvin put it, "that the Prophet spoke of some child who was born at that time, by whom, as an obscure picture, Christ was foreshadowed."[141] This view has become a dominant view in recent years among Christians who seek to dismiss the criticisms of the Orthodox Jew while maintaining the truth of the gospels. Even such conservative names as John Walvoord hold to it.[142] Gleason Archer believes this view best explains the use of the word עַלְמָה (alma) saying "'almah was an ideal term for the twofold aspect of the Immanuel prophecy."[143] Nevertheless, it should be obvious that the birth of Isaiah's son could not be what the prophet had in mind for, as Albert Barnes himself admits "it is clearly implied here, that the sign should be such as JEHOVAH alone could give."[144] Could not anyone have a child if she was not a virgin?

This returns us to the first view. Namely, that the "sign" is a the virgin birth of the Messiah. The Orthodox Jew objects to this view on several grounds. The first point, that עַלְמָה (alma) should not be translated "virgin," has already been refuted. The second argument applied against the gospel view is that the birth of the Messiah, many centuries still future, could in no way be considered a "sign" to Ahaz (7:11)![145] The criticism appears sound at first but ignores the fact that Ahaz had already rejected the sign God had given him[146] and declared that he would not "test" the Lord (7:12). Thus, as Robert Govett says, "as Ahaz had *refused* the miracle, the miracle was no longer to be vouchsafed to *him*."[147] The prophecy, says Matthew Henry, was "a sign to the house of David."[148] This is proven, as Scofield remarks, by verse thirteen which addresses the prophecy not to "the faithless Ahaz, but to the whole 'house of David.'"[149]

John Lightfoot summarized the entire prophecy by saying that "the Lord will not quite cast off the house of David, till a virgin have born a son, and that son be God in our nature."[150] To quote Calvin, "for on what did the deliverance of Jerusalem depend, but the manifestation of Christ?"[151] It is evident that the "Messiah must be of the seed of Eve, that is to say, he must be human, a man. An angel cannot be Messiah."[152] As Ironside observes, "the 'Seed of the woman' is a most significant expression and refers to the Virgin Birth of the Messiah. All others born into the world are definitely of the seed of man, but the great Deliverer was to come only through the woman."[153]

So the best view should be the one held by the Jews and Christians of antiquity. The "sign" should be, as John Wesley believes, solely a prophecy of the Messiah of the distant future.[154] This is further proved by his name; Immanuel.

The Son, Immanuel

Was Isaiah's son called Immanuel? Was Jesus called by this name? If not, what does the title Immanuel mean?

The Hebrew name Immanuel literally means "God with us." עם (*im*) means "with", נו (*anu*) means "us," and אל (*El*) means God. None of Isaiah's sons were called by this name, nor could they have been. Jesus on the other hand, although not formally given the name, was most literally Immanuel for, as Novatian said, "He is 'God with us.'"[155] Augustine believes the prophecy is proof that "God should be born Man,"[156] and Lactantius declared, "by this name the prophet declared that God incarnate was about to come to man."[157]

Those who deny that the Messiah is God incarnate cannot explain this title unless it be an ordinary name, and if it is an ordinary name, then the fact remains that no man of significance has ever formally received this name. It is either a name or a title, and if a title, it can refer only to one; the Messiah, who must be "God with us."

The Power of Damascus

Those who believe in the dual fulfillment that Isaiah 7:14-16 also attempt to connect 8:3-4 to Christ, saying that Christ received the power of Damascus. Interestingly enough, even those who do not believe in a dual fulfillment have often attributed the power of Damascus to Jesus, but is this necessary? Does the prophecy of Damascus refer to Christ at all?

Tertullian believes that the Magi represented the power of Damascus.[158] Likewise, Irenaeus says "the magi when they had seen, adorned, and offered their gifts ... departed by another way, not now returning by the way of the Assyrians, 'For before the child shall have knowledge to cry "'father'"' or "'mother'"' He shall receive the power of Damascus and the spoils of Samaria.'"[159] However, one wonders what passage Tertullian and Irenaeus are referring to for 8:4 actually reads, "before the boy knows how to cry out 'My father' or 'My mother,' the wealth of Damascus and the spoil of Samaria *will be carried away before the king of Assyria*." Jerome calls it spiritual Damascus and spiritual Assyria.[160]

In fact, this is an illustration of the problems caused by merging two incompatible prophecies. The prophecy of Damascus clearly refers to Isaiah's son and *not* the prophecy of the virgin's son. Isaiah is told specifically to "name [his son] Maher-shalal-hash-baz; for before the boy knows how to cry out 'My father' or 'My mother,' the wealth of Damascus and the spoil of Samaria will be carried away before the king of Assyria" (8:3-4). That prophecy was fulfilled "in 732 B.C. when Tiglath-Pilaser III destroyed Damascus."[161] On this account the Orthodox Jew is entirely correct. The wealth of Damascus and Samaria are to be carried off by "the king of Assyria," not the child spoken of in Isaiah 7:14-16.

In short, the prophecy of Damascus is a separate prophecy from the sign of the virgin birth. It is not quoted by Matthew and does not apply to the life and times of Jesus. It is an entirely separate chapter in the Bible because it is an entirely different prophecy!

Perpetual Virginity?

One final question may be addressed as to the theory of the perpetual virginity as taught by the Catholic Church. Since there are other passages that speak to this issue, I will only briefly address it here.

First, all agree that Matthew was the husband of Mary. Sex is the consumation of marriage. If Matthew never consumated the marriage after Jesus' birth, then they could not rightfully be said to be married.

Second, the angel does *not* forbid Matthew from having intercourse with her *after* the birth of Jesus. Matthew 1:25 only says that Joseph "kept her a virgin ***until*** she gave birth to a Son." Nothing is said of what happened afterwards, but seeing as how he is rightfully called her husband the marriage must have been consumated. And so we may agree with the Catholic father Saint Jerome when he said, "she was known [sexually] after she gave birth."[162]

Astrology in Matthew?
Matthew 2:2

"Where is He who has been born King of the Jews? For we saw His star in the east, and have come to worship Him."

The Magi only appear in the Bible in these few passages and yet their appearance is somewhat contentious, for a number of debates erupt around their appearance. The most acute is whether or not they were astrologers and, if they were, does this not prove that the Bible approves of astrology? Some say it does. Yet the response is that even though the Magi were astrologers, this neither approves the legitimacy of astrology nor the practice thereof. The debate here is, therefore, one of astrology itself. Attached to this debate is the question of how the Magi came to know of the Messiah and his birth at all; especially if astrology is neither true nor sanctioned by the Bible as some affirm.

Other debates related to the Magi are addressed elsewhere. Here only the debate as to the identity of the Magi, how they came to know of Jesus, and of their apparent use of astrology will be discussed.

The Magi

The first part of the question is "who were the Magi?" Tradition ascribed kingship to them and yet nothing in the Bible bestows such a title to them. H.A. Ironside believes that this tradition arose from a desire by some church fathers to place the prophecy of Psalms 72:10 at the first coming.[163] In fact, it is clear that the prophecy corresponds to the Second Coming of Christ. Let us consider that passage:

> "Let the kings of Tarshish and of the islands bring presents; the kings of Sheba and Seba offer gifts. And let all kings bow down before him, all nations serve him" (Psalms 72:10-11).

This cannot refer to the first coming, for the Magi are explicitly said to come "from the east" (Matthew 2:1). However, of these three nations referred to in the Psalms, and ascribed to the Magi by tradition, none can be legimately said to be "from the east." Sheba and Seba are to the south in southern Arabia and perhaps part of Ethiopia. Tarshish is a sea port city to the *west* of Israel! How then can they be said to be the kings of these countries? Moreover, had they been kings they would doubtless have brought a large entourage (as in Tissot's famous painting below), but the Bible says nothing of the sort.[164] Additionally, the Bible seems clear that they all came from the same country; not multiple countries (cf. Matthew 2:12). More importantly, they are called "Magi."

James Tissot – The Magi - 1894

The "Magi were primarily known as the priestly-political class of the Parthians."[165] These Parthians roughly correspond to modern day Iran. According to Herodotus the Magi were Median priest.[166] These priests were "the astrologers, interpreters of dreams, medical men, necromancers, etc."[167] Yes, they did practice astrology,[168] and were said to be "experts in the study of the stars."[169]   They were also monotheistic, being descended from the Zoroastrianist sect.[170]   This religion was, in fact, a blend of Judaism's monotheistic principles and the old Persian religions. Its "prophet" arose at a time when the Jews were in exile in Persia,[171] thus it does seem apparent that Judiasm was an influence upon him, although the religion itself retained many of the old pagan traditions of Persia. Among those traditions were astrology and other divination practices forbidden in the Bible. That is why the words *magic* and *magician* are derived from the very name "Magi."[172]

Nevertheless, if it is honestly acknowledged that these Magi practiced divination and astrology, even having claimed to have been guided to Bethlehem by a star, then the question of the Bible's view of astrology, and even divination, must be addressed, for it is a legitimate inquiry. Let us, therefore, examine these issues individually.

Astrology in the Bible

Some astrological practitioners claim the Bible not only does not forbid astrology but go so far as to say that astrology is practiced in the Bible. Of course some of the arguments are frivolous such as the sometimes used internet myth that Jesus' references to the end of the "age" refer to the coming of the "age of the Zodiac." Any serious student of the Bible knows that the "age" to which Jesus referred is synonymous with the "time of the gentiles" (Luke 21:24) and has nothing to do with astrological "ages," to which Jesus never makes a single references. Nevetheless, there are some passages to which astrologers point as affirmation of their practices. Let us examine all the relevant passages.

Passages "for" Astrology
The passages usually quoted "in favor" of astrology in the Bible are Genesis 1:14, Judges 5:20, Matthew 2:1-2, and Luke 21:25. Of course an examination of these passages reveals nothing of the sort. Consider Genesis 1:14 which reads, "Let there be lights in the expanse of the heavens to separate the day from the night, and let them be for signs, and for seasons, and for days and years." Now the astrologers take all references to "signs" as proof of astrology, but we must first, with all honesty distiquish between astro*logy* and astro*nomy*. The stars are obvious a sign "and for seasons and for days and years." This is simple astronomy. We can tell the seasons and times by looking at the stars, but astro*logy* is much more than astronomy. Astrology is a system of beliefs, one might say a theology, about the stars. It is therefore invalid to quote astronomical verses as proof of astrology's assersions.

The second verse referred to by astrologers is Judges 5:20. The passage says "the stars fought from heaven, from their courses they fought against Sisera." First and foremost, there is nothing in the context to support an astrological reading of "the stars fought from heaven." This is a "song of Praise" which describes the battle in poetic terms.[173] Stars in such passages often refer to angels, implying that the angels were fighting for Israel. Contextually there is nothing to infer that the solar alignment of the stars had anything to do with the victory, and there is no mention of the stars "aligning" as one would expect if the passage were referring to astrology.

Luke.21:25 says "there shall be signs in the sun, and in the moon, and in the stars." This, astrologers say, it a clear reference to astrological signs, or is it? Any student of the Bible knows that the "signs" to which Luke 21 referred are described specifically in the book of Revelation. They could be referred to as "omens" and there is nothing in the Bible to deny that God can, and does, send omens in the sky. Nevertheless, this argument again fails to distinguish between astrology and astronomy. Astrology is a specific philosophical, even theological, interpretation of the stars, constellations, and their effect upon our "fates" or "destinies." This is what the Bible rejects. Astronomy, and even omens sent by God, are not rejected. This is the same debate into which we enter with the Magi and which will be discussed in greater detail below.

Finally, Matthew 2:1-2 is, of course, the passage under discussion. Having looked at these passages it is clear that nothing explicitly makes reference to astrology, as opposed to astronomy, and one of them is actually symbolic of the angels in heaven and does not refer to the solor stars or constellations at all. Now let us examine the passages against the practice of astrology.

Passages Against Astrology

Now the astrologer lists the four passages above as "proof" of the Biblical endorsement of astrology, but the passages which speak against astrology are far more clear. Leviticus 19:26 and Deuteronomy 18:10-12 both forbid the practice of divination. Of course, divination, as the term was applied in those days, did include astrology. Nevertheless, the astrologer might argue that there is nothing in those commandment to explicitly forbid astrology. That said, two other passages make stronger and more clear arguments against.

Jeremiah 10:2-3 warns the people, "do not be terrified by the signs of the heavens, although the nations are terrified by them, for the customs of the peoples are delusion." In this case the "customs" of those who are in awe of "the signs of the heavens" appears to be that of astrology, but Isaiah 47:13-14 is even more explicit, calling the practice by name.

Isaiah 47:13-14 says, "let now the astrologers, those who prophesy by the stars, those who predict by the new moons, stand up and save you from what will come upon you. Behold, they have become like stubble, fire burns them; they cannot deliver themselves from the power of the flame; there will be no coal to warm by." Here the astrologers are called by name, and mocked as God's wrath is forewarned upon the people of Babylon.

Conclusion

Astro*nomy* and astro*logy* are two different fields. There is no doubt that astrologers are accute astronomers, but an astronomer is not necessarily an astrologer. There is an old saying, "a Ford is a car. Not all cars are Fords." Having said this, it is true that the Magi practiced astrology and the Bible itself declares that they were guided to Israel by a star. Consequently, we cannot so easily dismiss the use of astrology in this case. A closer examination is necessary.

The Sign of the Messiah

The Bible does not tell us exactly how the Magi came to Israel. It only tells us that they were guided by a "star." Although there has been much speculation upon this and what constellations might have guided them, we are reminded that the Bible "does not say stars – but star."[174] It is not an astrological constellation or alignment of stars (plural) but a single solitary star. How did a "star" guide them? Many theories exist to explain this. The great Christian astronomer and scientist Johan Kepler[175] speculated that it could have been a comet or meteor,[176] but if this were so, it does not provide a complete answer. Why does a comet tell the Magi that the Messiah is to be born in Israel? The answer may be a combination of things.

The Royal Star

Erasmus suggested that what the Magi saw was "the star that the prophecy of Balaam had shown would arise."[177] This "royal star"[178] is described in Numbers 24:17-19, but it is really a star?

> "I see him, but not now; I behold him, but not near; A star shall come forth from Jacob, and a scepter shall rise from Israel, and shall crush through the forehead of Moab, and tear down all the sons of Sheth. And Edom shall be a possession, Seir, its enemies, also shall be a possession, while Israel performs valiantly. One from Jacob shall have dominion" (Numbers 24:17-19).

The "star" appears to be Jesus Himself, and not a real star at all, for the "One from Jacob" is synonymous with the "star from Jacob" and the "sceptre from Israel" which all acknowledge is the Messiah. Erasmus is here separating the star from the Messiah, making it the sign which the Magi saw. It is possible that this is what the Magi saw?

If this were true it would be interesting that a pagan and disobedient prophet like Balaam prophesied an event that would guide pagan priests to come honor the Messiah. In both cases it is clear that gentile salvation is foreshadowed. Even those who were then worshipping the stars were called to Him who can redeem them from their sins.

Regardless of whether or not this was what Balaam prophesied, the fact is that "in the years 5 to 2 B.C. there was an unusual astronomical phenomenon. In these years ... the dog star rose heliacally, that is at sunrise, and shone with extradodinary brillance."[179] Most scholars agree that Jesus was born between the end of 5 B.C. and early 4 B.C. A few attempt to place Jesus' birth earlier,[180] but the weight of evidence favors late 5 B.C. or early 4 B.C.

Of course we cannot know what star it was that the Magi saw, but we do know they were guided by a star, so the greater question is why the appearance of a star, whether the dog star or something else, would lead them to believe that a Messiah was to be born in Israel. This is the part of the story that too many astrology advocates neglect.

The Prophecy of Daniel
Stanley Toussaint calls the Magi an "honorable class of astrologers ... acquainted with Old Testament prophecies."[181] He believes, as do others, that they were acquainted with prophecies of Daniel.[182] There is no doubt that the Zoroastrians were influenced by Judaism during the time of the exile in Persia. The "prophet" Zarathushtra himself arose in Persia at the time that many Jews were serving in the Persian courts.[183] Shortly before Cyrus the Great had even read the prophesies of Isaiah[184] and retained Daniel the Prophet as a high court official. Consequently, some suggest that the Magi could have "worked out the great time prophecy of Daniel"[185] or some other prophetic writings.[186]

There seems no doubt that many in Judea were expecting the coming of the Messiah. The Qumran community (known best for the Dead Sea Scrolls they collected) expected the Messiah was to be born sometime between 3 B.C. and 2 A.D.[187] Some theologians believe that Daniel predicted the birth of the Messiah, but did he? Many believe that Daniel's prophecy was about the death of Jesus and not his birth.

I will not repeat the lengthy debate found in my previous volume, *Controversies in the Prophets*, but I shall here repeat my conclusions. Daniel 9 prophesies the time until the Messiah would come. Although some, such as the church fathers Tertullian and Hippolytus, date the prophecy of Daniel 9 to the birth of Christ.[188] However, this cannot be true. First, the prophecy is about the time when the Messiah will be "cut off and have nothing" (vs. 26). To be born is not to be cut off. Instead an angel brought tiding of great joy (Luke 2:10) and Mary greatly rejoiced (Luke 1:46-56). Isaiah had predicted the happy event (Isaiah 7:14) and wisemen from afar came to worship the child of prophecy (cf. Matt. 2:1-12). Nothing in the text seems to imply being "cut off" or "having nothing" (vs. 26). Indeed, the wisemen even brought gifts worth great wealth (Matt. 2:11). Secondly, and more importantly, the numbers do not work out correct.

Without reentering the debate (see *Controversies in the Prophets* and/or *Controversies in Revelation* for a full discussion of this debate) it need only be stated here that the prophecy of Daniel 9 takes us from the second decree of Artaxerxes in March, 444 B.C. to the very week that Christ was crucified in early April, 33 A.D. The chart below details this view and shows the numerical calculations are accurate:

Hebrew/Chaldean Calendar (360 days)	Gregorian Calendar (365 days)
483 years x 360 days = 173,880 days	173,880 days / 365 days = 476.38 years

483 years x 360 days = 173,880 days
 	
Edict given in early March 444 B.C.
 	
Christ crucified April 3, 33 A.D.
	Specifically:
	   173,740 days = 476 Gregorian years
	+ 116 days in leap years
	+ 24 days between early March (when edict was given) and early April (when Christ was crucified)
	= 173,880 days or exactly 483 Hebrew years
	                      from the edict to the crucifixion!

483 years x 360 days = 173,880 days Edict given in early March 444 B.C. Passover week begins March 30, 33 A.D.	Alternately shown as: 476 x 365.24219879 days per year in the Gregorian calendar = 173,855 days + 25 days between March 5 and March 30 = 173,880 days or exactly 483 Hebrew years from the edict to Passion Week!

Consequently, while the Magi may well have been acquainted with some of the Jewish prophets, it is not likely that Daniel's prophecy was influential in their decision in and of itself. Knowing that the Messiah would be "cut off" in thirty to forty years certainly made people anticipate His birth, and Isaiah, as well as other Biblical prophets said a great deal about the coming Messiah, but by themselves the prophecies cannot explain how the Magi knew exactly when the Messiah would arive. One other key is needed.

The Legends of Asia-minor
I am reminded of the legends of the Aztecs who believed that a white god would come to liberate them from the brutality of their oppressors.[189] At the same time that those prophecies were spreading Cortez and his soldiers landed on the shores of Mexico. Although Cortez denied being a god, he led hundreds of thousands of Tlaxcalan Indians in a revolution against the Aztec empire. Now no one believes that the prophecies of the Aztecs were truly accurate, and yet there is no doubt that God prepared the people of Mexico for what was to come. God often uses even pagan "prophets," such as Balaam, to achieve His ends. The same was true in the Middle East at the time of Christ.

Lord Rawlinson noted that Cuniform inscriptions found on astrological tablets reported that a great king would arise in the west to bring peace.[190] As astrologers there can be no doubt that the Magi knew of this prophecy and were expecting it. The pagan historian Suetonius further records that "there had spread all over the Orient an old and established belief that it was fated at that time for men coming from Judea to rule the world"[191] and Tacitus said "there was a firm persuasion that at the very time the east was to grow powerful and rulers coming from Judea were to acquire a universal empire."[192]

In short, God prepared not only the Jews but also the unbelieving gentile world for the coming of His Son. The legends of Asia-minor prove that Jesus was not only for the Jews but for the whole world. God was preparing all for the reception of His Son.

Conclusion

Some theologians dismiss the astrology of the Magi by simply saying that "in those ancient days all men believed in astrology."[193] Of course we must distinguish between astrology and astronomy, but there is no doubt that the Magi were astrologers. Does this serve as an endorsement of astrology? No. God uses us all, just as God used the pagan prophet Balaam. God does not discriminate, but neither does He approve of our practices anymore than He approves of our sins.

God meets us where we are. That does not mean that God wants us to stay where we are. He wants us to come to where He is. This is part of the lesson of the Magi. They foreshadow gentile salvation and demonstrate that the Jews were not the only ones to whom Jesus came. While Herod tried to murder Jesus, pagan astrologers came to worship Him. Salvation had come "to the Jew first but also to the gentile" (Romans 1:16).

The Magi and the Shephards
Matthew 2:1-12 – Luke 2:8-20

"Where is He who has been born King of the Jews? For we saw His star in the east, and have come to worship Him ... they came into the house and saw the Child with Mary His mother; and they fell down and worshiped Him; and opening their treasures they presented to Him gifts of gold and frankincense and myrrh."

"And in the same region there were *some* shepherds staying out in the fields, and keeping watch over their flock by night. And an angel of the Lord suddenly stood before them ... they came in haste and found their way to Mary and Joseph, and the baby as He lay in the manger."

The image of the Magi together with the shepherds in the manger is ingrained upon the minds of all who have ever watched a Christmas movie or television special, but the critic here sees a contradiction. The Biblical scholar agrees ... to a degree. It is not a Biblical contradiction so much as it is a contradiction within the Hollywood interpretation; an interpretation which was created for artistic reasons more than Biblical accuracy.

The first thing we notice is that Luke records the story of the shepherds in the manger and says nothing of the Magi whereas Matthew speaks of the Magi and says nothing of the shepherds. Certainly if both were present at the manger then this would be a problem, but there is good reason to believe that the Magi did not arrive until weeks, some say a year, after Jesus' birth.

First, "in Matthew it is a house where the child is found, in Luke there was no room at the inn"[194] so they had to stay at the barn or manger. In addition to the difference in location, some argue that "the child must have been about a year old"[195] for when Herod sought to slaughter the children of Bethlehem he ordered all children under two years of age to be killed "according to the time which he had ascertained from the magi" (Matthew 2:16). If Jesus had only just been born then why kill two year old children? Could Herod have been concerned that his soldiers would mistake Jesus for an older child? My older brother did not learn to walk until he was two years old, whereas I was walking at nine months. A soldier is not a nanny, so Herod wanted to make sure that no child was left alive. Nevertheless, it is argued that the Magi's journey must have taken some time and hence when Herod attempted to ascertain the "time" the star appeared, he obviously *assumed* that the child was born at that time. Finally, Luke records that Jesus was presented to the Temple "when the days for their purification according to the law of Moses were completed" (Luke 2:21-38). However, after the Magi visit Joseph, Mary, and Jesus fled to Egypt (Matthew 2:13-15). They then remained there until after the death of Herod. This, it is argued, does not allow time for the presentation at the temple unless the Magi appeared much later.

Now in fairness, this scenario, though well accepted throughout the scholarly community does have some problems. For one thing, Herod died in 4 B.C., the same year that most scholars place the birth of Christ Jesus. God's wrath upon Herod for the crime at Bethlehem was immediate and severe. He died a horrible death, having been subjected to a disease which even resulted in "his privy-member [being] putrified, and produced worms" or maggots.[196] It is for this very reason that some attempt to push the birth of Christ back to as early as 6 B.C.[197] but why? Would Joseph and Mary be living in Bethlehem for a year or more when the registration for the census need only take a week or two? Moreover, Luke declares that after the Temple ceremony "when they had performed everything according to the Law of the Lord, they returned to Galilee, to their own city of Nazareth" (Luke 2:39). How then is it that the Magi appear at Bethlehem rather than Nazareth? It is logical that Joseph and Mary would have rented out a house after Jesus' birth so that Mary could recover and so that they might wait for the period of purification to be complete, but would they have waited over a year when their home was in Nazareth? The registration for the census would not have required them to stay indefinitely and it would not be practical for Rome to require such.

Logically, the Temple ceremony could have taken place after the flight to Egypt, since Herod died only a few months (if that long) after their flight. Consider the words of Luke carefully. It says "when the days for their purification according to the law of Moses were completed, they brought Him up to Jerusalem to present Him to the Lord" (Luke 2:22). Now the Law of purification is as follows; "she shall remain in the blood of *her* purification for thirty-three days; she shall not touch any consecrated thing, nor enter the sanctuary, until the days of her purification are completed" (Leviticus 12:4). So she could *not* have taken her son to the Temple for *at least* a month after Jesus' birth. It does not say *how long* after the days of purification were complete. Although some claim that Jesus must have been presented immediately, there is *nothing* in the Law of Moses which deliniates a time constraint. It is possible that the Temple ceremony did take place after the flight to Egypt, as seems to be indicated by their return to Nazareth rather than Bethlehem.

Having said this, there is no doubt that the Magi did not arrive at the manger, but after a time when Joseph and Mary had rented out a house. How long transpired here is unknown. If Jesus was born in late winter of 5 B.C. or early 4 B.C. as believed by most,[198] then there was as much as four months between the birth of Christ and the death of Herod. Can all these events fit into this narrative? The answer is a definitive, "yes."

The "Twelve days of Christmas" as celebrated in the east reflects the tradition that the Magi arrived on January 6, twelve days after Jesus' birth. This is perfectly consistent with the narrative. Herod's order for children two years and under was to insure that Jesus was killed for they did not have birth records in those days and had no way of knowing exactly how old a child was. Since it is hard to tell a child's age simply by looking at them, all children younger than two were ordered killed to insure the child did not escape. Finally, it is not logical to assume that Joseph and Mary had to stay in a stable for weeks. They had come to register for the census and no other reason. Because Jesus was just born it would not be good to travel back to Nazareth so soon, thus they found a house to rent out as soon as possible. It was there that the Magi appeared twelve days later. Mary and Joseph were probably planning on moving on as soon as Mary was strong enough, so it is not likely that they would have stayed in Bethlehem more than a month anyway. Finally, Herod's orders make clear that he believed the baby was probably still in Bethlehem. He wanted to leave no stone unturned.

A complete chronology of the events could be as follows. Jesus was born, by tradition (for the sake of argument I do not debate this here, but see

"When Was the Census? [Questions on the Birthdate of Jesus] Luke 2:1" for a critique),[199] on December 25. If the Magi then arrived twelve days later on January 6 as accepted by eastern Christians, the flight to Egypt may have taken place in late January. Herod's death was in April of that same year, 4 B.C., allowing Joseph and Mary to return after "the days for their purification according to the law of Moses were completed" and present Jesus to the Temple. They could easily have presented Jesus to the High Priests by the end of May which was well within the law and consistent with the Biblical accounts (See chart "Sequence of the Nativity Events" under Luke 2:22-39). They would then have returned to their native home in Nazareth as Luke explicitly says. This is all perfectly consistent with the Bible, with tradition, and with history.

A Misquote of Micah?
Matthew 2:6 – Micah 5:2-4

"You, Bethlehem, Land of Judah, are by no means least among the leaders of Judah; for out of you shall forth a ruler, who will shepherd My people Israel."	"But as for you, Bethlehem Ephrathah, *too* little to be among the clans of Judah. From you One will go forth for Me to be ruler in Israel."

This passage is actually a quotation by the rabbis who were telling Herod about the prophecy of the Messiah. Some see an obvious contradiction between the quotation and the actual verse, but this must be examined from two perspectives. First, we should remember that Matthew is quoting the priests here and thus his purpose is to accurately record what they said, not necessarily whether or not they were right. Having said that, Christians and Jews are in agreement as to the prophecy itself so it is not sufficient to dismiss the quotation as mere "Midrash interpretation."[200] We must, therefore, examine the passages in context.

It must be acknowledged that no Rabbi denied that the Messiah was to be born in Bethlehem. This is not some theory adopted by Christians to fit the birth of Christ but an ancient Rabbinical tradition. As Matthew Henry said, "it was universally known among the Jews that Christ should come out of the town of Bethlehem."[201] Here, as in John 7:42, the rabbis allude to the Aramaic Targum's loose translation of Micah 5:1, "out of you shall come forth before me the Messiah."[202] The quote by them is a paraphrase and not an exactly word for word quote, but this does not fully solve the problem. The rabbis said "You, Bethlehem, Land of Judah, are by no means least" whereas Micah actually said, "you, Bethlehem Ephrathah, are little." So we are faced with the seeming contradiction of whether or not Bethlehem is "by no means least" or is "little." Some, said Matthew Poole, "read [Micah] as an interrogation, 'Art thou little?' Which ought to be resolved by a negative, Thou art not little, and so reconcile

Matt. ii. 6."[203] But there is a better answer which is not really hard when we acknowledge that the rabbis were paraphrasing Micah.

To this very day the modern Jewish translation of Micah 5:1 read that "one shall come forth [from Bethlehem] to rule Israel for Me." That Bethlehem was indeed a tiny city and a small clan "too little to be counted among the clans of Judah" is denied by none, but here the rabbis emphasize that because the Messiah comes from Bethlehem she should not consider herself small for, in fact, she was "by no means the least." The priests were contrasting the greatness of Bethlehem with her actual size. Given that it was a paraphrasistic rendering of the prophecy and not an actual quote of Micah this makes perfect sense.

Too much has been said over the technical "contradiction" of their quotation rather than acknowledging the great irony of history and prophecy. Although Bethlehem was indeed "too small to be counted among the clans" God chose her to be great for from her would come the Messiah. As Saint Jerome remarked, this is "a sentiment in harmony with that of the apostle. 'God hath chosen the weak things of the world to confound the things which are mighty.'"[204] Bethlehem is, therefore, "by no means the least" but greatly honored indeed. The actual quote from Micah supports the Biblical account, for it reads in full;

> "'As for you, Bethlehem Ephrathah, *too* little to be among the clans of Judah, from you One will go forth for Me to be ruler in Israel. His goings forth are from long ago, from the days of eternity.' Therefore, He will give them *up* until the time when she who is in labor has borne a child. Then the remainder of His brethren will return to the sons of Israel. And He will arise and shepherd *His flock* In the strength of the LORD."

This is the prophecy which both Jew and Christian agree demonstrates that the Messiah would be born in Bethlehem. Bethlehem, though small, would become great among all the clans of Judah, for the Messiah was to born there! As Tertullian pointed out, no other "leader" has ever come from Bethlehem since.[205] How could they? Bethlehem is now a Muslim city! Could the Messiah be born in Bethlehem today? No. He was born two thousand years ago in a humble town of a humble clan in a humble manger.

A Misquote of Hosea?
Matthew 2:15 – Hosea 11:1

"What was spoken by the Lord through the prophet might be fulfilled, saying, 'Out of Egypt I call My Son.'"	"When Israel *was* a youth I loved him, and out of Egypt I called My son."

Matthew takes this as a prophecy of Jesus. He calls it a prophecy of Christ's return from Egypt where he fled as a child to escape Herod's wrath. "Out of Egypt I called my Son." Within the context of Matthew, the application seems appropriate and logical. The problem is that the passage is a quotation of Hosea 11:1 whose immediate context is one of judgment upon Israel. God is reminding Israel of her former days when she was a slave in Egypt and how God liberated her. So was Israel the son called out of Egypt, or was Jesus?

Bible scholars, past and present, are divided as to how to take Matthew's application. John Calvin, for example, takes this solely as a "comparison" by Matthew[206] and completely rejects any literal prophetic application.[207] Others argue for a symbolic or typological meaning.[208] Still others, like Matthew Henry, merge the typological view with a prophetic view, saying "the words have a double aspect, speaking historically of the calling of Israel out of Egypt and prophetically of the bringing of Christ thence."[209] This view is best represented by the words of John Wesley, "Israel the first adopted son was a type of Christ the first-born. And the history of Israel's coming out was a type of Christ's future coming out of Egypt."[210] Still, a third view is prevalent; a literal dual fulfillment.

I will breifly define dual prophecy for those unfamiliar with the term. Prophecies sometimes have dual fulfillments or what Dwight Pentecost calls the "law of double reference."[211] This means that some prophecies have two applications; the one close and immediate, and the other distant and future.[212] Many examples can be found in the Old Testament (*see Controversies in the Prophets* for more). This is one. Hosea is speaking to the Jews of his day in an immediate context of Israel, but the larger application is to the distant future of God's Son, Christ. How do we know this?

It is ironic that Saint Jerome, one of the biggest spiritualizers in Christendom history, actually provides us with the best argument for a literal application. He notes that the Hebrew text uses the singular word for "son"![213] While the Orthodox Jew would doubtless respond that Israel is being referred to as a singular entity[214] this argument is fundamentally flawed for when Israel is referred to the collective sense it is referred to as she in the feminine form (cf. Isaiah 1:21, 54:6, 66:7-8, Jeremiah 3:6-9, 12:8, 33:16, Lamentations 1:1-10, Ezekiel 16:48, 19:2-5, to name but a few)! Even the Targum, which represents Jewish interpretation, wrongly uses the plural form of sons here,[215] because they know that Israel can only be a "she" if used in the collective sense. In short, if Israel was the only literal subject of the prophecy then it would either have used the plural form of sons or the pronoun she as it does elsewhere else including Hosea! The "son" is singular because it refers quite literally to the Messiah, although the primary context does indeed agree with Israel's captivity to Egypt in times past.

To quote John Gill, the passage refers not only to Israel but also to Christ "not by way of allusion ... or as the type ... but literally."[216] This was the

41

view of the apostle Matthew and the choice of using the singular form of "son" substantiates the apostle's statement. The "son" has a dual meaning for both Israel and Christ.

The Slaughter of Children
Matthew 2:16-18

"When Herod saw that he had been tricked by the magi, he became very enraged, and sent and slew all the male children who were in Bethlehem and in all its environs, from two years old and under."

The story of Herod's slaughter of the innocents is ingrained upon the memory of every child. It typifies the barbarity and cruelty of the puppet king of Israel who feared that a small child would someday usurp his throne. It is also a story that secular Bible critics believe never happened. Desperate to attack any event in the Bible that cannot be verified from secular sources, the critic argues that this is a pure myth, but is it? Furthermore, what does the prophecy of Ramah have to do with the slaughter of the children in Bethlehem? These are the two controversies of Matthew 2:16-18.

The Slaughter of the Innocents

The Bible critic claims that the story of the slaughter of the innocents is a fable made up by the apostle Matthew. They offer no evidence except for the "similarity" of the account with that of Moses and the inherently weak evidence from silent argument, saying that Josephus would surely have recorded the incident had it truly happened. In fact, any serious scholar who has ever read Josephus knows that the Biblical account rings true. Why then did Josephus not record this event? Let us examine the facts.

On the similarities between Moses and Jesus' birth, they are just that, similarities. The differences far outweigh the similarities. It should serve as no surprise that there are similarities in the story for the student of history knows that slaughting children to prevent future heirs or a rising slave population was not a rare or unheard of event in antiquity. Such deeds occurred throughout history. It is, therefore, no surprise that there are similarities in the stories. Have the critics forgotten yet another similar incident recorded in 2 Kings 11:1? The claim that Matthew borrowed from the story of Moses is like claiming that George Washington "borrowed" the story of the American Revolution from the Cromwell Revolution! Revolutions happen. Dictators had no qualms killing innocent children. Indeed, it was the "safest" way to insure their throne rather than wait until the children were old enough to start their own uprising. It is also why children were invariably slaughtered upon the conquest of various cities and providences throughout the ancient realm. The kings wanted to insure that the children did not grow up to avenge their parents.

What then of Josephus' "silence" on the issue? Part of that has already been answered. These events were *not* rare. They were somewhat common. Beyond this fact, nevertheless, lie other reasons. For one thing, it has been duly noted that the "slaughter of infants two years or less in a town of the size of Bethlehem (population ca. 300) ... would be ... a comparatively minor incident"[217] in Herod's reign. Josephus was not writing an exhaustive history.

Bethlehem itself was only two hours distant from Jerusalem.[218] It was "a small and obscure village"[219] at the time. "Even today only about 20,000 people live there."[220] Estimates on how many children were killed in the slaughter vary. Some say "Bethlehem was not a large town, and the number of the children would not exceed from twenty to thirty babies."[221] Note that this number includes "Bethlehem and *all the neighborhood.*"[222] With only around three hundred people living in Bethlehem we should not expect much more than a dozen children that age. Including the environs of Bethlehem, the number thirty seems a fair number for the maximum number of children killed.[223] Now obviously this is not trivial, but let us examine exactly what Josephus does say about Herod.

Aside from the great many atrocities commited by Herod of the years, Josephus writes about the approaching death of Herod. This is significant for it sheds light on Herod's mindset and offers clues as to why the event of Bethlehem took a back seat to Herod's other plots at that time. There should be no doubt that the slaughter of the innocents took place in early 4 B.C., probably less than a month after Jesus' birth. Herod would die three to four months later in April. During that time Josephus records that Herod was stressed because he knew that he would die without mourning and that the people would have a festival to celebrate his death, so he sent out orders to the "whole nation"[224] that every prominent family head should come to Jerusalem and the death penalty was pronounced on any who refused. When they arrived they were promply arrested and thrown in the Hippodrome where orders were left that on the day of Herod's death they should all be slain in order that their might be weeping and sorrow in the land of Israel on that day! This Josephus records in both *Antiquities of the Jews*[225] and in *War of the Jews.*[226] Should we be surprised that with the imminent death of thousands of prominent families hanging over their heads, Josephus should neglect the slaughter of twenty to thirty children?

The Bible critic, as usual, acts not as a juror but as a defense lawyer, trying deperately to cast doubt upon the eyewitness' testimony, but the objective juror weighs all the evidence. If the critic wishes to make an argument from the silence of Josephus then I shall make an argument upon the silence of the ancient Bible critic for *no* Bible critic of antiquity ever denied the historicity of this event.

In short, the slaughter of the innocents was one of a series of events by Herod late in his life when he was slaying any and all whom he felt threatened his reign. Some have dared to say that this was "a just punishment of Bethlehem for their treatment of the blessed virgin and her young child, by inhumanly refusing to entertain her"[227] while others have called these children martyrs.[228] The event, never denied by any historian or critic of ancient times, rings true and is in perfect keeping with the facts laid out in Josephus' abridged history of Herod.

Jeremiah 31:15

Matthew further says "that which was spoken through Jeremiah the prophet was fulfilled, saying,

> "A voice was hear in Ramah, weeping and great mourning;
> Rachel weeping for her children, and she refused to be comforted; because they were no more."

Some translations read "Jeremy" rather than Jeremiah because the original Greek uses Jeremy, but "'Jeremy' is a translation of the Greek form of Jeremiah."[229] The quotation itself is from Jeremiah 31:15 but the passage does not appear to have anything to do with Bethlehem at all! Some, like MacArthur, sees the prophecy solely as typological,[230] meaning that it is a prophecy which serves as a symbol or comparison but does not have anything specifically to do with Bethlehem. Stanley Toussaint, however, takes another approach arguing that "Matthew never in chapter two says a *prophecy* is being fulfilled. In guarded language he writes that the events occured that *the words spoken through the prophets might be fulfilled*."[231] This argument seems to be a semantic one though it is one which does not really answer the question. How can the prophets words be fulfilled if the prophecy has nothing to do with Bethlehem? Is this an example of the "law of double reference."

A careful examination of the entire prophecy of Jeremiah provides a better explanation and demonstrates that Matthew's application is a valid in the proper context. Jeremiah chapter thirty-one begins with the simple promise, "I will be the God of all the families of Israel, and they shall be My people" (vs. 1), and in verse twelve, "they shall never languish again." But Israel did languish again. For 1900 years they languished among the nations, scattered from Russia to the Americas. For this reason verse eight declares, "I will gather them from the remote parts of the earth." Now it is important to note that the return to Israel under Cyrus was hardly "from the remote parts of the earth." Only in 1948 did the Jews literally return "from the remote parts of the earth." It is for this reason that H. A. Ironside believes this to be a prophecy of the "tribulation period" of the book of Revelation.[232] Nevertheless, it is apparent that there are Messianic overtones to the prophecy which ends with the promise of a "new covenant" in verses 31-40. Consequently, Jeremiah 31's ultimate fulfillment takes place in connection to the Messiah. It is in that context that Matthew refers to the slaughter of children in Bethlehem.

In verse sixteen the Lord tells Rachel, "restrain your voice from weeping, and your eyes from tears." The immediate promise was the first return of the Jews from Babylon, but the larger fulfillment is in the redemption of Israel which takes place after their second exile, but whose covenant blood (see next section below) was first shed at the first coming. Henceforth, there are dual references to both the first coming of Christ and the ultimate restoration of Israel in the End Times.

Consequently, the prophecy is actually a grand overview of Israel and its people and God's promise of restoration. Ramah itself was a city near Jerusalem and "it was here that the Jewish captives were assembled in chains."[233] Thus the initial prophecy makes an allusion to the weeping of mothers for their children who were being deported to Babylon, but there are clearly elements of the prophecy which relate to the Messiah and God's promise to restore the people of Israel. Jesus' birth was the first step in that process, so Matthew applies Ramah's weeping to the children of Bethlehem (a city not far from Ramah and probably part of a region sometimes known by that name). This is an example of the "law of double reference" and in keeping with the nature of Matthew's argument.

Conclusion

No serious scholar in the past ever doubted the atrocity of the slaughter of the innocents. Herod's character is well established in history and such deeds were common place. Similar events are recorded not only in Exodus 1 and 2 but also in 2 Kings 11:1 as well as countless events in ancient "secular" history.

Gustave Dore – Massacre of the Innocents

45

Matthew's quotation of Jeremiah is made in the context of Jeremiah's prophecy about the redempion of Israel which would come through the Messiah. The application of Ramah to Bethlehem is then acceptable in the context of a dual fulfillment.

The slaughter of the innocents demonstrates that Herod recognized Jesus was the Messiah and feared loosing his throne. In his fit of fear and madness the dying old man sought to slaughter everyone he viewed as a threat and such is recorded by Josephus. The fact that Josephus does not record each and every example of this attempt to suppress future heirs or usurpers is irrelevant for Josephus did not write exhaustively. Herod's last deed in life was to order the execution of quite literally thousands of prominent family members throughout Israel! The slaughter of the innocents cannot be denied ... or forgotten.

Prophecy of the Nazarene
Matthew 2:23

"He departed for the regions of Galilee, and came and resided in a city called Nazareth, that what was spoken through the prophets might be fulfilled, 'He shall be called a Nazarene.'"

Here again is a quotation by Matthew that critics call suspect. The biggest problem is that the prophecy does not appear to be in the Old Testament. No where are the words "He shall be called a Nazarene" found in the Scriptures outside of Matthew. Critics, of course, use this passage in a number of ways to cast doubt upon the Old Testament canon or upon Matthew's credibility, but neither arguments are valid. The Old Testament canon had clearly been well establish by the time of Jesus (see Appendix B in *Controversies in the Pentateuch* for a detailed discussion). The real debate is to what and whom was Matthew referring?

We must first acknowledge that Matthew "does not say '*by the prophet*,' ... but '*by the prophets*' meaning no one in particular."[234] Says John MacArthur, "because Matthew speaks of the *prophets*, plural, it seems that several prophets had made this prediction, though it is not specfiically recorded in the Old Testament."[235] But this is not a sufficient answer in itself. Linski has pointed that "no λεγων precedes οτι, which shuts out not only a direct quotation but also an indirect prophetic utterance."[236] He suggests, as do others, that Matthew is referring to the "the general character of the prophecies"[237] and that it "cannot refer to *one* prophet."[238] MacArthur compares Matthew's quotation to the book of Jude which draws upon extra-Biblical legends,[239] but this is still not a sufficient answer. It can be agreed that Matthew is not referring to a single prophet or quoting from the Old Testament, but he is obviously quoting *something*. What?

One possibility is a touchy subject. As Christians we believe that every prophecy of the Bible is inspired and the Word of God, but are their extra-Biblical prophecies? This notion disturbs some for there are certainly a plethora of false prophets and heretics throughout history. From Nostradomus to the Millerites there are those who have imitated the Biblical gift of prophecy and been found sadly wanting, and in so doing leading many astray. Consequently, many Christians refuse to acknowledge that prophecy can exist beyond the Bible.[240] In fact, Jude 14 specifically quotes an extra-Biblical prophecy! Balaam was a pagan prophet who uttered both false, and sometimes true, prophetic words. God has sometimes chosen to speak through pagans as he did with Balaam, but here it is the "prophets" who prophesy and not pagans. To what could Matthew refer?

According to Jewish tradition Adam, after being cast out of Eden, prophesied that the world be destroyed once by water, and once by fire.[241] This prophecy is found in Josephus but not in the Bible. So also it would appear that the Jews had long accepted, by multiple prophets, that there was a prophecy that "He shall be called a Nazarene." That this tradition is not longer extant is of no significance, for the historian is well aware that only the tiniest fragment of ancient books have survived to the present. Nevertheless, many disagree with this and look for the prophecy, in a general sense, in the Old Testament. In order to find the answer one must ask the natural question, "what does the prophecy mean?"

To this end several theories have originated as to the meaning of the prophecy and its connection to the Old Testament prophets. Each has its own strengths and weakness, leading some to take the plural of "prophets" as proof that all the theories have an element of truth, but no one in particular, is true. Let us examine them:

1. Jesus was of the Nazirite sect

Numbers 6 outlines the law of the Nazirites. These were men or women who made "a special vow, the vow of a Nazirite, to dedicate himself to the LORD." The actual Hebrew word is *nazir* (נָזִיר) which mean "separated one"[242] or "conscrated" one.[243] However, it is by no means certain that the name Nazareth is derived from this word. In fact, some argue that Nazarene is derived from *natzar* (נָצַר) meaning to "watch" or "keep."[244] The argument is that because *netzer* (נֵצֶר), from *natzar* (נָצַר), means "branch,"[245] the reference is to Isaiah 11:1. This theory will be addressed more fully below. Here it is only necessary to point out that because the word "Nazareth" is not found in the Old Testament, its actual etymology is unknown. John Calvin argued that "Matthew does not derive Nazarene from Nazareth"[246] at all, but by way of "allusion."[247] He believed that Nazarene came from "the word נזיר [which] means holy and consecrated to God."[248]

47

If we accept this, as seems acceptable from a linguistic standpoint, then there still remain problems. The Nazirite sect was restricted by their vows in the Law of Moses. According to Numbers 6 a Nazirite for the duration of his vow was forbidden to drink wine, to cut his hair, or to touch dead bodies. Critics have pointed out that Jesus did drink wine,[249] not only in Cana (John 2:1-10) before the start of His ministry, but also in Matthew 11:19 and at the Last Supper. Furthermore, it is argued that Jesus came into contact with dead bodies in several instances, but this is a poor argument. Ignoring the fact that Jesus resurrected those dead, sometimes without even touching them (cf. John 11:43), Samson was also a Nazirite but he not only came into contact with the dead, but personally sent many to their deaths! Obviously, the fact that Jesus resurrected the dead was not a violation of the law if Samson's causing men to die was not a violation of the law! As for Jesus' hair, we cannot say whether or not he truly had long hair as depicted in art and film, but if He were a Nazirite then He would have had long hair.

It seems then that the only real problems with this theory are whether or not Nazareth is derived from *nazir* (נָזִיר) and, more importantly, whether or not Jesus' use of wine serves as proof that He was not a true Nazirite. While it might be tempting to dismiss the wine, it does not seem that Jesus would violate a clear Law of Moses. Even though His critics accused Him of dismissing the Law of Moses, Jesus Himself affirmed that He did not come to abolish the Law, but to fulfill it (Matthew 5:17)! Thus even though we cannot dismiss this theory out of hand, for Jesus did vary with traditional *Mishnah* in regard to the Law's interpretation, neither can we affirm it. Is there an answer?

One variant on the Nazirite theory is the idea that Samson was a type of Christ.[250] According to this view, Samson, and Joseph as well,[251] were archetypes who represented Christ. Jesus was then called a Nazarene as the fulfillment of that typology (see notes on typology in *Controversies in the Epistles* for more). According to Matthew Poole, Joseph also was a Nazirite based on Genesis 49:26. In the Hebrew, the same word, *nazir* (נָזִיר), is found in speaking of Joseph.[252] Translation, however, vary. The ASV, RSV, and King James translate that Joseph was "separate" from among his brothers. Other translations are less literal, saying he was a "prince among his brothers" (NIV), "set apart from his brothers" (NRSV), or "distinguished among his brothers" (NAS).

In any case, it is not clear that Samsom was a type of Christ. Unlike Joseph, who would indeed make a better typological argument, Samson was an immature, violent, stubborn, and sinful warrior. Although one can draw allusions to his faith and service to God, Samson is a better example of God's grace among sinners and His willingness to use all of us, even when we are far from spiritual giants. He makes a poor archetype for Jesus, the sinless savior of the world who meekly died on the cross for our sins.

Jerry Falwell's commentary rejects this entire view saying, Nazarene is "from the city of Nazareth. It should not be taken to mean that he was a Nazirite."[253] Nonetheless, it has much in its favor. Certainly, it has strong advantages, but it also has strong disadvantages. Traditionally this has been the popular and historically attested view. From a strictly textual basis, it seems more than acceptable even if it is far from perfect. Is there a better alternative?

2. Jesus was the "branch" (from the Hebrew Netzer) of Isaiah 11:1

Arguably the most popular view among modern day evangelicals is the idea that Nazareth derives from the word *netzer* (נֵצֶר) rather than *natzar* (נָצַר) as discussed above. The relevance is that if Nazareth is connectd to *netzer* (נֵצֶר), meaning a "branch," than this would be "an allusion to Zech. iii.8, vi.12, Jer. xxiii.5 and more directly to Is. Iv.2; xi.1."[254] What does the prophecy of Isaiah 11:1 say? It says that "a shoot will spring from the stem of Jesse, and a branch from his roots will bear fruit." There are none that deny that the prophecy of Isaiah 11 is about the Messiah. He is introduced as a "shoot" or "branch" and thus many evangelicals have been eager to tie this prophecy to Isaiah.

If true it would answer all the questions. Why does Matthew say "prophets" rather than "prophet"? Because the "branch" is alluded to in Zechariah and Jeremiah as well as Isaiah. Why can we not find a prophecy which says "He shall be called a Nazarene"? Because Matthew is quoting a loose translation or *midrash* based on these prophecies! Few, if any, doubt that Isaiah 11:1, Jeremiah 23:5, Zechariah 3:8 and 6:12 refer to the Messiah. In fact, the Jewish Tanakh translation of Zechariah 6:12 actually reads, "a man called the Branch." This theory then seems solid until we look in the Hebrew and see that the word of "branch" in Zechariah 6:12 is not *netzer* (נֵצֶר) but *tzemach* (צֶמַח)! *Tzemach* (צֶמַח) also mean "branch" from *Tzamach* (צָמַח) meaning to "sprout forth." [255] Is this relevant? Yes, for we remember that the connection is through "Nazarene" from Nazareth! He is not called a "Zemachene" but a "Nazarene." Now some might say that this is splitting hairs, and it is true that because Matthew refers to "prophets" rather than a single prophet, the prophecy or perhaps *midrash* to which he referred could easily have amalgamated the synonyms together.

At first glance this appears the strongest view, but its etymology is suspect and it offers no proof that such a *midrash* ever existed. We must assume that it existed, but cannot offer proof. One might say, we have to take it on faith. Should we? Let us examine one last view before deciding.

3. Jesus was despised and rejected

Another alternate theory rest on the definition of *nazir* (נָזִיר) which, the reader will remember, means "separated one." The difference between this view and the first is that this term is taken not as a reference to the Nazirites, but as a form of reproach.[256] Taken from Psalms 22:6-9 and Isaiah 53 the word Nazarene is

49

presumed to be a variant for being despited[257] or humbled.[258] As John Wesley said, "he shall be despised and rejected, shall be a mark of public contempt and reproach."[259]

Theologically, the view seems sound and fits in perfectly with the context of John 1:46 in which it was asked, "Can any good thing come out of Nazareth?" However, this certainly seems far from an expectation that the Messiah would be a Nazarene. How could the prophecy be about the Messiah being a Nazarene if the people were shocked to see anything good from a Nazarene? Even though this view does draw a connection between Nazareth and Nazarene (which the other views fail to do in a substantive way) it is still a weak argument. The idea that it is synonymous with the Suffering Servant of Isaiah 53 fits well theologically, but it does not fit exegetically. Outside of John 1:46 there is no evidence of this application contextually. It is a good theological argument but a poor textual one.

Now aside from these views, a few other minor variants have been scattered throughout history. Erasmus' unique spin is found in his paraphrase of the gospel wherein he says, "in the Hebrew language Nazareth takes its name from a flower, because it was here that the purest little flower, consecrator of all virginity, was conceived by a virgin."[260]

Which of these views is best? At first glance the first view seems strong since Jesus was clearly consecrated to service with God. The problem is that it cannot fully explain Jesus' use of wine or the apparent connection to Nazareth. The second view seems strongest overall, particularly in light of Zechariah 6:12 which could be validly translated as "He will be called a 'Branch.'" If the ancient Jews substituted *netzer* (נֵצֶר) for *tzemach* (צֶמַח) then it might literally read, "He will be called a Netzerite"! Given that the Greek *Septuagint* translated "branch" into Greek with the word *anatole* ('Ανατολὴ) which means "One Rising from the Sun" or "One from the East" it is not out of question to see Jewish tradition making such a substitution! This only illustrates that Jewish *midrash* was not always literal, and was, in fact, often not. Both *netzer* (נֵצֶר) and *tzemach* (צֶמַח) mean "branch" so it is hardly unlikely that a *midrash* might have translated Zechariah 6:12 as "He shall be called a Nazarene." The fundamental flaw with this view is that it is pure speculation and has nothing to support it. Moreover, like the first view, it does not explain the connection to Nazareth.

Despite Calvin's claim that "Matthew does not derive Nazarene from Nazereth"[261] it seems apparent that Matthew is drawing a parallel for his gospel explicitly says that Jesus "resided in a city called Nazareth, *in order that* what was spoken through the prophets might be fulfilled." Any view which completely dismisses this cannot be valid.

Having taken all of this into consideration, it is likely that Matthew is quoting an extra-Biblical prophecy which no longer exist outside of the

50

quotation in Matthew. The prophecy may well have been *midrash* connected to the "prophets" as supposed in the second view, but it cannot have been taken solely from those passages; not even Zechariah 6:12. Now the appearance of prophecy outside of the Bible should not be alarming, for as I illustrated above, God used many people, including the pagan prophet Balaam for His Will and purpose. The prophecy was recorded by Matthew and serves its purpose. That the reference is apparently extra-Biblical should be of no more concern than of Jude's quotations from the Book of Enoch, but that is a debate reserved for Jude.

The Temptation of Christ
Matthew 4:1-10 – Mark 1:12-13 – Luke 4:1-12

"Jesus was led up by the Spirit into the wilderness to be tempted by the devil. And after He had fasted forty days and forty nights."	"And immediately the Spirit impelled Him *to go* out into the wilderness. And He was in the wilderness forty days being tempted by Satan."	"Jesus, full of the Holy Spirit, returned from the Jordan and was led about by the Spirit in the wilderness for forty days, being tempted by the devil."

Several aspects of the temptation appear before us. The first is simply that of chronology. While this is not important to the average reader it is important to the historian and inerrantist. More significant is the question of Satan's authority. Did Satan really even have the power to offer Jesus the kingdoms of the earth? If not, then how could it be a temptation at all? And what of fasting? If fasting is supposed to bring one closer to God, then how it is that Jesus was at His weakest after forty days? Or was He?

Chronology

"Chronology is the backbone of history."[262] This famous quote is known to every good historian. It is important because it allows us to connect events to one another instead of having a series of seemingly unrelated isolated events. Unfortunately, it is not always easy to construct solid chronologies from antiquity. Like a police investigator, the historian must examine all the eyewitness accounts to try to construct a fair chronology. While this is not always possible, it usually helps shed light upon certain facts within the accounts. In the case of the temptations it is fair to say "there is nothing very remarkable in Luke putting in second place the temptation which Matthew places last, for the Evangelists had no intention ... to keep an exact order of events."[263] Certainly, historians often arrange events topically, rather than chronologically, but the Bible critic is quick to jump on such chronological problems as "proof" of error. Consequently, I will briefly address the chronology of the temptation in the wilderness.

The first question is when did the temptations occur? There has been a common tendancy by historians to place the temptations before the events of John 1:19 – 2:11.[264] Since John does not address the temptations at all, it is often assumed that they must have taken place "immediately" (Mark 1:12) after the baptism of Christ, but what does "immediately" mean in the context of a person's life? If we are recording a history of three and a half years or more, as Mark was doing, then it hardly seems fair to assume that "immediately" must mean the very next day. Certainly a few days, perhaps a week, is sufficient time to fit the context of Mark's remarks. This seems most likely for two reasons. First, John 1:35 explicitly states "the next day" after concluding the story of John the Baptist. The "next day" after what? Obviously, the context seems to imply the day after Jesus' baptism (1:29-34). John then recounts the events of the first week after the baptism in detail, specifying, "the next day" (1:35; 43) and "on the third day" (2:1).

Some will argue that the baptism is not specifically mentioned in John 1:29-34 and therefore argue it could have happened earlier. They further argue that the calling of the apostles had to take place after the temptation. Both arguments fail. The baptism of Jesus is not mentioned specifically in John at all, but the reception of Jesus by John fit perfectly with His baptism and is John's attempt to not repeat what had already been told by Matthew, Mark, and Luke. The baptism can logically fit only here in John's gospel. Moreover, the calling of the apostles did take place instantaneously. When we read in Matthew of the calling of Peter (Matthew 4:18-22) it might seem that Peter had already known or at least met Jesus. It does not seem logical that he would take up and leave his job, family, and life for a man he had never even met before. Thus we may have in John the initial meeting of the first few disciples, but they were not formally called to leave until after the temptation. Although not certain it is more than plausible.

Another evidence for my chronology is the fact that Jesus specifically told His mother Mary at the wedding in Cana, "My hour has not yet come." It is for this reason that Jesus did not initially want to turn the water into wine! But if He had already been tempted and started calling His disciples then would not His ministry have begun? It seems logical to assume that Jesus left for the wilderness about a week after the baptism. When He returned, He called those disciples He had already befriended and began his ministry immediately afterwards.

Now the second chronological issue is that of the order of the temptations and when they took place. Generally, it is assumed that "Matthew preserves the original order."[265] This is in part the fact that Matthew uses "chronological devices" such as his use of "then" (cf. Matt. 4:5) to describe the the sequence of events.[266] Such sequential words are absent from Luke. Some argue that "for the sake of climax [Luke] delayed till last the temptation located here [4:5-6]."[267] Certainly this would be logical as Luke was arranging the temptations topically. H.A. Ironside argued that "the tests were threefold; appeal to the body, the soul, and the spirit."[268] Luke may have then wished to arrange the temptations so they would fit this topically.

The Kingdoms of the Earth

One of the most famous of the temptations was when Satan promised Jesus "*all*" the kingdoms of the earth (Matthew 4:8, Luke 4:5-8). Now one question this prompts is, "are they his to give?" If not, then how is it a temptation? If they are, then is Christ not sovereign? This very paradox is crucial to understanding much of history from a Biblical point of view. Did God relinguish His sovereignty over the earth in the Garden of Eden? Does Satan have authority over the earth? Neither answer is sufficient in itself.

Some, like Irenaeus, believed Satan lied when he declared he had the power to deliver the kingdoms to Christ,[269] but if he lied would Jesus not understand this? Could Jesus not know to whom the kingdoms of the world were bequeathed? 2 Corinthians 4:4 calls Satan the "god of this age" and John 12:31 calls him the "ruler of this world." In each case the emphasis is upon *this* world, or more literally "age" (αιωνος). It is a temporary state. Because man has rejected God, man has *voluntarily* surrendered *his* sovereignty (for sovereignty over the earth was given to us in the Garden of Eden) over to Satan. Here Satan is offering to relinquish that sovereignty to Christ before the appointed time. In other words, Jesus will one day rule the earth as King and Lord, but had Jesus accepted the sovereignty of the earth at that time then all of us would be lost for redemption and salvation would only come through Jesus' sufferings, death, and resurrection. In short, it was a great temptation because it was a choice between, as John MacArthur puts it, "enduring the long, bitter, humiliating, and painful road to the cross"[270] or taking the world as it was at that very time. Had Jesus chosen not to take the road to the cross, the world would be His Kingdom already, but we would all be lost. Jesus chose the right path even though it meant painful torment and the patience of thousands of years.

John Darby noted that "the world is the bait that Satan can offer that we should follow him."[271] It is the prize that Satan holds, and it is all that he can offer. Satan cannot offer us anything of eternal value, but as temporal beings who seem to see nothing beyond our nose, his temptation seems as great and powerful as anything imaginable. Jesus saw beyond the temporal and looked into eternity. He chose to long hard road for our sakes, and chose to remain loyal to the Lord Creator of all.

Fasting

A final cursory issue is that of why, if fasting is supposed to bring us closer to the Lord, is a time when we are most susceptible to temptation? The answer is that fasting brings us closer to the Lord by making us appreciate the basics of life and to rely on Him rather than material things, but at the same time our flesh is carnal and when it cries for food, there will obviously be a temptation to eat. In the same way, our flesh is often at odds with our spirit so that when we deny the flesh to grow in spirit, our flesh will cry out. This is where the temptation comes. If we survive the temptations, then we will be closer to God.

Summary

It is not without merit to mention that "according to rabbinic tradition, the coming of the Messiah to mark the deliverance of Israel would be indicated by His appearance on the temple roof ... 'in the hour when the King Messiah cometh, He standeth upon the roof of the sanctuary.'"[272] Consequently, it is significant, and somewhat symbolic, that when Satan took Jesus to the temple roof for one of His temptations, he was making an allusion to prophetic traditions about the coming of Christ. He was tempting Jesus not only to test God at the temple, but to tempt Jesus into believing that He might be fulfilling prophecy, when He would have been rejecting prophecy!

The temptations of Christ then have unique appeal to Himself and His role in history. What might not seem a temptation to us (throwing one's self off a high roof, for example) was to Jesus a great temptation. Jesus might have claimed the entire world without having to take the torturous road to the cross. This temptation accounted for the two of the temptations, and the most challenging.

Contraditions in the Beatitudes?
Matthew 5-7 – Luke 6

"Blessed are the poor in spirit, for theirs is the kingdom of heaven. Blessed are those who mourn, for they shall be comforted. Blessed are the gentle, for they shall inherit the earth. Blessed are those who hunger and thirst for righteousness ..."	"Blessed *are* you *who are* poor, for yours is the kingdom of God. Blessed *are* you who hunger now, for you shall be satisfied. Blessed *are* you who weep now, for you shall laugh. Blessed are you when men hate you ... for behold, your reward is great in heaven ..."

As the reader can see, it is not the substance of the sermons which is in conflict but the wording. The inerrantist believes that every word of the Bible is inspired by God and accurate, so even wording could theoretically create a problem or contradiction among the texts.

This "problem" is actually a simple one. Although the subject of the sermons are the same, they are clearly said to be *different* sermons to different people. The first is a sermon on *the mount* (Matthew 5:1). The second is the sermon on *the seashore* (Luke 6:17). Jesus was a missionary and evangelist. Unlike pastors who speak to the same audience every week and have a different sermon every week, an evangelist has the same message he must deliver to a multitude of people over a span of time. Since all agree the substance of the sermons are the same, the exactly wording is not problematic as they were not the exact same sermon.

Matthew 5:13 – See Mark 9:49-50

Abolish the Law?
Matthew 5:17-18

> "Do not think that I came to abolish the Law or the Prophets; I did not come to abolish but to fulfill."

There are many who believe that Jesus was the end of the law. Misquoting Paul, they say "Christ is the end of the law" (Romans 10:4). Of course, the entire sentence reads, "Christ is the end of the law for righteousness to everyone who believes." I do not need to read the State Penal code to find out if recreational drugs are legal in Texas for I do not use "recreational" drugs. If someone is studying the laws to find out what he can "get away with," then he is probably planning something unethical, if not illegal, but the righteous man does not need to consult law books to do what is right.

This is the crux of the debate. Does Paul mean that the law is dead to the Christian? If I sin does not the law still convicts me. Christ can pardon our sins, but he does not license our sins. I will say more of this in *Controversies in the Epistles*, for here is a debate on Jesus' remarks and not Paul's, but is sufficient to say that the devout Christians believes Paul was in perfect agreement with Christ, and few think of Christ as a strict legalist. If anything, Paul is generally viewed as more of a legalist than Christ! So how does this remark fit in with the words that follow? Was not Jesus contradicting their laws? Did not Jesus break the law and several occasions?

On one side of the argument are those believe that the law is dead. These argue that because "the phrase *the Law and the Prophets* was always understood to refer to the Jewish Scriptures"[273] Jesus was simply saying that the Bible is not abolished.[274] Nevertheless this is an insufficient argument for the Torah is called the Law for a reason; it is Law! The Law was the foundation for Israel and without the foundation a structure cannot stand (cf. Matthew 7:26-27). The fact that the Bible meticulously records the Law only further enhances this fact. Besides, why would anyone believe that Jesus had come to nullify the Bible itself? But Jesus was often accused of nullifying the Law. It is, therefore, significant that Jesus begun his sermon by clarifying "*do not* think that I came to abolish the Law." In prefacing his remarks with this statement the Lord was anticipating that some would misrepresent His remarks in this manner. Indeed, the words that followed are often presented with the phrase "you have heard it said ... but I say to you ..." Is this not a revoking of the Law? No. If Jesus had been referring to the written law He would have invariably used the term "it is written." By saying "you have heard" he was clearly referring to "oral or scribal law."[275] Jesus was not revoking the Law of Moses, but explaining that God judges by the heart. Obeying the statutory laws does not make one righteous, for God looks to the heart.

What then is the relationship of the law to which Jesus was speaking? Part of this will be addressed in the ensuing passages, but here it is Jesus' declaration that the Law is not to be abolished but "fulfilled." R.H. Linski once remarked that "'to fulfill' does not mean 'to develop,' as though the Old Testament contains only the germs or rudiments."[276] As John Calvin said, there is "agreement of Law and Gospel."[277] What Jesus is refuting is the oral tradition and interpretation of the law. It was the traditions of the Jews ("you have heard it said") and not the written law that Jesus was accused of violating. Of course this requires that we understand the differences. What is the "law"?

Division of the Law

John MacArthur, who believes that *all* the law is still valid, divides the law into three divisions; "the moral law was to regulate the behavior of all men; the judicial law was for Israel's operation as a unique nation; and ceremonial law was prescribed to structure Israel's worship of God."[278] Such a division is acknowledged by most scholars. So to which part is Jesus referring? Some, like John Wesley, say Jesus is only referring to the "the moral law."[279] Others believe that the entire "law is binding on the followers of Jesus to the end of time."[280] Let us look at these divisions individually and see how Christ regarded them.

Moral Law
William Barclay described the law of Moses as "great broad principles."[281] Every *just* law is founded upon great moral principles. Even today laws are divided into two categories in American jurisprudence. These are *mala in se* and *mala prohibita*[282] which mean, respectively, "inherently bad" and "bad by prohibition." Laws which are *mala in se*, such as murder and rape are inherently evil so that ignorance of the law is no excuse or defense. *Mala prohibita* are laws such as speed limits which must be posted since no one would inherently or morally know whether a speed limit is 30 mph or 40 mph. The moral law is therefore *mala in se*. Every great society has always had laws against murder

56

and stealing. No one can claim that such prohibitions are null and void. The Bible's great moral principles will remain throughout time.

Indeed, the Bible has laid the foundations for many great laws and nations throughout history. Some are unaware that many of our own laws here in the United States came word for word from the Bible. The testimony of two or more witnesses, for example, is found in Deuteronomy 17:6 where it is said that no one shall be sentenced to death without "the testimony of two or three witnesses." Such "great broad principles"[283] are for all eternity and Jesus affirms them repeatedly.

Judicial Law

What MacArthur calls "judicial law" has been called by various names, but in each case it refers to those laws that establish a country and its borders and defend it. Laws on citizenship, immigration, establishment of a military, courts, and the like are all essential to a country's existence in a hostile world. The United States Constitution serves in this capacity. In the case of Israel, the *Torah*, or Law, also established rules for the governing of Israel, for the establishment of courts, the priesthood, and rules of service. All such laws are obviously valid for that government, but can we expect that England or America or any other nation might be required to establish a Tabernacle as Israel did? Are these laws still valid outside of the nation of Israel?

On this there is dispute. Some hold that we should emulate the law of Israel in the establishment of government as well as in the moral laws of Moses. For the sake of brevity I will only say that there can only be one Israel. Certain aspects of Israel's "constitution" (for lack of a better word) can be emulated, but Israel remains unique in history. Its "constitution" is therefore unique to its role in history and the dispensations of God. We cannot expect that every nation must follow every aspect of the laws which pertain to Israel's government and nation.

Ceremonial Law

Ceremonial Law is similar to Judicial Law in as much as it pertains to the unique role of Israel in regard to Temple (or Tabernacle) worship. It is significant to note that even today in Israel it is impossible for the Orthodox Jew to obey *all* of these laws since there is no longer any temple. The laws relate to the Temple itself and the worship of God in the temple or tabernacle. Ceremonial cleanliness is one such example. Did Jesus support such laws as eternal? That too is debatable. Contrary to the dietary law of ceremonial cleanliness, Jesus Himself, while the Temple still existed, "declared all foods clean" (Mark 7:19). Thus, it would seem that Jesus Himself did distinguish between moral law and ceremonial law (but see endnote).[284]

Tradition

Now a fourth division of the Law not found in the Bible as a part of Scripture is oral law and/or tradition. The modern Jewish Talmud is, in fact, a collection of the traditions and interpretations of the Law that form the basis of modern Jewish life. Consider, for example, that the Bible says nothing about cheese burgers and yet to this day in Israel you cannot find cheese burgers. Why? The reasoning is based not upon Exodus 23:19; 34:26; and Deuteronomy 14:21 ("you are not to boil a young goat in the milk of its mother") but upon the tradition which suggests that even unknowingly mixing the milk (via a dairy product) with meat could unknowingly lead to the violation of this prohibition and would still be a sin. Therefore, in order to prevent an unknowing sin, no dairy products can be eaten with meat products.

These are the laws which Jesus criticized. This is to what Jesus referred when he said "you have heard it said." These are also the laws of which Jesus was accused of violating. This is an important distinction to make, for Jesus never violated the moral laws of Moses, nor even the ceremonial laws (even when Jesus declared all foods clean, He was not referring Temple worship).[285] A careful reading will show that in each instance where Jesus was accused of breaking the law, he was in fact violating only their tradition upon the law, and not the true Mosaic law! Here in the Sermon on the Mount Jesus is explaining the spirit of the law while critiquing the Jewish leaderships' traditions and interpretations of it. This will become evidence in the controversies which follow.

Fulfillment of the Law

If Jesus did not abolish the law, then what does it mean to "fulfill the law"? Tertullian, in describing "the commandment that the law should be fulfilled,"[286] seems to engage in double talk, saying, "if the gospel has not fulfilled the law, then all I can say is, the law has fulfilled the gospel."[287] Even the *Liberty University Bible Commentary* says, "the New Testament gospel is not contrary nor contradictory to the Old Testament law; rather it is the ultimate fulfillment of the spiritual intent of the law."[288] True enough, but what does this really mean? It is not enough to say that Jesus was the fulfillment of the law. How does Jesus fulfill the law? How is the gospel the fulfillment?

Eramus touched upon the answer more appropriately when he said "what the law promised is now being made manifest, what it predicted is being done, what it foreshadowed is being set out before the eyes of all, what it tried to accomplish but could not is now revealed in its fulness."[289] More specifically, "it was in His death and resurrection that Jesus espcially fulfilled the Law, He bore the curse of the Law (Gal. 3:13)."[290]

A thorough reading of the law shows that it is far more than just a set of rules and regulations. It was also a guide. In Galatians, the apostle Paul laid out in great detail how the law was intended to lead us to Christ and back to God. Step by step Paul shows that the law convicts us of our sins and demonstrates that someone *must* pay the price for our sins. We must either pay the price for our own sins, or we may accept that Jesus paid the price for us, and granted us a pardon.

Jesus was most literally the fulfillment of the Law because He was the lamb of God (John 1:29, 36). Ever since Abraham's son was spared, it was God who would provide the ultimate sacrifice (Genesis 22:8). That sacrifice was Christ. Therefore, to say "the gospel" is the fulfillment of the Law is not entirely sufficient, for it was most literally *Jesus Himself* who was the fulfillment of the Law. When Jesus said that He came to fulfill the Law, He meant it most literally by His death on the cross, and through His resurrection eternal life.

Summary

Marcion was a heretic who denied the Law was applicable to the Christian. Tertullian in refuting Marcion asked, "what business, therefore, had you to erase out of the Gospel that which was quite consistent in it?"[291] A judge can grant a pardon to a criminal, but he cannot pardon someone who is not guilty. It is the law which places us before the judge. Without the law, there is no need for a judge, nor a savior!

C.I. Scofield summarized Christ's fulfillment of the law as follows:

"(1) He was made under the law (Galatians 4:4).
(2) He lived in perfect obedience to the law (John 8:46; Matthew 17:5; 1 Peter 2:21-23).
(3) he was a minister of the law to the Jews, clearing it from rabbinical sophistries, enforcing it in all its pitiless severity upon those who professed to obey it (e.g. Luke 10:25-37) but confirming the promises made to the fathers under the Mosaic Covenant (Romans 15:8).
(4) He fulfilled the types of the law by His holy life and sacrificial death (Hebrews 9:11-26).
(5) He bore, vicariously, the curse of the law that the Abrahamic Covenant might avail all who believe (Galatians 3:13, 14).
(6) He brought out by His redemption all who believe from the place of servants under the law into the place of sons (Galatians 4:1-7).
(7) He mediated by His blood the New Covenant of assurance and grace in which all believers stand (Romans 5:2; Hebrews 8:6-13) so establishing the 'law of Christ' (Galatians 6:2) with its precepts of higher exaltation made possible by the indwelling Spirit."[292]

As John Walvoord said, "although the Mosaic law, as a dispensation, was to end at the cross, its moral and spiritual implications were to be fulfilled in later dispensations, including the kingdom."[293] Christ and the Law are perfectly compatible. Without the one, the other is ineffective. The Law condemns, Christ redeems. The Law passes judgement, Christ grants pardons. If we nullify the Law, we nullify Christ. If we acknowledge that the Law condemns us, we seek His pardon and redemption. Christ was literally the fulfillment of the Law.

Pluck Out Thine Eye?
Matthew 5:21-48

"If your right eye makes you stumble, tear it out and throw it from you; for it is better for you to lose one of the parts of your body, than for your whole body to be thrown into hell."

This is but one example of seemingly harsh statements by Jesus in which he appears to advocate self mutilation and/or other severe measures. It, and those like it, are often misquoted by both Bible critics and religious cults alike. Even many true Christians misunderstand the context of Jesus' remarks. Men like Tertullian, ignoring Jesus' previous remarks, declared that "'eye for an eye, and tooth for a tooth' has grown old,"[294] but in so saying he neglects the entire point of Jesus' remarks.

Several approaches have been taken in regard to these passages. Some argue that Jesus was merely being hyperbolical[295] and reject a "crude literalism."[296] They argue that Jesus was merely using "expressions" to "teach self discipline"[297] whereas men like Valerius Maximus *denies* it was hyperbolical at all.[298] Both views ignore the context.

While most today, like Erasmus of old, hold that Jesus "said these things to instruct by analogy"[299] this is not a sufficient answer. Stanley Toussaint says that "it is not to be taken literally because the tearing out of an eyeball or the severing of a hand or foot would not remove the cause of the offense"[300] and he is correct to an extent, but he seems to miss the entire point even while reaching the same conclusion. In other words, *if* our right eye caused us to sin "the logical thing to do would be to pluck it out" but "the right eye is not the source of sin, the heart of man is that source."[301] We must agree with R.H. Linski that "Jesus is not contradicting or correcting Moses"[302] but rather, as Ironside affirms, "correcting the faulty positions of the rabbis."[303]

This is the missing context. Jesus' sermon did not refute Mosaic law, but the old rabbinic tradition of Moses' law. If sin was caused by our eye then the logical answer would be "the excision of his own wicked eye"[304] but Jesus did "not mean that we are to ... cut off parts of his own body, since the nature of the limbs is not evil."[305] God looks to the heart. The teachers of Jesus' day were looking at external things. Throughout Jesus' sermon this evident. John MacArthur states that "in saying, 'but I say to you,' Jesus was not contrasting His teaching with that of the Old Testament but with the rabbinic tradition."[306]

Liberty University's Study Bible shows an apt chart in which the law is compared to the spirit.[307] The Rabbis were looking to the law, whereas Jesus was looking to the spirit.

THE LAW	THE SPIRIT
Murder	No anger
Adultery	No lust
Divorce	Commitment
Oath Taking	Speak the Truth
Retaliation	Forgiveness

This chart shows that there is perfect consistency with the teachings of Jesus and the Mosaic law, but it shows how different things can appear when we look to the heart rather than to external deeds.

As discussed in the previous debate upon Matthew 5:17-18, there is a specific context here to which Jesus is referring. He is not telling people that they must cut our their eyes or hack off their limbs to attain heaven, but rather he is speaking to a certain mindset; that of legalism. The Law condemns. Jesus brings life. One can choose the hard road which would include self mutilation, or can choose a *better* way ... Jesus Christ!

By pointing out that God judges by the heart, and emphasizing the harshness of the Law, Jesus was also illustrating the folly of attaining salvation through our own righteousness. Unfortunately, many refuse to accept this. Every time I read this passage I am reminded for the story of a Catholic Priest who castrated himself in order to avoid the sin of lust![308] Out of desperation he dismemebered himself because He did not understand that Jesus offers a better way. I am also reminded of a person close to me who literally denied he had ever sinned (though Romans 3:23 disagrees) and quoted the final passage of this section, wherein Jesus said, "you are to be perfect, as your heavenly Father is perfect" (Matthew 5:48). He seemed to be saying that he lived up to this call, but he once again missed the point. Scofield suggested that "the word implies full development, growth into maturity of godliness, not sinless perfection."[309] Perfection is an ideal to strive for, but it cannot be acheived through our own efforts, but only through Christ. It is Christ who redeems us, and Christ who perfects us.

Christ is therefore offering us two ways. We can strive for perfection through self mutilation and self deprecation or we can choose the way of repentance and faith in Christ Jesus! Any serious reading of these passages should make it clear which is the better way. The Law condemns us, but Christ brings us life eternal.

Matthew 5:32 – See Matthew 19:9

Matthew 6:9-13 – See Matthew 26:26-29

Christian Judgment
Matthew 7:1-5

"Do not judge so that you will not be judged. For in the way you judge, you will be judged; and by your standard of measure, it will be measured to you."

This is surely one of the most misquoted passage in the Bible; often by the very people to whom Jesus was speaking. It warns us that we will be judged by the same standards that we set upon other people, but does that mean that it is wrong to judge anything?

The Bible teaches several things about judgment, but in order to understand these teachings we need to distinguish between the different types of judgment, for judgment can refer to one of several things. The fact is that from the time we wake up in the morning until the time we fall asleep at night we have made countless judgments; some good, and some most probably bad. To judge is to make a decision about something. We pass judgment upon both the seen and unseen; upon the known and unknown. This is where the dilema lies. Let us examine the different types of judgments.

Judging Right from Wrong / Judging Actions
This sort of judgment is commanded by God. Proverbs 31:9 demands "open your mouth, judge righteously, and defend the rights of the afflicted and needy." If we do not judge righteously, how can we defend the weak or innocent? If we are afraid to judge between right and wrong we ultimately contribute to the evil in the world. Politicians must judge everyday whether or not a course of action will hurt or harm the people he is sworn to defend and protect. Obviously, most politicians make the wrong judgment, but we are commanded to make the right one. This is why Zechariah said, "These are the things which you should do: speak the truth to one another; judge with truth and judgment for peace in your gates" (8:16).

John MacArthur has pointed out that "those who hold to strong convictions and who speak up and confront society and the church are branded as violators of this command."[310] Indeed, the student of history knows that the Reformers, abolitionist, and the modern day pro-life movement have all been branded as judgmental hypocrites, condemning Catholic peasants, the slave holder, or the poor woman who chooses to have an abortion. History, however, has shown that these judgments are right and true. Freedom exist today because men stood up against injustice.

So we agree that this commandment of Jesus "does not forbid the judging of actions or evil."[311] As Irenaeus said, "the meaning is not certainly that we should not find fault with sinners, nor that we should consent to those who act wickedly; but that we should not pronounce an unfair judgment on the dispensations of God."[312]

I am reminded of the ancient Persian king Cambyses who punished a wicked judge by having him skinned. He then made a seat cover out of the skin and placed it over the "judgment seat" where all judges sat when making their decisions. Thus each judge sat upon the skin of a wicked judge, so all judges would be constantly reminded to be fair.[313] Consequently, such a barbaric pagan ruler as Cambyses seems to have understood better than many today the importance of judging, but judging fairly and righteously.

Judging Motives / Judging the Heart
King David understood what it was like to be judged by men, even though he also knew full well the depth of his own sins. In Psalms 109:31 he said, the Lord "stands at the right hand of the needy, to save him from those who judge his soul." The *soul*; this is what only God can judge, but what men judge all the time. "We are not to judge the inner motives of another."[314] Nor are we to pass "unjustifiable condemnation"[315] upon a sinner.

Those who judge our motives and hearts condemn themselves. This is part of what Jesus meant in the succeeding sentence where he says, "in the way you judge, you will be judged; and by your standard of measure, it will be measured to you." Notice two things. First, Jesus is acknowledging that everyone judges. He is therefore not forbidding thought (for to outlaw all judging would be nothing less). Second, Jesus is declaring that we will be measured by the same measuring stick which we use on others. It is, as Erasmus declared, "distorted judgment" ... "everyone should be a very acute judge of his own wrongdoings, more lenient of the faults of others."[316] Unfortunately, those who condemn us often do the very things they condemn us for. Is not the agnostic quick to judge a Christian caught in sin, despite the fact that the agnostic sees nothing wrong with sin? This is the "self righteous, hypocritical judging"[317] which Jesus condemned. It is "judging a fellow disciple out of self-righteousness"[318] rather than out of a sense of concern or love.

Now there remains another form of judgment. It is closely related to this, but I differentiate it from this kind of judgment for several reasons. It relies not necessarily on hypocrisy or the judging of ones' heart so much as bigotry and fear. This is something I learned when I attended a church where I became the victim of such judgments.

Prejudging / Passing Judgment
Prejudice is not unique to any class of people. Race, color, creed, sex, party affiliation are all just examples, but people within the same group can be just as guilty. We are too often quick to prejudge people. The popularity of psychology has made this all to popular, and even trendy. After all, psychology is notorious for prejudging people. I have seen this many times, and there are

many examples I could site personally, but I will only mention one; the worst case I have experienced.

Many years ago I began to attend a new church. I noticed that the people were suspicious of strangers and the church even had more security than most banks, but realizing that some attacks on churches have taken place more frequently over the years, I pushed these concerns to the back of my head and did not think of it, for I did have some good friends there at the church. Later, however, I made the mistake of asking a pretty young girl out on a date. She did not answer; she just ran off. Next week the pastor called me into his office and told me that church was not for dating. I agreed not to speak to her again, and I did not, but soon gossiping began. I do not, to this day, know exactly what all the gossip was about, but it increased and it was obvious that people questioned me for the simplest of things. After being denied church membership I asked for an appeal to be heard by the elders. I had friends at the church who could attest for me, and I wanted the right to answer whatever accusations were being made against me. Months passed and finally the pastor simply told me never to come back. I received no hearing, no appeal, and no chance to defend myself. I was condmened without hearing and without evidence. I was condemned without trial. In short, I was prejudged as an outsider who didn't conform to whatever they wanted.

The apostle Paul dealt with this same problem. In Romans 14 the apostle speaks of the debate concerning those who eat food sacrificed to idols. This controversy will be addressed fully in *Controversies in the Epistles*, but here it is relevant only to point out that Paul warned believers:

> "The one who eats is not to regard with contempt the one who does not eat, and the one who does not eat is not to judge the one who eats, for God has accepted him. Who are you to judge the servant of another? To his own master he stands or falls; and he will stand, for the Lord is able to make him stand ... But you, why do you judge your brother? Or you again, why do you regard your brother with contempt?" (14:3-4, 10)

It is this "sense of condemning"[319] others for things we do not understand or agree with that condemns ourselves. We pass judgment upon someone rather than passing judgment upon the action. Paul took a stand on the debate over food sacrificed to idols but he condemned neither side of the debate. He judged the doctrine, but loved the people on both sides of the debate.

Summary

Jonathan Edwards once said, "the hearts of men are naturally all full of the same corruption ... he that is most in censuring others for malice is a very malicious man ... a self-righteous and pharisetical man."[320] Hippolytus, the church father, told us that the heretics were judgmental, and not those who judge them.[321] This is often the case. We see many times in the New Testament where Jesus' enemies passed judgment upon Him and condemn Jesus for the very things they do.

Cyprian saw this passage as being about forgiveness.[322] Tertullian declared, "He has not prohibited judging, but told us how to do it."[323] Ironside may have summarized it best, saying, "it is a question of motives. There are circumstances when the people of God are commanded to judge ... but we are not to attempt to sit in judgment upon the hidden springs of action."[324]

The Centurion
Matthew 8:5-13 – Luke 7:2-11

"And when Jesus entered Capernaum, a centurion came to Him, imploring Him, and saying, 'Lord, my servant is lying paralyzed at home, fearfully tormented.' Jesus said to him, 'I will come and heal him.' But the centurion said, 'Lord, I am not worthy for You to come under my roof, but just say the word, and my servant will be healed. For I also am a man under authority, with soldiers under me; and I say to this one, "'Go!'" and he goes, and to another, "'Come!'" and he comes, and to my slave, "'Do this!'" and he does it.' ..."

"And a centurion's slave, who was highly regarded by him, was sick and about to die. When he heard about Jesus, he sent some Jewish elders asking Him to come and save the life of his slave ...

"Now Jesus *started* on His way with them; and when He was not far from the house, the centurion sent friends, saying to Him, 'Lord, do not trouble Yourself further, for I am not worthy for You to come under my roof; for this reason I did not even consider myself worthy to come to You, but *just* say the word, and my servant will be healed' ..."

Here the critic argues that there are conflicting testimonies. In Matthew it appears to imply that the centurion came to Jesus personally, whereas Luke says it was friends of the centurion who came and implies that the centurion never personally met Jesus. Is this not a contradiction?

Like the defense lawyer in a court of law, he argues that the eyewitnesses are giving conflicting testimony and, therefore, cannot be trusted, but we are like jurors who examine the testimony before passing judgment. This is standard practice for any police investigator. When two or more witnesses *appear* to give conflicting testimony it is the job of the detective not to discard their testimony outright, but to see whether or not there is a logical way of reconciling the testimonies. For example, if one eyewitness describes a blue car leaving the scene of the crime and another a red car, it is possible that there actually *two* cars present. The detective must examine all possibilities. The defense attorney does not care; and neither does the typical agnostic.

Some even question whether or not this was really a centurion. Robert Mounce believes that he was only a "Roman official" since "Galilee was not under Roman occupation" as of yet.[325] Nevertheless, there is no doubt that the Roman empire had men stationed throughout the empire. Herod was a puppet of Rome and none of Palestine/Israel could truly be said to be independent of Rome, so we have no reason to reject the testimony of either Matthew or Luke in this regard.

As to the question of who spoke to Jesus (the centurion or his emissaries) the answer is rather simple, although many, including some Christian scholars, have come up with elaborate, and unnecessary, solutions. Some, for example, argue that the centurion first sent representatives and then later came personally after the representatives failed,[326] but this would not be consistent with Luke's assersion that the centurion sent friends out to tell Jesus, "I am not worthy for You to come under my roof" (7:6). Gundry tries to get around this by arguing that Matthew changes the chronology of Matthew as part of some sort of Matthean "motif."[327] In fact, there is no reason to believe this. The answer is far more simple.

John Wesley believed that the centurion "spoke the words that follow by his messengers. As it is not unusual in all languages, so in Hebrew it is peculiarly frequent, to ascribe to a person himself the thing which is done, and the words which are spoken by his orders."[328] John Calvin likewise argued that "Matthew quite reasonably attributes to him what was done at his request and in his name."[329] This makes perfect sense for "what a man does through agents he may be said to do himself."[330] Is this not what messengers are for? Do they speak their own words? "This centurion actually came to Jesus through some Jewish intermediaries."[331]

That this is the case it obvious to any student of history. A king's messenger delivers the words spoken by the king. When a peasant returns home to inform his wife, "the king said our taxes will be increased this year," his wife does not answer, "you met the king! You liar, it was just his servant. Don't pay the taxes!" The words spoken were indeed those of the centurion. Matthew was not writing an exhaustive and detailed history of everything which happened, but recording accurately and faithfully what transpired. Luke, who was a historian, tried to be more technical in his record, but both are equally true.

What is lost on such debates is the true meaning of the passage. It was the fact that the centurion, a man of high esteem, considered himself unworthy of Jesus. Charles Spurgeon noted that "a sense of unworthiness is very desirable and commendable"[332] in the eyes of the Lord. This is the point too often lost.

Outer Darkness and the Believer
Matthew 8:12

"The sons of the kingdom will be cast out into the outer darkness; in that place there will be weeping and gnashing of teeth."

Three verses speak of "outer darkness"; here in Matthew 8:12, in Matthew 22:13, and in Matthew 25:30. One's first inclination is to ascribe the passages to hell, and Catholics have traditionally ascribed this verse to purgatory, but most have probably never heard of a third theory which was popular in the nineteenth century and has experienced a recent resurgence among some evangelicals. This is the view that "outer darkness" speaks of what has been termed "Millennial exclusionism."

Millennial exclusionism is the doctrine that "unsanctified believers" will be excluded from the Messianic kingdom on earth. Most Millennial exclusionists believe that outer darkness refers to a place where the unsanctified believers will reside during the Millennial kingdom (see notes on Revelation 20 in *Controversies in Revelation* for a full discussion of the Millennial kingdom). Consequently, some have termed this belief a sort of "Protestant purgatory",[333] something ardently denied by its advocates. They state that "unlike the Catholic [purgatory], future chastisement of unfaithful believers is not for the *purpose* of earning final, positional salvation. It is discipline."[334] Thus he is inadvertently admitting the similarities, save that the "*purpose*" (emphasis is his own) is different. To this Sir Robert Anderson said that they "fall back upon the old heresy of a purgatory of some kind; though with pharasaical blindness they assume that the better sort of Christian will escape the fiery discipline."[335]

What arguments do the Millennial exclusionists make to support this thesis? The majority of their arguments are theological strings, tied together from different passages. Chuck Missler, for example, sites many passages which speak of rewards for faithful believers and loss of rewards for unfaithful believers. He then quotes Colossians 3:24 which says we must know "that from the Lord you will receive the reward of the inheritance." He then draws the inference that we can *loose* this inheritance![336] The main inference seems to be that there is only one reward which we can loose; that of inhereting the Kingdom of God!

Exegetically, they argue that the "sons of the Kingdom" can only refer to "believers."[337] They further argue that "outer darkness" is a place outside of the Millennial kingdom, but not purgatory nor any other place of punishment.[338] However, this argument fall apart on three different levels.

First, Jesus was marveling at the faith of a gentile (vs. 10). He was contrasting the faith of the gentile with the "sons of the kingdom." Who are these "sons of the kingdom"? Clearly they are the Israelites to whom the kingdom was promised. Missler himself admits that they are Israelites, but then argues that they are "Jewish believers."[339] Nonetheless, to say that Jesus was contrasting a believer with other believers makes no contextual sense here. The Jews were expecting Jesus to bring the kingdom to them, but instead it will come to those who believe, such as the gentile centurion. Jesus was constrasting faith and faithlessness, not maturity and immaturity.

The second major problem is that while Chuck Missler is careful to say that this place of "outer darkness" is not a place of punishment, he carefully avoids the obvious implications of "weeping and gnashing of teeth." What does one envision when he hears of "gnashing of teeth"? Try to gnash your teeth. If you have ever done this, it is apparent that it is a reaction to physical pain. This is why doctors used to give people something to bite upon when performing surgery. In the days before anesthesia there were few ways to deaden the pain (one being alcohol). Consequently, the only way to keep someone from gnashing his teeth was to give him something upon which to bite. "Gnashing of teeth" implies pain. It can refer to nothing else.

Finally, to speak of any place where the Holy Spirit resides as a place of "darkness" is unbiblical. Since Millennial exclusionists argue that these "sons of the kingdom" are true believers who are saved by grace (albeit unsanctified ones) then it follows logically that they *must* have the indwelling of the Holy Spirit, but if Christ is the "light of the world" (John 8:12; 9:5) then it is nothing short of heresy to claim that any place in which the Lord dwells should be spoken of as a place of "darkness." Everywhere in the Bible wherein darkness is spoken of it is spoken of as a place where God is not present. I challenge the Millennial exclusionists to find a single passage where God is spoken of as dwelling in the darkness. He cannot find such a passage.

Now the only other places where "outer darkness" is mentioned are in two parables; the parable of the wedding feast (Matthew 22:1-13) and the parable of the five talents (Matthew 25:14-30). In both of these passages Millennial exclusionists insist that the parable speaks of unsanctified believers rather than unbelievers, but a close examination of the passages shows the opposite.

In the parable of the wedding feast (Matthew 22:1-13) the king had invited many to his wedding, but when they did not come, "the king was enraged, and he sent his armies and destroyed those murderers and set their city on fire" (v. 7). He then invited anyone else who would come, but when one of the original invitees appeared without proper dress he was cast into outer darkness. Once again, the Millennial exclusionists believe that these are "unsanctified believers." Missler argues that because the one cast into outer darkness is called "friend" then "He knew him as a 'comrade,' a fellow participant, or a follower."[340] However, the exegesis is forced to say the least. Consider that the king "sent his armies and destroyed those murderers and set their city on fire" (v. 7). This man was bound hand and foot (v. 13) and cast into the place of "gnashing of teeth." That this speaks of fiery judgment is even admitted by Millennial exclusionist J.D. Faust who says "many Christians will not be clothed with practical holiness in their bodies as they come into contact with the fire at the judgment seat."[341] Hence the Millennial exclusionists wants to say this is only "discipline" upon the unsanctified and that God will not actually "punish" us, and yet here the "fire at the judgment seat" is attributed to believers!

Lastly, consider the parable of the five talents (Matthew 25:14-30). The Millennial exclusionists point out that in this parable all the slaves are entrusted with money from their master and the one who does not earn interest is cast into outer darkness. Now one might be tempted to accept this as "unsanctified believers" if it were not for the fact that the parable does not end here, but rather Jesus continues with the imagery of the "sheep and goats" (v. 32). If we read the verse through continuously it should be apparent that there is no break, no change in topic, and no shift in conversation. Jesus said, "throw out the worthless slave into the outer darkness; in that place there will be weeping and gnashing of teeth. But when the Son of Man comes in His glory, and all the angels with Him, then He will sit on His glorious throne. All the nations will be gathered before Him; and He will separate them from one another, as the shepherd separates the sheep from the goats" (vv. 30-32). Now all agree that the goats are unbelievers who are sent into damnation, for Jesus declared that "these will go away into eternal punishment" (v. 46). How then can this be "unsanctified believers"? It is not possible to separate the two stories, for they are one and the same story. The parables are the same story, told in succession by Jesus. The imagery here is not of "unsanctified believers" but of unbelievers who have rejected the Lord.

Much more could be said of this, but the subject of judgment, rewards, punishments, and exclusion from the Millennium is a debate far beyond this passage. It is sufficient to say that while it is true that we will not have the same rewards, and that we may not all be kings in the Millennial kingdom (though this does not infer that we cannot serve with Christ in some other way), it is nothing short of heresy to claim that God will cause "weeping and gnashing of teeth" in a place of "outer darkness." The imagery in the Bible is very clear. This place of "outer darkness" is a place where Christ is absent, where there is pain and suffering ("gnashing of teeth" in itself is proof of this fact). The Biblical parables make "outer darkness" parallel to an army setting their city on fire (22:7) and to "eternal punishment" (v. 25:46). "Outer darkness" cannot in any way be accepted as an abode for "unsanctified believers" without denying that Jesus paid the price for all our sins on the cross. There is a great difference in saying that we will not all have the same rewards and/or honor and in saying that the unsanctified believers must suffer in "outer darkness" for a thousand years. This is nothing short of a Protestant purgatory and heresy.

Peter's Mother-in-Law
Matthew 8:14 – Luke 12:53

"When Jesus came into Peter's home, He saw his mother-in-law lying sick in bed with a fever."

Because of the modern Catholic teaching on the celibacy of the priesthood, and the fact that they believe Peter to be the first pope, some Catholics deny that Peter was ever married. Nevertheless, here it is affirmed that Peter was married, for one cannot have a mother-in-law unless one has a wife. Ironically, the Catholic Bible Douay-Rehims translates this as "his wife's mother." Now the official response to this by the Catholic church is to attempt to make a technical distinction between dogma or doctrine and Catholic "discipline."[342] They admit that priests were allowed to marry for centuries and then deny that it is technically forbidden today, a fact easily refuted by Catholics and Protestants alike. Moreover, they argue that Peter's wife had already died by the time he was an apostle. As proof they note that Peter's wife is not mentioned here; only his mother. However, a reading of 1 Corinthians 9:5 disproves this argument as well. The fact is that Peter was married. Moreover, even in the Catholic church many priests were free to marry until the brutal reign of Pope Gregory VII who forced married priests to divorce. Those who didn't were castrated and/or their wives were forcibly dragged off and tried as prostitutes or, if they were fortunate, placed in convents.[343] The Catholic church has never since renounced its position on this matter. Much more could be said of this, but it is sufficient here to simply state the fact that Peter was married.

"Let the Dead Bury Their Dead"
Matthew 8:22 – Luke 9:60

"Jesus said to him, 'Follow Me, and allow the dead to bury their own dead.'"

This is one of the "hard sayings" of Jesus. By "hard sayings" it means that the saying seems inconsistent with or "hard" in comparison to Jesus's teachings. Too often these "hard sayings" are dismissed by theologians in one way or another. This is unfortunate. We cannot and should not simply dismiss or trivialize these "hard sayings" of Jesus simply because they do not appear to fit our interpretation of Jesus' teachings. Let us examine this, the first of the "hard sayings."

There have been many attempts to minimize or even dismiss the hardness of Jesus' remarks. For example, Erasmus argued the man's request was a "pretext"[344] to "settling an estate" and being "concerned with an inheritance."[345] This view is also suggested by John MacArthur.[346]

Nonetheless, there is no evidence of this at all. A sincere exegesis should take the passage more at face value rather than trying to find a way out of the difficulty. Traditionally there have been three primary interpretation of this passage. First, is the view that Jesus was speaking of the spiritually dead. The second is that the man wanted to wait until a traditional the mourning period was over. The third view is that this is an ancient idiom. Each view will be examined closely.

Spiritually dead

By far the most popular view, espoused by evangelicals, Catholics, and most others is that Jesus was speaking of the "spiritually dead." John Wesley said that the man's father was "dead to God."[347] Albert Barnes argued that "men of the world are dead to religion"[348] and even the *Liberty Bible Commenty* says it "probably means let those who are spiritually dead bury the physically dead."[349]

Evidence for this argument is lacking. Cyprian attempted to justify the view by saying, "he had said his father was dead, while the Father of believers is living,"[350] but this seems weak to say the least. It is not the Father in heaven on whom the son was waiting for burial, but his own father. Is God not the God of all? Others say it means to "look of the future [and] ... leave a dying cause behind"[351] but all are pure speculation.

Advocates of this view are many ranging from the aforementioned John Wesley,[352] Albert Barnes,[353] and the church father Cyprian[354] to R.H. Linski, Warren Wiersbe, John MacArthur, F.W. Farrar, Gleason Archer, and even H.A. Ironside as well as countless others. Despite such prestigous support, there are many reasons to reject this view.

Aside from the lack of evidence of this position it is inconsistent with Jesus' teachings. Are we not being sent out in the world to bring the spiritually dead life? Is it not Jesus who restores life to those who are spiritually dead? Are we to judge who can and cannot be saved, even within our own family? Does not Paul say that whoever cannot take care of his own family cannot care for the family of God (cf. 1 Timothy 3:5)?

The fact is that this position is merely an attempt to soften the harsh words of Jesus and make them "spiritual." However, Jesus words *are* spiritual, so why must we "spiritualize" the meaning of a passage to make it spiritual? This process of spiritualizing passages which don't suit our own preconceptions is common among the self professed liberal theologians but frowned upon by evangelicals, and yet evangelicals are sometimes guilty of this as well.

Mourning Period

Another view designed to soften the blow is the idea that the man's father had actually already been buried but that "Jewish tradition required that a person mourn for the deceased father or mother for a period of thirty days."[355] It is claimed, therefore, that he wanted to wait until this period of over. The man's comment presumably entailed the tradition of applying spices on a body after it had already been interred, much in the same way that the Marys were going to apply spices to the body of Jesus after His burial (cf. Mark 16:1; Luke 23:56–24:1 [although this is suspect][356]).

Now this theory is intriguing, and even possible, but does not answer the fundamental question, nor is it evident from the text itself. Whether we claim that it was an "ailing father"[357] who was near death, or a father who was already dead, to suggest that Jesus, even to make a point about the "spiritually dead," would forbid a man from waiting a short period to bury his dying (or already dead) father is exactly the very proposal which these theologians are trying to get around! How ironic then that they are ultimately suggesting that very thing!

Idiomatic Saying

A final proposal is that this is a "proverbial saying otherwise known to us."[358] Indeed, when dealing with history this is not uncommon at all, and many times provides incredible insight into the words of Jesus. In this case, it appears to be an idiomatic saying from the Middle East, allegedly still used in some parts of Asia Minor.

We must remember that Israel was a Patriarchal society. Even to this very day in countries like India the Patriarchal society is still common. Families lived to together until the Patriarch died. Only then would the family split, and even then it would be only the brothers that divided the household. Daughters who married were taken into the Patriarchal family of her husband.

According to William Barclay, a Syrian missionary to Turkey reported to him that this very saying remained in use in Turkey, and was idiomic way of saying, "after my father dies."[359] In other words, he wanted to fulfill his duties under Patriarchal society until his father passed away. Jonathan Edwards paraphrased the passage as saying, "let me stay till my aged Father is dead ... after he should be dead, he would be willing to follow."[360] John Walvoord concurs.[361] If this is true then Jesus' remarks fit perfectly with his declaration that "I came to set a man against his father, and a daughter against her mother, and a daughter-in-law against her mother-in-law" (Matthew 10:35; cf. Luke 12:53).

Although a minority viewpoint this is well supported by the facts. It is adopted by men such as John Walvoord and others. It is also enlightening inasmuch as it sheds light on Jesus' remarks in a more literal way. Jesus said "everyone who has left houses or brothers or sisters or father or mother or children or farms for My name's sake, will receive many times as much, and will inherit eternal life" (Matthew 19:29; cf. Mark 10:29). Here he says the same thing in a more dramatic way.

Summary

Tertullian took the command of Jesus literally, arguing that "in Leviticus, which concerns the sacerdotal office, and forbids the priests to be present at the funerals even of those parents. 'The priest,' says He, 'shall not enter where there is any dead person; and for his father he shall not be defiled'"[362] (see Leviticus 21:1). Others have tried to brush off the controversial remark by saying that Jesus was simply referring to the "spiritually dead." John Calvin spoke from the middle saying, "anything which diverts us from a straight course, or hinders under, will savour only of death."[363]

The truth is that this is not Jesus' only controversial remark regarding the leaving of one's father or mother for the sake of the cause. The statement "bury my father" is almost certainly an idiomatic saying from the Middle East meaning that the man wished to fulfill his patriarchal duties under the society and wished to wait until his father's death before serving in ministry. That might be many years. Jesus, however, declared elsewhere that we must leave our father and mother if necessary for his sake (Matthew 10:35; Luke 12:53) and those who do "will receive many times as much, and will inherit eternal life" (Matthew 19:29; cf. Mark 10:29). Thus these words of Jesus are in perfect keeping with this teaching. They are "hard" but true. Jesus was not forbidding the man from attending his father's funeral, but telling him that He must follow Jesus now, and not some distant year in the future. We do not know what tomorrow will bring, so the time wasted waiting for tomorrow is time lost for the gospel. There is a sense of urgency in evangelism, and this was a point not lost on Jesus and His disciples.

The Maniac
Matthew 8:28-34 – Mark 5:1-20 – Luke 8:26-39

"When He came to the other side into the country of the Gadarenes, two men who were demon - possessed met Him as they were coming out of the tombs. *They were* so extremely violent that no one could pass by that way ..."

"They came to the other side of the sea, into the country of the Gerasenes. When He got out of the boat, immediately a man from the tombs with an unclean spirit met Him, and he had his dwelling among the tombs. And no one was able to bind him anymore, even with a chain ..."

"Then they sailed to the country of the Gerasenes, which is opposite Galilee. And when He came out onto the land, He was met by a man from the city who was possessed with demons; and who had not put on any clothing for a long time, and was not living in a house, but in the tombs ..."

73

There are two different debates here. The first is the question of where this event took place. Matthew describes it as the country of Gadarenes where as Luke and John call it the country of Gerasenes. The second question is whether there were two demon-possessed men as Matthew states or whether or not there was only one as Mark and Luke imply. The issues here are not really that difficult but require an understanding of testimonial witnesses. Sir Robert Anderson, former chief inspector of Scotland Yard, once remarked that (as all good detectives do) "when in my official life I have found a conflict of testimony between persons of known integrity. I have always sought some way of reconciling them."[364] This is not, as the Bible critic suggests, some desparate attempt to reconcile false testimonies but standard police work. Two people remembering the exact same event will recount different aspects of that event which may appear on the surface to be in conflict, but which make perfect sense when the whole facts are brought to life. So is the case here.

The Country
Readers of the King James Bible are at a loss to even understand the debate, for their Bible reads "Gadarenes" in perfect unison with Mark and Luke. This is because the Majority text used by the King James also had Gadarenes.[365] In fact, not only do the majority texts (most ancient and medieval Greek copies) contain this reading but so do the ancient codices *Sinaiticus* and *Washingtonius* (also called *Freerianus*).[366] In fact, of the most important ancient texts, the *Vaticanus* and *Ephraimi* are the only strong witnesses to the reading of "Gerasenes."[367] Now I shall not engage here in a debate upon the science of textual criticism[368] (the reader may refer to my appendices for some this debate), but I shall point out that the reading of Gerasenes is not as troublesome as some make it out to be. Here is why.

"Gergesa and Gadara were towns near each other. Hence the country between them took its name, sometimes from the one, sometimes from the other."[369] These are the simple words of John Wesley. They are true and accurate. Gadara and Gergesa were only twelve miles from one another.[370] The furtherest outskirts of Gerasa lay thirty miles inland whereas Gadara's furtherest point from there lay six miles inland.[371] Gadara itself was separated by a gorge[372] and the land around it took the city's name, encompassing a much larger area.[373] According to some, the fact that the demoniac was "born in the city ... but not living there now"[374] further clarifies the alleged discrepancy. Gadarenes and Gerasenes were in the same region. One might even call them twin cities. Ironside called them synonyms.[375]

Consider that to this day, the city of Richardson, Texas lay in both Collin County and Dallas County. The county line cuts straight through the city of Richardson. So a person would be true and accurate to say that he lives in

Richardson, in Texas, in Collin County, and perhaps even Dallas County (assuming his house lay on that invisible line as well)! Thus there is no great difficulty in these statements.

The Demoniacs

A larger problem appears to be whether or not there was only one demoniac or two. Some see a problem or conflict between these testimonies. Some, like Robert Gundry even argue that Matthew was trying to make an emphatic point and thus "compensates" by "doubling" the demoniac.[376] He calls this a "compensatory doubling" for effect![377] Of course another word for this would be "liar." Either he was telling the truth, he was mistaken, or he was a liar. Let us see which is the true case.

I previously alluded to the detective analogy of Sir Robert Anderson. Since we are dealing with a similar circumstance where two or more eyewitnesses *appear* to give a conflicting testimony, the analogy is valid. Let us say that two witnesses describe a bank robber driving off in a car. One says the car was red while another says it was blue. Is one mistaken? Is one lying? A defense attorney will make that argument, but a police investigator will follow up with more questions. Could there have been *two* cars?

This is most likely the case here. The gospel writers are not giving an exhaustive history, nor do they claim to be. Mark and Luke only mention one "but do not state that only one was present."[378] John Wesley suggests that Mark and Luke fixated on "the fiercer of the two"[379] but, as even Linski admits, "the latter do not say that there was *only* one."[380] "Mark does not specifically limit it to one. Probably one stood out as the leader."[381] This is perfectly logical. The Bible critic, like the defense lawyer, will try to shift the burden of proof to the witness by stating that there is no proof of this, but neither can he find any irreconcilable differences which would be required to dismiss an eyewitness testimony.

Demons or Disease?

There is another issue which is becoming more commonly discussed in recent years. Since the adventy of "Christian psychology" we see more and more Bible commentaries and preachers who seek to remove the spiritual aspects of the Bible and replace them with pseudo-science. Denying that demoniacs are real, they compare the descriptions found herein with various psychiatric manuals and suggest that these men were suffering from schizophrenia or some other psychiatric disease. Now I will not here debate the merits, or lack thereof, of psychiatry other than to point out that psychiatry consistently fails to distinguish between etiology and physiology (cause and effect).[382] On that basis alone it is a pseudo-science. Nevertheless, even if psychiatry is a perfectly valid and legitimate science, the fact remains that we have here not only the testimony of

Matthew, Mark, and Luke, but of our Lord Jesus Christ Himself! This was no mere "'disease."

John MacArthur has said that "many people who are diagnosed as mentally ill are actually demonized."[383] Even many Christian psychiatrists and psychologists agree that mental disorders cannot be blamed in many instances. Kurt Koch and Alfred Lechler, himself a psychiatrist, have lectured on the dangers of confusing disease and occult subjection.[384] In their research they encountered many, even secular psychiatrists, who felt that the problems of some of their patients was spiritual in nature. One neurologist said that "6% of the inmates in my psychiatric clinic are not so much suffering from mental illness as from occult subjugation or even demonization."[385] To misdiagnose demoniacs and "banish [them] to the realm of mental illness [is] a terrible mistake to make."[386]

In the case of the story recorded here in Matthew, Mark, and Luke, "the transference of demons to animals is ... a phenomenon ... completely unintelligible from the psychiatric point of view, even though it is admitted today that animals can suffer from various kinds of neuroses."[387] In other words, we must either consider Jesus and the apostles to themselves be hallucinating, to be liars, or we must accept that demon possession can exist.

A final word on this subject. In my own studies at a neuropharmochology course at U.T.D. a clinical psychiatrist was lecturing in class and admitted that when all the tools of his trade failed, he would, as a last resort, refer the patient to a priest, pastor, rabbi, or some other religious figure. He confessed that this tactic usually worked, and worked better than most of the tools used by clinical psychologists. Another psychiatrist phrased it even better, saying, "If I were able to obtain forgiveness for the sins of the patients in my clinic, I would be able to discharge half of them tomorrow."[388] Ironically, he may never even know how true he really is. Most "mental illness" is really spiritual in nature. It is through Jesus that we can obtain the forgiveness of sins, and the story told here in the synoptic gospels confirms that even the worst and most oppressed of all can be redeemed and freed through our Lord and Savior, Jesus Christ.

Summary

In these various accounts of the demoniac we have differing, but not contradictory eyewitness and second hand accounts of what transpired. The objective reader should be more like a juror than a defense attorney who is determined only to see the outcome of the case one way. A juror, however, is interested in truth. We who seek the truth cannot dismiss testimonies out of hand as do those who hate the truth. If the apostles lied, then time would have rooted them out. If, however, they have proven honest in other matters, there is no reason to reject their testimony here in a matter which is of no great significance in the first place.

Mark and Luke only mention a single man because he was the focus of the story, but nowhere do they deny that a second man was present. Gadarenes and Gerasenes were twin cities located the same region, twelve miles from city center to city center. That is closer than Dallas is to Fort Worth, although Dallas/Fort Worth is often abbreviated to "DFW." No contradiction is found here either. The two accounts differ only inasmuch as witnesses differ on what they felt was most important to the telling of the story, but nothing in these accounts is irreconcilable with the other. The jury is out, and the witnesses are born out.

Matthew 9:18-26 – See Mark 5:21-43 and Mark 5:25-34

The Twelve Disciples
Matthew 10:2-4 – Mark 3:16-19 – Luke 6:13-16 (Acts 1:13)

"Now the names of the twelve apostles are these: The first, Simon, who is called Peter, and Andrew his brother; and James the *son* of Zebedee, and John his brother; Philip and Bartholomew; Thomas and Matthew the tax-gatherer; James the *son* of Alphaeus, and Thaddaeus; Simon the Zealot, and Judas Iscariot, the one who betrayed Him."	"He appointed the twelve: Simon (to whom He gave the name Peter), and James, the *son* of Zebedee, and John the brother of James (to them He gave the name Boanerges, which means, "Sons of Thunder"); and Andrew, and Philip, and Bartholomew, and Matthew, and Thomas, and James the *son of* Alphaeus, and Thaddaeus, and Simon the Zealot; and Judas Iscariot, who betrayed Him."	"He called His disciples to Him and chose twelve of them, whom He also named as apostles: Simon, whom He also named Peter, and Andrew his brother; and James and John; and Philip and Bartholomew; and Matthew and Thomas; James *the son* of Alphaeus, and Simon who was called the Zealot; Judas *the son* of James, and Judas Iscariot, who became a traitor."

Some have seen a problem with the name Thaddaeus in Matthew and Mark whereas Luke (and Acts, also written by Luke) have Judas "of James." Critics scoff at those who say that Thaddaeus is the same person, but a survey of Greek and Hebrew names makes this apparent (as will be shown to the reader below). More intriguing is the question of whether or not this Judas Thaddaeus was the brother of Jesus.

Here is a quick overview of the apostles list in the synoptic gospels:

Matthew	Mark	Luke / Acts
Simon Peter	Simon Peter	Simon Peter
Andrew, Peter's brother	Andrew	Andrew, Peter's brother
James, the *son* of Zebedee	James, the *son* of Zebedee	James
John, James' brother	John, James' brother	John
Philip	Philip	Philip
Bartholomew	Bartholomew	Bartholomew
Matthew	Matthew Levi	Matthew Levi
Thomas	Thomas	Thomas
James *the son* of Alphaeus	James *the son* of Alphaeus	James *the son* of Alphaeus
Simon the Zealot	Simon the Zealot	Simon the Zealot
Thaddaeus	**Thaddaeus**	**Judas *the son* of James**
Judas Iscariot	Judas Iscariot	Judas Iscariot, the traitor

When we examine the original twelve apostles we note several things. First, at least two pair were brothers, possible three, and another may have been Jesus' brother. Simon Peter and Andrew were brothers (Matthew 10:2; Luke 6:14) as were John and James (Matthew 10:2; Mark 3:17). It should also be noted that Matthew Levi was also a son of Alphaeus (Mark 2:14; Luke 5:27) and thus may have been the brother of James, the son of Alphaeus. It is noteworthy that in Matthew's gospel the name James, the son of Alphaeus, immediately follows that of Matthew, just as Andrew's follows Peters and John's follows James. That "the son of Alphaeus" is only used to distinguish this James from the James the son of Zebedee is obvious, thus there is no reason for Matthew to list either his own heritage or that of John. Although by no means certain, it is a strong possibility.

Also worthy of mention is the theory that Judas "of James" is the brother of Jesus. This, however, I will reserve for debate after confirming that he is, in fact, the same Thaddaeus as mentioned in Matthew and Mark.

That the apostles had nicknames and were known by other names is apparent. Simon (probably Simeon in Hebrew) is explicitly said to have been given the name "Peter" by Jesus (Mark 3:16). Peter is Πετρος (*petros*) from the Greek word Πετρα (*petra*) meaning "rock"[389] (see notes on Matthew 16:18). He was also called Cephas (1 Corinthians 1:12 and others), the Aramaic word for "rock" (כֵּיפָא).[390] Likewise, John and James were dubbed "the son of Thunder" (Boanerges) by Jesus from the Hebrew construct of בְּנֵי (*bene*) meaning "sons of" and רֶגֶשׁ (*regesh*) meaning "tumultuous."[391] Matthew too is called Levi in Mark 2:14 and Luke 5:27. Now comes the question of Judas "of James" and whether or not he is the same as either Thaddaeus or Jude, the brother of Jesus or both.

Judas is the Greek version of Judah, which was among the most common names in Israel due the fact that Judah was the largest of the twelve tribes of Israel. It is hardly surprising then that someone named Judah would use a second name and/or surname to distinguish himself from his peers. This is also why Judas Iscariot carried the name Iscariot. In the King James Bible Thaddaeus is explicitly called a surname of Labbaeus. This reading, found in a few ancient manuscripts and the majority text served as the basis of the King James Bible, but most ancient copies read only Thaddaeus. In either case, Thaddaeus does not appear to be a proper name found among the Jews. It has all the marks of a nickname, much as Peter and other apostles were nicknamed by our Lord. There is dispute as to the actual meaning of Thaddaeus, however. D.A. Carson believes Thaddaeus comes from a root "roughly" meaning "beloved."[392] Joseph Thayer believes that it come from תַּדַּי (*thadday*) meaning courageous.[393] Merill Unger believes it is from תּוֹדָה (*thodah*), meaning to praise or to give thanks.[394] Unger believes that his full name was Judas Labbaeus, surnamed Thaddaeus.[395] There seems no real reason to reject this and no evidence to suggest otherwise.

The greater problem is whether or not this Judas Thaddaeus was also Jude the brother of James the less (Jude 1:1). The reader will note that the New American Standard Bible puts the word "son" in italics. This is because the Greek actually reads only Judas "of James." Now the normal meaning of this is "son of" but tradition holds that this Judas was one and the same as Jude (a shortened version of Judas or Judah). It is possible that "of James" could mean "brother of James" rather than the normal "son of James," although this translation would be uncommon. The strongest argument against this is the fact that Luke uses the specific word "brother" (αδελφος) in regard to Andrew (Luke 6:14). If Luke uses "brother" (αδελφος) for Andrew why would he not use it for Judas? The likely answer is that this Judas Thaddaeus is the "son of" a man named James, and not the brother of James the less.

One final note is needed on the reading Simon "the Cananaean" (sometimes erroneously rendered Canaanite). Cananaean is, in fact, a synonym for the Zealots. This is why many Bibles go ahead and translate it as such. They are one and the same. So the gospels are agreed that twelve apostles were:

1	Simon (Simeon), lovingly surnamed "Peter" to distinguish him from the other Simon
2	Andrew, the brother of Simon Peter
3	James, the son of Zebedee, called by tradition "James the greater"
4	John, "the apostle of love" and the brother of James the greater
5	Philip
6	Bartholomew
7	Matthew Levi, the tax-collector
8	Thomas, sometimes called by tradition "doubting Thomas"
9	James *the son* of Alphaeus, sometimes called by tradition "James the less"
10	Simon the Cananaean or Zealot
11	Judas Labbaeus, surnamed Thaddaeus to distinguish him from Iscariot (probably not Jude)
12	Judas Iscariot the traitor, later replaced by Matthias or the apostle Paul (but see debate in Acts)

The Staff
Matthew 10:9-10 – Mark 6:8 – Luke 9:3-5

"Do not acquire gold, or silver, or copper for your money belts, or a bag for *your* journey, or even two coats, or sandals, or a staff; for the worker is worthy of his support."	"He instructed them that they should take nothing for *their* journey, except a mere staff—no bread, no bag, no money in their belt."	"Take nothing for *your* journey, neither a staff, nor a bag, nor bread, nor money; and do not *even* have two tunics apiece."

This is another case of an *apparent* contradiction. At first glance it appears irreconcilable, but when we examine the context, the solution is easy. Consider that Jesus even told them not to go back for clothes or food. Are we to assume that they were naked? Are we to assume that they were to starve to death? Of course not. Jesus was telling them that "they were to go as they were."[396] "He that had one might take it; they that had none, might not provide any."[397]

This answer may appear *too* simple for some taste, but let us examine the facts carefully. In Matthew and Luke we have a quotation from Jesus. In Mark we have a general summary. In Matthew the specific words spoken are "do not acquire." In Greek the word is κτησησθε (*ktesesthe*) which is the subjunctive of the root word κταομαι (*ktaomai*). This word means to "acquire" or "to *procure* a thing *for one's self*."[398] In the subjunctive, that is exactly what it means.[399] It means not to go and procure what they did not already have. This is apparent by the emphasis on "extra" staff or "two tunics." One author even suggests that the "two" should modify not only the word "coat" but also "sandals and staff."[400] Grammatically, this is a valid argument. Logically, it is common sense. He was not, after all, asking them to travel barefoot.[401] "The Twelve are not to provide new sandals and a new staff in view of the four but are to go with the sandals and staff they already have."[402]

Despite these facts, some have sought other explanations. Gundry claims the gospel writers are employing "intensification."[403] William Barclay suggests that that the command was in response to the Talmud which forbids a staff in the Temple.[404] He says that Jesus was saying "you must treat the whole as your Temple of God."[405] Jonathan Edwards' Bible contains a note referenceing Numbers 2:18.[406] Of course this doesn't really answer the question. Still others argue that there is a difference in the staff spoken of my Mark and that of Matthew and Luke. John Calvin, for example, argued "Matthew and Luke mean the heavy sticks, which would be a burden to carry, but Mark means the light stick."[407] The *Liberty University Bible Commentary* says that "the meaning of Mark 6:8 is perhaps that they were to have one walking stick between the pair."[408]

One comment may be made on Mark's use of the word "except." The Greek is most literally translated as "if not." While this is the idiomatic way of saying "except," it doesn't always translate into English properly. It is an indication that "in Mark 6:8-9 the Twelve were to take (αιρω) a staff and sandals"[409] but "they are not to acquire (κταομαι) these things"[410] if they did not already have them. "In both accounts Jesus is prohibiting elaborate preparations for their journey."[411] So Mark "does not contradict Matt. x.10, where they are only forbidden to 'procure' a staff for their journey. They might take their staff if they possessed one."[412] This is the natural meaning, for no one suggest that Jesus was telling them to go naked and barefoot although they were also forbidden from going to "procure" more clothes or sandals for the journey.

Matthew 10:23 – See reference under Matthew 16:28

Christ Divideds Men
Matthew 10:34-39 – Luke 12:49-53

"Do not think that I came to bring peace on the earth; I did not come to bring peace, but a sword. For I came to 'set a man against his father, and a daughter against her mother, and a daughter-in-law against her mother-in-law; and a man's enemies will be the members of his household.'"	"Do you suppose that I came to grant peace on earth? I tell you, no, but rather division; for from now on five *members* in one household will be divided, three against two and two against three. They will be divided, father against son and son against father, mother against daughter and daughter against mother, mother-in-law against daughter-in-law and daughter-in-law against mother-in-law."

These harsh words are controversial because the appear to fly in the fact of Jesus' teachings concerning love and family. Indeed, these very words were used against Christians when we fed to lions and brutally persecuted by the ancient Romans.[413] The ancient pagan Roman historian Tacitus tells us that Christians were persecuted "for their hatred of mankind."[414] One can see why liberal theologians are quick to dismiss these words as not being authentic to Jesus. Even Donaldson and Roberts, editors of the Ante-Nicene Fathers, believe that Luke 12:50 was corrupted by "heretics,"[415] but cite no evidence to support this. In so doing they have justified the very attacks used by those who killed us.

81

The truth is that "context" is the word that draws fierce looks of anger and disgust from some Bible critics. I have literally seen some critics scoff at the very word, but context is the key to any legitimate interpretation. Only by taking words out of context can we twist the words. What then is the context?

John Wesley argued that "this is not the design, though it will be the event of His coming, through the opposition of devils and men."[416] Others have said that "the gospel would bring division" because of the local cults.[417] Indeed, Christianity has been persecuted for two thousand years. To this very day Christianity remains an illegal and/or restricted religion throughout most of the world.[418] An estimated 70% of all religious persecution today is directed against Christians. Cyprian declared that "we ever provoke the enemies of truth."[419] Tertullian likened this division to the separation of spiritual and carnal man,[420] saying that Christ "came to send fire on earth."[421]

Further context indicates that Jesus was not only warning us of opposition from pagans but also making a stern command that "nothing is to be preferred to the love of God and Christ."[422] John MacArthur states that "becoming a Christian requires affirming the lordship of Christ to the point where you are willing to forsake everything else."[423] While some rightly have a problem with MacArthur's view of "Lordship-salvation" the general remark is valid. Christianity was not intended to be an easy choice. It is choice which involves risk of loosing the love of one's very own family. To this day, even in America, and especially abroad, some families will disown their child for accepting Christ. We are called "intollerant" because we reject other religions (as if they accepted ours), and because we reject the traditions of our forefathers (assuming you are not from a Christian country). The way of Christ is not easy, but difficult. Jesus said, "the gate is small and the way is narrow that leads to life, and there are few who find it" (Matthew 7:14). This is a view not well tolerated by the majority, thus the sword of truth (cf. Hebrews 4:12) divides men and brings about conflict. When we choose to follow the Lord, we must be willing to accept that our own families will reject us. That is the price of following Jesus.

Lowly or Humble?
Matthew 11:29

"Take My yoke upon you, and learn from Me, for I am gentle and humble in heart."

This translation is not controversial, but it should be. We live in a generation which views "self-esteem" and other *self*ish ideology as sacrosanct. Consequently most see nothing wrong with calling one's self "humble" even though this would, at one time, be considered the height of irony. That is why the King James Bible, the ASV, RSV, and all other older translations correctly translate this as "lowly" rather than "humble."

The Greek word is ταπεινὸς (*tapeinos*). Thayer's Greek Lexicon translates this word as "lowly, of low degree."[424] Alternately it can mean to be "low in spirit,"[425] hence humble. Zondervan's *Complete Vocabulary Guide*, used widely in seminaries today, translates this word as "poor, subservient" or even "downcast one."[426] Yet another modern Biblical Greek dictionary lists "down-hearted" and even "lacking in confidence" as its meaning.[427] Now I do not mean to infer that "humble" is not a valid translation, for it is, and such is also listed in all the dictionaries above, but once upon a time people understood that a humble man does not call himself humble. He might call himself "lowly" or "poor" or "of low degree" but he does not call himself humble for to do so would be anything but humble. This point is lost on too many raised on the popularity of modern Christian psychology and its emphasis upon self worship, self esteem, and other selfish ideology. The point which Jesus is making is that He is "lowly in heart" and soul. That spirit is what makes for love and compassion. Pride makes for vanity, sin, and hatred. Therefore, even if following Christ is hard (cf. Matthew 10:34-39; Luke 12:49-53), Jesus' yoke is gentle. That is what Jesus said.

Can Satan Cast Out Satan?
Matthew 12:22-29

> "The Pharisees heard *this*, they said, 'This man casts out demons only by Beelzebul the ruler of the demons.' And knowing their thoughts Jesus said to them, 'Any kingdom divided against itself is laid waste; and any city or house divided against itself will not stand. If Satan casts out Satan, he is divided against himself; how then will his kingdom stand? If I by Beelzebul cast out demons, by whom do your sons cast *them* out? For this reason they will be your judges.'"

This passage is controversial primarily because it has been used by cult leaders and even pagans to argue that they must be from God. After all, even pagan priests claim to cast out demons, or do they? Jesus Himself made a curious remark when he said, "If I by Beelzebul cast out demons, by whom do your sons cast *them* out?" Now if their sons cast demons out, were they followers of Christ? No. This infers something else. Was Jesus really saying that only true believers can cast out demons or was He challenging the Pharisees to prove that his acts were against the will of God? We must consider two things in this regard.

First, although pagans claim to cast out demons, there are countless accounts where such incidents only led to worse oppression. Merrrill Unger said that "their object is not to liberate the victim but to deceive and enslave him."[428] In other cases some professionals have observed that the man who cast out the demons actually becomes possessed himself;[429] thus the victim is freed, but the priest has become possessed. In such cases it is clear that Satan's kingdom is not divided.

Second, Jesus clearly thrust the Pharisees accusations back in their face by asking them "by whom do your sons cast" out demons. This was Jesus' way of saying that the Pharisees were employing double standards. They accuse Jesus of casting out demons by Beelzebul but did not accuse their own sons of doing so, though both were casting out demons. He was challenging them to prove their logic and to show that Satan was not dividing against Himself, but in so doing, could He not also have been implying that some, at least pretend to, cast out demons that are not truly of God?

On this point I will not offer a definitive answer save to say that not all who claim to cast out demons are to be believed. Demons are deceivers and if they can deceive by leaving a man, by pretending to leave, or by possessing the very men who are performing the excorcism, then they triumph. The apostle Paul once declared, "But even if we, or an angel from heaven, should preach to you a gospel contrary to what we have preached to you, he is to be accursed!" (Galatians 1:8). So also 1 John 4:1 warns us :

> "Beloved, do not believe every spirit, but test the spirits to see whether they are from God, because many false prophets have gone out into the world. By this you know the Spirit of God: every spirit that confesses that Jesus Christ has come in the flesh is from God; and every spirit that does not confess Jesus is not from God; this is the *spirit* of the antichrist, of which you have heard that it is coming, and now it is already in the world" (vv. 1-3).

So Jesus is not telling us to blindly believe any who claim to cast out demons. He was challenging His critics to prove their assertation that the Devil's work was being done when it was clear that Jesus was bringing about great change for God. Such passages should be taken in context and not used to issue a blanket acceptance of all exorcisms.

Did the Pharisees Receive A Sign?
Matthew 12:38-39 – Mark 8:12-13 – Luke 11:29

"Then some of the scribes and Pharisees said to Him, 'Teacher, we want to see a sign from You.' But He answered and said to them, 'An evil and adulterous generation craves for a sign; and *yet* no sign will be given to it but the sign of Jonah the prophet.'"	"The Pharisees came out and began to argue with Him, seeking from Him a sign from heaven, to test Him. Sighing deeply in His spirit, He said, 'Why does this generation seek for a sign? Truly I say to you, no sign will be given to this generation.'"	"As the crowds were increasing, He began to say, 'This generation is a wicked generation; it seeks for a sign, and *yet* no sign will be given to it but the sign of Jonah.'"

No sign but the sign of Jonah. This famous prophecy predicts the death and resurrection of Jesus, but it also begs the question; didn't the Pharisees already see many signs? If so, then why would Jesus say they will receive no signs? The answer is actually very relevant today; particularly in the secular west.

It has been noted that among the great many signs already wrought by Jesus was a resurrection (Matthew 9:24-26)![430] Of course, the Pharisees had already just dismissed some of these miracles to demonic activity just a few paragraphs earlier (Matthew 12:22-29). Thus "'a sign to see' is an objection to the signs Jesus has thus far wrought."[431]

It has further been pointed out that such request among the Jews were not unusual. Ancient Jewish literature is filled with request for signs similar to those of Elijah.[432] The Pharisees expected lightning from heaven, earthquakes, and/or similar "proofs" to be issued forth at Jesus' command, but John Calvin stated that while many ask for signs, even as Gideon did, "Christ does not directly censure the scribes for asking for a sign but because in their ingratitude to God they maliciously spurn His many wonderful works."[433]

Tertullian said that the Lord "enjoins 'giving to everyone that seeks;' and yet he refuses to give to those 'who seek a sign.'"[434] The relevance of this today is obvious. In the secular west, we are used to hearing the mocking atheist blind to the miracles all around him, claiming magots and slugs are his distant cousins, and demanding that God strike him dead if He exist (but fully prepared to say how cruel and malicious God would be if He actually did strike him down). Such mocking baffoonery is what Jesus met. Despite all His miracles, His critics dismissed them in one way or another and demanded a "sign" which would suit their own tastes, even as critics continue to do so to this very day. I am reminded of the comic strip B.C. where the character is praying as asking God, "How do we know you even exis ..."? He is immediately interrupted by the parting seas, thunderstorms, earthquakes, and a stone rolling away from a now empty tomb. The character then says, "okay, okay ... I give up! Evertime I bring up this subject, all we get is interruptions!" He does not see any "signs" because he does not *want* to see them. Conversely there are many cults which rely on "signs," real or otherwise is irrelevant, to deceive people. This is the paradox. God is interested in faith, not signs. To reinterate, God gives many signs "'to everyone that seeks;' and yet he refuses to give to those 'who seek a sign.'"[435]

Matthew 12:40 – See "When Was Jesus Crucified?"

Matthew 12:46-50 – See Mark 3:31-35

Matthew 13:2-9 – See Luke 8:4-15

Parables and the Bible
Matthew 13:10-15

"I speak to them in parables; because while seeing they do not see, and while hearing they do not hear, nor do they understand."

Jesus often spoke in parables. These parables form an important part of Jesus' teachings, yet sadly some treat history as if it were parable and distort the meaning and purpose of parables in Jesus' ministry. It is important to understand therefore what parables are and how they are used by Jesus, as well as to distinguish between parable and history.

The later should not be hard, for when Jesus spoke in parables He said so. Contrary to the jest and sarcasm of the self-professed liberal theologian Jesus never spoke a parable without telling people he was speaking in parables. Moreover, it is clear that even in parables, the words had meanings; specific (literal) meanings. That is why the apostles asked Jesus what the parables meant; because there is an objective meaning. There is a right and wrong answer. It is therefore necessary to understand why Jesus spoke in parables and how one should interpret parables.

Why Jesus Spoke in Parables

This is the very question the disciples asked Jesus:

"The disciples came and said to Him, 'Why do You speak to them in parables?'

"Jesus answered them, 'To you it has been granted to know the mysteries of the kingdom of heaven, but to them it has not been granted. For whoever has, to him *more* shall be given, and he will have an abundance; but whoever does not have, even what he has shall be taken away from him. Therefore I speak to them in parables; because while seeing they do not see, and while hearing they do not hear, nor do they understand. In their case the prophecy of Isaiah is being fulfilled, which says;

"'You will keep on hearing, but will not understand; You will keep on seeing, but will not perceive; For the heart of this people has become dull, With their ears they scarcely hear, And they have closed their eyes, Otherwise they would see with their eyes, hear with their ears, and understand with their heart and return, and I would heal them'"" (Matthew 13:10-15).

To the secularist this seems like nonsense. To the liberal theologian this is mystic. To the believer it makes perfect sense. Symbols, and parables specifically, are not subjective as the liberal theologian claims. Symbols have specific meanings. A cross represents Christianity. A dove represents peace.

Context may render a slightly different meaning, but there are clear and specific (literal) meanings. The skeptic does not understand. To the secular man the cross is an instrument of torture. They will never understand how a Christian can look at a cross and see a symbol for life eternal. It is beyond their means, because they proceed from another prejudice. So also, the man who does not know Christ cannot and will not understand the true meaning of a parable in his heart. He might understand the symbolism, but he cannot understand its meaning; just as he cannot understand the message of the cross.

This method of teaching also has two other strong benefits. First, it allowed Jesus to speak openly against the hierarchy of his day. Although they understood, at least in part, that He was speaking about them on occasion, they could not move against Him on the basis of parables. They could not prove His words treasonous. Second, and more importantly, it allows even the newest of believers to be able to understand the message on a basic level. Unlike theological seminaries where theological terminology and intricasies are bandied about (even as my critics sometimes accuse me of doing), Jesus spoke to the common man on level that he could understand. He did not speak about Calvinistic predestination, but the sovereign will of God. He did not speak about a dispensational premillennial kingdom, but about the Kingdom of God coming to the people of Israel in due course. Nor did He speak of the perspicuity of Scriptures, but rather of the clarity that the Word of God speaks to those who believe and listen.

Interpreting Parables

The liberal mocks the literal interpretation of Scriptures by appealing to the parables and saying that Jesus did not turn into a loaf of bread when He said "I am the bread of life." Such childishness garners a few chuckles but shows both the ignorance of the Bible mockers and their inability to show any consistent interpretive methodology. *Any* legitimate exegesis of *any* work must be consistent and objective, rather than subjective and inconsistent.

The first question is, "are parables allegories?" Perhaps there is no "fundamentalist" or literalist more stringent than E.W. Bullinger, but among Bullinger's more famous works is a thousand page book describing a consistent and logical interpretation of the symbols in the Bible. In that book he describes a parable as "a story with a hidden meaning"[436] which is, in terms of interpretation, a *"continued Simile* – an illustration by which one set of circumstances is likened to another. It consists in *likeness*, not in representation, and therefore is not a continued *Metaphor*, as some have said; but a *repeated Simile.*"[437] In other words, the story is not a mere fairy tale, but it represents something real and literal which Jesus wanted to convey to His followers. Another text on hermeneutics suggests that "it seems likely that all these allegorical [interpretations] have little to do wtih the original meaning of the parable."[438] Some have even stated outright that "parables are not allegories."[439] What does all this mean?

Simply put it means that parables, like everything else in the Bible have specific and clear meanings that are not left open to subjective interpretations. The so-called liberal theologians deny this. They make the Bible open to subjective meanings. One of the pastors I was raised under used to say "this means something different to everyone," but when Jesus taught His disciples He gave it only one meaning, not many. Jesus taught there is a right and a wrong answer. The parable of the sower is a prime example and is debated under Luke 8:4-15. A serious examinion of parables illustrates the importance of interpreting the parables in a consistent methodology.

Summary

It is significant that Jesus not only identified every parable He spoke as a parable but that He explained its meaning to His disciples. Two things can be inferred from this. First, if He was not telling a real and literal story, He made sure His followers knew it. He did not deceive His followers or make up fairy tales. The Bible is true and literal history and whenever a parable is told, Jesus identified it as such. Second, by explaining its meaning to the disciples Jesus was affirming that the meanings of parables are not subjective. They have a specific and clear meaning. As such we should not go beyond what Jesus said as some high allegorists have done. Parables contain some of the most important and blessed teachings of Jesus' ministry and so we ought treat them with the highest respect and not add to Jesus' words.

The Parable of the Sower
Matthew 13:2-9; 18-23 – See Luke 8:4-15

John the Baptist Beheaded
Matthew 14:1-11 – Mark 6:14-29 – Luke 9:7-9

"The daughter of Herodias danced before *them* and pleased Herod, so *much* that he promised with an oath to give her whatever she asked. Having been prompted by her mother, she said, 'Give me here on a platter the head of John the Baptist.'"

"The daughter of Herodias herself came in and danced, she pleased Herod ... and the king said to the girl, 'Ask me for whatever you want ... up to half of my kingdom.' ... and she said, 'The head of John the Baptist.'"

"Now Herod ... was greatly perplexed, because it was said by some that John had risen from the dead ... Herod said, 'I myself had John beheaded; but who is this man about whom I hear such things?' And he kept trying to see Him."

88

John Waterhouse – Judgment Seat of Herod – 1887

There is not a great deal of controversy here so much as misunderstanding. The daughter of Herodias is not named in the gospels, but it is Josephus, the ancient Jewish historian, who tells us that her name was Salome.[440] This Salome should not be confused with the Salome found at the tomb of Christ with the two Marys (Mark 15:40; 16:1). Josephus further confirms the relationship of Herodias and the unlawful marriage which John criticized.

The only other issue which occasionally crops up is the question of blame (a question all too popular in this generation). It is clear that Herodias was the one who schemed with Salome to deliver up John the Baptist's head, and yet "Matthew lays the blame at Herod's door."[441] Of course this is no surprise. Herod himself admits "I myself had John beheaded" (Luke 9:9). He was tetrarch and he was himself responsible even though it was Herodias and Salome who plotted the crime.

The First Feeding of the Multitudes
Matthew 14:13-21 – Mark 6:32-44 – Luke 9:10-17 – John 6:1-13
See Matthew 15:32-39

Feeding the Dogs
Matthew 15:21-28 – Mark 10:25-28

"A Canaanite woman from that region came out and *began* to cry out, saying, 'Have mercy on me, Lord, Son of David; my daughter is cruelly demon-possessed.' ... He answered and said, 'I was sent only to the lost sheep of the house of Israel ... It is not good to take the children's bread and throw it to the dogs.'"	"The woman was a Gentile, of the Syrophoenician race. And she kept asking Him to cast the demon out of her daughter. And He was saying to her, 'Let the children be satisfied first, for it is not good to take the children's bread and throw it to the dogs.'"

This is another of the "hard sayings" of Jesus, and it is understandable, for the same Jesus who came to save *all* men here appears to be saying that he came only for the Jews and that gentiles are but "dogs." Obviously, this passage is among the more controversial in the gospels. To this end some scholars through the ages have tried to soften Jesus' remarks by implying that dog was a term of affection such as that used of a pet.[442] They insist that dog is "not necessarily a derogatory term."[443] Even H.A. Ironside suggested that Jesus meant it as "puppies."[444] Now such arguments ultimately do nothing for the discourse, for even if "dog" were not a derisive term (and it obviously is), it does not change the fact that Jesus was apparently refusing to cast demon's out of her daughter because she was a gentile. We must deal with this issue rather than trying to soften the words of Jesus.

Another argument used to dismiss the harsh words of Jesus is to emphasize that Jesus was simply testing her faith.[445] The *Liberty Bible Commentary* notes that Jesus wanted to "test the woman's faith"[446] or her "splendid faith,"[447] as another put it. Ironside said "it was meant to manifest the true attitude of her soul."[448] Now it will be conceded that since Jesus did give her what she asked for, it is apparent that this is true, but this is not a sufficient answer in and of itself. Regardless of whether or not He was testing her faith (He was) we must deal with the statement itself, for Jesus does not lie.

First, it has been pointed out that "the Jews called all Gentiles" dogs.[449] This was not unusual in itself. John MacArthur reminds us that the Canaanites were supposed to be wiped out by Joshua,[450] but the Israelis failed in that task. Most significant is the fact that, as Charles Spurgeon said, the woman "did not at all dispute it, but yielded the point."[451] Instead of denying that she was a dog, she (not Jesus) likened herself to a pet who begs for scraps at the table. What then does this mean?

John Calvin remarked that despite His comments, "the faith she had conceived in the goodness of the Messiah."[452] She did not react negatively to His statement but continued to believe in the righteousness of Christ. MacArthur said she showed five qualities of faith : repentance, direction, reverence, persistence, and humility.[453] Others say she showed love, faith, an indomitable persistence, and the gift of cheerfulness.[454] In other words, through this gentile "dog" Jesus wanted to show the people of Israel what true faith looks like and show that such faith is rewarded.

A second point to be made out of this is inferred by Tertullian who said "not yet had He 'cast to the dogs the children's bread.'"[455] What does he mean by this? Jesus clearly stated that He was sent "to the lost sheep of the house of Israel." Anyone familiar with the history of Christianity knows that the gentile Church did not truly develop until the time of Saint Paul, and even then there was a great debate among the apostles as to whether or not gentile converts had to convert to Judaism before they could become Christians (cf. Galatians 2). This is actually an important point which touches upon the doctrine known as dispensationalism. Specifically, has God forsaken the Jews as a race or will God keep His promises to Israel as a nation regardless of their faithfulness or faithlessness?

This debate will not be resolved in this passage, but the short answer is that the Church age is distinguished by Jesus from Israel and the age in which He was living. Several times in the book of Romans Paul stated that the gospel was given "first to the Jews, and then also the Greek" or gentile (Romans 1:16; 2:9-10). Jews and gentiles are thus distinguished even in the Church age, and yet the same Paul says "there is no partiality with God" (Romans 2:10)! This debate will be expanded in *Controversies in the Epistles* and cannot be answered here. It is sufficient only to say that Jesus' ministry was indeed to Israel. It was Paul who was sent to the gentile world. Thus Jesus does distinguish between the two even though He loves all equally. This division is, in part, because "the first will be last, and the last first" (Matthew 19:30; Mark 10:31). The Jews were the chosen race, but "I was found by those who did not seek me, and called those who are not a nation" (Isaiah 65:1; Romans 10:20). But if the *last* (gentiles) were the *first* to accept Christ, then the Jews (*first* chosen) will be the *last* to accept the Messiah, but they *will* be saved. God has not, and never will, forsake Israel.

The Second Feeding
Matthew 15:32-38 – Mark 8:1-21

"'Where would we get so many loaves in *this* desolate place to satisfy such a large crowd?' And Jesus said to them, 'How many loaves do you have?' And they said, 'Seven, and a few small fish.' And He directed the people to sit down on the ground; and He took the seven loaves and the fish ... And they all ate and were satisfied, and they picked up what was left over of the broken pieces, seven large baskets full. And those who ate were four thousand men, besides women and children."

"'How many loaves do you have?' And they said, 'Seven.' And He directed the people to sit down on the ground; and taking the seven loaves, He gave thanks and broke them, and started giving them to His disciples to serve to them ... and they ate and were satisfied; and they picked up seven large baskets full of what was left over of the broken pieces. About four thousand were *there;* and He sent them away."

This is no contradiction between these two passages, nor between the four accounts of the feeding of five thousand. In both accounts here the four thousand are fed with seven loaves and a few fish, and the remains filled seven baskets. The the first feeding all four gospels agree that there were five loaves, two fish, and the remains filled twelve baskets. However, some have seen problems between the feeding of the five thousand and the feeding of the four thousand. It is not uncommon to hear some people, ignorant of the fact that there are two separate feedings, claim that four thousand and the five thousand are the same account confused by the gospel writers. Of course, the fact that both feedings are recorded in Matthew and Mark easily discounts this argument.

A second contention is the question of how the apostles could ask, "'Where would we get so many loaves in *this* desolate place to satisfy such a large crow," if they had already fed five thousand earlier. The answer to this is equally easy for Jesus Himself remarks:

"'Do you not remember, when I broke the five loaves for the five thousand, how many baskets full of broken pieces you picked up?' They said to Him, 'Twelve.' 'When *I broke* the seven for the four thousand, how many large baskets full of broken pieces did you pick up?' And they said to Him, 'Seven.' And He was saying to them, 'Do you not yet understand?'" (Mark 8:19-21).

92

It is neither unreasonable, nor faithless, to question whether or not Jesus would repeat the miracle performed before the five thousand. Furthermore, the question asked by the apostle was "how?" He did not deny that Christ could repeat the miracle, but asked "how" the people should be fed. Jesus gave them the answer and they followed his instructions. Finally, it should be noted that even when the ancient Jews saw Moses part the Red Sea, they still lacked faith. Seeing is not believing. That saying is a myth. Faith is of the heart.

<h2 style="text-align:center">Was Peter the First Pope?
Matthew 16:18</h2>

> "You are Peter, and upon this rock I will build My church; and the gates of Hades will not overpower it. I will give you the keys of the kingdom of heaven; and whatever you bind on earth shall have been bound in heaven, and whatever you loose on earth shall have been loosed in heaven."

This passage is the passage used by the Catholic Church to support the doctrine of the papacy and the idea that Peter was the first pope. Protestants, with equal vigor, reject this in its entirety and almost to a man believe that the "rock" was not Peter, but Jesus Himself. I will not repeat the countless thousands of scholars, Catholics and Protestants, who repeat these views, for no one contests that these are the stubborn views of both. On the contrary, I will endeavor here to show both are in error.

<h3 style="text-align:center">The Rock</h3>

The first question is who or what is "the rock" to which Jesus refers. Traditionally Catholics have insisted that it none other than Peter himself while Protestants have reacted to the other extreme declaring Christ alone can be the rock and no one else.

The argument for both proceeds from the original Greek. The words are literally, "You are *Petros* (Πετρος) and on this *petra* (πετρα) I will build my church." *Petra* (πετρα), of course, is the Greek word for rock. Thus it seems apparent that Jesus is making a word play on Peter's name and, therefore, that Peter himself is that rock of which Jesus speaks. Many Protestants deny this voraciously. They argue that *Petros* (Πετρος) and *petra* (πετρα) are different words. Loraine Boettner argued that because *Petros* (Πετρος) is a masculine word and *petra* (πετρα) is feminine, the two cannot be the same.[456] James McCarthy argued that *Petros* (Πετρος) is properly a stone and *petra* (πετρα) properly a bedrock, saying, "What Jesus said to Peter could be translated 'You are *Stone*, and upon this *bedrock* I will build my church.'"[457] However, even if we assumed this to be true (and it will be discussed in detail momentarily) the above sentence is grammatically incorrect for we would have an untransitional shift. "This" *must* have an antecedent. If the antecedant of *petra* (πετρα) is not *Petros* (Πετρος), then what is it? Boettner and McCathy wish to refer it back to Christ Himself. Is this possible?

First, it is in error to claim that *Petros* (Πετρος) and *petra* (πετρα) are different words. In Greek proper names *all* have the sigma at the end. Because Peter is a man, the rendering of his name will obviously be masculine. This does not change the fact that it is, as a famed Greek lexicon states, "an appellative proper name" stemming from *petra* (πετρα).[458] It's definition does not differ from *petra* (πετρα) except inasmuch as it is a proper name.[459]

Second, Peter is the name given to Simon, the son of Jonah by none other than Jesus Himself (cf. John 1:42). It was Jesus' pet name for Simon and it is clear that in this verse Jesus is making a word play on Peter's name; a fact Boettner even admits.[460] The question is, therefore, what does the word play mean and what is the "rock"?

Some Protestants, like Matthew Poole, readily admit that this is so, arguing that rock is used in the sense of "a steady, firm believer."[461] Others, note that Jesus is called the foundation repeatedly in Scriptures, and Boettner even notes that "some of the church fathers, Augustine and Jerome among them, gave the Protestant explanation of this verse."[462] He is correct. However, there is a problem with this, and it is not a small one. The passages in which Jesus is called the foundation do *not* use the word *petra* (πετρα) as implied by Boettner and others. In each and every passage where Jesus is referred to the word is "cornerstone." This is a *different* word in Greek.

Matthew 21:42, Mark 12:10, and Luke 20:17 all quote Isaiah 28:16 which reads, "I am laying in Zion a stone, a tested stone, a costly cornerstone *for* the foundation, firmly placed. He who believes *in it* will not be put to shame." The word in each of these passages is *lithon* (λιθον) coupled with *kephalen gonias* (κεφαλην γωνιας). *Lithon* (λιθον) means "stone" and *kephalen gonias* (κεφαλην γωνιας) means "chief corner." Together they mean the "chief cornerstone." Nowhere is the word *petra* (πετρα) used. Acts 4:11 also uses *lithos* (λιθος), saying "this is the stone [λιθος] which was set at nought of you builders, which is become the head of the corner."

The strongest proof is found in Ephesians 2:20 where the apostle Paul declares that the universal Church is "built upon the foundation of the apostles and prophets, Jesus Christ himself being the chief corner *stone*." In this passage the "chief cornerstone" is one word, *akpogoniaiou* (ακρογωνιαιου) which is composed of the root *gonias* (γωνιας) found in the previous passages, meaning "corner." Note then that Ephesians not only declares that Jesus is the cornerstone, but also says that the church is built upon the foundation of the "apostles and prophets"! Thus it appears that Scriptures distinguish between a cornerstone (λιθον κεφαλην γωνιας) and a foundation rock (πετρα).

94

So it is clear that while Jesus is the cornerstone, Peter, and the other apostles, are foundations as well, but not cornerstones. The analogy is actually perfect, for a building cannot stand without a cornerstone. The central foundations, represented by the *petra* (πετρα), are necessary to keep the floors from caving in, but the building itself stands on its cornerstone which is Jesus Christ, and Jesus Christ alone. Protestants are thus *theologically* correct, but Catholics are *gramatically* correct. The real question is not whether or not Peter was the rock spoken of here, for he is, but what Jesus meant by it.

The Keys of the Kingdom

Having established that Peter is indeed the "rock" of which Jesus speaks, the next question is what do the keys of the Kingdom represent and do they bestow papal authority on Peter and/or his "successors"?

Everyone is familiar with the imagery of Saint Peter standing at the pearly gates of heaven with the keys. In popular imagery he alone can open the gates and let someone enter. Of course this imagery goes far beyond what is spoken of here, and implies that Peter, rather than Christ, has the very keys to salvation itself! Moreover, the Catholic Church not only bestow this authority on Peter but also upon all his "successors" although none are mentioned, or even alluded to, within these passages.

According to the official *Catechism of the Catholic Church* article 553, the keys of the kingdom represent "supreme authority"; not just authority, but *supreme* authority. Matthew Henry, on the other hand, says "the Old Testament promises relating to the church were given immediately to particular persons, eminent for faith and holiness, as to Abraham and David, which yet gave no supremacy to them, much less to any of their successors."[463] Moreover, one is want to find anything in this passage which refers to successors at all.

Let us consider first whether or not Peter was given *supreme* authority. Jesus does say that "whatever you bind on earth will be bound in heaven, and whatever you loose on earth will be loosed in heaven" but this is not the only place where that phrase is found, for in Matthew 18:18 Jesus repeats these exact same words to *all* the disciples, and some believe that Jesus was even speaking to *all* believers.

Certainly it is clear that Peter was not the only one to receive this authority. Furthermore, the apostle Paul clearly recognized no superiority of Peter over himself. After his conversion he states "I did not immediately consult with flesh and blood, nor did I go up to Jerusalem to those who were apostles before me" (Galatians 1:16-17) but rather "when Cephas [Peter] came to Antioch, I opposed him to his face, because he stood condemned" (Galatians 2:11). Paul goes on to explain this confrontation; "I said to Cephas [Peter] in the presence of all, 'If you, being a Jew, live like the Gentiles and not like the Jews, how *is it that* you compel the Gentiles to live like Jews?'" (Galatians 2:14).

Make no mistake, this was a personal insult to Peter. To suggest that a Jew was living like a gentile was a slap in the face. It is like calling a pastor or priest today a pagan. This clearly illustrates that Paul did not see Peter as having any supreme authority over him.

Finally, if Peter was the first pope it is odd that he never claims such authority or appears to exercise it even when the apostles were voting on a replacement for Judas Iscariot. Instead they all voted on the successor to Judas, choosing Matthias (Acts 1:26). This passage, therefore, does not appear to bestow any supreme authority upon Peter, and what authority was bestowed upon him was also given to the other apostles equally (Matthew 18:18).

Summary

The founder of the Church of Rome was not Peter, but Paul. It was Paul who was the "apostle of gentiles" (Romans 11:13). It is not insignificant that he does not address his Roman epistle to Peter. Furthermore, when he concludes his letter he sends greetings from all those known to the Romans which include such names as Timothy, Lucius, Jason, Sosipater, Tertius, Gaius, Erastus, and Quartus (Romans 16:21-23) but *not* Peter. If Peter was in Rome at that time it is odd Paul does not even mention him and if Peter was known to the Romans as their bishop, why does he not even send greetings? In fact, no ancient historian calls Peter a bishop of Rome. It is true that he did visit Rome and died in Rome (a fact denied by too many Protestants), but never is he called a bishop. Moreover, if such a thing as the papacy did exist, why would its head be Rome rather than Jerusalem? Shouldn't Peter have been the bishop of Jerusalem instead?

The simple fact is that too many theologians, both Catholic and Protestant, engage in what theologians sarcastically call *eisegesis* as opposed to *exegesis*. They read *into* the text what they want to find, instead of taking *out of* the text what is actually there. Textually, it is clear that Jesus is making a play of Peter's nickname. He is a "rock" and he, as well as the other apostles (Ephesians 2:20), are *a* foundation, but Jesus is the *cornerstone*. Jesus is the immovable rock, but that rock is properly a stone (*lithon* - λιθον) or cornerstone (*kephalen gonias* - κεφαλην γωνιας). Peter is merely a rock (*petra* - πετρα).

The authority given to Peter in this verse is also given to the other apostles (Matthew 18:18) and nothing implies any supremacy over the other apostles. Paul, in fact, showed no submission to Peter on several occasions, even publically challenging him (Galatians 2). Finally, there is nothing whatsoever in the text to infer a succession of apostles as claimed by the Roman Catholic Church. The passage is a testament to Peter and his faith and shows the divine authority God bestowed upon His apostles, but nothing more can be read into this passage. There is no papal supremacy found herein and no succession of apostles to the modern day.

Matthew 16:21 – See comments under "When Was Jesus Crucified?"

The Coming Kingdom
Matthew 16:28 – Mark 9:1 – Luke 9:27

"There are some of those who are standing here who will not taste death
until they see the Son of Man coming in His kingdom."

This is a highly controversial passage which involves a multitude of
issues. Was Jesus implying that His Second Coming will take place before all
of the apostle's died? Was He saying the Kingdom would come to earth before
then? Did one of these things happen? If not, was Jesus mistaken? The very
questions prod at certain theological assumptions. Just as Catholics read the
papacy into Matthew 16:18, so here dispensationalists, covenant theologians,
preterists, progressive dispensationalists, and many other theological ideologies
are read into the passage. All told there are no fewer than seven major theories
on the interpretation of this passage and most relate in one way or another to the
theological assumptions of the interpreter. Nevertheless, removing these
assumptions does not provide as much assistance as usual, for the curious
coupling of "who will not taste death" with the "Son of Man coming in His
kingdom" cannot be so easily resolved and should not be neglected.

Seven Theories

Leon Morris has counted seven predominant interpretations of this
passage.[464] Now seven is a favorite number of Christian theologians, but at least
one more could be added to the number, hence I list eight views. These theories
are recounted here in order of the chronology of events to which they refer and
are not organized by favorites.

A word before examining the views is prudent. It is wise to keep in
mind *two* critical parts of the passage. First, "there are some of those who are
standing here who will not taste death." This implies that there are some who
will taste death. Second is that they will see "the Son of Man coming in His
kingdom." Note "in His kingdom." This is no mere appearance as in Matthew
10:23 but a coming "in His kingdom." Any correct view must account for both.

Theory #1 : The Transfiguration
The theory of the Transfiguration is the view that the prophecy was about the
events of the Transfiguration which took place shortly afterwards. Tim
LaHaye's Study Bible probably best defines the view by saying;

"Verse 27 speaks of the second coming of Christ. In order to encourage
His disciples to keep a heavenly perspective. Jesus promises to

demonstrate a glimpse of His second coming to some of them. This promise was fulfilled in the Transfiguration."[465]

This view is by far the dominant view of most evangelical Christians. It is supported by scholars ranging from R.A. Torrey[466] to Stanley Toussaint[467] to George Peters[468] to Warren Wiersbe[469] and many others, but is it correct?

The argument in favor of this interpretation is that the events of the Transfiguration show the manifest powers of Jesus and offer a glimpse of the kingdom to come. Further, R.A. Torrey argues textually that "there should not be a chapter division where Matthew 17 begins."[470] He suggest that "the words were spoken as a prophecy of the Transfiguration, the account of which immediately follows the closely connecting conjunction 'and.'"[471] However, ancient Greek did not use periods or puntuation marks. Consequently, different conjunctions served that purpose. The Greek word *kai* (και) although correctly translated "and" in most cases, is also the word often used to designate a new sentence or even paragraph.[472] Thus its appearance here is hardly proof that the events of the Transfiguration is a fulfillment of the previous passage.

The biggest problem with this view is that it seems to neglect entirely the statement that "there are some of those who are standing here who will not taste death." Wiersbe says that "this statement would be fulfilled within a week on the Mount of Transfiguration"[473] but if that is so then how does those "who will not taste death" fit? "Some" of the disciples? Only three went to the mount of Transfiguration, but the statement was "some ... will not taste death."

In an attempt to reconcile this problem with the Transfiguration view Bruce Chilton argues that "those not tasting death" refers to Moses and Elijah, not the apostles.[474] Although innovative it does not fit the context at all. First, neither Moses nor Elijah were standing there are the time. Second, the context clearly implies some of the apostles *would not* die, and therefore some of the other apostles *would* die, before the event occurred.

Sir Robert Anderson asked rhetorically, "should we need the words of 2 Peter i. 16-18 to convince us that it was fulfilled at the Transfiguration?"[475] If these words do not imply a "remote event"[476] then we should have expected several apostles to have died in the week before the Transfiguration. If not, then Jesus' statement was irrelevant and sensational.

Theory #2 : The Triumphant Entry
A too often neglected minority view is that Jesus was referring to the Triumphant entry.[477] In some respects this is a good view for it was a "coming" and it is most likely the fulfillment of Matthew 10:23, which some connect to this passage. Moreover, it manifest His kingship in accordance with the prophecies of Zechariah and others. There is no doubt that the Triumphant Entry was a prophetic event. Unfortunately, it falls short inasmuch as it ignores both the fact that some of the apostles would apparently "taste death" and the fact that Matthew 16:27 clearly refers to the Second Coming. Now some could

argue that the postponement of the kingdom explains why Matthew 16:27 and 16:28 are differentiated, and this is plausible. The Cross postponed the kingdom which Jesus was bringing at the Triumphant Entry, but we must still deal with the question of those who "would not taste death."

Theory #3 : The Resurrection and Ascension
The third event which took place after these words which some attribute to the prophecy is that of the Resurrection and Ascension. John Walvoord, no allegorist in any sense of the word, declared that "after the Cross would come the glory of the resurrection and the coming kingdom."[478] John Calvin also believed that the "manifestation of heavenly glory which Christ inaugurated at His resurrection"[479] was the fulfillment of this prophecy.

At first glimpse this appears solid. One apostle had died (Judas Iscariot) and Christ certainly manifested His kingdom powers, but there are problems to be sure. First, "how is 'to come' ($\epsilon\rho\chi o\mu\alpha\iota$) to be associated with his resurrection and ascension?"[480] Can we take the "coming" as the resurrection? Furthermore, if we take Walvoord at his word then Walvoord is clearly deviating from his dispensational roots for is he stating that Jesus' kingdom had already come? If the Messianic Kingdom is still future, as Walvoord believes and states many times, then the "coming" of His kingdom does not appear to fit the events of the resurrection.

There is also a problem with the time table as well. It is true that Judas Iscariot had died, but all the other apostles remained, thus we still have trouble with the word "some." Some is not many nor is it few. Logically, we would expect at least two or three of the apostles to have died for this statement to make sense, but only one false apostle had died while all the others remained. Eleven out of twelve does not fit "some."

Theory #4 : Pentecost
The next event is that of the Pentecost. Men such as John MacArthur believe that the coming of the Holy Spirit constituted the fulfillment of this passage.[481] Others, like Albert Barnes, have also supported this view. However, it is not without problems as well.

First, it requires a "spiritualizing" of the kingdom.[482] Second, it is not truly a coming of Christ. To quote Dwight Pentecost, "The Son of Man did not come then. He *sent* the Holy Spirit."[483] The words "Son of Man" cannot be interpreted as the Holy Spirit, for they are specific to the Kingly Messiah and not the Counselor. It can refer only to the second person of the Trinity. Third, we again have the problem of the "remote event."[484] All but Judas the Traitor were alive at Pentecost, thus again calling into question the relevance of Jesus' remark if this were indeed of what Jesus spoke.

Theory #5 : The Destruction of Jerusalem

Almost two thousand years have passed since the Pentecost and yet Jesus has not yet returned. What event then could have transpired over these years, not recorded in the Bible, which might have been a fulfillment of this prophecy? An all too popular view, particularly among those who reject a literal kingdom or a literal Second Coming, is that Jesus was referring to the destruction of Jerusalem.[485]

Although this view has correctly been called "nightmare exegesis"[486] by most evangelicals it is not without strengths. At first glance it appears to fit with the comments of Matthew 16:27 involving judgment for the destruction of Jerusalem was certainly a judgment upon Israel. Further it is clear that "some" of the apostles had died years before this event while others were still living. As tempting as these strengths may be, the view falls apart upon close examination.

First, to connect the "coming" of the "Son of Man" with the coming of a pagan emperor to slaughter the Jews of Israel is not only typical of Preterists and allegorists, but tantamount to blasphemy. When Jesus comes to judge, He will not use pagan persecutors of the Christian faith to execute His judgment. It is not Titus who will come with judgment, but "the Son of Man." This is the Second Coming and not the fall of Jerusalem. While it may have been *a* judgment, it is not the judgment brought by "the Son of Man."

Second, it must allegorize the kingdom of God to the extreme. "What does this catastrophic event have to do with the coming of the kingdom?"[487] asks Toussaint. To this Linski can only answer that the "kingdom" is a rule in our hearts,[488] but even if we accepted such an allegorical interpretation, it still begs the unanswered question, "What does this catastrophic event have to do with the coming of the kingdom?"[489] Sir Robert Anderson rhetorically asks if the apostle's thought the destruction of the Jerusalem was what Jesus really had in mind when he prayed "Thy Kingdom Come."[490] Obviously, no sincere exegete believes that this event was the "blessed hope" (Titus 2:13) to which all believers clung!

Theory #6 : The Gospel / The Church

William Barclay declared that "it is the mighty working of His kingdom that Jesus is speaking."[491] In other words, it is the gospel, or some say the Church, of which Jesus was speaking. Some, like C.H. Dodd even saw this passage as a parable and argued that the kingdom had already come.[492] To this D.A. Carson remarks, "it introduces an insurmountable problem in Matthew, where the particle is *erchomenon* ('the kingdom of God *coming*')."[493] The kingdom had clearly not come at that time. If it came years later with the Church then we have the same problems evident in the view that the "coming" took place at the Pentecost, when the Church was formed. This view is essentially an extension of the Pentecost view, but more broad in its interpretation, and therefore less specific in its exegesis.

Theory #7 : Evangelism

This view differs only slightly from the above view but is still even more generic. Says D.A. Carson, "it seems best to take 16:28 as having a more general reference–viz., not referring simply to the resurrection, to Pentecost, or the like, but to the manifestation of Christ's kingly reign exhibited after the Resurrection in a host of ways, not the least of them being the rapid multiplication of disciples."[494] This view is, therefore, an attempt to take the strengths of some of the previous views and weave them into a single view, but in so doing it also takes the weaknesses of each of those views and weaves them together. Thus this offers no real alternative.

Theory #8 : The Second Coming

There is an event which remains yet future, to which Matthew 16:27 explicitly refers. That is the Second Coming, and contextually this seems the strongest view in light of His words, but it is also the most difficult interpretation for it is clear that *none* of the apostles, let alone "some," still live. To this end, atheists and Bible critics and other mockers say that Jesus and the apostles must have anticipated the Second Coming in their lifetimes. If so, then that means Jesus was wrong! Or does it?

Some have claimed that "no expectation of the final advent of Christ is involved in these words of Jesus"[495] but that seems strained, for the previous passages clearly make allusions to it. Others have suggested that because there is a difference in "ignorance and error"[496] Jesus was merely *ignorant* of when He would return, rather than incorrect. The problem with this remark is that Jesus does not claim ignorance. He claims to *know* that "there are some of those who are standing here who will not taste death." To this end, some have said that "ii Peter i.16-18 is not without relevance."[497] Indeed, it is relevant, but only to the Second Coming, not to the question of who will "taste death." No matter what we do we cannot, as Sir Robert Anderson reminds us, "neglect" that passage.[498] How then can this be reconciled?

There is a view which is related to the controversy of John 21:22-23 which could be put forward in defense of this theory. Namely the theory that the Apostle John was raptured and did *not* die. I refer the reader to John 21:22-23 for a more detailed debate, but here I will merely summarize that some believe that John never died.[499] Legends surrounding Jesus date back to the earliest of times and all confirm that John lived almost to the second century. He even escaped death at the hands of the Emperor Domitian who had him boiled in oil, and yet he miraculously survived, a fact recorded in most all history books.[500] Some believed that John never died at all, but will return with Elijah at the end of days.[501] Such a legend, if true, could explain to what Jesus was referring, except that it should actually have read "there *is* **one** standing here who will not taste death." It does not. Consequently, this theory does not help.

Summary

The reader can see that none of the views are without significant problems. Indeed, Sir Robert Anderson, in his book *Misunderstood Texts of the Bible*, refutes many of these views but never actually tells you which view, if any, he advocates. I too am inclined to such a stance, for while some are stronger than the others, none are sufficient to stand out from among the others. Most must interpret "kingdom" "as a metaphor to mean 'royal majesty' or 'regal splendor' in much the same way that *sceptre* has long been used figuratively to represent royal power and authority."[502] While this statement is true, it does not fit the context which follows a vivid description of Judgment at the Second Coming and of the "coming of the Son of Man." Symbolism is only acceptable with a specific context or else it becomes subjective and even meaningless.

Let us begin by rejecting the weakest views and looking more closely at the remaining. We can safely eliminate view #5 since we must reject the idea that the prophecy of the "Son of Man" refers to a pagan emperor. Views #6 and #7 rely on heavy spiritualizing without justification. Their exegesis is ambiguous and subjective and its own advocates cannot point to specific prophetic fulfillments. View #4 is tempting, but the phrase "Son of Man" can only refer to the second person of the Trinity and cannot be applied to the Holy Spirit with any credulity.

This leaves four views, all of which have some severe problems, which cannot be ignored. Here is a brief summary of the views with their strengths and weaknesses highlighted:

View	Strengths	Weaknesses
Transfiguration	1. Its close connection to the passage. 2. It appears to manfiest the kingdom powers of Jesus.	1. It neglects that "some" of the apostles would "taste death" beforehand. 2. The events at the Transfiguration hardly appear to reflect the "coming." 3. Matthew 16:27 is clearly about the Second Coming.
The Triumphant Entry	1. It was a "coming" of the king. 2. It manifest His royalty and Messiahship.	1. It neglects that "some" of the apostles would "taste death" beforehand. 2. Matthew 16:27 is clearly about the Second Coming and mentions no postponement.
Resurrection and Ascension	1. It manifest the kingship of Christ. 2. One of the apostles had died.	1. The death of one apostle does not fit the fact that "some" of the apostles would "taste death" beforehand. 2. The resurrection does not seem to fit the context of "coming." 3. Matthew 16:27 is clearly about the Second Coming.

View	Strengths	Weaknesses
Pentecost	1. The coming of the Holy Spirit would constitute the "coming." 2. One of the apostles had died.	1. It requires an unnecessary spiritualizing of the kingdom. 2. The Holy Spirit was not the "coming" of Jesus but was "sent" by God. 3. The phrase "Son of Man" properly refers to the Second Person of the Trinity alone, not the Holy Spirit. 4. The death of one apostle does not fit the fact that "some" of the apostles would "taste death" beforehand. 5. Matthew 16:27 is clearly about the Second Coming.
The Destruction of Jerusalem	1. It fits the context of judgment from Matthew 16:27. 2. "Some" of the apostles had "tasted death" while "some" still lived.	1. It is blasphemy to equate a barbaric pagan emperor with the "coming of the Son of Man." 2. It allegorizes the kingdom to the highest extreme possible. 3. It renders the "blessed hope" of Jesus' Second Coming as one of the darkest events of Israeli history.
The Gospel / The Church	1. The "kingdom" is manifest in God's Church / the Gospel. 2. One of the apostles had died.	1. It requires an unnecessary spiritualizing of the kingdom. 2. It suffers the same problems as the Pentecost view (e.g. "Son of Man" etc.). 3. Only one apostle had died; the Traitor Judas. 4. It relies on ambiguous exegesis.
Evangelism	1. The "kingdom" is manifest through many events in history.	1. It It requires an unnecessary spiritualizing of the kingdom. 2. It suffers the same problems as the Pentecost and Gospel/Church views from which it borrow so much. 3. It relies on ambiguous exegesis.
The Second Coming	1. It is a literal reading of the "coming of the Son of Man." 2. It is consistent with Matthew 16:27.	1. It completely rejects the fact that "some" of the apostles would "taste death" beforehand. 2. It *assumes* Jesus was either in error or ignorance.

Notice that all remaining views have trouble dealing with the statement, "there are some of those who are standing here who will not taste death." One possible explanation is that because of the postponement of the kingdom Jesus was to show a glimpse of that coming in glory of the Son of Man. If so, then this would favor the Transfiguration. The Resurrection theory also benefits from this interpretation, although less so.

The Triumphant Entry, though neglected and even omitted by some interpreters, deals alternately with the problem. It is clear that the Triumphant Entry was prophesied in Zechariah (see notes on Matthew 21:2) as the true king entered Jerusalem. However, the death and resurrection delayed or postponed the innauguration of His kingdom. One might view it as a King in exile, but His followers continue to promote His kingdom to come. It is possible then that that postponement might also postpone the fulfillment of this passage, but only if John, as legend says, was raptured. If this is so then even the last view still holds up.

Sometimes it is wiser to withhold comment than to leap to an assumption. I tend to favor one of these four views, but cannot affirm which. All have problems which should not be dismissed, but to these I will add a ninth view which may offer a solution. Perhaps the vision of John on Patmos, found in the Book of Revelation is a fulfillment in itself, for John clearly lived to "see" the "Son of Man coming in His kingdom." Might Paul or Peter have had similar visions, as recorded in the epistles? Perhaps this constitutes a ninth view.

My conclusion is to quote a saying of Jesus. "Let the reader understand."

The Transfiguration
Matthew 17:1-9 – Mark 9:1-14 – Luke 9:28-36

"Six days later Jesus took with Him Peter and James and John his brother, and led them up on a high mountain by themselves. And He was transfigured."	"Six days later, Jesus took with Him Peter and James and John, and brought them up on a high mountain by themselves. And He was transfigured before them."	"Some eight days after these sayings, He took along Peter and John and James, and went up on the mountain to pray. And while He was praying ... behold, two men were talking with Him; and they were Moses and Elijah."

At the Transfiguration three of the apostles saw Jesus in all His glory. It was a glimpse of the majesty to come. "What the disciples beheld there was the type of His glorious second coming as the Son of Man in His Kingdom"[503] It was also a time when Jesus was counseled by Moses and Elijah, the two greatest prophets of the Old Testament. It was a time of preparation for Jesus who knew what was to come. John Calvin suggested that it proved He could have been immune to death and thus "He was subject to death because He wished to be."[504]

Now some have questioned the role of Elijah in prophecy and this question is addressed in the next section below. Here I shall only address the critics who claim that Luke contradicts Matthew and Mark in their account of the story. Whereas Matthew and Mark stated that the Transfiguration was "six days later" Luke says it was "some eight days." How is this reconciled?

The alleged problem touches upon an issue which will be addressed under "When Was Jesus Crucified?" Nevertheless, the issue is not so complicated here so I will repeat it here. Matthew and Mark both state six days later. However, Luke, the only gentile author in the New Testament, spoke "based on a Greek way of speaking and means 'about a week later.'"[505] Note the word "about." The Greek word ὡσεί ('osei) is literally translated "as if, as it were, like" or "about." It is not an exact time but an approximation, and according to ancient Greek (see discussion under "When Was Jesus Crucified?") "Luke wrote that this event occurred 'about eight days after' (Luke 9:28), which includes the beginning and ending days as well as the six days between."[506]

Thus there is no contradiction between Matthew/Mark and Luke. The only difference is that Luke was used to speaking in Greek idioms and was approximating the time, whereas Matthew and Mark were being specific in their timetable.

Was John the Baptist Elijah?
Matthew 17:10-13 – John 1:19-21

"And His disciples asked Him, 'Why then do the scribes say that Elijah must come first?' And He answered and said, 'Elijah is coming and will restore all things; but I say to you that Elijah already came, and they did not recognize him, but did to him whatever they wished. So also the Son of Man is going to suffer at their hands.' Then the disciples understood that He had spoken to them about John the Baptist."

"This is the testimony of John, when the Jews sent to him priests and Levites from Jerusalem to ask him, 'Who are you?' And he confessed and did not deny, but confessed, 'I am not the Christ.' They asked him, 'What then? Are you Elijah?' And he said, 'I am not.'"

There is a prophecy in Malachi 4:5-6 which says that Elijah, who had been translated to heaven without experiencing physical death, would return to pave the way for the coming of the Lord. In Matthew Jesus declares that "Elijah is coming and will restore all things" but also "that Elijah already came." Jesus calls John the Baptist Elijah and yet in John we see that John denied being Elijah. To the Bible critic this is nonsense, but to the believer this is an important issue and two different alternatives have been offered.

One of the most popular views is to take Luke 1:17 which says that John the Baptist "will go *as a forerunner* before Him in the spirit and power of Elijah" and emphasize "the spirit and power" as to infer that "John was not the literal Elijah, but he was the Elijah that the prophecy spoke of, the one who was

105

to (and did) prepare the way for the Messiah, Jesus."[507] This view is accepted by such notables ranging from John MacArthur[508] to the more liberal Albert Barnes.[509] Erasmus called John "a certain Elijah"[510] and John Calvin even called "crass" the idea that the literal Elijah would *ever* return.[511] He claimed that Malachi's prophecy has "been twisted awry."[512] But did not Jesus say "Elijah is coming and will restore all things"? If these were Jesus' words and if Malachi specifically identifies the man as "Elijah *the* prophet" and just "one like Elijah" then should we so easily reject the literal view? Even the *Liberty Bible Commentary* claims that "John did minister in the spirit of Elijah (Lk 1:7) and was ever called Elijah by Christ (Mt 17:12), but he was not literally Elijah,"[513] but if Jesus called him Elijah, not "one like" Elijah, why should we deny it? Because John did? That leads to the question of why John denied it.

Logically, John's brain could have no memory of his previous life. A baby's brain is born without memory. Contrary to popular myth, memory is not stored in a particular area of the brain at all. Rather we sort through the billions of neurons in our brain to "remember" which were active in the past. In other words, the five senses activate certain neurons in our brain. Out of the billions of neurons the exact same combination of neurons will never be active twice in our lifetimes. Consider the visual stimulii alone. Add to this feelings, taste, smell, hearing, and even emotions and thoughts are added to this mix. This is why deja vu is common. We *feel* like we have been there before, but we haven't. This allows our brain to "remember" a virtually infinite number of memories whereas a computer's memory is quickly taken up and filled to its capacity. All of this is to say that John could not "remember" what his body had not experienced. The fact that he did not know he was Elijah does not nullify that Jesus clearly said he *was*.

Note Jesus did not say he was a "certain Elijah"[514] or that he was "the spirit of Elijah"[515] but that "*Elijah* already came, and they did not recognize him" (Matthew 17:12). As John Walvoord said, "the evidence that John the Baptist at least in part fulfilled the prophecy of Elijah is clear, but a future appearance of Elijah is debateable."[516] "Debatable"? Why? Both Jesus and Malachi say "Elijah *is* coming and *will* restore all things" (Matthew 17:11). Stanley Toussaint suggest that just as the "the coming of the Kingdom is also postponed and future"[517] so also is Elijah. Malachi clearly refers to the "great and terrible day of the Lord" (Malachi 4:5). This must be the Second Coming. If Elijah is to prepare the way for the Lord and if there are two separate comings of the Christ, why not two separate comings of Elijah? Jonathan Edwards noted in his Bible that Elijah was called the "Tishbite." He also noted that the "word signifies a restorer, or converter."[518] Indeed, this is no small irony for Elijah is just that. Jesus said "among those born of women there is no one greater than John" (Luke 7:28) and yet it was Elijah to whom Jesus was speaking on the mount of Transfiguration!

In short, just as there are two comings of the Messiah, Elijah was to come to prepare the way for both. He came as John the Baptist before the first coming of Christ and he will return, literally, before the Second Coming.

Matthew 18:1-5 – See Luke 9:46

The Exception Clause for Divorce
Matthew 19:9

"And I say to you, whoever divorces his wife, except for immorality, and marries another woman commits adultery."

It is no secret that Christianity disdains divorce. Here Jesus even calls it adultery "except for immorality."[519] Some, however, even reject this clause as an "exception clause." They argue that Jesus did not advocate or accept divorce even in cases of adultery. The argument is as follows.

First, it is said that the "immorality clause" applies only to a man and women in the betrothal or engagement period and not marriage.[520] They point out that Joseph and Mary were not yet married when Joseph "resolved to divorce her quietly." Consequently, they see this as a breaking of the engagement only. The problem with this part of the argument is that "when used in the context of a man and wife, the common meaning of *apoluo* was always divorce – not merely separation or the breaking of an engagement."[521] No legitimate argument can be made from this alone.

The second point they make is that the Greek word *porneia* (πορνεια) properly refers to fornication rather than adultery. Thus they argue that "the use of '*porneia*' must surely be talking about the betrothal period and not marriage."[522] While this argument is stronger than the first, the fact is that there is no proof that the word *porneia* (πορνεια) is used of the betrothal period for they were already treated as married. That is why Greek uses the same words to describe Joseph and Mary as are used of married couples, thus all translations call him her "husband," rather than fiancé. Moreover, *porneia* (πορνεια) is defined in the Greek-English Lexicon as "illicit sexual intercourse in general."[523] Hence, it is a broad general term for sexual misconduct. Consequently, adultery can be said to be *porneia* (πορνεια) but not all *porneia* (πορνεια) is adultery. Furthermore, the law of Deuteronomy 24:1 states that a divorce can be obtained if a husband, after marriage, discovers some "indecency" in her. In other words, if he discovers on their wedding night that she was not a virgin and had committed fornication in the past, he can divorce her. Thus the use of the word *porneia* (πορνεια) may actually be in keeping with the law of Deuteronomy 24:1.

The final argument is that adultery was punishable by death in the Old Testament. Thus Jobe Martin says, "Stoned, dead, people do not get divorced."[524] He believes this nullifies the idea that Jesus was speaking of married couples, but he errs in two major ways. First, the law *also* called for stoning during the engagement period. It says "if there is a girl who is a virgin engaged to a man, and *another* man finds her in the city and lies with her, then you shall bring them both out to the gate of that city and you shall stone them to death" (Deuteronomy 22:23-24). Therefore, the law does not distinguish between the two. This leads to the second flaw in the argument. Joseph resolved to "divorce" Mary *because* he was a "righteous man" (Matthew 1:19). Is it not better and more forgiving to divorce a husband or wife than to have them executed? Jobe correctly points out that the theme of Matthew 18 is forgiveness, but conveniently forgets that divorce is a merciful alternative to the stoning to which he refers!

A final comment is necessary. We were reminded earlier that Jesus Himself said He did not come to abolish the law (Matthew 5:17). Some claim that Jesus was doing just that since the Law allowed for divorce, but a careful reading of Deuteronomy 24:1 states that the divorce certification is only for "indecency." It explicitly says he can issue a divorce certificate "because he has found some indecency in her" and lists no other grounds for divorce. Consequently, Jesus is again affirming the law rather than contradicting it. Divorce has *always* been distasteful to God. Malachi 2:16 states, "'I hate divorce,' says the LORD, the God of Israel." Jesus is reminding the Jews that they, like our modern day lawyers, have perverted the law into something it is not. Jesus' statement, "whoever divorces his wife, except for immorality, and marries another woman commits adultery" is in perfect keeping with His law and that of Moses.

The Rich Man
Matthew 19:16-30 – Mark 10:17-31 – Luke 18:18-30

> "'If you wish to be complete, go *and* sell your possessions and give to *the* poor, and you will have treasure in heaven; and come, follow Me.' But when the young man heard this statement, he went away grieving; for he was one who owned much property. And Jesus said to His disciples, 'Truly I say to you, it is hard for a rich man to enter the kingdom of heaven. Again I say to you, it is easier for a camel to go through the eye of a needle, than for a rich man to enter the kingdom of God.'"

These controversial remarks have been trivialized by modern upper class Americans, distorted by asthetic monks, and perverted by modern socialists. All extremes must be rejected. First, notice that Jesus began His remarks by saying, "if you wish to be complete." The Greek word there is sometimes translated as "perfect." Jesus was not making the selling of his possessions a prerequisite to salvation, but to perfection. The issue is one of sanctification, not salvation. Moreover, in Matthew 6:21 Jesus said, "where your treasure is, there you heart will be also." It is clear that this man's heart belonged to gold and it is for that reason that he was asked to give it up.

Nevertheless, to deny that Jesus' following remarks imply much more is to trivialize the remark. Surely the saying "a camel through the eye of a needle" is ingrained upon the consciousness of every young child raised in a Judeao-Christian culture. Indeed, this "proverbial"[525] saying of Jesus became "in common use among the Jews, and still common among the Arabians."[526] We cannot dismiss this remark as too many are apt to do. One commentary reads, "the salvation of the rich sinner is just as miraculous as the salvation of a poor sinner. Both are only possible with God."[527] A true statement, but one which trivializes Jesus' remarks here.

The church father Cyprian saw this not as an edict, but as a statement of fact wherein the rich destroy themselves. "If rich men did this, they would not perish by their riches ... nor could he be overcome by the world who had nothing in this world whereby he could be overcome."[528] Another has said, "the difficulty lies in making the choice between caring for his wealth and caring for the things of God ... it is not that riches per se are a barrier to salvation, it is simply that they pose peculiar temptations to the rich man's spiritual welfare."[529] So it was cause and effect rather than a prohibition by the Lord. Money corrupts (cf. 1 Timothy 6:10). This was the lesson.

This "hard saying" of Jesus thus is about sanctification. "If you would be perfect" or "complete" was the preface to the remarks. Salvation is by faith alone, but the love of money creates an obstacle to love of God. Salvation is possible, but money is a stumbling block to faith. It has been noted that "hardly (Gr *dyskolos*) implies with extreme difficulty, though not hopeless."[530] Too many, in an attempt to justify our materialism, have illustrated that salvation is not denied to the rich man, but ignore that riches create such an obstacle to faith that Jesus compares this to threading the eye of a needle with a camel. One look at the fall of some television preachers who lived in the lap of luxury should demonstrate this remark. So also King Solomon in all his glory turned away from the Lord because of his wealth and riches (although he did repent and was saved). Let us therefore take warning and not trivialize the words of Jesus.

The Petition to Christ
Matthew 20:20 – Mark 10:35

"Then the mother of the sons of Zebedee came to Jesus with her sons, bowing down and making a request of Him. And He said to her, 'What do you wish?' She said to Him, 'Command that in Your kingdom these two sons of mine may sit one on Your right and one on Your left.'"	"James and John, the two sons of Zebedee, came up to Jesus, saying, 'Teacher, we want You to do for us whatever we ask of You.' And He said to them, 'What do you want Me to do for you?' They said to Him, 'Grant that we may sit, one on Your right and one on *Your* left, in Your glory.'"

There two aspects of this debate. The first is obviously the question of who made the petition to Jesus, but the second is the question of the petition itself and of the role of pride.

The argument involving the claim of contradiction is the same as another one addressed previously. If a messenger is relaying the words of the king it may be justly said to be the words of the messenger or the words of the king. There is no contradiction in these statements. John Calvin said, "it is probable that when their shame prevented them from asking, they cunningly brought in their mother who could ask more boldly"[531] but "that the wish came from themselves may be gathered from the fact that Christ replies to them and not to their mother."[532]

The real debate is over the request itself, for it is interesting that this request was made by two of the closest apostles to Jesus. At the mount of Transfiguration only three apostles were allowed to escort Jesus to the meeting with Elijah and Moses. Those three were Peter, James, and John. Yet despite their high status among the apostles Jesus rebuked the apostles and told them that "whoever wishes to become great among you shall be your servant, and whoever wishes to be first among you shall be your slave" (Matthew 20:26-27). It is also interesting that the apostles' request came immediately after Jesus declared "the first shall be last, and the last first" (Matthew 20:16). They did not seem to understand that "personal ambition is not a factor in the eternal, sovereign plan of God."[533]

Some believe that the apostles "were still looking for a temporal kingdom."[534] However, whether this is true or not is irrelevant. An earthly kingdom or a heavenly kingdom makes no difference to the qualities which Jesus is looking for in his disciples. Humility is what makes one great.

God humbled Himself to the point of dying on a cross as if He were a common criminal (Philippians 2:8). He was born in a manger, of humble beginning, worked as a carpenter, rode into Jerusalem on a donkey, and died on a cross. Humility is the key to greatness, not ambition. The Bible calls Moses the most humble man on earth (Numbers 12:3) and yet he was not even able to speak publicly so that Aaron had to be his spokesperson, yet no one but Elijah and John the Baptist ever came close to being as great as Moses. Many other examples could be cited. George Washington remains one of the most humble leaders in history, and one of its greatest. He was a devout man of God and the only truly indispensible man of the American Revolution. Thus, humility is what the apostles needed to learn before they could claim greatness. The lesson was that "whoever wishes to become great among you shall be your servant, and whoever wishes to be first among you shall be your slave" (Matthew 20:26-27).

Healing of the Blind
Matthew 20:29 – Mark 10:46 – Luke 18:35-43

"As they were leaving Jericho, a large crowd followed Him. And two blind men sitting by the road, hearing that Jesus was passing by, cried out, 'Lord, have mercy on us, Son of David!' The crowd sternly told them to be quiet, but they cried out all the more ... Jesus stopped and called them ... Moved with compassion, Jesus touched their eyes; and immediately they regained their sight and followed Him."

"Then they came to Jericho. And as He was leaving Jericho with His disciples and a large crowd, a blind beggar *named* Bartimaeus, the son of Timaeus, was sitting by the road. When he heard that it was Jesus the Nazarene, he began to cry out and say, 'Jesus, Son of David, have mercy on me!' Many were sternly telling him to be quiet, but he kept crying out all the more, 'Son of David, have mercy on me! ... he regained his sight and *began* following Him on the road."

"As Jesus was approaching Jericho, a blind man was sitting by the road begging. Now hearing a crowd going by, he *began* to inquire what this was. They told him that Jesus of Nazareth was passing by. And he called out, saying, 'Jesus, Son of David, have mercy on me!' Those who led the way were sternly telling him to be quiet; but he kept crying out ... Jesus stopped and ... Jesus said to him, 'Receive your sight; your faith has made you well.' Immediately he regained his sight."

Here is yet another example of three version of the same story; all accurate and true, but none exhaustive or complete. Strangely enough even Christian scholars have devoted much time to "resolving" the alleged difficulties, although a close examination shows that no difficulty exists except inasmuch as none of the accounts is exhaustive. All tell a part of the story. None tell the entire story. A true contradiction must, therefore, contain irreconcilable differences and not just gaps in the stories.

Two difficulties are presented. The first is the question of how many blind men were present. Mark and Luke mention one blind man, Mark even naming him. Matthew, however, mentions two. As elsewhere this problem is easily resolved for as Mark and Luke are not exhaustive accounts it is apparent that "Mark and Luke mention only one man ... who apparently was spokesman for the two."[535] Thus while they only reference one man, "they did not say that there was no more than one."[536] Police detectives are trained to understand that no witness will recount every single detail, thus sometimes leaving a false impression. This is why they interogate witnesses over seemingly insignificant details. This is a prime example. The accounts are the same, save that, as Linski (no die hard conservative) says, "Mark's account offers more detail."[537]

111

Despite this, some have argued that these are actually three entirely different accounts of four different men![538] Gundry notes the "similar miracle"[539] of Matthew 9:27-31 and then procedes to make the outlandish assumption that this is "Matthew's second version of Jesus' healing two blind men."[540] There is no justification for this claim or the absurb accusation of one Bible commentary that "Matthew's tradition was confused."[541] The simple fact is that there were two blind men present; one was named Bartimaeus who did all the talking and so he was the one mentioned by Mark and Luke, but the second man still remained.

The second "discrepancy" is whether or not Jesus was "leaving" (Matthew 20:29) Jericho or "approaching" (Luke 18:35) Jericho? John Calvin, noting that Mark says, "they came to Jericho. And as He was leaving Jericho", argues the blind men called out as Jesus entered but could not be heard and so they waited until he left[542] or perhaps that Jesus was testing their faith and so waited until He left to answer.[543] If this is the case then Luke's comment that he first cried out to Jesus as they were approaching is correct, but Jesus did not answer him until they were leaving as Matthew affirms. This is certainly possible, but a far more easy explanation is likely.

"There were two Jerichos. The Roman city lay a mile east of Herod's winter headquarters (also called Jericho) ... Luke's attention would be on the Herodian city."[544] This is the position held by most archaeologists and scholars.[545] Although critics will scoff, there is an Old Mexico and a New Mexico in America separated only by a inivisible line. Moreover, the ancient historian Josephus tells us that Rome divided Israel into eleven toparchies. One of these toparchies was Jericho.[546] Thus Matthew may have been referring to the region or toparchy whereas Luke was referring specifically to the city of Jericho. This makes the best sense. To this very day, there is an "Old Jerusalem" which lies within the city of "Jerusalem." If someone does not know the city or geography they might make the mistake of confusing the two. So also the critic mistakes the two Jerichos for one and finds error where is none.

The Triumphant Entry
Matthew 21:2 – Mark 11:2 – Luke 19:30 – John 12:12-15

"Jesus sent two disciples, saying to them, 'Go into the village opposite you, and immediately you will find a donkey tied *there* and a colt with her; untie them and bring them to Me.'"	"[Jesus] said to them, 'Go into the village opposite you, and immediately as you enter it, you will find a colt tied *there,* on which no one yet has ever sat; untie it and bring it.'"	"He sent two of the disciples, saying, 'Go into the village ahead of *you;* there, as you enter, you will find a colt tied on which no one yet has ever sat; untie it and bring it.'"	"Jesus, finding a young donkey, sat on it; as it is written, 'Fear not, Daughter of Zion; Behold, your King is coming, seated on the a donkey's colt.'"

Here is the famous event which was prophesied in Zechariah 9:9.

"Rejoice greatly, O daughter of Zion!
Shout *in triumph,* O daughter of Jerusalem!
Behold, your king is coming to you;
He is just and endowed with salvation,
Humble, and mounted on a donkey,
Even on a colt, the foal of a donkey."

The significance of the event is in the humility of the king and savior of the universe. To quote John Wesley, "the prince of peace did not take an horse, a warlike animal"[547] but a donkey. The donkey, of course, is looked upon as the comic version of a horse. It is small and weak compared to the war horses that kings would normally ride upon. Such triumphant entries of kings were filled with pomp. The king would ride upon a white stallion while red flowers or similar items were thrown out in front of the rider. Contrast the humility of Jesus' entry with the pomp of an earthly king such as that shown in the painting by Frank Dicksee (see next page).

This is the lesson we should take from these passages, and yet it is not surprising that some see problems. Some question the reference to a donkey and a colt in Matthew and John, pointing out that neither Mark nor Luke mention the donkey at all. Once again we have the same logic flaw. Just because Mark and Luke do not mention the colt's mother does not mean that it was not present. A colt, or a foal, is a young donkey which has not been castrated and, as Mark and Luke say, "on which no one yet has ever sat." It's mother was brought so that the colt would follow more easily (for donkeys can be very stubborn, especially when separated from their mother). Logically, there is nothing in these passages which contradict one another. It is the classically flawed argument that all references must be exhaustive, which they are not.

The larger issue is not an important one in terms of the story or events itself, but a chronological issue. I have elsewhere quoted the famed historian who said, "chronology is the backbone of history."[548] Much of this will be discussed in greater detail under "When Was Jesus Crucified?" The question of when the Triumphant Entry took place will be dealt with briefly here.

Three views are expressed. Some believe Jesus entered Jerusalem on Saturday, some on Sunday, and others on Monday. The first view, that of a Saturday entry, is the least supported.[549] This idea is based solely upon an interpretation of Matthew 12:40 which is debated under the section "When Was Jesus Crucified?" Suffice to say that its advocates claim that Jesus must have been crucified on Wednesday. However, this contradicts John's testimony that "Jesus, therefore, six days before the Passover, came to Bethany" (John 12:1) and then "on the next day" (John 12:12) Jesus entered Jerusalem at the Triumphant Entry. This means that the Triumphant entry was five days before Passover and, therefore, no early than Sunday and no later than Monday.

Frank Dicksee – The Two Crowns – 1900

By tradition Palm Sunday is the time when Jesus entered Jerusalem. John 12:1-3 explicitly states that Jesus entered Bethany six days before passover, which would be Saturday, Nisan 9 (the Hebrew calendar month). John 12:12 then appears to place the Triumphant Entry "the next day." However, some argue that the events of John 12:9-11 took place Sunday[550] and then John 12:12 was on a Monday.[551]   On what basis do they make this assumption?

John MacArthur is probably the most popular advocate of this position.[552] His reasoning is based on two evidences. First, he notes that this would elimate the problem with the so-called 'silent Wednesday'[553] of which we *appear* to read nothing in the gospels.   The second argument is based on typology.   If Jesus was the Lamb of God (John 1:29, 36; Revelation 5:6; 6:9; 7:17; 14:10; 15:3; 19:9; 21:23; 22:1, 3) then His sacrifice should coincide with the sacrificial law of Moses which included the slaying of the Pascal Lamb which took place at Passover.   This typology is generally agreed by most scholars but MacArthur, and others, point out that the sacrificial lamb was selected on the tenth day of Nisan (Exod 12:2-6)[554] which they say would fall on a Monday of that year.[555] Thus he says, "continuing that perfect fulfillment, He was then crucified on Friday the fourteenth of Nisan as the True Passover Lamb sacrificed for the sins of the world."[556]

There are two problems with his thesis. First, the "silent Wednesday" is not necessarily silent even if the entry was on a Sunday. Matthew and Luke do not offer a complete exhaustive record of chronology (see notes on "The Last Supper"). This is clear because Mark, who gives a more complete chronology, explains that Jesus and the disciples left for Bethany after looking over the temple "since it was already late." It is then the "next day" when Jesus returns to the temple and chases the money changers out (Mark 11:12-15). Thus the driving of the money changers from the temple took place on Monday as MacArthur correctly believes but the Triumphant Entry was late Sunday evening. This agrees with the view that the events of Mark 14:1-11 were on Wednesday, "two days" away from Passover (14:1). The Last Supper was then Thursday night (but see notes on "The Last Supper" and chart under "When Was Jesus Cruficied?").

This does, however, beg another question which is dealt with in more depth later. I will simply state my conclusion here. If Wednesday was "two days" from Passover (Mark 14:1) then we must recognize that many Jews reconned the new day from sundown. In other words, if Jesus entered Jerusalem on Sunday after evening had come (implied by the words of Mark 11:11) then He would technically have entered Jerusalem on Nisan 10, in accordance with the typology, for Nisan 10 began Sunday evening at 6:00 PM (as per the Roman calendar in use today) and continued until Monday evening at 6:00 PM. Indeed, there is no doubt that Nisan 10 overlapped Sunday by the Roman calendar. This also explains the difficulties with a Thursday Last Supper (see notes below).

In short, it is best to conclude that Jesus came to Bethany "six days" before Passover (John 12:1) on a Saturday and entered Jerusalem "the next day" (John 12:12) in the evening after "it was already late" (Mark 11:11), which would be Sunday night by the Roman calendar but Nisan 10th by some Jewish reconnings. He looked around the temple and then left, returning the "next day" wherein he cleansed the temple (Mark 11:12-15, but see notes below). This fits all the facts, is in perfect keeping with the typology, and accepts that the ancient tradition of Palm Sunday was not an error by the earliest followers of Christ.

The Cleansing of the Temple
Matthew 21:12 – Mark 11:15-17 – Luke 19:45

"And Jesus entered the temple and drove out all those who were buying and selling in the temple, and overturned the tables of the money changers and the seats of those who were selling doves."	"And He entered the temple and began to drive out those who were buying and selling in the temple, and overturned the tables of the money changers and the seats of those who were selling doves."	"Jesus entered the temple and began to drive out those who were selling."

Once again, some attempt to read contradictions into this account by merging separate events including the cleansing of the temple recorded in John 2:12-17. Some even have the audacity to claim that the chronology of the synoptic gospels was wrong and "John corrected" the others.[557] However, "the cleansing of the Temple reported by John 2:13, etc., it is not the same as the one reported by the synoptics."[558] Even a cursory reading of John makes it clear that the first cleansing took place early during his ministry when he was "confronted by the authorities"[559] but by the time of the cleansing reported here "no one dares confront him."[560] It is quite clear that "the chief priests and the scribes were seeking how they might put Him to death; for they were afraid of the people" (Luke 22:2). This is why they did not confront him the second time. They feared the crowd of Jesus' supporters. There is no such hesitation in the first cleansing which John explicitly places at the beginning of His ministry.

A second complaint is that there is allegedly a contradiction between Matthew which presumeably places the cleansing on the first day and Mark which explicitly says the cleansing took place the second day (11:11). The answer is, of course, given by the very fact that Mark is explicit whereas Matthew is not. Matthew does not give an explicit chronology, but Mark says clearly that "Jesus entered Jerusalem and came into the temple; and after looking around at everything, He left for Bethany with the twelve, since it was already late" (11:11). He then returned the next day and it was then that He cleansed the temple. The argument here made by critics is the flawed argument that each account must give a complete and exhaustive chronology, which is a logical flaw. Even published historians do not do this. The chronology is clear enough and Matthew places no special interest on which visit to the temple the cleansing took place; only that it took place in the last week of Jesus' life.

116

The Cursed Fig Tree
Matthew 21:18-22 – Mark 11:11-21

"Now in the morning, when He was returning to the city, He became hungry. Seeing a lone fig tree by the road, He came to it and found nothing on it except leaves only; and He said to it, 'No longer shall there ever be *any* fruit from you.' And at once the fig tree withered."

"On the next day, when they had left Bethany, He became hungry. Seeing at a distance a fig tree in leaf, He went *to see* if perhaps He would find anything on it; and when He came to it, He found nothing but leaves, for it was not the season for figs."

Two issues are taken with these passages. One is yet another chronological puzzle with which some take issue. Did the fig tree wither "at once" or was it the next morning? The other issue is one of whether or not Jesus cursed the fig tree in anger, and if so, how does this effect His character and our own response to anger.

The time sequence is not particularly as troublesome some make it out to be. Historians are not always time specific and "at once" in the context of history can certainly be synonymous with the passing of a single day. Mark's chronology is clearly more complete as he records the curse and then states that they came back the next day to discover the fig tree withered (Mark 11:20). Matthew does record that they had lodged "overnight in Bethany" as in Mark's gospel,[561] so whether, as John Calvin states, Matthew "recalls the omission"[562] or whether or not the fig tree did indeed wither immediately but "was not observed immediately,"[563] as John Walvoord suggests, there is nothing in Matthew which indicates an exhaustive chronology. As Calvin said, "Christ spoke the word of malediction to the tree on the day after His solemn entry into the city. Mark merely notes, what Matthew had omitted, that the event was brought to the disciples' eyes on the next day."[564] This seems the most logical answer. Nonetheless, this same issue repeated by critics has been rebutted before. An exhaustive chronology is not required in any history. Only if the chronologies can be said to explicitly contradict one another can we call them into question, and here we have only Matthew's gloss of the event compared to Mark's more complete chronology.

A more personal attack is one made against the character of Jesus. Some, like Linski, simply respond that "the character of Jesus need not be defended."[565] Others feel that the cursing of the fig tree was itself an immoral act![566] But Albert Barnes has said that this act "does not imply anger"[567] in itself. Rather, as someone else said, it "was not the result of quick temper" but to teach a lesson.[568] "Profession without practice is condemned,"[569] and therefore the fig tree was withered to teach a lesson about faith to the apostles on the last week of Jesus' life.

Some have even argued suggest that "the tree symbolized the nation of Israel"[570] and hence interpret this as a prophecy of Israel's withering, but the context of Romans 11 is not only different, but so is the moral, for in Romans 11 the tree root always remains Israel and Israel is never uprooted or cast out. It's tree limbs are trimmed and new limbs may be grafted in, but the trunk remains forever Israel. The argument is, therefore, poor both exegetically and theologically. The only point to this event was one of faith.

While the critic will attack anything in the Bible, even a little story such as this, there is nothing in the text to imply that the story is not true and accurate. Despite this, some critics have gone so far as to declare that the parable of the fig tree (Luke 13:16-19) is mistaken for a real event here![571] Such frivolous attacks show desperation. The withering of the fig tree was intended to teach the apostles about "faith that moves mountains."

Matthew 22:13 – See Matthew 8:12

The Sadducees and the Resurrection
Matthew 22:23-33 – Mark 12:18-27 – Luke 20:27-45

"On that day *some* Sadducees (who say there is no resurrection) came to Jesus and questioned Him."	"*Some* Sadducees (who say that there is no resurrection) came to Jesus, and *began* questioning Him."	"Now there came to Him some of the Sadducees (who say that there is no resurrection) and they questioned him."

These passages begin a series of questions which are among the most controversial passages of the gospels in terms of angelology. The Sadducees are introduced here as those "who say there is no resurrection," but critics have questioned this. However, Josephus affirmed in *Antiquities of the Jews* that the Sadducees taught "that souls die with the bodies."[572] Further, Josephus implied that the Sadducees accepted only the Law of Moses, and rejected all the rest of the Scriptures.[573] This would explain Jesus' answer, which was based on the words of Torah (the Law of Moses). Jesus answered, "regarding the resurrection of the dead, have you not read what was spoken to you by God: 'I AM the God of Abraham, and the God of Isaac, and the God of Jacob'? He is not the God of the dead but of the living" (Matthew 22:31-32).

An examination of these words reveals two things. Jesus responded to their query by appealing to their own beliefs and their common ground. He did not debate the worthiness of Psalms, although He could have, but proved they were wrong with the words of Moses himself. Perhaps more important than this was also the manner of Jesus' interpretation. Jesus took the words of Moses in the most literal fashion possible. He argued that based solely on the use of the present tense verb, God was declaring that Abraham, Isaac, and Jacob are still living and not dead! Had they been truly dead, it would have read, "I *was* the God of Abraham, Isaac, and Jacob." Thus Jesus took the scriptures very literally, in contrast to the prevailing opinions of many in the church today.

It is worth noting that Josephus saw the Sadducees as amoral, declaring "they may act as they please"[574] since they deny "punishments and rewards in Hades."[575] Interestingly enough, Josephus also criticized the Sadducees for their conduct towards one another even in conversation and debate.[576] This seems apparent here as the Sadducees question to Jesus was clearly a sarcastic one, attempting to mock the belief in resurrection rather than legitimately debating the issue. The query was clearly a sarcastic one, but even in regard to the issue of marriage in heaven, Jesus did not completely ignore the question, but answered. That answer is among the most controversial in the gospels; not so much because of the answer itself, but because of the interpretations which people have attached to it. For that reason, it is addressed separately below.

Angels and Marriage
Matthew 22:30 – Mark 12:25 – Luke 20:35

"For in the resurrection they neither marry, nor are given in marriage,
but are like angels in heaven."

Here Jesus briefly responds to the sarcastic question of the Sadducees, but He does not go into deatil. The reasons for this shall become apparent. Nevertheless, human beings don't like unsolved mysteries. We love conspiracy theories, mysteries, and horror stories because they involve the unknown. We don't like being kept in the dark, and yet to a degree this is exactly what Jesus did. He did not spend countless hours telling us what heaven will be like or having us daydream about things which might distract us from our duty here and now. He did, however, give us glipses of eternity. Here we are *compared* to angels. Note, however, it is "not 'angels' but 'as angels.'"[577] The liberal depiction of men with wings playing harps comes from a complete misrepresentation of Jesus' words here. We will not become angels, but we will become "*like*" angels. Apparently that means we will "neither marry, nor [be] given in marriage." It is from these words in which some the most controversial interpretations, even wild interpretations, are taken.

We can readily agree that Jesus' statement infers that the system of "marriage, reproduction, and childbirth ... [are] intended for the earthly life only."[578] There will be no children or, consequently, families in the context of this earth. Those institutions are important to this life and should be revered in the highest degree, but eternity is different for in heaven there will be no death, nor new births. It is, therefore, natural that the *sacred* institution of marriage does not exist in eternal heaven. This in no way negates the *sacred* institution of marriage on this earth. It is merely a statement of fact, for marriage and childbirth are no longer needed in heaven. This is not, however, the controversy. On the contrary, this is agreed by most all. The controversy involves those who "go beyond what is written" (1 Corinthians 4:6) and declare that since marriage and childbirth no longer exist, "we would be sexless."[579] They declare that "in the bodily frame all that divided the sexes will be no more"[580] and we shall be "asexual as the angels."[581] Such are the words of Charles Spurgeon,[582] Warren Wiersbe,[583] and apparently Jerry Falwell.[584]

1 Corinthians 4:6 warns us no to "go beyond what is written." Logically, if we assumed that the absense of marriage means that "sex is forever obliterated there"[585] it would *not* logically follow that we will all become sexually neutered *its*. The most bizarre statement I have read, from Albert Barnes, still bewilders me for he declares that we will be equal "in a kind of intercourse" to angels but "it does not imply that they shall be equal in intellect."[586] Such wild speculation clearly go far beyond what is stated by Jesus. Interestingly enough, however, many of these authors begin with fair assumptions. Take the church father Tertullian. He says:

> "As by not marrying, because of not dying, so, of course, by not having to yield to any like necessity of our bodily state; even as the angels, too, sometimes were 'equal unto' men, by eating and drinking, and submitting their feet to the washing of the bath, – having clothed themselves in human guise, without loss of their own intrinsic nature. If therefore angels, when they became as men, submitted their own unaltered substance of spirit to be treated as if they were flesh, why shall not men in like manner, when they become 'equal unto angels,' undergo in their unchanged substance of flesh the treatment of spiritual beings, no more exposed to the usual solicitations of the flesh in their angelic garb, than were the angels once to those of the spirit when encompassed in human form? We shall not therefore cease to continue in the flesh, because we cease to be importuned by the usual wants of the flesh; just as the angels ceased not therefore to remain in their spiritual substance, because of the suspension of their spiritual incidents. Lastly, Christ said not, 'They shall be angels,' in order not to repeal their existence as men; but He said, 'They shall be equal unto the angels,' that He might preserve their humanity unimpaired. When he ascribed an angelic likeness to the flesh, He took not from it its proper substance."[587]

In this he is not wrong, but Tertullian then draws the inexplicable conclusion that "no solicitude arising from carnal jealousy will, in the day of resurrection ... wound any"[588] "for you too, (women as you are), have the self-same angelic nature promised as your reward, the self-same sex as men."[589]

So Tertullian begins with a simple assumption and then carries it to an untenable extreme. So also the *Liberty Bible Commentary* correctly states that "to be as angels means that resurrected believers will have a glorified, non-mortal body, (capable of neither reproduction nor destruction). The reference is not intended to imply that glorified men become angels nor that all earthly family relationships are lost in heaven."[590] Such a comment is fair and reasonable and yet there is nothing in this statement which should lead to the conclusion that we will all become single asexual beings. I might be accused of sarcasm if I said this is the same thing as suggesting that we will all become transexuals, but the difference is minor, for is not a transexual someone who does not conform to normal sexual stereotypes? Is not a hermaphrodite someone with missing sexual characteristics or cross sexual characteristics. If males will become castrated and females loose their breasts, will we not then become transexual to a degree? This is clearly *not* of what Jesus was speaking.

Let us then look solely at the words of Jesus and the logical conclusions of those words. We will become, as MacArthur says, "like angels, equally spiritual in nature, equally deathless, equally glorified, and equally eternal."[591] From this we can conclude with John Wesley that the "incorruptible ... [have] little need of marriage"[592] since the current cycle of birth and death is no more. Hippolytus said, our bodies "grows not, sleeps not, hungers not, thirst not, is not weary, suffers not."[593] MacArthur suggests that there will not "be exclusive relationships in heaven, but everyone will be perfectly and intimately related to everyone else, including to the living God Himself."[594] These are *possibilities*, but beyond this nothing is said, nor should anything be said.

Finally, it should be said in passing that some, such as Erasmus[595] and MacArthur,[596] believe that the Sadducees denied the existence of angels as well as the resurrection. This seems to be case as Acts 23:8 states that "the Sadducees say that there is no resurrection, nor an angel, nor a spirit, but the Pharisees acknowledge them all." Nevertheless, it is noteworthy that when Jesus answered their words with words from Moses and by declaring that angels will be a "pattern"[597] for men in heaven, he was challenging the Sadducees denial of angels and the resurrection out of the lips of Moses, whom they believed.

Thus it may be said that Jesus affirms that in eternity the sacred institution of marriage will no longer exist and there will no longer be a need for child bearing or the raising of children. We will be patterned after the angels. We shall continue to love one another, including those who were our wives or children, but as an institution marriage will no longer be a necessity. It remains sacred on this earth for it is essential to our duties on this earth. In heaven we will have different functions and duties. Beyond this I will not go (1 Corinthians 4:6).

Love Your Neighbor or Yourself?
Matthew 22:39

"You shall love your neighbor as yourself."

121

The Bible warns that "in the last days difficult times will come. For men will be lovers of self, lovers of money, boastful, arrogant, revilers, disobedient to parents, ungrateful, unholy, unloving, irreconcilable, malicious gossips, without self-control, brutal, haters of good, treacherous, reckless, conceited, lovers of pleasure rather than lovers of God, holding to a form of godliness, although they have denied its power" (1 Timothy 3:1-5). This stern warning begins with the statement that this generation shall be "lovers of themselves." For centuries *self*ishness was considered a vice. The love of self was viewed as intrinsic. We must fight to think of others rather than just ourselves. All this changed in the 1960s. The "me generation" made selfishness a virtue by borrowing from atheistic psychologists. Today we are told by even the most conservative evangelical preachers, "love your neighbor as yourself means love yourself first"!

The self-esteem movement swept throughout the evangelical church in the 1970s. Although some resisted it, most churches and seminaries not only accepted it, but created their own psychology departments (ignorant of the fact that psychology does not even recognize the foundation of causal science or the fact that its founders, to a man, created psychology as a *substitute* for religion). Christian psychology introduced the Flower Child generation to the evangelical church. A few have challenged this cult of self worship. Dave Hunt and T.A. McMahon said, "the person who says, 'I'm so ugly, I hate myself!' doesn't hate himself at all, or he would be *glad* that he was ugly. It is because he loves himself that he is upset with his appearance and the way people respond to him."[598]

Now to the critic who will ask how it is good to hate one's self, I respond with Ephesians 5:29 which reads, "no one ever hated his own flesh, but nourishes and cherishes it." Self love is *intrinsic*. We only see the world through our own eyes because we are separated from God. This makes us, by definition, selfish. In another word, it makes us sinners. I can think of no one who has put the "self image" issue more in perspective than Hunt and McMahon when they say:

> "God made man in His own image. One thinks immediately of a mirror, which has *one purpose only*: to reflect a reality *other than its own*. It would be absurd for a mirror to try to develop a 'good self-image.' It is equally absurd and certainly unbiblical, for humans to attempt to do so. If there is something wrong with the image in the mirror, then the only solution is for the mirror to get back in a right relationship with the one whose image it was designed to reflect."[599]

Jesus is the solution to our problems, not selfishness. I lived in Plano when it was the suicide capital of the world. The people who were committing suicide was often rich, handsome, and popular. It was not enough, because they had no meaning in life. It is only God that gives us meaning, not self fulfillment or inner fulfillments as the trend has become to call such self gratifications. The problem with "self esteem" is the same as the problems with pride. John Piper put it best when he said, "boasting is the voice of pride in the heart of the strong. Self-pity is the voice of pride in the heart of the weak. Boasting sounds self-sufficient. Self-pity sounds self-sacrificing."[600] They are the flip side of the same problem; not self esteem but selfishness.

When Jesus says "love your neighbor as yourself" He was not commanding us to love ourselves, for that is intrinct. He was commanding us to love *others*. It is truly a wicked generation that takes the great commandments and turns them on their head to justify the selfishness of which 1 Timothy 3:1-5 so aptly warns. This is why the apostle Pauls states, "He died for all, so that they who live might *no longer live for themselves*, but for Him who died and rose again on their behalf" (2 Corinthians 5:15).

The Pharisees Condemned?
Matthew 23:1-36

"Hypocrites!"

Why is Jesus' condemnation of the Pharisees a controversy? Simply put, it is a controversy because it is so misunderstood and misrepresented by those who hate Christians. When I came to trust in Christ a person close to me would promptly call me a hypocrite anytime he got mad at me. He would always say "hypocrisy is the worse sin in the world!" Ignoring the irony of his remarks, it was readily apparent that he did not know a thing about the Pharisees, let alone the reasons for Jesus' anger towards them.

Let us begin with the sin of hypocrisy itself. In *Paradise Lost*, John Milton said, "Hypocrisy, the only evil that walks invisible, except to God alone."[601] This is a comment the hypocrite cannot even understand, and the great irony of those who project their own hypocrisy on others, for hypocrisy involves the heart and motives which only God knows. Jesus alone has the authority to call one a hypocrite, but why? Why was Jesus angry with the Pharisees?

This is the real irony of the debate. When we read the parable we see that the parable is not about hypocrisy but about abuse of power by those to whom it is entrusted. In the parable the Pharisees were the ones invited to the wedding. It was the Pharisees who were entrusted with the truth. In fact, it was the Pharisees who were closer in doctrine to Jesus than any other group. This fact shocks many, but it is true. As discussed a few pages ago, the Sadducees denied the resurrection and rejected the inspiration of the whole of Scripture. The Zealots were a militant group which sought to ussher in the Kingdom of God by physically overthrowing the Roman Empire. The only other major religious group in Israel was the Essene sect which some have argued was closest to Jesus.[602] Many even believe that John the Baptist was an Essene, but whether John the Baptist was an Essene or not the aescetic lifestyle of the Essenes was neither what Jesus taught to his followers, nor what he practiced except when fasting. There are similarities, to be sure, but Jesus did not preach a monastic lifestyle cut off from the world, but taught us to go out into the world and preach His gospel. No, it was the Pharisees who were doctrinally in line with much of Jesus' teachings. One Jewish author even declares that Jesus "taught the moral precepts of the Pharisaic school of Hillel."[603] Moreoever, the apostle Paul, in fact, was trained personally by Gamaliel (Acts 22:3), who was a the grand son of Hillel, the founder of the Pharisees.[604] To this day, Orthodox Jews are also considered the spiritual descendants of Hillel, yet many are unaware that Christianity's similarities to the school of Hillel.

It is precisely *because* the Pharisees were closest to the truth that they condemned for their rejection of the truth. The Pharisees were the ones to whom the Word of God seems to have been entrusted in Israel. Only the Essenses had as high a regard for the Scriptures as the Pharisees. It is for this very reason that Jesus called them hypocrites. As Jesus said, "to whom much is given, much is required" (Luke 12:48).

Who Was Zechariah ben Berechiah?
Matthew 23:34-35

"Upon you may fall *the guilt of* all the righteous blood shed on earth, from the blood of righteous Abel to the blood of Zechariah, the son of Berechiah, whom you murdered between the temple and the altar."

This ranks among the larger historical controversies in the Bible for Zechariah, son of Berechiah, is said by Jesus to have been slain in the temple self, and yet scholars hotly debate to whom Jesus was referring. There was a Zechariah slain in the temple as recorded in 2 Chronicles, but this man was apparently the "son of Jehoiada." The prophet Zechariah is said to be the son of "Berechiah" in the book which bears his name, but there is no record of his having been slain at all. Some have suggested other candidates as well. Which is true?

First, it must be stated from the outset that Zechariah was a very common name in Israel. Merrill Unger's *Bible Dictionary* list *twenty-eight* different Zechariahs mentioned in the Bible.[605] Moreover, history has recorded more than one man being slain in the temple. As sacred as the temple was, murders appear to have been committed there on several occasions. According to tradition, James, the brother of Jesus, was thrown down from the top of the temple mount and killed.[606]

Second, the argument that there is a textual error in the Bible is an argument which one will hear from advocates of various positions. They will state that "some mistake seems to have crept into the text"[607] and then procede to make this an all too easy excuse to simply disregard the evidence. Saint Jerome was one such scholar.[608] Many others could be cited as well, but the fact is that evidence for textual errors in any of the effected passages is weak. It is true that the phrase "son of Berechiah" is omitted in the *Codex Sinaiticus*, but that omission was actually corrected by its author in the margins![609] No other text even contains a hint of error in Matthew 23:35. Likewise, no evidence of alteration or omission exist in either 2 Chronicles 24:20 or Zechariah 1:1. It is, therefore, disingenuous to claim a textual error where no evidence exist simply because it creates a difficulty in interpretation. We must accept that the texts read exactly as they were written.

Ignoring the cynics who claim Jesus was ignorant, we may examine four serious theories. I list these in reverse order of popularity, and I do not arrange them in any personal order. Each view should be examined for consistency in three different areas. 1. An explanation of the title "Zechariah, son of Berechiah." 2. Evidence of their death in the temple. 3. An explanation of how the person fits contextually with the blood of prophets. Any legitimate interpretation must account for all three.

Theory #4 : Zechariah the father of John the Baptist
Because Jesus was speaking of the blood of the prophets throughout history, it is assumed by some that Zechariah, the father of John the Baptist, was the man to whom Jesus referred.[610] The fact that he was a high priest suggests the possibility that he could indeed be slain in the temple where he worked, had he incurred wrath because of his son. Unfortunately, the evidence ends here.

First, there is no evidence that Zechariah was the son of Berechiah. Second, there is no evidence that Zechariah was slain in the temple, and we might expect that Luke would have recorded such an event had it transpired. The evidence from silence is therefore silent on both sides of the argument. The greatest problem however is the context of Jesus' remarks. Although it is argued that Zechariah's death in Jesus' lifetime would match the blood of the prophets from Abel (the first martyr) to the last, it ignores the fact that John the Baptist, whom Jesus called the greatest of those born to women (Matthew 11:11), was martyred just a few short years earlier! Surely if Jesus were alluding to the last prophet slain in history up to that time, it would have been John the Baptist!

Despite its obvious appeal, this view is entirely speculatory. There is no evidence to demonstrate that it can fit any of the three requirements. We must look for a better solution.

125

Theory #3 : Zechariah ben Baruch

Many have found that "another Zechariah, the son of Baruch, or Barachiah, was slain by the Zealots in the midst of the Temple thirty-four years after this time."[611] This murder is recorded by Josephus and said to be at the hands of the Idumeans thirty-four years after Jesus was crucified![612]

William Whiston summarizes the problems with this view, saying:

> "Some commentators are ready to suppose that this 'Zarcharais, the son of Baruch,' was the very same person with 'Zacharias, the son of Barachias,' Matt. xxiii 35. This is a somewhat strange exposition; since Zechariah the prophet was really 'the son of Barachiah,' and 'grandson of Iddo,' (Zech. 1:1) and how he died, we have no other account, than that before us in St. Matthew; while this 'Zacharias' was 'the son of Baruch' ; since the slaughter was past our Savior spake those words, the Jews then had already slain him; whereas the slaughter of 'Zacharias, the son of Baruch,' was then about thirty-four years future: and since that slaughter was 'between the temple and the alter,' in the court of the priests, one of the most sacred and remote parts of the whole temple' while this was in the middle of the temple."[613]

This last comment speaks loudest. Jesus was not uttering a prophecy but referring to those "murdered" (34:31) in the past. Or was He? Some take, "I am sending you prophets and wise men and scribes; some of them you will kill and crucify, and some of them you will scourge in your synagogues, and persecute from city to city" (Matthew 23:34) as proof that this is a prophecy. However, the argument is that Jesus was prophesying his death, has many problems. To begin with, Jesus was speaking to the Pharisees and indicting them. How could he indict them on the murder of a man who had not yet died? The Pharisees would have reacted with laughter rather than anger. Moreover, there is no evidence that this Zechariah was a prophet or a follower of Christ. In fact, Josephus only calls him "one of the most eminent of the citizens."[614] Furthermore, the apostles were themselves being persecuted and martyred at this same time, so why would Jesus prophesy the death of an obscure man when James the Just himself had died being cast down from the temple![615]

Theory #2 : Zechariah the Prophet

"The word of the LORD came to Zechariah the prophet, the son of Berechiah, the son of Iddo" (Zechariah 1:1). So begins the book of Zechariah. Clearly the identification of Zechariah, the son of Berechiah, would appear to be obvious. Zechariah was a prophet and he was the son of Berechiah. The problem is that we have no evidence he was ever martyred, let alone matryred in the temple. Nevertheless, MacArthur, and many others, believes that he was indeed murdered in the temple.[616] Like William Whiston the only evidence he needs is the words of Jesus,[617] but this is somewhat trivial for the words of Jesus are what we are debating. We must provide evidence that this is indeed to what Jesus was referring. Let us examine the facts surrounding Zechariah and his life.

Matthew Poole dismissed this view, arguing that "there was no temple in his time."[618] In fact, the temple construction had begun during his ministry. Since we do not know when Zechariah died we cannot say that the temple had not been completed before his death. Moreover, the turbulent times during the construction of the temple and Zechariah's ministry do make for tempting circumstantial evidence but it is circumstantial at best. This was the time of Israel's re-establishment, not the time of its fall. There does not seem to be evidence that Zechariah was persecuted as were the prophets who led up to the fall of Jerusalem. Most importantly, if we are to make an argument from silence then the loudest argument from silence is the silence of tradition as to Zechariah's alleged martyrdom. Why would the alleged martyrdom of a great prophet like Zechariah not even warrant a mention by Josephus; particularly if it had been done in the Holy Temple defiling the sacred altar!

This view is therefore strong in the first point, but weak in its second. On the third, the view does seem to hold up well, for chronologically speaking Zechariah "was indeed the last of the Old Testament martyrs mentioned in the Hebrew Scriptures"[619] (assuming he was a martyr). Only Malachi followed Zechariah, thus making Zechariah the last of the Old Testament prophets to be slain *if* indeed he ever was slain.

Theory #1 : Zechariah the son of High Priest Jehoiada
In 2 Chronicles 24:20-21 the martyrdom of a priest named Zechariah is recorded as having taken place "in the court of the house of the Lord."

> "Then the Spirit of God came on Zechariah the son of Jehoiada the priest; and he stood above the people and said to them, 'Thus God has said, "'Why do you transgress the commandments of the LORD and do not prosper? Because you have forsaken the LORD, He has also forsaken you."'" So they conspired against him and at the command of the king they stoned him to death in the court of the house of the LORD" (2 Chronicles 24:20-21).

The event is also recorded in Josephus who says simply, "the king commanded that Zechariah, the son of the high priest Jehoiada, should be stoned to death in the temple."[620] One can see the similarities, but there are problems to be sure. On the first point there is much debate. This Zechariah is said to be the son of a high priest named Jehoiada and not Berechiah. One response to this is the fact that "giving new or additional names was a common practice among the Jews."[621] Thus some claim that Jehoiada had two names.[622] John Wesley is among those[623] as is John Calvin,[624] who said, "it is not absurd to suppose that his father Jehoiada received the same son of Barachiah as an honour."[625] This view, however, is not without difficulty for we are told that Jehoiada lived to be

127

130 (2 Chronicles 24:15). While his son could have been slain while Jehoiada still lived, it is commonly assumed that Zechariah was high priest at the time, and thus his father would have already died.

One solution to this problem is to assume that Jehoiada, or perhaps even Barachiah, was the grandfather of Zechariah.[626] This is based on the fact that the word "father" (*not* "beget" as used in Genesis) can mean forefather. So some say that Jehoiada was the grand-father and Barachiah the father[627] while other say that Barachiah was the grand-father.[628] John Walvoord is among the more famous advocates of this position.[629]

Nevertheless, having solved (presumeably) the problem with the name of Zechariah's father, there is the problem of his martyrdom for although both were slain on the temple mount, Jesus explicitly declared that Zechariah was slain "between the temple and the altar" whereas 2 Chronicles relates that this Zechariah was slain "in the court" of the temple. This is not a trivial issue for Jesus' remarks clearly indicate more than just a martyrdom but also a sacriledge rarely seen in history. Only a few times in history (Thomas Becket's murder for example) has anyone dared to commit murder in their own sacred house! The two stories, therefore, do not match up exactly.

On the final point, this view seems solid. 2 Chronicles is the last book in the Hebrew canon. This is because the Hebrew canon of the Bible is arranged differently than the Christians. The books are the same, but the arrangement is different. In the days of Jesus, 2 Chronicles would have been the last book of His Bible. Consequently, the death of Zechariah would match with being the last prophet whose martyrdom is recorded in the Bible.

Conclusion
When we examine these four theories and weigh them against the three central textual points of Jesus' remarks we are left to choose between Zechariah the prophet and Zechariah, son of Jehoiada. The relation to John the Baptist is pure conjecture without any evidence. The theory that this was some obscure Zechariah of the future is also conjecture without much support. In fact, it begs more questions than it answers, such as why Zechariah (an obscure man of history who may not have even been a believer) would be chosen over James the Just who was slain on the temple mount as well.

Choosing between the other two is not easy. The first point clearly favors the prophet Zechariah, whose book bears his name. The Zechariah of 2 Chronicles cannot be linked positively to any Berechiah and must be assumed. The second point, however, seems to favor 2 Chronicles, but when we examine it closely there is a clear difference between the temple court yard where he was stoned to death and Jesus' words that he was slain "between the temple and the altar" where no formal stoning could take place. Did they carry the stones into the sacred temple? Since the stoning was sanctioned by the king it was technically a legal execution and would have been done with some ceremony outside in the courtyard as the Bible states. Conversely, we must assume that

Zechariah the prophet met this fate, but the silence of even tradition speaks volumes against it.

The final point is contextual and both views fit it well. If we look at the canon of the Bible then 2 Chronicles was the last book of the Hebrew Bible and would serve to prove Jesus' point since Abel died in the first book and Zechariah died in the last. Alternately, if we look at history chronologically then Zechariah the prophet was the second to last prophet in the Bible, as only Malachi followed him before the New Testament era. If Zechariah was martyred, then he would be the last prophet of the Old Testament to have been killed.

As one can see, I am not one who is prone to interject his opinions upon the facts or adopt a view out of sentiment or emotion. I am honestly undecided between these two views. If a single tradition existed that Zechariah the prophet had died in the temple I would readily accept this view, but it seems hard to believe that not a single word has ever transpired about such a martyrdom if it did happen. That leaves us with 2 Chronicles whose account is problematic to the literalist, for Jesus did not say he died in the temple courtyard but specifically "between the temple and the altar." Did he run into the temple to seek santuary as he was being stoned? Perhaps they chased him into the temple, defiling the temple and sactuary. This conjecture may be best.

One thing we are sure of is that the Pharisees did not dispute that it happened, and it most certainly did. Our own ignorance of history is not proof that it did not happen, for the Pharisees were in a far better situation to know the truth, and it is a truth they never denied.

The Olivet Discourse
Matthew 24:4-14

"Do you not see all these things? Truly I say to you, not one stone here will be left upon another, which will not be torn down."

Because of the length of the Olivet Discourse I will break up the discussion into different sections. Here the primary discussion will be the historical / prophetic context of the discourse itself. In other words, have the prophecies of Jesus Christ now become history or are they yet to be fulfilled in the future? Such a question might seem frivolous to many, but in the counter-reformation a doctrine known as "preterism" emerged to counter those who claimed that the papacy was the anti-Christ.[630] Although not official supported by the Catholic church, preterism became popular among many Catholics and, ironically, many protestants have adopted this system of interpretation in recent years as well.

Put simply, preterism holds that all the prophecies of the Olivet Discourse (or at least most of them) as well as the prophecies of the book of Revelation were fulfilled in the first century after Christ, culminating with the fall of Jerusalem in 70 A.D.[631]   Since the words quoted above are clearly references to the destruction of the temple in 70 A.D. one is tempted to accept preterism at face value, but once anyone begins to read Jesus' words at length it is clear that the destruction of the temple is *not* related to the Olivet Discourse. It is for this reason that not everyone who believes Jesus is speaking of 70 A.D. in the Olivet Discourse can be classified as preterist.   Many, such as John Wesley, hold that the first section of the Olivet Discourse is about 70 A.D. whereas the later section is about End Times.[632] John Calvin also rejected a completely preterist interpretation, saying, "some wrongly restrict the destruction to the temple."[633]   Jonathan Edwards said that Jesus was speaking of "two events, one the destruction of Jerusalem and the works of God that accompanied it, the other the end of the world."[634]

So we have before us essentially three views. The futurist view that all the prophecies herein are of the end of days; the preterist view that holds that all these prophecies were fulfilled in the first century after Christ; and the mixed view which suggests that Jesus began by speaking about the fall of Jerusalem but then switched to last days at some point in the Olivet Discourse.

Wars and Rumors of Wars

It should clear that a passage of time has elapsed between Jesus' prophecy of the destruction of the temple in 24:2 and His "sitting on the Mount of Olives" when "the disciples came to Him privately" and ask about the End Times. Certainly the prophecy of Jerusalem's fall (which took place in 70 A.D.) piqued the apostle's curiosity, but one cannot rationally believe that the "end" took place in 70 A.D. That is why the words of Jesus must be "spiritualized"[635] to make them less than literal. John Wesley, for example, says that the end of which Jesus spoke was only the end "of the city and temple."[636]

Others, such as Warren Wiersbe[637] and John MacArthur connect these prophecies to the seals and trumpets described in the book of Revelation.[638] This is not, however, a commonly accepted view even among pretribultionsists (those who believe that all the prophecies relate to the end of days before the Second Coming of Christ). The reason is that Jesus refers to these first events (vv. 4-14) as "birth pangs." There have always been wars and rumors of wars. There have always been cults and heretics. There has always been lawlessness, but as these increase in frequency and intensity, as with a mother giving birth, the time for birth is growing closer.

Note that the "birth pangs" mentioned occur regularly throughout history. However, they are all growing more frequent and severe as time passes. Even many who erroneously associate these "pangs" with the judgment seals of Revelation have admitted that Jesus issued the warning in order that believers would "not be alarmed by these events. 'Such things must happen'; yet the End is still to come (v. 6). These are only 'the beginning of [the] birth pangs' that stretch over the period between the advents."[639]

The "birth pangs" are, therefore, not the first seven seals of Revelation but signs that precede the tribulation.[640] Wars, famines, earthquakes and the like will increase in both severity and frequency as the time of the Second Coming approaches. It is as the apostle Paul stated when he said, "the whole of creation itself groans and travails in labor pains until now" (Romans 8:22). History has proven that the frequency and intensity of natural disasters has progressively increased over the centuries. In the past few years alone the world has been hit by numerous hurricanes and tropical storms which were once relatively rare. Earthquakes in particular have increased dramtically. Over a decade ago, the *Fort Worth Star Telegram* reported that the twentieth century has recorded no fewer than 900,000 earthquakes![641] This is compared to only 2119 recorded earthquakes in the nineteenth century, and 640 in the eighteenth century.[642] These are the "birth pangs" of which Jesus spoke, not the judgments of the tribulation.

Despite this, John Wesley (a futurist), believes that the false Christs of whom our Lord spoke were those related to the fall of Jerusalem[643] but if this is so, who can the other elements of the prophecy relate to times past? Did not Jesus say that the gospel "shall be preached in the whole world as a testimony to all the nations" *first*? Surely the gospel had not even been preached unto all the kingdoms known to Rome at that time! To this Wesley and the allegorist can only say that it is "not universally"[644] the earth, but only the Roman earth. Even this seems insufficient for Christianity had hardly been preached even to all of the Roman earth at that time. Most people had never heard the gospel and of those who had heard of Christianity they knew nothing of it except that it was an obscure Jewish cult from Asia Minor.

Nothing in these first fourteen verses provides any definitive clues to the time of the prophecies' fulfillment except that *prior* to the end the gospel must be preached unto "all the nations." Only in modern times can this be said, and even today there are pockets where civilization is still just beginning to reach. It is my belief that even those small pockets must be reached *before* the end.

Conclusion

Nothing in these first fourteen verses can be said to justify the notion that Jesus was speaking of the Roman sack of Jerusalem. Indeed, it was not until the time of Constantine that anyone made such a claim of the Olivet Discourse as a whole. If Jesus were prophesying this event it would be strange indeed that not a single ante-nicene church father (those before Constantine's day) make this claim. Prophecy should not be so ambiguous to the believer.

It is sufficient to say that every church father quoted by preterists refer not to the Olivet Discourse or the book of Revelation, but to Matthew 24:1.

This prophecy is clearly distinct from the discourse which follows for 24:1 was spoken on the temple mount before many whereas the Olivet Discourse was spoken on the Mount of Olives to His disciples. The sole connection is that the prophecy of Jerusalem's fall piqued the apostle's curiousity for we must remember that the apostles did not yet realize that Jesus was to die on the cross. They fully expected that Jesus would usher in the Kingdom of God in their lifetimes. It was not until after the resurrection of Christ that they came to realize that a period of grace was to separate the first coming from the second. The gospel would *have* to be preached to "the whole world" and to "all the nations" (24:14). Were Jesus to have ushered in His kingdom at that time, we would all be damned. It is because of His grace that the kingdom has been delayed so that the gospel might reach *not some*, but **all** the world and **all** the nations.

Abomination of Desolations
Matthew 24:15-28

"When you see the *Abomination of Desolation* which was spoken of through Daniel the prophet, standing in the holy place (let the reader understand), then those who are in Judea must flee to the mountains."

"The Abomination of Desolation which was spoken through Daniel the prophet." These words connect the entire Olivet Discourse to the prophecy of Daniel. Since I wrote some thirty pages on Daniel's prophecy in *Controversies in the Prophets* I will not repeat the entire subject here but focus on Jesus' application along with a brief summary of Daniel and his prophecy of the seventy weeks and the abomination of desolation.

Daniel

The abomination of desolation is a prophecy of Daniel which takes place in the middle of a the final "week" of "seventy weeks" of years. Stephen Miller calls this prophecy "the most controversial verses in the Bible."[645] John Walvoord declares that they are "one of the most comprehensive and yet concise prophecies to be found in the Bible."[646] In these passages Daniel not only predicts the coming of the Messiah, but gives an actual timeline! Daniel declared:

"Seventy weeks [Hebrew-*shevim*] have been decreed for your people and ... after [sixty-nine] weeks [Hebrew-*shevim*] the Messiah will be cut off and have nothing, and the people of the prince who is to come will destroy the city and the sanctuary ... And he will make a firm covenant with the many for one week, but in the middle of the week he will put a stop to sacrifice and grain offering; and on the wing of abominations *will come* one who makes desolate, even until a complete destruction,

132

one that is decreed, is poured out on the one who makes desolate"
(Daniel 9:24-27).

The first problem is that the "weeks" to which Daniel refers are not
week *days* but week *years*. The ancient Jews divided everything by multiples of
seven rather than ten. We have decades, but the Jews had *shevim* (שְׁבֻעִים) or
"sevens," which is often translated as "weeks." So the seventy weeks were
actually seventy Jewish "septades" of seven years. Of course I made up the
word "septade" to substitute for decade since a decade is made up of ten years,
not seven, but the principle is the same.

The second issue is the fact that the ancients did not use the modern
365 a year calendar. Despite the protest of cynics, skeptics, and so-called liberal
theologians, all historians acknowledge that the modern calendar did not exist
until the time of Julius Caesar. The earliest calendar is believed to have been
comprised of twelve months alternating between 29 and 30 days a month
totaling 354 days. The ancient Jews are believed to have had used this calendar
at one time,[647] while the ancient Romans had a 355 day calendar.[648] The
Assyrians also used a similar calendar using a sort of leap month to correct the
conflict with the solar year.[649] Nevertheless, this method of calculation still
created too much a disparity between the lunar calendar and the solar calendar.
The ancient Chaldeans, or Babylonians, in turn created that 360 day calendar
that remained in effect for centuries.[650] This same 360 day calendar continued
to be used by the Persians when Cyrus conquered Babylon, at the time Daniel
still lived.[651] The first Greek to attempt to institute a 365 day calendar was
Thales[652] whose calendar would become the standard for Julius Caesar when he
created the Julian calendar,[653] later amended by Pope Gregory the Great; hence
the name Gregorian Calendar.

Therefore, if we take the *shevim* (שְׁבֻעִים) and multiply it by the 360 day
calendar in use in Daniel's time, we have a prophecy that can calculate exactly
when Daniel said the Messiah would come. I will not repeat the debate here
except to say that all the ancient Jews believed the Messiah was appear in days
when Jesus lived. The Dead Seas Scrolls, from the ancient Qumran
communities prove this.[654] Many of us believe that the prophecy literally takes
us to the very week, if not day, that Christ was crucified (see section "When
Was Jesus Crucified?"). However, the prophecy does not end here or it would
have no relevance to the Olivet Discourse, for according to Daniel there still
remained one *shevim* (שְׁבֻעִים) following the Messiah's death. This "week year"
or "septade" is then divided in half with the "abomination of desolation" taking
place at the midway point of the final week. This is the controversy I shall
address here. What is this final "week" and when does (or did) the
"abomination of desolation" take place? What is the "abomination of
desolation"? Was Jesus prophesying about the fall of Jerusalem in 70 A.D. or
events at the end of the age when the anti-Christ will rule the earth?

133

All are agree that with the death and resurrection of Christ the first sixty-nine *shevim* of Daniel are past history. We *may* even agree that the "the people of the prince who is to come will destroy the city and the sanctuary" (9:26) does indeed refer to the fall of Jerusalem in 70 A.D., but this event takes place **before** the final *shevim*, not *during* the final *shevim*. Preterist attribute the "abomination of desolation" to the fall of Jerusalem at this time and go to great lengths to show the similarities whereas futurist reject this in its entirety. Let us examine first the fall of Jerusalem itself.

The Fall of Jerusalem

In 64 A.D. the Roman procurator Florus seized gold from the Jewish treasury. That gold was supposed to be used for the sacred temple and the two revolutionary Jewish groups, the *Sicarii* and the *Zealots*, began an uprising. They assassinated Roman sympathizers among the Jews and attacked Roman troops and caravans. Roman soldiers marched on Palestine to regain control of the situation and by 67 A.D. general Vespasian had seized Galilee. He then marched down toward Jerusalem and the seige began in the spring of 68 A.D., but Vespasian was recalled to Rome and eventually named Emperor. In his stead Titus, his son, was named general and put in charge of the seige which was to last years. Jerusalem finally fell and the temple burned to the ground in 70 A.D., on the 9th of Av of the Jewish Calendar, the anniversary of the destruction of the first temple by Nebuchadnezzar. A few stragglers of resistance fighters continued to fight up until 73 A.D. when the last of the rebels committed suicide on the mountain fortress of Masada.[655]

Preterist like Karl Linski[656] and Albert Barnes[657] argue that the Roman war broke out three and a half years before the fall of Jerusalem, in 66 A.D. This is borrowed from the Nicene-church father Eusebius, who appears to be the first true preterist in regard to the Olivet Discourse.[658] Eusebius then claims that in 68 A.D., as the armies approached Jerusalem, the word of Jesus in 24:16 were fulfilled as the members of the Jerusalem Church fled the city to live in a city called Pella.[659] Preterist then count the destruction of the temple as the abomination of desolation and end the seventieth week of Daniel at the fall of Masada.

If we follow Eusebius' history then it is easy to see a superficial similarity. However, upon close examination the entire argument falls apart on three levels. First, the history does not match Jesus' prophecy, nor Daniels'. Second, the events of the Jewish War cannot be said to fulfill the purpose of Daniel's prophecy. Third, if the prophecy had been fulfilled then Jesus should have returned in 73 A.D. He did not. Let us examine these three areas carefully.

134

It has already been observed that the Jewish War began after Florus looted the treasury in 64 A.D., not 66 A.D. Eusebius takes a single event from a war which had been going on for some time and somewhat arbitrarily designates it as the beginning of the war. Josephus, however, clearly states that the war began under Florus in 64 A.D.[660]

Another problem is that Eusebius' attempt to connect the migration of Christians from Jerusalem to Pella does not fit the prophecy of Matthew 24:16 in which Jesus said, "those who are in Judea must flee to the mountains. Whoever is on the housetop must not go down to get the things out that are in his house. Whoever is in the field must not turn back to get his cloak. But woe to those who are pregnant and to those who are nursing babies in those days! But pray that your flight will not be in the winter, or on a Sabbath." These are Jesus' words, but the fact is that Christians did not flee to Mountains in 70 A.D.[661] and Pella is not mountainous.[662] It is a city in Greece near the sea!

Furthermore, the fall of Masada was not three and a half years later, but roughly 2 years and 8 months later. Prophecy does not deal in approximates, but in exacts. So strict is this rule that the Old Testament law calls for the death penalty upon anyone who utters a false prophecy (Deuteronomy 18:20-22)!

Yet another problem is how preterists define the abomination of desolation. Jesus describes the abomination of desolation as "standing in the holy place." Consequently, the abomination cannot be the destruction of the temple itself but must be something abominable to God that is placed in the temple. In antiquity the only thing designated as an abomination of desolation which had taken place in the temple was when Antiochus Epiphanes erected an idol of Zeus and slaughtered of a pig within the Holy Temple.[663] Even the murder of Zechariah does not appear to have been designated as an abomination of desolation by ancient Jewish historians, vile and sacreligious as the crime may have been. Consequently, the abomination must be something similar in nature, "standing" in the temple.

Some preterists claimed that Caligula fulfilled this prophecy when he attempted to place a statue of himself in the temple,[664] but the fact is that he did not succeded and died before his troops were able to carry out the atrocity. After his death, the troops were then recalled and the statue *never* appeared within the temple. Furthermore, the deed of Caligula clearly has no relationship to the fall of Jerusalem or to Daniel's prophecy of seventy *shevim*. As a result, most preterists rightly reject this argument. Instead most claim that the presence of the Roman imperial standard was the abomination.[665] This argument is also weak. First, if the standard was placed in the temple it cannot meet the requirements of the prophecy. Consider that the apostle Paul described the abomination by saying that the "man of lawlessness ... he takes his seat in the temple of God, displaying himself as being God" (2 Thessalonians 2:3-4).

Nothing remotely similar to this ever happened in 70 A.D. Secondly, it is not certain that the imperial standard was ever even placed within the temple which was burned to the ground. What is certain is that preterists seem to graspe at straws to try to make the prophecy fit history. Why?

All true preterists (as opposed to a few partial preterists) subscribe to a doctrine known as "covenant theology" or more specifically, "replacement theology." Because I deal with these theologies in more detail elsewhere[666] I will here only define the relevance in brief terms. Replacement theology argues that the church has replaced Israel in God's plan for the ages. They deny that physical "corporate" Israel has any place in the Lord's future plans. Consequently, they must make the fall of Jerusalem the ultimate fulfillment of God's prophecies regarding Israel. Such a system of theology clearly reads into the text, since Israel, as a nation, is mentioned repeated throughout prophecy. These theologians merely attribute all the prophecies of future Israel to the church. They view the revival of Israel in 1948 as a coincidence at best. One covenant theologian professor I studied under told me, to paraphrase, "I don't say that that country across the sea has no purpose but I cannot support everything they do and do not believe that they have a prophetic future." This is the true motive behind preterism, going all the way back to Eusebius (the first preterist of which I am aware) who viewed Constantine's empire (to a degree) as the ushering in of the kingdom.

Daniel's Prophecy

A greater problem with the preterist view is its relationship to the prophecy of Daniel. These prophecies cannot be separated since Jesus explicitly referenced Daniel 9 in His discourse. If we, therefore, take the prophecy of Daniel into account then we will see that the preterist viewpoint conflicts with both the beginning and end of the *shevim*.

According to Daniel, this final *shevim* begins with "a firm covenant" (9:27). This covenant is to last seven years, but can any preterist show any covenant Rome made with Israel at this time? Can they show any covenant at all? No treaty, no covenant, nor anything similar can be related to the beginning of the War of the Jews.

More importantly, Daniel declares that the end of the *shevim* signals "an end of sin ... atonement for iniquity ... [and] everlasting righteousness" (9:24) among other things. Preterist are quick to retort that Jesus did all that on the cross, but the cross takes place after the sixty-ninth *shevim*, not the seventieth (cf. 9:26)! In fact, it is *between* the sixty-ninth and seventieth *shevim* that Daniel says "the people of the prince who is to come will destroy the city and the sanctuary" (9:26)!

So it is easy to see that attempts to fit the fall of Jerusalem into Daniel's prophecy of the seventieth week (during which the abomination of desolation takes place) fail. Daniel explicitly says "the city and the sanctuary" will be destroyed *before* the covenant which begins the seventieth *shevim*. This is why scholars cannot even come to an agreement upon the exact prophecy. The famed Jewish theologian Rashi, for example, argued that the seventy *shevim* end with the destruction of the temple.[667] Others, like Metzudos and Rambam, agree,[668] but then all must admit that we still live in a world filled with wars, disease, suffering, and pain whereas the end of the seventy *shevim* should usher in an age of peace, righteousness, and justice. If we say that began on the cross then we should rightly place the end of the seventy *shevim* there, and not some 37 years later! If the cross was the end of the sixty-ninth *shevim* as Daniel indicates (9:24) then the seventieth *shevim must* precede the second coming.

The Olivet Discourse

What of the Olivet Discourse? The entire Olivet Discourse was in response to the apostle's question about "the sign of Your coming, and of the end of the age" (24:3). The mere fact that Jesus has not returned should be a hint that the events described in the Olivet Discourse have not yet happened. Consider, for example, Jesus' statement, "unless those days had been cut short, no life would have been saved; but for the sake of the elect those days shall be cut short" (24:22). Note carefully the words, "unless those days had been cut short, *no life would have been saved*." Could this have referred to Titus' army? Were those days "cut short"? Was all human life brought to the brink of extinction?

To be sure the destruction of Jerusalem was a severe and cruel blight upon the Jews, but history has seen far worse including the Holocaust. We should not take Jesus' words as exaggeration or hyperbole. They were words of *prophecy*.

The Future Abomination

If the Abomination of Desolation is not past, then what is it and when is it? We have already seen that the abomination takes place in the middle of the final *shevim* of Daniel's prophecy. We have further seen that this final *shevim* takes place *after* the destruction of the temple by Romans (9:26). There is clearly a gap between the sixty-ninth and seventieth *shevim*. This must be admitted even by the preterist, since thirty-seven years passed after Jesus' death and resurrection and the fall of Jerusalem.

That such a gap exist is admitted by all. The Epistle of Barnabas, one of the oldest non-Biblical church writings (which some believe was written by Barnabas, Paul's companion), states that "I find that a temple does exist"[669] in the 27th verse, but not in the 26th verse of Daniel. This can only be explained if the temple is destroyed and rebuilt in the interim. That is why so many believe that the temple of Jerusalem must be rebuilt before the end, and it at this time that the anti-Christ commits the Abomination of Desolation. Consider the words of the apostle Paul, "with regard to the coming of our Lord Jesus Christ ... let no one in any way deceive you, for it will not come unless the apostasy comes first, and the man of lawlessness is revealed, the son of destruction, who opposes and exalts himself above every so-called god or object of worship, so that he takes his seat in the temple of God, displaying himself as being God" (2 Thessalonians 2:1-4). Yet *no one* took his seat in the temple of God and displayed himself as being God in 70 A.D. This should be proof enough that Jesus and Paul were speaking of a time in the future when the temple will exist once again in the land of Israel.

I have written extensively on this subject in both *Controversies in the Revelation* and *Controversies in the Prophets.* I will, therefore, not repeat those pages, for they are many. It will suffice to say that after the temple had been destroyed by the Romans (as Jesus prophesied in Matthew 24:1) the ante-nicene church fathers agreed that Jerusalem would be restored and the temple rebuild. Irenaeus, who lived a hundred years after the temple fell, states that the future anti-Christ shall sit in the one true and literal temple of God and declare himself Christ.[670] So also Hippolytus, not long after, declares that when the anti-Christ comes he "shall build the city of Jerusalem and restore the sanctuary."[671] Terullian also held that the abomination takes place at the end of days, and not in the past destruction of Jerusalem.[672] Not until Eusebius in the days of Constantine do we see any exegesis attributing the Olivet Discourse to Titus and the fall of Jerusalem. The Abomination of which both Jesus and Paul spoke takes place in the middle of Daniel's last *shevim* (called the Tribulation by theologians) before the anti-Christ falls and the Messiah returns in glory. This Tribulation is described in the book of Revelation.

Conclusion

While Jesus was preaching on the temple mount, He had prophesied the fall of the temple. Much later that evening, the apostles had become curious. They did not understand the end of all things, so they ask Jesus about the time of the end. This "Olivet Discourse" did not relate to the fall of Jerusalem but was in answer to their querry. This is obvious by the fact that Jesus' discourse never even mentions the destruction of the temple or the diaspora of the Jews. On the contrary, it appears that Jesus returns to prevent the destruction of Jerusalem, not to cause it!

On one level it is understandable for some people to assume that the apostles understood all these things, but we must realize that the apostles did not even understand the death and resurrection of Jesus until after His resurrection. Consequently, they did not understand at that time about last days. It is therefore understandable that they inquired about it after Jesus' prophecy but it is a mistake to correlate the two. No Roman ever stood in the temple and declared himself God. Caligula's statue never even made it to the courtyard as the Jews prevented that abomination from taking place. We must, therefore, conclude that the events of which Jesus spoke take place not in 70 A.D. but in

138

the Last Days, which is what the apostles were asking about in the first place. Had the disciples asked about the destruction of the temple, He would have told them, but they asked about the End Times, and that is of what Jesus spoke; nothing else.

This makes far more sense than those who attempt to signal a shift in Jesus' discourse itself. Some, like John Wesley, believe that Jesus began by speaking about the destruction of Jerusalem, but then shifts to a discussion of End Times.[673] This view is even held some evangelicals,[674] but none seem to be able to justify this shift. Did Jesus arbitrarily jump over two thousand years of history without so much as a disclaimer? Although some see a "definite allusion" to Rome[675] it is the "revived Roman Empire" (see *Controversies in Revelation* for a full discussion of this) and not ancient Rome. As John Walvoord has said, the book of Revelation "coincides so exactly with this presentation" that it must be distant future.[676] Revelation itself was not even written until at least twenty-five years after the fall of Jerusalem. To suggest that the Olivet Discourse is past and not future "is the foolish, spiritualizing method, which does such violence to the Word of God."[677]

Matthew 24:31 – See Mark 13:27

The Generation
Matthew 24:34 (Cf. Mark 13:30 and Luke 21:32)

> "Truly I say to you, this generation will not pass away until all these things take place."

Preterists hold this verse up as proof that Jesus was prophesying the events of 70 A.D., for surely the generation to which Jesus was speaking has long ago passed away, or has it? To be sure this passage is problematic for many, but it is not as cut and dry as the preterist believes. This is apparent by the fact that there are no fewer than eight different interpretations possited by advocates from virtually all theological positions. Consequently, all deserve examination. Below is a brief overview. Debate will be reserved under "conclusion."

The Views

1. The Preterist View
The first view, already mentioned, that this is proof that all, or part, of the Olivet Discourse refers to the fall of Jerusalem[678] since no other event in that "generation" witnessed similar events. In fairness, this is the strength of the preterists' arguments, but it must still assume that an abomination took place, which they have been unable to demonstrate from history. Moreover, no serious student of the Olivet Discourse can claim that all the events Jesus described took place in those days; especially the Second Coming, for which we still wait!

2. *Double fulfillment*

The double fulfillment theory is common in prophetic interpretations; sometimes too common. It argues that the prophecy actually had two meanings; one in the remote future and a second (double fulfillment) in the far future.[679] Frequently, the remore or near fulfillment is not as literal as the second or far fulfillment. Thus the double fulfillment theory as applied to this passage is really a partial preterist view.[680]

3. *Current generation will* **begin** *to see these events*

Because Jesus compared some of these events to birth pangs which increase over time, it is has been suggested that Jesus' remark here is only meant to relay the fact that this generation would *begin* to experience these birth pangs, but that it would continue on until the time of the end.[681] Evidence for this is found in the use of the aorist tense, which is a kind of "indefinite tense" in terms of time sequence.[682] The problem with this view is that Jesus said "until all these things take place." Like the preterist view, we must assume that only *some* of these things had to take place in that generation, but not *all*.

4. *The Skeptic View*

The skeptic takes the preterist view with the exception being that he acknowledges that the prophesies of the Olivet Discourse did not take place in 70 A.D. and were not fulfilled. According to skeptics the fact that Jesus has not returned is simply proof that Jesus was wrong.[683] Of course, this is only true if the preterist view is true, so it is not a particularly powerful criticism of the Bible or of Jesus' prophecies.

5. *The Race View*

A rarely taught view is actually one of the strongest views. It argues that the Greek word γενεα (*genea*) "has in Hellenistic Greek the meaning of a race or family of people."[684] Some interpret this variously as Jewish race, human race, or sometimes even as the church,[685] but in each case it is a *race* or group of people.[686] This is not conjecture. Thayer's famed Greek lexicon list "generation" or "age" as *fourth* among possible translations. The first, when used as a verb, is to give birth to someone or something. The second is "a race of men."[687]

Basically, a γενεα (*genea*) is a group of people and its exact translation is governed by the context. This is also true of the Hebrew and Aramaic words.[688] The word used in modern Hebrew translation of Matthew is דור (*dor*).[689] According to the famed Hebrew scholar William Gesenius, דור (*dor*) "often means a *race of men*."[690] Consequently, it is irrelevant whether Jesus was speaking Greek, Hebrew, or Aramaic. In any case, the word can easily be translated as "race."

140

6. The Allegorical View

The allegorical view borrows from the often misquoted verse, 2 Peter 3:8, where Peter says "with the Lord one day is like a thousand years, and a thousand years like one day." They thus attempt to connect this passage to the generation. The strength of the argument is that unlike most abusers of this verse, the context of which Paul speak is, indeed, the subject of the Second Coming. The problem, however, is that Peter is was saying, "The Lord is not slow about His promise, as some count slowness, but is patient toward you, not wishing for any to perish but for all to come to repentance" (3:9). The "generation" has no relation to this passage and its application to it does not answer the question or solve the problem. The verse does show that the Second Coming did not have to take place in their lifetime, to be sure, but it does not address what Jesus meant by "this generation will not pass away until all these things take place."

7. The Indefinite View

Another view similar to that of the allegorical view is that the generation is actually a general term for an indefinite time period.[691] Once again borrowing from allegorical interpretation of Scripture, this view attempts to displace the generation in question by applying a symbolic meaning to it, but this again neglects the real issue. The view fails to properly address exactly what Jesus meant by "this generation will not pass away until all these things take place."

8. The End Times View

Arguably the most popular view among evangelicals and futurists is that "the word rendered 'this' may with equal correctness be translated 'that.'"[692] In other words, it would read, "that generation will not pass away until all these things take place." So this view takes the generation as referring to the generation who lives at the End Times.[693]

Conclusion

Of the eight views, only two hold water, and both of those require a different translation from what is recorded in most Bibles. The preterist view cannot be accepted, despite its seeming favoritism in this passage. Because Jesus said "all these things," and not just "some" we cannot accept that the generation was that living in Jesus' day, nor can we accept the partial preterist view (the double fulfillment view). "*All*" of the things Jesus spoke must occur in relation to this γενεα (*genea*), not some. Only two views adequately address this issue. The race view and the end times view alone accept that *all* prophecies of Jesus must and will take place during the time frame of which Jesus spoke. A closer examination of these views should reveal the truth.

Seemingly the simplest answer is that Jesus was speaking of "the generation in whose lifetime all these signs occur."[694] Some, like John Calvin, say that "within 50 years"[695] of the "signs" the end will come, but this requires a technical interpretation of the signs and is dangerously close the heresy of dating the time of Jesus' return. Nevertheless, most reject any form of date setting, and this view is one which I accepted for many years, but it has problems which cannot be easily resolved. For one thing, although John MacArthur believes that the context clearly fits the last generation,[696] this seems a redundant remark. Of course the generation which sees the events will see the events! Why would Jesus assure the apostles that the final generation would see those events when He was desribing to the apostles exactly what the final generation would see? This is the crux of the problem. Jesus is making assurances to the apostles. Why?

It is true that the greek word 'αυτη ('*aute*) can mean either "this" or "that." It is properly an identification marker used for emphasis or as a pronoun.[697] In this respect the view is solid, but the alternate view is equally strong.

The root word γενεα (*genea*) literally refers to those who have been born. Even today we use the term "generation" to denote not so much a time period as a people (e.g. the X generation). This is admitted by preterists like Karl Linski who notes that in Psalms 12:7 the word generation is used in a more broad sense, as in "thou shalt preserve their *generation* forever."[698] Another preterist, Albert Barnes,[699] goes even further, admitting that the passage could be translated, "this race of men."[700] In other words, men like Dave Hunt see this passage as akin to Zechariah's prophesy about the "faithless generation" that would not pass away until the Christ appears in their midst.[701] However, there is a more promising application. Jesus was saying to the apostles and to the Jews in general that they *will not* pass away. He was promising the Jews that no matter what happens to them in the Great Diaspora (during which the holocaust took place), God would not let them die out. The Jewish *race* will survive even unto the fulfillment of *all* these things.

The Last Days and the Days of Noah
Matthew 24:36-44 – Luke 17:22-37

"But of that day and hour no one knows, not even the angels of heaven, nor the Son, but the Father alone. For the coming of the Son of Man will be just like the days of Noah ... Then there will be two men in the field; one will be taken and one will be left. Two women *will be* grinding at the mill; one will be taken and one will be left."

When Jesus compared "that day" to the days of Noah, He made one of the most controversial remarks of the entire Olivet Discourse; something which might seem hard to do given the controversial nature of the discourse. Was Jesus referring to the rapture? Was He referring to the Second Coming itself? If the Second Coming then how could it be said "of that day and hour no one knows, not even the angels of heaven, nor the Son, but the Father alone"? Does it not take place at Armageddon? Is this proof of the rapture? Surprisingly many advocates of rapture say "no." This is perhaps the most startling aspect of the controversy.

For the uninitiated, I will pause to discuss the rapture, which is itself one of the most controversial subjects of the New Testament. As before, I will only briefly address the general issue itself as I devote fifty pages to the issue in *Controversies in Revelation*. Here I will only summarize the rapture before discussing its implications in this passage.

What Is The Rapture?

The first question may rightly be: what is the rapture? Literally, the rapture refers to Christ taking living Christians from the earth and transforming our mortal bodies into immortal resurrected bodies. It is what happens to those who are alive when the Lord comes for them; to those who will not experience death. This much is generally agreed upon. Even early Protestant commentators such as Matthew Henry acknolwedge this event and call it "the rapture,"[702] although he was not a true futurist. So also even Saint Augustine referred to the rapture.[703] There is no doubt of its *existence* in the Bible, but there is great controversy as to its exact timing and meaning. Many take it to be synonymous with the Second Coming, but this theory appears problematic, as the reader will see.

The first explicit reference to the rapture occurs in 1 Corinthians where Paul debates those who denied the resurrection of the dead. He emphatically states that the dead will be raised and given immortal bodies. He then follows this discussion up by saying:

> "Behold, I tell you a mystery; we shall not all sleep, but we shall all be changed, in a moment, in the twinkling of an eye, at the last trumpet; for the trumpet will sound, and the dead will be raised imperishable, and we shall be changed. For this perishable must put on the imperishable, and this mortal must put on immortality" (1 Corinthians 15:51-53).

It should be noted that the term "sleep" here is used by Christ and the apostles to refer to death. Just as some today use respectful terms such as "pass away" or "his final rest," so the apostles referred to death as "sleep," for the dead are awaiting Christ, who will awaken them and give them a resurrected, immortal body. More important to the debate is the fact that Paul says we will not all "sleep"; that is "die." Thus those who are alive at this coming will also be taken to heaven in and given an immortal body. This is clarified by Paul in his first letter to the Thessalonians:

> "We do not want you to be uninformed, brethren, about those who are asleep, so that you may not grieve, as do the rest who have no hope. For if we believe that Jesus died and rose again, even so God will bring

with Him those who have fallen asleep in Jesus. For this we say to you by the word of the Lord, that we who are alive, and remain until the coming of the Lord, will not precede those who have fallen asleep. For the Lord Himself will descend from heaven with a shout, with the voice of the archangel, and with the trumpet of God; and the dead in Christ shall rise first. Then we who are alive and remain will be caught up together with them in the clouds to meet the Lord in the air, and thus we shall always be with the Lord. Therefore comfort one another with these words." (1 Thessalonians 4:13-18)

When Paul says "we who are alive and remain until the coming of the Lord," he is referring to the a translation like resurrection with the exception being that the one translated has not died. This event is universally called the rapture. The word itself is Latin and comes from Latin text. It has been discussed since the early church fathers where men like Epharim the Syrian declared that rapture would take place three and a half years before the Second Coming.[704] Saint Augustine appears to have seen it more or less synonymous with the Second Coming and made little distinction.[705] Nevertheless, he did acknowledge its existence, thus negating the extreme critic who claim rapture was an invention of the nineteenth century. The doctrine of the rapture itself is denied by very few. Those who hold to a literal interpretation of Scripture are in full agreement as to the general meaning of this verse. The fundamental question that has arisen in recent years is not "what is the rapture," but "when is the rapture?"

It is certain that this event is said to occur in connection with the coming of our Lord Jesus, but other Biblical passages lead the reader to believe that this rapture is separate from the Second Coming. This is most evident in Jesus' Olivet Discourse where He sometimes speaks of His return as "coming at an hour when you do not think He will" (Matthew 24:44) while at other times it is said that "the sign of the Son of Man will appear in the sky, and then all the tribes of the earth will mourn, and they will see the Son of Man coming on the clouds of the sky with power and great glory" (Matthew 24:30). In other words, does Christ return specifically at Armageddon or is it that the "day and hour no one knows, not even the angels of heaven, nor the Son, but the Father alone" (Matthew 24:36)?

There are essentially three dominant views on the rapture. These three views are defined by where they place the rapture in relation to the Tribulation or the final *shevim* of Daniel as recorded in the book of Revelation.[706] The first view of the rapture is called *pretribulational* rapture because it holds that the rapture will occur *before* (pre) the tribulation begins. The *posttribulational* rapture holds that the rapture will occur at the end (post) of the tribulation. *Midtribulational* rapturists believe that the rapture takes place in the middle of the tribulation, in close proximity to the Abomination of Desolation. Another variant of this is the "pre-wrath rapture" theory which places the rapture sometime in the latter half of the tribulation. A few other varaints also exist (see *Controversies in Revelation*).

The Days of Noah

The debate over the comparison to the days of Noah involves not only this question of timing, but also a question of whether Jesus is even referring to rapture at all, as opposed to His glorious appearing at the Second Coming. One might be surprised to learn that ultradispensationalists (very conservative pretribulationists) do not believe that this is a rapture passage at all.[707] Consequenlty, it is not fair to stage this debate as pretribulational versus post-tribulational. Rather the debate will be one of whether or not this is a rapture passage at all. Only then can the timing question be addressed.

The reader should note that Jesus begins this comparison by saying, "of that day and hour no one knows, not even the angels of heaven, nor the Son, but the Father alone" (Matthew 24:36). This statement alone seems strong enough to deny that Jesus is speaking of His return at the battle of Armaggedon. "For as in those days before the flood they were eating and drinking, marrying and giving in marriage, until the day that Noah entered the ark" (Matthew 24:37). As Dave Hunt noted, "they did eat, they drank, they married wives, they were given in marriage, they bought, they sold, they planted, they builded. That cannot be at the end of the Great Tribulation; the world is practically destroyed."[708]

Despite this many, like John MacArthur, argue that this is a reference to the tribulation.[709] He says "the perilous times, the abomination of desolation, the disruption of heavenly bodies, and the preaching of God's witnesses during the Tribulation will have no effect on the majority of men."[710] But one only has to read of the death tolls spoken of in Revelation to see the folly of such an assumption. Indeed, at least 70% of the population of the planet has already been decimated before that final battle. Can we really see daily live continuing as usual at a time when "no life would have been spared" (Matthew 24:22)?

Nevertheless, even men like John Walvoord argue that this is not the rapture.[711] They argue instead that the reference here is not to Noah being "taken" but rather the wicked being taken in judgment.[712] They declare that "the flood came and took them away",[713] but this argument fails the test. A flood does not pick and choose its victims! The flood indiscriminately killed all who were not aboard the ark. Rather "the ark was the shelter for Noah and his family and it certainly lifted them up above the judgment ... The day he was taken out, here comes the judgment."[714] This is exactly what Jesus said. Notice His words, "the day that Noah entered the ark" (24:38). The image is of Noah being taken away to be spared the flood. This is admitted by at least one post-tribulationist who says this "may suggest that just as Noah was saved by being taken away ... so believers "shall in the rapture.[715]

So the picture described here is not during the "dark and terrible"[716] days of the Tribulation but rather at a time of "false security."[717] This is reminiscent of Paul's words in 1 Thessalonians 5:3, "while they are saying, 'Peace and safety!' then destruction will come upon them suddenly like labor pains upon a woman with child, and they will not escape." Thus Dave Hunt is correct to state that "Christ said that His coming would be at a time of peace and prosperity."[718]

The only argument that is made to refute this claim is that of the ultradispensationalist who insist that the church cannot in any way, even cursarily, be found before Acts 2.[719] Consequently, they deny that rapture can be found in the gospels. However, this is classical eisegesis, as opposed to exegesis. The problem is that saying the Church is a mystery does not negate allusions to the Church age in prophecy. If I say that a man will visit you tomorrow, and the next day Billy Graham shows up at your door, his appearance remains a mystery. After the fact we may realize that it was Billy Graham that I told you about, but before he arrives, it remains a mystery *who* will show up at your door. The *Church* was a mystery; not the rapture.[720]

The picture found here is of suddeness, when the world is at peace and life goes on as usual. This has been admitted by numerous post-tribulationists, amillennialists, and others who reject the rapture theory but must confess that this is a picture of men taken "into God's immediate protection"[721] as John Wesley said. It is a "sudden and unexpected" event.[722] John Calvin believed in this "suddeness"[723] but attributed the *believers* being taken to persecution.[724] Cyprian compared the one taken to one who had been converted.[725] In each case, though rejecting rapture, they confess that it is the Lord who takes us into His presence to be spared the coming judgment.

One final proof of rapture may be gleaned from the parallel passage in Luke 17:24 where the Lord said, "For just like the lightning, when it flashes out of one part of the sky, shines to the other part of the sky, so will the Son of Man be in His day." Why is this coming compared to lightning? Because of its suddeness? No, for the rain comes first and we expect lightning to follow. Because it represents judgment? Perhaps, but there is another reason. If we follow the analogy closely we notice that lightning does not reside on earth after it appears. It appears briefly and then returns to the heaven. This is not Jesus returning to rule and reign as He does at the Second Coming. This is Jesus coming in the sky like a lightning bolt to claim His own and to call them up to Heaven. As quickly as lightning appears, it returns to the clouds. This is rapture; not the Second Coming.

Conclusion

Although at first glance it is tempting to take this as the Second Coming, it fails the test of any good analogy. The problem is that floods are not picky. They do not pick and choose their victims. When the flood came it would have taken everyone in the field. It would have taken everyone grinding at the mill. It is not the flood which took one and left the other; it is God! It is God who took Noah out to safety so that he would be spared the flood. It was God who took Lot and his family out of Sodom so that judgment could commence. So also it seems that God will take one away to safety and the other will be left to judgment.

The reader should note that there is a shift in the context of Jesus' remarks. He has already discussed the tribulation and the Second Coming. In verse 32 He then shifts to general warnings and parables concerning the end times. Here He is comparing believers to Noah and Lot who were spared God's wrath. However, I am greatly concerned that some who do not take this view are giving the enemy fodder. What will they say when rapture takes place? They will quote the Christian who declares that these were "taken away in judgment"[726] and use it to imply that the righteous are the ones left behind. The anti-Christ will set himself up in Christ's place.

The image presented here is one of ordinary life when the antediluvians and Sodomites were oblivious to the judgment to come. God came and lifted Noah and Lot out of the lands which were to be judged in order that they might be spared and destruction fell upon them. The book of Revelation describes the judgments of God in the final tribulation (or *shevim*). In that book, even in the midst of judgment, God is merciful and gives man a chance to repent, but the world becomes bitter and hardened and brutally persecutes those who do repent. "While they are saying, 'Peace and safety!' then destruction will come upon them suddenly like labor pains upon a woman with child, and they will not escape" (1 Thessalonians 5:3). This is the day of which Jesus speaks.

Matthew 25:30 – See Matthew 8:12

The Holy Communion
Matthew 26:26-29 – Luke 22:19-20

"While they were eating, Jesus took *some* bread, and after a blessing, He broke *it* and gave *it* to the disciples, and said, 'Take, eat; this is My body.' And when He had taken a cup and given thanks, He gave *it* to them, saying, 'Drink from it, all of you; for this is My blood of the covenant, which is poured out for many for forgiveness of sins.'"

The controversy over the Lord's Supper is perhaps one of the most ironic controversies in the Bible, for the allegorist takes this passage in the most literal fashion imaginable whereas the literalist accepts this strictly as a memorial. We might say that the allegorist become literalistic in this passage whereas the literalist becomes an allegorist (although the reader will see that this is not really the case).

The central issue is whether or not the bread literally transforms into the body of Christ as taught by the Catholic Church. Protestants unanimous reject this notion; some even calling it outright heresy.

According to the Catechism of Catholic Church the Eucharist, or Lord's Supper, is "the same sacrifice with that of the Cross" save that it is not bloody.[727] They hold that the bread literally transforms into Jesus' physical body and the wine literally transforms into the physical blood of Christ. This doctrine is called transubstantiation.[728] The Council of Trent said that "identical with the sacrifice of the Cross."[729]

This doctrine is considered offensive to Protestants because it seems to conflict with the teaching that Christ died once (Romans 6:10; 1 Peter 3:18) for all. Moreover, Hebrews 6:6 speaks of those who "are crucifying the Son of God all over again and subjecting him to public disgrace" as unable to be brought back to repentance again. These passages conflict with the doctrine that Christ's body is continually resacrificed over and over. Indeed, there is nowhere in the Bible where such a doctrine is taught. It must only be assumed based on Catholic tradition and upon the most rigid interpretation of this passage, but although it is considered a literal interpretation, it really is not at all. Taking one piece of a passage literally, and rejecting the rest is not literal at all. Consider John Calvin's remarks. He said, "Christ does not say, This is my blood, but *this cup is* ..."[730] Others have noted that "if the words of the Lord had intended to convey a transformation of the bread into His body they would have read, 'This has become my body.'"[731] In fact, the language used by Jesus here is the same as he uses elsewhere. McCarthy, for example, has shown where Jesus used the same words to describe Himself, saying, "I am the bread of life" (John 6:48), "I am the door" (John 10:9), "I am the true vine" (John 15:1)[732] and more.

A literal interpretation means that the Bible speaks of literal historical people, places, and events. Jesus literally walked on water, for such is described not as a parable but as a historical event. Here Jesus is offering a memorial. With John Wesley, we believe the bread "signifies"[733] His body, but "'My body' does not mean 'a piece of my body.'"[734] It is a memorial. Such appears to be the view of the earliest church fathers. Tertullian, for example, wisely said, "His body is reckoned 'as bread' because He is the bread of Life."[735]

The Lord's Supper (Chronological Debate)
Matthew 26:26-29 – Luke 11:1-3   See "When Was Jesus Crucified?"

Was the Last Supper a passover meal? This debate is closely related to the question of when Jesus was crucified and will, therefore, be debated in that section entitled, "When Was Jesus Crucified?"

The Betrayal of Jesus
Matthew 26:47-57 – Mark 14:43-50 – Luke 22:47-53 – John 18:3-12

"He who was betraying Him gave them a sign, saying, 'Whomever I kiss, He is the one; seize Him.' Immediately Judas went to Jesus and said, "Hail, Rabbi!" and kissed Him ..."	"He who was betraying Him had given them a signal, saying, "Whomever I kiss, He is the one; seize Him and lead Him away under guard ..."	"One called Judas, one of the twelve, was preceding them and he approached Jesus to kiss Him. But Jesus said to him, 'Judas, are you betraying the Son of Man with a kiss?'"	"Jesus, knowing all the things that were coming upon Him, went and said, 'Whom do you seek?' They answered Him, 'Jesus the Nazarene.' He said to them, 'I am *He*.'"

Two issues are presented in this debate. The first is whether or not Jesus was confronted by Jewish temple guards or by Roman soldiers. The second issue is whether or not Judas truly kissed Jesus. Some allege that John's account allows no such action and is, therefore, contradictory to the synoptic gospels. Other issues, such as Judas' payment and the apostle's use of a sword are addressed as separate controversies below.

The Soldiers

Matthew says that Judas was "accompanied by a large crowd with swords and clubs, *who came* from the chief priests and elders of the people" (26:47) and John says (according to the NAS) that there were "*Roman* cohort and officers from the chief priests and the Pharisees." It is assumed that Matthew depicts Jewish temple guards and that John sees Romans, but a close examination refutes this. It is most probable that the soldiers were a mixed group of Roman soldiers and Jewish temple guards.[736] The facts, as will be shown, substantiate this not only from the text, but also from history, for Roman soldiers were often used to supervise and oversee arrest by local authorities, even though they were not supposed to be actively involved in such disputes.

The first thing to note is that John alone identifies the soldiers. The synoptic gospels only refer to a large crowd which came "from the chief priests and elders of the people." It should further be noted that John's gospel does *not* use the word "Roman." This is a translation choice based on the meaning of σπεῖρα (*speira*). The Living Bible, however, reads "Jewish police" and mentions no Romans at all! Most translations correctly choose not to translate the ethnicity or nationality of the soldiers since John does not identify them, save that they were operating under the authority of "the chief priests and the

149

Pharisees." So who were they, and if they were Romans, why would Romans be following the orders of the chief priests?

John uses three words to identify the soldiers. The first is σπειρα (*speira*), the second is χιλιαρχος (*chiliarchos*), and the third is 'υρηρεται (*huperetai*) "of the Jews." These three were all present in the "crowd" of which Matthew speaks. The last is not difficult to translate. Ὑρηρεται (*huperetai*) are court servants or officers.[737] Coupled with "of the Jews" it is apparent that this last group were, indeed, "Temple Police, under the command of the Sagan, or Captain of the Temple."[738] The first two terms, however, are not common among the Jews. Σπειρα (*speira*) is a military group, usually translated as a cohort, which is a Roman platoon made up of 600 soldiers.[739] This word, when coupled with χιλιαρχος (*chiliarchos*), must be a Roman cohort. This is because a χιλιαρχος (*chiliarchos*) is the captian or leader of a thousand soldiers, taken from the word χιλιας (*chilias*) meaning a thousand.[740] This commander is of a higher rank than a Roman Centurion who rules over a hundred men. A decturian resides over ten men. Thus the chilarian ruled over a thousand soldiers. We might liken the decturian to a corporal, the Centurion to a sergeant, and the chilarian to a lieutenant.

It is, therefore, proper to translate this as a Roman cohort since the Jews had no such equivalent. We can then conclude that it was a "mixed mob"[741] consisting of both Roman and Jewish[742] soldiers. "The Roman soldiers carried swords and the Jewish temple police had staves (clubs)."[743]

The next question, however, is why Roman soldiers would be acting under orders from the "chief priests" of the Jews. Certainly the Romans and Jews were no allies! The answer is actually simple. It was the law. Under Roman occupation the Jews were allowed to have their own law and their own courts and even their own police, but the Romans would carefully watch and oversee all their actions without directly participating. The Roman soldiers were there to make sure that nothing got out of hand and to insure that no riots broke out. Given the number of riots that had taken place over the past few years, the tension between Jew and Roman was high. It is for that very reason that Pontius Pilate and the High Priest Caiphas engaged in political mind games with one another, as we will see (discussed under "Who killed Christ?").[744]

The Kiss

The synoptic gospels all record Judas betraying Jesus with a kiss. This was to be the signal, but many asks "why?" First, he knew there was to be a crowd and human nature being what it was, Judas was afraid to enter in and point fingers and call out Jesus. This is not unusual as any psychologists will tell you. Kissing each other on the cheek was a common form of greeting among friends in those days. Thus Judas' last act with Jesus was not one of true contrition, but of a guilty conscience. A man might betray his friend today and still hug him "goodbye." So Judas betrayed Jesus with a kiss. Or did he?

Bible critics point out that the apostle John does not recount this part of the story and some go as far as to say that "Judas could not get close enough to Jesus to kiss him."[745] While this is an overt exaggeration, John's account does cursorily appear to create difficulties for the kiss. It reads:

> "So Jesus, knowing all the things that were coming upon Him, went forth and said to them, 'Whom do you seek?' They answered Him, 'Jesus the Nazarene.' He said to them, 'I am *He*.' And Judas also, who was betraying Him, was standing with them. So when He said to them, 'I am *He*,' they drew back and fell to the ground. Therefore He again asked them, 'Whom do you seek?' And they said, 'Jesus the Nazarene.' Jesus answered, 'I told you that I am *He*; so if you seek Me, let these go their way'" (John 18:4-8).

Now the omission of the kiss is not in itself significant, for I have shown elsewhere that eyewitnesses often omit what they do not consider to be of primary importance. The synoptic gospels were intrigued by Judas' kiss, but John wanted to emphasize the reaction of the soldiers. Even in His arrest Jesus did not waver or fear and the soldiers knew there was something more to this man. Some even believe that Jesus' statement "I am" was a reference to His deity (see notes on John 8:58-59).[746]

In any case, the kiss of Judas is not inconsistent with John's account. Having studied criminal justice at one time, I know that police officers are always required to asks the identity of the man arrested even if they already know. "Are you ....?" So also the Roman soldiers present would have required some proof beyond Judas' signal. Judas may have kissed Jesus, but the soldiers were struct by the fact that Jesus knew He was being betrayed and offered no resistance. They were doubtless expecting Jesus to run and flee, whereas He stood by without fear, despite knowing what was to happen.

The most likely scenario is that the soldier's entered the garden expecting Jesus to flee. Jesus turned to the soldiers and asked, "Whom do you seek?" (John 18:4). Note that at this time John mentions Judas was among the soldiers. It is probably after this exchange that Judas approached Jesus and kissed Him as He said "I am." This also explains the second "I am" found in John 18:5 after He had already identified Himself once. The soldiers being struck by the exchange and by Jesus' fearlessness (as well as a guilty conscience) had fell back and Jesus declared one final time that He was the one they were looking for. It is at that point that Peter struck out in fear.

Conclusion

Once again, as with any eyewitnesses to an event, different authors give accounts which emphasize different espects of the event, but do not contradict one another. A piece of a jigsaw puzzle may not appear to fit until all the pieces are in place, but once they are in place, the piece fits perfectly. This is the job of

151

any good and objective police detective and it is the job of any honest historian. Unlike the revistionist historians who simply seeks to tear down what he doesn't want to believe, a true historian weighs the evidence and compares it with other eyewitnesses to get a clear and complete picture. The same is true of Biblical exegesis. Only if the pieces cannot fit do we declare the Bible in error, and such is not the case here ... or anywhere else in Scripture.

Live and Die By the Sword
Matthew 26:52

"Put your sword back into its place; for all those who take up the sword shall perish by the sword."

This well known passage has often been used politically as proof that Jesus was a passivist. In fact, political interpretations of Jesus are wrought with difficulty for many reasons. Nevertheless, the passage could certainly be interpreted in that manner so it is fair to evaluate the passage within that context.

Tertullian rejected the notion of Christians in military service,[747] while Origen was an outright pacivist.[748] Many of the early Christians sought martyrdom rather than freedom, and there is indeed reason to reject the doctrine that government (of any kind) will save us. The early Church did not see much hope in reforming Rome, let alone overthrowing it. Nonetheless, the Church was by no means unanimous in this. Many Christians did serve in military service and the first gentile convert was, in fact, a soldier (Acts 10). Moreover, the Old Testament, which Jesus declared to be full and valid (see notes on Matthew 5:17-18) is filled with war and violence. How then is to be reconciled with Jesus' remark?

It may first be noted that Jesus knew Peter had a sword before they entered the garden.[749] Jesus Himself told the apostles, "whoever has no sword is to sell his coat and buy one" (Luke 22:36). The apostles then did just that, bought two swords, and showed their swords to Jesus, to which He replied, "It is enough" (Luke 22:38). This event immediately preceded the incident at the Garden of Gethsamane. Why then does Jesus rebuke Peter?

Generally there have been three possible answers to this question. The first is that "private individuals are forbidden to take up the sword"[750] but that government institutions may continue to use the sword if used justly. John Calvin said that "we should make a distinction between the civil court and the court of conscience."[751] Certainly this view would be consistent with the decree of the apostle Paul to submit to government institutions and authority (1 Timothy 2:2, 1 Peter 2:12, etc.). Thus, it is argued, "this statement does not include those whom God delegates the sword (government and legal authorities) but those who, like Peter, arrogate the sword to themselves."[752]

152

A second view is that this "is a statement of fact, but cannot be taken alone to teach nonviolence in all situations."[753] It is a declaration that "the warlike will perish at the hands of the warlike"[754] but "Jesus was not philosophizing."[755] "His point was that those who commit acts of violence to achieve personal ends will face punishment by civil authorities, the sword representing a common means of execution in the ancient world."[756]

A final argument is that this was stated "as a caution to Peter"[757] and not as a law. Some hold that it was an allusion to his martyrdom.[758]

There is truth in all three view, but what is most clear is that "'Put up again thy sword' clearly revealed that His kingdom would not be brought in by force at that time."[759] Those who were looking for a Messiah that was going to overthrow the Roman empire were to be disappointed, and yet it was this very argument that Caiphas and others used to try Jesus before Pontius Pilate. Jesus, therefore, wanted the apostles to understand clearly that His kingdom on earth was not to commence at this time and it would not be brought about by revolution as the Zealots and Sicarii believed.

Matthew 26:50 – See John 18:3-12

Matthew 26:57 – See Luke 22:66

Peter's Denial
Matthew 26:69-75 – Mark 14:66-72 – Luke 22:56-62 – John 18:25-27

"And Peter remembered the word which Jesus had said, 'Before a rooster crows, you will deny Me three times.'"	"Immediately a rooster crowed a second time. And Peter remembered how Jesus had made the remark to him, 'Before a rooster crows twice, you will deny Me three times.'"	"Peter remembered the word of the Lord, how He had told him, 'Before a rooster crows today, you will deny Me three times.'"	"Peter then denied it again, and immediately a rooster crowed."

Minor apparent discrepancies appear in this accounts, but the biggest purported discrepancy is the fact that Matthew, Luke, and John all agree that Peter was to deny Christ three times before the rooster crows, whereas Mark seems to contradict this, saying "before the rooster crows *twice*" Peter would deny Him three times. A careful look at these passages will reveal no contradictions, but only a question of semantics.

The Cock Crowing

Starting with the more difficult issue of how many times the cock was to crow, Gleason Archer's sarcastic reply speaks loudest, saying, "we may be very sure that if the rooster crows twice, he has at least crowed once."[760] Dave Hunt more tactfully puts it another way. "Christ is not referring to a particular rooster crowing nor to some rooster crowing *once* but to that time in the morning know as 'the *cockcrowing*.'"[761] Anyone who has ever heard a cock crow know that they crow in rapid succession. The crowing is not a single crow but many crows in rapid fire succession. This "before the cock crows twice" is just an idiomatic way of saying "before the rooster crows." They are identical because the crowing is composed of many crows; not a single crow. This is why John Calvin said, "I have no doubt when Christ said to Peter, 'Before the cock crows,' He meant the cock-crowing in its various repetitions."[762]

Despite this seemingly easy semantic resolution the issue has caused difficulty for many. Some have argued that the original texts were tampered with and contained no contradiction. Indeed, it is true that ancient manuscripts do contain variants. For example, the famed *Codex Sinaticus*, one of the oldest *complete* manuscripts of the Bible, omits "twice" and "second" from Mark.[763] Nevertheless, the evidence that this is original is meager. The few manuscripts which agree with the *Sinaiticus* actually disagree between verse 30 and 72. One omits "twice" in 30 while retaining the "second" in 72, and vice versa. All other manuscripts, including the ancient manuscripts agreed with our translations. Mark is simply using a different idiom for the cockcrowing, and is probably quoting Jesus, whereas the others may have just been paraphrasing Jesus.

It should be noted that those who claim Mark copied from Matthew (see "Mark and Plagiarism? The Authorship and Date of Mark"), or vice versa, are at a loss to explain this alleged discrepancy. Surely if they were copying from one another, they would have agreed on such a "simple" point?

The Denials

The second issue is of the exact sequence of events. Some see a contradiction in the accounts, but the best way to examine these stories like a detective. Let us examine each denial separately.

The First Denial

Matthew declares that Peter was "sitting outside in the courtyard" when "a servant-girl" approached him (26:69). Mark also has Peter "below in the courtyard" when "the servant-girls of the high priest" approached him (14:66). Luke agrees, placing Peter near "a fire in the middle of the courtyard" when a "servant-girl" recognizes him (22:55). In these there is no difficulty. John, however, gives a more detailed account, which some believe creates a problem, for in John it appears that he was at the "door outside" of the court when the slave-girl recognized him (John 18:16). Nevertheless, a close examination is perfectly consistent with the other accounts.

When we read John's account we get a more detailed story of what transpired. The other gospels are abbreviated and only mention Peter as being outside in the courtyard, but we must ask *why* was he in the courtyard? The answer is revealed in John. He had initially followed Jesus into the court and was standing outside the door when the slave-girl, whom Mark identifies as a servant of the high priest (which she clearly is in John) recognizes him. However, John does not say that she instantly spoke up. He records only that she said to him, "you are not also *one* of this man's disciples, are you?" We might assume that he was still standing out the door when she said this to him, but the next verse makes it clear that Peter had, at some point, left to go warm himself by the fire in the courtyard, which would only be a few yards from the court door. It is likely that the woman, recognizing him, followed him out to the courtyard and confronted him there.

After Peter denied it the initial time, she appears to have gone to talk to other servants at the court, and other bystanders were also present. Gossip was obviously involved as Peter was sitting in the courtyard, near the door to the court, waiting to see what was to happen to Jesus.

The Second Denial
Having been confronted in the courtyard, near the entrance to the court, Peter doubtless heard the gossip and knew he had been recognized, so he moved further away, but still close enough to know what was going on in the trial. Matthew notes that Peter had moved "out to the gateway" when another person recognized him (26:71). Mark says he had moved "onto the porch" when "the" servant-girl (presumeably the same one) again told the bystanders that he was one of Jesus' disciples (14:68-69). Luke is not specific, only saying that another saw him and confronted him (22:58). Between these synoptic accounts there is no real difficulty for they all portray Peter as moving away from the fire and being confronted by several people. Matthew actually says that a servant girl was speaking to bystanders and Mark says that the same servant girl was speaking. Obviously when gossip is involved, many are speaking. The servant girls were together accusing him and he was obviously confronted by several people before denying Jesus the second time.

The greater problem in this second account is with John, who appears to have Peter still "warming himself" (18:25) when he was confronted. However, it has already been shown that after being recognized initially, Peter began to move away. The gossip and accusations were obviously following him around until he denied Christ a second time. So a complete picture shows that Peter was still at the fire then the servant-girl began to tell the others who Peter really was. His first denial was not enough for her and she began to accuse him before other servant-girls and bystanders. He obviously got up from the fire, walked over to the porch and further to the gateway, all the time being followed.

This is substantiated by Luke when he records that it was "a little later." The accusions did not instantly stop only to start again later. They were ongoing. Finally he denies Jesus a second time. This is a logical, plausible, and common sense interpretation. No court of law would hold that it is not a valid interpretation unless evidence can be shown that Peter was not followed by his accusers.

The Third Denial
As illustrated above, the accusers did not instantly become quiet at Peter's denial. The gossip and finger pointed continued. Because Peter wanted to stay close to Jesus he could not completely leave the area, so he merely wandered around the courtyard and its surroundings. Matthew, Mark, and Luke all record unnamed "bystanders" as having confronted Peter the last time (Matthew 26:73; Mark 14:70; Luke 22:59). Luke says that this final confrontation was about an hour after the first two incidents and specifies that the last accuser was a man (22:59). Although some have assumed that John's identification of "one of the slaves of the high priest" (18:26) is synonymous with the slave girl from before, the Greek uses the masculine form of the word "slave," indicating that it was indeed a man.

The objective reader can see that the only alleged discrepancies involve how many people were following Peter before his second denial and how many were accusing him. We must assume that only one person confronted him at one specific time immediately before his second denial. Nothing in the texts can support this. As with all eyewitness accounts, the authors give a short incomplete account which may omit certain aspects of the story. When we put them all together we get the complete picture. Peter was recognized at the door of the court and was followed out to the courtyard by the fire. He was confronted and began to move away to the porch and gateway but was followed by those who recognized him. He was confronted a second time by several people. Finally, after an hour, when Peter had perhaps hoped that he was no longer under suspicion, another man, a slave of the high priest, approached and again confronted him. Peter denied Christ a third time and the cock began its crowing.

Conclusion

As we have seen elsewhere, different accounts do not mean conflicting accounts. When the pieces of the puzzle are put together they form a perfect picture of what transpired. The gospels depict Peter as wanting to be by Jesus' side but lacking the courage to give up his life. He loitered around the court but denied he was a disciple. When the cock began to crow, it crowed multiple times. The idiomatic "second crowing" has the same meaning as the first, for the rooster crows in rapid succession. The Biblical story is complete and accurate.

Judas' Death
Matthew 27:3-10 – Acts 1:18-19

"Then when Judas, who had betrayed Him, saw that He had been condemned, he felt remorse and returned the thirty pieces of silver to the chief priests and elders, saying, 'I have sinned by betraying innocent blood.' ... And he threw the pieces of silver into the temple sanctuary and departed; and he went away and hanged himself."

"This man acquired a field with the price of his wickedness, and falling headlong, he burst open in the middle and all his intestines gushed out. And it became known to all who were living in Jerusalem; so that in their own language that field was called Hakeldama, that is, Field of Blood."

Elsewhere I have often used the analogy of a police detective reviewing differing accounts, and I have elsewhere stated that no such contradictions exist when the accounts are fully examined. On this occasion I must fully and honestly state that the resolution of the difficulty between these two verses is one that I have taken on faith alone do to the fact that I find the authors in all other areas to be credible and honest. I will not here claim that the critics are groundless in their attacks, for the two passage do indeed seem to be at odds with one another, but a resolution of the conflict is possible if we take ancient tradition as a viable witness. Let us address the issues separately.

Judas' Suicide

This is the most difficult issue, and in all honesty the only passage in the whole of the Bible which I can see as contradicting one another. Note that I do not say they *do* contradict one another, but only that I can *see* them in that way. Indeed, the apparent contradictions are obvious. The question is whether or not they can be reconciled with credibility.

Matthew records that Judas hung himself in a suicide over despair. Luke's account does not offer an exact account of what happened, but says that he fell upon rocks wherein his intestines fell out. Even many evangelicals have had problems reconciling these verses. Some have dared to speak of Matthew having relied on "creativity" and "revisions"![764] Such absurd conclusions should only be made after a man is convicted, not before!

Although we cannot be certain based strictly on the Biblical texts, there is an ancient tradition which offers a reconciliation of these passages. According to the tradition Judas hung himself with his girdle or similar article which gave way, causing his body to fall upon the rocks.[765] Others have said that "the limb broke under his weight"[766] or alternately that "the rope broke."[767]

157

The "varying traditions"[768] are all similar in nature, and the specifics are unimportant. What is significant is that all believe that Judas had hung "himself over the ledge, [and then] then fell into the valley below."[769]

Are such legends credible? Can we hold them to be reliable? Is this really plausible or just a hackneyed attempt to reconcile the irreconcilable? If we examine Acts, we will see that this tradition is entirely likely for Luke's account in Acts does not attempt to offer a history of Judas' suicide at all. Rather Luke's account is aside wherein God's wrath upon the "wickedness" of Judas is briefly mentioned. Matthew, however, offers a fuller history and shows Judas' despair. "Apparently his body was not discovered for some days, because it became bloated and his bowels gushed out."[770] Thus, "Acts 1:18-19 adds to our understanding."[771]

Such a tradition must be taken on faith, since it cannot be born out in the Scriptures alone, but what can be born out is the fact that Luke was a true historian (see notes on Luke 1:1-3) who researched his material and had almost certainly seen Matthew's gospel or even spoken to Matthew. If the account of Acts was truly contradictory to Matthew's then Luke would have known. The fact that he appears to see no difficulty is further indication that the tradition is true.

The Field of Blood

Another problem with these two accounts is less troublesome, but nevertheless confusing. Was the Field of Blood called so because it was bought with blood money or because Judas' blood was spilled upon it? Was the field bought with Judas' money or with the priests' money?

The money issue is simple. Judas threw the money back to the priests, but the priests refused to accept it. *They*, therefore, bought the field where Judas had died in *his* name. One can justly say the priests bought it as in Matthew, or that it was "acquired ... with the price of his wickedness" (Acts 1:18).

As to the name of the field, the resolution is similar. I remember once my father and mother arguing about why my brother's middle name was "Wayne." Mom remembered him being named after a certain relative on her side, whereas dad remembered he was named after one of his relatives. *Both* are true. It was a Field of Blood because it was payed for with blood money, because Judas' blood was spilled upon it, and because it was to be a graveyard. *All* are equally true. What better name can there be?

Conclusion

The issue of the name is not troublesome as names often have multiple etymologies. In fact, traditions about the Potter's Field are intriguing and could shed even more light on the name and its multiple facets. Some believe that the Potter's Field is located in the Valley of Hinnom which Jeremiah prophesied would be the "valley of slaughter" (Jer. 7:32, 19:11) and which was once an area where pagan human sacrifices took place.[772] As the burial place for Judas, it seems appropriate.

The tradition in regard to Judas' death also fits the test of validity. Although we must be careful to accept traditions which may or may not be true, there is no reason not to accept this one.

Interestingly enough, more debate over Judas and his motives has occurred than over his death. Erasmus merged the traditions[773] and believed Judas repented before his death,[774] but had he truly repented, he would never have committed suicide. Nonetheless, some claim that Judas only betrayed Jesus because "probably he thought Christ would have prevented [the crucifixion] by a miracle."[775] Various other theories and traditions have been bandied about for ages but these such traditions should be rejected because they conflict with Scripture and have no material support. The tradition of Judas' death, however, fits the Biblical stories and explains the apparent contradictions.

The Prophecy of the Shekels
Matthew 27:9

"That which was spoken through Jeremiah the prophet was fulfilled: 'And they took the thirty pieces of silver, the price of the one whose price had been set by the sons of Israel; and they gave them for the Potter's Field, as the Lord directed me.'"

Critics have argued that this passage errs in three ways. First, all commentators agree that the passage in question is actually from Zechariah 11:12-13.[776] So it is assumed that Matthew erred in calling it Jeremiah's prophecy. Second, some argue that silver coins were no longer in use in Jesus' day, and further, that they did not weight out the price of coins at that time.

The later arguments are simple to refute. First, it is simply untrue that silver coins were not in use. Silver coins, of varying kinds, were in use throughout Rome and continue in use to this very day. The exact silver content and mixture is irrelevant. This is akin to arguing that we no longer have copper pennies and, therefore, if anyone speaks of such he is either lying or erring. In fact, copper pennies are no longer made of pure copper, but even today they all have a small mixture of copper to keep the color. Even if no copper were used, it is still copper colored. To speak of "pieces of silver" is perfectly accurate. By the same token, speaking of "weighing out silver coins" is an idiomatic expression which in no way negates the meaning of literalness of the passage. This is grasping at straws.[777]

On a more serious note is Matthew's use of Jeremiah for a prophecy of Zechariah, which in turn, appears on the surface to have no relation to Judas. These will be examined separately.

Zechariah or Jeremiah?

Several different theories have been presented to deal with this problem. Some are obviously more worthy than others. It has been variously submitted that this is A) a scribal error[778] B) that Zechariah was Jeremiah's secretary[779] C) that the quote is "a composite quotation" of both Zechariah and Jeremiah[780] and D) that Jeremiah was properly the name of the scroll in which Zechariah is found.[781] In some of these cases, there is no doubt and yet that may not be a sufficient answer itself. Let us examine these views.

A Scribal Error?
I have previously noted that evangelical Christians have no objection to the fact that some scribes may occassionally make scribal errors or mistakes in their manuscripts. So long as the original manuscript is free from error and inspired as the inerrant Word of God there is no problem.[782] Of course this leads to the question of how we know what is and is not an error. This is addressed to some extent in Appendix C and I will not address it here. However, the question of whether or not our current manuscripts err in this passage is relevant and some scholars hold that they are.

The actual physical evidence for such a scribal error is practically non-existent. A few Syrian translations and a single manuscript dating to the twelfth century are the only manuscripts which read Zechariah rather than Jeremiah![783] Despite this meager evidence, some, like John Calvin, maintain that Matthew never wrote Jeremiah's name at all.[784] They argue that the Greek short hand for Jeremiah is 'Iriou' (Ιριου) but the short hand for Zechariah is 'Zriou' (Ζριου).[785] Consequently, they argue that a single letter stands between Zechariah's name and Jeremiah's name.

Regardless of such *theories*, there is not a single ancient Greek manscript which supports this thesis. Moreover, if the manuscript were merely in "error"[786] then a new problem would arise since the Zechariah passage, by itself, seems to have little relation to Judas or the Potter's Field. Surely there must be a better answer than to assume an error occurred where no evidence of an error actually exist.

Jeremiah's Secretary
Another theory is that Zechariah wrote what Jeremiah had said.[787] It is assumed that Zechariah was a secretary or amanuensis for Jeremiah. This view is promoted by men such as Warren Wiersbe.[788] However, the theory is without merit. Those who date the book of Zechariah to pre-exilic times do so based soley on this passage. No independent evidence exist to date Zechariah's writings to the days of Jeremiah.[789] Most are in agreement that Zechariah was written around 520 B.C., around a hundred years after Jeremiah's day.[790] Moreover, it is explicitly stated in the book of Jeremiah that Baruch was his

secretary (cf. Jeremiah 36), and not a man named Zechariah. This theory is pure assumption and cannot be supported exegetically or archaeologically.

A Composite Quotation

The last two theories offer the most merit. Many have noted that "there are significant differences between Zechariah passage and the quotation in Matthew."[791] Some call it a "a composite quotation" of Zechariah 11:13 and Jerermiah 18:2-3; 19:1-13; and 32:6-15.[792] Some even argue that it is nothing more than an allusion to Zechariah 11:12-13, saying "the words do not agree closely either with the Hebrew or the LXX"[793] but are taken from Jeremiah 32:6-9.[794] Both statements are exaggerations. Jeremiah records the purchase of the Potter's Field whereas Zechariah records a prophecy concerning thirty pieces of silver and a potter. The quotation is much closer to Zechariah than to anything in Jeremiah.

Nevertheless, it is possible that "Matthew had both prophets in mind but only mentioned the 'major' prophet by name."[795] If so, does this not cause a problem with this "fusing" of quotations?[796] In actually ancient Greek does not contain quotation marks at all.[797] Instead, the Greek word ὁτι (*hoti*), usually translated as "that," introduces quotations.[798] The Greek word λεγοντος (*legontos*), usually translated as "saying," also serves this same purpose, and is the word found here in Matthew. The problem is that these words can also introduce paraphrasitic statements. This is why not all quotations are exactly alike. Sometimes the author is paraphrasing rather than quoting. The translator must make the choice of adding quotation marks or translating it as a paraphrase. In this case, it should be a paraphrase.

The Name of the Scroll

A final argument is that the use of the name Jeremiah is because the words of Zechariah are found in the old scrolls under the name Jeremiah. This requires some explanation, but it is actually a sound, if suspect, theory.

The book of Daniel contains long segments and quotations from both Nebuchadnezzar, the ancient Babylonian king, and Cyrus the Great, the ancient Persian king. When we quote those passages we often say, "according to Daniel," even though the quotations are actually from Nebuchadnezzar or Cyrus. This is acceptable since it is from the book of Daniel. No one questions this.[799]

In ancient Hebrew, the books of the Bible were not arranged in the same way as today. They did not have *books* at all, but *scrolls*. Obviously a scroll could only be so big before it becomes impractical to carry around and open with ease. The Old Testament of the Bible was actually divided into three sections, called the *Torah*, *Navim*, and *Ketivim* (the Law, the Prophets, and the Writings). In turn these sections were divided into smaller scrolls. Isaiah is properly the first of the prophets, but being the longest book, it is believed that this scroll stood alone. John Darby and H.A. Ironside both believed that Zechariah was found in the scroll which began with Jeremiah.[800] Thus Jeremiah began what we call "the Prophets" scrolls.[801]   Consequently, it is argued that "because Jeremiah was placed first among the prophets his name was taken for the whole book, i.e. Jeremiah, instead of 'the prophets.'"[802]

This theory makes the best sense of any *if* it is true. The only problem is that we must assume first that Isaiah formed its own scroll, which is probably true. Second, we must assume that Jeremiah did *not* form its own independent scroll. As arranged in current Jewish Bibles, Jeremiah is indeed found next to the minor prophets, with Daniel being relegated to the *Ketivim* (the Writings). Ezekiel is also found grouped with the minor prophets. Unfortunately, there is no way of knowing for sure how the ancients divided the scrolls, only how they divided the Bible into sections. This view is therefore a viable option, but not one that has been proven.

Reviewing the theories, the final two make the most sense. It is likely that Matthew was primarily paraphrasing Zechariah, but with allusions to Jeremiah. It should be noted that this is, in fact, a paraphrase and not an exact quotation of either Zechariah or Jeremiah. In all probability, Jeremiah was the book which began the second scroll of *Navim* or "Prophets." His name would, therefore, be acceptable as the scroll title, even if the paraphrase is primarily from Zechariah. The greater question is not why Matthew refers to Jeremiah, but what relationship the prophecy has to Judas.

The Prophecy

The prophecy of Zechariah does not appear, at first glance, to have any relation to Judas Iscariot or the betrayal Christ. That is why some have gone so far as to call this a "symbolic prophecy."[803]   However, this is a cop out. Prophecy is prophecy. There may be a secondary application, but it must still have some relationship to the event it is prophesying or else it is not a prophesy at all. The truth is that too many gloss over the passages without examining the context. It is true that Zechariah's primary prophecy is not about Judas, but it *is* about Christ!

As I point out in *Controversies in the Prophets* even the famed medieval Orthodox Jewish scholar Kimchi freely admitted that Zechariah 11 constitutes a major messianic prophecy.[804]   When we read the entire prophecy, we see that it is a prophecy about the shepherds of Israel. Two staffs are given to the shepherds, and it is after the staff called "Favor" is cut to pieces (11:10) that Zechariah is told take thirty pieces of silver for wages earned and then "I took the thirty *shekels* of silver and threw them to the potter in the house of the LORD" (Zechariah 11:13). After this event is a prophecy which most take to be of the fall of Jerusalem, which took place around 35 years after Jesus' betrayal.

When we look at Zechariah's prophecies as a whole, they encompass the coming of the "good shepherd," His rejection, the fall of Israel, and the

Second Coming (see *Controversies in the Prophets* for a full discussion of the prophecies). The prophecy here fits perfectly with the scope of history Zechariah is unfolding. The pieces of silver were indeed thrown to the "potter in the house of the Lord" (Zechariah 11:13), for Judas "threw the pieces of silver into the temple sanctuary" (Matthew 27:5) and the priests in turn bought the Potter's Field (Matthew 27:7). This is Zechariah's prophecy in a very literal fashion. The passages in Jeremiah are only cursorily relevant.

It is worth mentioning that thirty silver pieces was the price of a slave.[805] So the Lord's life was purchased as if He were a slave. Such facts go beyond mere symbolism. The Lord literally laid down His life for our sins, being purchased as if He were a slave, and becoming a Servant to all men (cf. Matthew 23:11). The money was thrown into the temple quite literally as Zechariah said (Matthew 27:5) and used to purchase the Potter's Field. This is no mere "symbolic prophecy"[806] but a true prophecy of Juda's betrayal of our Lord.

Conclusion

Too many people are struck by Matthew's paraphrasitic quotation and his reference to Jeremiah. In fact, the prophecy is quite literal within its proper context. The staff called Favor was cut into pieces. At that time Zechariah was (in his vision) paid thirty pieces of silver which he threw into the temple for the potter. After this comes a prophecy of Israel's fall. Historically, this fits with what happened in Jesus' lifetime. Jesus was the "good shepherd" (Zechariah 13:7). When He was struck, when the staff called Favor was cut into pieces, the sheep were scattered (13:7) and Israel was broken (11:14). The price of that shepherd's life was valued at thirty pieces of silver, the price of a slave.[807] But the shepherd will return and many of the sheep will be saved.

When Was Jesus Crucified?
Chronology of the Last Supper, Crucifixion, and Resurrection

One of the most common and controversial of debates is over when Jesus was crucified and when He ate the last supper. Was this last supper the Passover meal or not? In turn, this leads to a question of when Jesus was resurrected.

Before entering this debate, I would like to make a simple analogy which will illustrate the problem so many have. It is a fact that at 8:46 a.m. a plane hit the north tower of the World Trade Center on September 11, 2001. At 9:03 a.m. a second plane hit the second tower. However, I was in Texas, in the central time, zone when this took place. When asked, I would say that the plane hit the tower at 7:46 a.m. Now technically, one might say I am in error, but from my perspective in Texas, it is 100% accurate. It *was* 7:46 a.m. *in Texas*.

By the same token, someone in California might say it struck at 5:46 a.m. while they were still asleep. Also factor that some places do not observe Daylight Savings Time. The point is that such testimonies do not *necessarily* conflict with one another, and may, in fact, lend support and credibility to each other's testimonies.

Just as I have elsewhere compared good exegesis to good police work in piecing together eyewitness accounts, so it is true here. The eyewitnesses do not so much contradict one another as they tell the chronology from a different cultural understanding. No *fact* in this debate is dispute. It is the piecing together of the facts which confuse people, and honestly, the literature I have read only serves to make it much more complicated than it really is. I will endeavor to simplify the issues rather than engaging in a lengthy and technical debate.

Finally, note that all three issues discussed here are interrelated. Consequently, each section is not independent of one another. All three sections are important if we are to get a complete picture of the chronology of Jesus' final week.

The Last Supper

When we address this controversy there are two crucial errors made. "The first and chiefest among the blunders which mark this controversy is that of confounding the Passover with the Feast of Unleavened Bread."[808] According to Leviticus 23:5-6 "in the first month, on the fourteenth day of the month at twilight is the LORD's Passover. Then on the fifteenth day of the same month there is the Feast of Unleavened Bread to the LORD; for seven days you shall eat unleavened bread" (cf. Numbers 28:16-17). Thus the the Passover and Feast were technically different although the terms Passover, and even Feast, were sometimes used generically for the entire period as in Josephus where he states that "we keep a feast for eight days called *the feast of unleavened bread*,"[809] but in fact, the Feast of Unleavened Bread is only *seven* days! Josephus is, therefore, counting the Passover as a part of the greater feast.

The second crucial thing to keep in mind is how day time was measured back in those days. I earlier made the analogy to different time zones. Add to this "Daylight Savings Time" and it would be easy to see how someone not familiar with our country and culture could be confused. Likewise, in those days Romans, like most in the word today, began the new day at midnight, but Jews began the new day either at sundown or at sunrise depending on what part of Israel they originated.[810] This fact is referenced by the ancient Jewish *Mishnah*.[811] Even to this day Orthodox Jews follow the Sadducees method of reckoning the new day from sundown, hence shops in Israel all close at 6 P.M. *Friday* in observance of the Sabbath, which is on Saturday. Conversely, Jews like Josephus counted the new day from sunrise.[812] Consequently, when we consider that Jesus' trial took place in the middle of the night we must recognize that some place this on the new day, whereas others would consider this as still taking place on the previous day. Did Jesus eat his last supper before sundown, or after? All these factors *must* be taken into account if we hope to have a legitimate understanding of the Biblical account.

Having studied and researched this issue, I can honestly say that Bible scholars have made the issue far more confusing than it should be. Much of the confusion comes from a failure to understand five crucial cultural aspects of Jesus' time. When we take those factors into consideration, the apparent contradictions are easily resolved. These factors are as follows:

1) A reference to Passover may either refer to Passover proper or to the entire Feast (Passover plus the Feast of Unleavened Bread), but not to the Feast of Unleavened Bread alone.

2) A reference to the Feast of of Unleavened Bread may either refer to the Feast of Unleavened Bread proper (excluding Passover) or to the entire Feast (including Passover), but may not refer to Passover alone.

3) There were three ways of reckoning a new day; Roman time at midnight. Sadduceean time at sundown. Phariseean time at sunrise.

4) Matthew, Mark, and Luke all count time by the Pharisees method (cf. Matthew 23:44-45; Mark 15:25, 33; Luke 27:45).

5) John reconned time using the Roman method (cf. John 19:14 following the cock crowing).

With these factors in mind, a close examination of the passages is in complete agreement chronologically. Before determining if Jesus' Last Supper was a Passover meal, and whether or not it was on Wednesday night or Thursday night, let us look at the crucial passages.

The Synoptic Gospels and John 19:14

The synoptic gospels all state that "on the first day of Unleavened Bread the disciples came to Jesus and asked, 'Where do You want us to prepare for You to eat the Passover?'" (Matthew 26:17. Cf. Mark 14:12, Luke 22:7). John, however, states that "it was the day of preparation for the Passover; it was about the sixth hour" that Jesus was tried by Pilate (see also notes on "At What Hour? Mark 15:25 – John 19:14").

Much has been made of this seeming contradiction and many explanations offered, but the problem is actually a simple cultural one. By law Jews were forbidden from shopping on Sabbath (Saturday) so all the preparations for meals and such had to be made on Friday. Thus the "day of preparation" is universally acknowledged to be synonymous with Friday.[813] In other words, it was not a day when they were preparing for Passover but "the day of preparation" (i.e. Friday) during Passover week.[814] It might be translated "it was the Friday of Passover week." Bearing in mind the five points made above, this statement by John is in perfect accord with the other gospels. It also proves that John used Roman time, rather than the Phariseean time as the other gospels do, for the cock does not crow at noon, but at sunrise, just before 6 a.m. The "sixth hour" in John is 6 a.m. and synonymous with the twelfth hour of Sudduceean time or the beginning of the new day in Pharisee reckoning.

John 13:1

"Now before the Feast of the Passover, Jesus knowing that His hour had come that He would depart out of this world to the Father." These words precede John's description of the Last Supper and are used by some to argue that the Last Supper could not have been a Passover since it was "before the Feast of Passover." This argument, however, is weak. First, it states that "before the Feast of Passover" Jesus *knew* His time has come. It does not say that the Last Supper was "before the Feast of Passover." In fact, since the sentence is "before" the Last Supper it was also "before Passover." This statement has no bearing on whether or not the Last Supper was a Passover feast.

John 18:28

"Then they led Jesus from Caiaphas into the Praetorium, and it was early; and they themselves did not enter into the Praetorium so that they would not be defiled, but might eat the Passover." This statement confirms that many, if not all, of those who were accusing Jesus had not yet eaten Passover. The question is then how could Jesus have eaten Passover?

Remembering that the Pharisees and Sadducees reconned a new day differently, this question is easily resolved. The priestly class were made of many Sadducees. Jewish historian Chaim Potok said of them, "not all the priests were Sadducees but all Sadducees were priests, aristocrats, and wealthy merchants."[815] Consequently, it is apparent that those who accussed Jewish were predominantly Sadducees who had not yet eaten Passover, even though Jesus, along with the Pharisees and many others, had already taken the Passover meal.

The Bread

A final argument used against Jesus having eaten Passover is based on the Greek word for unleavened bread. The word for unleavened bread is "ἄζυμα (*azuma*) whereas the generic word for bread is "ἄρτος (*artos*). Since the descriptions of the Last supper uses the word "ἄρτος (*artos*) rather than "ἄζυμα (*azuma*) it is assumed that this could not have been a Passover meal.

The problem is that this fails the basic logic argument "a Ford is a car; not all cars are Fords." Unleavened bread or ᾰζυμα (*azuma*) was most definitely *bread* or ᾰρτος (*artos*). One cannot assume that unleavened bread is not used here since "unleavened bread was commonly called 'bread.'"[816] This is circumstantial evidence at best.

Luke 22:15
Too often neglected in this debate is the fact that Jesus explicitly refers to the Last Supper as Passover. Here in Luke 22:15 He states, "I have earnestly desired to eat this Passover with you before I suffer" (Luke 22:15). This is the same meal in which the apostles had "found everything just as He had told them; and they prepared the Passover" (Luke 22:13). In Greek the words "the" and "this" are found therein. This is not a translation issue, but what Jesus actually said. It was "*the* Passover" and Jesus longed to eat "*this* Passover" with the apostles.

The only response that has been offered to this passage is "Jesus did make this last supper a sort of Passover meal (but not the real one). He wanted to have this special fellowship with his disciples, his friends, being painfully aware of the agony he would go through, only a few hours later."[817] Hence they must aruge that it was a Passover "of sorts" but not the "real Passover"? When one examines the arguments made against the straightforward interpretation of Luke 22:13-15 it becomes apparent that this actually based on a failure to understand that the pascal lamb was sacrificed for two days in succession because the Pharisees and Sadducees reconned Passover from different times.

This is where the difficulty lies. Passover was to be celebrated on Nisan 14. For the Pharisees, including Jesus and His apostles, Nisan 14 began on Thursday morning, hence Passover was to be eaten that night, but for the Sadducees Nisan 14 did not begin until sundown on Thursday and was, therefore, to be eaten before sundown on Friday. This is how Jesus could eat Passover and yet die on the cross at the exact time that the pascal lambs were being slaughtered!

Summary
As we have seen, all the difficulties and "contradictions" disappear when we take into consideration the culture of the day. First, "the Passover and the Feast of the Firstfruits were both connected with the Feast of Unleavened Bread, and sometimes, as here, the term 'Passover' stands for the entire observance."[818] This is confirmed by Josephus when he "applies the name Unleavened Bread loosely when he speaks of the feast as lasting 'for eight days.'"[819] Second, and most significantly, the Pharisses and Sadducees reconned the beginning of Passover differently. For the Pharisees, including Jesus and His apostles, Nisan 14 began on Thursday morning, but the Sadducees did not reckon Passover until after sundown on Thursday and, therefore, was eaten before sundown on Friday.

In this way Jesus ate Passover, as He explicitly states (Luke 22:15) and yet died on the cross at the exact time that the pascal lambs were being slaughtered.

The Crucifixion

Having concluded that the Last Supper was eaten Thursday night, before the Sadducees had eaten Passover, it is apparent that Jesus died on Friday, as the ancient tradition of "Good Friday" affirms.[820] However, some will not accept this based predominantly upon Matthew 12:40. The notion of a Thursday crucifixion, although in the minority, is supported by numerous credible scholars and theologians of evangelical persuasion including Dave Hunt.[821]

According to Matthew 12:40, "just as Jonah was three days and three nights in the belly of the beast, so will the Son of Man be three days and three nights in the heart of the earth." So it is argued that Jesus had to be in the earth Thursday, Friday, and Saturday nights. The problem with this is that if we assume that Jesus had to spend three nights in the grave then He would also have had to have spent three full days in the grave, but if He did not die until Thursday evening, He had only Friday and Saturday.

Ironically, their answer to this problem is the same one used by those of us who support a Friday crucifixion. It is a well know fact that any portion of a day counted as a whole day.[822] Morever, "a fractional part of a day or night [was reconned] as one day and one night."[823] This is not opinion, for we find many such occurrences in the Bible. Genesis 42:17-18, for example, records where Joseph was imprisoned for "three days" yet was released "on the third day" (cf. 1 Kings 20:29; 2 Chronicles 10:5, 12). Likewise 1 Samuel 30:12-13 states that David "had not eaten bread or drunk water for three days and three nights" yet when ask, David said that he felt sick "three days ago." Another critical passage is Esther 4:16 where she is told "do not eat or drink for three days, night or day" and yet in 5:1 "it came about on the third day that Esther put on her royal robes and stood in the inner court of the king's palace." Note that two of these passage actually refer to three days and three nights, yet in each the "third day" is when the time period had been fulfilled! Why then cannot Jesus' statement be treated in the same was as David and Esther's?

Finally, the Bible makes it clear that Jesus was crucified the day before the Sabbath. Mark 15:42 states that "it was the preparation day, that is, the day before the Sabbath" (cf. Luke 23:54). So also John records that Jesus was to be taken down from the cross before sundown "so that the bodies would not remain on the cross on the Sabbath" (19:31). As aforementioned, the term "day of preparation" or "preparation day" was also uniformly an idiom for Friday, the day before the Sabbath. Those who reject a Friday crucifixion can only claim that Passover was also considered a Sabbath, but offer no proof of this.[824]

To argue that Matthew 12:40 requires a full 72 hours to pass is not valid, nor it is clear that Jonah himself was in the belly of the beast for 72 hours. It does record that he was inside the beast for "three days and three nights" (Jonah 1:17) but it also records that David had not eaten for "three days and three nights" (1 Samuel 30:12) and Esther likewise was not to eat for "three days, night or day" (Esther 4:16), but on both occasions the "three days and three nights" were finished "on the third day" (1 Samuel 30:13, Esther 5:1). So there is no reason to believe that "three days and three nights" means a full 72 hours, nor that it requires three distinct nights anymore than David or Esther experience three distinct nights. The phrase is idiomatic for any portion of time composed of part of three different days. It could be anywhere from 26 hours to 72 hours. In this case, it is clear that Jesus was crucified on Friday (the first day and night), stayed in the earth on Sabbath (the second day and night) and Sunday (which included the dawn, but also that period of Sunday when it was still dark).

Thus the Bible depicts Jesus as dying on Friday, Nisan 14, at the "ninth hour" (Matthew 27:45-46, Mark 15:33-34, Luke 23:44) which coincides precisely with Josephus' remarks that on "the Passover, when they slay their sacrifices, from the ninth to the eleventh hour."[825] This is three o'clock by Roman time. So Jesus died when the pascal lambs were being slain in the temple, shortly before the Sabbath began (John 19:31).

The Resurrection

A final problem is that of the resurrection chronology. I will address alleged "contradictions" in the accounts elsehwere. Rather here I will only address the chronology itself. Matthew states that "after the Sabbath, as it began to dawn toward the first day of the week" (28:1) the Marys came to the tomb. Mark also says that "very early on the first day of the week, they came to the tomb when the sun had risen" (16:2, cf. 16:9). Luke and John also agree (Luke 24:1; John 20:1, 9). The first day of the week, of course, is Sunday "after the Sabbath" (Matthew 28:1). This has created some confusion among readers. Likewise, the phrase "after three days" (Matthew 27:3; Mark 8:31) has been seen as problematic since it is elsewhere said to be "on the third day" (Matthew 16:21, 17:24, 20:19, Luke 9:22, 1 Corinthians 15:4).

These issues again are easily resolved when we understand the language and culture, but I again draw the analogy of a reader unfamiliar with the United States reading about someone living in Phoenix, Arizona. At one time he says he is in the Mountain Time Zone while at another time he says he is in the Pacific Time Zone! Those who live in the United States understand that Phoenix, Arizona does not observe Daylights Savings Time, and therefore realize that there is no such contradictions. A similar issue exist here, as with the start of a new day in ancient Israel.

Matthew 27:3; Mark 8:31

The gospels states that Jesus would rise "*after* three days" (Matthew 27:3; Mark 8:31). Some see a problem with the word "after," arguing it is inconsistent with "*on* the third day" (Matthew 16:21, 17:23, 20:19; Luke 9:22, 18:33, 24:7, 24:21; Acts 10:40; 1 Corinthians 15:4), a phrase used by the very same Matthew! If we quote Matthew in full we will understand why.

The priests and Pharisees went to Pilate and said to him:

> "Sir, we remember that when He was still alive that deceiver said, 'After three days I am to rise again.' Therefore, give orders for the grave to be made secure until the third day, otherwise His disciples may come and steal Him away and say to the people, 'He has risen from the dead,' and the last deception will be worse than the first" (Matthew 27:63-64).

Now Harold Hoehner points out that "the phrase 'after three days' must have been equivalent to 'the third day,' or otherwise the Pharisees would have asked for a guard of soldiers until the fourth day."[826] This is clear because the same apostle who referred to "after three days" also declared that He rose "on the third day" (Matthew 16:21, 17:23, 20:19).

The issue is a simple linguistic one. "After" carries unspoken connotations. If we are talking about a day, we are talking about a 24 hour period. In modern English "after" may mean "after the entire 24 hour period is completed" but in ancient languages (not just Greek and Hebrew) it meant "after this period of time has begun." So "after Monday" might mean "Tuesday" in the modern world, but it meant anytime after Monday morning back in antiquity. It might be Monday afternoon or might be Thursday! It was surely "after Monday *began*." This is why the priests and Pharisees only required that the tomb be guarded "*until* the third day" (Matthew 27:64).

Matthew 28:1

Matthew states that the two Marys came to the tomb of Jesus "after the Sabbath, as it began to dawn toward the first day of the week" (28:1). This seems to fit the testimony of the other gospels as well. The problem is when we recall that Matthew, Mark, and Luke reconned the new day as beginning at dawn (cf. Matthew 27:45-46, Mark 15:33-34, Luke 23:44 or see notes above) this statement is confusing for Sabbath would not be over *until* the dawn.

Some have argued that the translation is bad. The ASV and Darby translation render this passage as "late on the sabbath day, as it began to dawn toward the first day of the week." The Greek actually reads, "'Οψε δε σαββατων" (*opse de sabbaton*). The Greek word 'οψε (*opse*) is literally rendered "after a long time, long after, late,"[827] and yet the same lexicon

170

states that in Matthew 28:1 it should be "'after the sabbath' ... an interpretation absolutely demanded by the added specification τῃ επιφοσκ. κτλ."[828] However, this "interpretation" assumes that the new day began at sundown rather than sunrise as it did among the Sadducees. Still, Mark declares that it was "very early on the first day of the week" (16:2, cf. 16:9). This makes it clear that the Sabbath was already over so the translation is not really the issue (although I do prefer "late on the Sabbath" as the proper translation). The real issue is how Jesus could be resurrected on Saturday if the new day did not begin until sunrise, for Jesus prophesied that He would rise "*on* the third day" which was Sunday, not the Sabbath!

Two explanations have been offered. The first is that Matthew was using the Sadducees' method of counting days. This works for the resurrection but creates problems for the crucifixion, as we have seen (cf. Matthew 27:45-46). The second explanation is better. Roger Beckwith states "Matthew shows that the two reckonings were not in rivalry with each other."[829] In other words, just as I will use Mountain Time when visiting Arizona, but keep in touch with my friends from Texas using Central Time, so the apostles were not unaccustomed to Sadducees' tradition which was the dominant tradition in Judea where they were at the time of the resurrection. Regardless of our translation, it is apparent that Jesus was resurrected sometime before dawn *after* Sunday had arrived. "Matthew is emphatic that the tomb was not empty until the third day (Matt. 12:40; 16:21; 17:23; 20:19; 27:63f.), which would not have begun before nightfall on Saturday"[830] according to Judean (or Sadducees) reckoning. Consequently, it not unusual for all of the apostles to use Judean time even though they kept the Galilean tradition for the Last Supper and general time keeping. Such instances are neither contradictory nor unusual, for we do it ourselves as in my illustration of the Time Zones.

That Jesus was resurrected on the first day of the week, Sunday, is attested by all the apostles and affirmed by tradition as well. This was three days, by ancient reckoning, after He was crucified on Friday afternoon. Too much has been made over the "three nights" of Matthew 12:40 but technically even this was true for He spent the first fill night in the grave as well as the second night. The third "night" could include early Sunday morning before the sun had risen. So whether "three days and nights" was idiomatic or should be taken in a strict literal fashion the apostles all agree that this was accomplished "on the third day" which was the "first day of the week." The use of Judean time is to be expected since they were in Judean, even though they retained Galilean traditions and spoke in general terms according to the traditions in which they were raised.

Conclusion

Much confusion has existed because of cultural misunderstandings. The evidence has been presented above and demonstrates that the gospels are all in perfect agreement with one another. When we understand the distinction between Passover, the Feast of Unleavened Bread, and the generic use of these terms; that the "day of preparation" was not an adjective but a noun synonymous with Friday; and that the ancient Jews reconned the new day from different methods (which no one can deny) we reach the following conclusion.

Passover was to be celebrated on Nisan 14. For the Pharisees, including Jesus and His apostles, Nisan 14 began on Thursday morning, hence Passover was to be eaten that night, but for the Sadducees Nisan 14 did not begin until sundown on Thursday and was, therefore, to be eaten before sundown on Friday. This is how Jesus could eat Passover and yet die on the cross at the exact time that the pascal lambs were being slaughtered!

Mihaly Munkacsy - Ecce Homo - 1896

The following chart shows the entire Passion Week of Jesus as measured by the three different time reconnings. Remember that Matthew, Mark, and Luke all used the Pharisees method whereas John used the Roman method. Add to this the fact that many of those who crucified Jesus were of the dominant Sadducees party and used their own Calendar days. The reader can clearly see that everything in the Bible fits perfectly together like the completed pieces of a jigsaw puzzle and we cannot help but feel a little proud at having completed the puzzle to see a perfect and flawless image.

Time Chart on the Passion Week

Roman Day	Sadducees Calender		Pharisees	Events of Jesus' Last Week
Saturday	Nisan 8	6:00 PM	Nisan 9	Jesus enter Bethany and visits Lazarus (John 12:1-11; Matthew 26:6-13; Mark 14:3-9)
		12:00 AM		
Sunday	Nisan 9	6:00 AM		Crowds gather as Jesus visits Lazarus (John 12:9). The priests plot to kill Lazarus (John 12:10-11)
		12:00 PM		
		6:00 PM	Nisan 10	The Triumphant Entry, the first visit to the temple, and return to Bethany (Matthew 21; Mark 11; Luke 19:29-44; John 12:12-19)
		12:00 AM		
Monday	Nisan 10	6:00 AM		Cursing the fig tree (Matthew 21:18-19a; Mark 11:12-14). The cleansing of the temple (Matthew 21:12-13; Mark 11:15-18; Luke 19:45-48)
		12:00 PM		
		6:00 PM	Nisan 11	
		12:00 AM		The fig tree withered (Matthew 21:19b-22; Mark 11:19-26)
Tuesday	Nisan 11	6:00 AM		A day of preaching (Matthew 21:23-23:39; Mark 11:27-12:44; Luke 20:1-21:4)
		12:00 PM		
		6:00 PM	Nisan 12	The Olivet Discourse (Matthew 24:1-25:46; Mark 13:1-37; Luke 21:5-36)
		12:00 AM		
Wednesday	Nisan 12	6:00 AM		"Silent Wednesay" - A day of preaching and ...
		12:00 PM		
		6:00 PM	Nisan 13	The Sanhedrim plot (Matthew 26:1-16; Mark 14:1-11; Luke 21:37-22:6; cf. Matthew 26:2 & Mark 14:1)
		12:00 AM		
Thursday	Nisan 13	6:00 AM		Preparation for Passover (Matthew 26:17-19; Mark 14:12-16; Luke 22:7-13)
		12:00 PM		
		6:00 PM		The Last Supper (Matthew 26:20-35; Mark 14:17-31; Luke 22:14-23)
		12:00 AM	Nisan 14	Preparations for His betrayal (Luke 22:24-38) Jesus at Gethsamane and His arrest (Matthew 26:36-56; Mark 14:32-52; Luke 22:39-53; John 18:1-12) Jesus brought before Annas (John 18:13-24) Jesus led to Caiaphas (Matthew 26:57-68; Mark 14:53-65; Luke 22:54; John 25:27)
Friday	Nisan 14	6:00 AM		The cock crows. Peter has denied Christ three times (Matthew 26:69-75; Mark 14:66-72; Luke 22:55-62; John 25:25-27) Jesus first brought to Pilate (Matthew 27:1-11; Mark 15:1-2; Luke 23:1-7; John 18:25-28) Jesus brought to Herod (Luke 23:8-12) Jesus returned to Pilate (Matthew 27:12-25; Mark 15:3-14; Luke 23:8-23; John 18:29-40) Jesus scourged (Matthew 27:26; Mark 15:15; John 19:1). Jesus condemned (Matthew 27:27-31 ; Mark 15:16-20 ; Luke 23:24-25 ; John 19:2-16)
			Nisan 15	Carrying the cross and Simon of Cyrene (Matthew 27:32-34; Mark 15:21-23; Luke 23:26-33; John 19:17)
		9:00 AM		Jesus placed on the cross (Matthew 27:35-44; Mark 15:24-32; Luke 23:33-43; John 19:18-27)
		12:00 PM		Darkness descends on the land (Matthew 27:45-49; Mark 15:33-36; Luke 24:44-45)
		3:00 PM		Jesus dies as earthquake shakes the temple (Matthew 27:50-56; Mark 15:37-41; Luke 24:46-49; John 19:28-30) Jesus buried (Matthew 27:57-60; Mark 15:42-46; Luke 23:50-54; John 31-42)
		6:00 PM		
Saturday	Nisan 15	12:00 AM		
		6:00 AM		
		6:00 PM	Nisan 16	Guards at the tomb (Matt. 27:61-66; M 15:47; L 23:55-56)
		12:00 AM		
Sunday	Nisan 16	6:00 AM		Jesus resurrected from the dead (Matthew 28:1-8; Mark 16:1-8; Luke 24:1-12; John 20:1-10)

Annas or Caiaphas?
Matthew 26:57-68 – Mark 14:53-65 – Luke 22:54 – John 18:13-24

"They led Him to Annas first; for he was father-in-law of Caiaphas, who was high priest that year."

Two problems are alleged in this passage. The first problem is not one of a contradiction, for all say that Jesus was led to Caiaphas at some point, but rather one of Peter's denial. I did not address this under Peter's denial for the issue is only cursory and those who are interested in this topic will find it more easily addressed here.

Basically, the problem is that Peter follows Christ while being pursued by his accusors who are continuously asking if he is a follower of Christ. However, in the accounts all appear to take place in a courtyard area and its surroundings where Caiaphas was conducting the trial. Only John mentions Annas, who sends him to Caiaphas, but John records that Peter was first confronted at Annas house. Is there an inconsistency here?

The answer is "no" for the apostle John explicitly states that Annas "was father-in-law of Caiaphas" (18:13). What most people fail to realize that in ancient times, and even in many places around the world today, families lived together even after marriage. The house might be expanded and enlarged to accomodate a larger family, but extended families all lived under one roof, so Jesus was tried in the same household; that of Annas and Caiaphas. It was one house, and to this day there is a church built over the archaeological ruins of Caiaphas' house which had a dungeon build underground to house prisoners such as Jesus.

The second problem is the allegation that Annas and Caiaphas could not both be High Priest. John says that "Caiaphas [was] the high priest that year" (John 18:13) but Luke mentions "the high priesthood of Annas and Caiaphas" (Luke 3:2) and elsewhere calls Annas the high priest (Acts 4:6). This problem is actually easily resolved.

We know that Annas was appointed high priest by Quirinius, the Roman governor of Syria in 6 or 7 A.D.[831] but he was deposed by Valerius Gratus, the Roman procurator of Judea many years later.[832] However, under Jewish law the high priesthood was a lifetime appointment. Consequently the Jews did not recognize the right of the Romans' to depose their religious leader. As a result Annas made his son-in-law, Caiaphas (John 18:13; Acts 4:6) the "official priest recognized by the Roman government"[833] but the Jews continued to look to Annas as the true high priest. Nepotism is, after all, nothing new. Thus Caiaphas was the high priest recognized by Rome, who confronted Pilate, while Annas was the high priest to whom the people first brought Jesus. Again, this is perfectly logical, consistent, and historically accurate.

174

Who Killed Christ?
Matthew 27:25

"And all the people said, 'His blood shall be on us and on our children!'"

This infamous quote is one that Jews are taught to shudder from and to reject as the ravings of an anti-semitic author. The problem is that Matthew was a Jew who was writing to Jews. The only gentile author in the New Testament, Luke, does not mention this quotation at all. While the Jewish extremist might dismiss this as a gentile forgery long after the time of Jesus, this cannot be so (see Appendix C for evidence on the authenticity of Scripture). Matthew wrote the gospel which bears his name and Matthew was a Jew.

Let me begin by saying that the most offensive jokes I have ever heard about Jews were from Jews in Israel. Jews do not mind poking fun at themselves, but fear anti-semitism from those that are not. In the same way Matthew was writing to Jews and reminded the Jews of this truthful quotation in hopes of stirring the conscience of his Jewish audience.

The real questions is not one of who wrote these words or whether or not they are accurate, for they are, but what does this mean? Are Jews "Christ killers"? Did the Jews kill Christ or was it the Romans? Perhaps it was a collaborative effort?

These questions were stirred up when Mel Gibson's *Passion of the Christ* appeared in movie theaters. They are also based on classic misunderstanding of the gospel, as well as of history. There are two essential things to understand in this debate.

First, Jews and gentiles together bear the burden. The whole world is guilty. In his speech to the Jews, Peter declared that it was "the gentiles and the peoples of Israel" (Acts 4:27) who were guilty. And yet the Jews responded to Peter that he was trying to bring the blood guilty upon the Jews (Acts 5:28). The reasons for this are as follows. God entrusted the Word to the Jews. The Jews are the chosen race, but unlike modern day politicians Jesus taught, "to much is given, much is required" (Luke 12:48). Elsewhere the Bible teaches those who are in a position of authority receive *greater* judgment than those who are not (cf. James 3:1). The Jews were expected to recognize the Christ (Messiah). The pagans were ignorant of Messiah and behaved as ignorant men, but the Jewish priesthood should have been the first to recognize him. Moreover, one of Jesus' quotes was that "many who are first will be last and the last will be first" (Matthew 19:30; Mark 10:31; Luke 13:30). This may reflect upon the prophecy of Isaiah 65:1-3 wherein he prophesies that God will be found by those who did not seek Him (gentiles). In short, Israel *will* be saved (Romans 11:26) but first the "fullness of the gentiles" (Romans 11:25) must be brought in so that all mankind (Jews and gentiles) will worship the Lord.

Antonio Ciseri - Ecco Homo - 1871

The second, and most important, thing to understand in this debate is that it is *good* for us that He did die! The Bible is perfectly clear that had Jesus not died (and been resurrected from the dead) none of us would be saved! He came to be that sacrifice which was promised to Abraham in place of Isaac. Consequently, to speak of a "Christ killer" is to fail to understand that Jesus came for the express reason of dying. *I* killed Christ, and yet He died *for me*. This is the paradox of God's love.

Having addressed the misconceptions which underlie the entire debate, it is necessary to rebut some of the arguments made on its behalf. The reason is that such arguments are not so much attacks against Mel Gibson's *Passion of the Christ* as they are against the historicity of the Bible. The chief among these accusations it that Pontius Pilate is presumeably protrayed as a just leader who was manipulated by Caiaphas. They stated that the real Pilate (implying the one in the Bible is not real) brutally oppressed the Jews and hated Caiaphas. So does the Bible present an accurate picture? Was Pilate a "puppet" to Caiaphas?

The problem with the argument is that it is anachronistic and misleading. *Obviously* Pilate was not a just man or he would never have had crucified Jesus. Josephus gives us a complete picture of Pilate as governor of Judea.[834] When Pilate first arrived he expected to crush resistance and force the Jews in subjection as the empire did in other lands, but with each rebellion and

176

riot, no matter how savage and brutal he was, Pilate discovered that the Jews only became more rebellious. Moreover, the emperor became very angry with his rule. By the time of Jesus (around 33 A.D.) Pilate was in a precarious position. The emperor had warned Pilate that he did not wish to see any more uprisings or rioting. Consequently, when we read the political tête-à-tête between Caiaphas and Pilate we actually see an intuiguing insight into their minds. Caiaphas implicitly threatened to riot if Jesus was not crucified while at the same time implying that Pilate would be committing treason against Rome if he did not crucify Jesus. However, the irony of this entire debacle is that under Jewish law Caiaphas could not execute Jesus, for He was innocent. Caiaphas then took Jesus to the one man he knew would have no problem killing an innocent man; Pontius Pilate.

That the entire trial was a farce is apparent by the "illegitimacy of the trial which was being conducted during the middle of the night."[835] Yet despite this, Jewish law would not condemn Jesus. Only under Roman law could Pilate execute a man he had himself declared innocent of all charges! Remember this; the very men who were responsible for Jesus' execution (both Jewish and Roman) had themselves exonerated Him of all guilt!

The Words on the Cross
Matthew 27:37 – Mark 15:26 – Luke 23:38 – John 19:19

"This is Jesus, the King of the Jews."	"The King of the Jews."	"This is the King of the Jews."	"Jesus the Nazarene, the King of the Jews."

For some reason I have never completely understood, some have made a great deal over the fact that the gospels have abbreviated the full inscription on the cross. They have argued that there is some sort of contradiction. Worse yet, some have attempted a long, unnecessary, and rather complicated scheme to explain the differences. According to this popular explanation Matthew and Luke followed the Hebrew-Aramaic[836] inscription on the cross, whereas Mark followed the Latin inscription, and John followed the Greek inscription.[837] The long and protracted arguments in favor of this often promoted theory will not be repeated here for a simple reason; they are unnecessary. When two explanations are possible, the simplest is usually (but not always) to be preferred, and yet for some reason the simple, and obvious, answer is ignored by too many.

If, with Sir Robert Anderson, we "assume, for the sake of argument, that the full inscription was 'This is Jesus the Nazarene, the King of the Jews'"[838] then we can plainly see that *all* the gospels are correct. An abridgment is not a contradiction. It is not only acceptable but essential for any historian. If every word and action were recorded without abridgment then even a simple hour long conversation would take up thirty pages or more of a transcript. The gospel authors wrote what was important and each fully agree that in Jesus was proclaimed "the king of the Jews" on a plaque reserved for the crimes of the accused. In other words, a prisoner's crimes would normally be written on a plaque above their cross. People passing by would then see what crimes the man committed and take warning from it, but in this case there is a strange and prophetic irony in the inscription too often overlooked.

What is important is that this ironic inscription proved to be a prophetic one. It is proof that God is the true author of history. Who else would have put into Pilate's depraved mind to mock the Jewish leaders he hated so much, while inadvertently acknowledging the true king of kings! Moreover, this inscription was written in all three of the dominant languages of the day. Latin for the Romans, Greek as the international language of Rome, and Hebrew / Aramaic[839] (John 19:20) for the locals in Judea:

~~~~~~~~~~~~~~~~~~~~~~~~
זהו ישוע מנצרת מלך היהודים
Hic est Jesus Nazarenus, Rex Judaeorum
Αυτο ειναι ο Ιησους ο Ναζωραιος, ο βασιλευς των Ιουδαιων
~~~~~~

Thus the king was proclaimed to all people.

The Prisoners on the Crosses
Matthew 27:44 – Mark 15:32 – Luke 23:39-43

"The robbers who had been crucified with Him were also insulting Him with the same words."	"Those who were crucified with Him were also insulting Him."	"One of the criminals who were hanged there was hurling abuse at Him, saying, 'Are You not the Christ? Save Yourself and us!' But the other answered, and rebuking him said, 'Do you not even fear God, since you are under the same sentence of condemnation? And we indeed are suffering justly, for we are receiving what we deserve for our deeds; but this man has done nothing wrong.'"

Matthew and Luke both record the men (plural) who were crucified with Jesus as mocking him while Luke *appears* to contradict that, saying that only one of them mocked Jesus while the other defended him. However, like most apparent contradictions in eyewitness accounts, the conflict is easily resolved when we look at the complete picture.

We know that they were on the cross for six hours. We also know that death can bring out the fear of God even in the worst of criminals. I have no doubt that *both* criminals initially mocked Jesus when they were first placed on the crosses. This fits with both Matthew and Mark. Luke, however, gives a specific account which probably took place near the end of their lives. Said Matthew Henry, "so many evidences were given in such a short time"[840] that "a blessed change [was] wrought in him."[841] On his deathbed one of the two criminals had a change of heart. Having seen that Jesus was no ordinary man and no mere false messiah, he was no longer mocking Jesus, but instead turned the Lord and asked forgiveness.

This was the lesson that Luke wanted to present. Even on one's deathbed, it is not too late to repent and turn away from sin. Jesus promised that man that he would be in Paradise that very day (Luke 23:43)! So while they had both ridiculed Jesus, one repented towards the end while the other remained proud and bitter in his heart. This is what the complete picture shows us.

The Last Words of Jesus
Matthew 27:46 – Mark 15:34 – Luke 23:46 – John 19:30

"Jesus cried out with a loud voice, saying, *'Eli, eli, lama sabachthani?'* that is, 'My God, My God, Why have your forsaken me?' And some of those who were standing there, when they heard it, *began* saying, 'This man is calling for Elijah.' Immediately one of them ran, and taking a sponge, he filled it with sour wine and put it on a reed, and gave Him a drink ... And Jesus cried out again with a loud voice, and yielded up His spirit."

"Jesus cried out with a loud voice, saying, *'Eloi, eloi, lama sabachthani?'* which is translated, 'My God, My God, Why have your forsaken me?' When some of the bystanders heard it, they *began* saying, 'Behold, He is calling for Elijah.' Someone ran and filled a sponge with sour wine, put it on a reed, and gave Him a drink, saying, 'Let us see whether Elijah will come to take Him down.' And Jesus uttered a loud cry, and breathed His last."

"And Jesus, crying out with a loud voice, said, 'Father, into Your hands I commit My Spirit.' Having said this, He breathed His last."

"After this, Jesus, knowing that all things had already been accomplished, to fulfill the Scripture, said, 'I am thirsty.' A jar full of sour wine was standing there; so they put a sponge full of the sour wine upon *a branch of* hyssop and brought it up to His mouth. Therefore when Jesus had received the sour wine, He said, 'It is finished!' And He bowed His head and gave up His spirit."

A great deal has been made over these seeming conflicting accounts of Jesus' final words. Bearing in mind the logic of our previous debates, let us examine these testimonies closely.

To begin with, Matthew and Mark *do not* state that these were Jesus *final* words. They were certainly among His last, but both explicitly state that Jesus "cried out" before dying. What words He cried out, we are not told. Thus Matthew and Mark agree with one another (but see below for the Hebrew-Aramaic debate). It is with Luke and John where they appears to be stronger conflict.

According to Luke, Jesus cried out with a loud voice (cf. Matthew 27:50; Mark 15:37) saying, "Father, into Your hands I commit My Spirit." He then says, "having said this, He breathed His last" (Luke 23:46). John, on the other hand said, "He said, 'It is finished!' And He bowed His head and gave up His spirit" (John 19:30). Specifically, John records that Jesus said these words after taking the drink. Luke omits the drinking. Logically, then we must assume that Luke abridged the final words, as did John. If we put them together, we get, "It is finished! Father, into Your hands I commit My Spirit."

Now let us put the complete picture together. Both Matthew and Mark record that Jesus cried out "Father, why have You forsaken Me?" Some thought He was calling out to Elijah (see notes under Hebrew-Aramaic for an explanation of this). Then both Matthew and John record that they brought water to Jesus to drink. John records that He had said, "I am thirsty." Finally, all agree that Jesus cried out in last breath. Most likely His complete words were, "It is finished. Father, into Your hands I commit My Spirit." These were Jesus' final words.

Did God Forsake Jesus?
Matthew 27:46 – Mark 15:34

"Jesus cried out with a loud voice, saying, '*Eli, eli, lama sabachthani?*' that is, 'My God, My God, Why have your forsaken me?'"	"Jesus cried out with a loud voice, saying, '*Eloi, eloi, lama sabachthani?*' which is translated, 'My God, My God, Why have your forsaken me?'"

As a young child raised in a liberal church I was used to hearing that the Bible could not be inerrant for Jesus was clearly "wrong" and "mistaken," or so I was told. Admittedly, this verse even confounded me as a young believer, new to the true faith, but in fact, Jesus was not mistaken. The whole point of the cross is that God did turn His back, for that one brief moment, on His own Son for our sakes. Jesus bore the punishments for our sins. He was offered as the sacrifice of atonement for us. Thus for that one moment in history, Jesus, the only innocent man, was abandoned to torture and death in order that we might live.

180

Did Jesus Speak Aramaic?

"Father, into Your hands I commit My Spirit." These were among the last words Jesus spoke, but Matthew and Mark differ in that Mark is quoted in Aramaic (Mark 15:34) while Matthew is in part Hebrew (Matthew 27:46).

To my surprise there is among scholarly circles a debate as to whether or not Jesus actually spoke Aramaic or Hebrew. "Surprise" because the question should not be too hard to answer. Unfortunately, the scholars who argue this point are not the scholars who are most familiar with Hebrew and Aramaic. Some conservatives believe that there is something holy in the Hebrew language itself, and thus have an aversion to the idea of Jesus speaking in Aramaic. Conversly, some liberals have an aversion to Jesus speaking in the language of Moses.

To understand whether or not Jesus spoke in Hebrew or Aramaic, and to understand why there is such confusion on the issue, one needs to understand the difference in Hebrew and Aramaic. The languages are, in fact, sister languages. Just as modern English differs from the language of King Arthur or even King James, the languages of Hebrew and Aramaic differ, but share the same common roots.

A Brief History of Aramaic

The word Aramaic is now used to describe the language of the Chaldeans of ancient Babylon. For many years, the language was merely called Chaldee, but recent scholars have objected to this term on the basis that the people of Chaldea actually spoke many languages.[842] We must remember that Abraham, the father of the Hebrew people, came from Chaldea (Ur of the Chaldees – Genesis 11:31). After the confusion of tongues at Babel, Hebrew remained one of the languages and was shared by some of the early Chaldean descendants. Abraham obviously retained this language, but the Jews and Chaldeans remained seperate, the language of the Chaldeans changed, even as English has changed, becoming noticeably different from the former.

It is very likely that Aramaic is of the same stock as Hebrew, but it branched off from Hebrew at some point. The primary differences are in slightly differening vocabulary and slightly different constructs of nouns, verbs, and adjectives. One difference was its written alphabet. By the time of the Jewish exile under Babylon Aramaic used a different written alphabet from Hebrew, although the actually letters are the same. For example, the Aramaic letter *aleph* is written as א in Aramaic but 𐤀 in ancient Hebrew (called paleo-Hebrew). This changed when the Jews were led into captivity by the Babylonians in the sixth century before Christ.

After being taken captive by the Babylonians, whose native language was Aramaic, it was natural for the Jews to adopt the sister language for everyday life. Hebrew remained the language of synagogues but the common people spoke the language of their captives; Aramaic. This was not difficult as the languages are extremely similar, even sharing much of the same vocabulary, save slightly different pronunciations and word constructs. For example, in Hebrew the word for "heaven" or "sky" is שָׁמַיִם (shamayim). In Aramaic it is שְׁמַיִן (shemayin). In Hebrew the word for "holy" is קָדוֹשׁ (qadosh). In Aramaic it is קַדִּישׁ (qadish). In Hebrew the word for "voice" is קוֹל (qol). In Aramaic it is קָל (qal).[843]

The more difficult problem was the alphabet itself. To that end the Jews adopted the Aramaic alphabet as their own. To this very day Hebrew Bibles, synagogues, and newspaper use the old Aramaic script rather than the script in which Moses wrote.

Aramaic-Modern Hebrew script	Paleo-Hebrew script
בראשית ברא אלהים את השמים ואת הארץ:	×4 ᗯ7Ⴝ⪽⪽ ⪽ⴴ9 ×7Wⴴ⪽9 Ɽⴴⴴⴴ ×⪽7 ᗯ7ᗯWⴴ

Genesis 1:1 as written in modern script (on the left) and as Moses would have written (on the right).

When the Jews returned from exile, one would expect that they returned to their native language of Hebrew, which was retained in the synagogues. However, this is where the controversy lies. The Jews obviously continued to use the Aramaic script for Hebrew and the Jews even made Aramaic translation of the Bible, called the Targums, which were in use throughout the time of Jesus. The Hebrew Bible in its original language remained, and no one denies this, but the appearance of the Targums and the retention of Aramaic script are but two evidences that the common tongue remained Aramaic; not Hebrew, even after the return from exile. Aramaic writings are found throughout Jesus' time, but so are Hebrew writings.

So the question is, did Jesus speak Hebrew or Aramaic? Some indications in the Bible say Hebrew, but others, just as strong, say Aramaic. Why? Which is correct? Is there a contradiction in the use of two different languages? Could Jesus have spoken both languages? If so, why? To some these questions are more important than whether or not the earth revolves around the sun.

Critical Passages to Consider
To determine whether or not Jesus spoke Hebrew or Aramaic we need to examine several critical passages in the Bible. Obviously the first are the quotations in Matthew and Mark, but there are a number of other passages which may give hints at Hebrew and/or Aramaic usage by Jesus. Those passages cannot be ignored if we hope to have a complete picture of Jesus' language.

Matthew's gospel records Jesus' words as *"Eli, eli, lama sabachthani?"* but Mark records them as *"Eloi, eloi, lama sabachthani."* The first thing that the reader will notice is that they are virtually identical. The only difference in the words is that Matthew uses the Hebrew *"Eli"* for "My God" whereas Mark uses the Aramaic construct *"Eloi."* Both use the Aramaic word *"sabachthani."* Various theories have been presented on both sides of the argument to account for this.

Those who believe Jesus spoke in Hebrew point out that the Hebrew *Eli* could be mistaken for a shortened form of Elijah, since the observers thought that He was calling for Elijah.[844] They, therefore, insist that Matthew's Hebrew was the original. There are, however, two problems with this argument. First, "on the lips of a dying man's crying out in agony. *'Eloi'* could as easily be mistaken for Elijah as *'Eli.'*"[845] This is particularly true since Elijah in Hebrew/Aramaic is *Elihu.* A second problem is that *"'Eli'* may in fact support an Aramaic original, becase the Targum (written in Aramaic) to Psalm 22:1 has *Eli."*[846] So similar were Hebrew and Aramaic that the translators of the Aramaic Targum occasionally used common Hebrew words instead of Aramaic. This, however, leads to the third, and greatest problem. Namely, *"sabachthani,"* found in both Matthew and Mark, is Aramaic, not Hebrew. In Psalms 22:1, which Jesus is believed to be quoting, the Hebrew Bible contains the word *"azabthani"* (עֲזַבְתָּנִי), not the Aramaic *"sabachthani"* (שְׁבַקְתַּנִי).[847] The proper Hebrew is not *"Eli, eli, lama sabachthani"* but *"Eli, eli, lama azabthani."*[848]

The real question is why do Matthew and Mark differ. Those who believe Jesus spoke in Hebrew suggest that Mark used Aramaic because Mark was not an actual eyewitness and heard the quotation from someone speaking Aramaic.[849] However, it more likely that Matthew, who most probably wrote his gospel in Hebrew (see "An Eyewitness Account? The Authorship and Date of Matthew"), partially translated the Aramaic into Hebrew, though retaining the Aramaic *sabachthani.*

John 19:20

John states that the plaque on the cross was written in Hebrew. Doesn't this affirm that Hebrew was the language of the people?

Oddly enough, not all agree that John does say the plaque was written in Hebrew. Although the Greek word is Ἑβραϊστί (*Hebraisti*), even many Greek Lexicons state that this is a generic word for the Jewish language and actually refers to Aramaic or Chaldee.[850] In fact, the NIV actually translates this as "Aramaic" while the NAS and NRSV make a footnote saying, "Jewish Aramaic" but correctly retain "Hebrew" as the proper translation.

Basically, the argument is unwinnable either way, but it is also somewhat irrelevant. As stated earlier, the Jews retained Hebrew as their religious language even though the common people continued to speak Aramaic. This is similar to Catholics who speak Latin in Church even though it is a dead language. Having said that, anyone who could speak Aramaic could almost certainly speak Hebrew. Considering how short the sentence on the plaque was, it is somewhat frivolous to even attempt to distinguish between the two languages as the only difference would be minor spelling variations in the word "Jews" and the word for "this is." Everything else would be identical. Here is a side comparison of the two as they would probably have been written. The top one is Hebrew; the bottom one is Aramaic.[851]

זהו ישוע מנצרת מלך היהודים

דנו ישוע מנצרת מלך היהודין

Any linguist will tell you that languages change over time and often absorb new words and vocabulary. Consequently, the influence of Hebrew on Aramaic, and the influence of Aramaic on Hebrew, make the differences in such a short sentence negligible. It could be perfectly acceptable to say it was written in either Hebrew or Aramaic.

Aramaic Words in the New Testament
Many people have confused Hebrew and Aramaic words. This is in part because of their influence upon one another, but also because some simply pull out a Hebrew Lexicon and assume all the words found therein are Hebrew, when, in fact, Biblical Hebrew Lexicons include words of Aramaic origin which are also found in the Bible. These words are marked in the Lexicon, but the casual student will not bother checking the preface notes to see what the various symbols (indicating Aramaic etymology) mean. Consequently, it is common to see Hebrew only advocates claiming that words like "*sabachthani*" are Hebrew (see notes above), when they are actually Aramaic. Let us examine the words of Hebrew and/or Aramaic origin found in the New Testament.

Peter was not the apostle's given name, but a nick-name given by the Lord Himself. "Jesus looked at him and said, 'You are Simon son of John, you shall be called Cephas,' which is translated 'Peter'" (John 1:42). Peter is the Greek form from *Petra* (Πετρος), but Jesus actually called him by the Aramaic word *Cephas* (כֵּיפָה), meaning "rock." The Hebrew word for rock would be *sela* (סֶלַע).[852]

The early church would end their prayers with the word, "maranatha," meaning "our Lord come!" This word is found in 1 Corinthians 16:22 at the end of Paul's epistle. It is not a Hebrew word, as some believe, but a construct from the Aramaic *marana atha* (מְרָנָא אֲתָה).[853]

In Matthew 5:22 Jesus refers to the insult, "racca." This word comes from the Aramaic *rayqa* (רֵיקָא).[854] The Hebrew word would be *rayq* (רֵיק).[855] Thus the Aramaic form appears to be the form used here.

184

In Mark 5:41 Jesus resurrected a child from the dead. He spoke to her body saying, "*talitha cumi*," meaning "young girl, rise!" Now *cumi* (κουμι) is the same in both Hebrew and Aramaic (קוּמִי), meaning "rise." However, the term for maiden, or young girl, *talitha* (ταλιθα) is a distinctly Aramaic word, *telitha* (טְלִיתָא).

Another distinctly Aramaic word is Jesus' command in Mark 7:34 wherein He performs another miracle and cures a man's hearing. Jesus looked up to heaven and said "*ephphatha*" (ἐφφαθα), meaning "be opened!" This is from an Aramaic command, referred to as the *ethpaal imperitive*, of the Aramaic. In Aramaic it is *ethphathah* (אֶתְפְּתַח).[856] While the Hebrew and Aramaic root words are the same, *patah* (פָּתַח), the imperitive in Hebrew is rendered differently from Aramaic. The Hebrew, found in modern Hebrew translations today, is *'ipathah* (אִפָּתַח). Obviously, Mark is using the Aramaic form, not the Hebrew.

In addition the name Gabbatha found in John 19:13 is from the Aramaic word *gabetha* (גַּבְּתָא) meaning a raised place or elevation.[857] The Hebrew word would be *gab* (גַּב).

Several other words believed to be of Aramaic origin are included below under "*Words of Mixed Etymology*."

Hebrew Words in the New Testament

While it is clear that there are Aramaic words in the New Testament, it is equally clear that there are Hebrew words as well. An honest debate should not neglect these words or fail to account for them.

The word Messiah is usually translated into the Greek as *Christ* (Χριστος), but there are two instances where it is transliterated into Greek from its original form as *Messias* (Μεσσιας). These are found in John 1:41 and John 4:25. This word, of course, is Hebrew and is found, among other places in the Old Testament, in Daniel 9:26 as a prophecy of Jesus, the Messiah (מָשִׁיחַ). It is distinctly Hebrew, meaning "the Anointed One."

As Jesus entered Jerusalem, the people were shouting, "Hosanna!" (Matthew 21:9, 15; Mark 11:9-10; John 12:13). This word is a compound from the Hebrew *hoshiya na* (הוֹשִׁיעָה נָּא), found in Psalms 118:25, meaning "save us, please."

In Matthew 1:23 the apostle quotes Isaiah 7:14 wherein Jesus is called Immanuel, meaning "God with us." This Hebrew word is a compound from *im* (עִם), meaning "with", *anu* (אָנוּ), meaning "us", and *El* (אֵל), which is short for Elohim (אֱלֹהִים) or "God."

The word "corban" found in Mark 7:11 is also a Hebrew word found in Leviticus, and elsewhere. It is properly written *qarban* (קָרְבָּן) meaning a "dedicated gift."

185

Another Hebrew word is *cummin*, the name of a spice still in use today in the middle east. It is found in Matthew 23:23 and comes from the Hebrew word cammon (כַּמֹּן).

Other Hebrew words also occur in the New Testament. For example, the term Sabbath is obviously a Hebrew term found in the Ten Commandments. The personal name Satan, found in 1 Chronicles 21:1, is also Hebrew. *Sikera*, referring to "strong drink" (Luke 1:15), is also a Hebrew word; not Aramaic as some claim.

Finally, some claim that the nick name "sons of Thunder" found in Mark 3:17 is Aramaic, but Thayer's Greek Lexicon says that the Greek *Boanerges* (βοηνεργες) comes from the Hebrew words *benay* (בְּנֵי) *regesh* (רֶגֶשׁ).[858] Thus, it is Hebrew rather than Aramaic, even though the Aramaic is similar.

Words of Mixed Etymology the New Testament

Some words are the same in both Hebrew and Aramaic. Other words have become a part of Hebrew, but are actually of Aramaic etymology. Still other words are very similar, making the transliterations into Greek hard to determine the origin of the word. Such words make it hard to confirm which language was being spoken, but give remarkable insight into the influence of one language upon another. Contrary to the hard liners who believe that languages are fixed, the Hebrew student realizes that Moses' language differed to some degree from that of Abraham and Abraham's from that of Malachi. Although Hebrew has shown the remarkable ability to remain more static than most languages, it has changed over the years, just as English has changed.

For example, the Hebrew word for "father" is אָב (*ab*), but the Aramaic is אַבָּא (*abba*) which is what Jesus called His heavenly Father in Mark 14:36. Now some will point out that אַבָּא (*abba*) is a term of affection used to this very day but Jews in Israel, and this is true enough, but it is only a half truth for the word is still of Aramaic origin and it is used primarily of children. It is translated in modern Hebrew as "daddy"[859] or "pappa",[860] terms which no Orthodox Jew would use to refer to the sovereign God Almighty.[861]

The word *mammon* (μαμων) is found in both Matthew 6:24 and Luke 16:13. Some Bibles actually translate this directly as "riches" or "money." According to Thayer's Lexicon, it is transliterated into Greek from Aramaic word is *mammona* (מָאמוֹנָא).[862] The modern Hebrew equivalent is *mamon* (מָמוֹן) but that word is not found in the Old Testament. The Old Testament instead uses the Hebrew word *asher* (עֹשֶׁר). Thus is appears that the modern Hebrew word is actually one of Aramaic etymology which was not in popular use until after the exilic period. The form found in Matthew conforms to the Hebrew, but the word itself is of Aramaic origin.

Another example is Rabbi and Rabboni. The term Rabbi is a Hebrew term of respect for a teacher and is found many times in the Bible, but Rabboni is the Aramaic form found in Mark 10:51 and John 20:16. "Rabbi" is often found in both Hebrew and Aramaic writings, but "Rabboni" is distinctly Aramaic, and yet it is used by the same authors who elsewhere use "Rabbi." This is another example of mixed use where one or both of the languages used common terms.

Yet another word of mixed origin in the New Testament is the word of Passover. In Hebrew it is *pesach* (פֶּסַח). In Aramaic it is *pischa* (פִּסְחָא). The Greek uses the transliteration *pascha* (πασχα). Thus it is appears that the apostles used the Aramaic form rather than the Hebrew form of the word, but this cannot be certain since it would be extraordinary for a Greek word to end in a *ch* (χ).

This same issue is apparent in several names which advocates claim are Aramaic, but in reality the difference between the Hebrew and Aramaic words is solely the aleph (א) or "a" at the end of the word. Since Greek names only end in a select few letters, the use of an alpha at the end of the words does not necessarily prove Aramaic origin, although this is possible. These names include Gethsemane, Golgotha, Tabitha, Akeldama, and Bethseda.

Other words are the exact same in both Hebrew and Aramaic, such as *amen* (αμην / אָמֵן), which is usually translated as "truly," and from which we end our prayers.

Summary

If we exclude the personal names, the New Testament contains approximately twenty words of Hebrew or Aramaic origin. Here is a breakdown of the words.

Hebrew	Aramaic	Both	Probably Aramaic
Immanuel	Sabachthani	Rabbi	Abba
Messiah	Ephphatha	Cumi	Mammon
Sikera	Rabboni	Amen	Pascha
Hosanna	Racca		
Cummin	Talitha		
Corban	Cephas		
Sabbath	Maranatha		
Satan			

We can see that out of the twenty-one words, eight are Hebrew, seven or Aramaic, three words are used in both Hebrew and Aramaic, while three more words are most likely of Aramaic origin. In short, roughly half of the words are Hebrew and the other half Aramaic. Now some might argue that this is a case of one of the gopsel writers translating the Hebrew into Aramaic, but cannot be true for if we examine these words as they are broken down into the different gospels we will find another curiosity.

	Matthew	Mark	Luke	John
Hebrew	5	4	3	4
Aramaic	4 (2)	6 (2)	2 (2)	3 (1)
Common to Both	1	2		1

* Numbers in brackets are *additional* "probable Aramaic" words.

So we can see that even within the gospels, the use of Hebrew and Aramaic words is roughly divided 50-50%. Even Matthew, whom most believe wrote his gospel in Hebrew, retains a number of Aramaic words. Each author seems split between the use of Hebrew and Aramaic. Why? The answer should be obvious. Hebrew and Aramaic are sister languages whose influence upon one another is felt to this day. Because the sacred Scriptures were predominantly written in Hebrew (several chapters are actually written in Aramaic), the Jews were careful to retain the purity of the Hebrew language, but the common people, as they do today, adopted changes and influences from their surrounding culture. *Both* languages were spoken, and Jesus could most certainly speak both.

Conclusion
There are those who claim that the entire New Testament was written in Hebrew and that Jesus spoke Hebrew, and Hebrew alone. Alternately, there are those who insist that Jesus spoke Aramaic and Aramaic alone, believing Matthew was originally written in Aramaic (the rest of the New Testament in Greek). As we have seen, *both* are completely wrong.

Jesus could most certainly speak both Hebrew and Aramaic. There is also little doubt that He, and the disciples, were also well versed in Greek. It would not be surprising if some of them could even speak Latin. Too many Americans in particular assume that one must be highly educated to speak foreign languages, but that is because we are spoiled in America and, frankly, a little lazy. Anyone who has traveled to the poor countries of the world knows that there are those who can neither read nor write, but can speak multiple languages. Considering the similarities between Hebrew and Aramaic, there is little doubt that all the apostles, as well as Jesus, were fluent in both, and doubtless mixed languages in their speech as part of the common tongue.

To get a firm graspe on this, I ask the reader to think about the fact that J.R.R. Tolkien first gained fame by translating *Sir Gawain and the Green Knight* from Old English into Modern English. Even the Middle English of Wycliffe's famous Bible translation is hard for many to comprehend. Let us look at a randomly selected passage:

> "Treuli, treuli, Y seie to thee, whanne thou were yongere, thou girdidist thee, and wandridist where thou woldist; but whanne thou schalt waxe eldere, thou schalt holde forth thin hondis, and another schal girde thee, and schal lede thee whidur thou wolt not." (Wycliff).

188

"What I'm about to tell you is true. When you were younger, you dressed yourself. You went wherever you wanted to go. But when you are old, you will stretch out your hands. Someone else will dress you. Someone else will lead you where you do not want to go" (NIRV).

The debate about Hebrew and Aramaic is misplaced. Hebrew remained the language of the Bible and the Synagogues, but Aramaic was the common language of the people. Even those who spoke in Hebrew mixed their vocabulary with the sister language of Aramaic. This is hardly surprising since Aramaic is an offshoot of the original language of Abraham; Hebrew.

The Centurion
Matthew 27:54 – Mark 15:39 – Luke 23:47

"Now the centurion, and those who were with him keeping guard over Jesus, when they saw the earthquake and the things that were happening, became very frightened and said, 'Truly this was the Son of God.'"

There is no contradiction in the accounts. The controversy is far greater than that. The question is whether or not the Roman Centurion was affirming the diety of Jesus Christ or echoing his pagan heritage, for the Greek does not contain the definite article "the." As a result, a certain religion has translated this passage as "Truly this was a son of God." Of course, the Greek does not contain the indefinite article "a" either! So what does it mean and was the Centurion professing true faith in Christ or merely stating a fact?

The Greek reads literally, "this man was son of God." It has neither the definite nor indefinite article. There is no "the son," nor is there "a son." Now since Greek does not have an indefinite article, it has been argued that the absence of the definite article is proof that indefinite is intended. Thus "a god" would reflect the sentiments of a pagan Roman. Nevertheless, as convincing as this may sound there are several reasons to reject this.

In terms of the Greek grammar itself, the absence of the definite article does not mean an indefinite is intended. For one thing, proper names do not carry the article.[863] "Θεου υιος is like a proper name ... hence, has no article."[864] Furthermore, in Greek the definite article is not necessary in many instances, even as we do not specify "the" for every noun in a sentence. Once it has been established that we are talking about "the" subject, the article is no longer needed. As Leon Morris explains, "with Θεου υιος we have another example of the anarthrous predicate preceding the verb : it denotes 'the' Son, not 'a' son."[865]

Logically, there is another reason to reject the translation of "a son." If we are to take this as "a son" to reflect a pagan notion, then should not "God" be

189

plural rather than singular? If this were truly the reflection of a pagan thought, then it should be "a son of *the gods*." It is not. The word for God is singular.

The final reason to accept this as "the Son of God" is the testimony of Luke. Although Luke does not quote this statement, he does quote part of the Centurion's remarks, saying, "when the centurion saw what had happened, he *began* praising God, saying, 'Certainly this man was innocent'" (Luke 23:47). Now why would a pagan be "praising God"? Clearly if the Roman Centurion was praising God then He was acknowledging God Almighty! Once again, the word for God is in the singular, not the pagan plural.

This is the view of evangelicals throughout the ages, because it is the proper translation. From Erasmus[866] to Calvin[867] and even Origen[868] all agree that this is a declaration of faith. Some, like MacArthur, have even gone so far as to say that "he spoke for his men as well"[869] but this is inference at best. There is no indication of what the others thought, but the Centurion himself is clear.

Is this the same Centurion who is recorded in Acts 10? We cannot say, for this Centurion is not mentioned by name. All that we can say is that Luke himself said, "When the centurion saw what had happened, he *began* praising God!" This statement alone should is proof that he was acknowledging that Jesus was *the* Son of God.

Matthew 27:63 – See "When Was Jesus Crucified?"

Roman or Jewish Guards?
Matthew 27:65-66 (28:11-15)

"Pilate said to them, 'You have a guard; go, make it *as* secure as you know how.' And they went and made the grave secure, and along with the guard they set a seal on the stone ... some of the guard came into the city and reported to the chief priests all that had happened."

The first question might be, "why is this relevant?" Aside from the false accusations of anti-semitism, there is relevance as it relates to the historical evidences of the resurrection (see Appendix B - "The Resurrection"). The question of whether or not these were Jews or Romans is not so easily answered. There is evidence to support both sides, and both have merit.

Those who argue that the guards were Jewish make four points. Those who argue that the guards were Roman also make four points. All eight points seem equally strong. The evidence for and against each are so evenly spread that it is hard to decide between the two without bias. Nevertheless, I will endeavor to do just that. The relevance of the answer is prevalent primarily in debates about the resurrection, but since I discuss this in the Appendix B I will not debate it here. Suffice to say that I believe that whether the guards were Jewish or Roman, the evidence strongly supports the resurrection account.

Roman Guards	Jewish Guards
The majority text uses the "imperitive of command" (ασφαλισασθε) implying the soldiers were his to command.	Some modern translations follow good ancient text which uses the middle aorist tense (ασφαλισασθαι) implying the soldiers were the priests' to command.
There was a seal upon the door. A Roman seal would be expected to be guarded by Romans.	The guards reported to the priests, not to Pilate.
The guards were bribed and promised protection from Pilate. Why, unless they were Pilate's guards?	The priests said "*if* this should come to the governor's ears" but if they were Romans guarding a Roman seal, how could it *not* come to his ear?
The Greek word for guard is κουστωδια (*koustodia*) used primarily of Roman soldiers.	Pilate was not likely to acquiesce to Caiaphas twice.

In we are honest with ourselves, then it would seem that the evidence is pretty evenly balanced. An examination of these evidences may help shift the weight to one side or another.

The Greek Text
There are three words in these passages which can be used to support opposing positions. The first is the verb "you have" (εχετε). The second is the word "guard" (κουστωδια). The third is the verb "make secure" (ασφαλισασθε).

Εχετε
According to D.A. Carson the word εχετε (*exete*) "could be imperative ('Take a guard,' NIV), but it is more likely indicative ('You have a guard of soldiers,' RSV; cf. KJV)."[870] Josh McDowell believes that it is affirmatively the imperitive command,[871] but the problem is that on rare occasions Greek uses the same form for different tenses. Consequntly, both the imperative and the indicative use the ετε (*ete*) ending. As a result we cannot tell whether or not Pilate was saying "take a guard" as in the NIV, NLT, and Tyndale translations, or whether Pilate saying "you have guards" as in all other translations. If the later, then Pilate may have been flippantly saying "you already have guards. Your own!" Given the strained history of Pilate and Caiaphas, and the sarcastic (but prophetic) use of "King of the Jews" by Pilate on Jesus' plaque (John 19:19-22) it does not seem that Pilate would have been so eager to placate Caiaphas a second time. Interestingly enough, the modern Hebrew translation renders this as indicative ("there is to you" - לָכֶם), not imperative.[872]

Κουστωδια
Perhaps the strongest argument for Roman soldiers is the use of the word κουστωδια (*koustodia*), from whence we get "custodian," for "guard." This word, it is said, applies to Roman guards.[873] However, this is unclear for of the two words used for guards in the New Testament, φυλακας (*phulakas*) being the other, both are used of Romans for the primary reason that the Jewish temple

police are only mentioned specifically a few times. In those cases it refers to the "captain of the temple" (cf. Acts 4:1; 5:24) who was the head of the temple guards. Consequently, it seems a stretch to argue that κουστωδια (*koustodia*) can only be used of Romans. Terms such as Centurian or Decturian are explicitly Roman, but a κουστωδια (*koustodia*) and a φυλακας (*phulakas*) are both guards. The only difference is that κουστωδια (*koustodia*) is of Latin origin, and hence seems to be favored by the Romans, whereas φυλακας (*phulakas*) is Greek. The use of Latin etymology therefore supports the Roman guard argument, but not conclusively.

Ασφαλισασθε

The last word of relevance is the word for "make it secure." The majority text, along with a good number of ancient manuscripts reads ασφαλισασθε (*asphalisasthe*) which is an "imperitive of command."[874] Although not conclusive by any means, it might imply that the guards were his to command; "Go and secure the tomb!" However, many of the best ancient manuscripts actually read ασφαλισασθαι (*aphalisasthai*) which is middle aorist infinitive. This would loosely be translated as "go and secure it for yourself." The middle voice implies that it is done for "one's self"[875] and hence Pilate wanted no part of it. The manuscripts which support this include the *Sinaiticus*, *Ephraimi*, *Bezae* and *Washingtonius*, all famous ancient manuscripts, especially the *Sinaiticus*.

What does all this mean? Frankly, by itself it is inconclusive. When we consider that the book of Matthew was originally written in Hebrew (see "An Eyewitness Account? The Authorship and Date of Matthew") the Greek words may not be as helpful as we wish, although I have elsewhere concluded that Matthew translated *his own* work, and hence chose these very Greek words. It is probably, however, that Pilate was not being particularly compliant and his words may reflect a sarcasm regardless of whether the guards were Roman or Jewish.

The Bribe

After the resurrection of Jesus, the guards, whether they be Roman or Jewish, were terrorized by what they saw (Matthew 28:4). They fled to city and "reported to the chief priests all that had happened." Those who believe that these were Jewish guards argue that the fact that they reporting to the priests rather than Pilate proves they were Jewish, but those who hold that they were Romans respond:

> "They came to the high priest because he had influence with the Roman authority and because it was the only possible way to save their necks. The high priest had tried to bribe them (which would have been a mockery if they had been Temple police). He gave them money and

told them what to tell the people. When the news reached Pilate, he said he (the high priest) would keep them from being killed."[876]

Now while I have the greatest respect for John McDowell, this argument if flawed on several levels. First, Caiaphas and Pilate were enemies, not friends. The trial proves this. It was a classic political tête-à-tête between two people who hated each other. To expect that Caiaphas would have the political pull to get Roman soldiers out of trouble with Pilate seems far fetched. Second, McDowell says that "would have been a mockery if they had been Temple police"[877] which is true, but this implies that it would not be a mockery to bribe Romans? Of course it would. Bribery is a mockery and the high priest was mocking the laws of Israel when he chose to bribe men in order to hide the truth. Corruption was not new to the priesthood anymore than it was new to Roman government.

The only support this passage lends to those who believe the guards were Roman is the fact that they were promised protection from Pilate. This obviously indicates that Pilate was involved in some way. However, the statement of the high priest, "if this should come to the governor's ears" (Matthew 28:14), indicates that there could be a possibility that Pilate would never hear about it at all! *"If"*? The only way that Pilate might not hear of the incident (considering that a Roman seal was broken - see notes below) is if the guards were Jewish and the disciples said nothing (which they obviously did).

Finally, the story which the priests told the guards to spread is that the "disciples came by night and stole Him away while [the guards] were asleep." This too implies Jewish soldiers for, as Frank Morison commented, "the penalty for sleeping at the post of duty was death, and neither Annas nor Caiaphas, nor any other member of the Jewish camarilla had the power to protect a single Roman soldier from the wrath of Rome."[878] Hence the story could only have been circulated if the soldiers were Temple guards under the authority of the high priest.

In short, if the guards were Romans it is not likely that the enemy of Pilate would be able to provide much protection. If, on the other hand, the guards were Jewish, then the high priest could play the game of politics. "Why didn't you use Roman guards? Does Caesar know? We are just poor helpless subjects of the great Roman empire." How could Pilate answer such questions? Would he try to execute Temple police over the matter? Probably not, but if Roman guards failed to protect a Roman seal, they would be subject to immediate execution,[879] particularly if their story was that a bunch of peasant disciples broke into a sealed tomb, blocked by a two ton stone (see Appendix B), and stole the body out from the noses of the empire's own soliders!

The question of the bribery by the high priest strongly favors the Jewish guard theory, but it too is inconclusive. If the Greek word κουστωδια (*koustodia*) favors Roman guards then this passage favors Jewish guards. The evidence seems well balanced at this stage.

The Seal

The appearance of a seal on the tomb entrance (27:66) is often considered among the strongest evidence that the soldiers were Roman. Since Rome was occupying Israel, it seems natural that the seal used would have been Roman. If this is so then we would be hard pressed to believe that Pilate left Jewish soldiers to guard a *Roman* seal. This evidence appears to be the strongest in favor of Roman soldiers. Let us examine it briefly.

While Israel did have it own seal these official seals could only be used by King Herod, with the possible exception of high priests on Temple property. To place a seal on a tomb would normally require the authority of either Herod or Pilate. Herod, of course, had no interest in the debacle (Luke 23:7-15) and was not involved after he released Jesus. Pilate, on the other hand, was consulted by the high priests. He gave them his permisssion to "make [the tomb] as secure as you know how" (27:65). This would have included the official seal of Rome. Although it is possible that a Temple seal was used, the most logical assumption is that Pilate granted the seal when he gave permission to the priests to guard the tomb.

Now if the official seal of Rome was placed on the tomb it would be improbable that Pilate would place Jewish guards at the site, rather than Roman soldiers. Still, because of the animosity between Caiaphas and Pilate we cannot rule this out, but it does not seem highly likely. Consequently, the appearance of an official seal at the tomb seems to support Roman soldiers.

Conclusion

The Greek words seem to *slightly* favor Roman guards primarily on the weight of the Latin etymology for "guard." On the other hand the guards' bribe at the hands of the priests seems to strongly favor the use of Jewish guards, but is again inconclusive. The evidence from the use of a seal favors Roman soldiers, but with reservations.

In brief review, the Greek language does not truly give us an indication of the ethnicity of the soldiers, with the possible exception of the word κουστωδια (*koustodia*). This word, meaning "guard," is of Latin origin and hence some believe that it would naturally refer to Roman soldiers. Nevertheless, only terms like Praetorian or Centurian should truly be restricted to Roman soldiers. A "guard" is a "guard"; nothing else.

The bribe attempt and the discussion it involves implies not only that the guards were under the priests authority but more so that Pilate might not become aware of what happened. Such a thing would be unthinkable unless the guards were Jewish.

Finally, the use of a seal at the tomb required government approval. That was given by Pilate, which implies the use of a Roman seal. It seems extremely unlikely that Pilate would have placed a Roman seal at the tomb without Roman soldiers to guard it.

My ultimate conclusion is this : If Matthew cared whether or not the soldiers were Jews or gentiles, he would have said so. He didn't care. He had no interest in twenty-first century politics or concerns over alleged anti-semitism. After all, Matthew *was* a Jew, and once more, he was writing *to* Jews. He wished only to convict his own people of their sins and call them to repentance even as the prophets of the Old Testament did. It is for that very reason that he wanted to highlight the false "rumors" spread by the priesthood and to affirm that Jesus had in fact been raised from the dead.

The Resurrection Accounts
Matthew 28:1-8 – Mark 16:1-10 – Luke 24:1-24 – John 20:1-29

"Now after the Sabbath, as it began to dawn toward the first *day* of the week, Mary Magdalene and the other Mary came to look at the grave ... the angel said to the women, 'Do not be afraid; for I know that you are looking for Jesus who has been crucified. He is not here, for He has risen.'"

"When the Sabbath was over, Mary Magdalene, and Mary the *mother* of James, and Salome, bought spices, so that they might come and anoint Him. Very early on the first day of the week, they came to the tomb ... he said to them, 'you are looking for Jesus the Nazarene, who has been crucified. He has risen; He is not here.'"

"But on the first day of the week ... they found the stone rolled away from the tomb, but when they entered, they did not find the body of the Lord Jesus ... *the men* said to them, 'Why do you seek the living One among the dead? He is not here, but He has risen.'"

"Now on the first *day* of the week Mary Magdalene came early to the tomb, while it was still dark, and saw the stone *already* taken away from the tomb ... she stooped and looked into the tomb; and she saw two angels ... where the body of Jesus had been lying."

When I was in my twenties, I studied criminal justice at Collin College. I had wanted to become a police officer. This is one reason for my affection of Biblical apologist Sir Robert Anderson, the former chief inspector of Scotland Yard. He took the same deductive approach to Biblical criticism as he took to crime scene investigation. The Bible critics, however, behave not as police investigators but as criminal defense attorneys, trying to create contradictions and confusions where there are none. Nowhere is this more obvious perhaps than in the accounts of the resurrection.

Four differening accounts are given by the gospel authors. They reflect different eyewitness accounts, but as I have shown elsewhere, differing does not mean contradictory. Each author recounts specific selective events which, when put together, create a full and complete picture of the events. Let us break down the issues and examine them individually.

A Complete Timeline of Events
The chronology of the events surrounding the Resurrection are the most confusing. This is not surprising as any investigative detective will tell you. When investigating a crime scene and talking to eyewitnesses, the first thing the detective must do is put together a timeline of what happened. Without a proper timeline, the case falls apart. This is why O.J. Simpson got away with murder. The police did a bad job and the prosecution covered for their police by creating a different timeline than was originally presented. In essence, the prosecution gave O.J. Simpson his alibi by creating an inaccurate timeline![880] Here also, the Bible critic attempts to create a false timeline, thereby convicting the Bible of contradictions.

I have found that the best approach to deal with many of the alleged contradictions and problems is to first present my timeline and let the reader see if the facts fit the conclusions. After showing my timeline, I will then address specific questions and accusations about inconsistencies in the timeline and/or accounts. Remembering that a good detective must take all eyewitnesses into account *before* assuming one or more of them is wrong and/or lying, I have taken the Bible verses exactly as written, and arranged them together chronologically as follows:

Sequence Series	Biblical Passages
1 Prelude	And behold, a severe earthquake had occurred, for an angel of the Lord descended from heaven and came and rolled away the stone and sat upon it. And his appearance was like lightning, and his clothing as white as snow. The guards shook for fear of him and became like dead men. (Matthew 28:2-4)
2 Initial approach	Now after the Sabbath, as it began to dawn toward the first *day* of the week, Mary Magdalene and the other Mary came to look at the grave (Matthew 28:1). When the Sabbath was over, Mary Magdalene, and Mary the *mother* of James, and Salome, bought spices, so that they might come and anoint Him. Very early on the first day of the week, they came to the tomb when the sun had risen. They were saying to one another, "Who will roll away the stone for us from the entrance of the tomb?" Looking up, they saw that the stone had been rolled away, although it was extremely large (Mark 16:1-4). But on the first day of the week, at early dawn, they came to the tomb bringing the spices which they had prepared. And they found the stone rolled away from the tomb, but when they entered, they did not find the body of the Lord Jesus (Luke 24:1-3). Now on the first *day* of the week Mary Magdalene came early to the tomb, while it was still dark, and saw the stone *already* taken away from the tomb (John 20:1).
3 Mary Magdalene goes for help	So she ran and came to Simon Peter and to the other disciple whom Jesus loved, and said to them, "They have taken away the Lord out of the tomb, and we do not know where they have laid Him." So Peter and the other disciple went forth, and they were going to the tomb (John 20:2-3). But Peter got up and ran to the tomb (Luke 24:12a).

4 The angels in the tomb	While they were perplexed about this, behold, two men suddenly stood near them in dazzling clothing (Luke 24:4). Entering the tomb, they saw a young man sitting at the right, wearing a white robe; and they were amazed (Mark 16:5).
5 The angels speak to the remaining women	The angel said to the women, "Do not be afraid; for I know that you are looking for Jesus who has been crucified. "He is not here, for He has risen, just as He said. Come, see the place where He was lying. "Go quickly and tell His disciples that He has risen from the dead; and behold, He is going ahead of you into Galilee, there you will see Him; behold, I have told you." And they left the tomb quickly with fear and great joy and ran to report it to His disciples (Matthew 28:5-8). And as *the women* were terrified and bowed their faces to the ground, *the men* said to them, "Why do you seek the living One among the dead? "He is not here, but He has risen. Remember how He spoke to you while He was still in Galilee, that the Son of Man must be delivered into the hands of sinful men, and be crucified, and the third day rise again" (Luke 24:5-7). And he said to them, "Do not be amazed; you are looking for Jesus the Nazarene, who has been crucified. He has risen; He is not here; behold, *here is* the place where they laid Him. "But go, tell His disciples and Peter, 'He is going ahead of you to Galilee; there you will see Him, just as He told you.'" They went out and fled from the tomb, for trembling and astonishment had gripped them; and they said nothing to anyone, for they were afraid (Mark 16:6-8).
6 The other women inform the apostles	And they remembered His words, and returned from the tomb and reported all these things to the eleven and to all the rest. Now they were Mary Magdalene and Joanna and Mary the *mother* of James; also the other women with them were telling these things to the apostles. But these words appeared to them as nonsense, and they would not believe them (Luke 24:8-11).
7 Peter and John appear at the tomb with Mary Magdalene	The two were running together; and the other disciple ran ahead faster than Peter and came to the tomb first; and stooping and looking in, he saw the linen wrappings lying *there;* but he did not go in. And so Simon Peter also came, following him, and entered the tomb; and he saw the linen wrappings lying *there,* and the face-cloth which had been on His head, not lying with the linen wrappings, but rolled up in a place by itself. So the other disciple who had first come to the tomb then also entered, and he saw and believed. For as yet they did not understand the Scripture, that He must rise again from the dead. So the disciples went away again to their own homes (John 20:4-10). But Peter got up and ran to the tomb; stooping and looking in, he saw the linen wrappings only; and he went away to his home, marveling at what had happened (Luke 24:12).
8 Mary Magdalene at the tomb alone	Now after He had risen early on the first day of the week, He first appeared to Mary Magdalene, from whom He had cast out seven demons (Mark 16:9). But Mary was standing outside the tomb weeping; and so, as she wept, she stooped and looked into the tomb; and she saw two angels in white sitting, one at the head and one at the feet, where the body of Jesus had been lying. And they said to her, "Woman, why are you weeping?" She said to them, "Because they have taken away my Lord, and I do not know where they have laid Him." When she had said this, she turned around and saw Jesus standing *there,* and did not know that it was Jesus. Jesus said to her, "Woman, why are you weeping? Whom are you seeking?" Supposing Him to be the gardener, she said to Him, "Sir, if you have carried Him away, tell me where you have laid Him, and I will take Him away." Jesus said to her, "Mary!" She turned and said to Him in Hebrew, "Rabboni!" (which means, Teacher). Jesus said to her, "Stop clinging to Me, for I have not yet ascended to the Father; but go to My brethren

| | and say to them, 'I ascend to My Father and your Father, and My God and your God.'" Mary Magdalene came, announcing to the disciples, "I have seen the Lord," and *that* He had said these things to her (John 20:11-18). |

Now the reader will see that I have broken the gospel accounts into a series of eight different time sequences. This is the timeline of the events at the tomb. In order to answer questions about alleged inconsistencies within this timeline, I will address each sequence separately. This allows us to better look at each issue individually without confusing the events.

Time Sequence #1 - Did the Women Witness the Stone Being Rolled Away?
Mark, Luke, and John all make clear that the stone had already been rolled away when the women arrived at the tomb. However, some see a problem with Matthew's remarks on the subject, for he says, "Mary Magdalene and the other Mary came to look at the grave. And behold, a severe earthquake had occurred, for an angel of the Lord descended from heaven and came and rolled away the stone and sat upon it. And his appearance was like lightning, and his clothing as white as snow. The guards shook for fear of him and became like dead men" (Matthew 28:1-4). This, it is argued, implies that the women witnessed the earthquake and removal of the stone as well as the angel sitting upon the stone.

First, let it be said that I do not blame English translations, for context should be sufficient to prove that the remarks about the earthquake constitute a separate clause describing *why* the tomb was already empty by the time the women had arrived. Nonetheless, it is abundantly clear from the Greek text, that the earthquake was a past event, before the women had arrived. The clause should be distinguished from the appearance of the Marys and seen as an explanation of what had transpired earlier that night. This was no mere "symbolic dramatization" of an earthquake[881] but an actual event which struck fear into the soldiers who had fled the tomb and were nowhere to be found when the Marys arrived.

Perhaps the English translations would be more clear if they had used parentheses to separate the clause. A better translation might be, "Mary Magdalene and the other Mary came to look at the grave. And behold, a severe earthquake had taken place (for an angel of the Lord had descended from heaven and came and rolled away the stone and had sat upon it. And his appearance was like lightning, and his clothing as white as snow. The guards had shook for fear of him and became like dead men)." All this took place early that night after the Sabbath, by local reckoning, had expired.

Time Sequence #2 - What Time Was It and Who Went to the Tomb?
I have already addressed the chronology of the new day to some extent under "When Was Jesus Crucified." Nevertheless, some still see a conflict between the various accounts as to whether or not "it was still dark" as John 20:1 states or whether or not "the sun had risen" as Mark 16:2 says. Logically, all four

accounts affirm that it was on early Sunday morning around dawn. Albert Barnes believes that "the word *dawn* is of necessity in the original. The words there properly means, as the first day *approached.*"[882] John Wesley believed that "they had set out while it was yet dark ... but by the time Mary had called Peter and John, and they had viewed the sepulchre, the sun was rising."[883] This is common sense. It is always darkest before the dawn, so the saying goes. The events described in the gospels took place over at least an hour or more in time. The question is not one of contradiction, but specific chronology.

There are some scholars, like John Darby, who believe that the women originally went to the tomb to apply spices Saturday evening after the Sabbath was over by Sadducee time, and later returned the next morning to apply more spices.[884] Thus John Calvin argued that "Mark [is] referring two different things to one context."[885] Robert Gundry concludes that "Matthew obliterates this temporal shift"[886] and that the first approach to the tomb was "Saturday evening."[887] Others reject this, saying "he is not speaking of the time immediately after the Sabbath, for that would commence at sunset."[888]

In all honesty, such speculation is not necessary. When we piece together the various accounts, it does appear that they made more than one trip to tomb, for Mary went to retrieve Peter and John and returned with them later, but the initial approach to the tomb was just before sunrise. Since they started out walking when "it was still dark" (John 20:1) it is only logical that after they had arrived "the sun had risen" (Mark 16:2). This is consistent with Matthew's assersion that it was as "it began to dawn toward the first day of the week" (28:1). So also Luke affirms that it was "at early dawn" (Luke 24:1). Here there is no logical contradiction. The initial events at the tomb described in all four gospels took place sometime between 5:30 and 6:30 AM on April 5, Sunday morning, 33 A.D.

Another question often asked, is "who went to the tomb?" In John's account he mentions only "Mary Magdalene" (John 20:1) as coming to the tomb. Matthew says that "Mary Magdalene and the other Mary came to look at the grave" (Matthew 28:1). Mark states that "Mary Magdalene, and Mary the *mother* of James, and Salome, bought spices" to the tomb (Mark 16:1). Luke gives an even fuller account, apparently identifying "Mary Magdalene and Joanna and Mary the mother of James; also the other women with them" (Luke 24:10). Now it is not surprising that atheistic and radical Islamic websites have called this a hopeless contradiction, but we must remember the basic rule of logic in eyewitness accounts; they are not exhaustive accounts. Unless John said *only* Mary Magdalene had went to the tomb there is no contradiction to other eyewitnesses who provide a more complete list. As John MacArthur states, although Salome and Joanna were there "Matthew focuses only on the two Marys."[889] John focuses on Mary Magdalene. By looking at all the accounts, we can get a more complete picture.

Once again, we have a part of the picture presented by each gospel, written for the purpose of telling the story about the risen Savior. Luke is the only gospel author who wrote as a historian, so it is not surprising that his account gives a fuller list of those women who were at the tomb.

Time Sequence #3 - Mary Magdalene Goes for Help
This event is omitted by all but John who devotes most of the chapter to her and Jesus' appearance to her. This is not surprising since Mark affirms that Jesus "first appeared to Mary Magdalene" (Mark 16:9).

This event (Mary's seeking help from the apostles before the angels appeared to the other women) helps explain much of the confusion by those who erroneously group Mary Magdalene with the other women who remained behind at the tomb while she went to fetch help. The only question which this does not answer is why Luke 24:12 implies that all the women had informed the apostles rather than just Mary.

This is explained in much the same way as the other "conflicts." Luke is not giving a specific timeline at this point. He tells us that the women went and told the apostles what had happened, and then, as an aside (much like the description of the earthquake in Matthew 28:2), he tells us that Peter had gone to the tomb. In fact, Peter had probably left with John before the other nine apostles even heard what had happened. If this is true then Luke's statement, "now they were Mary Magdalene and Joanna and Mary the *mother* of James; also the other women with them were telling these things to the apostles" is a summary statement of how the apostles had first come to know of these events, and should not be taken as chronological. This is apparent by the use of δε (*de*), translated "now," rather than the usual conjunction και (*kai*). According to Richard Young's *Intermediate New Testament Greek* textbook this conjunction can be used to "shift to parenthetical material."[890] This is almost certainly the case here. As with Matthew 28:2 (see above) this is a parenthetical remark which does not attempt to connect the events into a timeline. It is simply a summary statement that all these women, at one time or another, relayed the information to the apostles and this is how they came to know of the empty tomb.

Time Sequence #4 - What the Women Saw. Angels or Men at the Tomb?
Several questions have been asked in regard to what the women actually saw at the tomb. Some ponder: 1) was the angel sitting on the stone (Matthew 28:2) or in the tomb (Mark 16:5; Luke 24:4; John 20:12)? 2) did the women see the angels in the tomb immediately (Matthew 28:5; Mark 16:5) or later (Luke 24:4)? 3) was there one (Mark 16:5; Matthew 28:5) or two angels (Luke 24:4; John 20:12)? 4) were they angels (Matthew 28:5; John 20:12) or men (Mark 16:5; Luke 24:4)?

The first question has already been answered; the angel on the stone was a parenthetical remark, referring back to the earthquake and the fear of the soldiers. It is not, therefore, necessary to explain how one person walked from here to there. So Matthew has skipped ahead to when the angel spoke to the women, but does not bother to explain that the angel had moved from the stone to the interior of the tomb for explaining such needless things would make the story both cumbersome and boring.

The second question is also easy to answer. Matthew and Mark do not provide an exhaustive chronology and saw no need of explaining that the angels were not visible immediately upon entering the tomb. Luke, however, makes this clear when he states, "while they were perplexed about this, behold, two men *suddenly* stood near them" (Luke 24:4). Note the word "suddenly." This indicates that the women did not initially see the angels. Matthew and Mark abbreviate the chronology, but in no way contradict this account. It is most likely that after the women had entered the tomb and saw it was empty Mary Magdalene then ran for help. At that time the angels "suddenly" appeared to the other women.

The third question once again touches upon the issue of exhaustive accounts versus abbreviated ones. The fact that only one angel is mentioned does not preclude the fact that a second may also be present. Only if Mark had said that there was *only* one could be assume there to be a contradiction. Nevertheless, John Wesley takes a different approach, arguing that "only one of them had appeared sitting on the stone without the sepulchre, and then going into it, was seen with another angel, sitting, one where the head, the other where the feet of the body had lain."[891] Thus he believes the second angel had still been on the stone and moved into the tomb to join the second. This is also a plausible explanation.

The final question is more of a technical one, for angels almost always appear in the form of men. Ever since Abraham entertained three men, one of whom the Bible identified as "the Lord" (Genesis 18:1-2) angels have appeared to men in human form. Hebrews even declares that "some have entertained angels without knowing it" (13:2). Consequently, these were angels who appeared in the form of men. Both are therefore correct.

Time Sequence #5 - The Angels' Speak - Did the Women Obey?
One interesting criticism leveled by Bible critics and asked by curious believers is the apparent contradiction between Mark's statement that the women "fled from the tomb, for trembling and astonishment had gripped them; and they said nothing to anyone, for they were afraid" (Mark 16:6-8) and the other gospels which make clear that they did tell the apostles and "all the rest" of Jesus' associates (Luke 24:9).

This is indeed a fair question, but not a particularly troublesome one. We must remember that Mary Magdalene was not a part of the group that fled from the tomb. She had already gone to retreive Peter and John and arrived later. It is most likely that the women were indeed afraid and did not tell anyone for some time.   They were frightened but soon came to their senses, remembering that the angels had themselves told the women to "report these things to the eleven" (Luke 24:9). In terms of my timeline, it is probable that the women met up with Mary Magdalene after she had seen the risen Christ, and it was then that they went together to inform the rest of the apostles as implied in Luke 24:12.

Still, there is another scenario presented by some. According to one theory the women had come separately. Thus, by this theory there were actually at least two different groups of women who appeared at the tomb. It would, therefore, be no contradiction to say that one group fled the tomb and *did not* tell anyone while another group did.[892] Support for this is largely inference, but interesting inference. Joanna, mentioned in Luke 24:10, was the wife of Herod's household manager (Luke 8:3) and as such would not have wanted Herod to know what had happened. The problem is that Joanna was among those who told the disciples (Luke 24:10). She was also a known follower of Christ, so it is likely that Herod already knew of her association with Jesus. Herod's encounter with Jesus was one of curiousity rather than animosity (Luke 23:8).

My original thesis is obviously the one I prefer and makes more sense contextually. The women were scared initially and did not tell anyone, but later (perhaps after meeting up with Mary Magdalene) they recovered their strength and went to tell the apostles, even as the angels had instructed them to do.

Time Sequence #6 - The Apostles Informed
This has already been addressed to some extent in the sequence above, but to summarize here, all gospels agree that the apostles were informed by the women. John adds that it was Mary Magdalene had informed Peter and John who then went to the tomb. The other women went to inform the remaining apostles who did not believe them. The statement of Luke 24:12 is parenthetical only, for Peter and John were most likely at the tomb with Mary Magdalene when the other women reported the events to the remaining disciples.

Time Sequence #7 - Peter and John at the Tomb
The apostles looked inside the tomb while Mary waited outside. There is no controversy here except perhaps some as to the identity of the unnamed apostle. I have already identified him as John, but in fact he is never called by name and neglected in Luke's account. Why? How do we know this is truly John?

Throughout the gospel of John, he refers to himself in the third person and never actually calls himself by name. In fact, the gospel of John is the only gospel that never once mentions the apostle John by name. This is believed to be on account of his humilty. In John 19:26 this same anonymous disciple was the one to whom Jesus entrusted his mother Mary. This disciple is universally accepted to be John with whom Mary lived thereafter. He is also called affectionately by theologians, "the apostle of love."

Some have argued that John's gospel is a contradiction of Matthew 28:9. They argue that Jesus' first appearance was in Matthew 28:9 and that this took place at the first trip to the tomb. This is actually bad exegesis. Matthew clearly states in verse eight, "they left the tomb quickly with fear and great joy and ran to report it to His disciples." Consequently, the appearance of Jesus in verse nine takes place *after* "they left the tomb quickly with fear and great joy and ran to report it to His disciples." The argument is therefore disingenuous.

Herbert Schmalz - Resurrection Morn - 1895

According to my own timeline, the appearance of Jesus in Matthew 28:9 takes place after His appearance to Mary Magdalene[893] and after the disciples had originally heard the news and disbelieved it (Matthew 28:8; Mark 16:9-11; Luke 24:9-12). This is consistent with the eyewitness reports and consistent with both a logical deductive and inductive approach to evaluating eyewitness accounts.[894]

Conclusion
The various accounts of the Resurrection, like all eyewitness testimonies, describe the exact same event from different perspectives with various information omitted by the different witnesses. This is true of any history and/or eyewitness account.

A fair study of the gospels leads to the conclusion that "each account supplements rather than contradicts each other."[895] A complete picture may be gleaned by putting the accounts together, which is called "harmonization." I have devoted a section of Appendix A to the harmonization of the gospels and a large section of Appendix B to the historical support for the resurrection accounts. Here I have merely hoped to demonstrate the unity of the gospels in regard to the resurrection accounts.

In summary, the vast majority of problems with alleged inconsistencies and/or contradictions with the gospel accounts are resolved when we factor in the fact that Mary Magdalene left the other women at the tomb to go retreive help from some of the apostles. We therefore have two separate groups who approached the tomb that Sunday morning. The first group, with whom Magdalene had originally come, remained at the tomb and witnessed what is recorded in the synoptic gospels, whereas Mary Magdalene had gone to get Peter and John who returned to the tomb and witnessed what John records in his gospel. The accounts are consistent and in full agreement with one another.

Matthew 28:17 – See Luke 24:33

The Trinity in the Great Commission
Matthew 28:19

"Go therefore and make disciples of all the nations, baptizing them in the name of the Father and the Son and the Holy Spirit, teaching them to observe all that I commanded you; and lo, I am with you always, even to the end of the age."

The Great Commission is the centerpiece of Christian evangelism, and yet it is not without some controversy in itself. The use of the Trinity is questioned by Arians, but there are other issues as well which should be addressed briefly. For example, was this a commission to all the earth? Why are they to be baptized? So also the secularist connects this Great Commission with the conquest by Spain and other Catholic countries around the world. Saint Augustine's decree "compel them to come to Christ"[896] became a battle cry for the military conquest of nations by European countries. These criticism and debates have served to belittle and deride the "Great Commission" which stands to this day as the foundation of Christian evangelism around the world. How then do we answer such questions?

Evangelism
Obviously Saint Augustine was not the author of the Bible. Our forefathers in America believed in religious freedom precisely because we believe, as Jesus taught (cf. Matthew 5), that God judges by the heart. Martin Luther once said, "a mind convinced by force is a mind not convinced at all." Rhetoric about the

Crusades or Conquistadors (which are themselves half truths) are irellevant to the words of Jesus. Nevertheless, we still hear cries from the liberal base in America that missionaries are intent upon destroying the culture of a particular people.

It is not my intent here to defend the spread of the gospel against such frivolous accusations, but to answer those critics within the Church who have minimized the Great Commission through bad exegesis. For example, one German theologian has argued that because the verb "go" in Greek is a participle, and only "make disciples" is an imperitive verb, then it should be translated "make disciples as you go,"[897] thereby negating any commission to missions in particular. This rather absurd argument is neither good exegesis of the Greek nor logical interpretation. He is correct to note that "make disciples" is an imperitive command in Greek, but going out into all nations is required in order to this. It is true that not all Christians are called to be missionaries, but the attempt to belittle missionary activity such as that commissioned herein is absurd. We are all ordered to "make disciples." We are further commissioned to do so throughout "all the nations" which by necessity requires "going" there at some point. The gospel is "good news" to all the world.

Baptism
The Great Commission includes a call to baptize believers. Now some believe that baptism is essential to salvation itself! Others, such as many in the Church growth movement today, have such little emphasis upon it that church members are never even asked if they have ever been baptized or want to be baptized. The former make baptism as much a part of the gospel as Jesus while the later minimize baptism so as to increase their membership numbers. Both are wrong.

I will deal in depth with the subject of baptism in my discussion in the book of Acts to be found in *Controversies in the Acts and Epistles*. Consequently I will only say here that there is nothing in this text to fix baptism to salvation. Baptism is a symbol of one's conversion to Christ and should be undertaken whenever possible as a visible way of demonstrating that faith, much as circumcision was to the Jews, but no Jew is damned because he was not circumcised and no Christian is lost because he has not been baptized. To quote D.A. Carson, "baptizing ... [is] not the *means* of making disciples, but [it] characterizes it."[898] For a full discussion of this debate see *Controversies in the Acts and Epistles*.

The Nations and the Church
Interestingly enough, the commission calls for us to go out into "all the nations" and yet here again replacement theologians and hyperdispensationalists fight among each other to exclude one or more group of people.

The replacement theologians emphasize "all nations" as if "all" excludes Israel. They argue that because Israel had rejected Jesus "Israel has forfeited her place, and now the preaching of the Gospel must be kept from her."[899] Essentially their linguistic argument is based solely on the fact that the word for nations here is also the word used for gentiles.[900] While it is true that εθνος (*ethnos*), from which we get the word "ethnic," can be translated "gentile," it is properly "nation." It is only translated "gentile" when it is contrasted with Israel and/or the Jewish people. "The nations" stand against Israel; "the nations" persecute the Jews; "the nations" make war on God, etc. In these contexts, the word may be translated "gentile," but to argue that "*all* nations" excludes Israel is wishful thinking by the replacement theologians. One might almost call it anti-semitic. This is especially true since it was the apostle Paul who became the "apostles to the gentiles" (1 Timothy 2:7). Obviously the other apostles were preaching to Israel and did not venture out beyond the borders of Israel until after Paul's conversion and success. It could properly be said that the Pharisees and Sadducees pushed the apostles to other nations, but they had initially preached solely to the Jews of Israel and the apostle Paul even declared that the gospel must be presented "to the Jew *first*, and also the Greek" (Romans 1:16; 2:9-10).

Conversely there are some ultradispensationalists who take the other extreme. They argue that because the church did not yet exist and is a mystery it is Israel to whom the Great Commission is given. Now while I agree that Israel had not been forsaken, it is the height of absurdity to suggest that Israel has been promulgating the gospel for the last two thousand years. It is the Church which has done so. Have we stolen their commission? Some very strong dispensationalists disagree saying, "although technically the dispensation of grace (or the church) had not yet commenced, the program of God had already changed focus from the nation of Israel to the nations as a whole."[901] This makes sense. If the ultradispensationalist argues that the commission was to Israel and its mantle was only picked up by the church after the coming of the Holy Spirit, then the ultradispensationalist starts to sound suspiciously like the replacement theologian!

"*All* nations" means "*all* nations" and not just some. We can neither exclude Israel, nor the nations at large. The gospel is for all, not some. We are all God's children and the Bible makes clear that God does "not want anyone to perish but for all to come to repentance" (2 Peter 3:9). This is the ultimate purpose of the Great Commission; to spread the news of salvation; to let the whole world know that they can be saved through Christ Jesus our Lord.

The Trinity

Every ancient manuscript contains the words, "baptizing them in the name of the Father and the Son and the Holy Spirit." There is zero evidence that these words were not in the original or that they are not an accurate quotation of our Lord Jesus. Nonetheless, the Arian (those who deny the trinity) reject these words as evidence of the doctrine of the Trinity. Their evidence for this is the fact that the apostles appear to have only baptized "in the name of Jesus." "Proof" of this is found in Acts 2:38; 8:16; 10:48; and 19:5, but a careful reading of these texts shows that these passages are merely summaries. They state only that people "were baptized in the name of the Lord Jesus" (19:5) but do not give us the exact words spoken by the apostles. Nevertheless, even if this were so, it is hardly proof that Jesus did not say that we are to baptize "in the name of the Father and the Son and the Holy Spirit" as *all* manuscripts affirm.

D.A. Carson has objected to the argument on the logical grounds that "there is no evidence we have Jesus *ipsissima verba* here."[902] In English, he means that there is no evidence that Jesus was commanding that we follow a ritual formula when baptizing. He was not commanding that the apostles repeat the exact same words, only that they be baptized in the name of our Lord, whom Jesus is clearly identifying as "Father and the Son and the Holy Spirit"! In short, the fact that the apostles *may* have only baptized in Jesus' name could be used as evidence *for* the Trinity rather than against it. Since none can deny that these are the words of Jesus, we may conclude that if the apostles took His words as an affirmation to baptize in Jesus' name, then the apostles must have seen the Father and Holy Spirit as one with the Son.

Here then is an explicit reference to the Trinity. That the doctrine of the Trinity is a Biblical teaching is defended in *Controversies in the Epistles*, but here lies evidence from the lips of our Lord Jesus Himself, and in the Great Commission itself.

Conclusion

The Great Commission is the frontpiece of evangelism. It is not a cry for conquest or the destruction of civilizations as extremists claim, but a cry to spread the good news of salvation to the ends of the earth and beyond. It is proof that salvation is offered to one and all, and no one who seeks the Lord may be denied access to Him. As the words of the Scriptures state, "whoever calls upon the name of the Lord shall be saved" (Acts 2:21).

Summary of Matthew's Gospel

Matthew is a favorite among many. His gospel was written predominantly to Jewish believers and features more quotes from the Old Testament and prophecy than any of the other gospels. Some believe that Mark and/or Luke consulted Matthew's gospel before writing their own (but see notes in Appendix A). Whether this is true or not, Matthew is one of two gospels which was written by one of the apostles and an eyewitness to the events described therein. It is also most likely the first gospel written and the reason that it stands first in our New Testament.

3

The Synoptic Gospels - Mark

Mark is the shortest and most concise of the gospels. Unlike Matthew, Mark was not an apostle and not an eyewitness to the events he describes. He was, however, a close associate of the apostles Paul (cf. Acts 12:25; 13:5) and Peter (1 Peter 5:13). He was also the brother of Barnabas (Colossians 4:10). His full name was John Mark and he served with both Peter and Paul in Rome (cf. Colossians 4:10; Philemon 24; 1 Peter 5:13; 2 Timothy 4:11). According to tradition John Mark was sent to Alexandria Egypt by Peter where he became its bishop.[903] Having been a young man when he met Peter and Paul, he was still serving in Egypt up until the earliest days of the second century when the Trajan persecution took his life. He is said to have been burned to death[904] (although a conflicting tradition says he died under Nero).

Ancient traditon says that Mark was "the interpreter of Peter"[905] and some ancients even went so far as to sat that Peter personally authorized the gospel.[906] As a companion of Peter, John Mark certainly had access to first hand accounts of the life and times of Jesus. This is not, however, without controversy, for the similarities to Matthew's gospel have led to differing theories. Some say that Mark "borrowed" from Matthew, while others claim that Matthew "borrowed" from Mark. Neither place too much stock in the theory that Mark gained his source information from Peter. Such a debate seems to trivialize Mark's work, so is necessary to answer such criticisms. Why are there so many similarities? If there were not so many similarities, would not the critic argue that the gospels "do not agree"? Such is the irony of Biblical critics. It is condemned if it does, and condemned if it doesn't. Let us examine these criticisms closely.

Mark and Plagiarism?
The Authorship and Date of Mark

That Mark wrote the gospel is unanimous among all early sources. There is no evidence to reject it. Considering the popularity of Peter and the fact that most consider Mark to have been written with Peter's assistance, it is unlikely that Mark would have received such unanimous credit over a man of Peter's stature unless it were true.

Its composition has been commonly dated between 60 A.D and 68 A.D.,[907] but this is by no means unanimous. Some scholars believe it was actually the first gospel written as early as 45 A.D.[908] This is based predominantly on the assumption that Luke and/or Matthew "reflect" Mark's gospel.[909] Nevertheless, this is suspect. Mark could certainly have been written before 60 A.D., but ancient tradition variously date it close to the time of the apostle Peter's martyrdom under Nero. Some, like Irenaeus, claim it was written afterwards, but others argue it had already been completed and approved by Peter.[910] Equally strong is the argument that its placement as the second gospel is because it was the second gospel written. Since Luke was almost certainly written around 60 A.D. (see next chapter), this would mean Mark's gospel was composed sometime in the 50s. It is safe to say that the gospel of Mark was written sometime between 50 A.D. and 68 A.D., probably closer to 55 to 60 A.D.

This leads to the inevitable question as to whether or not Mark "borrowed" from Matthew or whether or not Matthew "borrowed" from Mark, if either! Since this is debate at length in Appendix A, I shall abbreviate the debate here. While it is almost certain that both Mark and Peter had seen Matthew's gospels, the differences only make sense if Mark was not copying from Matthew (nor Matthew from Mark). One more logical explanation is that Peter and Mark saw Matthew's gospel and when reading it, Mark would ask Peter his own recollections of the event. Harkening back to my court of law analogy, eyewitnesses may remember and emphasize different things, but when they are in court and hear one another's testimony, they naturally tend to focus on the same things which are being discussed in court. So also, having read Matthew's gospel it is natural that Mark would ask for Peter's own description of the event. This alone can explain why Matthew and Luke stand "against" Mark in regard to those passages where the critic *claims* they are in contradiction. The critic is again trying to have it both ways. He claims that Mark and/or Matthew copied from one another, but then seems to imply that they were bad copyists, as the differences are used as an attack upon their historicity! So we may well ask the Bible critic, "if Matthew copied Mark then why do they 'disagree' on some points"? The answer can only be that they are two distinct and recollections of the same event. As with all eyewitness testimony, they may emphasize different aspects, abridge the complete story, or omit chronology which might confuse readers comparing the two accounts, but each is 100% accurate and true as we have seen.

In short, Mark was written by the companion of Peter and Paul, having spoken with Peter about the events he may have read in Matthew. His gospel is a short and concise gospel meant to be disseminated to the gentiles, whereas Matthew's gospel was focused on Israel and the Jews. Thus Mark may have been the first to write a gospel especially for the gentile reader.

A Historical Error?
Mark 2:26

"He entered the house of God in the time of Abiathar *the* high priest, and ate the consecrated bread, which is not lawful for *anyone* to eat except the priests."

This is a reference by Jesus to 1 Samuel 21:1-6, but in that passage it says that Ahimelech was name of the priest in the temple. Some have, therefore, argued that this is a mistake or error on the part of Mark (or even Jesus). In fact, there is no error as the Bible makes explicitly clear that Ahimelech was the son of Abiathar (2 Samuel 8:17; cf. 1 Chronicles 24:6). So it would seem that Ahimelech was a priest (not high priest) serving in the temple the day David arrived "in the time of Abiathar *the* high priest" (Mark 2:26). No contradiction or "error" can be found in this remark. Or can there?

The Problem

1 Samuel 22:20 records that "one son of Ahimelech the son of Ahitub, named Abiathar, escaped and fled after David." This is the Abiathar who most believe became high priest after Ahimelech's murder.[911] If this is the case then when David ate consecrated bread would have been before Abiathar was high priest and not "in the time of Abiathar the high priest," or so it is argued. The problem with this argument is manifold.

First, the term "high priest" is never mentioned in the book of Samuel. Ahimelech was called a "priest," nothing else. There is only one high priest, but many priests. Secondly, there is an Ahimelech who is explicitly said to be the son of an Abiathar (2 Samuel 8:17; cf. 1 Chronicles 24:6) whereas the Ahimelech of 1 Samuel 21-22 is said to be the son of Ahitub (1 Samuel 22:20) and the father of Abiathar. Third, some claim that this Abiathar was fourth generation from Eli[912] but Eli became high priest at least 170 years earlier![913] Since Eli was already an adult when he became high priest, we would have to assume that *at least* five generations had past; probably six or seven. Finally, 2 Samuel 8:17 says that "Zadok the son of Ahitub and Ahimelech the son of Abiathar were priests" after David had already become king but 1 Samuel 22:17-20 says that only Abiathar survived the slaughter. This leads to question of whether or not we are actually looking at more than one Ahimelech and/or Abiathar.

It is not uncommon to see children named for their grand father or ancestor. In the genealogy of Zadok, the son of Ahitub, we read in Chronicles, Ezra, and Nehemiah that there were two Zadoks, two Meraioths, two Amariahs, two Ahitubs, and three Azariahs in the same lineage. Remember that in genealogy the Hebrew word for "son" can be used of grandsons, great-grandsons, or indeed any descendant. Likewise, "father" can refer to a forefather.[914] Now the Hebrew word יָלַד (yalad), translated "to beget", can only refer to the immediate biological father, but 1 Chronicles, Ezra, and Nehemiah all use בֶּן (ben) which simply means "son of" or "descendant of."

Both Zadok (2 Samuel 8:17) and Ahimelech (1 Samuel 22:12) are called a "son of Ahitub." However, it does not seem likely that they were

211

brothers since Zadok was serving under David after the slaughter of Ahimelech. How then could be serving alongside a man who had died? Obviously, the Ahimelech "son of Abiathar" found in 2 Samuel 8:17 was not the same as the Ahimelech "son of Ahitub." They were certainly related, however, so since Ahimelech's lineage is not recorded (for Josephus believes the extinction of his family was prophesied to Eli for his sons' sins)[915] we can look to the lineage of Zadok to see if there are any clues.

1 Chron. 6:4+	1 Chron. 6:50+	1 Chron. 9:11	Ezra 7:1+	Neh. 11:10+
Eli*	Eli*		Eli*	
Phinehas	Phinehas		Phinehas	
Abishua	Abishua		Abishua	
Bukki	Bukki		Bukki	
Uzzi	Uzzi		Uzzi	
Zerahiah	Zerahiah		Zerahiah	
Meraioth	Meraioth		Meraioth	
Amariah	Amariah			
Ahitub	Ahitub			
Zadok	Zadok			
Ahimaaz	Ahimaaz			
Azariah				
Johanan				
Azariah			Azariah	
Amariah			Amariah	
Ahitub		Ahitub	Ahitub	Ahitub
		Meraioth		Meraioth
Zadok		Zadok	Zadok	Zadok
Shallum		Meshullam	Shallum	Meshullam
Hilkiah		Hilkiah	Hilkiah	Hilkiah
Azariah		Azariah	Azariah	
Seraiah			Seraiah	Seraiah

* Eli is not mentioned by name.

Now here we see that there were multiple Zadoks, Meraioths, Azariahs, and even Ahitubs. Could not Abiathar and/or Ahimelech have been named for their grandfathers? There are two possibilities here. The first is that Abiathar was named for his grandfather who was serving as high priest at the time Ahimelech was murdered. However, since Zadok is said to be priest alongside Ahimelech after David was already king (2 Samuel 8:17; cf. 1 Chronicles 24:6) and since 1 Samuel 22:17-20 records that the priests were killed except for Abiathar, it could be that this Ahimelech, who is called the son of Abiathar, was named after his grandfather who had died in that persecution. If this is so then Zadok was not killed earlier either because Saul spared a few priests or because he was either too young to have served in the priesthood, which may be the preferred explanation owing to the fact that his eldest brother had served some years earlier (1 Samuel 14:3). In either case, the later argument more sense, but the former could explain Mark's quotation.

212

Possible Solutions

There have been six essential explanations for this problem. They range from pure speculation to intiguing theories to logical arguments. It is hard, however, to know for sure which is the correct position since we lack a genealogy of Ahimelech or a complete list of high priests in the time of Israel. While we may not be able to prove which theory is correct, neither can the critic prove that Abiathar was *not* high priest at the time of Ahimelech, even as Jesus said.

The Textual Theory

Walter Wessel has argued that the name Abiathar may not have been in the original manuscript of Mark because his name was omitted by both Matthew and Luke.[916] He also points out that Abiathar's name is missing from "several" ancient manuscripts.[917] In fact, the only ancient Greek manuscripts which lack Abiathar's name are the codex *bezae* and *washingtoniaonus*.[918] Abiathar's name is found in older manuscripts including the ancient Papyrus 88 ($\mathfrak{P}^{88}$).[919] Thus it is highly unlikely that the name Abiathar is an error of a later copiest which is why every translation of the Bible correctly contains his name.

It is even less likely that the Old Testament books erred as others have suggested.[920] Despite Henry Swete's allegation that there is "confusion" about Abiathar in the Old Testament[921] the book of Samuel does not confuse the two, nor is there the slightest evidence that the names were transposed in 1 Samuel 8:17 as some argue.[922] Such wild speculation must be rejected without evidence of some kind. 1 Samuel 8:17 is just more evidence that we have assumed there could only be one Ahimelech, one Abiathar, etc., even though it has been illustrated above that children were often named for their grandparents.

A variant of this theory is one which suggests that Mark had been originally written in Aramaic and originally read "*abba* Abiathar," meaning "father of Abiathar." Because of the similarity of *abba* and the first part of Abaiathar's name it is suggested that abba was accidentally dropped out.[923] Once again, however, there is not the slightest evidence of this. It is pure unbridled speculation. We cannot assume that an "error" or omission has crept in when no textual physical evidence of such exist.

The Functional High Priest Theory

If, as is generally believed, Abiathar was the son of Ahimelech, then "Abiathar may have been assisting his father"[924] and would have been his successor.[925] Lenski argued that "father and son were both present when David came to Nob ... Abimelech, the father, soon died and Abiathar, the son, became high priest."[926] That Abiathar was present is obvious. The question is what role he played in the priesthood. According to Matthew Poole if "Abiathar assisted his father in the execution of the office"[927] he could be considered the *de facto* high priest.

The problem with this argument is that it is not certain that Ahimelech was high priest. He is called only a "priest" (cf. 1 Samuel 21:1). This argument must, therefore, assume that Ahimelech was high priest and that Abiathar was already in training to replace him.

The Father-Son Theory

Merrill Unger has offered an intriguing, if speculative, theory similar to that above, but which would more accurately explain the seeming inconsistencies in the account of Samuel. He says that "the best explanation seems to be that Abiathar, who was becoming quite old toward the latter part of David's reign, had his eldest son Ahimelech assume the heavy responsibility of the priesthood, and who, accordingly, was actually considered as the functioning high priest in place of his father."[928] Of course, Unger probably meant to say "Saul's reign," since David had not yet assumed the throne, but his theory is intriguing.

In support of this theory is 1 Samuel 4:4 wherein the sons of Eli were performing the functions of the aged Eli. If this is theory is true it would explain why Ahimelech is called the son of Abiathar and why Abiathar was high priest at that time. The problem is that Ahimelech was apparently murdered before David had assumed the reigns of government (1 Samuel 22:17-20). This makes Unger's theory less probable.

The Family Name Theory

It has been shown in the genealogy above that families often named their children for grandfathers or other famous family members. Since Ahimelech and Abiathar have no full genealogy recorded in the Scriptures, we cannot know for sure, but the difference between the account of 1 Samuel 21-22 and 2 Samuel 8:17 lend strong credibility to the fact that Ahimelech, or even Abiathar, were named after their grandfathers. This accounts for the confusion on the part of many scholars.

The Translation Theory

Some have suggested that the translation is what causes the difficulty rather than the words of Jesus. Walter Wessel argues that it might be translated "in the time of Abiathar, the one who [later] became high priest."[929] Matthew Henry said that "in the days of Abiathar the high priest" could equally be translated as "just before"[930] Abiathar became high priest.

The Greek is actually a very simple short phrase. It says "επι 'Αβιαθαρ αρχιερεως" which is most literally translated "on Abiathar high priest." Obviously, επι (*epi*) cannot be translated here as "on," its primary meaning. What are the other meanings of επι (*epi*)? They are "*upon; over; at; by; before, the presence of; when, under, at the time of; in the passage about.*"[931] Such is the complete primary definitions of επι (*epi*) found in *A Concise Greek-English Dictionary of the New Testament*. Notice some of the meanings.

"In the presence of Abiathar the high priest."

"When Abiathar was high priest."

"Under Abiathar the high priest."

"At the time of Abiathar the high priest."

"In the passage about Abiathar the high priest."

Most translations opt for "when" or "under" or "in the time of," but the other two make the most sense. Abiathar was a witness to the events as he was most certainly present when his father was serving David. The identification of Abiathar as high priest is simply to designate him apart from the other Abiathar. Do we not still call George Bush "Mr. President," even though he is no longer President? Do we not refer to past events of "President Barak Obama" even though he was not yet President?

Thus "in the presence of Abiathar (who later became the) high priest"[932] is favored by many including John Wesley,[933] and is a valid translation. Nevertheless, there is one other translation option which I have listed separately as it constitutes another theory. Technically, it is still a translation issue, but it deserves to be considered distinctly.

The Citation Theory

As shown above, "in the passage about" is listed in the Greek-English dictionary as a possible translation of επι (*epi*). This is because versification did not yet exist. If the apostles wanted to cite Scripture they could only refer to the name of the book, the prophet, or "in the passage about." Thus Jesus was telling the listeners where the passage in Samuel existed by declaring "in the passage about Abiathar,"[934] the one who became "high priest."

This is the view taken by men like Warren Wiersbe who said, "it is likely that our Lord used 'Abiathar' to refer to this Old Testament *passage* about Abiathar rather than to the man."[935] It is also arguably the best theory, although "in the presence of" should also be considered. Ultimately the context is what should govern the translations.

Conclusion

These are the dominant theories. Some other theories exist, such as Jonathan Edwards assertion that the term "high priest" was "generic" and the "equivalent of a 'chief priest.'"[936] Nonetheless, the best answer may a composite of some of the better theories. There is no doubt that the translation is misleading in English text. The earlier translations such as Wycliffe and Darby make it more clear that Jesus is not necessarily saying that Abiathar was serving as high priest at that exact time. It may be a quotation of "the passage about" Abiathar since versification did not yet exist. It may also be that Abiathar was the *de facto* high priest, assuming that his grand-father was not of the same name and still serving.

While we may not be able to prove which theory is correct, neither can the critic prove that Abiathar was *not* high priest at the time of Ahimelech. It is certain that Abiathar was present when these deeds took place, and this is probably all that "ἐπι 'Αβιαθαρ αρχιερεως" is meant to convey. Reading anything else into the text, particularly a techinical chronological argument is erroneous. This would be tantamount to claiming that anyone who refers to the American Revolution as taking place in the days of the President George Washington is in error. George Washington was not yet President, but he is known by that title and the American Revolution most certainly did take place in his day as he participated in. So also Abiathar "a high priest" was present when David took the consecrated bread.

Mark 3:13-19 – See Matthew 10:2-4

Mark 3:23-26 – See Matthew 12:22-29

Did Jesus Have Brothers?
Mark 3:31-35 (cf. Matthew 12:46-50 – Luke 8:20-21 – cf. Mark 6:3)

> "Then His mother and His brothers arrived, and standing outside they sent *word* to Him and called Him. A crowd was sitting around Him, and they said to Him, 'Behold, Your mother and Your brothers are outside looking for You.' Answering them, He said, 'Who are My mother and My brothers?' Looking about at those who were sitting around Him, He said, 'Behold My mother and My brothers! For whoever does the will of God, he is My brother and sister and mother.'"

Catholics believe in the perpetual virginity of Mary. Protestants believe that Mary was a virgin when Jesus was born, but that she had other children by Joseph after Jesus' birth. There is nothing impure or evil in lawful marital sexual intercourse. This in no way diminishes or belittles the Virgin Mary's chasity. The question is, therefore, whether or not these were Jesus' actual brothers who had come to greet him.

The Catholic church has offered two dominant theories to explain their teaching in light of this verse. The first view is the weakest. It says that this was Mary's sister who was also called Mary.[937] They argue that there is no Hebrew or Aramaic word for aunt or cousin and hence were also referred to as mothers and brothers.[938] However, this is not true. The Hebrew word for cousin is דּוֹדָן (*dodan*) and the Hebrew word for aunt is דּוֹדָה (*dodah*), found in Exodus 6:20, Leviticus 18:14, and 20:20.[939] Furthermore, it seems far fetched, to say the least, to suggest that Mary had a sister named Mary. What parent gives both of their daughters the same name? A better variant of this view is that Mary came with some of Jesus' cousins, but it has been shown that the Jews did have a word for cousins, so this explanation is insufficient.

A slightly better alternative offered up by Catholics is that these were actually Jesus' half-brothers by Joseph from another marriage.[940] While this is theoretically plausible it is not only wild speculation but seems to conflict with

216

Scripture, for nowhere is there the slightest hint that Joseph was a widower or that he had other children. The picture we see in Matthew and Luke is of two young people in love and engaged to be married. This theory does not come from exegesis but from a desire to defend Catholic tradition on the perpetual virginity of Mary. However, the chasity of Mary is not in doubt. It is the question of her perpetual virginity and this doctrine conflicts with Scripture.

Now according to some Mark 6:3 is proof that Mary had only one son, for some men called Jesus "*the* son of Mary" rather than "a son of Mary."[941] Nevertheless, this is an inherently weak argument, for in common language use we apply the definite article not to specify that there is only one son but to specify "*that*" son to whom the speaker is referring. Moreover, the entire verse reads, "is not this the carpenter, the son of Mary, and brother of James and Joses and Judas and Simon? Are not His sisters here with us?" Thus it is clear that they were not saying Jesus was the only son of Mary. It is not good exegesis to infer that the speaker is attempting to designate whether or not Jesus was an only son when no such intimation can be found in the context. In fact, Mark 6:3 is strong evidence in favor of the fact that these were Jesus' brothers and sisters.

One final argument made by supporters of the Catholic tradition is to ask why, if these were His brothers, "did Jesus set aside their filial obligations and place his mother in the charge of John?"[942] To that Warren Wiersbe offers the obvious answer. "Our Lord's half-brothers were not believers."[943] Although one may have become a believer after Jesus' death and resurrection, at the time these men were clearly not believers and probably somewhat jealous of their half-brother. Jesus wanted to leave the care of His mother to someone who trusted and believed in Him.

Ultimately, the proof that these were the actual step-brothers (for we agree that Joseph was not Jesus' biological father) is the fact that the Bible calls Joseph and Mary *husband* and *wife*. Sex is the consumation of marriage. Even in the Catholic Church a marriage can be annulled if it has not been consumated. Why? Because by Catholic law (as well as all other religious marital law) the marriage never actually took place *unless* it was consumated. Joseph could not be Mary's husband unless they had consumated the marriage.[944] There is nothing impure about sex within the confines of marriage. Matthew says "Joseph awoke from his sleep and did as the angel of the Lord commanded him, and took Mary as *his wife*, but kept her a virgin *until* she gave birth to a Son; and he called His name Jesus." (1:24-25). This verse make it clear that Mary was "*his wife*" and that she remained a virgin "*until* she gave birth" to Jesus; not afterwards.

Now an interesting sidenote is the assertation by some that they were disrespecting Jesus by interrupting him and "having no desire to come in" the house.[945] This argument is made presumeably to soften Jesus' apparent refusal to meet with them, but the Bible does not actually say whether Jesus granted their request or not. The point of the passages was only to illustrate Jesus' spiriutal lesson on the brotherhood of man and His love of his disciples. Jesus most probably did meet with Mary and his brothers who did not enter without permission as a courtesy, for in *any* culture it is disrespectful to enter a person's house without permission!

In summary, the doctrine of the perpetual virginity of Mary is a relatively late development not found in the Bible. She was a virgin when Jesus was born because Jesus was the Son of God, not Joseph. However, Joseph did take her as his wife, and the consumation of marriage is sexual union. This is why Matthew makes clear that she was "kept her a virgin *until* she gave birth" to Jesus (1:25). These were Jesus' literal step-brothers, the sons of Joseph and Mary.

The Parable of the Sower
Mark 4:1-9 – See Luke 8:4-15

Mark 5:1-20 – See Matthew 8:28-34

Jairus' Daughter
Mark 5:21-43 – Matthew 9:18-26 – Luke 8:40-56

"My little daughter is at the point of death; please come and lay Your hands on her, so that she will get well and live."	"My daughter has just died; but come and lay Your hand on her, and she will live.'"

Some alleged discrepancies are highlighted in these parallel passages. In Matthew's account the event seems to take place in his house while Mark allegedly places the event "by the seashore" (5:21). Second, it is questioned whether or not Jairus said his daughter was "at the point of death" (Mark 5:23) or "had just died" (Matthew 9:18).

The Setting

Mark says that "when Jesus had crossed over again in the boat to the other side, a large crowd gathered around Him; and so He stayed by the seashore" and then Jairus approached Jesus (5:21). In Matthew, it is argued, the setting is different and Jesus appears to be having dinner at Matthew's house (9:10). How is this resolved without speculation?

First and foremost, if we read the entire sentence in Mark 5:21 we see that Jesus "stayed by the seashore." How long did He stay? Was Matthew's house near the seashore? We are not told. We cannot *assume* that Jairus approached at that exact moment, for we are not told. Nor can we *assume* that Matthew's house was far from the shore. It is apparent that the Pharisees were not all standing inside Matthew's home. They were standing *outside* his home, which we may conclude must have been near the "the seashore."

One problem is that the NIV translation (which I have often defended) appears to insert chronology where it is not present in the original Greek. They do so to make a more polished sounding narrative, but this can be misleading as it is here. The parallel passage in Luke offers to explicit chronology and yet the NIV translates Luke 8:41 as *"then a man named Jairus, a ruler of the synagogue, came and fell at Jesus' feet."* This creates a chronological connection between the previous passage and this one, which is misleading. D.A. Carson has said that the NIV's translation of *"kai idou* in Luke 8:41 should not be rendered 'just then'."[946] He is correct, καὶ ἰδου (*kai idou*) is most literally translated as "and behold" as in the King James version. It is one way in Greek of starting a new subject. There is no time correleation between 8:40 and 8:41.

The setting is not explicit in any of the gospels, least of all in Luke's abbreviated version. We only know that Jesus had been staying (for how long we are not told) "by the seashore" and that he had eaten at the house of Matthew before being confronted by the Pharisees (9:9-17). It is poor exegesis to read a strict chronological setting into the text when none is offered. Consequently, we cannot see these passages as contradictory in this regard.

Jairus' Daughter
Matthew records that Jairus told Jesus "my daughter has just died." Mark says, "my little daughter is at the point of death." Luke does not tell us his words, but does say that "someone came from the house of the synagogue official, saying, 'your daughter has died; do not trouble the Teacher anymore'" (Luke 8:49). How are these to be reconciled?

There are three things to be considered. First, Jairus had come to seek Jesus' help because he knew Jesus could heal her, but after she died, another synagogue official went to him to tell him it was too late. Thus it is apparent that she died at some point between Jairus' initial appeal and His having arrived at Jairus' house. Second, it is by no means certain that Matthew should be translated "just died." The Greek reads, "ἡ θυγατηρ μου ἄρτι ετελευτησεν." The Greek word τελευταω (*teleutao*) means "to finish, to bring to an end" or "to die."[947] It is found in what is called the aorist tense. Earlier I mentioned that is what is called an "indefinite tense" which does not exists in English.[948] It is usually used for narrative purposes, and it does not prove that his daughter was already dead but rather than she was "being brought to an end," "being finished," or "near death." The translation "just died" is inferred from the adjective ἄρτι (*arti*), meaning "just now."[949] Furthermore, since Matthew does not elsewhere specify that she had died, translators feel it is justify to say that she was already dead. Nevertheless, a better translation might be "she is even now dying" or "at the brink of death." This is perfectly consistent with Mark's statement, "το θυγατριον μου εσχατως εχει." Εσχατως (*eschatos*) means "last"[950] and εχει (*exei*) means that she was *approaching* her end. That fact that Mark uses a different word is of no consequence since the statements begin with the Greek preposition ὅτι (*'oti*) which can either introduce and exact quote, or, as in this case, a paraphrase.[951] Moreover, if he was speaking in Aramaic then Matthew and Mark are both translations into Greek. This is the reason that the wording is sometimes different from one gospel to another. They are paraphrases and/or translations, rather than exact quotations.

Of course, an alternative, or more simplistic explanation, could be that Mark is quoting Jairus as he first approached Jesus while Matthew quotes Jairus after the official arrived to inform him of his daughter's death. Jairus did not give up but continued to plead with Jesus. This is also plausible, although the more technical answer is the preferred answer.

Ilya Repin – Raising of Jairus' Daughter – 1871

Summary
Matthew's home was apparently located close to the Sea of Galilee. This is not surprising since a tax collector could doubtless afford better accomodations than most. As Jairus approached he pleaded with Jesus, knowing that she was at death's door. Eventually an official of the Synagogue came and informed him that her daughter had already died, but he did not give up, but believed in Jesus who was able to raise her from the dead.

Power, Healing, and Omniscience
Mark 5:25-34 – Matthew 9:20-22 – Luke 8:43-48

"A woman who had had a hemorrhage for twelve years ... thought, 'If I just touch His garments, I will get well.' Immediately the flow of her blood was dried up; and she felt in her body that she was healed of her affliction."

There are no apparent contradictions which need to be addressed. Rather there are two major theological issues which cry out in this passage and remain a divisive issue to this very day. The first is the question of her healing and the "power" which had "gone forth" from Jesus. The second is the question of whether or not Jesus was omniscient. Did He not know who had touched Him? If so, why asks? John Calvin summed up the problems when he said, "it might seem absurd that Christ poured out His grace without knowing whom He was helping. There is also some difficulty where He says, a little later, that He realized that power went out of Him, as though it were just flowing out, not by way of free gift."[952] These are the questions which must be addressed.

Power and Healing
The controversy here is one of how God chooses to heal and of what constitutes faith. This woman's desire to be healed simply by touching Jesus' garment has been called "a superstitious view of Jesus"[953] or that "her faith seemed to be mixed with a measure of superstition."[954]

In the New Testament healing always takes place through Jesus. He, or His apostles, are always shown as the instruments of healing and faith in Jesus is the primary ingredient. In pagan religions, however, healing powers are seen as a form of magic which can be transmitted through various objects, often called a talisman. Here is a woman who is healed simply by touching Jesus' garment, and in so doing "power" left Jesus, seemingly (so say some) without His knowledge or consent. If true this would appear to conflict with the normal Biblical teaching on healing and faith.

The Power that Had Gone Out
The first subject of this debate is Mark's curious remark that Jesus perceived "that the power proceeding from Him had gone forth" (5:30). This relates to the question of ominscience, which will be dealth with separately, but it also relates to the question of the nature of this "power." It has been noted that "many touched the garments of Jesus, and no power went out from him to them."[955] Why was it so with this woman?

In the early church Irenaeus refuted heretics who connected her healing to the mystic power of Aeon.[956] Thus it is clear that some in the early church were influenced by pagan religion and belief in magic. They made Jesus out to be a sort of "magnetic medium."[957] This is also a heresy which stems from a false view of "power" which has too often become incorporated into some "Word churches" today. Some modern day "faith healers" teach that they are "channeling" the "power" of God, but channeling is not a Christian belief; nor is the doctrine that the "power" of God may be exercised apart from God and His agent Jesus Christ. How then can this be explained?

The answer is actual simple and it is a quirk of the English language. The Greek word used here is δυναμις (*dunamis*) from which we get the word "dynamite." It is correct to translate it as "power" but that is often misleading for the Biblical word used for "miracle" is also δυναμις (*dunamis*). They are one and the same. The "power" of which Mark is speaking is not some mystic "power" dispensed through a talisman, like a piece of Jesus garment, but rather that a "miracle" had taken place. My own translation might be "Jesus, knowing that a miracle had taken place by Him ..." sought to make the miracle public by calling the woman out.

Superstition or Faith?

This second problem, her alleged superstitious approach to Jesus, is resolved in one of several ways. First, most evangelical scholars agree that "it was her faith that was effective, not the superstition mingled with it."[958] Faith, not mysticism, was what led God to heal her. Nevertheless, this is not a sufficient answer in itself. Walter Liefeld seems to give a more complete answer when he says, "the intrusion of Hellenistic ideas and superstitions may indeed have influenced her action; but Jesus did not quench the 'smoldering wick' (Matt 12:20) of her faith; instead, he fanned the flame."[959] In other words, "accept the one who is weak in faith" and do not pass "judgment on his opinions" (Romans 14:1). There are many instances in the Bible where God used practices and people who were not godly for His own aims. Even the pagan prophet Balaam was used by God (Number 22-24), though Balaam was eventually slain for fighting against Israel (Numbers 31:8). So also God often spoke to pagan kings through dreams (Genesis 41; Daniel 2).

Sometimes we evangelicals become overly concerned with correcting the error of the weak instead of helping them to grow in faith slowly but surely with a guiding hand. It is necessary to correct error, but not at the expense of faith. This is the subject Paul deals with in deal in Romans 14 (see *Controversies in the Epistles*) and it is something which to this day is constantly misunderstood by people on both sides. It is sufficient to say that while God healed this woman despite her going about it the wrong way, Jesus felt the need to stop her before she left so that she might understand. This leads to the question of Jesus' omniscience.

Omniscience

Because the woman did not confront Jesus or speak to Him, but was healed by merely touching His garment, as well as the fact that Jesus sought her out, has led to the question of whether or not Jesus is omniscient. Was she truly healed without Jesus' knowledge? To this even the somewhat liberal minded Lenski replies, "to say that this outgo of power from Jesus was without conscious volition on his part is to misconceive the entire operation of power. It is always under the control of Jesus' conscious will."[960] Is Jesus omniscient? The overwhelming majority of Christians believe in the doctrine of Trinity (for those who question it, see discussions under the gospel of John, particularly John 1:1), so we believe that Jesus was the second person of the Trinity, God incarnate. Logically, if God is omniscient and Jesus is God then Jesus must be omniscient. Correct? Not *necessarily*. This is the real debate.

Jesus is the second person of the Trinity, but He was also 100% human. As such His physical body would have limitations except where God the Father chose to revoke those limitations. In other words, we may conclude that Jesus knew as much as God chose to reveal to Him, and that may be the equivalent of omniscience, but we cannot assume that *if* Jesus was unaware, He was somehow less than than God incarnate. It is apparent from Matthew 24:36 that Jesus' knowledge was limited in at least one area when he declared, "of that day and hour no one knows, not even the angels of heaven, nor the Son, but the Father alone." Thus the real question becomes "was He unaware?"

The truth is that the only reason anyone questions Jesus' awareness of the event is the fact that Jesus sought her out. I have already answered Calvin's question concerning the "difficulty where He says, a little later, that He realized that power went out of Him, as though it were just flowing out."[961] The "power" of which is spoken should be taken as a verbal use of the word miracle. It could be translated, "Jesus knew that a miracle had taken place by Him." So "there is assuredly no doubt that He healed the woman knowingly and willingly."[962] Why then did He seek her out?

John Martin believes that Jesus' asking who had touched His garment "does not imply He was ignorant of the situation."[963] When Jesus stopped the woman, He may have been seeking a way to give her the opportunity to reveal herself. Says one commentator, "she needed to know that it was her faith, not her superstitious belief, that had caused God to heal her."[964] Of course some do believe that God the Father healed the woman without Jesus' knowledge[965] although this argument is really negated by the explicit statement of Mark 5:30 that Jesus "knew" or "perceived." The motive for Jesus' actions was to give her strength of faith, for she was clearly weak in faith.

This is the most popular and attested view throughout history. Lenski said that His "action in making the woman reveal herself is taken for the sake of the woman ... and ... the people.[966] Warren Wiersbe said, "He dealt with her publicly not only for her sake, but also for the sake of Jairus."[967] John Darby had said that "faith makes the believer humble about his wretchedness; the woman wished to remain hidden"[968] but, as H.A. Ironside said, Jesus "desired her to confess before all the miracle that had been wrought."[969]

There may be another reason for Jesus' calling her out. In Greek, the word for healed is σεσωκεν (*sesoken*), from the root word σωσω (*sozo*), which literally means "to save."[970] Hence some believe that it is salvation that Jesus had in mind.[971] She was called out in order that she might know that it is faith in

Jesus by which she has been literally "saved," both physically healing and spiritual salvation.

Conclusion

Here we have the story of a woman who was weak in faith and desperate to be cleansed. She knew that Jesus could heal her, but was afraid to approach Him or asks for His help, so she chose to seek His healing in a manner which may have been influenced by superstition, but by which the Lord still chose to heal. Romans 14 discusses the faith of the weak, and we should not be overly concerned with her superstitious sentiments. We should not use this passage to promote a superstitious understanding of Jesus; nor should we be hesitant to deny that Jesus meets us where we are. If we weak of faith, He lifts us up and makes us stronger. This is what Jesus did in this instance.

As to the translation of "power" going forth from Jesus as if He were merely channeling mystic energy, the Greek makes it clear that it was a "miracle" which had taken place "through Jesus." A slightly paraphrasistic rendering of Mark 5:30 might be, "Jesus, knowing that a miracle had taken place by Him sought out the woman" in order that it be made known to all. The word for miracle and power are the exact same. It was not a mystic power, but the power of God. The Holy Spirit is not a force, as some heretically say, but a person; the third person of the Trinity. Thus it is *God* who healed her, and God who saved her.

Jesus' Brothers and Sisters
Mark 6:3 – See Mark 3:31-35

I have discussed this previously, but this passage deserves special mention inasmuch as it shows that Jesus was disrespected because he was from a common family of low birth. These "brothers and sisters" therefore must have been from his immediate family or else the criticisms would make no logical sense. This is further evidence that Jesus did indeed have step-brothers and step-sisters.

Mark 6:14-29 – See Matthew 14:1

Mark 6:32-44 – See Matthew 14:13-21

Mark 8:1-21 – See Matthew 15:32-38

Mark 8:12-13 – See Matthew 12:38-39

Mark 9:1-13 – See Matthew 17:1-13

Mark 9:33-37 – See Luke 9:46

Jesus and Hell
Mark 9:43-48

> "Hell ... the unquenchable fire, where their worm does not die, and the fire is not quenched."

Those who deny the reality of Hell often accuse those who do of distorting the Bible and message of Christ. Henry Swete even claims that in this passage "the question of the eternity of punishment does not come into sight"![972] Yet few people realize that it was Jesus Himself who taught more about the doctrine of Hell than all the rest of the Bible combined. It is true that the subject of hell is relatively minor in the broader score of Jesus' teachings, but the fact is that over 90% of the instances of Hell and/or Hades come from the lips of Jesus Christ.

It is Jesus who taught more than any of His disciples about the reality of hell and eternal punishment. Despite this, some have made a point of the fact that there are three different words translated as "hell," and each presumeably have different meanings. These words are *sheol* from the Hebrew שְׁאוֹל, *hades* from the Greek ᾅδης, and Gehenna which is also a Greek word (γέεννα). In order to gain a better understanding of the doctrine of hell and Jesus' view of it, it is necessary to examine these words individually and then see in what context Jesus uses theses words.

Sheol

The first word is from the Hebrew word *sheol* (שְׁאוֹל). There are sixty-seven instances on the Old Testament where the word *sheol* is left untranslated by the NAS Bible. This is a wise decision for *sheol* appears to be a more generic term that can refer to hell, but can also refer to a general abode of the dead. This fact, in itself, is controversial.

Some have suggested that Revelation does not depict the wicked as being cast into hell until the end of the ages. They, therefore, argue that the dead are all kept in *sheol* and divided into two groups; the righteous and unrighteous. This doctrine cannot be compared to purgatory (although some Catholics will see *sheol* as synonymous with purgatory) but to a temporary abode of the dead. One might liken its two halves to a temporary heaven and hell. Is this scriptural?

The first instance of *sheol* is found in Genesis 37:35 where Jacob was mourning for Joseph, whom he believed to be dead. He said, "surely I will go down to *Sheol* in mourning for my son." This generic term is common and is usually used of the dead. The King James, NIV, and many others translate *sheol* as "grave" here and elsewhere. However, the term takes on darker means in Numbers 16:30-33 where the grave is said to snatch the wicked and take them

225

"alive to *sheol*." Still more sinister is Deuteronomy 32:22 where God declares, "for a fire is kindled in My anger, and burns to the lowest part of *Sheol*, and consumes the earth with its yield, and sets on fire the foundations of the mountains." In both of these instances *sheol* could still be translated simply as "grave" but the King James translates the first as "the pit" and the second instance in Deuteronomy as "hell."

The most clear depictions of *sheol* as a place of the wicked are "Psa. 9:17; Prov. 23:14; in which *Sheol* can only mean the abode of the wicked, as distinguished from and opposed to the righteous."[973] Nevertheless, even these passages are somewhat ambiguous. Based solely on these passages it is hard to differentiate between hell and the grave. Hebrew grammarian William Gesenius said that "I have no doubt שְׁאוֹל is for שְׁעוֹל a hollow, a hollow and subterranean place" in which "the dead are gathered together."[974] Some call it simply the "netherworld."[975] Of this there is no doubt. *Sheol* (שְׁאוֹל) is more than just "the grave." It is an abode of the dead. The problem is that the Hebrew Scriptures are not clear in distinguishing *sheol* (שְׁאוֹל) from heaven or hell as we know them today. It is an abode of the dead, but nothing is manifest as to whether the dead here are suffering, in Paradise, or gathered together in a general abode until Judgment Day. The Hebrew word is sometimes taken as "grave" (NIV), "death" (the Living Bible), or "hell" (KJV), but it is more often then not left untranslated (NAS, ASV, RSV, NRSV, Tanakh). The Greek *Septuagint* translates the word as ᾅδης or *hades*. It us therefore prudent to examine the use of *hades* (ᾅδης) in the New Testament and Jewish literature.

Hades

Some reject *hades* (ᾅδης) as a literal place of the dead, in no small part because the Greek *Septuagint* uses the word *hades* (ᾅδης) which was been traditionally associated with Greek mythology and "orcus, the nether world, the realm of the dead" as found in Homeric poems.[976] Obviously, the idea that the Bible borrows from Greek mythology is disturbing, but it is also untrue. The fact that someone mentions "hell" does not presuppose that his view of Hell is borrowed from Dante's *Inferno*. In the same way there is no doubt that Homer and the Greeks had their own views of *hades* (ᾅδης), but that does not make the word synonymous with Homeric theology! That would be ridiculous.

The doctrine of hell as we know it was fully formulated before the time of Jesus. It can be found in Jewish literature such as the book of Enoch. In *Enoch* hell is clearly the abode of the fallen angels where punishment is to be meted out. Likewise, in the *Apocalypse of Zephaniah* Hades is described as the wicked half of a land of the dead which was divided into two halves. The one side is where the righteous reside, called Abraham's Bosom, and the other is Hades where those who are destined to eternal punishment reside. This teaching is supported by many evangelical to this day such as Merill Unger.[977]

226

However, some take a strong objection to this view, for the *Apocalypse of Zephaniah* also is said to have a sort of angelic ferryman, reminiscent of Greek mythology[978] and foreign to the teachings of Jesus. The response is that the Greeks may have taken and perverted the teaching passed down to them from the times of Noah, rather than the Jews "borrowing" it from the Greeks. Consequently, the central question is not what others taught, but what does the Bible teach.

The New Testament uses the word *hades* (ᾅδης) ten times. It occurs four times in the gospel, twice in Acts, and four times in Revelation where is it distinguished from death, but spoken of as death's companion. In Revelation 20:13-14 Hades itself is cast into the lake of fire which is eternal. This implies two things; that Hades is properly distinguished from Hell (the lake of fire) but also that Hades is destinted to be cast into hell for eternal torment. This is consistent with the teaching that Hades is a sort of temporary Hell in *Sheol* awaiting the final judgment of Revelation 20. The teachings of Jesus are more clear on this subject.

In Luke 16:22-24 Jesus tells a parable which seems to affirm this doctrine. He says;

> "Now the poor man died and was carried away by the angels to Abraham's bosom; and the rich man also died and was buried. In Hades he lifted up his eyes, being in torment, and saw Abraham far away and Lazarus in his bosom. And he cried out and said, 'Father Abraham, have mercy on me, and send Lazarus so that he may dip the tip of his finger in water and cool off my tongue, for I am in agony in this flame.'"

This fits very much with the imagery of the *Apocalypse of Zephaniah* where the abode of the dead are divided into Hades and Abraham's Bosom (also called Paradise). Nevertheless, once again the critic will cry out that this is just a parable and not a true story, as if that somehow nullifies the meaning. Therefore, a final quotation from Matthew 11:23 (cf. Luke 10:15) should be made, for there Jesus is speaking to those who have rejected Him, saying "You will descend to Hades; for if the miracles had occurred in Sodom which occurred in you, it would have remained to this day." This further indicates that Hades is a place of punishment.

Gehenna
As alluded to above, most scholars believe that "one should always distinguish between gehenna and hades."[979] This is because, unlike Hades, Gehenna is always described in the most negative of terms. Γέεννα (*Gehenna*) is found eight times in the New Testament. Every one of those citations is from the lips of Jesus Christ Himself. In the Sermon on the mount it is referenced numerous times as a place where the wicked reside and are apparently tormented. After

all, if it is preferable to cut off one's appendages rather than to go to Gehenna we must assume that Gehenna is an unpleasant place. The most vivid description of Gehenna is from this passage in Mark where it is described as "the unquenchable fire, where their worm does not die, and the fire is not quenched."

The Greek word Γέεννα (*Gehenna*) is actually a transliteration from the Hebrew word for the "valley of Hinnom" which was rubbish heap where "fire burned contiuously and worms multiplied throughout the debris."[980] It is also the place where children were once offered as burnt sacrifices to the god Moloch (2 Kings 23:10; Jeremiah 7:31, 19:2-6).[981] Some say that the "children were roasted to death in the red-hot iron arms of" Moloch's statue.[982] Others that the children were merely offered as burnt sacrifices (cf. Jeremiah 7:31, 19:5). In either case, Ahaz set up sacrificial altars for Baal and Moloch at Hinnom and "when the valley had been so declared unclean and had been so desecrated it was set apart as the place where the refuse of Jeruslaem was burned."[983] For this reason, critics argue that the image of Gehenna was simply that; an image. Of course this only begs the question. If Gehenna is an image of something, it is not a good image. If the imagery is for a place of "unquenchable fire, where the worm does not die, and the fire is not quenched" then we must assume that it is a place where we do not want to go. To dismiss Gehenna as a mere fable is to dishonor Jesus. The image of Gehenna is clearly one of Hell.

Nevertheless, some have argued that the words "unquenchable fire" were added by someone else,[984] but offer *no* evidence, for there is none to give. That the words are authentic is apparent by the fact that "unquenchable fire" and the "worm does not die" are phrases "repeated four and three times respectively."[985] There are not glosses or additions but are found repeated times in each and every single manuscript! The only reason to reject this is if one does not want to accept that "Hell is not temporary."[986] Those who argue that there is "perhaps no *material* fire"[987] must make this simply an illustration, but an illustration of what? Erasmus wanted to translate the passage more allegorically as the "worm of regret"[988] but in the end admits that the fire is real and Gehenna is Hell.[989]

Eternal Punishment

In addition to the passages cited above there are many other passages which do not use the word "hell" but which clearly speak of a place of eternal punishment. Says Merill Unger:

> "There are many phrases in which the overshadowing idea [of hell] is present with great distinctness, such as 'unquenchable fire,' 'torment in fire and brimstone,' 'the smoke of eternal,' 'the lake which burneth with fire and brimstone,' 'where the worm does not die,' 'the place prepared for the devil and his angels.'"[990]

To this may be added several passages from Revelation such as the "lake of fire" (20:10-15) and others. It is frivolous to dismiss such passages as mere imagery for a place which will not really be so bad or which is not eternal. It is clear that the Bible, and Jesus in specific, taught that there is a place of final judgment where the wicked will suffer for eternity.

Conclusion

It is apparent that *sheol* (שְׁאוֹל) is an abode of the dead divided into two halves. The one half is called Abraham's Bosom or Paradise where the righteous reside until the day of judgment; the other half where the wicked reside until their eternal fate. Hades is sometimes synonymous with Sheol, but Gehenna appears to always be synonymous with Hell or its temporary counterpart in Sheol. Thus Gehenna is always a place of torment; Hades is sometimes used simply of the abode of the dead, but at other times it is more specifically identified with the second half of Sheol where the wicked await their eternal punishment.

In both cases, the abode of the wicked is eternal. It may be conceded, as some believe, that although all are not equally punished or tormented in hell,[991] hell is real and it is eternal. Joseph Seiss argues that "there is just gradation in the sorrows of the lost ... though all the finally condemned go into one place, they do not all alike feel the same pains, or sink to the same depths in those dreadful flames."[992] Nonetheless, their judgment is final and for all eternity (Hebrews 6:2). The doctrine of purgatory cannot be found here. In Sheol the dead await resurrection, "some to *eternal* life, but others to disgrace and *everlasting* comtempt" (Daniel 12:2).

Fire and Salt
Mark 9:49-50

"For everyone will be salted with fire. Salt is good; but if the salt becomes unsalty, with what will you make it salty *again?*"

To these words Matthew adds the words, "it is no longer good for anything, except to be thrown out and trampled under foot by men." (5:13). Following the discussion of Gehenna it is clear that those who do not survive the fires of testing are to be "thrown out and trampled." The question is what is this fire of testing and what is the imagery of salt?

Verse 49 must be taken and examined separately from verse 50. Although the two are obviously connected, the salting with fire image stands apart from the image of saltiness. It is, therefore, best to look at the verses separately before merging the imagery.

Salted With Fire

It has been said that there are as many as fifteen or more different interpretations of Mark 9:49,[993] with many of these being variants of one another. Since many of the views are offshoots in one form or another, I have listed below the most popular and plausible views known to me. The first is really an argument often implemented into one of the other theories, and its therefore listed first.

View # 1 : Sacrificial Fires

Most ancient copies of Mark contain the verse as cited above, "everyone will be salted with fire." However, because that appears to be such a hard verse to interpret some ancient codex contain marginal notes and variants. The importance is not in what the original text of Mark read (for few doubt "everyone will be salted with fire" is authentic), but in how the ancients interpreted the verse.

The codex *Bezae* apparently attemped to "correct" his copy to read "every sacrifice will be salted with salt,"[994] thereby removing the difficulty of being "salted with fire," but this seems to have been taken from the codex *Alexandria* which contains the marginal note, "everyone will be salted with fire and every sacrifice salted with salt."[995] This appears to be lifted from Leviticus 2:13 where the Jewish priests are told "every grain offering of yours, you shall season with salt, so that the salt of the covenant of your God shall not be lacking from your grain offering; with all your offerings you shall offer salt."

It thus appears that at least some of the ancients saw this as a Jewish image of mankind as a living sacrifice (cf. Romans 12:1). In this context many have opted to interpret the verse accordingly. John Wesley said that everyone "shall be, as it were, salted with fire, preserved, not consumed thereby whereas every acceptable sacrifice shall be salted with another kind of salt, even that of Divine grace, which purifies the soul, (though frequently with pain) and preserves it from corruption."[996] John Nelson Darby also accepts this view.[997] However, neither explain what the imagery of fire represents. Wesley likens the salt to "Divine grace" but does not explain what the fire represents. As a result, many who accept this view are divided as to the exact meaning of the fire. Consequently, this view is often incorporated into one of the other views, as discussed below.

View # 2 : The Fires of Hell

The question of the salt is not so controversial as the question of the fire. Given that Jesus had just finished speaking about Gehenna and "the unquenchable fire" many, like Adam Clarke[998] and John Gill,[999] believe that Jesus is speaking of hell itself. Hence "everyone" refers not to everyone but to everyone who is sent to hell!

Weston Fields has gone to great lengths to argue that this seemingly strange analogy is actually a mistranslation into Greek from Hebrew, which he believes was the original language in which Mark wrote.[1000] He argues that the proper translation should be "everyone who is sent to hell will be completely destroyed."[1001] He makes this assertion based on the fact that the Hebrew word for salt, מֶלַח (*melach*), has a homonym whose root meaning he alleges can be translated as "destroy" or "vanish."[1002] Consequently, he argues that this verse should be translated as "everyone who is sent to hell will be completely destroyed."[1003] The problems with this interpretation, however, are many.

First, the homonym מָלַח (*malach*) actually means to "flee" or "vanish."[1004] This is far different from the context of "destroying." Second, Jesus did not say that the wicked will be "completely destroyed" in Gehenna but rather that they would suffer eternal punishment in "the unquenchable fire." To say that the wicked are "completely destroyed" sounds more like the doctrine of annihilationism. Third is the question of whether Mark was originally written in Hebrew, Aramaic, or Greek, which I will not venture into at this point, for the final point is the most important. Verse fifty is clearly and explicitly about *salt*. Verse forty-nine is a transitional verse between Gehenna and Jesus' teaching that we are the salt of the world (Matthew 5:13). To separate verse fifty from forty-nine would make Jesus' remark incomprehensible. Thus it is clear that Jesus was referring to salt and the translation is correct.

Although the context of Gehenna seems to favor this view, it has several problems. The first is that "everyone" should mean "everyone." To insert words not found in the text, as Weston Fields translation "everyone who is sent to hell"[1005] does, is poor exegesis. Moreover, as shown, the translation of Fields looses all continuity with the following verses which are clearly about salt and found in parallel passages in Matthew and Luke.

View # 3 : The Fire of the Holy Spirit
A better view is that the fire represents the purification of "Divine Fire"[1006] or rather the Holy Spirit. The imagery is taken from Matthew 3:11 wherein Jesus promises a baptism by fire. Likewise, at Pentecost when the Holy Spirit came upon the apostles they were said to have "tongues as of fire" (Acts 2:3). Contextual evidence for this view also comes from the allusion to Levitical sacrifices.

The imagery fits but the context does not. Clearly although the fire should not be seen as the fires of Gehenna (as stated above) the context does demand some sort of relationship between the previous passages about Gehenna and the passages about salt. The transition from "the unquenable fire" to a "baptism by the fire" of the Holy Spirit is questionable. Perhaps there is a better alternative.

View # 4 : The Fires of Persecution
Another view is that the fire represents the purifying fires of persecution. Tertullian once famously said that "the blood of the martyrs are the seeds of the church." Walter Wessel argues that "the previous verses relate to the dedication of the various members of the body (hand, foot, eye) to God. These must be sacrificed, if need be, to enter the kingdom of God, Here in v. 49 the total self is

in mind ... this saying, which is preseverd only by Mark, must have had special meaning for the persecuted Roman church.[1007]

Although this view seems better than the last, it still seems somewhat disjointed from the warnings of Gehenna found in those previous verses. It seems that we are getting closer to the truth, but have not yet arrived, for the correct view must take the full context of verses 43-48. Here Wessel attempts to tie the "dedication of the various members of the body" into this passage, but he does not account for the warnings of Gehenna, which no believer shall ever experience.

View # 5 : Purifying and Refining Fires
Although the fires of persecution theory touches upon the answer, it ignores two main elements of the passages. It ignores the warnings of Gehenna and it ignores the word "everyone." In this respect Grassmick is correct to attempt to define to whom "everyone" refers.[1008] Some say that "everyone" refers to "everyone in hell," but this argument has already been refuted. It is reading words into the text which do not exist. Others say that "everyone" refers "to every disciples living in this hostile world"[1009] as Wessel does. Since Jesus was speaking to His disciples, this view is possible contextually, but not likely as it also reads words into the text which are not there. The final choice is the most obvious. Everyone is everyone.

If *everyone* is intended then the results of the fires differ. Zechariah likens God's testing as refining fires. He declares that He will send some "through the fire, refine them as silver is refined, and test them as gold is tested" (13:9) This is the imagery that fits best. Metals that are impure are melted and burned in the "unquenchable fire" but gold and silver are refined and made pure. Thus *everyone* will be tested in this life. The trials and tribulations of life will either purify us and bring us to God, or we will be burned up in the process and sent to Gehenna. This view maintains the context of the previous verses and provides a perfect transition to verse fifty.

Summary
A passage cannot be read in isolation. Jesus was discussing man's struggles with sin and warning of the fires of Gehenna. Now he takes an image from Leviticus and Zechariah, calling us the "salt of the earth" (Matthew 5:13) and declares that as the sacrifices offered to God in Leviticus we will all be "salted with fire." Those who are impure, like cheap metals, are burned up, but those who are made of silver or gold are refined and purified. This leads to the verse fifty where Jesus discusses the nature of this "salt of the earth."

The Saltiness

The ancient world did not have refrigerators. They had salt. Salt was the main food preservative in antiquity. Food was packed into salt to preserve it and slow its decay. It was also a seasoning, of course. However, salt gets its flavor from those very preservatives. Eventually the salt will be robbed of its preservatives and must be thrown out.

This is the image Jesus is painting. We are "the salt of the earth" (Matthew 5:13). We are the preservatives of the earth and all who live in it, but like salt, once it has lost its taste "it is no longer good for anything, except to be thrown out and trampled under foot by men" (5:13).

The question here is, once again, who exactly are the salt of the earth? Is it believers in Christ as Darby believes,[1010] or is it *everyone*? The problem with Darby's argument is that Christians will never be "thrown out and trampled under foot" by God. Christ died for our sins. Any interpretation of an analogy must take the whole analogy into account. This takes us back to verse 49. Are all men intended or just some? If everyone means everyone there, then so here must all men be considered salt, but not all salt is useful, for those that have lost their taste will be "thrown out and trampled under foot." These are the unbelievers. Remember that Jesus is speaking to a crowd of people. Some were true believers. Some were not. Jesus was, therefore, urging them to become like salt and preserve the Word of God and His testimony.

Conclusion

Taken in isolation these passages are problematic, but taken in the larger context, and compared with the parallel passages it is clear that Jesus was calling upon those who fear God not to desert their bodies to Gehenna, but to let the fires purify their souls and become like salt which preserves. The analogy taken as a whole is a beautiful one. It applies to all men, but only those who trust in the Lord and His Son will be refined like gold and preserve life salt. Even as a sacrifice is salted in the fire, so we are salt thrown into the fires. We shall either be burned up as a useless metal or refined like silver and gold. All these images found in the Bible (Leviticus, Zechariah, Matthew, Mark, and Luke) explain Jesus' analogy perfectly and present us with hope for the one who loves God and a warning for the one who does not.

<h3 style="text-align:center">Mark 10: 1-12 – See Matthew 19:9</h3>

<h3 style="text-align:center">Mark 10: 17-31 – See Matthew 19:16-30</h3>

<h3 style="text-align:center">No One is Good?
Mark 10:18 – Luke 18:19</h3>

"Jesus said to him, 'Why do you call Me good? No one is good except God alone.'"

Was Jesus denying that He was good? Since few, if any, believe that, many have concluded that this was "a veiled claim" to deity.[1011] If no one is good but God then it follows that either Jesus is not good, or Jesus is God.

This statement is actually similar to that found in Psalms 14:1-3 and 53:1-3. In those passages it is explicitly stated that "There is no one who does good, not even one." Romans 3:23 states that "all have sinned and fall short of the glory of God." Yet we also know that Jesus alone among all men was "without sin" (Hebrew 4:15). Since Jesus Himself affirms that these are no mere words of distress or exaggeration, His affirmation is a test. As Matthew Henry said, "herein our Saviour doth not deny himself to be God, but checked him who did not believe him such."[1012]

Matthew Henry believed "our English word God doubtless has affinity with *good*."[1013] Hence goodly and godly are connected, but some, such as John Calvin, denies that He was "hinting at His deity."[1014] He suggests that Jesus meant to say, "you are in error to call me a good Master unless you acknowledge that I have come from God."[1015] In other words, he argues that Jesus was challenging the man who was not a true believer in Christ.

Nevertheless, Calvin's interpretation, followed by many, is not sufficient. As a young immature believer I was always troubled by these words. How could Jesus say He was not good? The only answer is that Jesus was God incarnate, the second person of the Trinity; the Son. Jesus alone is good among men, not because He has "*come from* God," as Calvin said, but because He *was* God in the second person of the Trinity; the Father's only begotten Son.

Mark 10:35 – See Matthew 20:20

Mark 10:46 – See Matthew 20:29

Mark 11:2 – See Matthew 21:2

Mark 11:1-17 – See Matthew 21:12

Mark 11:11-19 – See Matthew 21:12-17

Mark 12:18-27 – See Matthew 22:23-33

Rapture or the End of the Diaspora?
Mark 13:27

"And then He will send forth the angels, and will gather together His elect from the four winds, from the farthest end of the earth to the farthest end of heaven."

This parallel passage to the Olivet Discourse of Matthew 24 takes place at the Second Coming of Jesus. Here the Lord sends "forth the angels, and will gather together His elect from the four winds." This is often interpreted as gathering those who will return with Jesus at the Second Coming, but the passage here in Mark adds "from the farthest end of the earth to the farthest end of heaven." The addition of "farthest end of the earth" implies mortals on earth. As a result some have argued that this is rapture, and therfore, proof of a post-tribulation rapture. Those readers who are unfamiliar with the rapture theory should consult primarily the Appendices in *Controversies in Revelation* (but see also *Controversies in the Epistles*). Here, for the sake of the uninitiated, I shall briefly define one of the most controversial and difficult doctrines of the entire Bible.

Rapture is when Jesus comes to *take his own* (believers) and transform them into their immortal heavenly bodies without their having experienced physical death. It's place is in conjunction with End Times but is distinguished from the Second Coming where Jesus returns *with His own* to the earth. The rapture is a taking of believers; the Second Coming is a return with believers from heaven. The controversy and the debate is over when this rapture takes place. Many believe that rapture takes place years before the Second Coming, but "post-tribulationism" argues that the rapture is virtually synonymous with the rapture. Therefore, they see this passage as proof that Jesus is "gathering together His elect ... from the farthest end of the earth" in rapture.

At first glance this does indeed appear to be strong support for post-tribulational rapture. However, there are several reasons to rejects this view. The first is that this view cannot explain the appearance of believers *on earth* at the Second Coming if they have all been raptured here minutes (even seconds) before the Second Coming. Who would be left to inherit the Millennial Kingdom? When Jesus returns He will rule over the mortal believers who remain alive at the end of the "tribulation" (the time of the anti-Christ). So how could He have raptured them moments earlier, for those raptured are now heavenly immortals like the resurrected dead?

A closer examination shows other reasons for rejecting this as a rapture passage. Deuteronomy 30:4 contains a prophecy wherein "if your outcasts are at the ends of the earth, from there the LORD your God will gather you, and from there He will bring you back." This prophecy refers to the End Times, and many believe that it is taking place this very day as Jews are returning to Israel, but Jews (and believers in general) are scattered all over the earth to this very day. When Jesus returns, all will be gathered together to the place of His return. Is this of what Jesus speaks? The evidence supports this view for the following reasons.

It has been said, "it is interesting that in the synoptic gospels it is the angels that's doing the gathering of the elect. And yet in clear rapture passages it is Christ Himself taking up His bride and not angels."[1016] In 1 Thessalonians

4:16 the rapture is described as when "the Lord Himself descends from heaven." "Notice it says 'the Lord himself will come down.' Paul [uses] an emphatic 'himself.' One commentator added 'The Lord himself (and no other) will come down.'"[1017] However, here in Mark it is angels who do the gathering, and not Jesus. With the rapture Jesus comes to gather believers, but with the Second Coming it is angels who gather and Jesus who returns with the resurrected dead and those who were raptured. The gathering done by these angels, therefore, is not rapture, but rather a gathering of the living believers together, and a bringing of them to Jerusalem.

Although there are clear similarities to rapture, the differences are too striking to be ignored or rejected. Moreover, post-tribulational rapture creates too many difficulties and contradictions to be ignored (see notes on *Controversies in Revelation*). This passage should, therefore, be taken not as rapture but as an angelic gathering of mortal living saints who will inherit the Millennial Kingdom under Jesus, who will rule with the raptured and resurrected saints (cf. 1 Timothy 2:12; Revelation 20:6).

Mark 13:30 – See Matthew 24:34

Mark 14:14-23 – See Matthew 24:15-28

Mark 14:30, 66-72 – See Matthew 26:69-75

Mark 14:43-50 – See John 18:12

Mark 14:53 – See Luke 22:66

At What Hour?
Mark 15:25 – John 19:14

"It was the third hour when they crucified Him."	"Now it was the day of preparation for the Passover; it was about the sixth hour."

I have addressed the different methods of keeping time in the ancient world under Matthew "When Was Jesus Crucified? Chronology of the Last Supper, Crucifixion, and Resurrection." The different time reconnings cannot be denied and are confirmed by comparing Tacitus, Macrobius, Pliny the Elder, Josephus, and others. However, I did not deal with the subject in depth and some still see a problem with the three hour time lapse between the trial and crucifixion. It is therefore prudent to discuss the issue in more detail.

A Textual Error?
A handful of relatively early manuscripts change John's gospel to read "third hour" so as to better fit with the synoptic gospels. Conversely, the rather late

ninth century codex *Koridethi* (Θ) replaces the "third hour" of Mark with "sixth hour" to match John's gospel. Examining the early manuscripts as a whole, however, there is no doubt that Mark read "third hour" and John read "sixth hour." Despite this fact, some who reject the "western reckoning"[1018] of John's gospel argue that a textual error must have taken place.

Citing an old textual theory by Eusebius, Gleason Archer notes that "the numeral 'three' was indicated by capital gamma, whereas 'six' was indicated by a digamma (a letter resembling our *F*). The copyist thought he saw the extra horizontal stroke and changed 'three' to 'six.'"[1019] Now it may be logical to assume that a copiest might mistake a digamma for a gamma, but it seems somewhat frivolous to claim that a copiest mistook a gamma (*Γ*) for a digamma (*F*). Of course, not only is this pure conjecture, and a poor one, "but this does not really solve the problem at all, because John 19:14 does not indicate the time Christ was crucified but only the time of His appearance before Pilate's judgment seat."[1020] Consequently, we must reject the textual theory as idle, and unnecessary, speculation.

Time Reconnings

As I have discussed earlier in some detail, there were different methods of counting time in antiquity. This is confirmed by an examination of Tacitus, Macrobius, Pliny the Elder, Josephus, and others. To this day the reader can go to any Synagogue in the country and ask them when the Sabbath begins. They will tell you it begins at 6:00, not midnight!

While Henry Swete rejects this argument, declaring that "the problem cannot be said to have been solved yet,"[1021] he offers no rebuttal of it. That John was using Roman time is apparent by the time of the cock-crow (for cocks do not crow at noon) and can be easily inferred in John 19:42 for "the next day, the Sabbath, would be at 6:00 P.M. according to Jewish time, and it was already past 3:00 P.M. Since burial was unlawful on the Sabbath."[1022] In other words, it is acknowledged by all four gospels that Jesus was buried before 6:00 P.M. on Friday. This fact in itself proves that the "sixth" hour of John *must* conform to Roman time, not Jewish time.

This means that John records the appearance of Jesus before Pilate at "about" 6 A.M. in the morning. Mark records that Jesus was crucified at 9 A.M. our time. This leaves about three hours for the trial and passion of Christ before He was nailed to the cross. Some see a problem with this time frame. Could it really have taken three full hours to transport Jesus to the cross, they ponder? Let is us examine the facts.

The Duration of the Trial

Could the final stages of Jesus' trial would have taken three hours? Critics suggest this is impossible and a contradiction. Of course, the charge is invalid for in the real world it takes time to transport a prisoner from the courtyard to the place of flogging and back again, let alone the carrying of the cross to Golgotha which would have taken anywhere from thirty minutes to an hour depending on which Holy site is the authentic one.[1023] Consider that films omit the tedium of walking from one place to another, preparing the cross, etc. Despite this fact, in Mel Gibson's film the actual screen time from Herod sending Jesus back to Pilate to the time Jesus was nailed to the cross was a full hour in *film time*! How much longer would it have been in real time?

Moreover, since John says "about" the sixth hour, we may conclude that it is a round number. Between the sixth hour and the seventh is a full hour, and Jesus could have appeared before Pilate anytime in this period, but apparently closer to the sixth hour. Furthermore, the first hour in Mark's gospel would be from 6 A.M. to 7 A.M. in Jewish reckoning, thus the third hour was apparently just before 9 A.M., rather than after 9 A.M. Consequently, between two and two and a half hours is *more* than sufficient for these events to have transpired. It is more than reasonable to assume that the trial, preparations, mocking of Jesus, carrying of the cross to Golgotha (during which he needed the assistance of Simon of Cyrene), and the assembly of the cross, nailing, raising of the cross, etc., would certainly have taken at least two and a half hours or more.

Conclusion

That John uses Roman time rather than Jewish time is obvious. The cock crows at sunrise, not noon. All gospels record that Jesus was buried before the Sabbath, which to this very day begins officially at 6 P.M. Friday evening. Thus John records that Jesus stood before Pilate at around 6 A.M. The final stages of His trial, mocking, preparations for crucifixion, and transportation to Golgotha would easily have taken two and a half to three hours. Thus John is in perfect accord with the synoptic gospels.

Mark 15:34 – See Matthew 27:46

Mark 15:39 – See Matthew 27:54

Mark 16:1-8 – See Matthew 28:1-8

Mark 16:9 – See Luke 8:2

The Ending of Mark
Mark 16:9-20

Many may not realize it, but some Bibles place these verses in brackets. The reason is because these passages are among one of only three consequential passages in the whole of the New Testament where serious scholars question their authenticity. Despite the frivolous claim of atheists, Bible critics, and

Jihadists, there are only three places anywhere in the New Testament where one might reasonably ponder whether these were the words of the author. Why? Is it true? Did Mark pen these words? If not, how did they come to be? Who wrote them? Are they inspired? All these are fair questions which I shall endeavor to answer.

The Textual Evidence

Mark 16:9-20 can actually be divided into two separate sections. These sections are treated differently because they appear separately among the ancient manuscripts. Section 1 consist of the entire passages from verse nine to verse twenty with the exception of "Section 2." Section 2 is a short passage reading "and they promptly reported all these instructions to Peter and his companions. And after that, Jesus Himself sent out through them from east to west the sacred and imperishable proclamation of eternal salvation." This passage is usually found as the last verse in most Bibles.

Section 1

The larger section of verses 9-20 is found in many ancient manscripts, including codices A, C, D, W, Θ, the majority text (𝔪) and is further cited by the early church fathers Irenaeus and Tertullian. However, they are notably absent from two of the oldest codices, ℵ and B. Moreover, the codex *Washingtonianus* (also called the *Freerianus*, designated as W) adds a lengthy discourse not found elsewhere. It reads:

> "And they excused themselves saying, 'This age of lawlessness and unbelief is under Satan, who does not allow what lies under the unclean spirits to understand the truth and power of God. Therefore reveal your righteousness now' – thus they spoke to Christ. And Christ replied to them, 'the term of years of Satan's power has been fulfilled, but other terrible things draw near. And for those who have sinned I was handed over to death, that they may return to the truth and sin no more, in order that they may inherit the spiritual and incorruptible glory of righteousness that is in heaven.'"

In addition the early church fathers Clement of Alexandria and Origen do not mention the passage, although it is assumed that they should.[1024] Finally, both Eusebius and Jerome state that the passages are missing from many of the Greek manuscripts at their disposal (and they had many more ancient manuscripts at their disposal than we do).[1025]

Conversely, "there are indications of its use in Hermas, and Justin appears to refer to v. 20, whilst v. 19 is expressly quoted by Irenaeus as the work of St. Mark."[1026] A few passages from these verses are also quoted by the patristic father Tatian.[1027] Both Justim Martyr and Tatian lived in the first century after the apostles; all of these authors lived long before Origen, Eusebius, and Jerome.

Section 2
The words "and they promptly reported all these instructions to Peter and his companions. And after that, Jesus Himself sent out through them from east to west the sacred and imperishable proclamation of eternal salvation," are not found in most ancient manuscripts. They are only found in codices L, Ψ, and a few late manuscripts; a few of which place the passage after verse eight. The passage is entirely absent from codices א, A, B, C, D, W, Θ, and the majority text (𝔪). For this reason, most Bibles do not contain this short verse. It is usually believed that the words were added "to soften the harshness of so abrupt a conclusion, and at the same time to remove the impression which it leaves of a failure on the part of Mary Magdalene and her friends to deliver the message which they had been charged,"[1028] which is the impression left by the omission of Section 1.

"Internal" Evidence
In addition to the textual evidence cited above, some have argued for the exclusion of these passages based on so-called "internal" evidence. I shall again reserve comment upon this "internal" evidence for later. Here I shall again merely cite the "evidence."

It is argued that there are as many as seven "internal" reasons to reject these passages, although not all seven reasons are accepted even by advocates. In fact, Bruce Metzger (who rejects these verses) lists only two,[1029] and some are deriviative of others. Nevertheless, they are as follows:

1. "The vocabulary and style of verses 9-20 are non-Markan (e.g. απιστεω, βλαπτω, βεβαιοω, επακολουθεω, θεαομαι, μετα ταυτα, πορευομαι, συνεργεω, ″υστερον are found no where else in Mark)."[1030]
2. "The transition from verse 8 to verse 9 involves an abrupt change of subject from 'women' to the presumed subject 'Jesus' since His name is not stated in verse 9."[1031]
3. "Mary Magdalene is introduced with a descriptive clause in verrse 9 as though she had not been menioned already."[1032]
4. "The narrative is concise and barren lacking the vivid and lifelike details so characteristic of Markan historical narrative."[1033]
5. "Mark would have been expected to include a Resurrection appearance to the discples in Galilee (14:28; 16:7), but the appearances in verses 9-20 are in or near Jerusalem."[1034]
6. "Matthew and Luke parallel Mark until verse 8 and then diverge."[1035]
7. "The bizarre promise of immunity from snakes and poisonous drinks is completely out of character with the person of Christ."[1036]

Now I will comment on these "internal evidences" below, but it should be apparent to the reader that I find such "evidences" inherently weak as they reflect more opinion than fact. I have quoted the authors exactly so that I might neither be accused of taking them out of context nor stating opinion as fact. Opinions of what "Mark would have been expected"[1037] to do are hardly "facts." So also criticisms of "bizarre promises"[1038] are based on opinions rather than facts (see discussion on "Snake Handling" under Mark 16:17-18).

An Evaluation of the Evidence
What are we to make of these evideneces? From the evidence cited above many have concluded that the verses are not authentic and were added to the text by others. If true, then the question is "why?" Unfortunately the answers offered only lead to more questions and few satisfying answers. An evaluation of the evidence cited is essential before we can reach any conclusions as to why the text came to be altered, *if* it was at all.

These controversial passages *are* found "in every known Greek MS. except" ℵ, B, L, Ψ, ℸ[12], and ℘.[1039] It is of interest to note, however, that "in B," codex *Vaticanus*, "the scribe has left a column blank after κατα μαρκον, which has been taken to mean that he was aquainted with a text of St. Mark which did not end at v. 8, although his own copy failed him at that point."[1040] In other words, even the scribe of codex *Vaticanus* realized that verse eight was not the true ending of Mark. Since all other ancient manuscripts include the verses and are quoted in part by at least two patristic fathers shortly after the apostolic times, there does not seem to be sufficient evidence to reject the passages based solely on textual evidence. What then of "internal evidence"?

The "internal evidence" is subjective. Of the seven arguments listed above, two may be rejected outright as pure conjecture and opinion based on what the critic believes Mark "would have been expected"[1041] to do or what sort of "bizarre promises"[1042] Jesus would not have made (see notes on Mark 16:17-18 for a more objective explanation). Such is not fact, but guess work.

Two more "internal evidences" can be dismissed on similar grounds. To argue that "Matthew and Luke parallel Mark until verse 8 and then diverge"[1043] is a simplification at best. This is particularly true since the nature of the relationship between Matthew, Mark, and Luke is hardly agreed upon (see Appendix A). The argument assumes the validity of the critic's opinion on the Synoptic relationship and an argument based on assumption is not a solid argument. It is inductive reasoning at best; not deductive reasoning.[1044] Likewise, although "style" may be important, it is not valid to describe a small select passage as "lacking the vivid and lifelike details so characteristic of Markan historical narrative."[1045] This is, again, opinion; not fact.

This leaves three arguments; two of which are essentially the same (the presumed change of topic from the "women" to Jesus and of Mary Magdalene), and thus can be addressed as a single issue. These *two* arguments therefore deserve the most attention.

First is the question of whether or not there is truly an "abrupt and awkward"[1046] transition from verse eight to nine. It is said that "Mary Magdalene is referred to as if she had never been mentioned before, yet she appears three times in the crucifixion, bural, and resurrection narratives."[1047] On this same line of reasoning it is further argued that the "presumed" subject is Jesus, but Jesus is not named in verse nine.[1048] Thus the verse is criticized for reintroducing Mary Magdalene, who had not been mentioned since verse one, while at the same time criticizing the passage for *not* reintroducing Jesus who was mentioned just two verses previous! The reality is that the failure to reintroduce Jesus can be used as "internal evidence" of its authenticity, for it actually assumes that the reader had bothered to read the previous two passages. Furthermore, this alleged "awkward" transition is *at best* an argument that a verse is missing between verses eight and nine; not that nine through twenty are not authentic. Once again, it must be concluded that the arguments here are more subjective opinions than facts.

Finally, one "internal evidence" remains. I have saved it for last because it *appears* to be the most damning. This is the argument that "nearly a third of the significant Greek words in verses 9-20 are 'non-Markan,' that is, they do not appear elsewhere in Mark or they are used differently from Mark's usage prior."[1049] Now at first glance this too sound superficial for an author's style and vocabulary will change depending on the subject and target audience. While the reader may immediately recognize my style of writing, he may not, at first, recognize my fiction novels or even my narrative history, for my style and vocabulary differs in those. And this, despite the fact that I have written thousands of pages, thus giving the reader a far more in depth look at my style and vocabulary than Mark, who wrote the shortest of the gospels and who left no other writings to which we can compare. How then can the critic look at such a relatively short book and conclude that "απιστεω, βλαπτω, βεβαιοω, επακολουθεω, θεαομαι, μετα ταυτα, πορευομαι, συνεργεω, [and]"υστερον"[1050] are "non-Markan" words? The very term "non-Markan" seems to be subjective.

The only reason why this argument bears any weight at all is because of the seemingly large percentage of differences. It has been argued that out of the 167 total words found in verses nine through twenty there are seventy-five "different significant words."[1051] Of course, on closer examination eleven of these words do occur in Mark, but are "used in a different sense."[1052] Moreover, when we start examining the words invidually, the argument starts to loose weight. Let us examine some of the words listed by Bruce Metzger as the primary differences.

The first word Metzger lists is απιστεω (*apisteo*).[1053] This word means "faithless" and comes from the word "faith," πιστεω (*pisteo*), found repeatedly throughout Mark. Moreover, the word απιστεω (*apisteo*) is found in 2 Timothy

2:13, but nowhere else in the writings of the apostle Paul. Are we to consider this word "non-Pauline" and reject it as authentic? Because απιστεω (*apisteo*) is rarely used in the Bible, it is poor evidence to say that its inclusion is evidence against authenticity. It would be better evidence if these were common words which appear no where else in Mark. Then, and only then, could we assume that Mark's personal style and vocabulary do not fit. Likewise, επακολουθεω (accompany) is another rare word. The same could be said of several other words. Rare words are, by definition, rare. They cannot be used as proof of another author.

Thus it must be said in all fairness that "internal evidence" by itself is nothing more than circumstantial evidence and often nothing more than personal opinion. Combined with physical evidence a jury can convict someone on circumstantial evidence, but rarely on circumstantial evidence alone. If we examine the physical evidence (textual data) then we find that only two of the most ancient manuscripts lack these passages, and one of those, the codex *Vaticanus*, indicates that the scribe knew his copy was incomplete.[1054] Even two patristic church fathers quote from the passages. Consequently, although it is obvious that the passages were missing from some manuscripts distributed in antiquity, it is equally certain that they *were* included in many others. Since even the critics admit that Mark almost certainly did not end with verse eight, it seems that the evidence favors the inclusion of these passages as Mark's own words.

Theories on the Text

What are we to make of these evideneces? From the evidence cited above many have concluded that the verses are not authentic and were added to the text by others, and yet they are included in every Bible translation. The question is "why?" Unfortunately the answers offered only lead to more questions and few satisfying answers.

Of the many views and theories presented, three are most popular and attested. The first says that the original ending to Mark was somehow lost and that verses 9-20 were added to make Mark's ending seem not so abrupt. This view I have rejected for the reasons outlined above.

The second view argues that Mark did indeed end his gospel at verse eight. William Barclay calls it a "Lost Ending" arguing that "it may be that Mark died, perhaps even suffered martyrdom, before he could complete his gospel."[1055] There is an early tradition that Mark wrote his gospel during the persecutions of Nero,[1056] but there is no traditon that his gospel was left unfinished, and yet so close to being finished! This hardly seems likely, especially since the weight of evidence seems to favor the verses' inclusion.

The last view, which follows, is best. As the scrolls were disseminated, copies were sent out to the various churches, some copies were damaged and the last part of the scroll torn off. Because of the persecutions, it would take time to receive new copies. In the meantime, those regions which did not receive a complete manuscript made their own copies which they disseminiated. In time, the complete copies were found and restored, but by this time there were now two versions of Mark's gospel being spread. One was complete. The other was incomplete. This created some confusion as not all copiest had the completed version. In time all new manuscripts included verses 9-20, which were authentic.

Conclusion

Mark 16:9-20 is one of only three honestly contested passages in the entire New Testament (I say "honestly contested" to distinguish it from atheistic and Jihadists websites which claim the entire New Testament to be fraudulent or having been tampered). Despite the lengthy debates and speculation the physical evidence supports its authenticity which is why it is included in every translation. Let us reduce these arguments and consider the fact on a more simplistic level. "Which is easier to conceive: a) that Mark left his Gospel unfinished and allowed it to be published ... or b) that Mark did finish his Gospel by writing v. 9-20, but that many copies later on omitted these verses? Which is the easier to conceive?"[1057] Add to this the inspiration of the Holy Spirit and we must accept that these are the words of John Mark.

Snake Handlers
Mark 16:17-18

"They will pick up serpents, and if they drink any deadly *poison,* it will not hurt them; they will lay hands on the sick, and they will recover."

This passage has been called a "bizarre promise"[1058] that Christ Jesus would never have made. Some outright reject the passage. On the other hand, "superstitious use of this verse has given rise to the snake-handling and poison-drinking sects of Appalachia."[1059] These two extremes seem to feed off of one another, for the critic who calls this promise "bizarre" assumes that it leads logically to the second extreme, but neither are logical or Biblical.

It seems that the critics of this verse have forgotten the story of the apostle Paul while he was shipwrecked on the island of Malta. It reads:

"But when Paul had gathered a bundle of sticks and laid them on the fire, a viper came out because of the heat and fastened itself on his hand. When the natives saw the creature hanging from his hand, they *began* saying to one another, 'Undoubtedly this man is a murderer, and though he has been saved from the sea, justice has not allowed him to live.' However he shook the creature off into the fire and suffered no harm. But they were expecting that he was about to swell up or suddenly fall down dead. But after they had waited a long time and had seen nothing unusual happen to him, they changed their minds and *began* to say that he was a god" (Acts 28:3-6).

Thus not only was Christ's promise fulfilled, but it lead to the dissemination of the gospel among the superstitious people of Malta. Moreover, Matthew Henry records that "ecclesiastical history" shows that forcing victims to drink poison was among the cruelties inflicted by the Romans, but many Christians seemed uneffected by the poisons, thus other means of torture and execution were devised.[1060] So we again see Christ's words were not only literally fulfilled, but assisted in the spreading of the gospel throughout the world.

Now some have argued that this was an apostolic promise only and that "this promise ... does not warrant voluntary snake-handling or drinking of posion, practices not attested in the earth church."[1061] Indeed, the voluntary handling of snakes could be compared to the temptation of Jesus in Matthew 4:5-7 where the devil quoted God's promise to protect His angels. Jesus' response was another Biblical passage, "You shall not put the Lord your God to the test!" (Matthew 4:7, cf. Luke 4:9-12). In the same way it would be a sin to voluntarily drink poison or let snakes bite you. This is tempting the Lord God!

So this passage, like the rest of Mark 16:9-20 is authentic and a promise which has been fulfilled, literally, in history. Reactionary theology is that theology which is made in reaction against a particular view. We should no more react against this passage on account of snake-handling cults then we should react against the doctrine of the Trinity on account of Catholicism (I speak as a Protestant)! Acts 28:3-6 was a fulfillment of this passage, as were miracles said to be wrought during the early persecutions of Nero. In each case, the victim did not voluntarily offer himself up, for this would be a violation of the law of God, but had the poison or snake cast upon them unwittingly or unwillingly. God kept His promise and protected the early apostles in these instances and used those miracles for the furtherment of His glory and the dissemination of the gospel.

Summary of Mark's Gospel

Mark, the traveling companion of Paul and Peter, wrote this, the shortest and most concise of the gospels. Unlike Matthew, which was written to the Hebrew people, Mark was probably written to target the gentile church. As such it would have been written in Greek as in all our ancient copies. No tradition exist to suggests that it was written in any other language, as is the case with Matthew. The only relationship which John Mark's gospel has to Matthew's is that he had almost certainly seen it and asked the apostle Peter his own recollections of the events. He did not, however, use Matthew as a guide or copy from Matthew as is evident by the very critics who argue, erroneously, that there are contradictions in his version of events and Matthew's.

The primary difference in Matthew and Mark is the order in which some of the events are listed. According to the apostolic father Papias, who was a young man when the apostle John was preaching and later exiled to Patmos, "Mark, being the recorder of Peter, wrote accurately but not in order whatever he [Peter] remembered of the things either said or done by the Lord."[1062] Papias thus argues that Mark wrote topically, rather than chronologically, although some believe the reverse is the case. Either way, the relationship between Matthew and Mark is nominal and there is no instance of "copying" or plagerism. Peter was a witness to the events which John Mark wrote. It is natural that Matthew and Peter would recollect many of the same events, especially if Peter had seen Matthew's gospel, as he most certainly did. The real question might be, "why is John's gospel so different," but that is a topic reserved for John.

Mark is then the shortest and most concise gospel written primarily to the gentile church. As such it was the first gospel disseminated to the gentile world at large in the Greek language. Matthew would later be translated into Greek by Matthew himself, but was at this time a Hebrew work targeting the Jewish people. This would explain why some thought Mark was the first gospel written, while others believed Matthew was the first. Matthew was the first, but Mark was the first written to the gentile church at large in their own language. It is a record of Jesus as passed on by the apostle Peter through John Mark, his colleague.

4

The Synoptic Gospels - Luke

Luke was a physician (Colossians 4:14) and travelling companion of the apostle Paul (cf. 2 Timothy 4:11, Acts). He was a gentile convert and the only author of a New Testament book who was not a Jew. Luke's gospel is actually the first of a two part history he wrote for a certain Theophilus (Luke 1:3, Acts 1:1). The first book is this gospel. The second is the book Acts of the Apostles.

Luke is unique in many ways. He wrote not as an eyewitness but as a historian. He explicitly says that he "investigated everything" (1:3) in researching his work. As such few doubt that Luke read Matthew, and possibly Mark. The correlation between Luke and those two gospels is one of research, but Luke includes much which is not present in those two works. Had he merely copied those works, his gospel would have been of little value, but instead Luke, a highly educated man (much like the apostle Paul but from a different background), spoke to and recorded the testimonies and anecdotes of eyewitnesses; most notably Mary, the mother of Jesus. This is apparent by the anecdotal, but important, stories of the shepherds (2:8-20) and of Jesus when he was a boy (2:45-49). These stories are ones which a mother would remember.

So Luke's gospel enriches our understanding of Jesus and the events of his life by writing as a historian rather than as an eyewitness. Together with Matthew, Mark, and John, Luke helps provide a more complete picture. In this way *each* of the four gospels presents aspects of Jesus' life which would be lacking if only one author had written a much longer gospel. Matthew writes *to Jews*, proving the prophetic credentials of Jesus. Mark wrote *to gentiles*, explaining his mission and goals for all man. Luke wrote *as a historian*, providing anecdotes and historical backdrops. John wrote *as a theologian* and eyewitness, teaching the reader about Jesus.

A True Historian?
The Authorship and Date of Luke

As a historian Luke provides much historical information missing from the narrative accounts of Matthew and Mark. We find references to dates, emperors, kings, and other chronological historical information. Ironically, this very fact has been used against Luke by Bible critics. Without the full facts at their disposal, the Bible critic argues that Luke was "wrong" or dishonest, but as we shall see it is the critic, two thousand years removed from the facts, who is in error. Why would Luke have provided false information which would have been easily exposed and of no major consequence to his story? He provides that information because it was verifiably true and because he wrote as a historian.

Few doubt that Luke wrote the gospel bearing his name. It is clearly written by the author of Acts (cf. Luke 1:3 and Acts 1:1) and the evidence that Luke wrote Acts is overwhelming. Several times he refers to the travels of Paul by saying "we" (cf. Acts 27:3-7). Ancient tradition is also unanimous in attributing the works to him.

When the gospel of Luke was written is also more clear than with Matthew and Mark. Since we know that Acts was completed in the early 60s when the apostle Paul was awaiting trial, and the gospel of Luke was obviously completed a few years earlier, we can safely assume that Luke's gospel was written around 60 A.D. Some have argued that it must have been written later, based on the *assumption* that Luke used Mark's gospel *and* that Mark was written during the persecution of Nero in the mid-60s.[1063] Others, say that Luke refers to the destruction of Jerusalem in 70 A.D. and, denying the prophetic element, argue that Luke must have written after 70 A.D. Of course this can be rejected outright since it based on numerous unproven assumptions and interpretations. Whether or not Luke used Mark is uncertain. He certainly had seen Matthew and perhaps even Mark, but even if he did use Mark, this would only be evidence for an earlier date of Mark's gospel (see notes on "Mark and Plagiarism? The Authorship and Date of Mark"). This is because one cannot fix Luke's gospel later than Acts. Acts explictly refers to this gospel as his "first account" (Acts 1:1). Since Acts ends before the persecutions of Nero, Luke cannot reasonably be dated later than 62 A.D. at the latest!

So most all agree that Luke was written by the travelling companion of Paul around 60 A.D. It was written from the perspective of a historian, having consulted with existing documents, records, and the testimonies of the apostles, Mary the mother of Jesus, and other eyewitnesses. It is the longest of the gospels (1151 verses as opposed to Matthew's 1071[1064]) and provides the most historical background into the life and times of Jesus Christ.

When Was the Census?
(Questions on the Birthdate of Jesus)
Luke 2:1

"Now in those days a decree went out from Caesar Augustus, that a census be taken of all the inhabited earth. This was the first census taken while Quirinius was governor of Syria."

This passage helps to better pinpoint the birth of Jesus, but it is also the target of Bible critics who claim that no such census ever took place. It is more than a little ironic that Bible critics use Luke's historical research against him. With less information available today than the men of Luke's time, the critic nevertheless claims that no such census ever took place. Before refuting this accusation, I would ask the critic why, if no such census took place, would Luke have made such a claim when it bears no importance to the gospel story? In a

248

court of law one is required to find a motive for a lie. What purpose would Luke have had to make up such an event, which would have been easily exposed? Of course the Bible critic is not interested in such logic. He is just interested in attempting to tear down whatever the Bible says in an attempt to make the reader question the authority and accuracy of the Bible. It is for that reason alone that I endeavor to answer this false allegation against Luke, and to fix the date of Jesus' birth.

As to fixing a date for Jesus' birth, it is well known that no one dated history from the time of Jesus until centuries after His birth. Under Constantine the birth of Christ started to become the standard for measuring history, but it is universally accepted that the date of Jesus' birth was miscalculated by at least a few years. Despite what some believe, this does not effect the date of the crucifixion, which is a separate issue. Nonetheless, the reader should not be confused at hearing scholars speak of Jesus' birth in 4 or 5 *B.C.* (meaning "before Christ"). This will become clear in the pages that follow.

The Historicity of the Census
The central problem is that Quirinius (Cyrenius in the Latin) is mentioned as governor of Syria from 6 to 10 A.D.[1065] and, further, a census is said to have taken place at that time.[1066] However, that is far too late to match Luke's account since Herod died in 4 B.C. This has led some to conclude that Luke was mistaken or confused in his facts. Critics have used this alleged "mistake" to cast doubt upon the entire story, but is it really a mistake?

Three possible solutions have been offered. Two are relatively simple explanations; the third requires serious debate about a period of history with which we have sparce information.

Theory # 1 : Copy Error
Some have supposed that a "corruption in the text of Luke" must have taken place over the centuries.[1067] Of course the answer to this is simple. Of the thousands of ancient manuscripts of our Bible (a hundred of which are *ante-Nicene* in origin) and the countless quotations by apostolic, patristic, and church fathers, not a single manuscript shows a hint of any such error. The only copy errors found in these manuscripts is over the spelling of Quirinius' name![1068]

There is never a valid reason to assume that a copy error has been made if there is *no* textual evidence to support such an error. This is purely hypothetical and weighs against common sense, for if such an error had been made, *someone* would have noticed. This argument must be rejected outright.

Theory # 2 : Mistranslation
A better argument is that the passage has been mistranslated. According to this theory the word πρωτη (*prote*) translated "first" could be translated "before" as done in John 15:18.[1069] Hence, the translation should allegedly read, "the census

249

was before that made when Quirinius was governor."[1070] Although this sounds promising, it is actually very weak. The word πρωτη (*prote*) means "first" and as such is translated by the NIV even in John 15:18, "if the world hates you, keep in mind that hated me *first*." Context allows translators to translate that passage as "hated me before you" but in this case the NIV actually has the most literal translation. In fact, Thayer's famed Greek Lexicon list only one definition for πρωτη (*prote*); "first."[1071] There is simply no logical, exegetical, or contextual reason to change the definition of πρωτη (*prote*) from "first" to "before." Moreover, it is obvious that they were going to Bethlehem *because* of the census.

Theory # 3 : Luke is Correct
If the first two theories are to be rejected, and they must be, then there are only two possibilities remaining; either Luke was right or he was wrong. Let us therefore examine the evidence.

Critics have argued that Luke's account is implausible based on four "facts." First, they claim that if such a census took place Joseph would not have had to travel to Bethlehem but to register in the current city of residence. However, that argument has been rebutted by the discovery of an Egyptian papyrus from the prefect of Egypt under Rome who required citizens to return to the city of their origin.[1072] This makes sense since anyone could claim to live in another city and move away at registration time. It would have been impossible in that day and age to keep track of everyone which is precisely why people were registered in the city of their birth and were required to return there.

Second, they claim that no census would have been conducted by Rome under Herod since Herod was suppposedly a soverign. Once again, this argument does not hold up. For one thing Rome did conduct censii in vassal states and one such census is recorded as having been conducted in Apamea, Syria by the very same Quirinius.[1073] Additionally, Tertullian records at least one census in Judea under Saturninus.[1074] Moreover, in 8 B.C. Herod fell into disfavor with Augustus and his autonomy was restricted. The people of Israel were even required to give an oath of loyalty to Augustus, indicating that Herod was no longer trusted completely by Augustus.[1075] Consequently, there is no reason to deny that such a census could have taken place.

The third argument critics utilize is the argument from silence. They say that no such census is ever recorded as taking place outside of the Bible. This argument is particularly weak, even if it is true (and that is suspect). Aside from the inherent weakness of an argument from silence over a census in an age where papyri are rarely extant, is the fact that the critics themselves must concede that Rome conducted a census every fourteen years.[1076] Since all acknowledge that a census took place between 6-10 A.D. it follows there must have been a "first" (2:2) census approximately between 9-5 B.C.! Says John MacArthur, "the argument from silence is undercut by the many censuses known to have been carried out at about that same time."[1077] Lastly, a census is hardly ground breaking historically noteworthy event unless there was something special involved, such as the riots which erupted in the census conducted after 6 or 7 A.D. Those riots are doubtless the only reason that Josephus saw fit to record the census at all![1078]

The last criticism is that Quirinius was supposedly not governor until 6 A.D. and therefore could not have conducted this census in Herod's time. This argument deserves the most attention, and the reader will find that criticism is not based on fact, but a lack of facts. The evidence, fairly interpreted, supports the Biblical account.

Let is begin by establishing the uncontested facts. 1) Herod died in either March or early April of 4 B.C.[1079] 2) The Imperial "legate" of Syria from 9 B.C. to 6 B.C. was Saturninus.[1080] 3) A census was apparently started in Judea under Saturninus.[1081] 4) Quirinius was Imperial "*consular*"[1082] of Syria from 6 A.D. to 10 A.D.[1083] 5) Quirinius is referred to in Luke as ηγεμονευοντος (*egemonehontos*), meaning "commander" or "leader" and not necessarily "legate" or "governor." 6) Luke says that this was the "*first*" census undertaken by Quirinius, implying that he conducted at least two.

From these uncontested facts, two possible conclusions have been reached. Some believe that "Quinrinius was twice governor of Syria ... from B.C. 4 to A.D. 1; the second A.D. 6-10."[1084] Others believe that Quirinius was not actually governor the first time but rather a "consular"[1085] who served under the supervision of Saturninus and later the Imperial legate Quintilius Varus, who served from 7 B.C. to A.D. 4.[1086] Let us examine these two possibilities.

There is no doubt that Saturninus served as "legate" or governor of Syria from 9 B.C. to 6 B.C. Some sources have Quintilius Varus as legate from 7 B.C. to A.D. 4[1087] but Gleason Archer makes careful note of the "one-year overlap in these two terms."[1088] This implies that either there was a transition of some sort, or that they actually had two different titles. The words "president," "governor," "mayor," etc., all have specific meanings in our society. Ancient Rome had different titles and administrative positions. Pontius Pilate, for example, is variously called "governor" by some but "procurator" by others. The official title for each is then open to debate. What were the differences in a "legate" and a "consular," between a "governor" and a "procurator"? It doesn't matter. They were all administrative leaders of Rome with authority given to them by the emperor.

This confusion is one of many reasons that historians have variously dated the governorship (or Imperial legate) of Quintilius Varus. Some believe he was governor from 7 B.C. all the way until A.D. 4.[1089] Others date his rule only from 7 B.C. to 1 B.C.[1090] And some believe he was only governor from 6 B.C. to 4 B.C.[1091] Some believe that there was a dual legateship of Syria[1092] while others believe that the apparent vacancy after 4 B.C. was in fact filled by Quirinius who served twice as governor of Syria.[1093] This confusion should not be surpirising to the student of antiquity knows our information is fragmentary and Syria was not the center of the empire. The information at our disposal does offer "strong corroborative evidence that such a preliminary enrollment was made during the *first* term of office of Cyrenius (Quirinius) as Governor of Syria."[1094] These words are from the the the liberal scholar Farrar, former Dean of Canterbury.

What we can infer from this "strong corroborative evidence" is that when Luke refers to "a 'first' [he] surely implies a *second* one sometime later."[1095] There is no confusion with the later census of Quirinius. Furthermore, Tertullian stated that "there is historical proof that at this very time a census had been taken in Judaea by Sentius Saturninus."[1096] This census coincided with the falling out of Herod's favor with Augustus sometime between 8 and 7 B.C. Since "several years would be required to complete such a census,"[1097] and history has recorded censii that have taken decades to complete,[1098] it is more than logical to assume that Quirinius was put in charge of the census and continued it after Saturninus was removed from office. Whether Quirinius was "consular" under Quintilius Varus or governor, as most modern translations imply (older translations differ),[1099] is irrelevant. The facts lead us to believe that Luke was 100% correct. How could he not be? Would not the critics of his day have immediately pointed out Luke's "mistake"? Would no one have noticed such a glaring error? To suggest that the modern historians knows more about the history of ancient Syria than a historian who lived in that era is ridiculous. He had more information at his disposal as is evident by modern scholars inability even agree on the length of Sentius Saturninus' term. Luke, the ancient historian, surely knew what he was talking about.

The Date of Jesus' Birth

History was not dated from the birth of Christ until many centuries later. Based on the evidence we now have at our disposal, most agree that Jesus was not born in 1 A.D. as we reckon history, but several years earlier. Exactly when? Let us examine the evidence, bearing in mind what has already been said.

The Bible makes clear that Jesus was born before the death of Herod who tried to slay the baby Jesus. We know that Herod died between March 12 and April 11 4 B.C. based on the testimony of Josephus.[1100] Further, since the census of Quirinius did not begin until probably 6 B.C. (even though the charge was apparently given to Saturninus originally, it was not until he was replaced that the census count began), then Jesus must have been born sometime between 6 and 4 B.C. There are other clues as well, but those are not as clear.

Some have argued that Herod's desire to kill everyone under two years of age (Matthew 2:16) is proof that the wisemen did not arrive until two years later and that Jesus was already a small child.[1101] I have addressed this in part under "The Magi and the Shephards Matthew 2:1-12 – Luke 2:8-20" and will again in "Did Jesus Flee to Egypt? Luke 2:22." Here it is only necessary to reply that Herod did not know when the child was born. He only knew when the star first appeared to the Magi (Matthew 2:7) and wanted to make sure that the child did not escape him. This is why he slaughtered every child who was two years or less. Also remember that a soldier cannot look at a child and tell if it is eighteen months or twelve months; at least most cannot. Again, Herod was not taking any chances. Since the Magi's trip from Parthia had doubtless taken many months or even a year, Herod may have assumed that the child had been born before they even departed. We simply cannot attempt to determine Jesus' age based on Herod's actions. The Bible depicts Mary and Joseph as still living *in Bethlehem* when the Magi arrived. It is not logical to assume that they were living there several years later since Luke 2:39 declares that they went to Nazareth in Galilee after the dedication of Jesus at the temple (cf. Matthew 2:22-23). Surely they would not have waited two years to dedicate Jesus at the temple!

Now since as early as Hippolytus in the second century tradition has variously ascribed the birth of Jesus to December 25 or, as in older eastern tradition, January 6.[1102] Ultimately the tradition came to be that Jesus was born on December 25 and that the Magi arrived twelve days later on January 6. Now there are many who deny this entirely, claiming that this was an attempt to merge Christmas with a pagan festival![1103] Most evangelical Christians reject the December 25 date, arguing that Jesus could not have been born in the winter. The argument is that shepherds would not be out tending flocks in the middle of a frigid winter.[1104] It is claimed that "the flocks ... were usually taken into the folds in November and kept in till March."[1105] Nevertheless, this argument is very weak. First, no one keeps sheep locked up in a barn for five months! Sheep cannot be kept locked up in a confined space for months at a time and it is unlikely that poor shepherds would have even had such massive barns as to accommodate a great many sheep. The criticism is anachronistic and projecting rich modern sheep farms upon antiquity. Second, Israel is not Canada. Although winter is obviously colder than summer, the winters in Bethlehem were not necessarily biting cold. We have no idea what the temperature was on that day. Moreover, the concern over the tradition of December 25 is misplaced, for it is not even certain that December 25 was a pagan holiday at all! Alexander Hislop argued that "the very name by which Christmas is populary known ... Yule-day – proves at once is Pagan and Babylonian origin. 'Yule' is the chaldee name for an 'infant' or 'little child.'"[1106] Hence, he cannot demonstrate that such a pagan festival actually took place on this day, but that the Babylonian title "proves" its pagan origin (never mind that the Babylonian language was Aramaic; the same language used by Jews at the time of Christ). Of course, even if this is true, it hardly proves that such a festival took place on December 25; especially since the tradition of a December 25 birthday preceded Constantine and a Christian Rome by at least a hundred years!

Now it is clear that we cannot prove what day Jesus was born. It is clear, however, that Jesus was born most likely within six months of Herod's death. His death has been pinpointed to sometime between March 12 and April

11 4 B.C. If we use six months as a thumb ruler, then Jesus would not have been born before September 5 B.C. at the earliest. Given that the Magi appeared in close proximity to the birth of Christ (see notes above and in "The Magi and the Shephards Matthew 2:1-12 – Luke 2:8-20") it more likely that Jesus was born about one month before Herod sought to slay the children of Bethlehem. It is further agreed that "the massacre probably took place some months before [Herod's] death."[1107] This would make Jesus' birth no later than January. Consequently, a December or January birth of Christ between the end of 5 B.C. and the early part of 4 B.C. is most likely and well supported. We cannot be dogmatic, but the facts fit this very well and no solid argument can be leveled against it.

Conclusion

This initial enrollment took place exactly as Luke, a meticulous historian, records. It allows us to more accurately date the birth of Jesus to between the winter months of 5 B.C. or the early part of 4 B.C. No legitimate facts contradict this, but rather support it. The history of ancient Syria is not solidified but there is no question that Quirinius served in several capacities in Syria both before and after his later governorship of 6 A.D. This census matches other enrollments at this time and fits the timetable laid out for censii in Rome after Herod's fall out with emperor Augustus.

Did Jesus Flee to Egypt?
Luke 2:22-39

> "And when the days for their purification according to the law of Moses were completed, they brought Him up to Jerusalem to present Him to the Lord ... When they had performed everything according to the Law of the Lord, they returned to Galilee, to their own city of Nazareth."

The account of Matthew describes the appearance of the Magi, Herod's wrath, and Joseph and Mary's fleeing to Egypt to escape Herod. Luke, however, omits all of these events. Naturally, the Bible critics claims that Luke would never have omitted such a thing if it had actually happen, and quote these passages as "proof" that there was no such hunting of Jesus, nor a flight to Egypt. They paint a picture of Joseph and Mary calmly going to Jerusalem to dedicate Jesus at the temple and returning to Galilee without a care in the world. Obviously, this argument falls apart upon closer examination.

Once again, the reader will be reminded that the gospels are relavively short histories of a man's life. Mark and John do not even record a single word about the birth of Jesus, so it is bad logic to *assume* that Luke must have recorded the flight to Egypt as Matthew did. It is also hypocrisy considering all the critics admit that Luke had seen Matthew's gospel! Would he so obviously "contradict" a book from which he was "copying"? Of course not! Logically, the facts fit very well, but there is dispute as to the exact chronological sequence of events. Let us take a closer look.

Sequence of the Nativity Events*

Roman Year	/ Month	/ Day	Events of Jesus' Nativity
5 B.C.	December	25	Joseph and Mary arrive late at night but cannot find room at an inn. They stay in a manger (Luke 2:7). Jesus is born and visited by the shepherds (Luke 2:8-20). The next day Joseph and Mary find a house to rent until Mary is recovered and the census registration is complete (cf. Matthew 2:11). The Magi appear in Jerusalem inquiring the whereabouts of the Messiah (Matthew 2:1). They set out to Bethlehem to find the child (Matthew 2:8).
4 B.C.	January	6	The Magi appear in Bethlehem to worship the Christ child (Matthew 2:11). They depart without returning to Herod (Matthew 2:12). Joseph and Mary are warned to flee to Egypt (Mattthew 2:13-14). Herod begins to realize that the Magi have deceived him. He sents orders to kill the children of Bethlehem (Mattthew 2:16). The soldiers carry out their duty and collect the census enrollment which would show the names of any children registered there that escaped death. Joseph, Mary, and Jesus' names were on it.
	February		Mary and Joseph arrive in Egypt.
	March	12	Herod falls violently ill (Josephus, *Antiq.* XVII.vi.5, *War* I.xxxiii.7). There is an eclipse of the moon verified by astronomers as March 12/13 (Josephus, *Antiq.* XVII.vi.4). Herod develops magots in his testicles from the acuteness of the disease, probably a kind of leprosy or gangrene (Josephus, *Antiq.* XVII.vi.5). Herod leaves orders to execute noble family members on the day of his death (Josephus, *Antiq.* XVII.vi.5). Herod executes his son Antipater (Josephus, *Antiq.* XVII.vii.1, *War* I.xxxiii.7). Herod dies five days later (Josephus, *Antiq.* XVII.viii.1, *War* I.xxxiii.8). The orders for execution are not carried out (Josephus, *Antiq.* XVII.viii.2).
	April	11	The Jews celebrate Passover after the death of Herod (Josephus, *Antiq.* XVII.vix.3). Joseph and Mary learn that Herod is dead and return to Israel (Matthew 2:19-21).
	May		Joseph and Mary arrive in Jerusalem and present Jesus at the Temple (2:22-38). Joseph and Mary leave to go live in Nazareth in Galilee (Matthew 2:22-23, Luke 2:39).

* The days for Jesus' birth and the Magi's appearance are traditional and used for illustration purposes only.

It has been argued that the law required Jesus to be presented to the temple as soon as possible and hence they would not have waited a year or more until they returned from Egypt. Further, they argue, if they had gone to Jerusalem before Egypt then Herod would have captured them, not to mention that Luke says they returned to Galilee (2:39). However, any careful reading of the texts disolves these arguments. According to Leviticus the law reads only that "she shall remain in the blood of *her* purification for thirty-three days; she shall not touch any consecrated thing, nor enter the sanctuary, until the days of her purification are completed." Thus there is no explicit time restriction upon presenting Jesus to the temple other than that Mary had to be purified *first*. Secondly, Joseph and Mary did not spend a year or more in Egypt for they returned immediately after Herod's death (Matthew 2:19-21) which was in March or April of the very same year. So Joseph and Mary most likely only stayed in Egypt for three to four months.

The "Missing Years"

Luke is the only author who includes anecdotes, provided by Mary, about Jesus' childhood. We read about Jesus being lost and found in the temple (Luke 2:42-51) but then read nothing else about His childhood until He begins His ministry some twenty years later. These so-called "missing years," as some have erroneously termed it, have become a tool used by some people to make unsubstantiated claims about Jesus as a means of luring unsuspecting Christians away from the faith.

One of the most popular theories put forth about the "missing years" is that Jesus traveled to India (or in some versions Tibet) and studied under a Guru. It has been promoted over the years in the east but also in the west. They argue that alleged "simlarities" between the Hindu (or Buddhist) tradition and Christianity are proof of Jesus' Hindu values. To this I usually answer my Hindu friends by saying, "if you truly believe this then why not read His own words as recorded by those who lived with, worked with, and died for Jesus; the Bible?" Unfortunately too many Hindus, although claiming to believe "all gods are one," are taught never to pray to Jesus. They ask me to pray to Jesus on their behalf but they will not pray to Jesus themselves. The reasons for this are beyond the scope of this book, but the point is that the Hindu priests themselves almost certainly know that Jesus never saw India. The evidences against it are plentiful.

Consider first that Jesus was a carpenter from a poor family. Traveling to India, even today, is not cheap. Even with the divide between east and west broken since the travels of Marco Polo and the swift transport of airplanes it cost me well over a $2000 to travel to India for a week, and I did not stay in a luxury hotel but the rather the cheapest I could find with a private bath. In Jesus' day travel would have involved hiring a large caravan with a small army of mercenaries to protect the caravan against robbers, bandits, and/or the Partians, with whom Rome was in conflict. Food would also have to be provided for a trip which would last for probably six months at least! The travel would have included the deserts of modern day Iraq and the vast mountains that lay between India and the west. The idea that a poor carpenter could have traveled to India is beyond reason. Travel between eastern and western kingdoms of this sort were rare and reserved for rich nobles and political emissaries. That is why the world knows the name of Marco Polo. It was he that first helped to break the invisible barrier that had spawned the ancient saying, "east is east and west is west and never shall the twain meet."

A second reason to reject this theory is the fact that Jesus was rejected by his relatives and friends in Nazareth because he was a commoner who had been raised in their town and had no special qualifications (cf. Mark 6:3). How could they have said this about someone who had traveled and studied in India? Surely, if it were true, Jesus would have been revered as a world traveler much as Marco Polo's fame spread.

Third is historical evidence. There is not a single tradition of Jesus having traveled to India or Tibet until the nineteenth century when Nicholas Notovitch claimed that Tibetan Gurus had records, which he never saw, alleging that Jesus had visited their monastery.[1108] Ignoring the fact that the monastery probably does not even date back to the first century or the fact that those records have now been said to have been "lost," it is apparent that a tradition 1800 years removed is not of as much value as the Scriptures written by those who lived with Jesus, and what they record is something quite different.

Jesus quoted Moses and the Hebrew Bible frequently. It is not uncommon to hear the gurus claiming that Jesus "borrowed" the saying "love your neighbor as yourself" from them, but He was, in fact, quoting Moses in Leviticus 19:18. Everything Jesus did and taught was in accordance with Hebrew Scriptures and Jesus Himself said "not the smallest letter or stroke shall pass from the Law" (Matthew 5:18). If Jesus was really a Hindu then He was also a liar for He taught that His words came from Moses and from the Scriptures. He never claimed to have learned from abroad nor did He teach Hindu doctrines. This is what makes the theories so offensive. It is not whether or not Jesus visited India, for their would be no sin in so doing as I have done and hope to do again, but in whether or not the words of Jesus are true and honest. If we accept that Jesus was a secret Hindu or Buddhist then we must also accept that He was a liar. The real proof that Jesus never visited India ultimately comes from the Hindu priests themselves for they warn their followers never to read the Bible nor pray to Jesus, although they are free to pray to any number of other gods. The truth is that they know the words of Jesus conflict with their tradition. Jesus was a Jew in both heritage and faith.

How Old Was Jesus?
Luke 3:1 – 3:23

"Now in the fifteenth year of the reign of Tiberius Caesar ... Jesus Himself was about thirty years of age."

The concern here is one of chronology; boring chronology. If Jesus was thirty years old, and He was born in 5 or 4 B.C., as stated above, then this would mean Jesus was was baptized in 27 A.D., but the fifteenth year of Tiberius was 29 A.D. Or was it? And if Jesus was baptized in 27 A.D. then how could He have died in 33 A.D. as prophesied? This chronological dispute is not one between Bible critics and Christians but between Christian scholars, and even this dispute between scholars does not take a decided battle between liberal and conservative or Catholic against Protestant, for there are evangelicals on both sides of the position, Catholics on both sides, etc. It is a question of the historical chronology of the Bible which is important to historians but of no major significance upon the Bible itself. Nevertheless, there is one reason that I will choose to discuss this debate to a fair degree. Namely, the fact that I have elsewhere defended the belief that the prophet Daniel predicts the very day that Christ would die on the cross, and that being April 3, 33 A.D. (see notes on Daniel 9:26-27 in *Controversies in the Prophets* for a full discussion).

There are three major reasons to reject a 27 A.D. baptism for Jesus. The statement "Jesus Himself was about thirty years of age" is not particularly troublesome. It is "about" thirty; not thirty. The Greek is "ὡσεὶ ἐτῶν τριακοντα" (*hosei eton triakonta*). ὡσεὶ (*hosei*) means "as it were," "like," "about," or "nearly."[1109] It is not exact, but approximate. In fact, it would be logical to say that Jesus could not have been exactly thirty or this word would never have been used at all. Had Jesus' baptism been in 29 A.D. He would have been thirty-two years old; hence, the use of ὡσεὶ (*hosei*) would be appropriate.

The second reason to reject 27 A.D. is the explicit statement of Luke in 3:1 that it was the fifteenth year of Tiberius. Every historian (ancient, modern secular, or religious) has dated the beginning of his reign to 14 A.D. However, advocates of the 27 A.D. date have pointed out that Velleius Paterculus noted that Tiberius was co-regent during Augustus' last two years.[1110] They, therefore, date Tiberius' reign from 12 A.D. rather than 14 A.D. The problem is that no historian reckons his reign in this way, so why would Luke? Moreover, the logic in this argument is equivalent to saying that George Bush Sr. was President in 1981. He was not. He was Vice-president! No one would count Bush's presidency from his years as Vice-president and no one counts Tiberius' reign from his co-regency with Augustus who was still emperor! Nor is this the only instance of a co-regency with an emperor, but never have any historians counted the reigns from their co-regencies. This is an attempt to escape the conflict with their system. It is not a proper reckoning of Tiberius' reign. Josephus counts twenty-two and a half years for Tiberius' reign, which does not include the co-regency.[1111] So also the Roman coins minted date his reign from the Roman year 767 (after the foundation of Rome, 754 B.C.) which is 14 A.D. Says Harold Hoehner, "there is no evidence, either from historical documents or coins, for [the co-regency theory] whereas there is abundant evidence Tiberius reckoned his first year after the death of Augustus."[1112]

The final reason to reject a 27 A.D. baptism is the strongest. Adocates of this position place the crucifixion in 30 A.D. as Passover only fell on a Friday in the years of 27, 30, 33, and 36 A.D.[1113] However, this leaves a ministry of only *two and a half* years! A ministry of at least three years is overwhelmingly accepted by advocates of all positions based on the Biblical narratives.[1114] Consequently, a 27 A.D. baptism would either make Jesus' ministry too short or extend it over five years! Neither can be the case.

In conclusion, the fifteenth year of Tiberius is reckoned as 29 A.D. by every ancient and modern historian. Since Jesus is said to be "about" thirty, but *not* exactly thirty (or else the word 'ωσεὶ would never have been used), we can conclude that Jesus was probably thirty-two years old at His baptism (depending on his birthday). Three and a half years later He would have been crucified on Friday, April 3, 33 A.D., the very day prophesied by Daniel as the day the Messiah would be "cut off and have nothing" (Daniel 9:26).

Luke 3:24-38 – See Matthew 1:2-17

Luke 4:5-12 – See Matthew 4:5-10

Luke 5:1-11, 27-32 – See John 1:35-42

Luke 6:14-16 – See Matthew 10:2-4

Luke 6:20-49 – See Matthew 5-7

Luke 7:2-11 – See Matthew 8:5-13

Forgiven Much, Love Much
Luke 7:47-48

"Her sins, which are many, have been forgiven, for she loved much; but he who is forgiven little, loves little."

Rasputin was known as the "mad monk." He was a perverted man who twisted this passage to mean that "salvation was most readily attained through sins of the flesh."[1115] His argument, in his own words, was "how can we repent if we have not first sinned? ... yield to [temptation] voluntarily and without resistance ... then we may afterwards do penance in utter contrition."[1116]

Here Jesus seems to say that those who have been forgiven much love much. Logically then is Rasputin right? Of course not, but the question does remain what the relationship between love and forgiveness may be. One problem is in modern English translations. Most translations incorrectly infer that she was forgiven *because* she loved much. The King James, NAS, RSV, Living Bible, ASV, and others all erroneously translate this passage as *"for* she loved much." This error is the polar opposite of Rasputin and implies that we merit forgiveness because of our love, despite the fact that the Bible clearly states "we love, because He first loved us" (1 John 4:19). This is obviously the case in this passage as Jesus explicitly deliniates. Consider his response to the Pharisee who objected to her actions:

> "'A moneylender had two debtors: one owed five hundred denarii, and the other fifty. When they were unable to repay, he graciously forgave them both. So which of them will love him more?' Simon answered and said, 'I suppose the one whom he forgave more.' And He said to him, 'You have judged correctly'" (Luke 7:41-43).

She loved Jesus *because* He loved her and forgave her. So it is with all of us as well. How then is it said "many sins are forgiven her, *because* she hath loved much" (Douay-Rheims translation)? The original Greek says nothing of the sort! Despite the massive number of translations which read *"for* she loved much" (King James, NAS, RSV, Living Bible, ASV, etc.) the normal word for "for" is γαρ (*gar*). Here, however, the Greek reads ὅτι (*'oti*). It's primary meaning is "that" or even "in order that." The causal relationship is almost the opposite of "for" or "because." Now in all fairness ὅτι (*'oti*) can, governing the context, be translated as "for" or "because" but that is wholly unjustified here for the following clause proves the cause and effect relationship is that forgiveness breeds love. It says, "he who is forgiven little, loves little" (v. 48) but if Jesus had intended to say "because" then it should have reads, "he who loves little is forgiven little."

It seems that too many translations have feared the Rasputin error and seek to make love a prerequisite to forgiveness, although Jesus was clearly teaching that God's forgiveness is the cause of the woman's love. This is correctly displayed in a translation I do not normally favor; the NRSV renders it best, saying, *"hence* she has shown great love."

Now if it is agreed that she loved Jesus because He forgave her and not vice-verse, then this brings us back to Rasputin's heresy. Should we not sin in order that we might love? If common sense is not a good enough answer then let us look at Jesus' analogy again. If a moneylender has forgiven a five hundred denarii debt and the debtor then goes back out and borrows another five hundred denarii which he promptly spends on selfish gain without the ability to repay, then he is not showing love but contempt. He is treating the moneylender as a fool for having forgiven the first debt. Let us never show contempt for God by repeating the sins for which we have been forgiven! Let us show our love for God even as this woman showed her love for all the sins she was forgiven.

I had always memorized this passage in my own little paraphrase, "he who has been forgiven much, loves much." It is because "God first loved us" (1 John 4:19) that we love. Apart from God there can be no truly unselfish love. We may love, but we always have a *reason* for loving. The only *unselfish* love (that without reason) is that which comes from God alone.

Was Mary Magdalene A Prostitute?
Luke 8:2 – Mark 16:9

"Mary who was called Magdalene, from whom seven demons had gone out."

Very little is actually said about Mary Magdalene in the Bible apart from her appearances at the tomb, showing her to be among the most loyal of Jesus' followers. However, early tradition (early second century) has read Mary into Luke 7:37-50 and later into John 8:3-11. Pope Gregory the Great in the sixth century is sometimes credited with being the first to claim that Mary Magdalene was a reformed prostitute when he said, "she whom Luke calls the sinful woman [Luke 7:37-50], whom John calls Mary, we believe to be the Mary from whom seven devils were ejected according to Mark. And what did these seven devils signify, if not all the vices? ... It is clear, brothers, that the woman previously used the unguent to perfume her flesh in forbidden acts."[1117] Now Gregory was, in fact, playing off of older traditions, but many reject those traditions in their entirety including Pope John Paul II who rejected that Mary Magdalene was ever a prostitute.[1118]

The tradition of Mary's "iniquity and infamy"[1119] can be traced back possibly as early as the second century, but no explicit mention can be proven. The Jewish Talmud also favors the theory of her immorality although not explicitly calling her a prostitute.[1120] Certainly she was, from the earliest of times, believed to have been a repentant sinner, for righteous virgins tend not to be possessed of seven demons. The problem is that gnostic religious cults (such as promoted by idiotic films like *The DaVinci Code*) have made Mary into a mystic priestess and wife of Jesus. In reaction against such absurd fabrications many have gone to the other extreme and attemped to make Mary into a virtuous saint. Both extremes are to be rejected outright.

Based on the Bible alone we can say little about Mary's background but we can say she had a past. Both Luke and Mark record that she had seven demons cast out of her; not just one. Although John Martin claims "often in Scripture the number seven is used to denote completion. Apparently Mary had been totally demon-possessed,"[1121] this is unfounded. Nor does he quote examples of this "completeness." What does "totally demon-possessed" mean anyway? Are others only 20% possessed? No, we must take Luke at his word. She had seven demons cast out of her.

Now some have said that "a devil would use her body for sexual gratification if our understanding of demonic behaviour and ability is correct."[1122] Although this is not necessarily true, it does seem logical. Most artists throughout the centuries have always depicted the men from whom Jesus cast out demons to have been naked. This was also based on the tradition that demons sought the humiliate their hosts and degrade them in every possible way. This, combined with the assumption that Mary was the woman of Luke 7:37-50, is doubtless what led to the tradition that Mary was a prostitute.

Henryk Siemiradzki – Christ and the Sinner (or) Christ First Meeting with Mary Magdalene – 1873

Now the question remains, "was Mary Magdalene a reformed prostitute"? We cannot say, but we can say that there is nothing wrong with showing the grace and love of our Lord and His ability to transform people's lives. I once met a woman who worked in the "adult" film industry as an actress. She was tired of the lifestyle and abuse and was seeking something more in life. She asked me a lot of questions about Jesus and when I told her that Mary Magdalene was once a prostitute (by tradition) she at first thought I was mocking her, but soon realized I was telling her that Jesus accepts all of us no matter what our past. I have not heard from that woman in years and have no idea if she ever accepted Christ but I still think about her.[1123] Although we should not accept tradition as fact without reservation, we also should not be afraid to show the transformative power of Jesus in the lives of people. Mary Magdalene was most certainly one of Jesus' most loyal followers and the first to see the resurrected Jesus. How great a testimony to transforming lives she can be!

Parable of the Sower
Luke 8:4-15 – Matthew 13:2-9 – Mark 4:1-9

"'The sower went out to sow his seed; and as he sowed, some fell beside the road, and it was trampled under foot and the birds of the air ate it up. Other *seeds* fell on rocky *soil,* and as soon as it grew up, it withered away, because it had no moisture. Other *seeds* fell among the thorns; and the thorns grew up with it and choked it out. Other *seeds* fell into the good soil, and grew up, and produced a crop a hundred times as great.' As He said these things, He would call out, 'He who has ears to hear, let him hear.'"

This parable is one of my favorites for it shows, in a simple analogy, how the human race will react to the gospel. It shows that there are four kinds of people. The first is the one who never accepts the gospel. Few dispute this. Like seeds that fall on roads, the Word of God takes no root and dies. The last is undisputed and represents the true believer in whom the Word of God takes root and blossoms and grows and produces fruit. The controversy is over the middle two. What do these represent? Or more specifically, do they represent a class of the saved?

The seed with shallow roots is that of which Jesus said "the one on whom seed was sown on the rocky places, this is the man who hears the word and immediately receives it with joy; yet he has no *firm* root in himself, but is *only* temporary, and when affliction or persecution arises because of the word, immediately he falls away" (Matthew 13:20-21; Luke 8:13; Mark 4:16-17). Now our imagery must be consistent. If the seed represents the Word of God sewn in our heart then it must be that if the seed dies, so does the Word. In this case it is apparent that this is someone who is not a true believer. This passage represents men like Larry Flint whom at first accept the Word only to turn away from it and hate those who sew it. They have "no firm root" so the seed dies and with it dies the man's soul.

The seed among thorns is different. Jesus said, "the one on whom seed was sown among the thorns, this is the man who hears the word, and the worry of the world and the deceitfulness of wealth choke the word, and it becomes unfruitful" (Matthew 13:22; Luke 8:14; Mark 4:18-19). Now many believe that these men are also lost, but the imagery here is different. Unlike the previous seed, this seed *takes root* and *does not* die. This means that the Word of God is not dead. However, it is "unfruitful." It is apparent that the seed which grows fruit is that which produces converts and spreads the Word. Those who believe that this group is not saved fail to distinguish between salvation and sanctification. They are in danger of teaching a veiled form of salvation by works. Certainly James declared that "faith without works is dead" (2:18-26) but this enters another debate (see *Controversies in the Epistles* for a full discussion of James). Suffice to say that the true believer must distinguish between saving grace and sanctification. We should produce fruit and we should be sanctified, but God's grace cannot be limited to the spiritually mature lest we deny that salvation is by grace, and grace through faith alone. If the seed lives, so does its host. This group of people are those who have received the grace of God but do little with it. They are choked off by the world and bear little fruit because they have become attatched to the world.

It is not for us to damn these, but to help cut away the thorns in order that they might grow and produce some of that needed fruit. If we simply burn the bush, we will destroy the seed along with it. A good gardener does not set fire to his field, but prunes the leaves and cuts away the thorns so that his flowers may grow and breath. So let us not be judgmental to the weak, but help them to be sanctified through our Lord and Savior Jesus Christ.

Luke 8:20-21 – See Mark 3:31-35

Luke 8:26-39 – See Matthew 8:28-34

Luke 8:40-56 – See Mark 5:21-43

Luke 8:43-48 – See Mark 5:25-34

Luke 9:3-5 – See Matthew 10:10

Luke 9:7-9 – See Matthew 14:1

Luke 9:10-17 – See Matthew 14:13-21

Luke 9:28-36 – See Matthew 17:1-13

The Greatest in Heaven
Luke 9:46, 22:24 – Matthew 18:1-5 – Mark 9:33-37
(Also see Luke 9:48 on "Child Like Fatih?")

"An argument started among them as to which of them might be the greatest."

There are passages which seem to imply that we will all be equal in heaven (cf. Galatians 3:28), but there are also passages which teach that there will be rank in heaven. Indeed, this is such a passage, but how? Does not Jesus chastize them for asking such a foolish question? This is the paradox we seem unable to understand. Jesus will bring low the haughty and raise up the humble. "The issue was not whether there would be rank in the kngdom but the nature and qualifiaction of such rank."[1124] Indeed, Jesus does not deny that there will be a greatest and a least in heaven, but teaches the apostles that they are wrong to seek glory among themselves. To this end He used a small child to illustrate His point.

Arguing about who will be greatest in heaven is not unique to the apostles. This pride is apparent in people throughout history including the church today. Far too many pastors think having the biggest church with the most members makes them more important than the pastor of a thirty member church or a hundred member church, but God sees things differently. None is greater than Jesus and yet He was born in a barn, of humble and poor parents, raised in a small village, of average looks and appearance (Isaiah 53:2), and died the most cruel and degrading of deaths!

In the Millennium the pastor who faithfully shepherded his flock of fifty will be given greater authority and blessings than the pastor who shepherded a church of two thousand but saw little fruit among those thousands. Who is the better shepherd? The one who had a small flock and knows each sheep and cares for each one's needs and insures than none stray from the flock and are devoured by wovles, or the one who cannot even count his flock, who does not know them by name, and does not even know if a sheep has left the flock and been eaten by wolves? The Lord says the first one is greater.

The principle that "the one who is least among all of you, this is the one who is great" (Luke 9:48) is one of the greatest precepts of Jesus. He who humbled Himself unto death on a cross (Philippians 2:8) expects that we too should be humbled. I am always annoyed by the Hollywood stars who are honored at awards and declare "I am so humbled!" Have we truly forgotten what humility means? It comes from the word "humiliation." That is what Jesus suffered on Passion week. The humble will be brought high and the proud brought low. This is why Jesus used a child for His illustration, but even that illustration seems to have been perverted. Let us examine Jesus' words carefully.

Child Like Faith?
Luke 9:48 – Matthew 18:3

"Whoever receives this child in My name receives Me, and whoever receives Me receives Him who sent Me; for the one who is least among all of you, this is the one who is great."	"Unless you are converted and become like children, you will not enter the kingdom of heaven."

Matthew is the only one who records Jesus' statement that we must "become like children." This statement has too often been used to imply that Jesus taught "simple faith"[1125] or "child-like faith," but this is nowhere in the context. It is "not foolish as children (1 Cor. 14:20), nor fickel (Eph. 4:14), nor playful (*ch.* 11:16), but, *as children, we must desire the sincere milk of the word*

(1 Pet. 2:2); as children, we must be careful for nothing, but leave it to our heavenly Father to care for us (*ch.* 6:31); we must, as children, be harmless and inoffensive, and void of malice (1 Cor. 14:20)."[1126] The context of the passage, as discussed above, is about "humbling yourselves as little children."[1127] There is not a single word about faith in the passages.

This often coined term, "child-like faith," has become a source of mockery among those who lie to their children about Santa Claus instead of teaching about the birth of Jesus Christ. It is a term found nowhere in Scripture. The purpose of Jesus' illustration was to show humility and was in response to their inquiries about who will be greatest in heaven. The passage teaches not that we must be naive like children but that we must be innocent like children. We must be humble and innocent in all things, trusting in the Lord and leaning upon Him. This is the meaning of Jesus' words.

Who Is With Me?
Luke 9:50 – Luke 11:23

"Jesus said to him, 'Do not hinder *him;* for he who is not against you is for you.'"	"He who is not with Me is against Me; and he who does not gather with Me, scatters."

Void of context this obviously appears to be a contradiction, but the contexts of the remarks are so evident that an atheist I was debating once could only respond "you people always talk about context." Yes, "we" do. Every statement has a context, and everything which is not in context is necessarily "out of context." Without context it is hard to interpret anything, which is the very reason that cult leaders, atheists, Jihadists, and "liberal theologians" seek to ignore or demolish context. Let us look at the contexts of the two passages in question, and bear in mind that the same author wrote both passages, so he was obviously aware of what he had written just two chapters earlier.

The first passage is Jesus' response to a specific question by John, who said, "Master, we saw someone casting out demons in Your name; and we tried to prevent him because he does not follow along with us" (Luke 9:49). Jesus replied in this case that although he was not following them, his actions were leading people to Jesus and showing the authority of Jesus and His name. The context is specifically about a man who was driving out demons in the name of Jesus. Jesus replied that the apostles should not prevent anyone from so doing.

The second passage is also about casting out demons, but the context is quite different and reveals an amazing consistency in Jesus' remarks. The Pharisees were reprimanding Jesus for casting out demons, declaring that He was "casting out demons by the hand of the chief of demons, Beelzebul" (11:15). To this Jesus replied the oft quoted passage by Abraham Lincoln, "any kingdom divided against itself is laid waste; and a house *divided* against itself falls. If Satan also is divided against himself, how will his kingdom stand?"

266

(11:17-18). It is then that he declares "He who is not with Me is against Me." In other words, Jesus' kingdom is not divided. Those who would divide the kingdom are His enemies. Those who assist the kingdom (as in the first passage) are not His enemy.

Thus in the first passage the man was helping Jesus even though He did not (yet) understand who Jesus was; indeed even the apostles did not fully understand yet. In the second passage, Jesus was responding to the Pharisees who were angry at Jesus for casting out demons. In the first instance a man was casting out demons in Jesus' name. In the second instance the Pharisees were in effect forbidding Jesus to cast out demons. Therefore the context yields an amazing consistency. In each the casting out of demons is an aid to the kingdom of Jesus and those who were against the casting out of demons were His enemies, whereas those who were casting out demons were His allies. There can be in no way a contradiction between these two passages, but rather an amazing unity and message; that Jesus' kingdom is never divided against itself!

Luke 9:60 – See Matthew 8:22

The Seventy
Luke 10:1-17

"Now after this the Lord appointed seventy others, and sent them in pairs ahead of Him to every city and place where He Himself was going to come."

The NIV, along with the Douay-Rheims, NLT, Wycliffe's translation, and the famed Latin Vulgate, read seventy-two. In either case, the question arises as to how and why Jesus chose these men after the apostles, and to what purpose they were created.

Seventy or Seventy-two?
The reading of "seventy" is supported by such ancient texts as the *Sinaiticus*, *Alexandrinus*, *Ephraemi*, the *Washingtonianus* (*Freerianus*), and the Majority text. With such strong support one is tempted to accept it readily, but when one examines the reading of "seventy-two" and its support, there is pause to question this. It is supported by papyri 45 and 75, the *Vaticanus*, and the *Bezae* (*Cantabrigiensis*). Now both papyri are actually older than any of the existing manuscripts which read "seventy." Papyrus 45 ($\mathfrak{P}^{45}$) dates to around 225 A.D.[1128] and Papyrus 75 ($\mathfrak{P}^{75}$) may even go back further to 175 A.D.[1129] Beyond these the *Sinaiticus* and *Vaticanus* are the oldest, dating to the time of Constantine. Of these manuscripts only the *Sinaiticus* reads "seventy."

Additional evidence (in the form of quotations or translations) from antiquity are also divided, but if we look solely at the physical textual evidence, we would immediately accept the reading of "seventy-two." So why do so many reject it?

According to famed textual scholar Bruce Metzger "the concept of '70' is an established entity in the *Septuagint* and in Christian tradition. The number of examples of '70' in the Old Testament is overwhelming: there are always 70 souls in the house of Jacob, 70 elders, sons, priests, and 70 years that are mentioned in chronological references to important events."[1130] He thus concludes that "it is astonishing that the reading ʹεβδομηκοντα δυο occurs at all in 10.1 and 17, and that it has such strong support."[1131] However, in making such a statement, he has inadvertently admitted that "seventy-two" should probably be the correct reading for it is perfectly logical to assume that the "two" could have accidentally dropped out and not been noticed by scribes familiar with the *Septuagint*, but it would be completely "astonishing" to see a "two" *added* to the text, let alone added by the most ancient and "strong support."[1132] Let us look at the reasons that seventy-two should be accepted beyond the textual support.

It is true that the Bible usually uses the number seventy, but in Revelation 21:7 the measurement of the sacred wall is seventy-two rather than seventy. Furthermore, there were seventy-*one* Sanhedrin, not seventy. Thus, seventy is not always supported. Moreover, there is an interesting fact often overlooked. Three, like seven, is often considered a holy number (as in the Trinity). There were twelve disciples. Twelve times three equals thirty-six. Because Jesus stated that these men were to travel in pairs (to provide protection, companionship, and perhaps in deference to Deuteronomy 17:6; 19:15)[1133] we should then multiply this by two, which in turn equals seventy-two.

Now it is apparent that "seventy" is the usual number found in Scripture, hence it is likely that the "two" was dropped either accidentally or on purpose, assuming that it should have been "seventy." Nevertheless, there is no logical explanation for how "seventy-two" came to be in the text if it was not there originally. Metzger himself considers this "astonishing."[1134] Consequently, although "seventy" may someday prove to be the correct reading, "seventy-two" seems to be the stronger supported both textually and logically.

The Purpose of the Seventy (Two)
What is more important than their exact number is the purpose for which they were made. Note that there is no authority to forgive sins, to appoint priests or bishops or any other hierarchical authority bestowed upon them. These are missionaries whose purpose is to spread the gospel. In verse 10:19 Jesus gives these men "authority to tread on serpents and scorpions, and over all the power of the enemy, and nothing will injure you." This is the only authority given unto them. They instructions are to spread to gospel and set a pattern of missionaries to come.

What is more significant is that these men were under the twelve apostles; not in an hierarchical sense but in the sense that they are disciples of the disciples. The importance, forgotten in an age of "bigger churches are better," is that for each apostle there are but six disciples. The pattern set is not that we should be out trying to grab the largest number of "converts" (see notes on Luke 17:11-19) but that we should nurture and disciple men who will in turn nurture and disciple others. If a single man "converts" 100 people he has done good, but if a single man disciples seven good men who in turn disciple seven good men each and those seven men each, then this man has not sewn the seeds for 399 "converts" but better yet, 399 disciples! Who has done better? And if half of the 100 converts of the first fall away because they had no firm foundation, then how much better the man who disciples? Whose harvest is greater?

Conclusion

Too often we forget the lessons which Jesus has taught about humility and discipleship. We seek to have 100 crowns for "converting" 100 people, but discipling creates far more converts, and far more disciples. A big church is not better than a small one, but usually worse. This is the fallacy of hierarchies, but also "megachurches" among Protestants. Each wants to be the biggest, but Protestants generally prefer the title "pastor" to "priest" because we claim to draw upon Jesus' imagery of a shepherd who pastors his flock. How then can we pastor sheep we do not even recognize as our own? If we do not even know the name of each and every member of our church *personally*, then how can we be an effective sherpherd?

There were twelve apostles who were discipled by Jesus Christ Himself. He then appointed seventy-two (or seventy) under them. The pattern is that of discipleship, not hierarchy. These men had no authority over church institutions nor power beyond ministering the gospel and obeying Jesus' commands. They were missionaries and should be the model for missionaries today.

Luke 11:23 – See Luke 9:50

Luke 11:29 – See Matthew 12:38-39

Luke 12:49-53 – See Matthew 10:34-39

Lazarus
Luke 16:19-31

"Now the poor man died and was carried away by the angels to Abraham's bosom; and the rich man also died and was buried. In Hades he lifted up his eyes, being in torment, and saw Abraham far away and Lazarus in his bosom. And he cried out and said, 'Father Abraham, have mercy on me, and send Lazarus so that he may dip the tip of his finger in water and cool off my tongue, for I am in agony in this flame.' ... 'If they do not listen to Moses and the Prophets, they will not be persuaded even if someone rises from the dead.'"

The story of Lazarus tells us a very important message. It tells us that people reject the truth because they choose to, not because they are ignorant or because of circumstances or for any other reasons. In fact, this story may even foreshadow the unbelief of the Priests, Sadducees, and Pharisees after the resurrection of Jesus, for it is clear that Pilate and the Priests were aware of the empty tomb and had even feared this very event. Guards were placed at the entrance to the tomb for this very reason (Matthew 27:63-65) and they too had even seen the risen Lord (Matthew 28:4)! As pagans the guards may have simply passed it off as dark magic. As montheists the Priests may have simply passed it off as a false demonic apparition. In both cases, they rejected the truth because they chose to. "'If they do not listen to Moses and the Prophets, they will not be persuaded even if someone rises from the dead" (16:31). These are the stern words of Jesus. Either we accept the truth or we don't. Nothing on earth will change a man's heart; only the Lord can change the human heart whenever someone calls upon Him (Joel 2:32; Acts 2:21).

Hades and Abraham's Bosom
Now the biggest controversy in this passage is the issue of of *hades*, Paradise, and Abraham's Bosom which I have previously addressed under "Jesus and Hell, Mark 9:43-48" and shall not repeat it here. However, some have argued that the story could be construed anachronistically. Says Walter Liefeld, "though Revelation 20:14 places the throwing of death and Hades into the lake of fire at the end of history ... in this story the rich man is already in a torment of fire."[1135] Thus Liefeld urges against building "an eschatology on it."[1136] Nevertheless, even if we grant that the point of the story is not eschatalogical the fact remains that we must assume that the fires of torment do not exist in *hades* prior to the final judgment. Since the passage specifically mentions Abraham's bosom (which appears to be a part of *Sheol*) it is apparent that *hades* and Paradise in *Sheol* do contain some form of blessings and punishment which exist even before that the Last Day.

A Parable or a True Story?
A secondary issue, which indirectly relates to that subject, is the question of whether or not this was a parable or a true story. At least one professor known to me believes that this is not a parable at all, but a true story. His reasoning is that 1) Jesus, contrary to His normal practice, never calls it a parable; and 2) Jesus specifically names Lazarus whereas none of His other parables give a name to the individuals in the story.

A Complete List of Biblical Parables

Parable[*]	Parables Specifically Identified as Parable	Parables Identified by Comparison
Wise and Foolish Builders		Matt. 7:24-27; Luke 6:47-49
The Sower	Matt. 13:3-23; Mark 4:1-20; Luke 8:5-15	
Tares among the Wheat	Matt. 13:24-43	
The Mustard Seed	Matt. 13:31-32; Mark 4:30-32; Luke 13:18-20	
Leaven	Matt. 13:33; Luke 13:21	
Hidden Treasure		Matt. 13:44
Costly Pearl		Matt. 13:45-46
The Dragnet		Matt. 13:47-50
Head of the Household		Matt. 13:52
The Unmerciful Slave		Matt. 18:23-35
Laborers in the Vineyard		Matt. 20:1-16
The Landowner	Matt. 21:33-44; Mark 12:1-11; Luke 20:9-19	
Marriage Feast		Matt. 22:1-14; Luke 14:16-24
The Fig Tree	Matt. 24:32-35; Mark 13:28-39; Luke 21:29-31	
The Ten Virgins	Matt. 25:1-13	
The Talents		Matt. 25:14-30
The Growing Seed		Mark 4:26-29
Watchful Doorkeeper		Mark 13:34-37
Good Samaritan		Luke 10:25-37[**]
The Rich Man	Luke 12:16-21	
The Faithful Steward		Luke 12:35-48
Barren Fig Tree	Luke 13:6-9	
The Lost Sheep	Luke 15:3-7	
The Lost Coin	Luke 15:8-10	
The Prodigal Son	Luke 15:11-32	
The Unrighteous Steward	Luke 16:1-13	
Lazarus		Luke 16:19-31[**]
The Persistent Widow	Luke 18:1-8	
The Pharisee and Tax Collector	Luke 18:9-14	
The Ten Servants		Luke 19:12-27[**]
The Good Shepherd	John 10:1-18	
The Vine		John 15:1-5

[*] Note : some take illustrations as parables and include them in lists of parables, but a true parable is a story, not merely an illustration. My list is restricted to true parables. However, illustrations would obviously fall under the category of "comparisons."[1137]

[**] Note : Luke does not here actually specify the comparison in words, thus this may be an exception (see discussion below).

Although hardly convincing in themselves, these arguments do bear some significant weight. The first point is actually the strongest, for unlike the claim of the "liberal scholar" or "Higher critics" Jesus never left the hearer to ponder or wonder about the nature of the story. Moses was a real person. He was named by name and quoted as a historical person and source of authority. The Bible portrays the parting of the Red Sea as history, not fable. However, whenever the Bible relates a parable for the purpose of teaching a moral lesson, it makes clear that it is a parable in one of two ways. The first way is to simply state that it is a parable. The second is by way of making a comparison, usually using specific qualifying words and phrases such as "everyone who hears these words of Mine and acts on them, *may be compared to* a wise man" (Matthew 7:24). Are there exceptions? The preceding chart is a complete listing of every parable in the gospels.[1138]

Now the reader will note that there may be a few exceptions. Aside from the passage in question, the most obvious is the story of the Good Samaritan. Luke is the only gospel writer who sometimes neglects to specify parables, although the parallel passages do (Luke 10:25-37; 14:16-24; 19:12-27; 21:29-31). Another possible exception is found in Matthew 24:45-51 and Luke 12:42-46, but is this really a parable? Although some call it the parable of the "Wise and Foolish Servants" there is no real story there. Instead, the parable of the Ten Virgins serves this purpose; to further illustrate Jesus' point. Consequently, the passages in Matthew 24:45-51 and Luke 12:42-46 do not constitute a parable but a simple illustration without a story.

Note also that the Unrighteous Steward (Luke 16:1-13) does not specify that it is a parable, and yet it can be proven via the fact that it is a continuation of the parables begun in 15:3 which are so designated. The question then is whether or not Luke 16:14-18 constitute a legitimate break in the narrative, requiring Luke to again specify that a parable is here intended. The answer is that we cannot prove it does. Furthermore, since Luke is the only gospel writer that does not always specify parables, we cannot prove this is not a parable based on this fact alone.

What of the second point? It is true that no other parable gives a name to the individuals of the story. This is because the characters are intended to be generic, thus representing different types of people in the real world. Why then is Lazarus given a name? The argument is that if Lazarus were intended to represent poor people then he would have remained a nameless poor person just as the rich man is nameless.

This argument is fairly convincing on the surface, but again amounts to circumstantial evidence alone. In short, the story of Lazarus may be a true story, but we cannot truly know since the story involves interaction with the head in *Hades*. Only the Lord knows if the story it true, and it is very likely that something like this has happened many times. We, therefore, have no reason to deny that it is a true story, but neither can we prove it. True or not, it is used by Jesus as an illustration in the same way that the parables are used.

Conclusion

Sometimes it is possible to get sidetracked by issues beyond the original context. While the story may be true and authentic, its purpose is the same as a parable. Its purpose is to show that the unbeliever rejects God not out of ignorance or circumstances, but out of a bitter heart. The atheist who demands proof of God already has it. He simply refuses to accept it. Even if Jesus Christ were to be raised from the dead, the unbeliever will not accept it! This is the proof of history. Signs, wonders, and even Jesus' resurrection from the dead were all passed off as demonic activity, trickery, or drunken illusions to those who refused to accept. Faith involves the spirit. The mind reacts to the spirit, but intellect is not the primary agent. The myth of "fact versus faith" is nowhere more obvious than in the mind of the atheist who accepts magots and slugs as his distant cousins but refuses to accept that gravity is an unseen force which cannot be disected, observed under a microscope, nor can its atomic structure be found, not can a chemical equation be created and yet it impacts every aspect of our daily life. So it is with God. Faith, whether in the believer or unbeliever, is the agent; intellect is the defensive agent.

The Ten Lepers
Luke 17:11-19

"Were there not ten cleansed? But the nine – where are they? Was no one found who returned to give glory to God, except this foreigner?"

There is no real controversy here, but I could not allow this passage to pass without comment, for here is a true story which illustrates why so many ministries today are working on a false premise. Namely, that bringing someone to the altar or that healing the sick produce true faith. Some (mega-churches) seek a large number of followers while others (signs and wonders minstries) seek to glorify God through healing services, and yet here Jesus healed ten men, but only one became a true follower of Christ. The others were grateful in their own way, but their motivations were selfish and their graditude was limited. True faith is found in the heart. We should keep this in mind when we are out seeking "converts." Our goal should be to show Jesus to people, but it is between them and the Lord; not us. Baptizing ten people does not mean we have made ten converts. Jesus healed ten lepers but only one gave glory to God.

A Kingdom in Our Midst?
Luke 17:20-21

"The kingdom of God is not coming with signs to be observed; nor will they say, 'Look, here *it is!*' or, 'There *it is!*' For behold, the kingdom of God is in your midst."

273

This passage is often translated as "Kingdom within you" and used to defend the doctrine of a "spiritual kingdom" as opposed to a literal Davidic kingdom following the return of Christ (as described in Revelation 20). The problem is that "this was addressed to the wicked Pharisees"[1139] and not the apostles or the church. As John Martin points out, "it would not make sense for Jesus to have told the Pharisees that the kingdom of God was within them as if it were some sort of spiritual kingdom,"[1140] for the Pharisees were the enemies of Jesus who were deliberately mocking Him and trying to instigate charges of treasons against Jesus. How then can this passage be explained?

The Translation Debate

Chiefly the debate revolves around the correct translation, although the various perspectives tend to choose their translation based on their own preconceived bias. "Within you" clearly seems to support some variation of a "spiritual kingdom" theory, but Greek lexicons also list "among you" or "in your midst" as viable translations.[1141] Since "the word 'within' (GR *entos*) is used in the New Testament only twice"[1142] it is not easy to determine based strictly upon grammar. Here is a look at how the various major translations have rendered it.

Tyndale Translation	"The kyngdome of God is with in you."
Wycliffe Translation	"The rewme of God is with ynne you."
King James Version	"The kingdom of God is within you."
Darby Translation	"The kingdom of God is in the midst of you."
Douay-Rheims Bible	"The kingdom of God is within you."
Geneva Translation	"The kingdome of God is within you."
New American Bible (Catholic)	"The kingdom of God is among you."
New American Standard Bible	"The kingdom of God is in your midst."
Revised Standard Version	"The kingdom of God is in the midst of you."
New Revised Standard Version	"The kingdom of God is among you." (footnotes "within you")
New International Version	"The kingdom of God is within you." (footnotes "among you")
New International Readers Version	"The kingdom of God is among you."
American Standard Version	"The kingdom of God is within you."
The Living Bible	"The Kingdom of God is within you." (footnotes "among you")
New Living Translation	"The kingdom of God is already among you."
Israeli Authorised Version	"The Kingdom of Elohim is within you."

The translation "within you" is found in the KJV, ASV, NIV, Tyndale, Wycliffe, Douay-Rheims, Living Bible, Geneva, and Israeli AV. "Among you," "in your midst," and similar translations include the NAS, RSV, NRSV, NIRV, Darby, NLT, and even the Catholic NAB. I say "even the Catholic NAB" because it is well known that this verse is used by many to support the Augustinian theory of the kingdom.[1143] The irony is that a number of the early Church Fathers did not take this approach. It is true that men like Origen took this allegorically as the "Spirit of God,"[1144] but the problem again arises as to why Jesus would say this to the Pharisees as if they had the Spirit of God. The Church Father Tertullian argued alternately, "who will not interpret the words 'within you' to mean *in your hands, within your power,* if you hear, and do the commandment of God? ... the kingdom of God lies in His commandment."[1145] This variant makes the kingdom more of an extension of the Mosaic covenant.

Neverthelees, even John Wesley, who believed that "it is a spiritual kingdom, an internal principle"[1146] himself admitted that "among you" is the proper translation.[1147] This only makes sense for Jesus would never have told the Pharisees that the Holy Spirit resided within them!

Of course the question still remains, what does "in your midst" mean? Several different nuances have been offered, but each stems from the fact that Jesus is the king and when the Pharisees rejected the king, they were rejecting His kingdom; the Davidic kingdom. The Jews had long believed that the Messianic kingdom would come when the Messiah came and crushed the Roman empire. Therefore, the Pharisees were attempting to entrap Jesus by getting Him to say that He would overthrow Rome, but Jesus wisely answered that the kingdom, which in some ways was to be synonymous with Israel, was "within their midst." If they wanted to see the kingdom they had only to trust its king, Jesus.

The Kingdom Views
Even if we accept that the proper translation is that the kingdom was "within their midst," we are still left with a variety of interpretations. Most of the interpretations reflect one's predisposed hermenuetic. In this case the kingdom hermeneutics are an outgrowth of the systems developed by "Covenant Theology," "Dispensationalism," "Progressive Dispensationalism," and even "Ultradispensationalism." These are discussed briefly below, but the reader should also refer Appendices E for a more detailed discussion of the various kingdom theologies. Here I will reserve comment for the exegesis of this passage alone.

What specifically does "in your midst" mean? How did this statement relate to the kingdom they were seeking and the one that Jesus was offering? There is the debate. The major theories are as follows:

View # 1 : A Spiritual Kingdom
The most dominant view throughout history has been that Jesus was speaking of a "spiritual kingdom."[1148] This view obviously favors the "within you" translation, but as already noted, it makes no sense that Jesus would have told his enemies that the "Spirit of God,"[1149] as Origen believed, was "within" *them.* Nevertheless, the theory is not completely without merit. Some strengths are apparent, but many more weaknesses. Let us examine them.

Strengths
The most obvious strength of this view are the initial comments of Jesus wherein He declares, "The kingdom of God is not coming with signs to be

observed; nor will they say, 'Look, here *it is!*' or, 'There *it is!*'" Said Matthew Henry, "it will have a silent entrance, without pomp."[1150] Many commentators have argued that this is proof that the Pharisees were looking for the "pomp and splendor" that accompanies "a secular kingdom to be set up in the world."[1151] Indeed, this aspect is true. Jesus' statement was a rebuff of the common belief that the Jews had at that time; namely, that the Messiah would come to overthrow the Roman empire and establish the Davidic kingdom.

In this respect, advocates of this position are correct to point out that Jesus was correcting their perception of the kingdom of God. Of course, too often this view looses sight of the fact that Jesus was speaking to the Pharisees who were obviously trying to entrap Jesus. They had expected Jesus to declare His kingdom would arrive and overthrow Rome at such and such a time and place, in which the Pharisees would have immediately gone to Pontius Pilate with proof of Jesus' treason against Rome. This is the context so often forgotten. The statement is a rebuff of the Pharisees. Consequently, "it would not make sense for Jesus to have told the Pharisees that the kingdom of God was within them as if it were some sort of spiritual kingdom."[1152]

Weaknesses
The weakness of this view are many. First, if the kingdom of God were solely a "spiritual kingdom" or even the Church, as Augustine taught,[1153] then Jesus' answer to the apostles in Acts 1:6-7 (the second book of Luke) would make no sense. For when the apostles asked, "is it at this time You are restoring the kingdom to Israel" Jesus did not deny it would happen, but instead declared, "it is not for you to know times or epochs which the Father has fixed by His own authority." He did not say that the kingdom has already come or that the Church was its fulfillment, but instead told them to proclaim to gospel to the ends of the earth.

This leads to the question of what is the gospel. Is the gospel the kingdom? Obviously the gospel is a message, and a message of salvation to which the kingdom is connected in some way, but the kingdom cannot be synonymous with the gospel itself. Rather the gospel is the proclamation of salvation! This will be addressed more fully in my next volume, but the point is that Jesus was not declaring the kingdom had already come. On the contrary, the very Lord's prayer that so many quote ritualistically in churches today, says, "Your kingdom come. Your will be done, on earth as it is in heaven" (Matthew 6:10; Luke 11:2). The Greek is not present tense, or past tense, nor would anyone claim that God's will is currently being done on earth as it is in heaven! Indeed, the apostle Paul called Satan the "god of this world" (2 Corinthians 4:4) and Satan offered Jesus all the kingdoms of the world as if they were his to give (Matthew 4:8-9)! It is apparent that whatever Jesus meant, the kingdom had *not yet* come "on earth as it is in heaven."

Summary
Whatever merit the "spiritual kingdom" view offers is muted by its single minded attempt to deny any reality to the kingdom as defined elsewhere in Scripture and to deny the promises God made to the Jews concerning the Davidic kingdom. As Sir Robert Anderson noted, "divine promises and prophecies are not like bank-cheques that become invalid by lapse of time."[1154] Whatever *unconditional* promises God made He will keep. Nevertheless, many of the Latin fathers did indeed seek to eliminate Israel from the equation by denying that a literal kingdom of David need ever be established. The irony is that such allegorist as Saint Augustine, while denying a literal earthly kingdom, used this "spiritual kingdom" as a means of justifying the earthly kingdom of Rome as a material extension of it. In other words, although the Augustinians of the Middle Ages argued that the belief in a literal kingdom of God on earth was "carnal" and heretical, even persecuting millennarians during the height of the Middle Ages, it was, in fact, the amillennial Augustinians who were materialistic and carnal by attempting to make the Holy Roman Empire into God's "visible" kingdom. Thus the "spiritual kingdom" theory actually became *the* central doctrine of the carnal materialistic medieval church! Clearly, the doctrine is flawed.

View # 2 : Postponement of the Kingdom

If the "spiritual kingdom" view is on one side of the debate, then the Postponement of the Kingdom view is on the polar opposite. According to this view, the kingdom promised to Israel was to be "postponed" until the time of the gentiles was complete.[1155] This is connected to the "gap" found in prophecy of Daniel 9 (see notes in *Controversies in the Prophets* for a full discussion).[1156] Consequently, although advocates accept that the kingdom will be eternal (as confirmed in Revelation 20-22), they believe that the kingdom's physical manifestation takes place at the Second Coming.

How does this fit "in your midst"? According to Stanely Toussaint, "His kingdom would not be gradual so that it can be observed in a slow metamorphosis" but sudden and immediate so that it may be said it is "in your midst."[1157] Other dispensationalist argue that the kingdom was in their midst inasmuch as the king, Jesus, was in their midst.[1158]

Strengths

Perhaps the strongest evidence is in that "the Lord Jesus never spoke of the kingdom entering people; He only said that people will enter the kingdom."[1159] The very "Lord's prayer" spoke of "may your kingdom come ... on earth" (Matthew 6:10). Likewise in Acts, Jesus seemed to confirm that a future kingdom would come to earth (Acts 1:67 – but see debate on Acts in *Controversies in the Acts and Epistles*). In a great many passages where Jesus speaks of the kingdom, He appears to be speaking about a physical kingdom of some kind on earth. Of course there are some passages which are used to refute this, but the majority seem to favor a real kingdom on earth with Jesus as king. This is admitted by the "liberal spirtualizer" Frederick Grant who says "the Kingdom of God was that which the prophets had announced, and for which all Israel waited. We must not think of it in the form it has now taken" (or rather the form in which Grant believes it has taken).[1160] In other words, although he believed that the kingdom was now strictly a "spiritual kingdom", but he acknowledged that Jesus and the Jews understood the kingdom in a literal sense. Grant believes that the kingdom was transformed into a "spiritual kingdom" but that we should not be so naive as to read this view into His comments which were addressed to a nation awaiting a physical Davidic kingdom to arise and overthrow Rome.

When we read prophecy in the Bible, and particularly the prophecy of Daniel 9, we see that although the kingdom of God encompasses far more than an earthly Davidic kingdom there can be no doubt that both the Prophet Daniel and Jesus expected this prophecy to occur literally at some point in the future. Any spiritual aspects of the kingdom are in addition to its literal aspects, but Jesus continuously spoke of the *coming* kingdom and the Apostle John prophesied its coming in Revelation 20-22.

Weaknesses

There is no doubt that the kingdom is more than just an earthly physical kingdom. Jesus Himself said that His "kingdom is not of this world" (John 18:36). Dispensationalist Sir Robert Anderson (who seems to favor this view) also states that we cannot assume "that 'the Kingdom of God' is merely a synonym for the millennial kingdom, an error which is exposed by the very first passage in which the phrase occurs in the Epistles. In Romans 14:17 we read, 'The Kingdom of God is not meat and drink; but righteousness, and peace, and joy in the Holy Ghost.' This reminds us of the Lord's words to Nicodemus. The world and its religion is the natural sphere, but the Kingdom of God is spiritual; and none can enter it, none can see it, without a new birth by the Spirit."[1161] Hence Sir Robert Anderson warns against taking the kingdom *strictly* in its physical manifestation.

Summary

The Kingdom of God is eternal. It embraces both heaven and earth, but its physical manifestation should not be dismissed. Daniel 9 prophesied a future Davidic kingdom for Israel and its people. Revelation describes this kingdom as lasting a thousand years (Revelation 20:4). When the Jews rejected Jesus, it is believed that the future kingdom was "postponed" until a future time, which co-incides with the Second Coming and the end of the Time of the Gentiles.[1162] Consequently, this view is the literal view of the coming kingdom without rejecting its spiritual aspects.

View # 3 : The "Already–Not Yet" View

The flaws of the "spiritual kingdom" theory and the alleged rigidness of the "postponement" view have led some to adopt what I have often termed the "both–and" viewpoint, which seeks to compromise between two opposing positions. Advocates, however, prefer the title, "Already–Not Yet." The term was coined by George Ladd, a covenant theology, and later adopted in a slightly modified form by progressive dispensationalists. Blaising and Bock, fathers of so-called progessive dispensationalism, call "the church an inaugurated form of the future kingdom of God."[1163] Ladd spoke of "fulfillment without consumation."[1164] In both cases, they expect a future kingdom, but also envision the kingdom as existing here and now in the church.

In its application to this passage, advocates may take either of the preceding interpretations. This is the "beauty" of "both-and" arguments; it allows flexibility to interpret different passages in a variety of ways. Of course this is also its biggest drawback.

Strengths

As with all "both-and" theologies, the theory hopes to take the strength from both other views. It acknowledges a physical earthly kingdom of the future, but also accepts the spiritual applications so apparent in many of Jesus' teachings. In this respect it appears to be the strongest view. Unfortunately, such "both-and" theologies tend not only to take the strengths of opposing views, but also their weaknesses as well.

Weaknesses

If the "Already–Not Yet" system takes its strength from opposing views, it also takes it weaknesses from them. The theory allows the reader to pick and choose and lacks consistency which should be expected in any good exegesis. Advocates can safely choose whichever view seems best to them at the time, but it is for this very reason that its credibility is questioned. Even if a "fundamentalist" is wrong, he is less likely to distort a particular passage if he is following a systematic, logical, and common sense exegesis. Liberal theology, on the other hand, tends to allow the reader's imagination free range in interpretation, thus he is more susceptible to wild fanciful interpretations at odds with what the original author intended.

Summary

The fundamental weakness of this view is its failure to implement a consistent and logical exegesis to all passages. Advocates of this view will vary greatly upon specific passages because it lacks such consistency. Ironically, this is part of the reason for its popularity. In allowing the reader to pick and choose, it helps the reader to escape difficulties in problem passages, but escaping a difficulty is far different from *solving* the difficulty.

View # 4 : Heralders of Kingdom to Come
There is a final view, which is sometimes considered an outgrowth of the "postponement" theory. However, it differs in some ways. Its main feature is in how it views the church and its relationship to the kingdom. This is the problem which plagues the above interpretations. Spiritualizers ignore the prophecies of the coming kingdom, Postponement advocates too often ignore the spiritual applications and have a hard time explaining the role of the Church in the kingdom, and Already–Not Yet advocates mix the two systems together into a hodgpodge that is inconsistent and sometimes contradictory.

In studying this issue, I looked to history. How are kingdoms formed? What constitutes a true kingdom? When I wrote the *Rise and Fall of the Holy Roman Empire* I was most struck by the fact that no two historians could even agree upon what the boundaries and limits of the empire truly were, for it was an empire divided among Church and State, and even within these two institutions were many divisions. Vassal kings often acknowledged the emperor in name only and paid no heed to his edicts or decrees. Others were subjected to every whim of the emperor, while still others bowed to the papacy as king, and offered little fealty to the emperor. How does this relate to the coming kingdom of Christ? That is the question. When we look at history we see that kingdoms embrace more than just physical territory. Even when kings conquered a territory it was not easy to subject the people of that territory to their rule. I will offer a brief example from history, and then explain its relationship to the kingdom of Christ. When William the Conqueror conquered the throne of England, he still had to bring the people under his rule and revamp England. The country would radically change under William, but it was not an easy change. First William wanted a census so that he would know how many subjects he had and how to allocate vassals, taxes, and other institutions throughout the land. People were thus sent out to the regions to take a census. The result of this "Doomsday Book" was conflict which would last many decades.

Here is the relevance to the kingdom of Christ. Jesus came to fulfill the prophecies of Daniel, Isaiah, and other great prophets, but He did not want to damn his very subjects to hell, which would have been the inevitable result of Christ's judgment had He not taken our sins upon Himself on the Cross. Many times He promised that the kingdom would come, but in the parable of the Wedding Feast, He made it clear that He would send out men to collect as many guests for the wedding as were willing to come. Like the census takers of William the Conqueror, the vassal Lords of the king must first proclaim the coming kingdom and prepare the way. The Church is not Israel, nor it is the kingdom of God, but it is like a vassal Lord, heralding the coming kingdom of which it is a part. The vassal Lord has the authority of the king, and is a part of His kingdom, but the kingdom has not yet come to the earth except in title and deed. William the Conqueror held the title of king, but he was not truly king until he exercised that authority over his subjects. So also Christ has not yet exercised His authority over the earthly realm, although it is His by right. We, the Church, are here to prepare the way in order that the people might not be caught unaware or unprepared on that day when Christ returns. It is for that purpose that we, the Church, exist. We are not the kingdom. We are the Heralders of that kingdom and of salvation. We are the Lord's vassals, and the earth is His inheritance.

Strengths

This view explains the apparent dichotomy between Jesus' statements. In some instances it is clear that He is speaking of an earthly Davidic rule such as that prophesied by the Biblical prophets of Old. In other places it is clear that Jesus' realm is not of this world and takes it authority from God alone. It explains how the kingdom can be spoken of as existing "in their midst" while at the same time promising that it would not come until the time of the gentiles is complete (cf. Luke 21:24). The king was present and the preparations for His coming kingdom had already been initiated, but its commencement was still future and will take place at the Second Coming of Christ.

Weaknesses

A weakness may be preceived in comparing Christ's kingdom and the kingdom of God to an earthly kingdom, but Jesus Himself in His parables made the exact same analogy many times. God communicates on our level so that we can understand. This is also the beauty of the mystery of God taking on human flesh in order that we might be able to grasp the infinite in a finite form. God is beyond our comprehension, and yet Jesus, as a human, was able to be one of us and live among us and show us *exactly* what love truly is. Consequently, such comparisons are only weak when they are carried to extremes, for we must agree that God's kingdom is not like man's.

Summary

The kingdom of God is an eternal kingdom whose realm includes both heaven and earth. However, the earth is not now subject to the king in the truest sense of the word. The Church is like a vassal Lord whose duty is to herald the coming kingdom and proclaim the gospel of salvation which guarantees entry into that kingdom. Salvation implies the necessity of being saved, but from what? Our sins make us a part of the kingdom of Satan, but only by being born from above can we enter the kingdom of God (see notes on John 3:3). Our job is to preach the gospel and prepare the way for the kingdom of God, even as

John the Baptist and Jesus Himself proclaimed, "Repent for the kingdom of God is at hand" (Matthew 3:2; 4:17)!

Summary : The Kingdom Hermenuetics

As the reader can see, most of these interpretations seem to fit a preconceived notion rather than flowing naturally from the text. While I discuss the kingdom hermenuetics in Appendix D, it is prudent to address them briefly here. First let it be said that all these hermenuetics are similar in most respects. They all accept that God works in history toward the ultimate goal of salvation through Jesus Christ. However, they differ in the details; particularly in regard to Israel and its purpose in history.

Covenant theology differs from its dispensational brothers in that it rejects any future for national Israel and the Jewish people. They hold that the Church has "replaced Israel." In Augustine's system, the kingdom of God was synonymous with the Church. It is for this reason that the Crusaders held they were expanded the "kingdom of Heaven" when they conquered Jerusalem.[1165] Of course most modern Covenant theologians do not accept this sort of extremist interpretation, but all hold that the Church is virtually, if not wholly, synonymous with the kingdom of God. Some Covenant theologians do accept that a Millennial kingdom will arise after the Second Coming, but other do not. This theology is sometimes called "Replacement theology" because it holds that the Church has replaced Israel in God's prophetic plan or eschatology.

Although Covenant theologians present dispensationalism as some sort of "new" theology which is radically divided among itself, this is fiction. Covenant theology and traditional dispensationalism are really different branches of the same tree. The tree is the system of theology which examines how God has acted in history. Despite minor differences developments in the theological system began to diverge primarily over one issue, and one issue only; has the Church replaced Israel? Since the time of the Church fathers this has been a divisive issue upon which scholars have differed for centuries, but with the rise of Zionism and modern Israel the debate has taken front stage. Dispensationalists are all of the branch which says, to one degree or another, that God has not forsaken Israel, nor has the Church permanently replaced Israel, but three different branches of dispensationalism debate to what extend this is true and how, if at all, this effects the Church.

Traditional dispensationalism maintains that Israel and the Church are two different things and must be looked upon differently. Traditional dispensationalists hold that prophecies of Israel apply to Israel. The Church is obviously a significant part of God's plan, but does not negate His promises to the Jewish people. After all, if God cannot bring the Jewish nation to repentance then how could He ever have brought the Gentiles to repentance either? If the gentile nations have been changed through Christ, shall God not do the same for Israel as He promised? A Jew can be a part of the Church in this age, but he

282

does not cease to be a part of God's promise to *the Jews*. The prophecy of Romans 11:26 is taken literally; not in that "every Israelite will be saved, but Israel as a nation will be saved,"[1166] as Sir Robert Anderson phrased it.

Hyper-dispensationalism is a branch of traditional dispensationalism which takes excesive views of the differences between Israel and the Church and God's dealings with each. I personally met one hyper-dispensationalist who held that only the epistles of Paul were written to the Church and that all the other books of the New Testament apply to the Jews specifically. He essentially made two different gospels; one for gentiles, and one for Jews which required the keeping of the law. Because hyper-dispensationalists never call themselves hyper-dispensationalists they often pose as "traditional dispensationalists." As a result, not only do Covenant theologians love to quote these men as poster childs for "traditional dispensationalism," but too many legitimate traditional dispensationalists have been influenced by some of the doctrines of hyper-dispensationalists (although not the teaching of two gospels, as alleged by critics). The result is that some have become disenchanted with dispensationalism, and that led to the rise of progressive dispensationalism in the 1990s.

Progressive dispensationalism attempts to moderate between the extreme hyper-dispensational theories and those of Covenant theology. In some respects, it was an attempt to harken back to the earlier dispensationalists, but it was also a compromise with Covenant theology. Borrowing from covenant theologian George Eldon Ladd, progressive dispensationalism adopts an "Already–Not Yet" theology in what they call "realized eschatology" or Ladd's "fulfillment without consumation." The system essentially attempts to accept both an allegorical interpretation of prophecies for the present age while accepting that there may be a literal fulfillment at the Second Coming.

Conclusion

How one interprets this verse depends greatly upon how they view the kingdom of God. Those who reject a literal kingdom of God at the Second Coming of Christ tend to interpret the verse allegorically as a kingdom within our hearts. Those accept the literal return of Christ and the establishment of a Davidic kingdom (cf. Revelation 20) tend to interpret "in your midst" as a reference to Christ, or to Israel as a nation. Israel was, after all, to be God's nation and a beacon of light unto the gentile world, but the Jews did not live up to this expectation and the Pharisees themselves challenged their very king! This is the view that best fits the context, for how could Jesus tell the Pharisees that the kingdom was it their wicked hearts? Moreover, even many a spiritualizer, such as Frederick Grant, admitted that we should look at the passages in the way in which the Jews of that would have understood it. Jesus was talking to the Pharisees and every Jew expected a Davidic king to rule the nation of Israel. "Where is this kingdom you promise?" asked the cynical Pharisees. Jesus replied, "in your midst." They had only to accept their king and live up to the promises they had made and the kingdom of Israel would have become the kingdom for which they waited.

The kingdom of God is the entire realm of which God rules. It includes both heaven and earth, but Satan is called the "god of this world" (2 Corinthians 4:4). The Apostle Peter calls us strangers and aliens in this world (1 Peter 2:11). We are but ambassadors of the Kingdom of God. Jesus is the rightful heir to the throne of David, but He has not returned to claim His place on the throne. Like any kingdom on earth, ambassadors represent the king and his kingdom wherever the king sends them. We, the Church, represent God and His kingdom on earth, but we are *not* the kingdom. The kingdom will come (future tense, as in the Lord's prayer) when Jesus returns, and not before then. This is a teaching consistent with Jesus' words and promises throughout the entire Gospels and the epistles of His disciples.

Luke 17:22-37 – See Matthew 24:36-44

Luke 18:18-30 – See Matthew 19:16-30

Luke 18:35-43 – See Matthew 20:29

Luke 19:28-41 – See Matthew 21:2

Luke 19:45-46 – See Matthew 21:12-17

Luke 20:27-45 – See Matthew 22:23-33

The Desolation of Jerusalem
Luke 21:20-24

"Jerusalem will be trampled under foot by the Gentiles until the times of the Gentiles are fulfilled."

I have already addressed the "Abomination of Desolation" under the parallel passage Matthew 24:15-28. However, this passage deserves special attention because it is the only place in the Bible where the term "times of the Gentiles" is used. This term bears significance for two reasons.

First, it is apparent that the "Abomination of Desolation" cannot be a prophecy about the fall of Jerusalem in 70 A.D. because 70 A.D. was not the end of gentile trampling, but *the beginning*. This is a prophecy about gentile domination of Jerusalem which began in 70 A.D. The larger prophecy is about the End Times and the return of Christ (see notes on Matthew 24:15-28). Consequently, the relevance here is to gentile domination which did not stop after the sack of Titus. Early in the second century a certain Bar Kochba

284

claimed to be the Messiah and started a new revolt against Rome.[1167] By 135 A.D. Hadrian had defeated the rebellion and in 138 A.D. he renamed Jerusalem "Colonia Aelia Capitolina."[1168] Historian Philip Schaff, himself a preterist, records that Jerusalem was "again destroyed"[1169] during that Bar Kochba rebellion when "more than a half million of Jews were slaughtered after desperate resistence."[1170] Following this the Jews were expelled from Jerusalem and the city became dedicated to the pagan god Jupiter.[1171] The expulsion of Jews and the permanent occupation of Jerusalem by Romans could hardly be seen as the end of Jerusalem's woes. Even before the Arabs swept across the middle east, Jerusalem remained a prize to be won. In 614 A.D. the Persian general Shahr-Baraz conquered Jerusalem and slaughtered most of its inhabitants.[1172] In 629 A.D. the emperor Heraclius reclaimed Jerusalem for the Roman empire,[1173] but just three years later a certain "prophet" named Mohammed died. His followers were destined to conquer the mid-east and Jerusalem along with it. By 637 Omar had conquered Jerusalem and the Dome of the Rock was eventually built where the Holy Temple of Solomon once stood.[1174] To this very day that Dome stands as a stumbling block to Jews who seek to rebuild the temple and is a thorn in the politics of Arab-Jewish relations. From this time until the modern age the trampling did not cease. I have recorded a larger history elsewhere and will not repeat it here.[1175] Nevertheless, even in the modern age, the gentile domination and trampling cannot be said to have ended. In 1947 the United Nations created a partition plan which would have divided Palestine between the Jews and Arabs.[1176] The Arabs, however, refused to accept the partition declaring the whole of Palestine belonged to them. They promised to "throw the Jews into the sea,"[1177] and further declared, "we will strangle Jerusalem."[1178] Seven nations, counting Palestine, invaded Israel[1179] but God was with Israel and by the end of the war, Israel had won its independence, but Jerusalem was still divided. A wall ran down the middle of Jerusalem. It was still a city "trampled" by gentiles. In 1967 Egypt again prepared to invade Israel and the Six-day war began, but again Israel prevailed. This time Jerusalem was in Jewish hands, except for the temple mount itself.[1180] The city's most Holy site to Jews remained in Muslim hands, and has to this day. Terrorism has become common place in Jerusalem; a city which remains populated by Palestinians in the western half. No honest person denies that Jerusalem has, and continues to be, trampled by gentiles. It seems that ever since Nebuchadnezzar invaded Jerusalem over 2600 years ago Jerusalem has been "trampled under foot by the Gentiles" (Luke 21:24). The destruction of Jerusalem by Titus was hardly the end of trampling, but one in a series of tramplings which continue to this very day. No logical person would, therefore, believe that Jerusalem is at peace, which begs the question, "if Jerusalem is still trampled then how could the times of the gentiles be said to be fulfilled?" Obviously that time has not yet come for the trampling must continue until

"until the times of the gentiles be fulfilled." The next logical question therefore is, "what is the time of the gentiles?"

This is the second issue; what is the time of the gentiles? The word gentile means only one thing: someone who is not a physical descendant of Jacob. It has no other meaning. The church is made up predominantly of gentiles. The world at large is predominantly gentile. The only ones who are not gentiles in this world are Jews, regardless of whether or not they accepted Jesus as the Messiah. So if the "times of the gentiles" must come to a close one day, what can this mean but that the time of the Jews will come? This is the controversy. Many, as arrogant as any Pharisee, presume that the Church has permanently replaced Israel and negated all the promises God made to the Jewish people. Yet here Jesus is clearly saying that there is a day when the "time of the gentiles" will be complete! Or does He?

One argument that is sometimes made is that the word "fulfilled" has multiple meanings. The Greek word πληρωθῶσιν (*plarothosin*) can be defined as "fulfilled, make full, bring to completion, complete, or accomplish."[1181] In each case the meaning involves the completion or end of a thing, not its beginning. The covenant theologian sees the church age as eternal. He must, therefore, see the "fulfillment" as the beginning of the church age. However, the apostle Paul warned us not to be arrogant (Romans 11:20) but fear the Lord, for "if God did not spare the natural branches, neither will He spare you" (11:20-21). Some would wish that God discard the natural branches (Jews), save a few token members, but this doctrine, prominent among Replacement theologians is diametrically opposed to the teaching of Scripture. Jesus used to say, "many who are first will be last; and the last, first" (Matthew 19:30; Mark 10:31). The Jews were the first to whom God made promises. We gentiles were but pagans who practiced human sacrifice, cannibalism, barbarity, and cruelties beyond imagination. It was God's pleasure to show His grace by transforming the barbaric cultures of the gentiles. If, however, he forgets the first, who were the Jews, then how can we expect God to keep His promises to us; the last. We accepted Jesus first, though we were last. The Jews, who are first (Romans 1:16; 2:10), will be the last to accept the Messiah, but they, as a nation, will accept Him.

Galatians 3:28 says there is "neither Jew nor Greek," but it is talking about equality in the eyes of God, and no more negates the distinction between Jew and gentile in eschatology than it renders men emasculated for declaring "there is neither male nor female"! No theologian can dismiss the importance of the passing of the "times of the Gentiles." This does not mean that gentiles loose our inheritance anymore than the institution of the Church means that the Jews have lost their inheritance (as many Covenant theologians so erroneously teach). God will give to each as He promised; both Jew and gentile. When Christ returns He will establish the Millennial Kingdom and the "times of the Gentiles" will be passed. This will not be the final eternal age, but it will be a time when God fulfills His promises of a Davidic kingdom for the Jews. The Church is like a gentile ambassador for the coming king. The temporal Millennial kingdom itself will be Israel. This is then followed by the eternal kingdom wherein both Jews and gentiles will be equal and where "He will wipe away every tear from their eyes; and there will no longer be *any* death; there will no longer be *any* mourning, or crying, or pain; the first things have passed away" (Revelation 21:4).

Luke 21:32 – See Matthew 24:34

Luke 22:19-20 – See Matthew 26:26-29

Luke 22:47-53 – See John 18:12

When Did Christ Appear Before Caiphas?
Luke 22:66 – Matthew 26:57 – Mark 14:53 (cf. John 18:13)

"When it was day, the Council of elders of the people assembled, both chief priests and scribes, and they led Him away to their council *chamber*."	"Those who had seized Jesus led Him away to Caiaphas, the high priest, where the scribes and the elders were gathered together."	"They led Jesus away to the high priest; and all the chief priests and the elders and the scribes gathered together."

Some have argued that this verse contradicts the accounts of Matthew 26:57 and Mark 14:53. However, Luke does not include the initial appearance which John 18:13 makes clear was before Annas, and not Caiaphas. Thus once again the critic takes an ommision (the appearance before Annas) and argues that Luke's gospel cannot allow for such an appearance. This is both illogical and dishonest, but see notes on Matthew 26:57.

Another criticism is made by adopting a time specific (and erroneous) interpretation of each passage and then saying they contradict. This old tactic can be easily disproven. According to the view, Matthew 26:57 says that on the night Jesus was arrested the priests and scribes were gathered together prior to Jesus being brought to the high priest but Mark 14:53 says the priests and scribes gathered together on the night of Jesus' arrest after Jesus was brought to the high priest while Luke 22:66 allegedly says the priests and scribes assembled the day after Jesus was arrested. Note how each "statement" is actually an interpretation of what the passage says, rather than an actual reading of the passages.

Note that Matthew and Mark actually say the same thing. Matthew says that they had "led Him away to Caiaphas, the high priest, where the scribes and the elders were gathered together." Mark also says "they led Jesus away to the high priest; and all the chief priests and the elders and the scribes gathered together." The critic here attempts to argue that Mark implies the elders had to gather together after Jesus was brought but that Matthew, using the past tense, implies they were previously assembled. Such a frivolous interpretation is typical of a defense lawyer in a court of law trying desperately to make witnesses appear as if they are contradicting one another, but common sense prevails. Matthew and Mark say the exact same thing. But what of Luke's assersion that it was "day"?

Luke 22:66 also states as Matthew and Mark that but adds that this was "when it was day." Now the reader will remember that Jesus was arrested in the dead of night and stood before Pilate around 6 A.M. He will also remember that the Romans began the new day at midnight, as we do, but Jews began the new day at either sundown or sunrise. Luke, of course, was a gentile and obviously considered a meeting at around 5 A.M. to be the new day. Even by Jewish reconning, the new day would begin at 6 A.M. Since this trial took place immediately before He was taken to Pilate it is common sense that Luke's account fits perfectly with Matthew and Mark's. The reader is referred to "When Was Jesus Crucified? Chronology of the Last Supper, Crucifixion, and Resurrection" above for a more detailed analysis of the chronology of the trial and crucifixion of Jesus.

Luke 22:34 – See Matthew 26:69-75

Luke 23:38 – See Matthew 27:37

Paradise and Hades
Luke 23:43

"Truly I say to you, today you shall be with Me in Paradise."

I have discussed in some detail the doctrines of Paradise and Hades under both Mark 9:43-48 and Luke 16:19-31. Here again the issue arises. Josephus used the word Hades as a generic term for the dead, both good and bad, where there are both "punishments and rewards in Hades."[1182] However, Paradise is the more specific term for the good part of Hades where the righteous await their resurrection. John Wesley calls this "the place where the souls of the righteous remain from death till the resurrection."[1183]

Thus the criminal who was crucified along side Jesus, even though he had formerly mocked Jesus just hours earlier, was promised salvation. Such a deathbed conversion is proof that Jesus transforms and can forgive us as long as we live, up until the very moment we die, if only we repent and place our trust in Him. This passage alone should contradict those strict hyper-Calvinists who deny that deathbed confessions are legitimate[1184] and serves as notice that it is never too late to repent. Having said that, we never know when we are to die. We could die this very hour in an accident or natural disaster. Indeed, it was a near death experience which made Martin Luther reevaluate his own life and realize that he was not ready to meet God. From that time onward he studied the Scriptures and became the alledged father of the Reformation. So too, we should look at our own life and decide whether or not we are truly ready to meet God should we die this very day.

Luke 23:47 – See Matthew 27:54

Luke 23:55 – See Mark 16:1

Luke 24:1-12 – See Matthew 28:1-8

When Did the Apostles Return to Galilee?
Luke 24:33 – Matthew 28:16 – Acts 1:3-4

"And they got up that very hour and returned to Jerusalem, and found gathered together the eleven and those who were with them."	"The eleven disciples proceeded to Galilee, to the mountain which Jesus had designated."	"To these He also presented Himself alive after His suffering, by many convincing proofs, appearing to them over *a period of forty days and speaking of the things concerning the kingdom of God.*"

Now I have no problem with those who are concerned over legitimate *apparent* contraditions, which are common in any eyewitness accounts. However, I little sympathy for the Bible critic who grasps at straws to create contradictions where none is apparent. Here Shabbir Ally, the anti-Christian Muslim cleric and Bible critic, suggests that Matthew's account demands that the apostles must have left *immediately*, although the text says nothing of the sort. As in previous sections I have discussed that omissions among eyewitness testimonies are not only common but logical. None claims to be an exhaustive account of every single action or the Bible would be the size of libraries counting tens of thousands of pages. Although Shabbir entitled his book "101 *Clear* Contradictions in the Bible," there is nothing *clear* about this misquotation, nor about the logic behind it. It is frivolous and only included here because the internet has helped to perpetuate many of the myths.

The Ascension
Luke 24:51 – Acts 1:9-12

"While He was blessing them, He parted from them and was carried up into heaven."

"And after He had said these things, He was lifted up while they were looking on, and a cloud received Him out of their sight."

This debate is similar to the previous in that assumes that Luke records a complete chonology of every event before the ascension and that, therefore, the ascension must have taken place on the *same* day as the resurrection! Bear in mind that Acts was written *by the exact same author* of Luke! The fact is that the gospel of Luke ends with a very brief summary statement which alludes to the ascension. It is does not tell us what happened in the forty days before His ascension because he intended on including that information in his second volume; the book of Acts!

Summary of Luke's Gospel

Luke may be considered a true historian's account of the life, death, and resurrection of Jesus Christ. He consulted with eyewitnesses, probably read the gospel of Matthew (and possibly Mark), and includes anecdotal information provided by Mary and others. The relationship between Luke and the other synoptic gospels is discussed under Appendix A. It is sufficient to say here that Luke was a travelling companion of the apostle Paul who wrote his gospel (and Acts) as a historian for a friend who wanted to know more about Jesus and the history of Christianity.

5
—
The Gospel of John

John's gospel is the most unique. It is the only gospel to mention most of the "I am" sayings of Jesus because it is the most theological of the gospels. John wrote not so much about what Jesus did, but about who Jesus was. For that reason his gospel is also the most clear about the deity of Christ. Although the other gospels also make the deity of Christ evident, it is John who emphasizes the relationship of the Father and Son from the very first passage. These factors help to make John different from the Synoptic gospels, and complimentary to them.

Since the rise of "critical," or rather skeptical, scholarship there has been much debate over why the Synoptic gospels tell similar stories of Jesus but the real question should not be why are Matthew, Mark, and Luke so similar, for they all record the same history of the same Son of God, but rather why is John so different? It is only logical that histories of the same man would recount the same events. Do not all histories of George Washington relate the story Valley Forge? Certainly they do! The question is, therefore, why is John's different? This is the irony of the debate. John's is different *because* he had read the other gospels and did not want to repeat unnecessarily much of what had already been told in the three previous gospels.

Matthew wrote for Jews, citing many Biblical prophecies from the Old Testament. Mark wrote for gentiles. Luke wrote as a historian. John wrote as a theologian. Together these four gospels complement one another and provide a full picture of Jesus; from the perspective of Jewish prophecy, from the perspective of gentiles who did not know God, from the perspecitve of history, and from a theological perspective. John, as the last of the gospels, completes the picture of Jesus and shows us not what Jesus was, but *who* He was.

The Authorship and Date of John

As always there are critics who claim that John did not write the gospel which bears his name and that it was a late writing far removed from the witnesses of Jesus. However, very few such sincere critics exist today for the discovery of the Rylands Fragments has silenced all but the dishonest critics; at least in regard to late dating of John's gospel.[1185] This fragment (also noted as $\mathfrak{P}^{52}$) is usually dated to about 125 A.D.,[1186] no later than 135 A.D.,[1187] and probably earlier. Given that the fragment shows the gospel had already been distributed as far as Egypt, most serious scholars believe this gospel could have been written no later than 100 A.D. when the apostle John was still living (he was the youngest of the disciples and lived until he was in his 80s or even 90s).

Ironically, "it is common today to find nonconservative scholars arguing for a date as early as A.D. 45-66"[1188] with conservatives date it between 85 and 95 A.D.[1189] This is, in part, because early tradition records, as Irenaeus said, that "John, the disciple of the Lord ... published a Gospel during his residence Ephesus in Asia."[1190] This would either be shortly before or after his exile to Patmos during the persecutions of Domitian in the early 90s. Furthermore, its placement as the fourth gospel is generally believed to be because it was the fourth gospel written.

Internal evidence also supports John in the late first century. The author gives detailed descriptions of certain places and architecture (cf. the five colonnades of the Pool of Bethesda in 5:2) which may indicate that the architecture was no longer in existence (as the Romans destroyed much of these colonnades in the 70 A.D. invasion) and needed to be described to the reader. It is also, of course, evidence that the author was alive and in Jerusalem before 70 A.D., hence an eyewitness. However, the most convincing evidence is the aside in John 21:23 where the author refutes a legend which said that John would not die (but see notes on John 21:23). If such a legend had arisen and needed to be refuted then it follows that John was already aged when he wrote his gospel.

Of course the fact that John is the author has been virtually unanimous throughout history. To be sure a few various alternate theories argued for someone else ranging from a Presbyter named John in the second century to Mary Magdalene (now popularized by gnostic conspiracists)! In fact there is no doubt that John wrote this gospel. It is affirmed by Polycarp who was himself a disciple of John[1191] and by virtually all other Church Fathers.

That John is the author is apparent in the text even though he is not specifically named (an act of humility, no doubt). "The beloved disciple" is the author (21:24) and his identity can be asertained from the gospel with certainty. Since John's authorship is not in doubt, I shall not repeat every internal evidence and passage, but shall merely summarize it simply. "The beloved disciple" was a member of Jesus' inner circle of three (cf. 20:2-10; 13:23-24; 19:26, 35). Of the three (Peter, James, and John), Peter is referred to in the third person many times, but John is never mentioned by name at all. James was the first to die a martyr in the 40s and could not have written the gospel. Finally, as aforementioned, John 21:23 recounts the legend that "the disciple" would not die. This is John and no other. All the other disciples had died a martyr's death.

Thus John, often called the "the Apostle of Love" wrote this gospel late in life, probably in the 90s. He did not want to repeat unnecessarily what had already been told in the three Synoptic gospels, but wanted to describe Jesus for who He was, as the Second person of the Trinity. His is a theological gospel, desribing the teachings of the Jesus in great detail and containing the famous "I am" passages. It is a gospel of love.

The Deity of Christ
John 1:1-5, 14-18

"In the beginning was the Word, and the Word was with God, and the
Word was God ... And the Word became flesh, and dwelt among us."

These beautiful words begin the gospel of John and one of the greatest
controversies of the Trinity. What do these simple words mean? As Genesis
began with the simple phrase, "in the beginning," so here John begins "in the
beginning." What follows defines who Jesus is, and it is for that very reason
that cults and heretics have tried to manipulate its meaning for two thousand
years. Here in this "simple statement ... is perhaps the clearest and most direct
declaration of the deity of the Lord Jesus Christ to be found anywhere in
Scripture."[1192] Is it any wonder that it is also one of the most controversial?

The Eternal Jesus?
John begins with the beginning, but "there is nothing older than the beginning"
(Saint Cyril).[1193] Consequently, "the Word had no beginning" (John Darby).[1194]
Since it is clear from verse fourteen that "the Word" is Jesus (see below) then
"Jesus was preexistent"[1195] as James Boice said. Indeed, "the Son is before all
time"[1196] and, as Chrysostom affirmed, "this expression, 'was in the beginning,'
is expressive of eternal and infinite being."[1197] "Here then we have the sublime
revelation that our Lord Jesus Christ is an eternal Being."[1198]

Now some heretics question this, arguing that Jesus was created first of
all beings, but was not eternal. However, Chrysostom objected that "was" and
"made" have nothing in common.[1199] Indeed, "the verb *was* does not express a
complete past, but rather a continuous state."[1200] Nowhere is Jesus spoken of in
John as having been created, but rather that the Word was already in existence
"in the beginning."

This calls into question the role of Jesus in creation. John 1:3 says,
"All things came into being through Him, and apart from Him nothing came into
being that has come into being." Compare this with Colossians 1:16 which
states that "For by Him all things were created, *both* in the heavens and on earth,
visible and invisible, whether thrones or dominions or rulers or authorities--all
things have been created through Him and for Him." Here John places Jesus "in
the beginning," thus "'Jesus Christ' was already in existence when the heavens
and the earth were created."[1201] More than that, however, the Pastor of Hermes
notes that "the Son of God is older than His creatures, so that He was a
fellow-councillor with the Father in His work of creation."[1202] This doctrine is
consistent with the teaching that God the Father was speaking to Jesus when He
said "Let Us make" in Genesis. Interestingly enough, "there is an ancient
Targum (translation of the Hebrew bible into Aramaic) in which God's speaking
is personified, or reified, as his *Memra* or Word."[1203] This Targum, the *Neofiti*,
reads in Genesis 1:13, "the Word of the Lord created ..."[1204]

Now more will be said of "the Word" and of His relationship to God the Father, but first it is important to address two key issues which arise in this debate. The first is the actual use and meaning of "the Word" to identify Jesus. The second is the question of Arianism (among the first Christian cults in history, followed by gnostics) and its mistranslation of this passage.

The "Logos"

The Greek word for "Word" is λογος (*logos*). "There is no doubt that by the *Logos* is meant Jesus Christ."[1205] This is made explicitly clear in verse fourteen, but while the *Logos* is clearly Jesus Christ, some have argued that its application to Jesus as a title implies that John was somehow promoting Greek philosophy, which Paul openly ridiculed (cf. 1 Corinthians 1:20-29)!

This tactic is acheived through a subtle infusion. It is pointed out that the modern word "logic" comes from the word *logos*, and that the ancient Greek philosophers sometimes used the word in the context of "reason."[1206] They then apply the "rationalist" (liberal) doctrines of the "Age of Reason" to the Bible.[1207] This absurdity is revealed by a closer examination of both history and language.

First, in philosophy "reason" was but one of many definitions.[1208] So even if we were talking about Greek philosophy it would still be dishonest to apply this definition to the word λογος (*logos*) without a qualifier. Second, "the term λογος never has a sense of *reason* in the New Testament."[1209] This is because the "Jewish and Greek conceptions of '*Logos*' were so different that they could not be fruitfully joined."[1210] These words, ironically, were uttered by a scholar who then proceded to try to do just that! Thus while admitting that the "Jewish and Greek conceptions of '*Logos*' were" completely different, he attempts to merge them together. Another "conservative" scholar attempts to connect λογος with stoic philosophers[1211] and then implies John "arbitrarily foisted upon Jesus" this term![1212] Of course, the Hellenistic use of λογος "does not prove, as is sometimes loosely suggested, that the term λογος was very widely current in this sense."[1213] Any Greek lexicon in the world defines λογος (*logos*) first and foremost as "word" and this is its meaning and translation throughout the Bible.[1214]

The most obvious reason to reject this is the fact that "John, of course, was neither a disciple of Heraclitus nor a follower of the stoics."[1215] The Bible makes perfectly clear that Greek philosophy (even that of the stoics) is inconsistent with the Biblical teachings on God (cf. 1 Corinthians 1:20-29). "Λογος is used of the 'Word of God.'"[1216] This is the clear meaning and context of the word. Indeed, Jesus is called the "Word of God" in Revelation 19:13,[1217] which was also written by John. Thus it is concluded without doubt that "the Word" is Jesus Christ and has no other meaning than that Jesus is the "Word of God."

Was the Word God? (Unitarianism and the Trinity)

"The Word was God." As John MacArthur once said, "that simple statement ... is perhaps the clearest and most direct declaration of the deity of the Lord Jesus Christ to be found anywhere in Scripture."[1218] It is for this very reason that Arians (those who deny the deity of Christ Jesus) deliberately mistranslate this verse. The New World Translation (official translation of the Jehovah's Witnesses) reads, "in the beginning was the Word, and the Word was with God, and the Word was *a god*." Thus they deny that the "Word was God" but rather apply to the Word the "title" of "a god" in the same context as Psalms 82:6 and John 10:34.

The argument used by Arians, such as the Jehovah's Witnesses, is that the Greek does not use the definite article ("the") before "God" and should be thus translated as "a God" rather than "God." Of course, there is no indefinite article ("a") in the Greek either. In fact, there is no indefinite article in Greek at all! Of course, there are many reasons to reject this dishonest translation. The reasons are listed here in no particular order.

1. As aforementioned, there is no indefinite article ("a") in the Greek. Furthermore, the absence of the definite article does not prove an indefinite one is intended.[1219] Greek language structure and declentions determine this factor as defined in the following comments.

2. "The God" is expressly stated in the previous clause of the same sentence. It would be bad grammer to repeat the definite article after it has already been defined. Think, for example, of this English sentence. "This year we are electing the President, and President Obama is running for re-election." Now add the definite article before each instance. "This year we are electing the President, and the President Obama is running for re-election." See how the sentence not only becomes redundant even contradictory. It implies that "the President" has already been elected, so why are we having another election? Now add the indefinite article as the Arians would do. "This year we are electing the President, and a President Obama is running for re-election." See how the sentence now becomes even more confusing as if there are multiple Presidents at a given time!

3. More importantly, as John MacArthur pointed out, "according to the rules of Greek, when the predicate nominative (God in this clause) precedes the verb, it cannot be considered indefinite."[1220] The "predicate nominative" is a fancy linguistic word referring to the definition of a subject. For example, a Greek textbook says "in the sentence, 'John is a man,' 'John' is the subject and 'man' is the predicate nominative."[1221] *However*, when the word "man" precedes the subject "John" it must be translated "John is the man." This is the case in Greek where is actually reads, "καὶ θεος ην 'ο λογος" [literally : "and God was the Word"]. Thus, "God *cannot* be indefinite.

4. Furthermore, in Greek, the definite article is used to identify the subject of the clause.[1222] In *The Basics of Biblical Greek*, William Mounce says,

"we know that 'the Word' is the subject because it has the definite article."[1223] If God has the definite article then it, and not "the Word," would be the subject. This would change the meaning of the sentence, as illustrated below.

5. Moreover, if the subject of the sentence were God rather than "the Word," then "the effect of the article, if inserted, would be to declare that God and the Word are co-extensive ... The Three Persons of the Godhead would thus be denied."[1224] William Mounce, in his Greek grammer textbook, says, "its lack of a definite article keeps us from identifying the *person* of the Word (Jesus Christ) with the *person* of 'God' (the Father)."[1225] Similarly, Frederick Godet said that "the word θεος, God, is used without an article, because it has the sense of an adjective and designates, not the person, but the quality."[1226]

6. An alternate of the above argument is that "it would be pure Sabellianism to say 'the Word' was 'ο θεος."[1227] This differs slightly from the previous argument, in that Sabellianism is the doctrine of modalism. In other words, it is the teaching that God transforms from one mode to another, but is never three distinct (or even two distinct) persons. Thus "this would identify the Logos with the totality of divine existence, and it would contradict the preceding clause."[1228] In either case, the definite article would actually be of as much use in denying the Trinity as the indefinite article, if it existed! This is why there is neither!

7. Aside from the actual Greek grammatical reasons for rejecting the Jehovah's Witnesses' translation are many exegetical and logical ones as well. For example, John Darby has pointed out "the Word had no beginning"[1229] but were not angels created? If Jesus was merely an angel, as the Jehovah's Witnesses maintain, then He would be created and yet here Jesus is in existence in eternity past and a participant in creation!

Any serious examination of the Scripture leads to the inevitable conclusion that John believes Jesus to be the incarnation of the one and only true God of Israel. Martin Luther saw the entire Trinity here, stating, "he states expressly that three distinct Persons dwell in that same single divine essence, namely, God the Father."[1230] However, Luther appears to have problems defining them with precision. He correctly defines the Word as "Jesus"[1231] but elsewhere as "Holy Spirit."[1232] So also Irenaeus said that "having first of all distinguished these three ... he again unites them"[1233] in this passage. Once again though, it is unclear to which he attributes the Holy Spirit. What is clear is that there are at least two separate beings. As James Boice made clear, "*with* God" (v. 1) "is an affirmation of Christ's separate personality."[1234] He was "with God" and "a companion," but He also "was God." Thus the inevitable conclusion is that "the Son is God."[1235] No translation can get around this fact, which is made all the more clear in verse fourteen.

"The Word Became Flesh and Dwelt Among Us"

Here in verse fourteen it is clear that "He who 'was God' became flesh."[1236] This is the incarnation of Jesus Christ. However, it is no surprise that these simple words remain controversial ones. If God became flesh, was He sinful? Could he be clothed in sinful flesh and not be sinful? Was Jesus truly a man in the flesh or did He have a phantom body? These are the questions which arose from the earliest heretics in history. On the one hand were the Arians who denied the divinity of Christ and on the other were the Docetists who denied that Jesus was truly a man. Verse one was written by John to prove the Arians wrong and verse fourteen was written to prove the Docetists wrong.

Such is the fundamental doctrine of all true Christian sects since the time of Christ. Even the notorious allegorist Origen maintained orthodoxy in saying, "while made a Man [He] remained the God which He was."[1237] Ignatius, one of the earliest Church Fathers, said that Christ was God "being incorporeal."[1238] Having said this, debate among the early heretics, and modern ones, continues as to what was meant by "flesh" and by the words "dwelt among us."

The word "flesh" is σαρξ (*sarx*) in Greek and refers to "flesh and blood." It is a physical body. Said Charles Spurgeon, "the Lord became bone of our bone, and flesh of our flesh."[1239] However, critics point out that "flesh" is used idiomatically in the Bible to refer to the sinful nature of man. The "sins of the flesh," is such an example. The apostle Paul often uses "flesh" in this manner, but it is clear that here "'flesh' denotes human nature, but not ... sinful nature."[1240] Thus many believe that σαρξ (*sarx*) "means more than merely acquiring a physical body"[1241] for Jesus was susceptible to the same temptations as us (Hebrew 2:18; 4:15), and yet He did not sin. It is for this reason that the heresy known as Docetism promoted "the idea of Christ as a mere phantasm, without human flesh and blood,"[1242] and it is for this reason that most believe John wrote these very words to refute that ancient heresy.

Still another ancient heresy is that of Eutyches who essentially argued that Christ was part man and part God. In an feeble attempt to combat this heresy Thomas Aquinas argued that the passage should read "assumed flesh" rather than "was flesh."[1243] This, he presumed, would negate the force of Eutyches' argument, which attempted to segregate the human and divine elements of Jesus. However, here, like Eutyches, Aquinas was attempting to mold the unphantomable God into Greek philosophy and understand the inifinite in a finite manner. H.A. Ironside addressed the issue in a less philosophical way, saying that the translation "made flesh," found in the King James and many others, should be rejected for "*became* flesh."[1244] Technically, this is the correct translation for the Greek word is "became" or εγενετο (*egeneto*). This negates the notion of Jesus having been "made" since He was eternal.

In each of these cases the problem is with temporal men trying to understand God in finite human terms. Jesus became a man in order to relate to us on our own level, but that does not mean that we can integrate the divine with Greek philosophy. We are only to understand that, as John Calvin said, "the eternal God 'appeared in a body' (1 Timothy 3:16)."[1245] Erasmus looked beyond the philosophical attempt to comprehend the Trinity in human terms and looked at the more sublime humility of love of God. "What is frailer than human flesh, or more despised? What is mightier than God, or more sublime?"[1246] and yet they were joined together.

This leads the question of God's "dwelling" among us. It is not "lived among us" but "dwelt." Why? What difference does this make? The Greek word is εσκνωσεν (*esknosen*) from the word σκηνη (*skene*) which means "tabernacle." Tabernacle is the name for the portable temple (for lack of a better word) found in Exodus 27:21; Lev. 1:1; and Num 1:1,[1247] to name but a few. It refers to the dwelling place of God. "'But will God indeed dwell on earth?' asked Solomon as he dedicated the temple."[1248] That passage is 1 Kings 8:27 and suggests that Solomon understood that God could not be confined to a temple, but it also foreshadowed something far greater. That God would literally dwell among us as a man in Christ Jesus!

Conclusions

The famed Desiderius Erasmus once said that "since the nature of God immeasurably surpasses the feebleness of human intelligence [and] ... its reality cannot be perceived by our senses, or conceived by our minds, represented by our imagination"[1249] God became a man so that we could understand and have a relationship with Him. Ephraem the Syrian put it even more simply, saying, "the Word came and clothed itself with flesh, so that what cannot be grasped might be grasped through that which can be grasped."[1250]

Many of the ancient heresies, which continue down to this day, are based on the erroneous attempt to understand omniscience and omnipotence in human terms. How can God be man and still be God in heaven? How can three equal one? How can one equal three? How can an infinite God be confined in a finite body? All these questions have lead to heretical answers because they all try to phantom the unphantomable. The entire point of the incarnation was that God lowered Himself to our level so that we could relate to Him, not so that we (as finite beings) could understand the infinite.

So here then is a clear reference to the Trinity. To paraphrase Irenaeus, John first goes into careful detail to "distinguish these three" and then "he unites them" together.[1251] This *Logos* is the Word of God. "When in the account of the creation, we read - 'And God *said*,' the reference is to the Son of God."[1252] The Word of God is the Son of God. This title, "'*Logos*' ... is applied to Him twice, as in 1[1] in reference to His eternal, divine life, and at 1[14] in reference to His incarnation."[1253] It can be none other than Jesus Christ and nothing less than the Word of God, the second Person of the Holy Trinity, God incarnate, come to dwell among us and live as one of us in order that we might know Him and find salvation through Him.

John 1:19-21 – See Matthew 17:10-13

Isaiah 40:3 and John the Baptist
John 1:23

"He said, 'I am *a voice of one crying in the wilderness, '"Make straight the way of the Lord,"'* as Isaiah the prophet said.'"

The context of the passage in Isaiah appears to be one in which the return of the Jews from exile is envisioned. Therefore, some have questioned its application to John the Baptist. How could John the Baptist be the fulfillment of this passage if the passage is about "the deliverance of the Jews out of Babylon"?[1254]

When reading the prophets it is clear that they did not write as a sort of future historian, but as a preacher giving warnings to the people of Israel of what was to come. Isaiah's prophecies were not simply about what was to happen, but why. More importantly, every prophecy, however dark and dire, also offered a seed of hope. That seed is always related to the Messiah. In other words, a prophecy about the Babylonian exile was tempered by promises of the coming Messiah. Contextually, this did not mean that the Messiah was to come immediately after the fall of Babylon, nor did any scholar, past or present, believe that was to be the case, but rather that just as the Jews were punished for their sins, so also would they be comforted by the Messiah.

Let me give an example. If I were writing a "prophecy" of America a hundred years before our country was born, I would not merely write a "futury" (future history), for the purpose of prophecy is to warn, chastize, and offer hope to the righteous. Thus, I might say, America will enter a bloody war with England. Twice she shall be invaded and twice repel the enemy, and yet it is America that shall save Britain when Germany invades her. Now the student of history knows that I am talking about three separate wars separated by hundreds of years. Before the events take place, we might assume that the events all transpire in close proximity to one another, but this is not always the case. This is why so many had not understood the difference between the first and second coming of Jesus. The Messianic hopes were so closely intertwined that few saw there were two separate appearances.

In this case, Matthew Poole is correct to say that while the passage in Isaiah "seems to be understood immediately of the deliverance of the Jews out of Babylon ... but ultimately and principally concerning their redemption by the Messiah, whose coming is ushered in by the cry of John the Baptist."[1255] Naturally, the atheist will scoff, but he is supposed to. The "coincidences" of history are too great to be dismissed easily, but the nature of prophecy is that it

299

is to be taken as a warning to the unbeliever, a comfort to the believer, and a mystery to the scoffer.

If we take the passage in Isaiah as applying strictly to the return from Babylon, then to whom would the prophecy refer? No one can answer. The Orthodox Jew can only say that it is the "Holy Spirit,"[1256] but cannot say anything beyond this. This is because the specific verse is a "comfort" verse which looks ahead to the coming of Elijah, whom Jesus identified as John the Baptist (see notes on Matthew 17:10-13 – John 1:19-21).

The Chronology of the Disciples' Calling
John 1:40-44

> "He found first his own brother Simon and said to him, 'We have found the Messiah' (which translated means Christ) ... The next day He purposed to go into Galilee, and He found Philip. And Jesus said to him, 'Follow Me.'"

Some claim there is a contradiction between the chronology of John's calling of the disciples and the synoptic gospels. However, the alleged contradications are, once again, based on fallacious *assumptions* rather than a complete narrative. Let us first look at the assumptions and then look at the passages in questions.

To begin with, the gospels are not complete unabridged histories, but short narrative histories. We have no reason to believe that Jesus walked up to two total strangers who were fisherman, called them and, without having met Jesus before, they decided to follow Him to the ends of the earth. This is *assumption*, not fact. It is logical to assume that Jesus had met and spoken to many, if not all, of the disciples before He went to be tempted. He then called the disciples after returning from the desert.

Now we only read about the calling of six of the twelve disciples. Matthew Levi's calling is the same in all, but Peter, Andrew, James, and John is where the critic sees contradictions, so let us examine these callings.

The Calling of the Disciples
In the accounts of Matthew and Mark we are only told that Jesus met Simon Peter and Andrew while walking by the Sea of Galilee and "immediately" they followed Him. Of course, this naturally brings to mind why, if Jesus had never met them before, two fishermen would "immediately" leave everything behind to follow a complete stranger (Matthew 4:18-22; Mark 1:16-20). Obviously, this was not their first meeting, nor does Matthew or Mark say that it was.

Luke's account is more detailed in that it gives an anecdote about having met Simon and having caught a great number of fish in the the lake of Gennesaret (Luke 5:1-11). Still John's account is even more enlightening, for John explains that Andrew (and one other unnamed disciple, probably John) was already a disciple of John the Baptist and had seen Jesus when we was baptized by John. He then followed Jesus and introduced Simon to the Lord.

When we put these three accounts together we may surmise the following: Simon and Andrew were friends with James and John; all of whom were fishermen by trade. Andrew and John (most likely) were already disciples of John the Baptist and then they saw Jesus baptized, they knew He was the one John had prophesied about, so they followed Him and introduced their brothers Simon and James. The incident at the lake of Gennesaret was probably closely related to this initial contact as well. When Jesus went to Galilee shortly thereafter the four men followed, but Jesus had not yet been tempted so He asked them to wait where they took up their trade at the Sea of Galilee. Following the temptation Jesus then returned from the desert and called Simon Peter, Andrew, James, and John from the Sea of Galilee and began His ministry.

This scenario makes perfect logical sense and accounts for all the eyewitness and testimonial accounts recorded in the gospels. There is nothing to suggests that this is not what happened. The critic must only *assume*, but cannot demonstrate.

The Chronology of the Wedding and the Temptation of Jesus
This leads to a similar chronological dispute concerning the wedding at Cana. This first miracle of Jesus is explicitly said to have taken place "on the third day" (2:1) after Jesus' baptism. Critics, of course, claim this contradicts Mark's statement that Jesus went to be tempted "immediately" after the baptism is diametrically opposed to John's statement. This rather frivolous argument assumes that "immediately" in the context of a person's life must mean within twenty-four hours, which is not a rational argument. I went to college "immediately" after I graduated High School, but this does not mean that I did not have a Summer vacation first.

Moreover, if the critic wishes to get technical, then it should be pointed out that the Bible actually says "immediately the Spirit impelled Him *to go* out into the wilderness" (Mark 1:12). It does not say "immediately he went out" but "immediately the Spirit impelled Him *to go* out." Obviously Jesus went to the wedding, which He must have known about beforehand, and left for the desert afterwards. He had known about the wedding even before His baptism, so He planned to get baptized, attend the wedding with His family, go to be tempted, and then return to start His ministry. During these few days between the baptism and the temptation, He met with several of the disciples and attended the wedding. That this wedding was before the temptation is not only clear from John's chronology but by Jesus' statement, "my hour has not yet come" (2:4). That hour was to come after His temptation at the beginning of His ministry.

301

Conclusion

It is not proper exegesis to assume chronology where none is explicitly stated. Historians often omit information which they feel is not relevant to the larger issue. A man's life is but a drop in the ocean of time. How much more can we draw from words like "immediately" in the context of a life?

A straightforward reading of the gospels, taken collectively, leads us to conclude that after Jesus' baptism, He met with several of the disciples, whom had been disciples of John the Baptist, and spoke to them. They followed Him to Galilee where He was to attend a wedding. After that wedding, Jesus went to be tempted in the desert, and when He returned He called the disciples with whom He had already forged a relationship.

Water to Wine?
John 2:1-11

"The headwaiter tasted the water which had become wine."

Several debates revolve around this first miracle of Jesus. The chronological debate was addressed alongside the "Chronology of the Disciples' Calling" in the section above. Naturalists who deny miracles claim some sort of sleigh of hand, which the Christian must reject as frivolous. It also makes Jesus out to be dishonest at best, and a charlatain at worst. The greater debate seems to be over the question of wine itself. Some believe that the drinking of wine is wholly wrong and a sin. They claim that this must have been grapejuice, rather than wine. However, this issue is not reserved to a few, as one might first be inclinded to assume.

R.A. Torrey argued that it was unfermented wine, and therefore intoxicating.[1257] He said:

> "He provided wine, but there is not a hint that the wine He made was intoxicating. It was a fresh-made win. Newly made wine is never intoxicating until, some time after the process of fermentation, the process of decay has set in. There is not a hint that our Lord produced alcohol, which is a product of decay or death. He produced a living wine, uncontaminated by fermentation."[1258]

Now this sounds logical at first, and I do not pretend to be an expert on wines or fermentation, but I am pretty sure that unfermented wine is grape juice and yet the Bible clearly refers to this as "wine." Indeed, many commentators have taken note of the fact that the people were "astounded by the high quality of the wine."[1259] This does not sound like grape juice.

Basically, it is true that many people cannot hold their liquor. Such people, when reformed, should not even be offered a tiny glass, for this is a temptation to them. Out of courtesy, respect, and love, we should never drink around such people, nor judge them (see comments on 1 Corinthians 8 in *Controversies in the Epistles*). Having said this, there is nothing in the Bible to suggest that drinking in moderation is a sin. It is, and has always been, traditional for Jews to have wine at weddings. Jesus did not condemn the tradition or say a single word against it. Neither did He get drunk. He, like most, had a simple glass of wine to commemorate and honor the wedding guests; nothing more. We should neither use this passage to condone drinking and hanging out at bars, nor to imply that drinking at social events is a sin, for this passage says neither.

46 years?
John 2:20

"It took forty-six years to build this temple, and will You raise it up in three days?"

This passages has been problematic for some because the forty-six years to which the Jews referred does not seem to accurately correspond to most chronologers view of history. The problem is not so much with the Bible as with archaeology and chronologers of history. As a result several different interpretations have arisen to explain this passage.

Jesus' Age?

The weakest theory is that the Jews were referring to the age of Jesus.[1260] Since Jesus was actually referring to the "temple of His body" it is argued that the Jews too were referring to Jesus' body, but this cannot be for several reasons. The most obvious is that verse twenty-one confirms that the Jews did not understand He was speaking of His body, and therefore assumed he was speaking of the Temple of Jerusalem. This is affirmed in both Matthew and Mark where one of the false charges leveled at Him by his accusers was that He had threatened to destroy the Holy Temple of Jerusalem (Matthew 26:61; 27:40; Mark 14:58; 15:29).

Additionally, we know that Jesus died when Pontius Pilate was prefect, but he left office in 37 A.D. Jesus, therefore, could not possibly have been forty-six years old as claimed. Many other evidences as to Jesus' relative youth are present throughout the gospels and have been addressed elsewhere in his volume, so I shall not repeat them.

Solomon's Temple

One argument is that this referred to Solomon's Temple, but this does not make sense in light of the context. They assumed that Jesus was threatening to destroy the Temple (cf. Matthew 26:61; 27:40; Mark 14:58; 15:29), but Solomon's Temple had already been destroyed centuries before! Moreover, as Harold Hoehner points out, "the demonstrative pronoun ουτος 'this' points to the actual temple that was existing there are that time."[1261] Additionally, the only evidence to support this theory, Biblical or extra-Biblical, is from the apocryphal "gospel of Nicodemus."[1262] No other evidence suggests that Solomon's Temple did indeed take forty-six years to complete.

Zerubbabel's Temple
Although the same points made against Solomon's Temple apply equally to Zerubbabel's Temple, it can be argued that Herod's Temple was simply and expansion of the existing Temple of Zerubbabel. Thus it could be argued that the Temple standing in Jesus' day was technically built by Zerubbabel. That would negate the force of the preceding arguments. Nonetheless, even if we attempt to merge Zerubbabel's Temple with Herod's the problem is not solved. Although there is an argument to be made on its behalf, the reader will see that the evidences weigh strongly against it.

On behalf of the view is it alleged connection to the prophecy of Daniel 9. In that prophecy there are seven *"shevim"* (a week of years, or seven years). Men such as the venerable Dr. Lightfoot believe that the prophecy is about the building of Zerubbabel's Temple.[1263] The forty-six years of John 2:20 are then said to correspond to this prophecy. However, there are several problems with this view. The obvious is that the forty-nine years of Daniel 9 must either be viewed as a rounding off of years (which is impermissible in prophecy) or that there must have been three years of preparations.[1264] Either is conjecture.

More critical is the fact that Daniel's prophecy begins with an edict. Although scholars do not completely agree on when that edict was given, there are only four dates proposed by scholars, none of which can be connected to the building of Zerubbabel's Temple. The various edicts suggested are Cyrus's edict in 539 B.C., the edict of Darius in 519 or 518 B.C., Artaxerxes' first edict in 457 B.C, and his second in 444 B.C. Subtract forty-nine years from each of these and you get 490 B.C., 470 or 469 B.C., 408 B.C., or 395 B.C. However, according to Jewish historian Martin Gilbert, Zerubbabel's temple was completed on the fourth day of Adar, 515 B.C.[1265] and Josephus said that it took seven years to build this temple.[1266] As the reader can see, none of this fits the prophecy of Daniel (for an extensive debate see *Controversies in the Prophets*).

Herod's Temple
The most prevalent view is that the Jews were speaking about "this" temple; i.e. Herod's Temple which was standing in Jesus' day. Nevertheless, this does not solve the debate entirely, for Josephus records that the Temple was in continuous construction and renovation up until around 63 A.D.[1267] It is, therefore, assumed that the forty-six years means that Temple construction began forty-six years before Jesus stood in that courtyard on that day. Archbishop Ussher pointed out that the *aorist* tense of the Greek word for "built" proves that construction was still ongoing.[1268] This is generally agreed by all, but the exact chronology is not agreed upon for the various dates found in

Josephus appear to contradict one another. For example, in *War of the Jews* Josephus states that "in the fifteenth year of his reign, Herod rebuilt the temple"[1269] but in *Antiquities of the Jews* he said it was "in the eighteenth year of his reign."[1270] Additionally, Josephus said that the Temple sanctuary was completed after eighteen months,[1271] and gives no date for the continuation of the Temple's expansion. Which date do we take? And do we count the building of the sanctuary or only the construction of the Outer Temple? Since the Sanctuary was built over Zerubbabel's Temple, can it really be considered a new Temple? Did construction on the Outer Temple begin immediately after the Sanctuary was finished? These are the questions which must be asked.

As to the question of fifteen or eighteen years, most scholars believe that the fifteen is in error. A few have argued that the fifteen refers to initial preparations for the temple, with the temple beginning actual construction in the eighteenth year. Although this is possible, most believe that the beginning of the Temple Sanctuary construction began beween the Hebrew month of Nisan 1, 20 B.C. and Nisan 1, 19 B.C.[1272] This roughtly corresponds to late March 20 B.C. to as late as March 19 B.C. Since the sanctuary was necessary for the religious function of Passover, it is logical to assume that the construction began after Passover so as to interfere with the feast as little as possible. Since Josephus records that the sanctuary was complete eighteen months afterwards, it is apparent that the sanctuary was ready by Passover 18 B.C. Subsequently, Herod began to build the outer temple sometime after that in his twentieth year. So we have to decide between 20/19 B.C. and 18/17 B.C. Equally great scholars exist on both sides of the argument. Thus all these questions have led to two interpretations within this larger view.[1273]

From 20 B.C. to 27 A.D.?

The reader will recall that scholars are divided as to whether or not Jesus was crucified in 30 A.D. or 33 A.D. Advocates of the 30 A.D. crucifixion date often use this verse to "prove" that Jesus' first year of ministry was 27 A.D.[1274] However, this view is not as straightforward as it might seem, nor is it as friendly to the view as is suggested.

If the Jews were referring to the sanctuary then temple construction began in 20 B.C. sometime after Passover.[1275] Forty-six years later, however, would not be 27 A.D. but 26 A.D. This is because 1) there is only one year between 1 B.C. and 1 A.D., but also because 2) no one is one year old until he has lived for one year. So the Temple would not be one year old until 19 B.C. (or even 18 B.C. if the Temple did not begin until 19 B.C.).

The greater problems have been addressed under "When Was Jesus Crucified? Chronology of the Last Supper, Crucifixion, and Resurrection" and "How Old Was Jesus? Luke 3:1 – 3:23" and will be repeated here, except to point out that this event followed shortly after Jesus' baptism which is explicitly said to be in the fifteenth year of Tiberius (Luke 3:1). Thus this event could not have taken place in 27 A.D. (see notes on Luke 3:1).

From 17 B.C. to 29-30 A.D.?

As aforementioned, the sanctuary itself was essentially Zerubbabel's but was refurbished and renovated in a year and a half by Herod. The rest of the Temple was truly Herod's Temple. The sanctuary was necessary for worship and, therefore, had to be completed as soon as possible whereas the rest of the Temple had work continuing upon it even after the days of Jesus. Consequently, when the Jews were referring to forty-six years they may have been either referring to the completed sanctuary or, more likely, to the continuous construction of the Temple outside the sanctuary as is evidenced by their remarks. Further, the use of the *aorist* tense in Greek confirms that the building of the Temple was an ongoing process. As a result, many believe that the dating of the Temple should begin after the completion of the sanctuary.

If this is true then we must still decide between 18 B.C. and 17 B.C. This is not an easy task since we do not know in what month Herod began construction, nor whether or not there was a lull between the completion of the sanctuary and the ground breaking on the outer Temple. However, famed Archbishop Ussher believes that Temple construction began in the winter months of 17 B.C.[1276] If so then the Jews could have said that the temple had been being built for forty-six years in 29 A.D. It's forty-seventh birthday would then be sometime in 30 A.D.

Conclusion

There seems no doubt that the Jews were speaking of the Temple standing in their day. When Jesus stood trial He was falsely accused of threatening to tear down the Temple (Matthew 26:61; 27:40; Mark 14:58; 15:29) which had stood for forty-six years. It is, therefore, to Herod's Temple that the Jews referred.

Unfortunately, there is a lot of misconceptions concerning Josephus' quotations which have made dating attempts all too subjective. Josephus himself seems confused as to whether construction began in the fifteenth or eighteen year of Herod, but in either case he says the Temple was completed after eighteen months. Consequently, it cannot be the Sanctuary to which the Jews were referring and Josephus gives no date as to the construction of the outer Temple. We can only assume that such construction began shortly after the completion of the Sanctuary. If this is true then it takes us to 30 A.D. which corresponds to the chronology of Luke 3:1. Independently, however, this passage is not strong evidence for the dating of Jesus' ministry since it involves assumptions about Josephus' dates which cannot be determined with any precise accuracy.

Born Again
John 3:1-3

> "Truly, truly, I say to you, unless one is born again he cannot see the kingdom of God."

True Christians have always believed in the necessity of being "born again." So much so that in times past there was no need to call one's self a "born again Christian." As R.C. Sproul once said, "'born-again Christian' is a redundancy. It's like speaking about 'an unmarried bachelor' or 'a three sided triangle.'"[1277] However, in an age where nominal Christianity reigns, Bible-believing evangelicals have always felt the need to distinguish ourselves from those who carry the moniker of Christ but have never so much as picked up a Bible or devoted a shred of their life to the Lord. Consequently, the term "born-again Christian" became popular in recent memory, only to loose favor after an unpopular President took the label for himself.

The real question is what does this mean in the context of Jesus' remarks. Clearly Nicodemus did not understand the initial remark and many today also fail to understand its meaning. To this end there are three related questions. 1. Who was Nicodemus? This relates the very question since it was Nicodemus whose questions elicited this answer. 2. What did Jesus mean by 'born-again'? 3. What does Jesus mean by "cannot see the kingdom of God"?, for this relates the second question, and yet is too often overlooked by expositors.

Nicodemus

Nicodemus is mentioned five times in the Gospel of John (three times in this chapter) and does not appear anywhere else in the Bible. However, he appears to be a man of some significance and some even debate whether or not he became a disciple based on John 12:42 and 19:39. He is described as a Pharisee and a "ruler of the Jews." Some believe that he may have been one of the Sanherdin (often described as a "supreme court" of Israel), but the Bible is silent on this beyond the fact that he was a "ruler."

Based on John 19:39 it is apparent that Nicodemus did eventually become a follower of Jesus. His appearance at night in that passage and here in 3:2 has suggested to some that he was afraid was being seen, for 12:42 states that the rulers who trusted in Jesus were afraid "that they would be put out of the synagogue." Since Jesus rebuked these leaders for loving "the approval of men rather than the approval of God" (12:43) many scholars have continued to debate to what extend Nicodemus was a follower of Jesus. Warren Wiersbe, for one, denied that Nicodemus was afraid to be seen with Jesus.[1278] It has been suggested that his night time visits were becase it was "a time when Rabbis studied."[1279] Obviously as a ruler of Israel, we would expect Nicodemus to be busy in the daytime, but neither side can prove their opinions.

Still other critics of the Bible have claimed that Nicodemus is a Greek name which would never be used by Jewish priests. They thus attempt to claim that this is a fabricated person invented by the gospel authors, but there are other Nicodemus' mentioned in both Josephus[1280] and the Talmud.[1281] Some even speculate the Nicodemus mentioned in the Talmud is the same as that of John's gospel.[1282]

So there is no serious question that Nicodemus was a ruler who lived at the time of Jesus. Whether he was a true disciple (as 19:39 suggests) or merely a sympathizer, he was clearly interested in hearing from Jesus. His response to Jesus' remarks also provide insight into the mind of the Jews at that time, as well as ours.

"Born Again"
It has been pointed out by countless commentators throughout the ages that, as Thomas Aquinas said, "the Greek rending is not 'again,' but *anothen* i.e. from above."[1283] Hence, "the word translated here *again*, means also *from above*"[1284] thus rendering Jesus' statement as "you must be born from above." Or does it?

The problem with this argument is that Nicodemus' "childish" response (as Calvin phrased it)[1285] makes no sense in that context. Why would Nicodemus confuse being "born from above" with entering "enter a second time into his mother's womb" (3:2)? That would make no sense. Frederick Godet stated that "the misunderstanding of Nicodemus is more easily explained, if Jesus said, in Aramaic : *anew*, rather than *from above*."[1286]

To this end many prefer the idea of being "born anew" implying, in John Darby's wordds, "a beginning again of life, of a new source, and of a nature – a life that come from God."[1287] Although this captures the idea of Jesus' teaching, it is best to retain the most literal translation "born again," which carries the same meaning and better explains Nicodemus' confusion.

Said Martin Luther, "a child which is to be born two years from now is still nonexistent" so it is with us "not yet reborn."[1288] Erasmus said it was not children of men a second time but children of God[1289] to which Jesus referred. It is a "renewal of the whole person"[1290] and much more than "only reformation of life."[1291] John Wesley said "to be born again is to be inwardly changed from all sinfulness to all holiness."[1292]

So we are born once in the flesh, but to see the kingdom of God we must also be born a second time; in the the spirit (see notes on John 3:5). This, however, leads to the question of what Jesus meant when He spoke of seeing the "kingdom of God." That debate is actually a far greater one, and yet one that is sadly ignored by many.

The Kingdom
The doctrine of the kingdom of God, of which much more will be said later and in the appendices, is among the great controversies of the New Testament. It is no small irony that its appearance here in connection with being "born again" is

ignored by so many. We naturally think of being "saved" but too often think only of being saved from Hell or from death. Here, however, we are saved *into* something. It is not merely a rescuing from Hell and death, but a salvation from death into life, or more specifically, into the kingdom of God. It is obvious, therefore, that an understanding of the kingdom of God is necessary to fully understand Jesus' remarks.

Since I devote a great deal of debate to the kingdom of God elsewhere (see in particular John 18:36 and Appendix D) I shall only briefly discuss the issue here in the context of Nicodemus for the "Messiah and the kingdom were inseparably associated in the Jewish mind"[1293] and it would be folly to read something into the passage which is not there. "Nicodemus certainly did not understand by the kingdom anything different from that Kingdom which the Prophets of his people had predicted."[1294] Nowhere is this fact more evident than as expressed by the "liberal spiritualizer" Frederick Grant who said that "the Kingdom of God was that which the prophets had announced, and for which all Israel waited. We must not think of it in the form it has now taken"[1295] (or rather the form in which Grant *thinks* it has taken). In other words, he is acknowledging that we must understand the kingdom in the context in which Nicodemus would have understood it, and that is of a literal kingdom of Israel ruled in Jerusalem by the Messiah!

How then can we not "enter the kingdom of God" if we are not born again? Those on the left see the kingdom solely as a "spiritual" kingdom with no physical manifestation whereas those on the right see that the earthly kingdom of Jesus will not come until after the Second Coming and will be inhabited solely (at its inception) by believers, thus no unbeliever will enter the kingdom to come. Others moderate between these two positions, but the fact that Jesus did not clarify the kingdom to Nicodemus implies that Nicodemus did not need instruction upon this issue. Certainly if there is a correction needed, Jesus did not offer one at this time.

Conclusion

The simple remark of our Lord, that we must be born "of the spirit" in order to see the kingdom of God, is a cornerstone of Christian belief. We must be born of the spirit. We are much more than physical beings, and without being made right with God, in His Spirit, we are eternally separated from Him. A man without a spirit is like a car without an engine. However attractive it may look, it will not run without an engine. Without being born of the spirit, we are mere empty shells and husks. If our bodies are like cars, then our souls (see *Controversies in the Epistles* for more on trichomy versus dichotomy) are like and empty gas tank. Only when we fill the soul with the Spirit of God can we achieve what God intended us to be.

Water and Spirit
John 3:5

"Unless one is born of water and the Spirit he cannot enter into the kingdom of God."

Amid the discussion of rebirth, Jesus said that one must be "born of water and the Spirit." This analogy has left many Christians to wonder what is meant by being "born of water." Essentially there are three dominant views, with subsets within those views. The chart below shows how these views relate to one another. Some see the water as the water of baptism. Others see it merely as a symbol for something. Still others believe that it represents physical birth which is thus contrasted with the spiritual birth.

Baptism	Symbol of ...	Physical Birth
Christian Baptism	Holy Spirit	
Baptism of John	Word of God	
Baptismal Regeneration	The Law of Moses	
Baptism as a Symbol		

Baptism

A great many have seen the water reference as a picture of baptism. This is particularly true of those who believe that baptism is essential for salvation. Thus baptism is elevated along side the spiritual birth as a requirement for salvation. Others do not take this strict stance, but still insist that baptism is the picture presented here. Frederick Godet, noting that Jesus had previously been baptized shortly before, even goes so far as to ask, how could this "possibly have designated on His lips anything else than baptism?"[1296] His view is shared by many over the years including such scholars as the famed John Lightfoot.[1297]

Of course this only begs the question. Unless one believes in baptismal regeneration (the doctrine that the man is reborn and regenerated spiritually only *through* the act of baptism) then to what could Jesus be referring? Most evangelicals agree that baptismal regeneration is a false doctrine, so what else could Jesus have been referencing? Indeed, "Christian baptism was not instituted, nor did the facts exists which it symbolizes, till the Lord died and rose,"[1298] so how could Christian baptism, let alone baptismal regeneration have been of what Jesus was speaking?

Although many insist Jesus was "almost certainly" speaking of baptism[1299] there is only one other baptism to which Jesus might have spoken; that of the baptism of John,[1300] which He had previously undergone. This is the view of many evangelicals,[1301] but it too falls short of the mark for John's "water-baptism is the picture of the burial of the old man, not a picture of a second birth."[1302] Not until the death and resurrection of Jesus did baptism take

310

on a new meaning, and one which is clearly distinguished from John's baptism in Acts 18-19.

A final argument is that baptism is itself a symbol, but this is redundant. The act of baptism is a symbol of death and rebirth in Christ, but if we say that it is a symbol here to be contrasted with rebirth then we must ask exactly what it symbolizes. This then leads us to the second major view.

Water as a Symbol

If water is a symbol then we may ponder, a symbol of what? Some argue that it represents the Law of Moses, but few hold to this today. To say the Law of Moses is a requirement of salvation is to condemn all those not under the law which the apostle Paul declares are all who have faith in Jesus (Romans 2-3; 1 Corinthians 9)! Two other possibilities present themselves.

Arthur Pink compares the "water" to the "water of life" in 4:14,[1303] which is then says is an "emblem" for the Word of God.[1304] This view has found favor among many evangelicals such as H.A. Ironside[1305] and C.I. Scofield.[1306] However, it is hard to distinguish the Word of God from Jesus (John 1:1, 14). He would be saying, "you must be born of Me and of the Spirit." Since Jesus and the Holy Spirit are two parts of the Holy Trinity, it may be feasible, but not likely. The alternative is that the water represents the Spirit.[1307]

In defense of this view some have noted that Hebrew parallelism (a form of Hebrew poetry used for emphasis and memory) would equate the water and Spirit in verse five with the flesh and spirit of verse six.[1308] Nevertheless, this is actually the problem. The water is parallel to flesh, not spirit. If it were then it would be a total redundancy. Jesus would be saying "you must be born of spirit and spirit" as opposed to verse six where He refers to both flesh and spirit. This is the true test of any legitimate symbolism. If we substitute the item being represented by the symbol, the sentence should still makes sense. In this context, this symbolic use for water appears to fail the test.

Physical Birth

There is one final view. The water from the birth sac has often been used to represent physical birth.[1309] Indeed, water was used as a euphimism in antiquity for birth.[1310] Many have resisted this interpretation as carnal, but it fits logically with the idea of being "born again." There is physical birth and then there is a second spiritual birth. Verse six parallels this, making it clear that "that which is born of the flesh is flesh, and that which is born of the Spirit is spirit." This view is the most straightforward and would have made the most logical sense to Nicodemus for the other views all seem anachronistic at best since Jesus' ministry was just beginning.

Conclusion

A man must be born of the spirit as well as the flesh. That a man is born of water (at birth) is taken for granted, but to this Jesus is adding a second birth;

that of the spirit. This takes into account the entire discourse to Nicodemus, for Christian baptism did not yet exist and John's baptism did not guarantee salvation (see Acts 18-19). The symbolic views are either redundant or refer to emblems which Jesus would make later in His ministry. Here it appears that Jesus is merely creating Hebrew Parallelism for physical birth and spiritual birth; the two births spoken of in verse three.

Who Has Ascended to Heaven?
John 3:13

"No one has ascended into heaven, but He who descended from heaven: the Son of Man."

Martin Luther once said that "this [is a] strange proclamation that pertains to Christ alone."[1311] It suggests that Christ has already ascended to heaven, though He had not yet died, but also that He descended from heaven. Obviously, this creates a few issues for some. First is the rather trivial argument by some Bible critics that Elijah had also ascended to heaven (2 Kings 2:11), thus "contradicting" Jesus's remark. Of course, a general statement does not negate single exceptions, but even if it did, the larger context of Jesus's remark would invalidate the criticism anyway for Elijah has not yet descended from heaven. Jesus both ascended and descended. This is the context of his remarks and the Jews fully understood what He was saying, even if many today do not. Jesus was affirming that "he is omnipresent,"[1312] which Elijah most certainly was not. Only God is omnipresent!

Despite this some Christians have had difficulties with this concept. Thomas Aquinas believed that only His "divine nature" came down from heaven[1313] whereas Hilary of Potiers believed that this "refers to his origin from the Spirit."[1314] In fact, Desiderius Erasmus was correct when he said that the Son of Man "has come down from heaven to earth but now dwells in heaven."[1315] And John Calvin said that "what correctly applies to one of his natures is applied to another of his natures."[1316] Augustine expressed it this way, saying, "in his nature as Son of God he was in heaven, but as Son of man he was still on earth and had not yet ascended into heaven."[1317]

In other words, "the actual presence of Christ in heaven, is already very positively contained in the *perfect* αναβεβηκεν, *has ascended*. This tense does not signify : has accomplished at a given moment the act of ascending ... but His 'is there.'"[1318] Jesus is omnipresent because Jesus is God incarnate, the second person of the Trinity of the One and only God of all the universe. Said Harold Ironside, "the wonder of it is this, that He who came down from heaven and had the power to ascend into heaven, was at all times the Son of Man in heaven, for He was omnipresent."[1319]

Are the Father and Son Equal?
John 5:19-26

> "The Son can do nothing of Himself, unless *it is* something He sees the Father doing; for whatever the Father does, these things the Son also does in like manner."

If Jesus hinted at His deity in John 3:13 He here angers the Jewish priests by making this even more clear. Despite this there are those who believe that these verses deny the deity of Jesus, for if He was God, how could He say "the Son can do nothing of Himself"? A fair question.

There have been three basic approaches to this by Trinitarians. I call these the "human limitation view," the "Will of Christ view," and the "equality with God view." Needless to say, some have taken more than one approach, since each of the views has some merit.

On the idea of human limitation, R.C. Sproul said that we must distinguish beween the "ontological Trinity," which is about "the fact God is three in one," from the "economic Trinity," which deals with the roles of each person of the Trinity.[1320] "Even though the Father and son are equal in power, glory, and being, nevertheless there is economic subordination of the Son to the Father."[1321] Calvin expressed this same argument in more basic and simple terms, saying that this can "only apply to the Son of God insofar as he is manifested in the body."[1322] This has been a popular interpretation throughout the ages, but it is one which Arthur Pink rejected in its entirety.[1323]

Pink believed that Jesus's statement showed only His desire to serve God and "was solely a matter of *will*."[1324] James Boice declared that Jesus was not a zombie[1325] and thus it was "a matter of the will."[1326] The Church father Cyril of Alexandria phrased it better, distinguishing between someone saying they "cannot carry an enormously heavy piece of wood" which would display weakness and saying "I cannot do anything" against my father's wishes.[1327] It is question of Jesus' desire to obey the Father, and not His inability.

Of course, even though will is a factor, there is an even more clear factor, and it is that fact which enraged the enemies of Jesus, for He was making Himself *equal* to God.[1328] By saying He could not do anything contrary to the will of the Father "He was assserting that His work was identical with that of God."[1329] The ironic answer is clearly the best answer. "His works are the works of the Father"[1330] and they are "in all respects equal in Godhead with the Father."[1331] Ironside best paraphrased this view, saying, "the Father can do nothing without the Son, the Holy Spirit can do nothing with the Son, the Father can do nothing without the Holy Spirit, the Holy Spirit can do nothing without the Father, and the Son can do nothing without the Holy Spirit."[1332]

This view is actually one of the oldest and best attested views. Saint Augustine declared that the phrase "cannot do anything of himself" shows "the works of the Father and the Son are inseparable."[1333] The Church father

Tertullian even equated this verse with proof that Christ made the earth.[1334] Even Calvin, who advocated the human limitation view, also felt that Christ was insisting "strongly that in this work there is no difference bewteen him and his Father."[1335]

The proof of this view is the the fact that His enemies protested strongly at this answer as heresy. "If [the Pharisees] had misunderstood Him, Jesus surely would have immediately and vehemently denied making such a claim,"[1336] but in fact, "Jesus did not deny the correctness of their interpretation."[1337]

There is an element of truth to the second view. As Robert Govett said, "the Son *can* do nothing for Himself! This is said of the *inner* neccessity arising from His divine nature. It is the incommunicable glory of the Creator, that He cannot change to evil."[1338] Nonetheless, the third view is best and keeps with the theme which Jesus was making in these passages. He was repeatedly speaking about the unity of the Father and Son. Jesus was always very careful in His words. He never said anything frivolously or loosely, for the Jewish heirarchy was watching Him closely. For this very reason, the remarks are very clear in that Jesus was expressing His unity with God the Father. This is one of His first hints at deity, although He would express this teaching more clearly as He approached the appointed time. Had He been more clear too early in His ministry, the priests would surely have silenced Him much earlier, but that day would come not come until the day appointed by God and prophesied by Daniel.

John 5:31 – See John 8:14

John 6:1-13 – See Matthew 14:13-21

John 6:44 – See also John 12:32

"They Shall Be Taught By God"
John 6:44-45

"No one can come to Me unless the Father who sent Me draws him ... It is written in the prophets, 'And they shall all be taught of God.' Everyone who has heard and learned from the Father, comes to Me."

Exegesis is reading "out" of the text. Eisegesis is a made up, but popular word among theologians, meaning to read "into" the text. Here is a passage that seems simple enough. Nonetheless, Calvinists, Arminians, devotees of Aquinas, and many others have read into the text words and meanings not apparent, or have they? Does "all" mean "all"? Who is teaching here? What does the "drawing" mean?

"No one can come to Me unless the Father who sent Me draws him." Some Reformers saw this "drawing" as "a gracious allurement."[1339] Calvinists, on the other hand, maintain that "Jesus wasn't simply saying, 'No one will come to Me unless the Father wooes them to Me. No, His meaning was much stronger."[1340] For Calvin was a compelling. R.C. Sproul openly criticized those translations that do not use the word "compel."[1341] In fact, the Greek word, 'ἑλκύω ('elkuo), can mean "attract" on the one side and it can also mean "to drag" on the other.[1342] Both translations are possible, thus nullifying the word itself as proof as one view over another. This is why virtually every translation rightly uses the more word "draw" rather than reading into the text one extreme or the other. In each case, the theologians are dragging their own debates into a passage which cannot be honestly used in favor of either extreme. It says that the Lord draws people unto Himself. That is what it means. Calvinists, Arminians, and others can continue their debate in more appropriate passages, but this is not one of them.

Traditionally the teaching passage has been viewed as the teaching of the Holy Spirit, as the Lord Bishop of Durham said.[1343] Barnes said, "it is by the teaching of His word and Spirit."[1344] However, if we distinguish between the persons of the Trinity then, as Erasmus stated, "the Father makes the heart ready to be taught."[1345] Wesley more ambiguously referred to "the secret voice of God."[1346] Aquinas went so far as to say that it is the Church to which the teaching is referred.[1347] However, all agree that "it is through the teaching of the Word that God draws people to the Savior."[1348] The Calvinists limit this by saying that "all whom God has taught do come to Jesus"[1349] but Lightfoot and others say "there is thus no thought here of a limited number of selected individuals; it is open to everyone to hear the Father's voice."[1350] So "those who come to the saving faith do so because they are supernaturally instructed by God."[1351]

Now not all agreed upon what passage Jesus' is quoting. Bede seemed to believe that there was an allusion to the prophecy of Joel 2:23, although this seems suspect to say the least.[1352] Still others believe that Jeremiah 31:34 is in mind, but Aquinas preferred Isaiah 54:13[1353] which reads, "All your sons will be taught of the LORD." This seems best as it is very close to Jesus' words, making it a paraphrase rather than an allusion.

Now there is a final view. Although the teaching does come "from the Father" there is a very literal prophetic application here as well. If "all will be taught by God" and if we take this in its most literal form, then we have here another allusion to the deity of Jesus Christ, for Jesus taught "all" to whom He preached, and He was most literally God incarnate, the Second Person of the Trinity.

Where then is the controversy? In this: that if "all" means "all" does this mean that "all" men or saved? Perhaps, as Arthur Pink said, "'all' *does not mean* 'all' ... but ... His elect"![1354] Calvin explicitly said that "the word 'all' must be limited to the elect."[1355] Once again, can we take either extreme? First and foremost, to draw either extreme we must connect the teaching of "all" to the acceptance of the gospel. Although there is obviously a connection, it is not logical to follow that because "all are taught by God" that "all" will receive it. Sir Robert Anderson believed that such arguments were missing the entire point. These words "are not, as commonly supposed, a limitation place upon the gospel; but they emphasize the solemnity both of preaching and hearing the gospel." [1356]

When we take the passage at face value without trying to read our own theology into the text, it is clear that Jesus is speaking about the preaching of the Word of God. It is also an indication that God must prepare the human heart to receive it, but there is nothing within these words to define any specific limitation, nor to infer a universal acceptance. Neither teaching (universalism and Calvinism) are not to be found here.

Quotation from Scripture?
John 7:38

"He who believes in Me, as the Scripture said, 'From his innermost being shall flow rivers of living water.'"

Critics of the Bible are quick to point out that some of the passages quoted in the New Testament are hard to find in the Old. They suggest either that the Bible has changed (they present no evidence of this – see Appendix in *Controversies in the Pentateuch*) or that the New Testament authors were wrong, misleading, or even dishonest. Such dishonest appraisals betray the critic at the most base of levels. Nevertheless, it is true that Jesus and the apostles sometimes paraphrased the Scriptures or even quoted from Midrashic interpretations of the Jewish Scriptures rather than quoting directly. To those unfamilar with the ancient Jewish culture this may seen confusing, but to those who are familar, it only makes sense. Jesus was, after all, speaking to Jews and they understood, even if the modern critic did not.

In this case Jesus quotes, "from his innermost being shall flow rivers of living water." Suggestions have ranged from Psalms 78:15-16 to Zechariah 14:8, but the context should eliminate those passages unless we take this more as an allusion than an actual quotation. This is in error.

Others have suggested that it is a composite quotation, which is a kind of paraphrase combining two or more passages which have the same theme and message. Three passages, all from Isaiah, would best suit this view. Isaiah 44:3; 55:1; and 58:11 all speak of water and spirit. Isaiah 44:3 declares, "I will pour out water ... I will pour out My Spirit." Isaiah 55:1 reads, "everyone who thirsts, come to the waters." Finally Isaiah 58:11 says that "the Lord will continually guide you and satisfy your desire in scorched places ... And you will be like a watered garden And like a spring of water whose waters do not fail." This final passage seems very close to Jesus' words, particularly in the context in which it is given.

316

Could Jesus's quote have actually been from a Midrash (an important Jewish book of interpretations) of Isaiah 58:11? Some Midrash remains to this day, but much of it is lost. We cannot say for certain if Jesus was quoting the Midrash or merely creating His own paraphrase of the passage, but the quotation itself in perfectly in context and in keeping with the manner of debate.

The Woman Caught in Adultery
John 8:1-11

"The scribes and the Pharisees brought a woman caught in adultery, and having set her in the center *of the court,* they said to Him, "Teacher, this woman has been caught in adultery, in the very act. "Now in the Law Moses commanded us to stone such women; what then do You say? ... 'He who is without sin among you, let him *be the* first to throw a stone at her.'"

This is surely one of the most famous stories in the entire Bible, yet few know it is also one of three of the most contested Bible verses in the New Testament. Contested because some say it was not written by John and others that it was never a part of the gospels until centuries after the gospels were written! The problem is more severe because this is not merely one of the countless fruitless and trivial attacks by Bible critics, but because many Bible believing evangelicals and conservatives also adhere to this.

Vasily Polenov – Woman Taken in Adultery – 1887

Is the story authentic? Did it really happen? If so, did John write it? Why do so many ancient manuscripts omit the verse from John? All these questions are legitimate questions which deserve an answer, and as always the truth will prevail.

Additionally, there is even more controversy over its interpretation. Often this passage is used to dismiss sin or teach libertarianism and criticize those who speak out against sin. Some use it to support a political agenda. Still others reject all these arguments.

Finally, there is the controversy over the woman herself. Who was she? Tradition has often ascribed her to be Mary Magladene, as depicted in Mel Gibson's *Passion of the Christ*. A number of Protestants reject this outright. Who is right and does it really even matter?

These are the controversies surrounding one of the most famous Bible stories in the entire gospels. Interestingly enough, these controversies often feed off of one another, as we shall see.

Is It Authentic?

The first, and most important, question is whether or not the story is authentic and true. Was it even written by John? This might seem a pointless question were it not for its curious omission from many of the oldest and best manuscripts known to exist! Why? Let us begin, as always, by examining the evidence itself.

The Evidence

This story is unique from a textual standpoint not only because it is absent from many ancient manuscripts but because where it is found, it is found in different places, and even gospels! It has been found in some manuscripts to be inserted after John 7:36 and Luke 21:38.[1357] Others "put it at the end of John's Gospel as a kind of postscript."[1358]

Although absent from most ancient manuscripts it is found in the Codex Bezae (one of the oldest Uncials) and both the Codex Ephraemi and Alexandrinus are actually "defective" at this point in the manuscript,[1359] meaning that the Uncial scrolls are damaged at this point, missing several pages or leaves. The Alexandrinus is otherwise a nearly perfectly preserved manuscripts, as is the Codex Bezae. Along with the Sinaiticus and Vaticanus, these five Codexes make the oldest Uncials in existence, so if we are completely honest then only two of the five oldest Uncials can be said to omit this passage with certainty.

Additionally, it is found in The *Apostolic Constitutions*[1360] which was written in the 3rd century,[1361] and later scholia and scribes said it was found in the "most ancient" manuscripts[1362] which no longer exist, thus giving second hand evidence that it did indeed exist in antiquity. Finally, Papias, who was himself a disciple of the apostle John, relates the story.[1363]

Below is a chart showing the important text and whether or not they contain the story. I have omitted those manuscripts and authors whose evidence is uncertain.[1364]

Omits the Passage	Contains the Passage
$\mathfrak{P}^{66}$ (2nd century)*	Papias (Early 2nd century)
$\mathfrak{P}^{75}$ (2nd or 3rd century)*	The *Apostolic Constitutions* (3rd century)
ℵ (4th century)	D (4th or 5th century)
B (4th century)	Earliest Latin translations.
W (5th century)	ᘈ (The majority texts)
Some early Syrian translations.	
A few medieval manuscripts.	

* Note that these two papyri can only confirm that the passage was not found after John 7:52; not that it was not found elsewhere as the papyri are both fragmentary manuscripts.

Evaluation of the Evidence

Now what are we to make of the evidence? Some, like John Calvin, rejected it outright[1365] as do some modern evangelicals like Merrill Tenney.[1366] The New English Bible even omits the passages![1367] They suggests that the sixty variants are at odds with "a true apostolic test"[1368] and list each of the medieval manuscripts which omit the passage to make the chart above look even more impressive (as well as adding Church Fathers who do not quote the passage).

In all fairness, if we were to judge the authenticity of the passage based solely upon this evidence, then we might well be compelled to reject it. However, there is compelling reason to believe that the passage is genuine. Indeed, even those who reject the passage as an authentic Johannine work accept it as a true story. Various theories have been offered for how it came to be placed in John, and who, if not John, did write it.

Before determining who wrote the passages, let us first decide if they are authentic to history. Oddly enough, even its most rigid critics tend to accept "that it was an incident which John was accustomed to narrate in his oral teaching, omitted indeed from the Gospel as originally penned by him; but afterwards inserted."[1369] One is inclined to ask why. If it is so evident (in their opinion) that it is not a part of John's original gospel, how can they support it as an authentic account? The answer they themselves give that its antiquity is unquestionable (indeed it is) and that it bears the mark of a true story. To this end, various theories have developed as to how this true story came to be a part of John, if it was not written by him. Some simply say that it was a "true apostolic tradition introduced by some later editor of the Gospel,"[1370] but this is not sufficient. If it was written by another (some have even suggested Mary Magadalene) then it might not do to have a one page "Gospel According to Mary" but why insert it into John?

Most argue that editors thought it would best fit in John's account, but John MacArthur takes the opposite view, saying that "its placement here disrupts the flow of thought in this section" which he believes is the Feast of Tabernacle.[1371] John Lightfoot argued that it belongs to Luke, saying, "the expressions 'the Mount of Olives' and 'the Scribes,' and the particles used are more in keeping with the earlier gospels than with John" and that the "resemblances to St. Luke's gospel are especially striking."[1372] Since one manuscript actually places this story in Luke's gospel, it is apparent that one cannot say that it was inserted *into* John without cause.

While critics are at a loss to show how the passage came to be inserted *into* John, there is strong evidence as to how it came to be *expunged* from John in some manuscripts. Saint Augustine believed that it was removed from John's gospels by legalists[1373] who objected to it its use "to justify the employment of gentle means in ecclesiastical discipline."[1374] This actually requires some historical background. During the persecutions of ancient Rome, most Christians were given the choice of sacrificing to Caesar or dying by cruel and horrid deaths. Following the persecutions there was strident and emotional debate among the early Church clergy as to how those "lapsed" Christians, who denied Christ to save their lives, should be treated.[1375] Should they simply be allowed to return to the Church? Should they be denied entrance into the church altogether? Perhaps they should have to undergo a rigid test of repentance? Some, we are told, were denied communion for as long as ten years.[1376] The fact that the ancient *Apostolic Constitutions* uses this passage to recommend leniency to lapsed sinners is evidence of this conflict. It is also explain why, as Augustine said, these passages were expunged from many Bibles.

Further proof that this may have been exactly what happened, is ironically evidence used by the detractors of this passage; namely, the fact that two of the oldest Codexes, Alexandrinus (A) and Ephraemi (C), have both been damaged at this exact spot in John despite the fact that the Codex Alexandrinus is a nearly perfect manuscripts everywhere else! Could those pages have been deliberately removed? In fairness, this is pure speculation, but it does serve to beg the question. Even the critics of the passage admit to its antiquity and authenticity, so why is the passage missing from so many ancient manuscripts? Augustine's answer seems the best and most logical.

That leaves us with the question of whether or not John truly did write the passage in question. Arno Gaebelein declared that "it is evident the text belongs here and is genuine."[1377] How is it evident? James Boice list four evidence. 1. It is found in Papias, a disciple or John. 2. If it is not authentic then "the change of thought ... is abrupt and unnatural."[1378] 3. Augustine's claim supports its authenticity. 4. "Wisdom."[1379]

The first evidence has already been discussed, as has the third. The second point deserves attention. Although critics claim that the vocabulary and style to not fit John and that it "its placement here disrupts the flow of thought"[1380] others have argued the exact opposite. Said Arthur Pink, "if our passage be a spurious one then we should have to pass straight from 7:52 to 8:12. Let the reader try this."[1381]

John 7:9 makes it clear that verses 7:1-7:52 all take place in Galilee. However, in 8:12 Pharisees suddenly appear as Jesus is speaking in the Temple in Jerusalem (8:20)! If this passage does not belong, for it alone explains the transition and Jesus' travel from Galilee to Jerusalem in verses 1-2, then how can the critic explain Jesus' sudden shift from Galilee to Jerusalem without a single word of transition! John 8:2 shows this event took place following[1382] the incident of chapter seven. If one rejects the story of the adulteress, then one must reject verses 1-2 as well, for every manuscript lacking the adulteress lacks verses 1-2 and vice versa. If John 8:1-2 belong, then so does the story of the adulteress.

Conclusion

When only one side of a case is heard it is easy to make the accused seem guilty. In the age of the modern media everyone should be familiar with this tactic. Countless news stories led us to believe that one thing had happened as if there was no room for doubt, but later facts leak out and eventually we realize that the exact opposite of what we were led to believe was true. The same is true of this passage.

When we examine *all* the facts, it is clearly apparent that the passage is not only ancient and authentic, but that it properly belongs in John's gospel where it was unsuccessfully expunged by some who sought to punish lapsed believers who had forsaken Christ during the difficult persecutions. In their anger at having suffered for the faith while the lapsed took the easy way out, they went so far as to try to expunge part of the Word of God in order that this passage might never be used again to call for leniency!

It is impossible to read from 7:52 to 8:12 without the story of the adulteress. The transition would not only be illogical but irrational as chapter seven takes place in Galilee and chapter eight takes place on the Temple Mount. The passage is found in one of the oldest Codexes, is referenced by John's own disciple Papias, and quoted in the ancient *Apostolic Constitutions* as evidence that lapsed Christians should be forgiven. It is authentic, true, and belongs where it is currently found, in John's gospel.

Writing in the Dust

Having determined that the story is authentic, it is then necessary to determine the meaning of certain aspects of the story. One of the most curious is that of Jesus' writing in the dirt. When confronted by the lynch mob (and as such it could well be described) Jesus at first appeared to ignore them, instead writing in the sand. What was he writing? What was the meaning and significance? Having examined hundreds of commentaries through the ages, I have found essentially seven different theories.[1383]

1. To Gain Time

Some have simply argued that Jesus' writing was "a mechanical action which would suggest only an unwillingness to speak on the subject brought before Him, and preoccupaton with his own thoughts."[1384] This is a psychological answer which does not appear to attach any real significance to the event in itself, but rather sees it as an extension of Jesus' psychological state.

2. Weeping

Some have said that this is a mere form of weeping. Jesus was showing His concern and sorrow over the event. Nevertheless, this too does not really answer the question as to what was written or, for that matter, why Jesus was writing.

3. A Line in the Sand

In Mel Gibson's *Passion of the Christ* the writing was filmed, perhaps more symbolically then literally, as Jesus drawing a line in the sand. He drew a line, symbolically daring them to cross over the line. As a work of film art, it is very effective but true only from a symbolic point of view. H.A. Ironside offered a similar symbolic argument, saying that Jesus was tell them that "they will come down to the dust of death eventually because of their sins."[1385] In either case, the Bible makes clear that this was not just a line in the sand, but an actual writing of some sort.

4. To Shame Them

Martin Luther said they "did not deserve a reply ... He does not deign to speak to them and answer them."[1386] Others have said more explicitly that Jesus sought to shame them. Certainly both answers are true, but again do not actually answer the question directly. What was Jesus' writing? That He wrote to shame them and that they did not deserve a reply is apparent, but the larger question remains. This answer is thus moving in the right direction, but lacks substance.

5. Writing His Response

Many commentators have simply said that Jesus was writing His response to them without actually saying what that response was. This is safe exegesis but not good exegesis. We may not be able to say exactly what Jesus was writing, but it deserves a better answer than merely that this was Jesus' answer.

6. The Writing of the Law

One of the better views that Jesus was showing them that "it was he himself who once wrote the Ten Commandments."[1387] This was the view of the Venerable Bede and Saint Augustine.[1388] It is argued that it was "the finger which wrote the law"[1389] which was writing in the dust. To extent this view touches upon the answer, but not clearly. Was Jesus simply writing the law they were misquoting? Or was He doing something more?

7. Writing Out Their Sins

The final theory seems the best. Saint Jerome held that it was a judgment against the accusers.[1390] This is supported by the fact that several manuscripts add the phrase "he wrote out the sins of each one of them"[1391] including one fifth century manuscript.[1392] Moreover, it has been pointed out that the Greek word "*kategraphen* (8:6) literally means 'to write against.'"[1393] If this is the case then Jesus was giving them fair warning. He ignored them, instead writing some form of judgment.

Conclusion

Each view has a measure of merit, but the last view alone makes sense in the context. They were testing Jesus, but they did not even deserve a reponse. Their act was a henious sin in itself, and so Jesus, by way of warning, "wrote against" them some form of judgment.

Crime and Punishment

The greater question here is of crime and punishment. However, because that issue is so important, and because these verses are often misquoted for political reasons, it is best to deal with that topic in a separate section below (see John 8:11).

Summary

These passages are among the most famous in the whole of the New Testament, and also among its most controversial and debated. Although it is one of the three most contested passages in the New Testament, it is almost certainly the authentic writing of John. Its ommission in many ancient texts is due to the severity of anger against lapsed Christians who had denied Christ in order to escape torture and death during persecution. This passage was excised in order to justify harsh disciplinary actions against those Christians by the survivors.

As to what Jesus was writing in the dust, we cannot say for certain, but it apparent that it was a warning and judgment of some kind. By not speaking immediately, the accusers were actually given a chance to leave and escape their judgment, but instead they stayed behind and continued to try to trap Jesus. That leads to the next great debate ... crime and punishment.

Crime and Punishment
John 8:11

"The Law Moses commanded us to stone such women; what then do You say? ... He who is without sin among you, let him *be the* first to throw a stone at her."

This passage has been infamously thrown around as an excuse for those suffering from a guilty conscience. Others have used it to justify the rejection of captial punishment and to support light punishment for criminals. This is not new. It is so old that some attempted to expunge the passage from John so that it could no longer be used to support such laxity![1394] However, both extremes are wrong, misguided, and based on poor exegesis. Let us examine the facts.

First, it is clear that the accusers were "saying this, testing Him, so that they might have grounds for accusing Him" (8:6). This was not a trial but a trap. No matter how Jesus answered, they hoped to have him guilty of some crime; "either of usurping the office of a judge, if he condemned her, or of being an enemy to the law, if he acquitted her."[1395] As Jonathan Edwards said, if He had condemned her they would accuse Him of "sedition, for the Romans had taken away the power of life and death from the Jews."[1396] On the other hand, if He had said that the law was wrong and she should not die, they could accuse Him of heresy for rejecting the law of Moses! In fact, it was they who were guilty of breaking both the law of Moses *and* the law of Rome!

Let us consider first what the law of Moses actually says. The actual Talmudic law itself is brief and does not even specify stoning at all.[1397] Leviticus 20:10 states that "if *there is* a man who commits adultery with another man's wife, one who commits adultery with his friend's wife, the adulterer and the adulteress shall surely be put to death." Note that it says "the adulterer and the adulteress." "Where was the man?"[1398] This is the first clue that this lynch mob was not acting in accordance with the Law of Moses. The man was absent. But there is much more, for Jewish law "insisted on much more rigorous standards of proof than those accepted elsewhere."[1399] The requirement of two or more witnesses is but one example (cf. Number 35:30, Deuteronomy 17:6-7, 19:5). Furthermore, according to Leon Morris Jewish law was so strict in its requirement of proof that "even lying on a bed together was not sufficient proof."[1400] They would literally have to be caught in the act by two or more witnesses. This is why divorce in the Law of Moses was granted for unfaithfulness (see notes on Matthew 19:9).

In short, "the woman was not brought before Jesus for formal trial"[1401] but rather she was used as a prop by a lynch mob for the express purpose of trapping Jesus. This is the reason Jesus was so angry. They "did not deserve a reply."[1402] Where were the accusers? Where was the man? Where was the judge? By telling them that the one "without sin" should cast the first stone, Jesus was challenging them. He was daring them, if you will. He knew they were bluffing, although some suggested that "without sin" actually meant that the men were guilty of adulterous afairs as well.[1403] Did they know this woman? Was she a prostitute (as some traditions state)? In Jewish law the one who cast the first stone *must* be the victim of the crime. In this case, it would have to be the husband or wife of one of the adulterers, but neither was present. Therefore,

"He who is without sin among you, let him *be the* first to throw a stone at her"! This was the challenge.

Obviously there is a lesson in here about love and forgiveness, but it is an error to read something political into the story. Jesus did not come to see government reform, nor did He come to overturn the Law of Moses (see notes on Matthew 5:17-18). He came to call the lost to repentance. If the law forgave criminals then we would live in total anarchy. However, it is not the job of the Church to enact the law. That is the job of government. This is why Protestants believe in a so-called "separation of church and state" (often misquoted by those who seek to abolish religious freedom). Church and state serve different purposes. It is a mistake to confuse the functions of the two. While there is a relationship between the two (and it is for this reason that the Constitution does not use the phrase "separation of church and state"), they perform different duties. Our job is to love and forgive. This is what Jesus did. He did not overturn the law, but upheld it in its highest form. Moreover, he spared the accusers death, for they had placed themselves under death by "bearing false witness" (the ninth commandment) against this woman. This is the lesson. It is not a political one, but one of love, forgiveness, and redemption.

Jesus' Testimony
John 8:14

"Even if I testify about Myself, My testimony is true, for I know where I came from and where I am going."

Some say that this is a blatant contradiction of John 5:31, and void of any context, it would appear to be just that, but any cursory examination of the context actually proves that Jesus is saying the exact same thing! How? Let us examine the passages in question.

In John 5:31, Jesus says, "if I *alone* testify about Myself, My testimony is not true. There is another who testifies of Me, and I know that the testimony which He gives about Me is true." Here in John 8:14 it might appear that he is saying the opposite, "even if I testify about Myself, My testimony is true, for I know where I came from and where I am going." Of course, anything which is not in context it necessarily out of context. That is how it works.

The quotation in John 5:31 is in the context of "a concession to the legal rule that man's testimony about himself is inadmissible as evidence in court."[1404] The Jews were challenging His authority because "self-testimony is not a valid testimony,"[1405] so Jesus affirmed that even *if* He testified alone, His testimony would be rejected, but "the witness or record He bore was not in *independence* of the father, but ... perfect accord therewith."[1406] *If* is a theoretical preposition that does not in any way contradict a *factual* statement.

Here in chapter eight, Jesus takes this a step further, noting that even *if* He did not have another to testify for Himself, that would not mean that He is wrong. Truth is truth and does not need a witness to it. "He had shifted His argument from the basis of abstract legality to the prinicle of His personal competence."[1407] Said R.C. Sproul, "He said His testimony was based on firsthand knowledge of heaven, for He had come from there and was going back there."[1408]

Lost in this debate is the larger meaning of Jesus's words. As Erasmus said, Jesus was saying, "I say nothing on my own authority, but on the authority of Him from whom I have been sent ... He cannot lie."[1409] The principle "was true of universally fallen of men ... but Jesus was not the *mere* man, or the *fallen* man. His testimony was the witness of One perfect in knowledge, and perfect in holiness."[1410] In this context Jesus was saying that He is "inseparably unified to the Father,"[1411] as John Wesley said. Indeed, "this is the very badge of Deity."[1412] This is the reason the Jewish heirarchy was so angry at Jesus. They understood Jesus perfectly. He was moving from hinting at His deity to His eventually outright acknoweldgement of it, which would lead directly to the Cross.

How Old Was Jesus?
John 8:57

"So the Jews said to Him, 'You are not yet fifty years old, and have You seen Abraham?'"

The subject of Jesus' true age is discussion under Luke 3:1 – 3:23. However, it is necessary here to address those who believe that this passage proves Jesus must have been at least in his forties, if they were saying he was not yet fifty. Merrill Tenney believes Jesus simply looked much older than his age,[1413] which may be possible. They most likely did not know how old Jesus was, even as we don't know how old the people around us are unless they are close family or friends. Since Jesus was in his mid to late thirties it would not be unrealistic to say that Jesus might have look in his forties. Nevertheless, there is a better answer provided by Matthew Henry.

Matthew Henry said "old age is reckoned to begin at fifty (Num. 4:47), so that they meant no more than this."[1414] This seems to make the most sense, for fifty obviously carried a connotation. Perhaps a man of fifty was considered wise. Even as we refer to anyone under a certain age as a "kid", even if he be a full grown adult, they appeared to attach some maturity to the age fifty. Since they almost certainly did not know Jesus's true age, this seems the best answer.

"Before Abraham was, I AM"
John 8:58-59

"Jesus said to them, 'Truly, truly, I say to you, before Abraham was born, I am.' Therefore they picked up stones to throw at Him; but Jesus hid Himself, and went out of the temple."

This is one of the most important verses in the Bible, and it is a statement that led directly to His crucifixion, yet many are oblivious to this passage and its meaning. Unitarians seem to trivialize its meaning and liberals render it mere symbolic rhetoric. What did Jesus mean when He said, "before Abraham was born, I am"? The Jews understood exactly. That is why they picked up stones to stone him (8:59). Jesus was using the very "incommunicable name of God"[1415] to declare that He was God incarnate! This was blasphemy to the Jewish priesthood and the primary reason for his trial and execution.

For the English reader this may not be clear to those not familiar with Hebrew or the Old Testament but this is "a distinct reference to Ex. iii.14"[1416] where God said to Moses, "I AM WHO I AM; and He said, 'Thus you shall say to the sons of Israel, "'I AM has sent me to you.""' Jesus did not say "I *was*" but "I AM"![1417] "The affirmation that He was none other than the Eternal One."[1418] Jesus assumed the very name of God as his own.[1419]

Once again, the Jews "were not in doubt of what he meant."[1420] They understood perfectly. As Erasmus said, "a mortal man seemed to be laying claim to eternal existence."[1421] Another commentator said that "by using the timeless 'I am' rather than 'I was' Jesus conveyed not only the idea of existence prior to Abraham, but timelessness, – the very nature of God himself (Exod. 3:14)."[1422] Jesus declared that He was "beyond time"[1423] for "eternal existence knows neither past nor future time."[1424]

Some have noted the similarities to Psalms 90:2[1425] where David declared, "before the mountains were born or You gave birth to the earth and the world, even from everlasting to everlasting, You are God." Here Jesus says, "before Abraham was, I AM." Jesus was "from everlasting to everlasting."[1426] This is the reason that they tried to stone Him. This is the real underlying reason they sought to execute Jesus. Previously, Jesus had dropped hints of His deity as the Messiah, but He was not yet ready to die. Now His time was coming, and Jesus was no longer dropping hints, but outright declaring that He, God the Son, had become flesh and dwelled among us (cf. John 1).

"Ye Are Gods"
John 10:34

"Jesus answered them, "Has it not been written in your Law, '*I said, you are gods*'? If he called them gods, to whom the word of God came (and the Scripture cannot be broken), do you say of Him, whom the Father sanctified and sent into the world, 'You are blaspheming,' because I said, 'I am the Son of God'?"

Having previously asserted His deity Jesus again draws the ire of the Jewish priesthood for implying the same. Here, however, Jesus reply has been distorted, corrupted, and misused by many, particularly in recent years. Some modern heretics have misquoted this verse to imply that we are "little gods" or "a God kind of creature."[1427] Kenneth Copeland even said, "you don't have a God living in you; you *are* one!"[1428] What then does this verse mean?

The passage is actually a quotation of Psalms 82:6-7. Jesus was quoting the passage to illustrate the frailty of the Pharisees attacks on Jesus, but it is the context of the Psalms which is relevant to any actually meaning and application of "gods" to mortal men. It is no surprise, therefore, that heretical preachers ignore the second part of the passage in question. It reads, "I said, 'You are gods, and all of you are sons of the Most High.' Nevertheless you will die like men and fall like *any* one of the princes." Notice that it is a chastizement! "You are gods ... but you will die like men." What kind of "god" is so helpless?

So, as Hunt and McMahon said, rather than being a good thing, it is a bad thing.[1429] The Lord is in a way mocking man who sought to become "like god" in the Garden of Eden (Genesis 3). The full context of the passage elaborates even more.

"God takes His stand in His own congregation;
He judges in the midst of the rulers.

How long will you judge unjustly
And show partiality to the wicked? Selah.

Vindicate the weak and fatherless;
Do justice to the afflicted and destitute.

Rescue the weak and needy;
Deliver *them* out of the hand of the wicked.

They do not know nor do they understand;
They walk about in darkness;
All the foundations of the earth are shaken.

I said, 'You are gods, and all of you are sons of the Most High.
'Nevertheless you will die like men and fall like *any* one of the princes.'

Arise, O God, judge the earth! For it is You who possesses all the nations."

Notice verse one refers to "rulers." It is thus commonly assumed that the passage was specifically referring to "Jewish magistrates"[1430] or judges. This position is the dominant view held throughout the centuries by men like Thomas Aquinas,[1431] John Calvin,[1432] John Lightfoot,[1433] H.A. Ironside,[1434] R.C. Sproul,[1435] Charles Erdmans,[1436] Albert Barnes,[1437] James Boice,[1438] Leon Morris,[1439] Warren Wiersbe,[1440] and John MacArthur[1441] to name but a few. They variously hold that the title "gods" was bestowed because they were "interpreters of divine law"[1442] or "because they ruled as His representatives."[1443] Desiderius Erasmus said, "God Himself has bestowed the honour of His name on those to whom the word of God was spoken."[1444]

Nonetheless, this is not the universal view. Some believe that the "gods" refer not to men at all, but to angels. This was the view of men like Origen.[1445] Robert Govett argued that "'the Congregation of God' – in the opening of the 82nd Pslam – alludes to what we see in Job i.6-8. The angels, or sons of God, assemble before Jehovah."[1446] He concludes, therefore, that "the Psalmist refers, I believe, to the angels who fell in Noah's day."[1447] The problem with this view is that verse seven speaks of the "gods" dying like men, but angels cannot die like men. Moreover, verse two condemns them for judging unjustly, but angels do not judge men. In fact, we will judge angels (1 Corinthians 6:3)!

So it seems best to accept that this passage is, indeed, attributing the title "gods" to mortal men, but the context makes it equally clear that this is not truly an honorary title as Erasmus believed,[1448] nor should we accept Athanasius's claim that it is an allusion to the idea that "he made Moses a god to Pharaoh."[1449] On the contrary, it seems that God is mocking the judges and rulers of the earth who have set themselves up as gods. In fact, the pagan rulers most literally called themselves gods and often demanded to be worshipped. The Egyptian Pharaohs were believed to be the incarnations of Ra and the Roman emperors demanded sacrifices to themselves. Here the Lord is mocking them, saying "you are gods ... but you will die like men, and fall like *any* one of the princes."

We must, therefore reject the idea that this was some sort of "divine power"[1450] or even Athanasius's metaphoric claim that, "He was made man that we might be made god."[1451] None of this is evident in the Psalms, and even less so in the words of Jesus which simply meant, "if it is permissible to call men gods because they were vehicles of the word of God, how much more permissible is it to use 'God' of him who *is* the Word of God."[1452] "The Jewish leaders understood clearly what He was saying! Some modern liberal theologians would water down our Lord's statement, but the people who heard it knew exactly what He was saying, 'I am God!'"[1453] When the Pharisees objected that this was blasphemy, "Jesus, observe, does not deny that He was God."[1454]

Thus another strong allusion to the divinity of Jesus has been perverted by some today to imply that we are divine! This is counter to the gospel and to the context of the very verse they are citing! Jesus was God incarnate, the Messiah. We are but men. If God mockingly calls men "gods" then what accusation can they bring against the Messiah, the Son of God? None!

Caiaphas' Prophecy
John 11:49-50

"It is expedient for you that one man die for the people, and that the whole nation not perish."

Caiaphas was the lead instigator in the trial and execution of Jesus Christ, and yet here is one of the great ironies of history. Although he said this with political expediency in mind, it was actually God who spoke through him and uttered one of the great truths of the Christian faith. John himself said;

"Now he did not say this on his own initiative, but being high priest that year, he prophesied that Jesus was going to die for the nation, and not for the nation only, but in order that He might also gather together into one the children of God who are scattered abroad" (John 11:51-52).

This is an example of God's sovereignty and His will being supreme over our own petty schemes, and is also an indication that God can speak through anyone. Bad men can say good things. In the end it is God who is supreme and it is His will that takes precedent over our own plans. Here the very man who instigated the murder of Jesus utters, by God's initiative, one of the great prophecies of the Bible; that Jesus died in order that we might not perish.

John 12:12-15 – See Matthew 21:2

Does "All" Mean "All"?
John 12:32

"I, if I am lifted up from the earth, will draw all men to Myself."

"I will draw all men to Myself!" What a marvelous proclamation by our Lord and Savior Jesus Christ: except that Calvinist Arthur Pink declares "'all' *does not mean* 'all' ... but ... His elect."[1455] Pink should be respected for his honesty in the matter, for Calvin himself said that "the word 'all' must be limited to the elect."[1456] The question is, therefore, does "all" mean "all"?

Such a question should be obvious to "all," but apparently is not. This very question hits to the very core of the Calvinist-Arminian debate. On the one hand, Calvinist like R.C. Sproul say, "Jesus wasn't simply saying, 'No one will come to Me unless the Father wooes them to Me. No, His meaning was much stronger."[1457] He then goes on to criticizes all transaltion for not using the word "compel"[1458] in John 6:44 although he does not seem to criticize those translations here in John 12:32 which uses the exact same word!

Conversely, men like Martin Luther, whom not even the most strident Calvinist would call Arminian, said that the "drawing" was but "a gracious allurement."[1459] In the one "'all' does not mean 'all.'"[1460] In the other, it but an enticing. Is either view correct? Is there another? Ultimately we must look at the issues of free will and sovereignty to understand the answer. We may find that the issue is not one of Calvinism versus Arminianism after all.

Calvinism and Arminianism Defined

For the newcomer to Christian theology, I will pause here briefly to define Calvinism and Arminianism. These two theologies are often considered to be violently opposing theologies, although they are, in fact, two different extensions of the same theologies, and both John Calvin and Jacob Arminus were from the same religious traditions and convictions save one : the nature of free will and the sovereignty of God.

Calvin believed that the sovereignty of God was such that man cannot have true free will. Although modern Calvinist will continue to debate to this day the extend of this belief, and of Calvin's assersion of it, the central tenant of Calvinism is that man is not truly free. Those who are saved were "predestined" by God and those who are not predestinted *cannot* be saved.

Arminius studied at Calvin's seminary but broke with Calvin over the issue of predestination.[1461] Calvinist argue that Arminians deny the sovereignty of God because they emphasize free will.

Both Calvin and Arminius summarized their views on the subject in "five points." I have listed these five points below in contrast to one another. The letters represent an acrostic employed by Calvinist (TULIP represents the five points shown below). I have created my own acrostic for Arminianism.

The Five Points of ...

	Calvinism[1462]		Arminianism[1463]
T	*Total Depravity* : Man is incapbable of good or of believing in Jesus unless God has regenerated him *first*.	S	*Sinfulness of Man :* Man cannot "do anything that is truly good" and therefore must be regenerated.
U	*Unconditional Election* : "Some receive the gift of faith and others do not receive it" solely by the mysterious will of God.	P	*Pardon Offered for All :* "Christ died for and obtained redemption and forgiveness of sins for all but these benefits are effective only for those who believe in Christ."
L	*Limited Atonement* : Salvation is only for "those, and only those, who were from eternity chosen" as the elect.	A	*Atonement for All Who Believe :* "God from eternity past determined to save all who believe in Jesus ..."
I	*Irresistable Grace* : "All those whom God has predestined unto life, and those only" ... receive God's grace which cannot be resisted.	R	*Resistable Grace* : God's grace is essential for salvation and offered to all but may be resisted.
P	*Perseverance of the Saints* : The elect "can neither totally nor finally fall away from the state of grace, but shall certainly persevere."	U	*Undetermined Perseverance* : We are saved through faith but whether man can fall away from the faith "must be more particularly determined out of the Holy Scriptures."

As the reader can see, each of the five points deal with the question of the relationship between free will and God's will. The Calvinist believes that God's will negates that of man. The Arminian believes that God's will allows for man's will. Each claims that you must either be a Calvinist or an Arminian, although neither actually explains *why*. Considering that the overwhelming majority of Christians, both Catholic and Protestant, are neither one, this seems a stunning claim, but it one constantly made nevertheless.

The Calvinist Debate's Roots

Calvinists invariably want to make the debate one about the sovereignty and predestination of God, which few doubt. How does God's sovereignty and man's free will co-exist, if at all? This is a legitimate debate, outlined below. However, it is disingenuous to say that this is the debate about Calvinism. It is not. In fact, the roots of Calvin's views on sovereignty and free will are older than the birth of Jesus Christ ... but *not* the Bible!

That John Calvin borrowed heavily from Saint Augustine is freely confessed by such ardent Calvinists as B.B. Warfield and Charles Spurgeon. Warfield declares that "the system of doctrine taught by Calvin is just ... Augustinianism."[1464] Spurgeon said, "Calvin derived it mainly from the writings of Augustine."[1465] What is not admitted, is that Augustine also borrowed his ideas, but not so much from the Bible alone, as from Greek philosophy which the apostle Paul so stridently criticized (cf. Colossians 2:8). To understand this debate, we must go back, ever so briefly, to the true origins of the debate. Sadly, that debate is *not* one found in the Bible.

Aristotle is sometimes considered the first philospher to originate the debate between what is now called "determinism" vs. free will. Others believe it can be traced to pre-Socratic philosophers like Heraclitus and Leucippus, but it is the Stoics who are universally accepted as the early formulators of the doctrine.[1466] Among the foremost of these was Alexander of Aphrodisias.[1467] Does man have free will or is he just a puppet, a cruel joke from the gods? Given the nature of the Greek gods, the real surprise is why this debate did not originate sooner. Consider that the Greek gods were notoriously cold and cruel. The original version of the movie *Clash of the Titans* depicted the gods as playing chess with men. Mankind was a kind of toy. This cold calculating view of the gods gave way to a debate among the ancient Greeks about the very nature of free will. Specifically, do we have it at all? The debate is obviously by no means a Christian debate. Even to this day secularists, darwnists, and particularly psychologists debate on the nature of determinism. For some we are products of our society, for others we are determined by our parents, by our genes, by evolution, or any number of other factors, including God.

There are literally hundreds of views of how we come to be who we are. Are we truly unique? Are we just complicated machines? These debates continue to rage in secular universities, leaving God out of the equation, of course. The question here, however, is whether or not Calvin's view on determinism and free will is truly any different. Whether it was Augustine or Thomas Aquinas, their views on free will were influenced by Aristotle and the Greeks as much as, if not more than, the Bible. This cannot be denied with credulity.

Sovereignty, Free Will, and the Doctrine of Universalism

Having determined that the issue of God's sovereignty and man's free will is the underlying issue, we may well ask if they contradict one another. The obvious answer is that they *can*, but that does not necessarily mean that they *do*. Where the two are in contradiction, God's will obviously prevails! But what about where they are not? Is there such a thing? For the Calvinist God cannot even offer us a chose between Coke and Pepsi, since we might choose wrongly! This is the irony of Calvinism. When the Bible says God wants "all" to be saved (cf. 2 Peter 3:9) they naturally see a conflict with those passages which make it perfectly clear that there *is* a Hell and not all *will* be saved. They decide, therefore, that "'all' does not mean 'all'"[1468] whereas the Arminian takes a different approach. Some Arminians (but not all) says Hell is but allegory and that "all" men *will* be saved (this is called the doctrine of Universalism).

Notice that *both* the Calvinist *and* the Arminian choose which passage is truly God's will and which passage must be amended. *Both* assume that both passages cannot be true! Why not?

Calvinist James Montgomery Boice himself clearly distinguishes between the "*sovereign* or *efficacious* will of God"[1469] and the "disposition of God"[1470] or what others call the "permissive will of God." In the later, it is what God desires, but not to the exclusion of the former. In other words, the Calvinist admits that God may want something which He does not make come to pass! How then is it that he rejects any notion of free will in regard to the five points of Calvinism?

Conversely, the radical Arminian (although not Arminius himself), believes that all men *will* be saved, not that God *wants* all men to be saved. He takes the other extreme of denying God's will in regard to punishing the wicked!

Notice that both proceed from the same false assumption. Both assume that there is a contradiction between the wills that cannot be resolved without diminishing one. This, however, is sheerly Aristotilean philosophy. If God wishes to give us a choice, it is He who gave us the choice. Certainly we are not completely free, as some claim. I can say that will be President some day, but in reality it is not entirely in my hands. Many men have willed to become President, but it did not happen. Nevertheless, that does not mean that we have no choice. We cannot choose what is not open to us. Proverbs 16:9 states that "the mind of man plans his way, but the LORD directs his steps." This verse demonstrates the true relationship between God's will and our will; between sovereignty and free will.

333

Consider the following. We love our pets. Most people love dogs and cats, but dogs and cats have a will of their own (particularly cats). They do not always obey. Why do we love them so much? Would not a machine or toy be better? No. Why? Because when they choose to love us, it makes that love all the more special. We love dogs because they are loyal, even though they may sometimes disobey us, or even bite us. Am I less than my dog? Is my will subject to my dog's will? Has my dog become my master? How absurd would such a claim be? How much more is God's love of us than ours for a dog? How much more freedom and forgiveness has God given to us, than we give to our dogs? Should I compare myself to a dog in God's eyes? Yes, for I am not even worthy of being called a dog, and yet my Lord loves me.

Conclusion

Dave Hunt compared Calvinism to a man holding "a rope 30 feet above a man at the bottom of a well and plead[ing] with him earnestly to take hold of it."[1471] If "all" men are not offered salvation, when of what value is the Cross? Our God becomes little more than the pagan gods of old, playing games with man.

The Bible declares that "the mind of man plans his way, but the LORD directs his steps" (Proverbs 16:9). In this respect, we are not completely free, and I praise the Lord for that very fact. However, it also affirms that God, in His *sovereign will*, has chosen to give us certain choices in life for which we are accountable. It is true that not "all" men will be saved, but "all" men are drawn to Jesus. This is what John 12:32 says and this is what it means. Every man has a spiritual longing; everyone. Only Jesus can truly fill that hole. Every man is drawn to it, but in order to receive it, we must deny ourselves (cf. Matthew 16:24; Mark 8:24; Luke 9:23). This is the dilemma. Sin and self are interrelated. Sin is selfishness. If we must deny ourselves then it is like denying who we are, at our most basic level. We must acknolwedge that we are not self sufficient and that we are lacking in ourselves. Many will choose self over God. The Lord has given us that choice and we are accountable for that choice. It is for this very reason that those gospel ministers who try to remove "obstacles" to the Cross, too often remove the one obstacle which Christ Himself laid before us!

Here in John 12:32 Jesus says, I, if I am lifted up from the earth, will draw all men to Myself." This is what it says, and this is what it means. "All" means "all," but it is God's predestined will that we must choose Him over our own selves. Therefore, all are drawn to Him, but not all will accept Him. This is God's sovereign predestined will.

John 14:7-15 – See John 5:19-26

The Holy Spirit
John 14:16-31

"I will ask the Father, and He will give you another Helper, that He may be with you forever."

The doctrine of the Trinity is a fundamental aspect of the Christian religion. It is also one of its most controversial. If we then divide the Trinity into its three parts, it is the Holy Spirit that has proven the most controversial of all. Few can deny that Jesus claimed deity. Several of the many passages have been addressed already. Here a new person is introduced. The person of the Holy Spirit. Who is this person? Is He also God manifested in Spirit?

The *Paraclete*
The Holy Spirit is identified here by the title *Paraclete* (παπακλητος) which is variously translated as Comforter (KJV, Tyndale, Wycliff, ASV, Darby), Helper (NAS, NKJV), Counselor (NIV, RSV) Advocate (NLT), and even Friend (NIRV). To this other commentators have added "strenghtener."[1472]

According to the Greek Lexicon, *Paraclete* (παπακλητος) literally means "summoned, called to one's side."[1473] It's primary definition is advocate, or "one who pleads another's cause before a judge."[1474] R.C. Sproul said that "'Advocate' gives us a good idea of what a paraclete is. In antiquity a paraclete was an attorney, basically a defense attorney."[1475] Warren Wiersbe believes "it means 'called alongside to assist.' The Holy Spirit does not work instead of us, or in spite of us, but in us and through us."[1476]

Thus the "advocate" is more than just a "counselor." He is not only called to comfort us but to assist us.[1477] His chief purposes for us are to comfort, to teach, and to aid.[1478] Moreover, as our advocate, he pleads for us to the Father on our behalf. The imagery is a perfect one. As sinners we are not worthy to even approach the judge, but the Holy Spirit, as our advocate, can approach the judge. He is, therefore, all of the above. He is a comforter, an advocate, a helper, a counselor, and a friend, but is He something more? Is He the Spirit of God indwelling within us?

The Council of Nicaea
Arianism is the name given to those who reject the belief in the Trinity. It takes its name from a man called Arius who lived at the same time as Constatine and challenged the centuries old doctrine. It is, therefore, ironic that modern day Arians claim that the doctrine of the Trinity can be traced to the Council of Nicaea called by Emperor Constantine in 325 A.D.

Arianism itself is descended from the gnostic cults which plagued early Christianity.[1479] Both the Trinity and the rejection of it were taught from the earliest days of Christianity. Over the centuries internal bickering over the doctrine continued and after Constantine's conversion these theological debates

335

became quite heated as fear of persecution died down. Consequently, Constantine called upon himself to convene a council of all the church of the empire to deal with the subject of Arianism.[1480]

Arians erroneously claim that the Trinity was an invention of the Council of Nicaea. In fact, the doctrine was taught by such ancient church fathers as Tertullian who noted that "He showed a third degree in the Paraclete, as we believe the second degree is in the Son."[1481] He further stated that there was "unity" in these three.[1482] There was God the Father, God the Son, and God the Holy Spirit.

The Council of Nicaea ultimately came to an agreement upon the Biblical doctrine of the Trinity. It did not formulate any new doctrines, but confirmed the doctrines and beliefs long held since the time of Christ. To this day the Nicene Creed is the only creed agreed upon completely by Catholics, mainstream Protestants, and the Eastern Orthodox churches.

God the Holy Spirit
Now the real question is not what the Council of Nicaea taught, but what the Bible teaches. That Jesus claimed divinity cannot be denied with credulity. What then of the Holy Spirit? Is God a duality or a Trinity? Although there are a great many verses which have been used to support the Trinity, we may conclude from this passage three things about the Holy Spirit.

1) The Holy Spirit is a "He"
Many believe that the use of the pronoun "He" rather than "it" proves that the Holy Spirit is a person. H.A. Ironside said, "Our Lord would never have used this masculine pronoun if He did not mean us to understand that just as God the Father is a Person, and God the Son is a Person, so God the Holy Spirit is a Person."[1483] Conversely, critics argue that the Greek word is "it" and not "He." This unfortunate debate is more techinical that it should be.

The first technical issue is the textual debate. Ancient copies of this passage already reflect possible dissention because some manuscripts do use the "neuter" case which is usually translated "it." Other ancient copies use the definitive "He." The "neuter" αυτο is found is such ancient and respected copies as the Codex Sinaiticus (א), Vaticanus (B), Washingtonianus (W), and an ancient papyrus ($\mathfrak{P}^{75}$). Moreover, it is reflected as a "correction note" in both the Codex Bezae (D) and another ancient papyrus ($\mathfrak{P}^{66}$). So also the majority text ($\mathfrak{m}$) seems to reflect this. Now while this might seem strong, there are good reasons to reject "it" as the proper translation. The first reason is the other side of the textual argument. Despite the seemingly strong evidence for "it" there is even stronger evidence for the masculine pronoun αυτον meaning "He." Most noteably is the fact that the most ancient manuscript available for this passage ($\mathfrak{P}^{66}$) reads αυτον. So also the ancient Codex Bezae (D) reads αυτον. Later scribes added a "correction" in the margin, but there is no doubt that the originals reads αυτον or "He." $\mathfrak{P}^{66}$ is of particularly significant since it is the oldest manuscript for this passage dating back no later than 200 A.D. as possibly as early as 130 A.D., not too long after the death of John Mark!

The second reason for translating this as "He" is the strongest. One does not normally refer to *any* spirit as an "it" to begin with, and even less so when that spirit is spoken of as having the characteristics of a person! This leads to the second point extracted from John 14.

2) The Holy Spirit Shows the Characteristics of a Person

It has already been demonstrated that the Holy Spirit is referred to as a *Paraclete* (παπακλητος) or Counselor. He is an Advocate. Neither of these positions can be maintained by a machine or an "it." The Holy Spirit is a sentient being demonstrating the capabilities of a person. His chief purposes are to comfort, teach, and aid us.[1484] All of these actions require the characteristics of a person.

Beyond John's gospel the Bible provides even more evidence of the characteristics of the Holy Spirit. John MacArthur has said that "scripture reveals that the Holy spirit possesses the attributes of persondood : intellect ... emotion ... and will"[1485] (cf. Rom. 8:27; 1 Cor. 2:11; Eph. 4:30). In Ephesians 4:30 it is apparent that the Holy Spirit can grieve. In Romans and 1 Corinthians the Holy Spirit is said to have thoughts and a mind capable of interceding on behalf of the saints. In all these cases, the Holy Spirit demonstrates the abilities and characteristics of personhood.

3) The Holy Spirit is of the "Same Kind" as Jesus

Jesus said " I will ask the Father, and He will give you another Helper." The word for "another" is αλλος (*allos*). This word literally means "another of the same kind", hence "the Comforter would be of the same quality and character as Christ's."[1486] He is *"another* Comforter."[1487] It is, therefore, clear that Jesus is comparing the Holy Spirit to Himself in more than a superficial way. He is a comforter, counselor, advocate, and helper *like* Jesus. That is saying a great deal.

From these three things, it is more than apparent that the Holy Spirit is a person equal to and "of the same kind" as Christ. Logically, the Holy Spirit cannot be viewed as any other than the very Spirit of God Himself indwelling with us. As such, He is clearly a third person of the Trinity.

Summary
Here Jesus has promised to send a comforter. "'I will ask *the Father.*' Can anyone not blinded by error deny that there are *two persons here*? And that a third is spoken of as sent?"[1488] These were the words of Robert Govett. It is indeed clear that this third person is the Holy Spirit, and that He is of the "same

kind" of Jesus and the very Spirit of God. He is intended to comfort us, to guide us, to counsel us, and to defend us.

How can anyone call the Holy Spirit anything other than God? Is there another Holy Spirit? If a spirit indwells within us is it not either God's spirit or that of a demon? The Arian sees the Holy Spirit as something inferior to what the Bible makes Him out to be. He is not an it. He is not a warm fuzzy. He is the Spirit of God comforting us.

On another note, it is "both interesting and important to observe that *eroto* is the word used *by our Lord alone of His own prayers to the Father ...* [and this] throws light on our Lord's own assertion of His Divinity, that He habitually used, to describe His own request to the Father, a word which cannot ordinarily be used of *our* request to God."[1489] So here we have a brief glimpse of the Trinity. God the Son prays to God the Father for "another of the same kind." This one is clearly described not as an "it" but as a "He," as a person; the third person of the Trinity. God, the Holy Spirit, indwells the believer on behalf of the Father and Son.

This is an important doctrine for several reasons. It is essential that we understand that God is not leaving us alone in this world. He is with us at all times. Furthermore, "if Jesus Christ were dwelling in your house you would not ignore Him, you would not go about your business as if He were not there."[1490] So also the Holy Spirit should remind us that God is watching us. When we sin, He is there to convict us. When we are sad, He is there to comfort us. When we are joyful, He is there to rejoice with us. He is with us at all times and we should act accordingly. This is why Paul could say, "do not grieve the Holy Spirit of God" (Ephesians 4:30). Instead we should act as if Jesus is standing next to us in everything we do, for in a real sense of the word, He is.

Is the Father Greater Than the Son?
John 14:28

"The Father is greater than I."

John 14:28 has created confusion among many for several reasons. First is whether or not this contradicts the statements of John 5:19-26 concerning the unity of the Father and Son. Indeed, here again Jesus declares that "I am in the Father and the Father is in Me." Thus, once again, Jesus declaration of deity riled the Pharisees to anger, but how can He then say "the Father is greater than I"? Secondly, if Jesus declared that He was equal to the Father in 5:19-26 then how can the Father here be said to be greater?

The Humanity Argument
The traditional answer is echoed by John Calvin who said that this statement should "only apply to the Son of God insofar as he is manifested in the body."[1491] It is the "humanity argument."[1492] However, Calvin himself seemed

inconsistent on this view for he elsewhere says "Christ is not speaking here either about his human nature or about his eternal divinity, but for the sake of our weakness he places himself between God and us."[1493]

Historically this has been the most popular argument. It has been posited from the earliest of times by names like Theodoret of Cyprus,[1494] Hilary of Potiers,[1495] Basil the Great,[1496] Didymus the Blind,[1497] and Saint Augustine.[1498] Indeed, the Catholic Fathers in particular espoused this view. Thomas Aquinas declared that "when he says the Father is greater than I, he does not mean I, as Son of God, but as son of man" in "his human nature."[1499]

Nonetheless, this is by no means a Catholic view. John Wesley said that this refers to Jesus "as he was man. As God neither is greater nor less than the other."[1500] Albert Barnes said that this is "not to compare his own *nature* with that of the Father, but his *condition*."[1501] Robert Govett said that "Jesus, by His incarnation, was made lower than the angels, to suffer death."[1502] Finally, Warren Wiersbe said that Jesus was "limited by having a human body. He voluntarily laid aside the independent excercise of His divine attributes and submitted Himself to the Father."[1503]

Obviously, there seems to be an element of truth in this argument, but it is not sufficient in itself. We say that the Father, Son, and Holy Spirit are equal, but if the Father were greater than the *human* Jesus, He would still be greater than *the Son*. So the question remains. How can Jesus be both equal to the Father and yet say the Father is greater?

The Hierarchy Argument

Another argument is that God the Father was greater in hierarchy among the Trinity.[1504] In this view, all three are equal in essense, but not in duty and function. R.C. Sproul uses more theological language to say the same thing when he declared that "the Father is greater than the Son, not in substance, but greater in the economy of redemption."[1505] Such trendy theological terminology may confuse some, and avoid imagery of a medieval hierarchy, but it is essentially the same argument.

This view too, goes back to the earliest of Church Fathers, although not as pronounced as the "Humanity argument." John of Damascus taught that there is no "superiority in any other respect except causation."[1506] Today Arthur Pink teaches that this refers only to the "official character and position"[1507] of the Father and Son.

This argument is a better argument that the "humanity view," for a private is not inferior to his sergeant nor the sergeant to his general, but each is subject to one another according to rank. The Father is the head of the family. In this respect, God the Father is the head of the Trinity and "greater" than the Son and the Holy Spirit, and yet all three are equally God. This is the nature of the Trinity. One God who is manifest in three persons.

Combination Arguments

Naturally, there are offshoots and variants, many of which combine part or all of the other views. James Boice, for example, accepts both the "incarnation" view and also that Jesus was "below the Father in terms of His outward Glory and official position."[1508]

Harold Ironside applies this not so much to his humanity as His humiliation upon the Cross, noting that "He takes the place of subjection."[1509] Indeed, Jesus humbled Himself so low that He was born a manger, the son of a poor carpenter, lolely, and humiliated at Calvary. In this respect Robert Govett also eches the sentiment to some extent, saying that "Jesus, by His incarnation, was made lower than the angels, to suffer death."[1510]

Still others seem to avoid the issue altogether, like Martin Luther who argues that "whether according to His essence He is greater or less than the Father ... here it is Christ's purpose to tell the disciples not to be afraid."[1511] This seems to dodge the question rather than answer it. His caution, however, is understandable for, to quote John MacArthur, this "has been twisted by heretical groups into an incorrect assertion of His inferiority to the Father ... the Lord was not speaking here of His essential nature as God, but of His submissive role during His ministry on earth"[1512]

Conclusion

The Arian claims this is proof that Jesus could not be God incarnate, but "could any mere man, unless insane or blasphemous use these words in comparing himself with God"?[1513] Indeed, it is because Jesus dared to compare Himself with the Father that the Jewish hierarchy sought Jesus' life.

In terms of the actual comment, it is clear that Jesus was not denying His deity, for He makes that amply clear in numerous passages. Rather He is preparing the apostles for His departure. He is, therefore, alluding to His death on the cross. In this respect it is apparent that Jesus was inferior in terms of His subjugation to the Will of God and in the Passion. All the arguments have an element of truth in them, but the hierarchal one explains the others. Because God the Father is the head of the Trinity, God the Son subjected Himself to the humiliation of the flesh and the tortures of the Cross for our sakes. This passage is not about inferiority, but about humility.

The Son of Perdition
John 17:12

> "While I was with them, I was keeping them in Your name which You have given Me; and I guarded them and not one of them perished but the son of perdition, so that the Scripture would be fulfilled."

Critics claim that there is no such Scripture in the Bible to be fulfilled. However, the passage is not quoting a Scripture passage but paraphrasing it.

Consequently, several passages have been suggested. The two primary passages cited most are Psalms 41:9 and 109:6-8.[1514] Some have even suggested an allusion to Psalms 69:26.[1515]

Psalms 41:9 reads, "Even my close friend in whom I trusted, Who ate my bread, Has lifted up his heel against me," but this is likely a reference to one of David's enemies. Nevertheless, it may have a secondary prophetic meaning alluding to the Last Supper wherein Jesus broke bread with Judas. Although John's gospel does not mention the Last Supper, this passage clearly takes place in close proximity to it. Many "Harmonies" places these words after the Lord's Supper while Judas was away meeting with the priests in secret.[1516]

Other scholars believe that the allusion is more apparent in Psalms 69 and 109. Said John Tenney, "A comparison with Peter's statement in Acts 1:20, after Judas's death, suggests that it was probably Psalm 69:26 or Psalms 109:6-8."[1517]

Psalms 69:26 says, "For they have persecuted him whom You Yourself have smitten, and they tell of the pain of those whom You have wounded." However, Psalms 109:6-8 appears the most prophetic of all these passages, saying:

> "Appoint a wicked man over him, and let an accuser stand at his right hand. When he is judged, let him come forth guilty, and let his prayer become sin. Let his days be few; Let another take his office."

Indeed, this very passage is quoted in Acts when the Apostles elect Matthias to replace Judas.

Now when we read the ambiguous remark, "so that the Scripture would be fulfilled" it becomes apparent that Jesus did not specify the passage, because he was probably alluding to multiple passages. This is not uncommon. If there are more than one passages, we may simple allude to the "prophecies of End Times" or something similar. Consequently, the very fact that Jesus did not specify a passage, or author, or make a quotation suggest that this is the same context. All three passages allude to, or specifically prophecy, the events of the betrayal by Judas.

Who Arrested Jesus
John 18:3-12

> "So the [*Roman*] cohort and the commander and the officers of the Jews, arrested Jesus and bound Him, and led Him to Annas first; for he was father-in-law of Caiaphas, who was high priest that year."

The word "Roman" found in the NAS is not found in the Greek. That is why it is placed in italics in the New American Standard. It is assumed, but not stated. It is also refuted by some. Why, they argue, would Roman soldiers take Jesus to the Jewish High Priest? If they had arrested Him, would they not have taken Him to Pilate immediately rather than waiting until the Jewish hierarchy requested? Would Roman soldiers even bother listening to the priests? All these arguments are sound, but do not necessarily lead to the conclusion that the Jewish temple police were the ones making the arrest. How then can we decipher this?

The situation is a political one; both then and now. Those claiming that it was the Jewish Temple police who arrested Jesus are accused of anti-Semitism whereas those who claim it was Romans are said to ignore the majority of the evidence in the gospels. That the Jewish priesthood was involved is obvious and attested by the Jewish authors of Matthew, Mark, and John, so the anti-Semitic argument can be dismissed, but were the Romans involved, and, if so, why? Why would Romans be involved in the politics of the Jewish High Priest, especially, given the animosity between the two groups?

Here I will take the unusual precedent of beginning with my conclusion. With Robert Govett I concur that "Jew and Gentile join to seize Christ."[1518] "In addition to the Roman soldiers, the temple police were also present."[1519] The evidence of this is clear. The "why" is of historical importance in understanding the trial and the politics behind Caiaphas and Pilate's *tet-a-tet*.

That "the arresting party consisted of both Jews and Gentiles"[1520] can be proven by the texts themselves. Luke 22:52 specifically mentions "the chief priests and officers of the temple and elders who had come against Him." Matthew (a Jew) remarks that "a large crowd with swords and clubs, *who came* from the chief priests and elders of the people." (Matthew 26:47; cf. Mark 14:43). Now the Jewish temple police carried clubs, so this fits with Luke's assersion that "officers [police] of the temple" were present. However, who are the ones with the swords? John mentions a captian. That word in Greek is χιλιαπξος (*chilarchos*). A χιλιαπξος (*chilarchos*) is commander of 1000 Roman soldiers.[1521] Consequently, his appearance "favours the view that 'the band' was a 'cohort'"[1522] or "Roman foot" as John Wesley called them.[1523]

Now the real question is why a Roman commander would be present at the night time arrest of a Jewish "heretic." Romans were not concerned with the petty religious squables of the Jewish High Priest, and it is clear that priests and officers of the Temple were present. Jesus was, in fact, taken not to Pilate at first but to the High Priest. Why?

The answer is found quite simply in Roman law. Subjugated nations were allowed to have their own laws, customs, and religion, so long as it did not interfere with Roman rule. Consequently, any arrest made by Jewish temple police had to be observed (but not conducted by) a Roman officer. It is probably that there were but a few Romans present at the arrest of Jesus. They were there officially as "observers" to insure that Roman law was obeyed. However, it was the priestly hierarchy that was behind the arrest as attested by all the gospels and ancient historians, whether Jewish or gentile. How Pilate came to be involved is another interesting political question and one which will be answered in the pages to follow.

Jesus Before the High Priests
John 18:13

> "[They] led Him to Annas first; for he was father-in-law of Caiaphas, who was high priest that year."

I have addressed the various issues regarding Annas and Caiaphas twice before. The first in the section on "Annas or Caiaphas? Matthew 26:57-68 – Mark 14:53-65 – Luke 22:54 – John 18:13-24" and the second under "When Did Christ Appear Before Caiaphas? Luke 22:66 – Matthew 26:57 – Mark 14:53 (cf. John 18:13)." In the first section I discussed the fact that Caiaphas was acting High Priest while Annas was technically the High Priest until his death, even though he was no longer acting in that capacity. As to whether it was Annas or Caiaphas' house, the answer is simple; it was both. John MacArthur notes that "it was common for several generations of a family to live under the same roof."[1524]

The greater issue is the fact that Jewish law would not let Jesus be convicted. It is for that very reason that Caiaphas contrived to try Jesus before Pilate, believing the Romans would crucify Him in order to avoid another riot. This political intrigue proves not only interesting but fits very well with a correct chronological understanding of history. Those who deny that Pilate would have been "intimidated" into crucifying Jesus are deliberating being anachronistic in their history. Pilate had been warned several times by the Emperor that he would not tolerate anymore riots or atrocities against the Jews. The political situation there was tense and tenuous. Pilates butchery early in his reign only antagonized the Jews rather than making them pliable as he had hoped.

The unique and even prophetic thing to take from this is the fact that Jesus was acquitted by the Jewish court, by Herod, and even by Pilate himself (Luke 23:4, 14; John 18:38, 19:6) and yet crucified nevertheless! This is important to remember, for even those who crucified Him recognized His innocence.

John 18:25-27 – See Matthew 26:69-75

"My Kingdom is Not of This World"
John 18:36

> "Jesus answered, 'My kingdom is not of this world. If My kingdom were of this world, then My servants would be fighting so that I would

not be handed over to the Jews; but as it is, My kingdom is not of this realm.'"

This passage counts in the top ten controversial passages in the New Testament, if not the entire Bible. It has been used by various groups, theologies, and sects to justify everything from the medieval church to the denial of a Second Coming of Jesus. How such diverse and opposing views can be extrapolated by the passage is unique, to say the least, and reminiscent of Erasmus' statement that "It is the generally accepted privilege of theologians to stretch the heavens, that is the Scriptures, like tanners with a hide."[1525]

The Views
Most Bible translations read simply "My kingdom is not of this world." Some take a more theological approach rendering it variously. The NIRV says, "My kingdom is not part of this world." The New Living Translation prefers, "My Kingdom is not an earthly kingdom." Each represents a theological slant. In fact, the best translation would be "My kingdom is not from this world."[1526] The Greek word is εκ (*ek*) meaning "from,"[1527] not εν (*en*) meaning "in."[1528]

It is important to understand that there are not two or three different views but many which in one way, fashion, or form, relate to many different theological biases. These biases range from covenant theology to historic dispensationalism to progressive, traditional, or hyper-dispensationalism to medieval Catholicism and even to those who deny Jesus has ever had, or ever will have, a kingdom. Consequently, it is futile to attempt to address the theologies underlying the many interpretations. Instead I prefer simple exegesis; which has actually been criticized by some.

I have broken the theories up into seven different interpretations, although several are offshoots or mergers of one or more of the others. The distinction is made in an attempt to simplify the issue and not to categorize all scholars into a single field. R.C. Sproul, for example, is quoted as an advocate of the *Universal Kingdom View* although he would also fit in with the *Future Kingdom View*. Likewise there is a fineline between the *Church Kingdom View* and the *Spiritual Kingdom View*. Many other examples could be cited. The distinctions sometimes involve certainly theological slants with which I will not deal in detail. My purpose here is exegesis, not theology.

The Spiritual Kingdom View
Undoubtedly one of the most popular views throughout history has been the *Spiritual Kingdom View*. This idea, that the kingdom is a "spiritual kingdom"[1529] as John Wesley said, was to a large extent a reaction against the medieval view, to which it is ironically very similar. Consequently, it is the view held by John Calvin who said that "in these words Christ ackowledges that he is a king"[1530] but a king of a "spiritual" kingdom.[1531] This view is the dominant view of Calvinists such as James Boice.[1532]

Martin Luther explained that Jesus was telling Pilate, "My kingdom does not injury to you"[1533] and that "I do not possess a kingdom in opposition to the emperor."[1534] While true, this does lead to the conclusion that Jesus' kingdom is entirely separate from the material world. This must be assumed.

The Church Kingdom View

Ironically, the dominant Reformed Protestant view above was a reaction against this *Church Kingdom View* which is based on the *same* flawed theology. Remember that while the Holy Roman Empire was clearly an earthly kingdom, the Church technically distinguished between the rule of the Church and the rule of the Emperor.[1535] Consequently, many medieval theologians also subscribed the *Spiritual Kingdom View* but it was Saint Augustine who explicitly made this "spiritual kindgom" synonymous with the church.[1536] He argued that Christ's kingdom was to be viewed as the people who reign in His name.[1537] Thus the irony of ironies is that the "spiritual" kingdom of the Church eventually became the earthly kingdom of the Holy Roman Empire.[1538]

Augustine rejected the Manichean heretics who saw the physical world as inherently evil,[1539] and thus argued that because the "spiritual" kingdom influences the earthly kingdoms, the Church was, for all intensive purposes, that kingdom. Obviously, the fruits of this heresy are apparent from medieval history. It is also a lesson in the dangers of interpreting Scripture theologically, rather than exegetically. The "spiritual" kingdom of Christ had become the earthly Holy Roman Empire by the hands of the Church's most allegorical interpreter!

The Heavenly Kingdom View

Another offshoot of the *Spiritual Kingdom View* is the *Heavenly Kingdom View*. Although technically sound, it often reads too much into the idea of Heaven and the Heavenly kingdom, hence it is heavily influenced by various theologies and their views upon Heaven and what constitutes a "heavenly kingdom."

Eusebius called Christ's kingdom "heavenly and angelic"[1540]; a view echoed by such great scholars as Desiderius Erasmus.[1541] It is also a view espoused by advocates of many of the other views in one form or another. Often associated with the *Spiritual Kingdom View* it is also held by men like H.A. Ironside, a dispensationalist, who maintains that "His kingdom will not be at this earthly order; it will be a heavenly kingdom set up here on earth."[1542]

It should be obvious that while calling Christ's kindgom a "heavenly kingdom" cannot be said to be in error, it is equally obvious that this may mean something entirely different to different people. Consequently, it is not of much help in regard to solid exegesis. Jesus's kingdom may be "heavenly" but how does this relate to the earth upon which Jesus was standing when He made the remark. Was He advocating a "spiritual kingdom" or a "future kingdom" or something else? The question remains.

345

The Future Kingdom View

Along with the *Spiritual Kingdom View* the *Future Kingdom View* has been the most popular over time. It may be simplified as "My kingdom is not now of this world."[1543] It is a future kingdom, not a present earthly kingdom.

Arthur Pink said that Jesus "warned Pilate that there was *another* world."[1544] This is the world to come; the future age. He explained that Jesus "did not say 'My kingdom is not *in* this world,' but 'My kingdom is not *of* this world.'"[1545] It was a kingdom *from* God[1546] in the future.[1547]

This is a perfectly logical possibility. As Jesus did not elaborate, there is room for interpretation, but the Bible clearly speaks of the age to come as a new world, even as we speak of pre-Democratic Europe as the "Old World." Thus the kingdom of Christ "will come later but *now* is not the time. [His] rule is now of a different nature. In this dispensation [Jesus] shall not have the earthly kingdom to which [He is] entitled."[1548]

The Universal Kingdom View

This view is an extension of the *Future Kingdom View* but shares some things in common with the *Heavenly Kingdom View* as well. R.C. Sproul summarizes this view very well when he says, "He did not say that His dominion and authority did not include this world or that His realm was a transcendent Spiritual Neverland. This is the same Jesus who affirmed, 'All authority has been given to Me in Heaven and on earth' (Matthew 28:18) ... Jesus said that He did not plan to establish a kingdom by force."[1549] In other words, Jesus' authority belonged to both heaven and earth (Matthew 28:18); a universal kingdom. Obviously, this ignores the issue of whether or not Jesus' earthly realm is currently in place, and thus the *Universal Kingdom View* is often held by advocates of almost every other position as well. It is not a "stand-alone" view.

It is worth nothing that even when Jesus denied His kingdom was of this world, he was admitting to being a king![1550] The RSV even translates "kingdom" as "kingship." Thus some have argued for "Rule fo God" as a valid translation.[1551] Finally, "it is interesting that Pilate called Jesus 'king' at least four times during the trial and even used that title for the placard he hung on the cross."[1552] Clearly Jesus was a king and never denied it. He had the "authority to reign"[1553] (as Chrysostom said) but was not completely exercising it *for our* sakes. Tertullian summarized it by saying, "though conscious of His own kingdom, He shrank back from being made a king."[1554] Was not yet His time?

This is a sound interpretation, but lacking in itself. As aforementioned, it is not a "stand-alone" theology. It must be coupled with one of the other views to make sense of the context of Jesus' remarks to Pilate.

The Kingdom Source View

The *Kingdom Source View* is another interpretation which is not a "stand-alone" view. It affirms that there is a difference in being *in* this world and being "*of* the world."[1555] Thomas Aquinas correctly stated that Jesus's kingdom "does not have its source from this world."[1556] It is an affirmation that the kingdom "does not derive its origin or its support from earthly forces."[1557]

As aforementioned, "of this world" is a poor translation choice. "The expression εκ του κοσμου, *of this world*, is not synonymous with εν τῳ κοσμῳ, *in this world*."[1558] The Greek word found in John 18:36 is εκ (*ek*) meaning "from,"[1559] not εν (*en*).[1560] John MacArthur, digging deeper into the meaning of εκ (*ek*) says that it literally means "out of the midst of" and thus "its source was not the world system, nor did Jesus derive His authority from any human source."[1561]

Robert Govett best represents this view when he said that "Heaven, not earth, is the *source* of our Lord's future kingdom."[1562] The proper translation should be "My kingdom is not from this world."[1563]

The "Both-And" View

I have generally been critical of *"Both-And" Views* in general, and no less here. However, I have also noted that several of the above views are not "stand-alone" interpretations. It is clear that both the *Universal Kingdom View* and *Kingdom Source View* are true, but only if combined with a correct view on the third point: namely, the relationship of Christ's kingdom to the earthly realm.

This is where many fail. Even many evangelicals fall back on the *Spiritual* or *Church Kingdom View* by saying that Jesus is speaking of a "reign rather than a realm,"[1564] but this is a cop-out. Whatever one is reigning over is necessarily their realm. You cannot have one without another. This is always the tactic of modern "liberal" scholarship. It attempts to ignore problems, rather than analysing them. It pretends that a problem will disappear if you pretend it is not there.

Conclusion

We must accept both the *Universal Kingdom View* and *Kingdom Source View* but only in conjuction with a third aspect which answers the question concerning the relationship of Jesus's kingdom to the earth. Matthew 28:18 states that "All authority has been given to [Jesus] in Heaven and on earth." So we must accept that the "earth" does enter the picture in some way. This leaves the first four views.

The *Spiritual Kingdom View* sounds good and "spiritual" but on a substantive level it is meaningless. Does the spiritual world not relate to the world in which we live? What is a "spiritual kingdom"? When pressed to explain what a "spiritual kingdom" is, they usually answer only that Christ reigns in our hearts. The context of the kingdom comment, however, goes far beyond reigning in people's hearts. The *Spiritual Kingdom View* has become a sort of cop-out for those who do not want to acknowledge any connection between Jesus's kingdom and the world in which we live (either present or future). It is insufficient to deal with the context of Jesus's remarks and offers no hope for the future history of mankind.

This view is held variously by Covenant theologians, many Catholics (as well as Protestants, particularly from the Reformed tradition), and so-called "liberal" theologians. It is a favorite position of amillennialists and preterists (see *Controversies in Revelation*).

The *Church Kingdom View* is an ironic outgrowth of the *Spiritual Kingdom View*. I say ironic because the *Spiritual Kingdom View* attempts to seperate the kingdom of God from any aspect of the material world, but the *Church Kingdom View* transfers the kingdom from "our hearts" to the Church. Because the Church lives in the real world and interacts with it, the *Church Kingdom View* has actually become the most political of all the views. It fails to distinguish between the visible and invisible Church and sees social activism and justice as an extension of Christ's kingdom. Consequently, while often responsible for great political movements its emphasis upon political solutions also led to the Middle Ages.

This view was strongly promoted by Saint Augustine and is popular among many Catholics, Reformed Protestants, social activists, Covenant theologians, and many of the other same groups as support the *Spiritual Kingdom View*. It is thus the ironic cousin of that view and suffers the same problems, but with the additional problem of placing too much faith in political solutions to man's problems. Exegetically, it is very weak.

The *Heavenly Kingdom View* has a degree of truth in it, but is only part of the truth. It seperates Christ's kingdom from the world by pointing out that Jesus's kingdom is from Heaven. The problem with this view is that while its source is Heaven and while Heaven is a *part* of that kingdom, it is not restricted to Heaven. Matthew makes clear that "all authority has been given to [Jesus] in Heaven *and* on earth" (28:18). Thus the *Heavenly Kingdom View* is a half truth which ignores the controversial part of Jesus's statement. Ignoring a controversy does not solve that controversy. This view is variously accepted by theologians of almost all persuasions.

The *Future Kingdom View* best fits the context of the prophecies of the Second Coming. This is why the view is espoused by pre-millennialists and dispensationalists of almost all persuasions (see *Controversies in Revelation*). It also fits the declaration of Jesus after His resurrection in Matthew 28:18. In isolation John 18:36 only says that His kingdom is not "from" this world. "The expression εκ του κοσμου, *of this world*, is not synonymous with εν τω κοσμω, *in this world*."[1565] In other words, it is "not of the same nature as earthly kingdoms."[1566] However, if *all* authority both on Heaven *and* on earth has been given to Jesus (Matthew 28:18) then we cannot ignore the prophecies of His Second Coming. Jesus was not standing before Pilate to lecture him upon prophecy, but to answer his query. Jesus' kingdom was no threat to Pilate or His disciples would have fought for Him. It is no small irony that in the famous novel *Ben Hur*, Ben Hur actually leads and army to liberate Jesus before realizing that Jesus did not wish to be rescued from the cross![1567]

When we consider all factors together, it is clear that Jesus was telling Pilate only that He had no desire to overthrow Rome at that time and that His kingdom was not a worldly kingdom. He was defending Himself against the lies of Caiaphas. Although all agree that Jesus had the *right* to rule, Tertullian noted that He surrendered that right to rule to be subject to the cross.[1568] The purpose of the First Coming is distinct from the Second Coming. Nevertheless, after His resurrection Jesus assured His disciples what He *would* come again (cf. Acts 1:11) and when He comes He will bring His kingdom with Him. No honest reading of the Olivet Discourse, prophecies of the Second Coming, or the book of Revelation can deny this. Jesus' kingdom is *from* Heaven but authority is over *all* creation, not merely Heaven, the Church, or even our hearts, but over all of God's creation.

The Scars in His Hands
John 20:27

> "Then He said to Thomas, 'Reach here with your finger, and see My hands; and reach here your hand and put it into My side; and do not be unbelieving, but believing.'"

Studies into crucifixion have been done to help us understand the suffering which Jesus went through on our account. Although there have been differing opinions as to whether or not Jesus died of a ruptured heart or asphyxiation, or something else, this is not the controversy, for medical examiners can only speculate without a body to examine. No, the controversy, though minor, is over a study conducted in 1932 by Pierre Barbet. In that study Barbet became the first man to suggest that the nails were not driven through Jesus' hands, but through his wrist.[1569]

Now this issue is hardly of paramount importance one way or another, but it has had peripheral impact upon some debates (see Appendix B and E). It has also been seen in recent twentieth century art as well. Oddly, and somewhat ironically, it is most accepted by evangelical Christians who profess to accept the Scriptures alone, but here abandon the words of John 20:27 for suspect medical research which has since been discredited by a number of Christian doctors.

The Evidence
French doctor Barbet's research became vastly influential in the fifties when it was translated into English. It won favor among evangelicals and has been echoed by many doctors since. I discuss the medical implications of the crucifixion under Appendix E and will not debate that here. It is sufficient to say that medical examiners are not in complete agreement, for there is no body

upon which to perform an autopsy. There is, however, evidence from both written testimony (such as the Scriptures) and archaeological evidence from ancient Rome which do provide some information on ancient crucifixions. Here I will discuss only the controversy over the nailing of the hands.

In Barbet's research he argued that the nails must have been driven through the wrist at a spot termed "Destot's space."[1570] According to this theory, the nail pierced through the center of the wrist, away from the main artery.[1571] Despite the widespread acceptance of this theory, it is flawed on several bases. Examining the arguments will show why.

1. Ligament Strengh.

The first reason Barbet rejected the palm area was based on the theory that the ligaments in the palms are not strong enough to support the weight of a person hanging upon a cross.[1572] The mathmatical calculations are too technical and not necessary here. It is sufficient to say that the amount of pull on each arm can be converted into force tension equivalent to weight in pounds.[1573] If the arms were stretched to 90° then the force tension per arm would literally be the equivalent of thousands of pounds of weight![1574] Obviously, this is impossible. When Jesus was hanging on the cross, His arms were more likely somewhere between a 60° and 70° angle. In these cases the pull would be roughly equivalent to the total body weight of Jesus (slightly more for 70°) but for *each* arm. The palms of the hand are sufficient to hold this weight.

Barbet, however, assumed a 75° to 80° angle, and thus more force tension which the palm could not sustain. It is easy to see that depending on what angle one assumes Jesus' arms were stretched too, it would be easy to claim that the hands (or even the wrists) ligaments are not strong enough to offer support. Nevertheless, without proof this is just assumption. Moreover, Barbet made a second mistake in this regard inasmuch as his research was based in part upon crucifying dead corpses.[1575] A corpse naturally is decaying and hence the ligaments will not be as strong as that of a living person. Both of these errors make the argument against the ligament strength of the palms weak.

2. The Shroud of Turin

Since Barbet believed that the palms were not strong enough to support the force tension he argued that a spot, known as "Destot's space" in the wrist, is strong enough to support being suspended upon a cross.[1576] He argued that the nail could be driven through this space without breaking a bone or cutting the main artery. Most, however, are unaware of his evidence for this theory. He actually drew his theory not so much from science or the Bible (although he attempted to support it from both), but from an ancient mystic "prophet" named Saint Brigit[1577] and from the Shroud of Turin which *appears* to show blood stains near the wrist area.

Since I discuss the Shroud of Turin in some depth in Appendix B I will not debate its authenticity or lack thereof here. Rather I will point out that not all are agreed that the Shroud depicts nail holes at the wrist. Frederick Zugibe argues that the nails would have been driven at an angle through the palm and emerging on the back side of the hand near the wrist joint.[1578] The apparent bleeding seen on the Shroud is obviously from the back side of the hand and thus it is unclear and inconclusive whether or not the Shroud depicts a hand or wrist wound. Consequently, the Shroud of Turin does not provide sufficient evidence for one view over another.

 3. History and Archaeology

 Another argument used in this debate is that evidence found recorded by ancient historians and by archaeological discoveries. One of the most famous archaeological discoveries was from a crucified man in Judea which dates to 7 A.D.[1579] This particular crucified body appears at first to support Barbet's thesis until we examine it more closely. Dr. Zugibe pointed out that the bones were scarred from the nail back further toward the arm itself but it was not at Destot's space.[1580] Nonethless, it is clear that this particular man was crucified by nailing his arms, not his hands. This is not unusual since historical records show that there was no one consistent method for crucifixion. Different soldiers in different parts of the empire utilized different methods. Some used nails, some merely tied the arms with ropes. Some used a X shaped cross, others the T cross or the traditional ✝ cross. Some used one nail for both feet, some used two nails for separate feet. Some nailed the hands, some the arms. As a result quoting historians upon a particular method of crucifixion is insufficient to prove that Jesus was crucified using the same method. Jesus *could* have been nailed through the wrists *or* the palms of the hands. Neither can be proven based on extra Biblical historical evidence.

 4. Art and Mystics

 As aforementioned Barbet developed his theory in part based on the mystic prophecies of a Saint Brigit but also by studying ancient art of crucified men. As is the case with history and archaeology, such evidence is not sufficient since crucifixions were not standardized. Art only depicts how a particular person believed it may have been done. Having said that, it is not without merit to point out that the vast overwhelming majority of art through the ages depicted Christ as having been nailed through the palms of the hands, and *not* near the wrist.

The Scripture

Ultimately the only evidence of any real merit in regard to the crucifixion of *Jesus* is that testimony of eyewitnesses recorded in the gospels. As the reader can see above, all other evidence is inconclusive and can be selectively used to support either position.

 The Bible itself uses the word χειρος (*xeiros*). This word is translated as "hand"[1581] : nothing else. It can be used metaphorically to refer to "help" as in a "helping hand"[1582] but every translation, and even all of its related words, refer to "hand." Consider, for example, χειρογραφον (*xeirographon*) meaning "*hand*-writing"[1583] or χειροποιητος (*xeiropoi'atos*) which means "skill," from "made by the *hand*"[1584] or even the word for "vote", χειροτονεω (*xeirotoneo*) which literally means to "stretch out the hand" as we do when voting (when we raise our hands to indicate support).[1585] All relate to the "hand" not the wrist. Many other examples could be cited. The Greek word for wrist is καρπος (*karpos*), not to be confused with the homonym καρπος (*karpos*) meaning "fruit."

The only argument which can be made against this is the fact that in Acts 12:7 the chains of Peter are said to be removed from his "hands" (χειρος). Since chains are tied to the wrists it is apparent that this particular passage uses "hands" in a loose sense of the word. Nevertheless, it does not make sense for the word hands (χειρος) to be used in two different contexts within the same sentence. John 20:27 reads, "Reach here with your finger, and see My hands (χειρας); and reach here your hand (χειρα) and put it into My side." Could χειρος (*xeiros*) seriously be expected to have *two* different meanings in the same sentence? The fact that the word δακτυλον (*daktulon*) is used for finger further substantiates that this is not possible, for χειρος (*xeiros*) is sometimes used in the loose sense of the word to refer to a finger, but here the proper word δακτυλον (*daktulon*) is used to avoid confusion. If Jesus had been nailed through the wrists, would He not have used the proper word for wrists as well?

Annibale Carracci - The Mocking of Christ - 1596

Conclusion

I once held to the belief that the nails were driven through Jesus' wrists. I was wrong. The theory won popular favor among evangelicals and has circulated ever since in contrast to the lasting opinion of literally almost two thousand years. The evidence in favor of the wrists thesis is inconclusive at best. In some cases it is just wrong. Like many theories in science it has become popular like a fad, but will probably fade with time as many theories do.

Would Peter Live to See the Second Coming?
John 21:22

> "Jesus said to him, 'If I want him to remain until I come, what *is that* to you? You follow Me.'"

One of the most unique elements in all of the gospels is this seemingly strange aside by John. He follows up these words with the following statement:

> "Therefore this saying went out among the brethren that that disciple would not die; yet Jesus did not say to him that he would not die, but *only*, 'If I want him to remain until I come, what *is that* to you?'"

Is this a prophecy? Was John *refuting* the prophetic interpretation of Jesus' words? No fewer than a half dozen theories have risen over the centuries in response to this.

The Theories

If the people of John's day were confused and misled by some as to the meaning of this seemingly innocent remark, then it is little wonder that so many different interpretations have been passed down through the centuries. A brief examination of the theories is prudent.

The Second Coming Thesis

It is clear from verse 21:23 that some in John's day believed that this was a prophecy that John would not die. Since Jesus has not come and since John did die, modern day Bible critics have argued that this is a false prophecy.

Obviously, 21:23 was written by John to insure that this false assumption was not accepted as fact. Jesus "did not say to him that he would not die, but *only*, 'If I want him to remain until I come, what *is that* to you?'" These words should be enough to refute this thesis, but Bible critics die hard. They argue that "*If I will*" is "no less admisible, for Jesus could not have presented as possible ... a thing which was impossible."[1586] Of course anything is *possible*, but that has nothing to do with the remark, as John clearly stated. Jesus *could* have returned, but did not. The argument is therefore irrelevant.

Nonetheless, critics argue that Matthew 10:23, 16:28, 24:34, Mark 13:30, and Luke 21:32 all suggest that Jesus would return during the disciples' lifetime. In fact, a close look at these passages says nothing of the sort. Matthew 10:23 is a prophecy to all believers, not just the apostles. Matthew 24:34, Mark 13:30 and Luke 21:32 I have addressed previously, as I have also done with Matthew 16:28. The reader is referred to those debates if he wishes more specifics. It is sufficient to say here that these are suspect interpretations read into the text to prove a thesis they themselves say is false! Thus, to quote Sir Robert Anderson, "the critic attributes his own errors to the Bible, and then precedes to refute them."[1587]

The Rip Van Winkle Thesis
Tertullian affirmed that John "underwent death."[1588] According to Theodore of Mapsuestia John died under Trajan in 106 A.D.[1589] With John's death the hope of those who believed that John would live to see the Second Coming perished, and yet out of that hope arose a legend which Saint Augustine related. In that story John, though buried, is but asleep awaiting the day that he would be awakened before the Second Coming in Last Days.[1590] John, it is said, is like a sort of ancient Rip Van Winkle who will awaken centuries later and will thus be alive when Jesus returns.

Although interesting it is not a view seriously supported by anyone today, but it has led to a similar offshoot which has garnered a few modern supporters. That is the theory that John was actually raptured much like Elijah and will return to the earth before the Second Coming, as described below.

The 2nd Prophet of Revelation 11 Thesis
In the book of Revelation there is a prophecy all-but universally accepted as predicting the coming of two prophets who will preach in Jerusalem before the Second Coming of Christ (see *Controversies in Revelation*). One of these prophets is almost always assumed to be Elijah based on Malachi 4:5 and several other passages. However, the identity of the second is unknown. Speculations, conjectures, and guesses have ranged widely, but the one which is relevant here is a rare view which holds that the second prophet is none other than the apostle John.[1591]

In addition to John 21:22, advocates of this position argue that Revelation 10:22 also predicts John's return when it John is told, "you must prophesy again concerning many peoples and nations and tongues and kings."[1592] Neither passage, however, is particularly clear in this regard.

This view is basically an outgrowth of the ancient "Rip Van Winkle thesis" as I have dubbed it. It is interesting and unique, but not particularly based on solid exegesis. It appeals to our love of mystery, but not to sound exegetical reading. It is better than the previous views, but not convincing.

The Last Apostle to Die Thesis

On a similar line to the Rip Van Winkle thesis is the most plausible argument that Jesus was merely prophesying that John would be the last living apostle. This has the benefit of at least being factual for he did not die until 106 A.D. if Theodore of Mapsuestia is to be believed.[1593] Nevertheless, its strength ends here. Nothing in the passage seems to refer to John's death, and thus it is hard pressed to argue that Jesus was prophesying of his dying last.

The Destruction of Jerusalem Thesis

With the death of John, another view arose. Since John obviously did not live to see the Second Coming, some began to argue that it was a prophecy, not of the Second Coming, but of Christ "coming" for "the destruction of Jerusalem"![1594] This is the accepted view of preterist (those who believe that all the prophecies of the New Testament were fulfilled at the destruction of Jerusalem),[1595] but its first appearance was around the time of Chrysostom who paraphrases this as, "until I come to destroy the Jewish nation."[1596] The view has appealed to anti-semitism as well as preterism, but was also popular in the Middle Ages and even among many Protestant Reformers like John Wesley.[1597]

Despite its seeming, if sporatic, popularity through the ages, it is one of the weakest views. For one thing "the Roman destruction of Jerusalem is never called the coming of Christ,"[1598] nor could it be by any rational system of exegesis or debate. Jesus is coming to save the world, not to destroy it. The pagan Roman armies are in no way synonymous with Christ. The judgment of God may or may not utilize human agents, but never is it referred to as a "Second Coming of Christ."

The Writing of Revelation Thesis

Another view is that "the Lord probably meant that John should be the last of His Apostles to pass from this earth, and that he was the chosen one who should behold in a great vision, as He did in Patmos, the end of the age, and the Lord's return."[1599] Connected to the Last Apostle to Die Thesis stated above, but with the added content of John's composition of Revelation. This, it is argued, makes sense because John *saw* the Second Coming in his vision of Revelation, even though he didn't technically live to see the *actual* Second Coming. Once again, this is speculative, although plausible.

The Non-Prophetic Thesis

The best is the view of the Apostle John himself. His remarks in 21:23 are a "conspicuous attempt to discriminate between truth and exaggerated rumor."[1600] It seems apparent that John did not believe this was a prophecy at all. John explicitly says "Jesus did not say to him that he would not die, but *only,* 'If I want him to remain until I come, what *is that* to you?'" R.C. Sproul summarized this as saying that "what happens to John is none of your concern. I'm not going to give a prophecy about each of you. Just follow Me."[1601]

This is the non-prophetic thesis. It says that Jesus "rebukes Peter's curiousity about John and presses upon him his own duty."[1602] The purpose was not to prophesy anything about John but, as Spurgeon remarked, "we are not to be curious as to what God is going to do with other people."[1603]

This is clearly the best thesis. The quotation begins with the word "if." By definition, this is not a statement of fact, and therefore not a prophecy. It is a conditional clause. It is "*if*," but "they had forgotten the *if*. The future of John was not their business."[1604] "Jesus is not represented as saying that it *is* is will that the Beloved Disciple would survive; but if it *was* His will, that was no concern of Peter's."[1605] Erasmus stated simply that John's life "did not concern Peter."[1606] The remark "was not an answer, but it was a rebuke ... what was to happen to John ... had no bearing on his responsibility."[1607]

Miscelaneous Interpretations

In addition to the views above there are many scattered miscelaneous views from people as would be expected. Saint Jerome, for example, read this simply as "until I come to call him to myself",[1608] thus making it synonymous with death itself! Such an ironic interpretation scarcely makes sense in the context, let alone being able to explain the obvious misunderstanding of people in John's day. Saint Augustine's ambiguous "mystical"[1609] argument having no relation to either apostle is not sufficient either,[1610] especially since he cannot even define to what this "mysticism" refers.

John Nelson Darby argued that Jesus was simply saying that "His ministry makes known the ways of God to the end,"[1611] but this again does not fit the context. Darby also translates the word "tarry" (or "remain" in modern translations) as "abide," implying faithfulness rather than physical life. John Lightfoot responds to this by saying that "if the word carried this meaning here, the misunderstanding in 21$^{.23}$ could not have arisen."[1612] He is right. We cannot ignore the context nor can we ignore John's own response to those who misunderstood what was being said.

Conclusion

The apostle John makes a point of clearing up misconceptions about Jesus' remarks. People love a mystery, and the longevity of John only fed rumors that he would live to see the return of Christ. Nevertheless, "John saw it as important that the point be cleared up ... it was necessary to make it clear that there was no prophecy that he would live right through the age."[1613]

This is the simple but true answer. Some theologians have a problem with Jesus' use of a conditional clause. John Calvin, for example, could not accept such a conditional statement from Jesus because of his own views on predestination. For Calvin there is no "if." He, therefore, argued that this is a mistake by the "ignorance of the transcribers."[1614] He offers no proof that the original text read anything other than what it now reads in *every* text in existence. Calvin's assumptions about predestination are not legitimate grounds for rejected the text. The use of a conditional clause should not be interpreted in a theological manner. It's purpose was to make a point, not to determine the time of Jesus' return or to imply indecision on God's part or to debate the efficacy of predestination. Any attempt to read into the text any of these things is a misrepresentation of what Jesus was saying. He was simply saying, "do your job, and don't worry about my plans for John."

Summary of John's Gospel

John is unique among the gospels. The last of the gospels to be written, it differs from the synoptics for that very reason. John did not write to add to what had already been written but to instruct his disciples in the theology of Christ, rather than focusing on the history which had already been written by Matthew, Mark, and Luke. Obviously there is overlap since all are based on the life of Jesus, but John's gospel bears a distinct theological mark.

John is often called the "apostle of love" and it is no surprise that his gospel is about the love of God. Some of the most famous Bible passages come from John. Its charm is also in its writing style. John wrote in simple language that few honest men could not understand if they so choose. Of course dishonest men distort his words as they do all others, but the simplicity of John and his focus upon Jesus' teachings and deity make this gospel stand out from others.

Appendix A

—

The Synoptic "Problem"

The synoptic gospels get their name from the fact that they often repeat the same events and stories. Synoptic stems from "synonymous" but is this even true? For literally centuries no one applied this term to the first three gospels. The similarities were believed to be solely due to the fact that they were all accounts of the same person and events. In recent centuries, however, critics ask why John's gospel does not repeat many of the same stories as the Synoptics? They argue that the synoptic gospels must have borrowed from each other and/or another common source.

The central problem with this entire debate is that it has the feel of lawyers arguing a case in the best interest of their client whereas the reader should be more like a juror, carefully weighing and examining all the evidence. Where there are similarities the critic argues that there must have been plagiarism, or interdependence. Where there are differences they argue that they cannot even agree! Yet *both* facts, argeements and divergences, can also be used as evidence that they did not rely on one another! What then are we to make of the synoptic gospels and John's uniqueness?

The "Q" Theory

"Q" is short for the German word "quelle" meaning "source."[1615] It represents a hypothetical non-extant (or rather non-existent) "source" for the synoptic gospels. The "Q" Theory is actually divided into at least two different branches. One suggests that all the synoptic gospels borrowed from this alleged "Q" source while the more popular variant argues that Matthew and Luke borrowed from both Mark and "Q."[1616]

On the surface the theory seems plausible and perhaps even acceptable, but some have pointed out that while :

> "There is a value in source criticism, but its danger has been in the readiness of critics to assume that the Bible writers merely copied ideas from other religions and cultures – that Moses cribbed his laws from the Hammurabi Codes, that the Jews borrowed their ceremonies from surrounding nations, that the prophets copied their visions from contemporary culture, and so on."[1617]

Additionally, Brian Edwards points out that such "source criticsm" formed the basis for the false and heretical teaching of the Documentary Hypothesis[1618] (see notes from *Controversies in the Pentateuch*). Does "Q" pose a similar threat to the authenticity and inspiration of the Bible? I will let the reader reach his own conclusions, but not without debating the efficacy of the theory.

It is worth noting that of the literally tens of thousands of manuscripts of the New Testament,[1619] some of which date back to the second century (or earlier – at least two manuscripts were when the apostle John and Mark were still living)[1620] not a *single* solitary copy of any such ancient "Q" document has ever been found. The evidence for this "Q" is indirect at best. References by some of the Church Fathers to "oracles"[1621] and/or other unidentified writings have been appealed to as proof of some ancient "Q" document, but others argue that the "oracles" refer to nothing less than the gospels themselves! There is no proof that such a "Q" document ever even existed, let alone that our gospels were copies or plagerized fragments of it. If "Q" ever did exist then it is most likely nothing more than the notes, or diaries, taken by the apostles themselves during the lifetime of our Savior Christ. Let us, therefore, look at a more plausible theoretical relationship between the synoptic gospels.

Hypothetic Relationships of the Synoptic Gospels

Why are there so many similarities among the synoptic gospels? This is a fair question, especially when we see some places where there is almost a word for word parallel. Nonetheless, the "differences" are equally important. If they were merely copying from one another or from a "Q" document, then the "differences" would be inexplicable. I have addressed many of these in the text of my book and will not repeat them here. Rather I will offer a more plausible argument for the relationship between the gospels.

First, I reject that notion that Mark was the first of the gospels to be written. For one thing, if we ignore the assumption that Matthew "borrowed" from Mark, the evidence for the dating of Mark's gospel points to somewhere between 60 and 68 A.D.[1622] This makes sense for the critics themselves admit that where one of the synoptic gospels stands "against" the other, it is almost always Matthew and Luke who stand "against" Mark, not vice-versa as we would assume if Mark was written first.[1623]

Second, we know that of the four gospels, two were second written by first hand eyewitnesses, and the other two were written by companions of the apostles as second hand accounts passed down from the apostles. Matthew and John were witnesses to the events. Mark and Luke were not. Luke admits to researching his information and there is no danger in assuming that Luke, the third gospel writer, has seen Matthew (and possibly Mark). However, it makes no sense to assume that Mark wrote first (against all evidence to the contrary). Matthew was an eyewitness and based on good evidence his gospel was written first sometime between 40 and 50 A.D.[1624] in Hebrew but later translated (by his own hand) into Greek around 60 A.D.[1625]

360

Third, we must understand that each of the gospels was written for a different audience and a different reason. Matthew, for example, offers extensive quotations from the Hebrew Tanakh (Old Testament) and was originally written in Hebrew (or possibly Aramaic) because it was written for Jews. Mark's gospel would actually be the first gospel written in Greek and for gentiles who were not familiar with the Hebrew Scriptures (Old Testament). Luke was the last of the synoptic gospels written and Luke wrote as a historian.[1626]

Fourth, Mark was a companion of Peter and Paul (cf. Colossians 4:10; Philemon 24; 1 Peter 5:13; 2 Timothy 4:11) and did not have to rely on people he did not know. He had the testimony of eyewitnesses with whom he travelled. Tradition ascribes Mark's gospel as being assisted by Peter himself.[1627]

The evidence for the four presuppositions above is strong (see notes on Matthew, Mark, and Luke for a more detailed defense) and does not rely on the *assumption* of who borrowed from whom. If we take these facts at face value then the relationship between the synoptic gospels becomes much more clear.

Matthew first wrote his gospel in Hebrew before he left for the mission field. The Hebrew gospel was disseminated among the apostles and Hebrews but gentiles did not yet have a Greek copy to read. Mark, the companion of Peter, was familiar with Matthew and consulted with Peter for his own opinions and recollections on the life of Christ. Mark decided to create a Greek gospel directed to gentiles unfamiliar with Judaism. Later Matthew translated his own gospel into the Greek while in the mission field. Finally, Luke, as a historian, fully admits to consulting with others which including reading the gospel of Matthew (and possibly Mark). Thus there is no "Q" document, unless it be the diary or notes of the apostles themselves. There is no mysterious lost gospel and no reason to believe such a thing ever existed. It is the figment of German theologians' imagination and not a single fragment of any such document has ever been found, in contrast to the 24,600 New Testament manuscripts[1628] (5700 ancient Greek copies).[1629]

Harmonization Difficulties

The gospels are all short histories of the life of Jesus. None even pretends to be an exhaustive or comprehensive biography. Consequently, the desire has arisen among many to tie the gospels together into a "harmonization."

Some have objected to harmonization attempts. Most of these criticisms come from the "left" and from critics who deny that the Bible is historical, and therefore object to applying legitimate historical scholarship to the Bible. Ideally a true "harmonization" is when the different accounts are placed side by side in chronological order. This is, in theory, what all true historians hope to do, and it is a noble effort, but it is also to one degree an impossibility. We can agree on a *general* harmonization, but an exact harmonization is not possible since the gospel authors did not always write chronologically, but topically.

One problem is that when the chronologies differ (for some portions of the gospels are sometimes arranged topically, not chronologically) some scholars *assume* that Mark's is the correct chronology based in the "Q" theory discussed above.[1630] This is poor scholarship. If a gospel is topical rather than chronological, it should be apparent based on circumstances within the text. It is poor judgment to simply assume that one author is chronological and another is not without good reason.

Good harmonies look for chronological markers within the text and gauge these against one another. Like Biblical archaeology,[1631] there are two types of markers. The first are absolute markers such as given dates (eg. Luke mentions the fifteenth year of the reign of Tiberius in 3:1). The second are relative markers which can range from the mention of a particular feast to simple relatives of time like "then" and "afterwards." These markers do not give an exact timeline, but do establish that one thing happened before or after another event. We can then compare these markers to those of the other gospels.

Obviously, since much chronology in the gospels uses relative time markers, there will be differences of opinions in regard to parts of Jesus' ministry. This is to be expected. The reader should not be overly concerned with which sermon came first or similar difficulties. The general chronology is solid and apparent in the gospels themselves. Consequently, harmonies are useful, but should not be taken at face value. They can be helpful when the reader is confused about certain events in Jesus' life and they are very beneficial in comparing the gospel's accounts of the same events. However, the serious Bible student should not rely on such harmonies too extensively as they are historical and theological attempts to reconstruct a "proper" timeline, and will be filled with certain assumptions which cannot be proven.

Conclusion

As someone once said, "the Synoptic propblem is no problem at all, and one is tempted to wonder whether it has been invented by those very academics in order to keep themselves in business."[1632] For literally centuries no saw any such "problem" with the synoptic gospels.

The "problem" arose when the deistic and even atheistic German "theologians" of the nineteenth century[1633] began to "deconstruct" (their own choice of words and a synonym for destruction) the Bible and remove what they assumed to be "myth." Like modern day defense lawyers, their objective is not to get the facts and fairly evaluate the evidence but to tear down all eyewitnesses that might harm their client and, having defamed all the evidence against their client, declare with a straight face that *no* evidence exist against their client. In this case, the victim is the Word of God, the criminals are the German "Higher

Critics", and the evidence against their biases is overwhelming. The first three gospels are similar because they are all based on the same *eyewitness* accounts. The influence upon on another was minimal. The greater question is why John's gospel was so different? The ironic answer is that John had read all three previous gospels and did not want to unnecessarily repeat what had already been said.

Appendix B

—

Apologetics and the New Testament

Apologetics is defense of a particular belief or faith. Contrary to propaganda, apologetics relies on facts, reason, and science to defend faith. This is not unusual but common sense, for the false, and dishonest, dichotomy of "fact versus faith" is one created by intellectually dishonest and insecure critics and atheists who are unable to defend their own beliefs. For example, Biblical archaeology is the largest field of archaeology on the planet. Obviously, it is not large because no evidence exist of the Biblical stories, but because there is so much evidence. Faith is whether or not Moses parted the Red Sea. However, it is a *fact* that Moses led the Jews out of Egypt. Even the pagan Egyptian historian Manetho admitted as much.[1634] Bible critics have weaved this false view of faith as something which is contrary to the facts, while presenting their own *interpretations* of selective facts as if they were synonymous with the facts themselves! This is disengenuous and intellectually dishonest.

The Relationship Between Evidence and Faith

As stated above, faith is whether or not Moses parted the Red Sea. Faith is not whether Moses led an exodus, which was confessed even by the Egyptian enemies of the Jews and all others until the rise of modern liberal criticism. Fact and faith are not necessarily mutually exclusive. If they were we would have no need of courts of law. The purpose of a trial by jury is to weigh and evaluate evidence beyond a reasonable doubt (not beyond a shadow of a doubt. Most of the time there is never enough evidence to say "beyond a shadow of a doubt"). This is because 90% of what we see in this world is a mixture of *facts* and the interpretation of those facts, which we believe on *faith*.

Did O.J. Simpson kill his wife? Did Mark Furhman plant to glove in his back yard? The evidence could support either, or *both*. People have formulated their own opinions based on faith in their interpretation of selective facts. The *complete* facts which *are* synonymous with "truth" are rarely known. Only in the most rare of circumstances are facts complete. Instead we have pieces of a jigsaw puzzle, but many of the pieces *are* missing. This is life. This is reality. This is the relationship of evidence and faith. This is what apologetics is about.

Now the theologian might argue that when the author of Hebrew 11:6 said "without faith it is impossible to please" God he was refuting apologetics. In fact, the author of Hebrews cited facts about history to support his faith in the God of Israel. Ultimately faith is trusting in something or someone. If you have faith in your wife, then you trust that she is not out sleeping with strangers. You have no *proof* that she is not, but you trust that she is not, because you have faith in her. In this example, a person's faith may be misplaced, but in our case, our faith is never misplaced in God.

Consider the words of the apostles in Acts 17:3, who we are told were "giving evidence that the Christ had to suffer and rise again from the dead." They did not expect that people would believe simply because they said so but because the evidence showed that Christ was the prophesied Messiah. Indeed, the prophecies themselves were evidence! Consider also the NIV translation of John 14:11 where Jesus said "believe on the evidence of the miracles themselves." Now evidence is not proof. Faith is still required, and this is the faith of which Hebrews 11:6 speaks. How much evidence do we need? How much faith is required? That is the question. Each person may required a different degree of each, but to say that evidence is contrary to faith is both dishonest and disengenuous.

Historical Evidences

Most atheists are honest enough to recognize that Jesus was a historical person, but the internet has helped to popularize a small minority of extreme atheists (or dishonest ones) who deny that Jesus even existed. This despite the fact that there is more historical support for the life and death of Jesus Christ than there is of Julius Caesar! How then can some atheists claim that even the existence of Jesus was myth? They employ the age old defense lawyer tactic of atttacking all the witnesses, Christian and pagan, and then pretending that the evidence (they have none) supports their defendant. I will briefly examine the main non-Christian sources which affirm the existence of Jesus Christ and His death under Pontius Pilate.

Talmud

The Babylonian Talmud is a collection of ancient Jewish writings. It is a sort of compendium of Jewish laws, customs, and history. It also contains several references to Jesus. One refers simply to "Yeshu the Nazarene [who] practised magic and led Israel astray"[1635] which many believe may be a reference to Jesus given that He was falsely accused of socerery and magic by His accusers (cf. Matthew 12:24; Luke 11:15).[1636] Yeshu, of course, is the Hebrew name Jesus. Since Greek has no "y" and no "sh" the "j" and "s" replace them. Also all proper names in Greek must end in a sigma, or "s."

The most clear reference, however, reads, "on the eve of Passover they hanged Yeshu the Nazarene."[1637] Atheists, in typical fashion, just claim that this was another Yeshu the Nazarene, but how many people named Yeshu (Jesus) do they seriously believe were hung on a cross "on the eve of Passover"? Combined with quotations from pagan Roman historians, who affirm that it was

Pontius Pilate who hung Him on a cross during the reign of Tiberius, no serious person can reject that Jesus was a real person.

Josephus

Perhaps the most controversial reference to Jesus outside of Christian sources is that of Josephus, the famous Jewish historian of the first century. A somewhat controversial figure himself (he is sometimes considered a traitor for abandoning the war against Rome and instead becoming a historian under Roman employment), Josephus makes the following comment about Jesus:

> "Now, there was about this time, Jesus, a wise man, if it be lawful to call him a man, for he was a doer of wonderful works, — a teacher of such men as receive the truth with pleasure. He drew over to him both many of the Jews, and many of the Gentiles. He was the Christ; and when Pilate, at the suggestion of the principal men amongst us, had condemned him to the cross, those that loved him at the first did not forsake him for he appeared to them alive again the third day, as the divine prophets had foretold these and ten thousand other wonderful things concerning him; and the tribe of Christians, so named for him, are not extinct at this day."[1638]

Since Josephus was a Jew who did not accept Jesus as Messiah, many critics have claimed that this passage must have been tampered with and added by Christians. Of course, it seems frivolous to claim that such an "addition" would escape the notice of the Jews for all these centuries or to ignore that not a single ancient Greek fragment of Josephus differs from these comments. However, some have pointed out that an Arabic translation does differ. What is interesting is that even the critics admits that while "the pronounced Christian traits of the testimonium" as absent, the majority of the testimony remains albeit with "a noncommittal attitude being taken up."[1639] Consequently, even the sincere critic admits that Josephus identified Jesus as a historical person who was crucified under Pilate and was the founder of the Christian religion.

Despite these facts, some atheists continue to attack the entry in its entirety arguing that Josephus, as a Jew, *would* never have been respectful of Jesus or *should* have said more about Jesus.[1640] Of course it is absurd to argue about what *should* have said, or psychoanalyse what we think he *would* have said. We have what he *did* say, and he acknowledges in every text copy in existence (including the Arabic) that there was a "Jesus ... [whom] Pilate ... had condemned him to the cross ... and the tribe of Christians, so named for him, are not extinct at this day."

Pliny the Younger

Pliny the Younger was a Roman Governor during the reign of Trajan who persecuted Christians. We have in our possession many of Pliny's correspondences with Trajan concerning the persecution of Christians and how to deal with the issue. If tradition is correct, then Saint Mark died in 106 A.D. during these persecutions.[1641] That same year Pliny wrote a letter to Trajan in which he told the emperor that he forced suspected Christians to "curse Christ, which a genuine Christian cannot be induced to do."[1642] The interesting part, however, is that Pliny soon began to wonder why the Christians were being punished at all.[1643] Although he viewed them as a superstitious cult, he affirmed to the emeperor that:

> "They were in the habit of meeting on a certain fixed day before it was light, when they sang in alternate verse a hymn to Christ as to a god, and bound themselves to a solemn oath, not to any wicked deeds, but never to commit any fraud, theft, adultery, never to falsify their word, not to deny a trust when they should be called upon to deliver it up."[1644]

Once again, as is the practice of the critic, it is claimed, without evidence, that this passage is forged by early Christians. Oddly enough, one conspiracy web site also claims that it could be not genuine because no early Christian quotes the passage![1645] Ignoring the fact that these same critics claim Christians forged this passage they never quoted, it is a frivolous argument since since literally no one denied the historical crucifixion of Jesus under Pontius Pilate until the modern era, and it would therefore be ridiculous to assume that the early Christians would be quoting pagan historians to prove what no one denied!

The fact that Bible critics are so intimidated by such a simple passage which in no way affirms the validity of the Christian faith shows their fear. They cannot even admit to the Christian character of the early Christians?

Sutonius
Acts 18:2 mentions that Jews were expelled from Rome for a time under the emperor Claudius (see *Controversies in the Acts and Epistles*). The pagan Roman historian Sutonius also recounts this event, saying that "as the Jews were making constant disturbances at the instigation of Chrestus, he expelled them from Rome."[1646] Later Sutonius briefly addresses the barbaric persecution of Christians under Nero.[1647]

The debate here is whether or not this "Chrestus" is a reference to early Christians who followed Christ or some other Jewish man named "Chrestus." Since I address this in detail in *Controversies in the Acts and Epistles* I will only address the question of whether or not this could be a reference who Jesus who had, by all accounts, already died. It is fully admitted that Sutonius was no expert on Christianity which he considered a "mischievous superstition."[1648] As a result, it is natural that he might have confused a riot started over "Christ" with the actual person of Christ (Chrestus) who he assumed was in Rome at the time. The greater argument here is simply that Sutonius affirms the existence of Christianity in the time of Nero. Critics can only say that his claim that

Christianity was "new" is proof that it had not been around for thirty years![1649] Thus they define "new" how they want to, even though Mormonism (which has been around for two hundred years) is considered a "new religion" this very day. Once again, the atheists go to extremes to deny the very existence of Jesus.

Tacitus

Probably the most famous pagan quotation of the historicity of Jesus is that of Tacitus. Tacitus is the most famous of all ancient pagan Roman historians. In his *Annals* of Roman history he makes the following remark about Nero and the persecution of Christians:

> "To relieve Nero from the infamy of being believed to have ordered the Conflagration, the fire of Rome ... he falsely charged with the guilt, and punished Christians, who were hated for their enormities. Christus, the founder of the name, was put to death by Pontius Pilate, procurator of Judea in the reign of Tiberius: but the pernicious superstition, repressed for a time broke out again, not only through Judea, where the mischief originated, but through the city of Rome also, where all things hideous and shameful from every part of the world find their center and become popular."[1650]

Some have tried so desperately to reject these words that they have argued that "Tacitus had no motive to investigate his information on Christ" and therefore, "he may have accepted information from Christians uncritically."[1651] Such attacks, reminiscent of desperation, are unfounded, especially when we see that these same critics accept almost everything else Tacitus said with unwavering faith. They single out his recognition of the historical personage of Jesus as the writings of a gullible idiot, but accept all else he wrote as well researched and authentic history!

Other critics argue that the words Christian and Christus (Christ) should be rendered Chrestians and Chrestus.[1652] Since Christ has been spelled as such, this might seem possible, but why would the critics make this argument? Because Chrestus was a proper name used among some Greeks and Romans. Thus they argue that this Chrestus was not Jesus Christ, but some other man. Like the argument for Sutonius above, it is frivolous since Tacitus makes clear that this man was "put to death by Pontius Pilate, procurator of Judea in the reign of Tiberius," that he was "the founder" of the religion, that it was diseminated first in Judea, and that it's followers were persecuted by Nero and falsely accused of starting the famous fire in Rome! Now how man people with the name or title Christus or Chrestus can be said to fit all these facts above? One! Jesus Christ.

Finally, it is unlikely that the word Christian was Chrestianos in the first place. If translated from Latin, it would literally mean "the useful ones" but why would Tactius apply such a label to people "he also referred to ... as 'hated for their shameful acts'"?[1653]

Others

In addition to these quotations, there are those of others, such as Lucian, but the most damning are perhaps not what Jewish and pagan witnesses said, but what they did not say. For example, Tertullian, the church father, wrote to the Roman senate in an attempt to defend Christianity against the charges levelled against it. What is interesting is not so much Tertullian's defense, so much as Rome's response.

In Tertullian's *Apology on Behalf of the Christians* he recounts the basic historical facts about Jesus, but in the reply Rome never disputes any of these essential facts![1654] Since Tertullian specifically mentions Pilate and a report Pilate made to Rome, the Roman Senate would have had that report. If it did not exist, they would not have ignored such an obvious lie or error by Tertullian. Instead they seem to accept for granted the basic historical facts about Jesus.[1655] This is why literally no one before the modern age disputed the historicity of the person known as Jesus. What rational person could? The honest historian of antiquity knows that there is more ancient historical evidence of the life of Jesus Christ than there is of Julius Caesar! If the critic disputes this then I urge him to use the *same standards* he applies to Jesus, and apply those to Julius Caesar. Since the critic "deconstructs" all first hand accounts as "biased" we must reject those. All second hand accounts must also be rejected according to "critical standards." Finally, remarks by Roman historians must be scrutinized as forgeries (despite no evidence of such) by later supporters of Julius Caesar. Now I ask the reader : what evidence is left?

No person in human history has had more written about him than Jesus Christ. Even if we reject all the writings made by Christian followers of Christ, there would still be more written about Jesus than almost any other person in human history. Why? Obviously, he was a real person whose influence upon the world is undeniable. The religion which *He* founded (and none other), has helped shape the modern world. From a pagan world of slavery and barbarity, the influence of Christianity slowly changed the world and was the impetus for abolitionism, modern democratic republics, the end of segregation, the establishment of universities, great hospitals, and many other great things in history. The question should not be whether or not the New Testament is based on history, but whether or not Jesus was truly resurrected from the dead.

The Resurrection

The apostle Paul once declared that "if there is no resurrection of the dead, not even Christ has been raised; and if Christ has not been raised, then our preaching is vain, your faith also is vain" (1 Corinthians 15:13-14). Without the resurrection Christianity is a lie. Without the hope of eternal life beyond death, all things in life are futile and all "is vanity and striving after the wind" (Ecclesiastes 2:26). On this we agree with the atheists. We also agree that the resurrection is not something which can be proven beyond a shadow of a doubt, but which requires faith. However, this does not mean that it is contrary to the facts or to evidence. Like most things in life, the evidence does not "speak for itself."[1656] The evidence does, however, speak to us, and the evidence suggest that the resurrection most likely did take place. Faith is required to believe, but evidence suggest that it is a well grounded faith. Unlike the blind faith of the atheist, our faith is founded upon a solid foundation; the resurrection of Christ.

Let us look at the evidence. The facts of the case which no honest scholar can refute are as follows:

1. Before the crucifixion, Jesus' disciples were scattered and afraid. Only John was by His side at the cross.
2. Pilate placed guards at the tomb to insure the body could not be stolen.
3. The body was missing on the third day. The guards were told to keep quiet.
4. The disciples risked death to proclaim the resurrection of Jesus.
5. The disciples spent the rest of their life in virtual poverty spreading the gospel to various nations.
6. All but one disciple was martyred for his faith in the resurrected Jesus.

What do these six points demonstrate? They constitute strong and solid circumstantial evidence for the resurrection. The critic will immediately answer, "Circumstantial? No one can be convinced on circumstantial evidence." In fact, this is not true. While most people are not aware of it, one can be convicted of a crime on circumstantial evidence, provided there is enough of it. Without finding the body (which is in heaven) we can never prove beyond a shadow of a doubt that Jesus was or *was not* resurrected, but the six points when examined carefully provide powerful evidence that He was. A simplified version of this argument has been dubbed by some the "Lunatic, Liar, or Lord" argument. Mocked for its use of circumstantial evidence, it is in reality the only evidence we have in existence today, and it cannot be discarded by those who *wish* to reject the evidence.

Let us examine these evidences separately and see what light they shed on the facts.

1. *Scattered Disciples*

The night of Jesus' trial and the day of His crucifixion is a dark day for His disciples. Of the twelve, one commited suicide (Matthew 27:5), nine are nowhere to be seen (apparently in hiding), and one followed Jesus to the trial but three times denied knowing Jesus out of fear (Matthew 26:58-76). Only John stood by Jesus at the cross (John 19:27).

Such actions are not unusual. Jesus was an innocent man being falsely convicted and executed in a way no criminal had been (scourging and crucifixion were rarely done together – it was usually one or the other). The disciples were scared and afraid for their own lives. The point is not that what they did was cowardly, but that it shows the disciples had believed all was lost. When things were darkest, they fled out of fear.

In short, it is apparent that before the crucifixion of Christ, none of His disciples believed He would be resurrected, and none had hope. They had given up all for lost. Something happened to change their mind.

2. *Guards at the Tomb*

Despite the fact that the disciples did not seem to understand the prophecy of Jesus' resurrection, the the chief priests and the Pharisees understood full well that Jesus had prophesied His resurrection from the dead. As a result they asked Pilate to post guards at the tomb to insure that the body was not removed (Matthew 27:65).

The precautions taken were quite strict. Whether we believe that the guards were Jewish or Roman, the security would be similar. If they were Roman guards then there were a minimum of four guards stationed at the tomb.[1657] Any guard who failed in his duty could be sentenced to death, and the death penalty was the only punishment for sleeping on duty.[1658] There was no leniency. Jewish guards would have been under the employ of Caiaphas who had conspired to kill Jesus and would have had twice as great a reason to protect the tomb than Roman soldiers who had no particular interest in Jewish theological debates. Furthermore, Jewish guard duty was no less strict that Roman. Paul Maier noted that Herod guarded Peter with four squads of soldiers (Acts 12:4) which were composed of four men each, making sixteen guards total.[1659] The Temple police were even "forbidden to sit down or to lean against something when he was on duty."[1660] Finally, the seal itself was the authority of Rome. An ancient inscription found at a similar tomb declared to all grave robbers a dire warning, saying, "the offender [will] be sentenced to capital punishment on charge of violation of sepulchre."[1661]

Last, but not least, the Roman seal was placed over a large stone which sealed the tomb. Such stones are estimated to have weighed between 1½ and 2 tons.[1662] The stones were not simply boulders placed in front of the entrance, but were stone slabs designed to roll into place. The photo on next page is a photograph of one of the sites which some believe could be the tomb of Christ. Whether this is His tomb or not, it is certainly similar to the one Christ would have been buried within. Notice how the stone groove is made. The rock slab would have fit in the groove. The right side of the groove is a lower elevation than the left side, hence gravity would allow the stone to slide into place when the stone was released. The circular edge shows the approximate size of the stone and where it set. Obviously the stone could not be moved without a great deal of help. How then did the women expect to roll the stone away so they could apply more spices (Mark 16:3)? The only way would have been with the help of the Romans who had levers and equipment available to roll the stone uphill along the groove. When the lever was removed (and placed in safe keeping) the stone would roll back into place, and no one could move it.

David Criswell © 2003

3. *The Empty Tomb*

The fact that the tomb was empty was universally accepted even by the enemies of Christianity. It is for this very reason that the high priest circulated the rumor that the disciples stole the body (28:13-15). One lawyer commented on the circumstances. "The absence of any sign that the tomb of Jesus became an object of interest to His contemporaries during the critical weeks and years following the Crucifixion"[1663] serves as proof that the tomb was universally acknowledged to be empty. Were it not, the enemies of Christianity would simply have presented the body. Instead, the rumor that the body was stolen was circulated. It is for this reason that "from the moment the women returned from the Garden, the tomb of Jesus passed, historically, into oblivion."[1664] Even the fifth century anti-Christian work of a hostile Jewish writer, known as the *Teledoth Jeshu*, admits the body could not be found.[1665] The tomb was empty and everyone knew it.

4. *Proclamation Amid Persecution*

As noted in the first point the disciples were scattered at the trial and crucifixion. Josh McDowell even went so far as to call them cowards.[1666] And yet a month later "something came into the lives of these very simple and oridnary people that transformed them [from] broken and shattered party"[1667] to the brave disciples who risked death itself for the proclamation of a risen Jesus. Moreover, one of Christianity's greatest persecutors, Saul, became arguably its most famous adherant, the Apostle Paul! Clearly *something* happened to transform the lives of these men.

5. *Poor Missionaries*

There was no television in ancient Rome. The apostles became missionaries and missionaries were the poorest of men. The apostle Paul worked as a tent-maker to support himself (Acts 18:3) and often stayed with friends when he was visiting a country (1 Corinthians 16:6). The apostles made no profit off of their preaching but lived and died as poor men whose riches lay in heaven. Obviously, they had no ulterior motives.

6. *Martyrdom*

Peter was imprisoned, Steven was stoned to death, James would be thrown down from the Temple to die. Indeed, all but John died martyrs, most meeting cruel tortures before their death. Even John was boiled in oil, although surviving.[1668] Such was the dedication of men who fervently believed in what they were preaching. This begs the question, "How could they have given so much if the resurrection was a lie?" They certainly were not lying, for no man dies for what he knows is a lie. Nor were they simply misguided or mistaken, for neither is worth laying down one's life. Were they insane? Their actions show no hint of mental instability nor do their writings reflect the mind of mentally disturbed individuals, but careful sincere men of devotion.

What do all of these points lead us to believe? Several options have been offered. They are *briefly* as follows:

I. *Wrong Tomb*

One supercilious argument is that the apostles went to the wrong tomb and mistakenly believed that Jesus had been resurrected.[1669] This is easily refuted by the facts above. Even the enemies argeed that the tomb was empty, hence the false rumors spread by the priesthood, not to mention the fact that the apostles were not imbeciles, let alone all eleven of them, plus the women!

II. *Unknown Tomb*

A variant of the above, except that this one assumes the tomb was always empty. Essentially, it argues that rather than the apostles going to the wrong tomb, the guards guarded the wrong tomb![1670] Perhaps even sillier than the "Wrong Tomb theory" this one makes the entire people of ancient Israel, including the Roman govenment, incompetent and stupid, as well as the apostles.

III. "Spiritual" Resurrection

A favorite of liberal theologians is the idea that Jesus' resurrection was "spiritual" and not physical.[1671] This argument ignores the fact that such a "spiritual resurrection" would leave a body behind. It rejects the testimony of the apostles and ignores the fact that the tomb was completely empty.

IV. Legend

This is a favorite among more sincere atheists and agnostics who acknowledge the historical basis of Christianity, but reject the resurrection. They claim that the resurrection was a legend which did not start until two decades or so later.[1672] However, this argument also fails to meet the criteria of logic given the facts above. Even after twenty years, the body would not be disolved or decayed beyond recognition. Bodies in ancient Israel were wrapped and treated with spices. Although by no means mummified, they would not deteriorate completely in only twenty years, hence the Jews would be able to point to the body of Christ. Moreover, it seems beyond credulity to believe that the apostles would believe such a thing twenty years later; let alone that the people would so gullibly accept such an event twenty years after the apostles had been preaching to the contrary! If they had not taught to the contrary, then it is an indication that it was not a late arising legend.

V. Hallucination

Ranging from drugs to mental disorders, some have argued that the apostles merely hallucinated the resurrection and empty tomb.[1673] Once again, this ignores that all agreed the tomb was empty. Unless we are expected to believe that the entire Roman and Jewish population and government of Jerusalem were drinking laced water then the idea is preposterous. Moreover, if the water had been laced, why would they all have the *same* hallucination?

VI. Body Stolen
a. By Disciples

That the body was stolen by the disciples was the story circulated by the priesthood (28:13-15), but it fails on numerous levels. I have already pointed out the impossibility of peasants overpowering armed guards, breaking the seal, and rolling away the stone without the proper equipment which only the authorities would have had (kept and guarded separately). Moreover, the motive for such a theft is nullified by the fact that the disciples lived in poverty, were persecuted, and gave their lives for their beliefs. No one does this for something they know is a lie.

b. By Authorities

This strange offshoot suggest that the authorities moved the body to prevent any such theft.[1674] Logically, this makes no sense. Would they not have presented the body as proof it was not resurrected? Would they have guarded an empty tomb for no reason? What possible motive would the authorities have to remove a body, knowing the disciples would claim it was resurrected! More than this, we are to believe that the authorities never bothered to refute the disciples' claims except to say that the disciples stole the body? Such an argument makes no logical sense at all and shows the desperation of the Bible critic.

VII. Sleeping
a. Passover Plot

One of the most famous theories, first presented in the 1965, was Hugh Schoenfield's "Passover Plot" in which he alleges that Jesus staged the events in order to present Himself as the Messiah.[1675] In this outlandish theory, Jesus faked His own death! The absurdity of this argument is far beyond the scope of this book, but can be summarized briefly by pointing out that faking a death on the cross, surviving the cross in the first place, fooling the Roman soldiers, not suffocating in the shroud and tomb, like Houdini getting out of the shroud, and escaping a tomb from the *inside* (it would be harder to move the stone from the inside than the outside!) are beyond logic. It shows the extremes to which some will go to deny the obvious. It may take faith to believe in the resurrection but it takes far greater faith to believe in such absurdities designed solely to escape the fact that Jesus was resurrected from the dead.[1676]

b. Misdiagnosed

An offshoot of the "Passover Plot" argues that Jesus did not deliberately fake His death, but that he had passed out and was mistakenly believed to have been dead.[1677] This theory is not plausible either. It still leaves the incomprehensible questions about how the soldier's could have been mistaken, how He could have lived through the crucifixion and spear in the side, how He could breath under a shroud for 72 hours, how He would escape the shroud, and how He could move the stone. This theory offers no real improvement over its illegitimate father; "The Passover Plot."

These have sometimes been simplified into the "Lunatic, Liar, or Lord" argument. In other words, all of these theories boil down to one of three issues. If Jesus or the disciples were insane, why did they not act insane. Their actions were not those of lunatics or madmen but of humanitarians who gave their lives for Jesus and for others. If they were liars, then why die for a lie? Why live your life in poverty travelling the world as missionaries for a lie? Lies are selfish and imply selfish motives, and yet the lives and deaths of both Jesus and the disciples shows a selflessness, not a selfish motivation. The only alternative left is that Jesus was Lord and that He was truly literally raised from the dead.

The Shroud of Turin

One of the most controversial of all artifacts from Biblical studies is the Shroud of Turin; not because atheists and Bible critics doubt its authenticity but because Christians themselves are divided over the issue despite its ability to confound twenty-first century scientists to this very day. Indeed, without the aid of computer technology no one has ever been able to duplicate the shroud, and yet many continue to maintain that it is a medieval forgery.

How is such a thing possible? Is the shroud legitimate? It is a medieval artifact? Why has no one been able to settle this issue? And why are Protestants so reluctant to admit its authenticity?

I will divide the debate into two sections : science and the Bible. Together, we should be able to provide and answer to this difficult question.

Science

Bible critics will state first and foremost that the Carbon dating of the artifact proves it is a medieval forgery dating to sometime between 1260-1390 A.D.[1678] I personally remember when the carbon dating news first hit the newspaper. I also remember the retractions published on the back page, hidden away days following the front page barrage. All archeologists know that for any artifact to be carbon dated it cannot be exposed to the open environment for any duration of time.[1679] The entire precept and principle of carbon dating requires that said artifact have been removed from the open envioronment, and hence contamination, for hundreds of years, yet here is an artifact openly admitted to have been worshipped and exposed to the enviornment for hundreds of years! Moreover, dating the artifact to the Middle Ages does not settle the scientific questions which this shroud poses; questions which befuddle scientists to this very day. Let us look at the major scientific tests which the shroud has endured.

Carbon Dating

As aforementioned, it is well known that some scientists using small samples and a special carbon dating technique called the accelerator mass spectrometry dated the shroud to 1260-1390 A.D.[1680] However, what is not as well known is that fact there are a myriad of problems with the samples, testing, and dating of the shroud.

First, there was more than one carbon dating attempt on the shroud. The only one which dated to the late Middle Ages is the also the only one hailed by the media, but at least one other carbon date yield a date of around 200 A.D.[1681]

Second, and more importantly, the most basic archaeology textbooks make it clear that no sample should be exposed to the enviornment for any duration of time. For example, the secular archaeology textbook *Archaeology: Theories, Methods, & Practice* states that for carbon dating to take place accurately without contamination:

> "All radiocarbon samples should be sealed within a clean container such as a plastic bag *at the time of recovery* ... cardboard labels inside can be a major source of contamination. The container should be placed inside another; one plastic bag, well sealed, inside another bag separately sealed can be a sound procedure for most materials ... wherever possible exclude any modern carbon, such as paper, which can be disastrous ... containers should be stored in the dark" (emphasis added).[1682]

Obviously *none* of these precautions were taken with the shroud which *all* admit has been exposed to the outside enviornment for hundreds of years. The purpose of all these precautions is to prevent contamination which can make carbon dating completely useless. "Margin of errors" in carbon dating apply only when there is little or no contamination. When contamination has occurred, the carbon date is of no value whatsoever. A brief history of the shroud reveals that it had been through a fire in 1532, was doused with water (a contaminate source), kept in a damp dungeon for many years, and was "man-handled many times through the ages. Since sweat consists of a lot of proteins which in turn contain carbon-12 and carbon-14, more carbon-14 invariably would make its carbon-14 date appear younger."[1683]

Moreover, after the fire which damaged the shroud patches of medieval cloth were used to make repairs to the damaged areas on the shroud. The history of the shroud is a history of hundreds of years of contamination. One only has to read the above quoted archaeology textbook's procedure for obtaining uncontaminated samples to see how absurd it is to claim that the shroud is not severely contaminated.

In short, although the carbon date favors the idea of a medieval fraud, the large amount of contamination renders the results completely invalid. The 130 year "margin of error" noted by the labratories assumed no contaminates, although those same labratories admitted to at least 20% contamination in their tests.[1684] Thus, the carbon dates are not useful in dating an artifact which has been exposed to the open enviornment for *at least* seven hundred years.

Finally, the proof that the carbon dates is in error due to contamination is the fact that recent research has found that the Templar Knights hid the shroud from the Muslims and from Saladin (1174–1193 A.D.) in the times of the Crusades.[1685] This means that the origin of the shroud could not possibly be later than 1100 A.D., 160-280 years *before* the date suggested by these fallacious carbon samples. The carbon date must be rejected as contaminated and egregiously false.

Negative Photography

The most interesting thing about the Shroud of Turin is that the image is not a regular picture or painting, as one would expect, but a negative image similar to modern film negatives, but these were not invented or known until 1822 when Jean Niepce presented the first photograph.[1686] For the young reader, used to digital cameras, I will briefly explain the older photographic technique. In simple terms, a thin liquid film is placed on a paper and enclosed in the camera without exposure to light. When the camera shutter opens for a fraction of a second, light enters the camera and the liquid film takes on the opposite (or negative) color of what the camera sees. These negatives are then converted to pictures by reversing the negatives and restoring the correct colors. In other words, black becomes white, and white becomes black.

What is astounding is that no one knew about this in the Middle Ages, or antiquity. Modern photography was discovered in the early 1800s, so if the image is a medieval forgery how did the forger even know about photographic negatives, let alone make one?

Since extensive examination and testing has revealed no ink or water colors or anything else used in painting (see *Iron Oxide Testing* below)[1687] scientists have continued to speculate to this very day *how* the image was made. The various theories presented are beyond the scope of a simple appendix, but it is sufficient to say that if we exclude modern computer technology (used to make replica of the shroud today) then of all the naturalistic theories presented, only one seems to have any support. That is the theory that the image could be made by an "extremely brief (in milliseconds) burst of radiant energy."[1688] Obviously, no medieval forger would be capable of doing this, nor have any modern scientists been able to duplicate this method. One can only imagine, however, what radiant energy a resurrection might produce.

3-D VP-8 Imaging

Perhaps the most fascinating scientific test produced on the shroud is something called the VP-8 Imaging. What this test does is to measure the "cloth to body distance"[1689] and to attempt to construct a three dimensional image from these measurement. What is fascinating, however, is the fact that, in the words of a member of the Shroud of Turin Research Project who conducted the tests, "the three dimensional attributes of the VP-8 shroud images cannot be reproduced by any artistic endeavor."[1690] To attempt to do so results in a distorted picture.

Once again, it is far beyond the scope of a short appendix to explain the technicalities of the tests, but its results are undeniable. This artifact alone defies all artistic and/or photographic endeavors. Once again, the only possible explanation seems to be that the image was produced by a short burst of radiant energy. This energy then distributed a different level of intensity based on the distance of a particular part of the body to the shroud. This intensity creates the "cloth to body distance"[1691] which alone allows the VP-8 3-D image modeling to construct a 3-D computer model.[1692] All other 3-D modeling must use different methods to supply assumed information not available on the actual painting/picture/photograph. Here, however, the intensity of the image supplied this information without added interpolation. In short, no artistic endeavor nor photograph made to this very day can replicate the shroud's results found in the VP-8 imaging. The tests again strongly support the fact that the shroud was not a forgery or artistic endeavor but was formed when something, somehow, created a burst of radiant energy. Perhaps something like a resurrection from the dead.

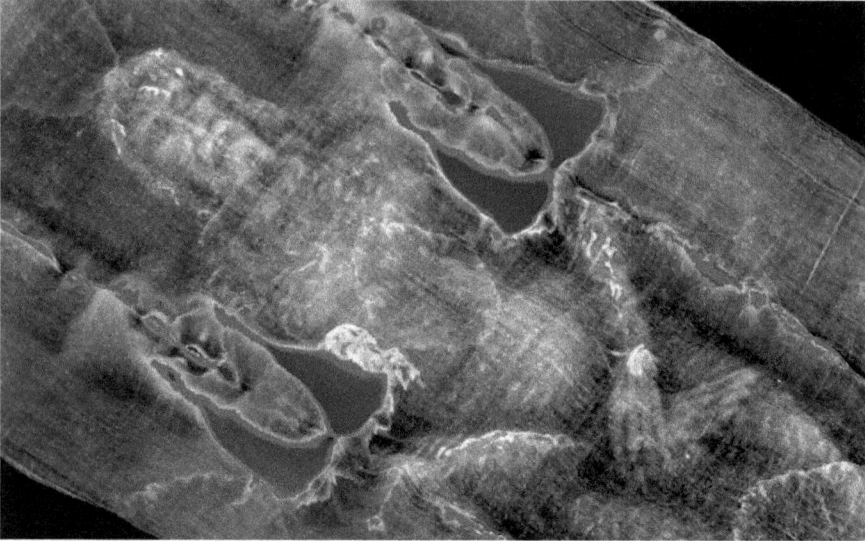

Used with permission – http://thierrycastex.blogspot.fr/ – Thierry CASTEX – 3D Processing © 2012

Iron Oxide Testing

If the shroud was made by human hands then it would have to have some form of ink, water colors, or some other kind of substance that would leave an image. Iron oxide is found in a kind of paint, so when one researcher suggested he had found iron oxide on the shroud X-Ray fluorescence tests were done to either substantiate or nullify this opinion.[1693] Without getting technical, iron is found in hemoglobin and hence, blood. The only way to know if this was trace iron from blood or from paint was to do a chemical analysis of the shroud. After prolonged studies it was agreed that there was no iron oxide from paint. There were, however, trace amounts of various chemicals found in blood. This led to the next question, and the next series of tests. Was it actual trace amounts of blood on the shroud?[1694]

380

Blood Samples

How can blood survive for two thousand years? A simple question with a simple answer. As blood decays, it leaves behind trace amounts of chemicals and elements which compose blood. Thousands of years will decay the chemical composition, but not trace amounts of the chemicals themselves. In science things break down to their basic elements, but the elements never disappear. So it is true with blood.

A grand total of thirteen different tests were run to determine whether or not there were trace elements of blood. Without describing these technical techniques, I will merely list them here with their results. The techniques and results listed by the Shroud of Turin Research Project were "X-ray fluorescence test, indicative reflection spectra, indicative microspectrophotometric transmission spectra, chemical generation of characteristic porphyrin fluorescence, positive hemochromogen tests, positive cyanomethemoglobin tests, prositive detection of bile pigments, positive demonstration of protein, positive indication of albumin, protease tests leaving no residue, positive immunological test for human albumin, microscopic appearance as compared with appropriate controls, and forensic judgment of the appearance of the various wound and blood marks."[1695]

The results of these tests were that there was, in fact, trace elements of blood on the shroud, but only on those sections of the shroud where blood marks appeared. The iron traces were from hemoglobin. Other trace elements also confirmed that the splotches contained traces of real blood, and yet the image itself was not created by blood.

Pollen Samples

Pollen settles on cloth. It is natural that trace pollen samples would be on the cloth, and would give us a clue to where the shroud has been. This is because pollen, like plants, are sometimes indigenous to certain areas. A total of fifty-eight pollen samples were tested and found on the shroud. Of those fifty-eight samples forty-five are found in Israel.[1696] The second largest sampling is twenty-five which can be found in the Middle East and in Turin,[1697] after which the shroud is named. Moreover, "only seventeen of the fifty-eight species grew in France or Italy. Practically all the rest were of non-European origin and in the Jerusalem area."[1698] Even more startling is that many of the Jerusalem species are now extinct and are only known because "these pollens have been found embedded as microfossils in the mud at the bottom of the Dead Sea and Lake Gennesareth by Israeli scientists."[1699]

In short, pollen samples demonstrate conclusively that the shroud of Turin was in Israel for a significant portion of its life. Furthermore, many of the pollen species are now extinct, meaning that the shroud resided in Israel before these species became extinct! Although we do not exactly when the pollen species became extinct, we do know that after the first Crusade Muslim warriors began to burn forest and defoliate Palestine in order to gain a strategic advantage over the Crusader forces.[1700]   This was the twelfth century, at least a hundred years before critics claim the shroud was made.   Also given that the Catholic church had lost control of Palestine long before the thirteenth century it is only logical to assume that the shroud resided in Israel centuries beforehand, maybe even over a thousand years earlier.

Eye Coin Analysis

The human eye cannot even perceive the image of the coins on the shroud, which covered Jesus' eyes, but a careful examination of the cloth does show a very feint image of coins. "Using a NASA-developed image analyzer" scientists could enhance the image and identify the coins "as leptons, struck in Israel in AD 29."[1701]   How a medieval forger would even know what a lepton looked like is as great a mystery as the shroud.   Consequently, this is more strong evidence that the shroud dates to sometime after 29 A.D.[1702]

Medical Analysis

Artist are just that; artist. Medical doctors look at things that normal people simply do not. For example, who would look at the shroud and notice that the head appears to be slightly pressed forward, as if the chin has dropped down to the neck. The answer is, a mortician. Dr. Frederick Zugibe believes that this is indicative of rigor mortis.[1703]   Some of the details of medical examiners' opinions on the shroud will be discussed under the Biblical sections, but it worth noting here that everything from the blood splotches on the hand to the scourge marks to orientation of the feet correspond not to an artistic rendering, but to what morticians would expect to see from a body wrapped and buried after a crucifixion.[1704]

Scientific Test	Evidence for Authenticity	Evidence Against Authenticity
Carbon dating		✓
Negative Image	✓	
3D Imaging Technology	✓	
Iron Oxide	✓	
Blood Samples	✓	
Pollen Samples	✓	
Eye Coin Analysis	✓	
Medical Analysis	✓	

The reader will immediately notice that of the eight major tests produced on the cloth only one (carbon dating) supports a medieval forgery and yet, despite its obvious failure to account for hundreds of years of contamination, it is usually the only test with which the general public is aware. The Hollywood owned major media outlets obviously have their own political agenda in mind. Nonetheless, the weight of evidence is strongly against any man, from *any* era, creating this shroud by artistic endeavors. The only method which scientists have been able to speculate might have created such a shroud (without modern computers – which still don't pass all the tests above) is by a short burst of radiant energy. Thus, science strongly supports that this could be part of the shroud which covered Jesus when He was resurrected from the dead.

The Bible
Protestant evangelicals, such as myself, will be quick to say that the only thing which matters is what the Bible says. Some have argued that the Bible *excludes* the shroud from being authentic. If I have a prejudice, this would be it, but does the Bible truly exclude the shroud?

Perhaps it is best to start by trying to understand the difference in the Protestant and Catholic perspective, for many assume that all Christians favor the shroud. This is far from the truth. Most Catholics favor the shroud but too many Protestants have an inherent bias *against* the shroud. Why? The first part of the answer is simply history. Protestants have an aversion to relics of any kind, which we often associate with idolatry. This is natural since the Middle Ages was a time when people were so obssessed with relics that people believed in relics such as the skull of John the Baptist and even a jar of the "Milk of the Virgin"![1705] The second reason is a better reason. It is simply the fact that we are reluctant to accept anything related to Jesus that does not come from, or is not in accordance with, the Bible. If the shroud is not medival then the first objection is nullified. The second objection is more important and must be examined before we can make a determination on the authenticity of the shroud.

Burial Shrouds in Ancient Israel
There are two main Biblical arguments made against the shroud. The first is that according old Israel law "no individual could be buried in fewer than three separate garments."[1706] John 20:6 is hailed as proof of this, as it mentions two separate linen cloths, neatly folded. Of the course the simple answer to this is that the Shroud of Turin was not the only linen cloth. The fact that the linens were not removed from the tomb, but left in place, also supports the idea that a follower of Jesus might well have taken the cloth and kept it. Why would they leave it in the tomb? This is especially true if the resurrection had left an image upon the shroud.

In short, there was certainly more than one cloth used to bury Jesus. This is not in doubt. The shroud is alleged to be only the larger cloth that covered the entire body. In fact, Zugibe believes the image on the shroud demonstrates that the hands and feet were bound.[1707] We can safely conclude then that there were probably at least five strips of linen used; one to wrap the head (John 20:7), one to wrap the feet (seen from the orientation of the feet on the shroud image), one to wrap the arms, one to wrap his waist, and one larger linen which covered the length of the entire body. Could other strips have also been used? Perhaps, but the Jews did not mummify their bodies, and we know that Jesus had to be buried within three hours because of the coming Sabbath, so five strips seems to be the logical answer and in keeping with the belief that the shroud is the larger body covering.

Was the Body Cleaned? A Morticians' Answer

A greater problem could be the assumption that the blood on the shroud is not in keeping with the tradition which required the washing of the body before burial (John 19:40).[1708] Because there are clear blood splotches seen on the shroud it is suggested that the body could not have been washed and one conservative author, whom I respect greatly, makes a straw man argument indicating that the shroud, if real, would have been the shroud used to wrap the body at the cross, and then refutes this false assumption by saying that "we have no reason to assume that reused this single cloth."[1709] Of course they did not, nor does anyone make such a claim. In fact, all agree that the body *was* washed before burial. So why are they blood splotches on the cross?

First we must be clear that they had less than three hours to wash, wrap, and bury Jesus in accordance with Jewish laws and customs. It is clear that Jesus had to be buried before sundown or it would be a violation of the Sabbath law. Some even believe that the women were brining spices to the tomb on Sunday (Luke 24:1) because they did not have time to do all the proper burial customs before Sabbath. Although some spices were used before burial (John 19:40) Luke's gospel makes it clear that after the burial "they returned and prepared spices and perfumes. And on the Sabbath they rested according to the commandment. But on the first day of the week, at early dawn, they came to the tomb bringing the spices which they had prepared" (Luke 23:56-24:1). Further evidence for the hurried burial is found in John 19:42 which states that "because of the Jewish day of preparation, since the tomb was nearby, they laid Jesus there." In other words, they did not have time to transport the body to a tomb further away.

Now I have already said that the body was washed. Why then is there a concern over the time of burial? Because the blood splotches are consistent with minimal bleeding of a corpse *after* a body has been washed but *before* the entire blood in the body had time to clot within the veins.[1710] In simple terms, if the body had been wrapped without washing then the entire body would have been covered in blood. Obviously the body was washed, but in washing the body, the clotted blood or scabs would be removed as well. On a dead body the blood would not naturally flow without circulation, but because the blood in the veins did not yet have time to clot or dry up, the moving of the body after wrapping would cause minimal blood flow and seepage, resulting in the blood splotches on the shroud.[1711]

Once again, the argument that the Bible precludes any blood from appearing on the shroud is invalid. It is clear both from the Bible and from the Shroud of Turin that the body had been washed *and* buried within three hours of Jesus' death on the cross.

Conclusion

The Shroud of Turin has confounded twenty-first century scientists to this very day. If it is a medieval forgery then the forger was a genius beyond human imagition, familiar with modern camera photography and negatives, scientific knowledge of plants and blood samples, and an astute historian able to replicate crucifixion victims with precision. The procedure with which this "forger" created this artifact is still unknown to this very day, unless it be some scientific technique utilizing radiant energy. Needless to say, this forger went to extra-ordinary lengths to forge a relic in a day when people readily believed in relics such as the Skull of John the Baptist and a jar carrying the "Milk of the Virgin."

As a Protestant evangelical I am naturally skeptical of such relics. Like many Protestants my bias is *against* the authenticity of the shroud. Nevertheless, there is nothing in the Bible which would invalidate this, nor is there any good reason to believe that the larger shroud, as opposed to the smaller wrappings, would not have been kept by family members and passed down through the generations. The shroud is another piece of evidence that Jesus was indeed raised from the dead. It is good to make sure that we are not touting evidence which will someday be discredited (thereby discrediting us), but nor should we merely mimic Bible critics who will never accept any evidence, no matter how great. I am of the opinion that the shroud is real, and until scientists can explain how a medieval forger could have created such a relic which passes all the scientific tests listed above, I will continue to hold that position.

Conclusion

No sincere critic can deny that the New Testament is based on historic facts. Until relatively recently in history all have admitted to the fundamental historic truths of Christianity including the enemies of Christ. Apologetics is the defense of the faith. It is not at odds with faith as some claim. Indeed, some Calvinists have argued that apologetics is a demonstration of a lack of faith and contrary to Christianity. These hyper-Calvinists reject that intellect is truly an obstacle to the faith, and in one respect they are correct. Intellect is sometimes a mask against faith, but not an obstacle. True intellect supports the truth of the gospel, and this is why apologetics is perfectly consistent with Christian evangelism and the Great Commission.

Apologetics does not need to rely on archaeology or science, although these are useful. History too is an apologetic. The great Sir Robert Anderson once commented that the testimony of the martyrs itself is a testament.[1712] Indeed, the deist dictator Napoleon once commented that his belief in God arose from the history of the Jews. Their very survival and history serves as proof of God's existence. Agnosticism claims to know nothing about God, but history and nature both cry out about the nature of God. Romans says, " For since the creation of the world His invisible attributes, His eternal power and divine nature, have been clearly seen, being understood through what has been made, so that they are without excuse" (1:20). Sir Anderson noted that "agnostics assume a double incompetence – the incompetence not only of man to know God, but of God to make Himself known."[1713] Yet God has made Himself known, through history and through nature, but most clearly through the Scriptures and specifically, through Jesus Christ our Lord.

Appendix C

—

The Authenticity of the New Testament

Having established that the New Testament is based on historical fact, the next logical question is whether or not the New Testament is a faithful transmission of the followers of Jesus or whether or not they are either late forgeries or alterations of the original texts.

Having addressed the issue of authenticity in the introduction of each gospel it is not my intention to repeat what all but the most liberal or atheistic of critics deny; that the disciples of Christ were indeed the authors of the gospels which bear their name. Rather I will discuss whether or not the original writings of the authors have been changed or altered and the formation of the Canon of the New Testament.

The Canon of the New Testament

The internet and books like *The DaVinci Code* have served to promote some absurd myths about the Bible and Christianity. One of those myths is the idea that the Bible somehow relates to the time of Constantine the Great. In fact, nothing could be further from the truth. The Bible had long been established, accepted, and canonized before Constantine was ever born. In fact, "the Council of Nicea did not address the issue of canonicity"[1714] for that issue had long been settled.

The "canon" is a term used to represent those books which have been recognized as the authoritative Word of God. Other books, while they may be instructive, useful, or historical, are not considered canon. Only those books in the canon are considered to be the infallible Word of God. So the question is, how did the canon come to be? As aforementioned, the Council of Nicea had *nothing* to do with the canon, because it was accepted centuries earlier. Let us look at the debate and the facts.

The Acceptance of the Canon

The primary questions concerning the canon are "when" and "how." We will begin with "when." As already mentioned, some attempt to argue that the canon was never settled until the time of Constantine. Even some evangelical publishers have blindly published books by "scholars" who argue for a late canon date based on suspect arguments. Lee Martin McDonald, for example, sites ancient authors who may have rejected part of the canon (even as some do today) or perhaps even accepted other books (even as the Mormons and others do today).[1715] Furthermore, if a church father quoted from an apocryphal book

387

(see below) he *assumes* that the church father accepted it as canon.[1716]   He nowhere proves this assumption.   Others argue that it was the Council of Laodicea in 363 A.D. which settled the canon.[1717]

Now some might wonder how this is a controversy at all.   Either the books are in the Bible or they are not! Right? Wrong. "Books" was we know them today did not exist in antiquity.   They used scrolls which were kept separate. A scroll could obviously be only so large. No one denies that all twenty-seven books of the New Testament existed in the early church, but so did many other books. Since "books," in the traditional sense of the word, did not exist until Constantine's time, it is easy for some to dishonestly argue that the canon did not exist until Constantine's time. However, the facts invalidates these claims.

As early as the second century we have a list of the canonical books. The discovery of the Muratorian canon in the nineteenth century demonstrated that the canon had most likely been accepted by the time of its composition, circa 170 A.D.[1718] Nevertheless, there are some problems with the Muratorian canon. For one thing the manuscript is damaged and so the first two books of the canon are not visible. However, the gospel of Luke is explicitly said to be the third gospel, indicating that Matthew and Mark were the first two gospels.[1719] Additionally, Hebrews, James, 1 and 2 Peter, and 3 John appear to be omitted.[1720] Still, some believe that they may have been in the document; its fragmentary nature being evidence that the books *could* have been listed.[1721] Alternately, the Muratorian canon includes the Wisdom of Solomon (an apocryphal Old Testament book) as among the canon of the New Testament.[1722] Consequently, some critics use these discrepancies as evidence that the canon was not settled.

The irony of the critics is their inate ability to contradict themselves. Consider that one author admits that there was "wide agreement"[1723] on the Scriptures under Diocletian's persecutions, but then goes on to claim that the canon dates to the time of Eusebius[1724] (a contemporary of Constantine). Of course, how could he deny that the Scriptures were not already "widely" agreed upon, for the emperor Diocletian not only persecuted Christians but actively sought to find and destroy "all copies of the Bible."[1725] To this end Christians were tortured until they revealed where their copies were hidden. Obviously, one cannot search out and destroy copies of the Scriptures if there was no Biblical canon!

The fact is that from earliest time the church fathers refer to the "Scripture"[1726] of New Testament authors. All twenty-seven books of the New Testament are cited *as* Scritpure by one or more of the fathers. The following chart shows all the major Uncials (complete "books" of the Bible, as opposed to individual scrolls popular in the early days of Christianity), apostolic fathers, and ante-Nicean church fathers (those who preceded Constantine and the Council of Nicea) who quote a specific book *as* Scripture. It is noteworthy that just because a church father did not quote a book does not mean that the book was not a part of Scripture. I, for example, did not quote from Titus in this book, and yet it is a part of Scripture. Nevertheless, the citations should prove that there was uniformity upon the canon from the earliest of times. I have also included those apocryphal books which are not a part of Scripture, but appear to be quoted as such from a few fathers (this will be explained in a section below). A more detailed explanation of the chart and its implications will follow.

Biblical Book	Primary Uncials	Books Quoted as Scripture Apostpolic Fathers	Ante-Nicean Church Fathers
Matthew	ℵ / A / B / C / D	Cl / Ba / Δ / Ig P / Ir / CA / M	J / Hp / Cy / N / M / T / L Mu
Mark	ℵ / A / B / C / D	Cl / Δ / Ig / P / Ir CA / M	J / Hp / Cy / N / M / T / L Mu
Luke	ℵ / A / B / C / D	Cl / Δ / Ig / P / Ir CA / M	J / Hp / Cy / N / M / T / L Mu
John	ℵ / A / B / C / D	Cl / Ba / H / Ig Ir / CA / M	J / Hp / Cy / N / M / T / L Mu
Acts	ℵ / A / B / C / D	Cl / Δ / H / Ig / P Ir / CA / M	J / Hp / Cy / N / M / T / L Mu
Romans	ℵ / A / B / C / D	Ba / Δ / Ig / P / Ir / CA / O / M	J / Hp / Cy / N / M / T / L Mu
1 Corinthians	ℵ / A / B / C / D	Di / Δ / H / Ig P / Ir / CA / O / M	J / Hp / Cy / N / M / T / L Mu
2 Corinthians	ℵ / A / B / C / D	Di / P / Ir / CA O / M	Hp / Cy / N / M / T / L Mu
Galatians	ℵ / A / B / C / D	Ig / P / Ir / CA O / M	J / Hp / Cy / N / M / T / L Mu
Ephesians	ℵ / A / B / C / D	Di / Ig / P / Ir CA / O / M	Hp / Cy / N / M / T / L Mu
Philippians	ℵ / A / B / C	Di / H / P / Ir CA / O / M	Hp / Cy / N / M / T / L Mu
Colossians	ℵ / A / B / C / D	Ig / Ir / CA / O / M	Hp / Cy / N / M / T / L Mu
1 Thessalonians	ℵ / A / B / C	P / Ir / CA / O / M	Hp / Cy / M / T / L / Mu
2 Thessalonians	ℵ / A / B / C	P / Ir / CA / O / M	J / Hp / Cy / M / T / L Mu
1 Timothy	ℵ / A / C / D	Di / P / Ir / CA O / M	Hp / Cy / N / M / T / L Mu
2 Timothy	ℵ / A / C / D	P / Ir / CA / O / M	Hp / Cy / T / L
Titus	ℵ / A / C / D	Di / Ir / CA / O / M	Hp / Cy / N / M / T / L Mu
Philemon	ℵ / A / C / D	Ir / O / M	L
Hebrews	ℵ / A / B / C / D	Δ / Ir / CA / O	J / Hp / Cy / M / T / L
James	ℵ / A / B / C / D	Ig / Ir / CA / M	J / Hp / Cy / M / T / L
1 Peter	ℵ / A / B / C / D	H / Ig / P / Ir CA / O	J / Hp / Cy / M / T / L Mu
2 Peter	ℵ / A / B / C / D	P / Ir / CA / O	J / Hp / Cy / M / T / L Mu
1 John	ℵ / A / B / C / D	Δ / H / P / Ir / CA O / M	J / Hp / Cy / M / T / L Mu
2 John	ℵ / A / B / C / D	Ir / O / M	Cy / T / Mu
3 John	ℵ / A / B / C / D	O	T
Jude	ℵ / A / B / C / D	Δ / CA / O / M	Hp / Cy / M / T / Mu
Revelation	ℵ / A / C / D	H / Pa / Ir / CA / O / M	J / Hp / Cy / M / T / L Mu

Table
Primary Uncials
ℵ = Sinaticus / A = Alexandrinus / B = Vaticanus / C = Ephraemi / D = Claromontanus (Bezae)

Table cont.
Apostolic Fathers

Cl = Clement of Rome / Ba = Epistle of Barnabas / P = Polycarp / Ig = Ignatius / Δ = Didache /
Ir = Irenaeus / Pa = Papias / H = Shepherd of Hermas / CA = Clement of Alexandria / Di =
Diognetus / O = Origen / M = Muratorian canon

Ante-Nicean Church Fathers

J = Justin Martyr / Hp = Hippolytus / Cy = Cyril / N = Novatian / M = Methodius / T = Tertullian /
L = Lactantius / Mu = Muraturian fragment

Apocryphal Books

Apocryphal Book	Primary Uncials	Apostpolic Fathers	Ante-Nicean Church Fathers
Hermas	ℵ / D	Ir	-
Barnabas	ℵ / D	Cl	-
Apoc. Peter	D	Cl	-
Acts of Paul	D	-	-
1 Clement	A	-	-
2 Clement	A	-	-
Didache	-	Cl	-

Looking at the preceding charts, several things should be apparent. First, every book in the New Testament was accepted as Scripture by one or more of the earliest church fathers. Second, the books which have the fewest citations are the smallest books, indicating that the lack of citations is not because they were not accepted was Scripture but because there was not as much material to quote (even as I have not quoted from 3 John in this book). Third, of the five earliest Uncials no book from the New Testament is found in fewer than four of them. Also note that some of these Uncials are damaged meaning that the missing books could have been there, although we cannot prove it. Four, no apocryphal book from the New Testament has more than three major sources! Five, the "Gospel is Thomas," which the "Jesus Seminar" placed alongside the four true gospels, is not cited by a single author, father, or Uncial! *No one* believed the "Gospel of Thomas" to be anything but a forgery.[1727]

Another intriguing proof that the canon had been settled long before Constantine is the fact that critics appeal to the heretic Marcion who compiled a canon of Scripture which omits some of the current twenty-seven books of the Bible, but neglect to mention that "Marcion formed his Bible in declared opposition to the holy scriptures of the church from which he had separated."[1728] In other words, Marcion's canon demonstrates only that he was in opposition to the canon which already existed!

In short, there can be no doubt that the twenty-seven books which comprise the New Testament were accepted as canon from the earliest of times. By at least the second century, the majority of Christians agreed upon the sacred scriptures, and some books were accepted from the time of their writing (cf.

2 Peter 3:16). Attempts to date the canon to Constantine's time or later are naive at best, and dishonest are worst. Modern day "books" date to that era, but the scrolls which comprise the Bible were accepted as Scripture from the time of the apostles and their disciples.

How Was the Canon Formed?

A fair question is "how was the canon formed?" The fact that this is not an easy question to answer should in itself refute those who claim that some church council formed the canon. Were this true the evidence would be undeniable. The problem is that before Constantine's time there was no unified church government throughout the land. This fact alone demonstrates that the acceptance of the canon (as shown above) was not the work of some council or church authority, but the work of the Holy Spirit.

It has been argued that the writings of the apostles were accepted from the very beginning as they were written.[1729] This is partially true, but not entirely. It is possible that Paul wrote more letters than have become a part of the Bible, and it is certain that some writings of the apostles, notably John's *Revelation*, were debated for some time before becoming accepted. The early church was not naive and were cautious to insure that no false or heretical forgery made it into the canon. Because there were no chuch councils or popes to rule on these issues, there was occasional division as evidenced by the church father's writings. This, however, only further substantiates that the guiding force was the Holy Spirit, for it seems certain that at least twenty-five of the twenty-seven New Testament books were accepted as canon by the end of the second century, and probably much earlier.

Entire books have been written upon the question of "how." Consequently, I will refer to reader to Randall Price's *Searching for the Original Bible* or similar work. For the purposes of this appendix I will merely summarize my conclusions. First, apostlic authority was the primary requirement for canonization, and no book which could not be demonstrated to have been either written by an apostle, or by a close associate of an apostle, would be accepted. Second, the book had to be inspired and instructive. As Paul stated, "All Scripture is inspired by God and profitable for teaching, for reproof, for correction, for training in righteousness" (1 Timothy 3:16). Finally, the church was careful to insure that nothing contrary to the teachings of Jesus (as indicated by those gospels accepted *from the beginning*) would enter into the canon. As a result, some books were held to be instructive and useful but *not* Scripture (see below). In other words, the Holy Spirit guided the early church and insured that only those works inspired by the Holy Spirit and by witnesses and disciples of the apostles would enter into the canon.

Apocryphal Books

The term "lost books of the Bible" is a term floated around by people with suspect motives and agendas. Some, like the sham "Jesus Seminar", count the fraudulent "Gospel of Thomas" as one of "five gospels" in order to cast doubt on the four authentic gospels, but none tell you that *no one* other than the gnostic cults has ever accepted the Gospel of Thomas. Nevertheless, books entitled "the Lost Books of the Bible" imply that there are indeed "lost books" which did not make into the Bible. Why? What are these books?

Many books are written today. It was no different in the days of the early church, but what comprised a Biblical book and a non-Biblical book? As discussed above, the first criteria is whether or not it was written by a disciple of Christ or someone connected to the apostles who had first hand knowledge of either Jesus or His apostles. *No* book could be accepted to the canon which did not meet this criteria, no matter how good a book it might be.

It is true that religious cults have always existed, and to that end there were cults which attempted to create their own Scriptures and their own "gospels." Nevertheless, *none* of these books were ever accepted by mainstream churches. Despite what the critics imply, there are only six books excluded from the canon which were ever truly considered for the canon. No other book, especially those of the gnostics, were ever even debated in the mainstream church. What of those seven books?

Of all the so-called "lost books" only six appear in any early Uncials, and only four are quoted among the apostlic fathers. These are the *Shepherd of Hermas*, *the Epistle of Barnabas*, *the Apocalypse of Peter*, *the Acts of Paul*, the epistles *1 & 2 Clement*, and the *Didache* or *"Teachings of the Apostles."*

The Shepherd of Hermas

The *Shepherd of Hermas* is essentially a long parable. It uses allegory to tell moral Christian messages and to represent the church. It is certainly of early Christian origin although probably not from the first century. Those few who did accept it as authoritative argue that the author was the Hermas mentioned in Romans 16:14, thus connecting the author to the apostle Paul.[1730] However, most of the church fathers believe it was written by the brother of the bishop of Rome, Pius I, in the second century.[1731] This fact alone would exclude it from the canon although it did engender respect from many. Athantasius, for example, considered *Hermas* to be "a most profitable book"[1732] but most definitely "not belonging to the canon."[1733] This widespread respect has often been used to imply its controversy, but in fact only Irenaeus quotes *Hermas* as "scripture." The book can be found in the Codex Sinaiticas and the Codex Bezae, but nowhere else is placed alongside Scripture. Considering how widespread the church had become by the time of Irenaeus it is apparent that very few accepted *Hermas* as scripture. Since there are those, to this very day, who differ on the Biblical canon (religious cults and "liberal" theologians, for example), the fact that Irenaeus seems to stand alone is a testament to the uniformity of the early church fathers.

The Epistle of Barnabas

After the *Shepherd of Hermas*, only the *Epistle of Barnabas* comes close to eliciting real controversy. The epistle is supposed by many to be the writing of the apostle Paul's long time companion, but the epistle nowhere makes this claim for itself.[1734]   Most believe that the epistle was written sometime between 70 A.D. at the earliest and 132 A.D. at the latest.[1735]   This makes the epistle among the earliest non-Biblical books, and explains why it is so popular, but like the *Shepherd of Hermas*, respect for its antiquity and content does not lend support to any claim for canonicity.   It is found in both the Codex Sinaiticas and the Codex Bezae alongside *Hermas* but quoted only by Clement of Rome as possible scripture.   Again, considering how widespread the church and the scriptures were at this time, this is meager support to argue against an established canon.   The *Epistle of Barnabas* is a book indicative of early Christian thought, but not a part of scripture, nor does its author even make this assertion.

The Apocalypse of Peter

The *Apocalypse of Peter* was not written by Peter, but is acknowledged to be a forgery written in the second century.   Nonetheless, because of its proximity to the early church it was popular among some in the early church.   It obviously draws its inspiration from the book of Revelation, but differs from it in numerous ways.   A great deal of *Peter's Apocalypse* is a vision of hell and a description of the punishments bestowed on people for various sins.   Those punishments often correspond to their crimes.   For example, unrepentant mothers of abortion must wade in the blood and corpses of dead children.   This book is found only in the Codex Bezae and quoted as scripture only by Clement of Rome.   No other church father calls its scripture, nor is there any real support for its inclusion in the canon.

The Acts of Paul

First mentioned by Tertullian in the second century, but not as a canonical work, the *Acts of Paul* is a collection of traditions about Paul as well as containing the "third epistle" to the Corinthians (see below).   The traditions include the story of Peter being crucified upside down.   The Acts is dated to the middle of the second century and is nowhere cited as scripture by any church father.   Nevertheless, it is found in the Codex Bezae.   It has never been accepted as a part of the canon.

The 1st and 2nd Epistles of Clement

Clement is generally believed to be Clement of Rome.   Various traditions make him either the second of fourth bishop of Rome.[1736]   Some church fathers believe that this Clement was Flavius Clemens, the emperor Domitian's cousin and former consul, who was martyred by the emperor around 96 A.D.[1737]   Others argue that he was the Clement mentioned in Philippians 4:3, but this is less likely.[1738]   If it were the Clement of Paul's epistle then he would be from Philippi, not Rome.   It also seems unlikely that this Clement was Clemens who died in 96 A.D. since tradition, if it to be accepted, makes Clement the pope from 91 A.D. to 101 A.D.[1739]   In any case, his proximity to the apostles and the tradition that he learned from the apostles themselves have made the epistles very popular among the early church, but despite this fact, they are nowhere cited as scripture, nor do the epistles make claim to spiritual authority.[1740] Of the texts cited above, they are found only in the Codex Alexandria. It is also worth noting that some church fathers rejected 2 Clement as genuine.

The Didache or "Teachings of the Apostles"

The *Didache* has been described as "a church-manual of primitive Christianity."[1741] It is divided into two sections. The first is considered a "moral treatise" while the second "gives directions affecting church rites" such as baptism, prayer, and fasting.[1742] The author is unknown and the *Didache* is nowhere called canonical by the early church except via Clement of Rome's extensive quotations from it.

One may have noticed that Clement of Rome factors into five of these seven "lost books." Clement, of course, was not an apostle, but allegedly tutored under one of the apostles. Two of the seven were his epistles (actually the second may not have been his at all) and it is in those epistles that he alone refers to three other books as Scripture. If we reject Clement's opinions then only the *Shepherd of Hermas* is cited by any apostolic father as scripture. No other apocryphal book is quoted as anything more than "a profitable" but non-canonical book.[1743]

Other books which have been presented as "lost books" include the *Third Epistle of Paul to the Corinthians*, the *Epistle of Paul to the Laodiceans*, the *Gospel of Thomas*, and even the *Gospel of Judas*!

The Third Epistle of Paul to the Corinthians

The *Third Epistle of Paul to the Corinthians* is an extract taken out of the *Acts of Paul* (see notes above). It is suggested that it may be a letter referred to in 1 Corinthians 5:9 or even 2 Corinthians 7:8. Certainly it is an indication that not everything written by Paul was made a part of Scripture. This is not troublesome since only those books inspired by the Holy Spirit are to be considered canon. *If* this epistle is genuine, and many doubt it, it is a useful epistle and instructive, but not inerrant or inspired, and therefore is not a part of the canon.

The Epistle of Paul to the Laodiceans

Colossians 4:6 says, "When this letter is read among you, have it also read in the church of the Laodiceans; and you, for your part read my letter *that is coming* from Laodicea." Like the missing letter to the Corinthians, it is clear that not everything Paul wrote became a part of Scripture, nor should they have. The epistle here is alleged to be one of those missing letters, although most all agree that this letter is a forgery. Not only is it not accepted by any mainstream church father but they actively oppose it. This is because the letter is believed to be a forgery used to promote false and heretical doctrines. This is also why it is listed as Scripture by a few early gnostic cults and by the heretic Marcion. The Muratorian canon explicitly rejects the epistle as a forgery.[1744]

The Gospel of Thomas

The gnostics were one of the earliest Christian cults in Christendom. This "gospel" was attacked as a gnostic forgery and as heretical by Hippolytus and other church fathers, even including the "liberal" allegorist Origen.[1745] It has never been included in any list of canons discovered. There is no question as to its late gnostic origin. Depite this it has been hailed as a "lost gospel" by modern Bible critics and cults, even being the basis for some of the conspiracies in books and movies like the *DaVinci Code*. In fact, no serious scholar believes this "gospel" was written by Thomas or even that it dates to the first century as some critics claim.[1746] The irony is that the same critics who will date Thomas to the first century without a shred of evidence, reject the true gospels as dating to the first century. Such dishonesty would not even be worthy of mention were it not for the rise of gnosticism popularized by secular Hollywood.

The Gospel of Judas

Another gnostic "gospel," this forgery dates to the late second century or possibly much later. Containing a dialoque between Jesus and Judas, who betrayed Christ, it is apparent that the "gospel" is used to promote heresies about Jesus, and sympathizes with the traitor of Jesus. No one has ever accepted it as authentic or canonical. Once again, it would not be worth mentioning at all were it not for the National Geographic channel airing gnostic propaganda disguised as new.[1747]

Conclusion

The Biblical canon was closed and complete by sometime in the second century. Although there were dissenters and hold-outs who did not agree completely on the canonitical books, all twenty-seven books of the New Testament were accepted by most mainstream churches, and long before Constantine the Bible was as it is now so that when the emperor Diocletian sought to eradicate the Bible, he knew exactly what books to look for. The uniformity of the Biblical canon from early church is itself a testament to the fact that it was the Holy Spirit, and not some church council, that moved men to accept the inspired works of the New Testament.

The Authenticity and Transmission of Text

Critics claim that the Bible has been substantially altered since it was originally written, and even deny that the Bible was written in the early dates to which it is credited. In short, they claim that the Bible cannot be trusted in what it says. They ask, without wanting an answer, "how can we know what is authentic and what is not?" Many of these critics subscribe to what is called "higher criticism," but contrary to their claims it is the "higher critics" who disregard facts for unsubstantiated theories. *Textual criticism* is the *science* or study of the transmission of ancient texts. Textual criticism relies on *facts* such as the findings of the Dead Sea scrolls and witnesses to ancient scribal practices.

Textual criticism is the science by which we can say with confidence that the Bible is authoritative in that it faithfully transmits the original authors words in all substantive and important matters, as the reader will see.

Having said this, it is true that all scholars, whether liberal or conservative, agree that scribes make occasional mistakes in the transmission and copying of texts. The issue is not whether or not any errors can be found in the texts, but whether or not we can determine what errors exist and whether or not these errors have become incorporated into our modern text.

It is easy for the skeptic to mislead people into believing that we are left to ponder what the original texts said with phony numbers, dishonest representations, and lies about antiquity, but by studying the facts it becomes easily and readily apparent that with very few exceptions, scribal errors are not only easy to detect but the original remains faithfully recorded elsewhere, for there were many scribes and many texts made. We do not rely on a single scribe or a single document but the works of many men from different places in different times. Moreover, the scribes were not the only people to see or read the texts, thus the work of the scribes would be exposed to outside examination and scrutiny. While the critic portrays the scribes as dishonest and unethical men, history shows to the contrary. The scribes believed that what they were doing was sacred, and hence they tried faithfully, with fear and trembling, to reproduce copies without error. The proof of this follows.

Surviving Texts
Critics will make a point of saying that we do not have any of the original manuscripts the apostles wrote. They deliberately ignore that we do not have the original manuscripts from *any* book in antiquity, nor could you prove it if we did. Can anyone reading this tell me what the apostle Paul's handwriting looks like? If not, then you could not prove we had the original even if we did! Moreover, even after the invention of the printing press one could easily asks, "do we have the original plates?" The answer would probably be "no."

How then can we know what was originally written. Obviously, as copies are spread out across the world, it becomes harder and harder to "forge" or alter the original without making it vastly different from other copies distributed elsewhere. Even a vast conspiracy would not be able to co-ordinate alterations of copies across the east and west, across multiple countries and continents, or across different language translations. Consequently, the more copies one has, the easier it is to determine if mistakes or alterations were made, and how series these alterations may have been made. It may even be possible to determine which is the original and which is the alteration by comparing the different texts (see next section).

In regard to the New Testament there has been what some have called "an embarrasment of riches"[1748] and an "abundance of textual evidence"[1749] unparralleled in antiquity. The riches are composed of two parts. First is the sheer number of ancient manuscripts from all over the various parts of the known world and in many different languages and translation. Second is the antiquity of the manuscripts. In fact, while we cannot honestly claim to have any "original autographs" we can say with fair certainty that we have at least one manuscript (probably two or three) which date to a time when apostle John, and probably John Mark, were still living!

The oldest manuscripts known to exist are papyri 32 ($\mathfrak{P}^{32}$), 45 ($\mathfrak{P}^{45}$), 46 ($\mathfrak{P}^{46}$), 52 ($\mathfrak{P}^{52}$), 64 ($\mathfrak{P}^{64}$), 66 ($\mathfrak{P}^{66}$), and 75 ($\mathfrak{P}^{75}$).[1750] All of these manuscripts are dated to before 200 A.D. However, scholars are reluctant to date most of these before then because of the difficulty in proving such a date. Nonetheless, there is good evidence to date at least three to the early second century, or even before then.

Papyrus 46 ($\mathfrak{P}^{46}$) is formally dated to around 200 A.D.[1751] as are most all papyri which are suspected to be second century, but which cannot be proven with certainty. Nevertheless, paleographer Young Kyu Kim argued that based on the style of Greek lettering (which changes over time, just the modern letter "s" used to be written as "ʃ") it should be dated to "Later First Century."[1752] The only arguments used against this dating is that "$\mathfrak{P}^{46}$ is a perfectly ordinary copy"[1753] and that "it must have taken some time for the nine Epistles that are preserved in $\mathfrak{P}^{46}$ to have been collected."[1754] On this basis Metzger rejects a date of 80 A.D. for the manuscript, but nowhere does he provide evidence for dating it later than the first part of second century. If we then accept Metzger's silent admission that Kim's thesis is sound save the time needed for preservation, and we acknowledge that such collections are found in the early second century, then we would have no reason to reject $\mathfrak{P}^{46}$ as dating somewhere between 100 and 115 A.D.

Papyrus 52 ($\mathfrak{P}^{52}$) is among "the oldest copy of any portion of the New Testament known to be in existence today."[1755] It dates to at least 125 A.D. if not before.[1756] Additionally, Papyri 66 ($\mathfrak{P}^{66}$) is yet another second century document which Herbert Hunger, director of the papyrological collections at the National Library in Vienna, dates to the early second century.[1757]

Now if tradition is to be believed the apostle John died in the time of emperor Trajan at age one hundred.[1758] Traditional also makes John a teenager at the time of Jesus' ministry. Since Trajan ruled from 98 to 117 A.D. and because Jesus died in 33 A.D. we may conclude that John was no more than twenty at this time. Eighty years later would be around 113 A.D. Of course one tradition or another have both John and John Mark dying in 106 A.D.[1759] Although I do not suppose that John wrote $\mathfrak{P}^{46}$, $\mathfrak{P}^{52}$, or $\mathfrak{P}^{66}$ is apparent that the New Testament can make a closer claim to the autographs than any other writing of antiquity in history. It is of interest to note, however, that both $\mathfrak{P}^{52}$ and $\mathfrak{P}^{66}$ are papyri of John's gospel. It is inconceivable that forged and/or altered copies of John's gospel would be circulating at a time when John still lived without his raising a hand in objection! Surely, the manuscripts we have lend credibility to the fact that we have authentic replicas.

The chart below compares the Biblical texts with all other major works of antiquity (none of which the critics doubt to be authentic).[1760]

Author/Book	**Ancient Manuscripts**			
	Oringally Written	Earliest Existing Copy	Difference	# of Copies
Homer's *Iliad*	900 B.C.	400 A.D.	500	643
Euripedes	5th Cent. B.C.	Circa 1000 A.D.	1500	9
Herodotus	5th Cent. B.C.	1st Cent. A.D.	400	75
Sophocles	5th Cent. B.C.	Circa 1000 A.D.	1400	100+
Thucydides	5th Cent. B.C.	900 A.D.	1300	20
Aristotle	4th Cent. B.C.	Circa 1000 A.D.	1400	5
Demostenes	4th Cent. B.C.	900 A.D.	1300	200
Plato	4th Cent. B.C.	900 A.D.	1200	7
Julius Caesar	1st Cent. B.C.	900 A.D.	1000	10
Lucretius	60 B.C.	1550 A.D.	1600	2
Livy	59 B.C.-17 A.D	350 A.D.	400	27
Tacitus	Circa 120 A.D.	1100 A.D.	1000	20
Suetonius	Circa 140 A.D.	950 A.D.	800	200+
The New Testament	40-95 A.D.	100-150 A.D.	25-50	5700+

Obviously the wealth of textual data belongs to the Bible before any other book of antiquity. Ironically this has become a double edged sword for critics will count the number "errors" by scribes at around 200,000 while neglecting to mention that of 5700 manuscripts and the 7958 verses (averaging very roughly 25 words per verse) in the New Testament (totalling over one billion words in all) these "errors" not only represent a tiny percentage of the New Testament, but, as we shall see, only around 40 verses are truly in doubt, and less than a dozen make any real difference to the texts, two of which are here in the gospels which I have addressed (see notes on Mark 16:9-20 and John 8:2-11).

Analysing the Scribal Errors
How can I say that 40 of the 7958 verses in the New Testament are in doubt? Actually, I believe the number is far fewer, but not all scholars are as conservative as I am, so in fairness it is worth examining how we arrive at these conclusions. It has already been demonstrated that there is a wealth of information about the New Testament from various countries, languages, and people very early in Christian history. Copies do not get disseminated quickly or easily in antiquity. *If* the Bible were altered then we would expect to find one of several things. First, we might expect a passing of centuries before copies are discovered such as implied in the *DaVinci Code* and other anti-Christian conspiracies. Since this is not the case, and far from it, we can discount this. A second thing we might look for would be substantial differences in various copies of a certain country or region as opposed to those of another (the same

might be true of translations into other languages). In this case, it is argued that there are differences, but as we shall see the differences are linguistic, minor, and easy to distinguish.

The four major textual designations are the Byzantine textual tradition, the Alexandrian textual tradition, the Western textual tradition, and the Caesarean textual tradition.[1761] Nonetheless, contrary to the what the critic wishes, these textual "traditions" are extremely close. The greatest differences between these arise from linguistic and educational differences. For example, the Alexandrian tradition has a tendancy to alter quotation of the Old Testament from the author's translation to conform to the famed Greek *Septuagint* translation so well known in Alexandria.[1762] The modern day equivalent would be if an author quoted the New American Standard Bible translation, but a copy distributed in England changed the quotations to all be from the King James Bible. Another example of alterations made by one of these "traditions" is the use of synonyms for outdated words.[1763] For example, a famous verbal spar erupted once in Eusebius' time over a priest who substituted the then modern word for "bed" or "pallet" for the antiquated Biblical word found in John 5:8.[1764] Such fights, however, only show how great was the desire to be faithful to the original text. Moreover, an examination of the types of errors and mistakes found in these manuscripts also serves to demonstrate how easy it is to spot the errors from the original text!

Errors of Sight
There are various kinds of errors of sight, all of which are easy to catch. For example, the Greek letters Λ and the Δ look very similar. Sometimes a scribe may mistake one letter for another as in Acts 15:40 where the Greek word ΕΠΙΛΕΞΑΜΕΝΟΣ (*epilaxamenos*) meaning "having chosen" is mistakenly taken for ΕΠΙΔΕΞΑΜΕΝΟΣ (*epidaxamenos*) meaning "having received" in the Codex Bezae.[1765] Other examples are when a scribe sees the same word in close succession and accidentally skips over the first appearance of the word. In these instances a short sentence or clause may have been omitted, but it is, once again, easy to catch the mistake in the manuscript.

Errors of Writing
These errors could be summarized simply as ancient *typos*. Misspelled words or poor penmanship which might then be mistaken for something else typify these types of errors. Obviously there are the easiest to spot and of no significance.

Errors of Hearing
Sometimes scribes would have a copy read to them rather than reading it themselves. On occasion there will be words which sound very similar or have similar endings. Various diphthongs, for example, may be confused for one another. Again, these are usually pretty obvious and easy to catch. One

example is from papyrus 46 ($\mathfrak{P}^{46}$) in which νεικος (*neikos*) meaning "conflict" is mistaken for νικος (*nikos*) meaning "victory."[1766]

Errors of Memory

A common error is when a reader looks at the text and then begins to write the copy from his mind he may forget trivial things like word order (particularly if he is tired). A common error found is the fact that some texts often read "Jesus Christ" while others read "Christ Jesus." Most of these errors make no difference in the meaning or translation of a text, and are easy to recognize.

Misunderstanding

Misunderstandings can fit in with some of the errors listed above but can also include things such as misunderstanding common abbreviations which were often used by scribes. For example, θεος (*theos*) meaning "God" is sometimes abbreviated simply as θς (*ths*), which can easily be mistaken for ος (*os*) which is a relative pronoun.[1767] Thus "God" is mistakenly replaced with the pronoun "He."[1768] Such instances are again obvious and insignificant.

Grammatical Changes

Another common change is the substitution of words or grammar for more modern (for the time of the writing) ones. The use of synonyms to replace words was common. As mentioned above, John 5:8 is an example of where a later Greek word for "bed" or "pallet" was substituted for the more antiquated one used by Jesus.[1769] A modern day parallel is the updating of English grammar in newer translations. Since no one uses "ye" or "thou" anymore, "you" is used to replace those words. The same thing took place with Greek copies. Nevertheless, by looking at textual traditions and using a basic knowledge of *Koine* Greek, these instances are also quite easily recognizable and insignificant.

Intentional Changes

All of the changes or errors listed above are either accidental errors or minor changes in grammar and vocabulary. Here, however, we come to those changes which are of importance for these would be deliberate changes to the text. Note that of all the "errors" and "changes" to which the critic appeals, these actually represent the tiniest of percentage of the discrepancies. Moreover, these alterations are often even easier to spot because of the plethora of diverse manuscripts, textual traditions, and translations available. Any serious alterations to the original apostles' manuscripts would have to have been done while the apostles were still living, and they would surely have objected! Indeed, as aforementioned, we have at last two manuscripts which date to the time when two of the gospel authors were still alive![1770] Consequently, this tiny percentage of alterations among the hundreds of thousands of verses known to exist in ancient manuscripts is insignifact; particularly in light of the fact that no doctrine of the Christian faith rest upon a single passage, but many passages!

So it should be obvious that the claims that we cannot know what the original texts of the apostles contained are frivolous. Only forty verses are seriously contested by any but the most atheistic or liberal of critics. Of these forty only four are of any real significance; two of which are here in the gospels (see notes on Mark 16:9-20 and John 8:2-11).

Summary
The wealth of textual copies available of the New Testament is unparalleled in history. No book in antiquity compares to the "embarassment of riches"[1771] available for the New Testament. It is for this very reason that critics attempt to exploit textual variants ("errors") found in these texts while neglecting to mention that the sheer volume of information available to us makes it easy to detect well over 99% of these mistakes, and no information leads us to believe that the Bible handed down to us today was intentionally altered. Let us compare the Biblical debate to that of other works of antiquity.

Homer's *Iliad* is among the most famous works of antiquity. No scholar denies that we have is a faithful copy of what he wrote. However, of the 15,600 lines that make up Homer's classic, 764 lines are in question[1772] whereas "of the approximately 20,000 lines that make up the entire New Testament, only 40 lines are in question. These 40 lines represent one quarter of one percent of the entire text and do not in any way affect the teaching and doctrine of the New Testament."[1773] Consider that "these 764 lines [in Homer's *Iliad*] represent over 5% of the entire text, and yet nobody seems to question the general integrity of that ancient work."[1774] The 40 lines of the New Testament represents less than on half of one percent of all the verses in the New Testament or .005%. No serious person can deny that we have faithful reproductions of what the apostles wrote.

Conclusions

There has been much talk about the "historical Jesus" among so-called "liberal scholars" but how can we discover the true "historical Jesus" if we reject the historical documents written by those who actually knew and lived and worked with Jesus? These "scholars" claim to want to know the "real" Jesus by rejecting the writings of those who did know the real Jesus. They attempt to replace true history with their own imagination. They make Jesus into their image without any witnesses, while scorning the witnesses and testimony of the apostles left to us in the New Testament.

Former Chief Inspector for Scotland Yard, Sir Robert Anderson, said of the "higher critics" who reject the gospels, "if the case could be brought before any serious judicial tribunal it would be 'laughed out of court.'"[1775] He noted that, "as usual with experts, the critics look only at one side of the question."[1776] When examining the Bible from a legitimate critical viewpoint Anderson said, "I am not assuming that the Evangelists were *inspired*, but merely that they were competent and trustworthy witnesses."[1777] He did believe that the Bible was inspired, but his *faith* in the inspiration of the Bible was not based on ignorance, but knowledge.

Sir Anderson said that "our belief in God tends to a belief in the existence of a written revelation."[1778] The Bible is that written revelation. History proves this. What we have are what the disciples wrote. What we read is what Jesus taught to His followers. What we *know* about the Bible is why we have *faith* in what it says. No man's beliefs are 100% fact nor 100% faith. This is the great lie that insecure agnostics and critics present. They *assume* miracles cannot happen and declare this to be a fact. They then reject all facts that do not fit this assumption. They operate on faith but claim to operate on facts. The honest Christian knows that his faith is a question of trust. Every man has a different level of trust. Certainly God will reward those who have a higher level of trust in Him, but this does not make our faith in Him contrary to the facts, but in accordance with them.

A man has *faith* that his wife is not cheating on him. He does not *know* this, but his faith is based on what he does know about his wife. If his wife slept around a lot before their marriage, his faith might be misplaced, but if his wife was a virgin on their wedding night he has good cause to believe in her faithfulness. Fidelity before marriage is a good indicator of faithfulness after marriage. Yes, we can sometimes misplace our faith, but that faith is not based on ignorance. Because we know the Bible is true and accurate in all that can be examined, we have faith that it is true and accurate when it speaks of what cannot be examined. I *know* that Moses led the Jews out of Egypt (a fact even admitted by the pagan Egyptian priest Manetho).[1779] I have *faith* that Moses parted the Red Sea. I *know* that Jesus was crucified, dead, and buried under Pontius Pilate and that His body disappeared on the third day. I have *faith* that He was resurrected from the dead. Faith is what pleases God, ignorance displeases God. The two are at odds with one another. Our faith is based on God's faithfulness and the truth of His word, for "without faith it is impossible please God" (Hebrews 11:6).

Appendix D
—
Distinctive Titles in the Gospels

There are two seperate groups of titles used in the gospels upon which some theologians have tried hard to make clear distinctions, while others have tried equally hard to equate as synonyms. The first group of titles are those of the "Son of Man" and "Son of God," both of which are used of Jesus. The second group of titles are the "kingdom of heaven" and the "kingdom of God." Although these issues have been touched upon the main text of the gospels, it is necessary to address the issues more fully here.

"Son of God" and "Son of Man"

One of the most unique facts about Jesus and the doctrine of the Trinity is the belief that Jesus was both God and man. He most literally both the "Son of God" and the "Son of Man," but there is more to this than simply this fact. They are titles, and both have a distinct meaning and use.

Son of God

The term "Son of God" or "sons of God" can be found directly in reference to only three things. Angels are referred to as the "sons of God" repeatedly in the book of Job and in Genesis (but see notes on Genesis 6:2-4). So also Adam is referred to as a son of God (Luke 3:38). Finally, of course, Christ is given this title throughout the New Testament. But what of Jesus' disciples? Are we not also called sons of God? Technically, we are always identified as adopted sons (Romans 8:15, 23; 9:4; Galatians 4:5; Ephesians 1:5) or "sons of the resurrection" (Luke 20:36). In each of these cases, "sons" is qualified. The reasons for this distinction are important if we are to understand the importance of the title as applied to Jesus.

Adam and the angels were both made by the direct hand of God. All mortal men since Adam (save Christ) have been made by God, but only through the medium of the sperm and egg. We are sons of man. We are human in every sense of the word. However, Jesus is the exception. He is most literally the "Son of God" because the seed did not come from Joseph or any other man but from God directly without sexual intercourse. Jesus, like Adam and the angels, came into this world by the direct hand of God. Thus this title alone makes Jesus much more than a mere man as some liberals claim. It is for this very reason that the Jewish hierarcy sought to kill Jesus, for the very title was blasphemy to them (Luke 22:70-71; John 19:7) and worthy of death on that basis alone.

Only the Messiah could properly lay claim to this title, and no mere mortal man could apply the words to himself without charges of blasphemy being brought against him (Luke 22:70-71; John 19:7). By accepting this title and applying to Himself, Jesus was claiming to be more than a man; He was calling Himself the Messiah, who alone among men of that age could rightfully accept the title.

Son of Man

The term "Son of Man" is also a distinctive term. However, it is not a synonym for "Son of God." The term could be used of any man, but as a title it had a specific, and Messianic, usage. Daniel 7:13 is a prophecy about the coming Messiah. It reads:

> "Behold, with the clouds of heaven One like a Son of Man was coming, and He came up to the Ancient of Days and was presented before Him. And to Him was given dominion, glory and a kingdom, that all the peoples, nations and *men of every* language might serve Him. His dominion is an everlasting dominion which will not pass away; and His kingdom is one which will not be destroyed" (Daniel 7:13-14).

This is a clear prophecy of the Second Coming of the Messiah. The title is repeated in the book of Revelation (1:13; 14:14). It directly connects the prophecy of the Messianic kingdom with the title "Son of Man." The fact that the term "Son of Man," rather than "Son of God," is used here is worthy of note, but Jesus' use of the term is even more important. Of the eighty-four usages found in the gospels, all but one are by Jesus in reference to Himself, and the one is when the Jewish critics were mocking His use of the title, saying "who is this Son of Man?" (John 12:34).

Gleason Archer remarked that it is only when Peter made the declaration that the "Son of Man" was "the Christ, the Son of the living God" (Matthew 16:13-16) that "Jesus commended him for this confession of faith and conferred on him the 'keys of the kingdom.'"[1780] Sir Robert Anderson stated that "'Son of Man' is a Messianic title which is never used in [the New Testament] save in relation to the Messianic Kingdom."[1781]

The importance of the term is two-fold. First, it is clearly a Messianic title with which the Jews were very familiar. It is a distinctive title for the Messiah Himself. Second, it is in contrast to the other title for the Messiah, "the Son of God." It is evidence of both the humanity and deity of Christ. He is called the "Son of God" which no mere mortal man can lay claim to (short of adoption or resurrection) but He is also called the "Son of Man." He is both man and God. These titles, therefore, represent Jesus' claim to be Messiah, but also His claim to be God made flesh (John 1:14).

The Kingdoms of Heaven and of God

There are two other titles found in the New Testament; more controversial than the last. The terms "kingdom of heaven" and "kingdom of God" are used by Jesus repeatedly throughout His ministry. Some claim that they are syonyms. Some claim they are entirely different. Others claim that they overlap and are different aspects of the same thing. The answer is not a simple one. Some make the kingdom into a mere allegory or even a synonym for the church. Others, on the opposite extreme, make a rigid distinction between the terms "kingdom of heaven" and "kingdom of God" so that one may enter one, but not the other.

Throughout Jesus' ministry He spoke constantly and repeatedly about the kingdom. Indeed, the terms "kingdom of heaven," "kingdom of God," and kingdom without a qualifier are used just over a hundred times in the New Testament, and yet the word "church" is found only three times (Matthew 16:18; 18:17). The problem grows when we learn that the term "kingdom of heaven" is used 32 times in the Gospels, but *only* in Matthew. Moreover, when "kingdom" is used without a qualifier it is found roughly 16 times, but half of those are again found in Matthew. Thus "kingdom of heaven" is exclusive to Matthew while the phrase "kingdom of God" is found in all the gospels. Still more intriguing is that the word "gospel" is actually found 19 times in the gospels, but only six times with a qualifying genitive. In four of these it is the "Gospel of the Kingdom" (Matthew 4:23; 9:35; 24:14; Luke 16:16).

Thus the kingdom is fundamental to Jesus' message and His gospel. Perhaps we should start with that gospel. We use the word today as synonymous with the message of Christianity and Jesus Christ, which is true enough, but in the gospels the word actually has a more specific meaning. Ευαγγελιος (*evangelios*) is the Greek word for "gospel." It literally means a bearer of good news.[1782] It is from whence the word "evangelist" comes. Etymologically it is a contraction of "good" and "messenger." Ευ (*eu*) is a prefix making something "good." Αγγελιος (*angelios*) is the word for "messenger" from which we get "angel." However, its meaning is more technically that of a king's messenger, or in the case of angels, God's messengers. This is relevant because it tells us something about the kingdom, for in antiquity there was no internet, no phone, nor a printing press for a mass media. When a king died and new king was crowned the king's messengers would travel from town to town to proclaim the new king and/or any new edicts he may have passed. Jesus said "the kingdom of God is near" (Luke 21:31). He did not say "the kingdom of God is here." Instead He sent out messengers, evangelists, to proclaim the good news of the coming kingdom. This means that the kingdom, at least in the larger sense of the word, was a future Messianic kingdom. We are messengers and ambassadors of that kingdom, but "our citizenship is in heaven" (Philippians 3:20). The current kingdom of the world belongs to Satan (cf. 2 Corinthians 4:4; Matthew 4:9; Luke 4:7).

This was said because it is prefatory, for if we are to understand the kingdom we must understand the larger picture. Jesus did not speak of the kingdom as something which was then present but something which was "near" (Luke 21:31). In the larger sense there can be no doubt that He was speaking of the same Messianic kingdom of which Daniel prophesied and which the Jews were eagerly awaiting. The question remains, however, "how do the terms 'kingdom of God' and 'kingdom of heaven' relate to the larger kingdom of which Christ spoke?" Breaking down the interpretations may help us to better evaluate the different perspectives and come to a better conclusion.

One oddity I have discovered in researching this issue is that an individual's interpretation of the difference, or lack thereof, between the "kingdom of heaven" and the "kingdom of God" seems to have no relation to one's theological slant. Dispensationalists, covenant theologians, and even millennial exclusionists are all divided on the issue. Many millennial exclusionists make a careful distinction between the "kingdom of heaven" and the "kingdom of God" so that the entering of the one does not necessarily relate to the entering of another, but then other millennial exclusionists make their arguments based on the assumption that they are the same! This will be discussed below, but it is necessary to eliminate all preconceptions before examing the texts.

The Synonymous View

A common view is that "kingdom of heaven" is synonymous with "kingdom of God." George Peters favorably quoted the a nineteenth century Bible dictionary which said, "there is reason to believe not only that the expression 'Kingdom of heaven,' as used in the N.T., was employed as synonymous with 'Kingdom of God,' as referred to in the Old Test., but that the former expression had become *common* among the Jews of our Lord's time for denoting the state of things expected to be brought in by the Messiah."[1783] In other words, the terms were viewed as synonyms for the Messianic kingdom promised by the prophets of the Old Testament; particularly Daniel. However, George Ladd believed to contrary, arguing that "both 'the kingdom of God' and 'the kingdom of the heavens' are seldom used in Jewish literature *before* the days of Jesus."[1784] In either case, it is clear that in the days of Jesus, the terms were commonly accepted without explanation.

It has been pointed out that the "genitive" use of the phrases ("of heaven" and "of God") should be understood as "belonging to" God or heaven.[1785] Mal Couch, although he distinguishes between the two phrases, believes that "in all instances, the expressions *kingdom of God* and *kingdom of heaven* refer to the coming millennial reign of Christ on earth."[1786] Thus all are agreed that in the context of Jesus' time, both of the phrases referred in some way to the coming Messianic kingdom prophesies in the Old Testament.

The question is whether or not these expressions have a secondary meaning which distinguishes one from another or from the Messianic expectations of the Jews. The evidence that they are one and the same include 1) the fact that only Matthew uses the term "kingdom of heaven," 2) that the parallel passages to Matthew's passages about the "kingdom of heaven" use the term "kingdom of God," and 3) that nowhere does Matthew make a distinction between the "kingdom of heaven" and the "kingdom of God."

Let us begin with the first point. *Nowhere* is the phrase "kingdom of heaven" used except in Matthew. If the "kingdom of heaven" is distinct from the "kingdom of God" then we would have to assume that this major teaching of Jesus was completely ignored by every other New Testament writer. Of course advocates of the distinction do claim to have an answer, but that will be addressed under *the Distinction View*. It is sufficient to say that even if there is a distinction, it is a distinction made only by Matthew. A close examination of Matthew's use of the terms in the chart below may yield some clue.

Matthew's Use of Kingdom Terms

"The Kingdom of Heaven"	"The Kingdom of God"	Undefined "Kingdom"
Matthew 3:2		
Matthew 4:17		Matthew 4:23
Matthew 5:3		
Matthew 7:21		
Matthew 8:11-12		Matthew 9:35
Matthew 10:7		
Matthew 11:11-12	Matthew 12:28	
Matthew 13:11-52		Matthew 13:19
Matthew 16:19-28		Matthew 16:28
Matthew 18:1-4		
Matthew 18:23		
Matthew 19:12-14	Matthew 19:24	
Matthew 19:23		
Matthew 20:1	Matthew 21:31-43	Matthew 20:21
Matthew 22:2		
Matthew 23:13		Matthew 24:14
Matthew 25:1		Matthew 25:34
		Matthew 26:29

The reader will be immediately struck by the fact that "kingdom of God" is found only three times in Matthew, and one of those appears to be parallel to "kingdom of heaven" found in the previous verse (19:23-24). In that passage Jesus says, "Truly I say to you, it is hard for a rich man to enter the kingdom of heaven. Again I say to you, it is easier for a camel to go through the eye of a needle, than for a rich man to enter the kingdom of God." Thus the famous passage seems to identify entering the "kingdom of heaven" very clearly with entering the "kingdom of God." So clear is the parallel that one must conclude that if the rich man cannot "enter the kingdom of heaven" then neither will he "enter the kingdom of God." If there is a distinction, neither Matthew nor Jesus make any mention of it here.

The second evidence is stronger still, for when we examine parallel passages, we find that Mark and Luke use the phrse "kingdom of God" in the same instances where Matthew uses "kingdom of heaven." Consider the following chart.

Parallel Passages

Matthew	Mark	Luke
3:2 : "Repent, for the kingdom of heaven is at hand." (cf. 4:17 & 10:7)	1:15 : "Repent, for the kingdom of God is at hand."	10:9 : "Repent, for the kingdom of God is at hand."
5:3 : "Blessed are the poor in spirit, for theirs is the kingdom of heaven."		6:20 : "Blessed *are* you *who are* poor, for yours is the kingdom of God."
8:11 : "Many will come from east and west, and recline *at the table* with Abraham, Isaac and Jacob in the kingdom of heaven."		13:29 : "They will come from east and west and from north and south, and will recline *at the table* in the kingdom of God."
13:24 : "The kingdom of heaven may be compared to a man who sowed good seed in his field."	4:26 : "The kingdom of God is like a man who casts seed upon the soil."	
19:23 : "It is hard for a rich man to enter the kingdom of heaven."	10:23 : "How hard it will be for those who are wealthy to enter the kingdom of God!"	18:24 : "How hard it is for those who are wealthy to enter the kingdom of God!"

Notice that not only do Mark and Luke substitute "kingdom of God" for "kingdom of heaven" in the call to repentance, the beattitudes, and elsewhere, but the passage concerning "outer darkness" (Matthew 8:11-12), with which millennial exclusionists (see below) make such an important theological distinction, is paralleled in Luke 13:29 with the phrase "kingdom of God." This is discussed in more detail under *millennial exclusionism*, but the point here is that the two phrases are again used synonymously.

The final argument is that Matthew nowhere attempts to make a distinction. If the phrases were distinct we might expect that Matthew would clarify the difference, if any. This is especially true in Matthew 19:23-24 where the two expressions are used interchangeably. Would Matthew really use these expressions interchangeably without defining the differences between them? And what would we make of the eight references to the "kingdom" which do not use a "qualifying possessive genitive"?[1787] Would he leave the reader wondering to *which* kingdom he was referring? This only makes sense if the two phrases are identical.

The Distinction View

There are others who believe that the expressions "kingdom of heaven" and "kingdom of God" cannot be identical, even though they are similar. J. Dwight Pentecost says that they are "two aspects" of the same kingdom, "the eternal and temporal."[1788] This view says that the "kingdom of heaven" is specifically "any type of rulership God may assert on earth at a given period."[1789] For Merrill Unger "the 'kingdom of God' is evidently a more comprehensive term than the 'kingdom of heaven.'"[1790] Thus, as Lewis Sperry Chafer said, "the kingdom of heaven is no other than the rule of God on earth" or rather the Millennium as opposed to the larger "kingdom of God."[1791]

There is an old saying. "A Ford is a car; not all cars are Fords." This is basic logic. Consequently, it is permissible to argue that the "kingdom of heaven" is a part of the "kingdom of God," while not all of the "kingdom of God" is connected to the "kingdom of heaven." Or is it the reverse? This is the problem. There is an attempt by these authors to make a careful distinction between the two terms, but when it comes to defining them exactly, they cannot seem to do it consistently.

There have been several different attempts to clarify exactly how the two term differentiate from one another. Dwight Pentecost believes that the kingdom has taken various forms throughout history.[1792] He sees the kingdom in ancient Israel, in the modern age, being "formed through the preaching of the gospel," and in the future Millennial kingdom.[1793] In this respect some dispensationalists echo the sentiments of covenant theologians and allegorists. This is not to say that Pentecost is wrong, but to point out that there is simply no consistency even among similar theological groups when it comes to interpreting the distinction. Thus, while they argue that there is a careful distinction which must be approach "cautiously"[1794] they apply the terms rather loosely. The dominant variants are as follows.

1. The Kingdom of Heaven as the Church

Probably the oldest *distinction view* is that the "kingdom of heaven" is synonymous with the church. They see the church as executing God's will on earth. However, there are many problems with this view. Sir Robert Anderson notes that if a man must be born again to see the kindgom of Heaven (John 3:5) then "still more incongruous would it be to say, 'he cannot see the Church.'"[1795]

This is the test of good exegesis. If we are claiming that the "kingdom of heaven" is the Church then we should be able to substitute the word Church where "kingdom of heaven" appears, but it becomes readily apparent that this is not possible. Moreover, the very doctrine is dangerous as it attributes the kingdom to the material visible church. This is why the term "kingdom of heaven" was used during the medieval Crusades ... and this by allegorists who considered it nothing short of heresy to claim that the Millennial kingdom of Christ would rule so "carnally" on earth!

It may be fair to say that the invisible church is a small extension of God's kingdom, but it cannot logically or exegetically be synonymous with either "kingdom of heaven" or the "kingdom of God."

2. The Kingdom f Heaven as the Millennial Kingdom

Mal Couch argued that "in all instances, the expressions *kingdom of God* and *kingdom of heaven* refer to the coming millennial reign of Christ on earth. This kingdom then goes on into eternity."[1796] This is the polar opposite view of fellow dispensationalists Dave Hunt who sees the millennial reign in no way connected to the kingdom.

The problem seems to be not so much of a distinction between "kingdom of heaven" and "kingdom of God" so much as our failure to distinguish properly between the Millennial kingdom and the eternal kingdom. In fact, Dave Hunt openly says that "the millennium is not the kingdom."[1797] He rejects the application of the kingdom to the millennial reign in any sense. He argues that "the millennial reign is not the 'government and peace' which the Bible says will never end ... certainly 1000 years is not endless, and war cannot be equated with peace."[1798] Since the Millennial kingdom ends in a war (Revelation 20:7-9) Hunt rejects the kingdom application to the millennium.

Dave Hunt further noted that "flesh and blood cannot inherit the kingdom of God" (1 Corinthians 15:50),[1799] but it is clear that there will be mortal children born in the Millennial kingdom, even though the inheritance refers to resurrected believers (I discuss this in further detail in *Controversies in Revelation*). Does this prove that the Millennium cannot be a part of the kingdom? Or are we to distiguish between resurrected inheritors and mortal citizens.

Between these two extremes are men like Lewis Chafer who claimed that the "kingdom of heaven" refers to the Millennial kingdom whereas "kingdom of God" is the larger and more comprehensive term.[1800] This is one of the most popular views, but if it is to accepted then each and every instance of "kingdom of heaven" found in Matthew *must* refer to the Millennial kingdom; there can be no exceptions. How then do they explain Matthew 11:12?

Matthew states that "from the days of John the Baptist until now the kingdom of heaven suffers violence, and violent men take it by force" (11:12). How can this be the Millennial kingdom? How can violent men "take" the Millennial kingdom "by force"? If it is answered that this is the final battle of Revelation 20:9 then I would respond that they neither succeed in "taking it by force" nor is that day "now." This is the real stake in the heart. Jesus said "until now ... violent men take it by force." Although there is a future Millennial kingdom which is clearly a part of the "kingdom of heaven" the two cannot be synonymous for the "kingdom of heaven" was in existence at that very time! If part of that kingdom could be seized by force then we are led to believe that Israel and/or the church formed a *part* of the "kingdom of heaven" just as it forms a small part of the "kingdom of God."

In this respect, Dwight Pentecost is correct to argue that the kingdom has manifested itself in forms throughout history.[1801] Israel is not the kingdom, nor is the church the kingdom, nor is the Millennial reign the kingdom, but all are extensions of the kingdom inasmuch as they are under the authority of God and His kingdom.

Thus while many have argued that "the care with which Matthew differentiates 'the kingdom of heaven' from 'the kingdom of the Father' wherever it is found in his tradition suggests that we approach this distinctive Matthean use cautiously"[1802] advocates of this position consistently fail to do that very thing.

3. Millennial Exclusionism

Millennial exclusionists are those who believe that the 1000 year reign of Christ spoken of in Revelation 20 is reserved for sanctified believers alone. They interpret verses like Matthew 8:12 as proof that immature or unspiritual believers will be cast out of the Millennium. They believe that all believers will be saved, but not all will receive the blessings of the kingdom.

Many, but not all, Millennial exclusionists adhere to the second position. They take the "kingdom of heaven" as the Millennial kingdom and, with Chuck Missler, define the "kingdom of God" as "all-inclusive."[1803] However, some take the exact opposite view, arguing that the "kingdom of God" is the Millennial kingdom and "kingdom of heaven" is the larger all-inclusive word. To this latter argument, Sir Anderson refutes it by saying:

> "Exclusion from the millennial kingdom, we are told by some, will be the penalty imposed on Christians who lapse into immoral practices ... this assumes, however, that 'the Kingdom of God' is merely a synonym for the millennial kingdom, an error which is exposed by the very first passage in which the phrase occurs in the Epistles. In Romans 14:17 we read, 'The Kingdom of God is not meat and drink; but righteousness, and peace, and joy in the Holy Ghost.' This reminds us of the Lord's words to Nicodemus. The world and its religion is the natural sphere, but the Kingdom of God is spiritual; and none can enter it, none can see it, without a new birth by the Spirit. This is a truth of present and universal application. 1 Corinthians 15:50, which refers to the future, is a still more decisive refutation of the error. There we read that 'flesh and blood cannot inherit the Kingdom of God'; that is, can have no place or part in it. But, as we all know, 'flesh and blood' — men in their natural bodies — will be in the millennial kingdom."[1804]

Now the irony is that Sir Anderson accepts the former proposition, comparing the terms to England and the British Empire.[1805] Nevertheless, I believe it has been properly demonstrated that neither proposition is sufficient. Since I have addressed most of the arguments of Millennial exclusionists under Matthew 8:12 I will address only Matthew 7:21 and the application of this passage by exclusionists.

Matthew declares that "Not everyone who says to Me, 'Lord, Lord,' will enter the kingdom of heaven, but he who does the will of My Father who is in heaven *will enter*." Because Millennial exclusionists see the "kingdom of heaven" exclusively as the Millennial kingdom, they believe that this is a reference to believers being barred from the kingdom. They assume that everyone who says "Lord, Lord" is a true believer, even though they know that there are many false believers, cults, and heretics among us to this very day. In short, they must assume that Jesus is referring not to fake believers or cults or heretics, but to true saved believers in Christ. Nonetheless, this assumption is easily refuted by the words of Jesus Himself when He answers these men, saying, "I never knew you; depart from me, you who practice lawlessness" (7:23). Notice the severity of Jesus' words; "I *never knew* you." No believer, not matter how unsanctified or immature will be denied by Jesus. In fact, Jesus makes it very clear that He will never forsake us (Hebrew 13:5) or deny us.

In 2 Timothy 2:13 Paul says, "if we are faithless, He remains faithful, for He cannot deny Himself." Notice that He is faithful even when we are not. Even if we sin, He is there for us and will never deny us. Nowhere does Jesus say to the believer "I never knew you; depart from me", for if He did He would be denying Himself (2 Timothy 2:13)!

Conclusion

I have been very open to this issue for many years. I have struggled with it myself, but I am currently of the persuasion that "kingdom of heaven" and "kingdom of God" are synonymous with the larger ruler and reign of God, encompassing, but never exclusive to, Israel, His church, and the Millennial kingdom. There are five reasons that I currently hold to this position; several of which have never been answered or refuted by advocates of the other positions.

1. No logical or exegetical argument has explained why Matthew, and only Matthew uses the phrase "kingdom of heaven" unless it be personal preference, which indicates that it is a mere synonym for "kingdom of God." No other explanation has been offered that explains this fact.

2. No fewer than seven different parallel passages in Mark and Luke substitute "kingdom of God" where Matthew has "kingdom of heaven." The fact that the terms may overlap is a possible explanation, but insufficient without context.

412

3. Matthew 19:23-24 uses both phrases in the same sentence and referring to the same thing. Hence, in this passage denial of entrance into the one (kingdom of heaven) is synonymous with a denial of entrance into the other (kingdom of God)! The two expressions are used interchangeably.

4. Matthew, who alone uses the expression "kingdom of heaven," refers to the gospel on several occasions as the "gospel of the kingdom" (4:23; 9:35; 24:14) without a qualifier (e.g. "gospel of the kingdom of God"). If we accept that this kingdom is restricted solely to the Millennial kingdom then we must accept that the gospel itself is restricted to the Millennial kingdom; which, of course, no one does. The logical answer then is that this kingdom is synonymous with the larger "kingdom of God." If this were not so then Matthew would have had to use a qualifier, saying "gospel of the kingdom of God" so that His readers would not be mislead.

5. Finally, Jesus Himself declares that the "kingdom of heaven" was present both in His day when He declared that "from the days of John the Baptist until now the kingdom of heaven suffers violence, and violent men take it by force" (11:12). Obviously the Millennial kingdom has not yet arrived and yet the "kingdom of heaven" was being beseiged in days of Jesus. This indicates that the "kingdom of heaven" is much more than just the Millennial reign (which is but a part of it).

Conclusion

The terms "Son of God" and "Son of Man" express not only the divinity of Jesus, but His Messianic credentials. He was most literally both the "Son of God" and the "Son of Man," but the latter is a Messianic title found in the book of Daniel. Both titles are equally accurate and true.

The expressions "kingdom of heaven" and "kingdom of God" are not as easily resolved. Despite objections from some the best answer seems to be that they are synonymous terms, with Matthew preferring the expression "kingdom of heaven" rather than "kingdom of God," preferred by the author gospel authors. The greatest proof of this is in Matthew 19:23-24 when it says, "Truly I say to you, it is hard for a rich man to enter the kingdom of heaven. Again I say to you, it is easier for a camel to go through the eye of a needle, than for a rich man to enter the kingdom of God." So it is apparent that the rich man can neither enter the "kingdom of heaven" or the "kingdom of God" which are used synoymously in Matthew. Various parallel passages also make it hard to present the "kingdom of God" as a broader term than "kingdom of heaven." Finally, Jesus Himself remarked that the "kingdom of heaven" had been and even then was presently under seige by the forces of darkness (Matthew 11:12), making it evident that the "kingdom of heaven" cannot be exclusive to the Millennium.

These expressions are important in understanding Jesus and His kingdom. It proves the Messianic credentials of Jesus and emphasizes both His humanity and divinity. It further shows that His kingdom cannot be restricted to a thousand year reign, but is eternal.

Appendix E

—

A Medical View of the Crucifixion

One of the most basic doctrines of the Christian faith is that Jesus suffered and died for our sins. Centuries earlier Abraham had taken his son to be sacrificed (as the pagan tribes in Canaan had done) on Mount Moriah but God stopped him. "God will provide Himself the lamb" the sacrifice, we were told (Genesis 22:8). Jesus is repeatedly depicted as the "Lamb of God" (John 1:29, 36; Revelation 5:6; 6:9; 7:17; 14:10; 15:3; 19:9; 21:23; 22:1, 3). To that end the sacrifice of Jesus has always been a cornerstone of Christianity. The cross represents that sacrifice, but the tortures that Jesus endured for us went far beyond the cross. The book of Isaiah specifically prophesies "by His scouring we are healed" (Isaiah 53:5). The entire Passion of Christ was the debt that Jesus paid for our sins. It is therefore relevant to look briefly at that Passion from the perspective of a doctor.

Although examinations of the Passion have always been a preoccupation of some scholars, one of the earliest and most influential books to examine the Passion from the perspective of modern medicine was Pierre Barbet's *A Doctor at Calvary* originally written in 1937. To this very day the work is echoed by scholars and medical doctors, although some have disputed some of his findings (see "The Scars in His Hands – John 20:27" for more). Not all agree, for example, on whether Jesus was nailed through the palms or wrists, or whether he died of asphyxiation or a burst heart, but I will repeat here as briefly as possible what most scholars do agree upon, and touch upon what controversies are necessary.

The Garden

Luke 22:44 records that Jesus' "sweat became like drops of blood, falling down upon the ground." Medical doctors have observed such a rare medical condition called *hematidrosis*.[1806] This is when the blood vessels near the sweat glands burst. It is caused by severe anxiety and fear.

This fits with the emotional distress which Jesus had that evening. He knew that He was about to bear the punishment of the whole world upon His shoulders. He even ask if this burden might be lifted from Him, but fortunately, He did what we too often fail to do. He ended His prayer by saying "not My will, but Thine be done" (Luke 22:42).

Following Jesus' arrest in the Garden He was originally taken to a Jewish court for trial where He was beaten (Matthew 26:67). If the Shroud of Turin be legitimate, then Jesus' nose was apparently broken during the beating. Nevertheless, Jewish law would not allow them to condemn an innocent man

415

and Jesus was found not guilty by the Jewish court. Consequently, He was taken to the Romans, knowing that they were not above executing the innocent.

The Scourging

Jewish and Roman law differ on scourging. Many see scourging as merely whipping as was often the case under Jewish law, but Jewish law also restricted the number of lashes to 39 (Deuteronomy 25:3). The Romans, however, had no such restrictions. In fact, scourging could often be done until

William Bougereau - The Flagellation of Christ - 1880

the victim was dead. One very realistic part of Mel Gibson's *Passion of the Christ* was the depiction of the scourging whip. The Romans tied little sharp pieces of bone and metal to the whip. The pieces would "dig deep into the flesh, ripping small blood vessels, nerves, muscles, and skin."[1807]

As aforemention, Roman law did not restrict the number of lashes. Once again, if the Shroud is an accurate indication then Jesus was scourged between 100 and 120 times![1808] What Gibson's film did not show was that such scourging was often accompanied by "bouts of vomiting, tremors, seizures, and fainting fits."[1809] Scourging was so severe that Romans often used it to inflict the death penalty by itself. Pilate had been warned by his wife not to crucify Jesus (Matthew 27:19) thus his original intent was to appease the accusors of Jesus (Luke 23:16; John 19:1). Only when the scourging failed to satiate the assembled mob did Pilate send Jesus to be crucified.

The Mock Coronation

The Roman soldiers were under no obligation to mock Jesus as the King of the Jews. This was an act undertaken on their own. The act, however, bears significance in that it not only typified Jesus' humble existence as King of the Jews, but it added significantly to the torture which He endured for our sakes. The thorns found in Judea vary but each had long pricks which could be upwards of an inch or more. Because of the thorns, the soldiers could not merely press the crown upon Jesus' head with their hands. They literally pushed it on with a fork like stick, shoving the thorns deep into Jesus' skull. According to one doctor, the effect is like an "electric shock lancinating across the sides of His face."[1810]

In addition to the crown of thorns, the soldiers put a robe upon his back. As the blood from the scourging dried, the blood would have gripped the threads of the robe. When the robe was ripped off it would be like ripping off a giant band aid and reopened the scourging wounds. It would have felt like an electric shock covering his whole body.[1811]

The Mock Coronation proved a perfect compliment to the Triumphant Entry. Instead of the triumphant entry upon a stallion and a bed of roses, Jesus rode in upon a donkey over Palm leaves. His coronation was with a crown of thorns. Such was the life the King born in a manger.

The Way of the Cross

Prisoners were required to carry their own cross to the place of execution. However, the victim did not carry the entire cross as often seen in paintings and films, for it could have weighed anywhere from 150 to as much as 300 lbs.[1812] Instead, the condemned carried their cross bars which would have weighed between 50 and 100 lbs. Because of the significant loss of blood and brutality which Jesus had already undergone, it would impossible for Jesus to have carried the cross (Matthew 27:32). He was simply too weak.

Given the punishment and torture which Jesus had already endured, even walking would have been a difficult and painful task. When Jesus attempted to carry His cross He would have fallen many times. According to one doctor "every time Jesus tripped and fell, lancinating pains would radiate across his face and scalp and pricipitate severe pains in all of his muscles and joints."[1813] This is why Simon of Cyrene was eventually pressed into service to carry Jesus' cross. All of this indicates that the amount of torture Jesus had already endured was far beyond what normal prisoners were subjected.

The Nails

I have devoted a section of the maint text to addressing this issue (The Scars in His Hands - John 20:27). Here I will merely summarize the medical aspects regardless of whether the nails were driven through his hands or wrists. Namely, the fact that when the nails were driven through the palms it would have punctured or grated against nerve endings. These nerve endings would cause excruciating pain not only when the nails were being driven into his hands, but also every time Jesus moved or took a deep breath upon the cross. This is true regardless of where the point of penetration took place.

The Crucifixion

The person was transfixed to the cross in such a way to make breathing difficult. His body would be draped so that his rib cage pressed down against the lungs. In order to take a breath, Jesus would have to have pulled his body up with his hands while pushing up with his feet at the same time. This would cause the nails to rub against the median nerves causing burning pains and sometimes muscle spasms. This made breathing a painful act in itself. The victim of crucifixion would sometimes die of asphyxiation (suffocation), sometimes of the elements, or sometimes from something else. There were many ways in which death could overtake a cruficixion victim.

It was also not uncommon for a crucifixion victim to have insects "light upon or burrow into the open wounds or the eyes, ears, and nose of the dying and helplesss victim."[1814] Crucifixion was a slow lingering death that could take up to three or four days to die. Nonetheless, because the Sabbath was fast approaching and Jewish law forbade things such as crucifixions on the Sabbath, Rome obligued by breaking the legs of most crucifixion victims who were still alive shortly before Sabbath. This would cause the rib cage to collapse completely down on the lungs and cause the survivor to suffocate within a few minutes as the outstretched arms are not strong enough by themselves to pull the body up for long. However, we know that when the soldiers came "to Jesus, they saw that He was already dead, they did not break His legs" (John 19:33). Instead they pierced him with a spear to make sure he was dead. The result of this wound is surely the most intriguing aspect of the death of Jesus.

The Death of Christ

We are told that Jesus had already died before soldiers broke the legs of the other two prisoners. To make sure that Jesus was dead "one of the soldiers pierced His side with a spear, and immediately there came out blood and water" (John 19:34). This fact has led medical examiners to postulate the exact cause of Jesus' death. What was it that killed Him? Fourteen theories have been put forth by doctors over the years. A brief examination of them is prudent.

Thee of the theories all relate to the hypothesis that Jesus was killed in one way or another as result of the spear, but since John makes it clear that Jesus had already died these theories may be safely discarded.

The final eleven theories are all technical variations of one of two major hypothesis. One of these two major divisions assumes that Jesus died of asphyxiation. The other one is that Jesus died of a heart attack. Shock to the heart from the strain of his injuries and torture can easily cause a heart failure. The heart simply stops beating under the pressure and strain. Many of the theories attribute Jesus' death to a heart attack caused by one or more factors brought on by the scourging and crucifixion, but other theorists suggest that it was more than shock or heart failure. They believe that Jesus' died of a ruptured heart.

The asphyxiation theory does not properly explain the appearance of blood and water mixed, but if the heart ruptured or burst there would be both blood and water mixed. Although there are other possible explanations, the idea that Jesus' heart burst is an important one because it has theological significance. Why? Because a heart burst is also called a "broken heart."

Some doubt that Jesus could have died of a heart rupture because he was a young man in good physical condition, but this ignores many factors, including the trauma caused by torture and, more importantly, emotional distress. A ruptured heart is often caused by emotional distress. That is why the term "broken heart" is used so often. Jesus literally bore the burden for the entire world upon His shoulders. His sweating of blood in Gethsamane shows the extent of his emotional stress. All the gospels record that Jesus cried out with a loud voice immediately before He died. "It is finished!" (John 19:30). Such indicates that Jesus knew He was dying. He did not suffocate, for a suffocating man does not cry out. Furthermore, a man with a heart attack rarely speaks. A man whose heart has burst may cry out as he feels his heart rupture and His blood flow out of the heart.

The importance of this fact is this: despite hours of torture beyond human endurance, Jesus did not die of suffocation, exposure, or any other external cause, but ultimately He died of a broken heart. He endured more than we can imagine for our sakes. Some cringe at this warm and fluffy teaching, but it is true spiritually, medically, and logically. It fits the facts revealed in the gospel, and it shows how great was the love of Jesus.

One doctor commented "anyone with a medical background cringes and wonders conversely how He lasted for as long as He did."[1815] The answer is *because He loves us*." Peter said it best, "He Himself bore our sins in His body on the cross, that we might die to sin and live to righteousness; for by His wounds you were healed" (1 Peter 2:24; cf. Isaiah 53:4, 12).

General Scripture Index

ENDNOTES

1 Sir Robert Anderson, *The Critics Criticized* Pickering & Inglis (London, England) 1904 pg. 153

2 So called "skeptics" go out of their way to discount "secular" or non-Christian references to Jesus. Sometimes their attempts to reject the historical reality of Jesus are laughable. Not even those who fed us to lions ever denied the basic historical backdrop of the Christian faith. We were accused of everything from cannabalism to homosexuality, but never did *any* persecutor of the Christian faith deny that Jesus was a real carpenter who was tried and executed in Judaea under Pontius Pilate on the eve of Passover over a religious dispute! (See Appendix B).

3 There is not a single church father who accepts this "gospel of Thomas" as anything other than a forgery (F.F. Bruce, *Canon of the Scriptures* IVP Academic [Downers Grove, Ill.] 1988 pg 200).

4 The "Five Gospels" publication was the outgrowth of the so-called Jesus Seminar wherein extreme liberal theologians (some atheists) gathered together to vote on which Biblical text were accurate and which were not. In the end they could agree only that "love thy neighbor" was authentic, discounting everything else as exaggeration or lie. They offered no proof. They offered no evidence other than their own assumptions about the "historical Jesus" as if the Biblical Jesus were not historical. They then published their findings in the *Five Gospels* which included the known fraud "the Gospel of Thomas" which all agree was not written by Thomas at all! Such frivolous and unethical tactics display the bias and lack of objectivity to be found among Bible critics today.

5 Sir Robert Anderson, "Daniel in the Critics' Den," *The Collected Works of Sir Robert Andreson Vol. II Anderson on Biblical Criticism* Fortress Adonai Press (North Carleston, SC) 2011 pg. 33

6 Edwin R. Thiele, *The Mysterious Numbers of the Hebrew Kings* Kregel Publications (Grand Rapids, Mich.) 1983 pg. 33

7 Sir Robert Anderson, *The Bible and Modern Criticism* Pickering & Inglis (London, England) 1907 pg. 222

8 Ibid. pg. 130

9 Ibid. pp. 142-143

10 Sir Robert Anderson, "Misunderstood Texts of the Bible," *The Collected Works of Sir Robert Anderson Vol. 2* op. cit. pg. 264

11 Robert Gundry, *A Survey of the New Testament* Zondervan (Grand Rapids, Mich.) 1994 pg. 161

12 Such arguements were common in the liberal church where I was raised. The Bible was not taken as serious history, and often was a mere prop on stage, seldom used in the sermons.

13 Merrill Tenney, *New Testament Survey* W. B. Eerdmans (Grand Rapids, Mich.) 1985 pg. 149

14 Ibid.

15 Louis Barbieri, "Matthew," *The Bible Knowledge Commentary : New Testament* John F. Walvoord & Roy Zuck, eds., Victor Books (Wheaton, Ill.) 1986 pg. 15

16 Thieleman J. Van Braght, *Martyrs Mirror* Herald Press (Scottsdale, PN) 1660 pg. 91

17 John Foxe, *Acts and Monuments Vol. I* Religious Tract Society (London, England) 1883 ed. pg 97

18 Merrill Tenney, *New Testament Survey* W. B. Eerdmans (Grand Rapids, Mich.) 1985 pg. 150

19 Ibid.pg. 151

20 Barbieri, op. cit. pg. 16

21 C.I. Scofield, *First Scofield Reference Bible* A.C. Gaebelein (New York, NY) 1917

22 Merill Unger, *Unger's Bible Dictionary* Moody Press (Chicago, Ill.) 1957 pg. 706

23 Gundry, op. cit. pg. 161

24 Ibid.

25 Irenaeus, "Against Heresies," III. i. 1., *Ante-Nicene Fathers Vol. I* Alexander Roberts & James Donaldson, eds., Charles Scribner (New York, NY) 1886

26 Barbieri, op. cit. pg. 16

27 Gundry, op. cit. pg. 161

28 Van Braght, op. cit. pg. 91

29 Unger, op. cit. pg. 706

30 Papias, "The Fragments of Papias," *The Apostolic Fathers* J.B. Lightfoot & J.R. Hammer, eds., Baker Book House (Grand Rapids, Mich.) 1984 pg. 529
31 Barbieri, op. cit. pg. 15
32 Ibid.
33 Merrill Tenney, *New Testament Survey* W. B. Eerdmans (Grand Rapids, Mich.) 1985 pg. 150
34 R.C.H. Lenski, *The Interpretation of St. Matthew's Gospel* Augsburg Publishing (Minneapolis, MN) 1943 pg. 38
35 Unger, op. cit. pg. 706
36 Some insist that Hebrew, and not Aramaic, was spoken, but these are usually people who think of Hebrew as the "Holy language" and do not want to think of Jesus speaking in anything but Hebrew. All evidence suggest that Aramaic was in popular use from the time of the Babylonian exile, although the official language of the synagogue remained Hebrew.
37 Gundry, op. cit. pg. 159
38 http://www.nypost.com/p/news/regional/item_KJXdKMwZqBgHPdXXdGWnEP
39 William Barclay, *The Gospel of Matthew Vol. 1* Saint Andrew Press (edinburgh, Scotland) 1956 pg. 2
40 Leon Morris, *The Gospel According to Matthew* Wm. Eerdmaans (Grand Rapids, Mich.) 1992 pg. 21
41 Quoted in John Nelson Darby, *The Collected Writings of J. N. Darby Volume 19 Expository # 1* Believer's Bookshelf (Sunbury, Penn.) 1971 pg. 82
42 Ibid.
43 John Lightfoot (1859) [1663], *Horæ Hebraicæ et Talmudicæ*, 3, p. 55, http://philologos.org/__eb-jl/luke03.htm.
44 A.C. Gaebelein, *The Gospel of Matthew Vol. 1* Our Hope (New York, NY) 1910 pg. 19
45 Leon Morris, op. cit. pg. 22
46 Darby, *Collected Writings Volume 19 Expository # 1* op. cit. pg. 82
47 John Calvin, *Calvin's Commentaries : A Harmony of the Gospels Matthew, Mark, and Luke Vol. 1* Wm. Eerdmaans (Grand Rapids, Mich.) 1972 pg.53
48 Ibid.
49 R.A. Torrey, *Difficulties in the Bible* Whitaker House (New Kensington, PA) 1996 ed. pg. 163
50 Gleason Archer, *Encyclopedia of Bible Difficulties* Zondervan Publishers (Grand Rapids, Mich.) 1982 pg. 316
51 Gundry, *Matthew* op. cit. pg. 18
52 H.A. Ironside, *Expository Notes on the Gospels of Matthew* Loizeaux Brothers (New York, NY) 1948 pg. 11
53 John Wesley, *Explanatory Notes Upon the New Testament* Abraham Paul (New York, NY) 1818 pg. 154
54 F. W. Farrar, *Texts Explained* F.M.Barton (Cleveland, Ohio) 1899 pg. 2
55 Ibid.
56 Albert Barnes, *Barnes' Notes on the New Testament One Volume ed.* Kregel (Grand Rapids, Mich.) 1962 pg. 2
57 http://aramaicnttruth.org/downloads/outside/Aramaic%20Jesus%20Genealogy.pdf
58 Barbieri, op. cit. pg. 18
59 D.A. Carson, "Matthew," *The Expositor's Bible Commentary Vol. 8* Frank Gaebelain, ed. Zondervan Publishers (Grand Rapids, Mich.) 1984 pg. 66
60 Clement of Alexandria, *Ante-Nicene Fathers Vol. II* Alexander Roberts & James Donaldson, eds., Charles Scribner (New York, NY) 1886 pg. 334
61 Robert Mounce, *New International Bible Commentary : Matthew* Hendrickson Publishers (Peabody, Mass.) 1985 pg. 8
62 Morris, *The Gospel According to Matthew* op. cit. pg. 24
63 Mounce, op. cit. pg. 8
64 Jerry Falwell & Ed Hindson, eds., *Liberty Commentary on the New Testament* Liberty Press (Lynchburg, Virginia) 1978 pg. 5

65 W.F. Albright & C.S. Mann, *The Anchor Bible : Matthew* Doubleday & Co. (Garden City, NY) 1971 pg. 5

66 John Whitcomb & Henry Morris, *The Genesis Flood* Presbyterian & Reformed (Grand Rapids, Mich.) 1961 pp. 481

67 Joseph Thayer, *Thayer's Greek-English Lexicon* Baker Book House (Grand Rapids, Mich.) 1977 pg. 113

68 Lenski, *Matthew's Gospel* op. cit. pg. 38

69 Stanley Toussaint, *Behold the King* Kregel Publishers (Grand Rapids, Mich.) 1980 pg. 40

70 Matthew Henry, *Matthew Henry's Commentary* Vol. 5 Hendrickson Publisher (Peabody, Mass.) 1991 ed. pg. 3

71 Carson, "Matthew," *Expositor's Bible Commentary Vol. 8* op. cit. pg. 67

72 Toussaint, op. cit. pg. 41

73 Farrar, op. cit. pg. 1

74 John Walvoord, *Matthew : Thy Kingdom Come* Moody Press (Chicago, Ill.) 1974 pg. 18

75 Gundry, *Matthew* op. cit. pg. 19

76 Toussaint, op. cit. pg. 41

77 Irenaeus, *Ante-Nicene Fathers* Vol. I Alexander Roberts & James Donaldson, eds., Charles Scribner (New York, NY) 1886 pg. 453

78 John MacArthur, *The MacArthur New Testament Commentary* Matthew 1-7 Moody Bible Instituted (Chicago, Ill.) 1985 pg. 3

79 Calvin, op. cit. pg.53

80 Lenski, *Matthew's Gospel* op. cit. pg. 33

81 Cf. Norman Geisler, ed., *Inerrancy* Academie Books (Grand Rapids, Mich.) 1980

82 Robert Gundry, *Matthew* Wm. B. Eerdmaans (Grand Rapids, Mich.) 1982 pg. 16

83 John Gill, *Expositions of the Old Testament* Vol. 1 William Hill Collinridge (London, England) 1852 pg. 33 as cited by James Ussher, *Annals of the World* Master Books (El Cajon, CA) 2003 ed. pg. 21

84 John Wesley, *Explanatory Notes Upon the New Testament* Abraham Paul (New York, NY) 1818 pg. 10

85 Warren Trenchard, *Complete Vocabulary Guide to the Greek New Testament* Zondervan (Grand Rapids, Mich.) 1992 pg. 138

86 Ibid. pg. 177

87 http://biblicaldiscipleship.org/content/relationships-and-bible

88 Ibid.

89 Carson, "Matthew," *Expositor's Bible Commentary Vol. 8* op. cit. pg. 74

90 Cited in Ibid.

91 As noted above Matthew first wrote his gospel in either Hebrew or Aramaic and addressed it to the Jewish community whereas the other gospels were written in Greek and addressed to the church in general.

92 *The Aramaic Bible Vol. 11 The Isaiah Targum* Michael Glazier Inc. (Wilmington, Del.) 1988 pg. 17

93 Alexander Roberts & James Donaldson, eds., *Ante-Nicene Fathers* Vol. III William B. Eerdmans Publishers (Grand Rapids, Mich.) 1999 pg. 161

94 Ignatius, *Ante-Nicene Fathers Vol. I* op. cit. pg. 57

95 Irenaeus, *Ante-Nicene Fathers Vol. I* op. cit. pg. 451

96 Philip Schaff, ed., *Nicene and Post-Nicene Fathers Second Series Vol. VII* Charles Scribner (New York, NY) 1892 pg. 78

97 Philip Schaff, ed., *Nicene and Post-Nicene Fathers Second Series Vol. VI* Charles Scribner (New York, NY) 1892 pg. 370

98 Abraham Ibn Ezra, *Commentary on Isaiah* Society of Hebrew Literature (London, England) 1873 ed. pg. 41

99 Martin Luther, *Luther's Works Vol. 16 Lectures on Isaiah 1-39* Concordia House Publishing (St. Louis, MS) 1958 pg. 84

100 Ibid.
101 John Lightfoot, *The Whole Works of the Rev. John Lightfoot Vol. II* J. F. Dove (London, England) 1822 pg. 250
102 Matthew Poole, *A Commetnary on the Holy Bible Vol. II* Hendrickson Publishers (Peabody, Mass.) no copyright listed pg. 341
103 John Wesley, *Explanatory Notes Upon the Old Testament Vol. III Psalms LXIII – Malachi* Schmul Publishers (Salem, Ohio) 1975 pg. 1964
104 C. H. Spurgeon, *The Treasury of the Old Testament Vol. 3 : Psalms CXIII to Isaiah* Zondervan (Grand Rapids, Mich.) 1951 pg. 426
105 John Gill, *Expositions of the Old Testament Vol. 3* William Hill Collinridge (London, England) 1852 pg. 761
106 John Nelson Darby, *The Collected Writings of J. N. Darby Volume 30 Expository # 2* Believer's Bookshelf (Sunbury, Penn.) 1971 pg. 188
107 C.I. Scofield, *First Scofield Reference Bible* A.C. Gaebelein (New York, NY) 1917 ref. Isaiah 7:13
108 Poole, *Vol. II* op. cit. pg. 341
109 William Genenius, *Gesenius' Hebrew and Cahaldee Lexicon to the Old Tesament* Samuel Tregelles, trans., Baker Books (Grand Rapids, Mich.) 1847 (1984 ed.) pg. 633
110 Poole, *Vol. II* op. cit. pg. 341
111 Alexander Roberts & James Donaldson, eds., *Ante-Nicene Fathers Vol. III* William B. Eerdmans Publishers (Grand Rapids, Mich.) 1999 pg. 336
112 Philip Schaff, ed., *Nicene and Post-Nicene Fathers Second Series Vol. VI* Charles Scribner (New York, NY) 1892 pg. 370
113 Saint Cyril of Jerusalem even argues that *na'arah* should usually be translated as virgin for in Deut. 22:27 he says "doth it not speak of a virgin?" and on 1 Kings 1:4 he argues that she was a virgin since she was chosen for the king (Philip Schaff, ed., *Nicene and Post-Nicene Fathers Second Series Vol. VII* Charles Scribner [New York, NY] 1892 pg. 78).
114 Genenius, op. cit. pg. 633
115 Jerome, *Post-Nicene Fathers Second Series Vol. VI* op. cit. pg. 370
116 A.J. Rosenberg, ed., *The Book of Isaiah Vol. I with Rashi Commentary* Judaica Press (New York, NY) 1982 pg. 67
117 H. A. Ironside, *Expository Notes on the Prophet Isaiah* Loizeaux Brothers (New York, NY) 1952 pg. 46
118 It is generally believed that Matthew wrote in Hebrew, or possibly Aramiac, and not Greek. This was recorded by Papias and quoted by Eusebius. Cf. Eusebius, *Church History* Kregel (Grand Rapids, Mich.) 1999 ed. (3:39:16) pg. 130
119 Ibn Ezra, *Isaiah* op. cit. pg. 42
120 Cyril, *Post-Nicene Fathers Second Series Vol. VI* op. cit. pg. 78
121 Tertullian, *Ante-Nicene Fathers Vol. III* op. cit. pg. 161
122 Darby, *Volume 30* op. cit. pg. 188
123 Gill, *Vol. 3* op. cit. pg. 761
124 Rosenberg, *Isaiah Vol. I* op. cit. pg. 67
125 Cyril, *Post-Nicene Fathers Second Series Vol. VII* op. cit. pg. 78
126 Ibn Ezra, *Isaiah* op. cit. pg. 41
127 Luther, *Vol. 16* op. cit. pg. 85
128 John Calvin, *Calvin's Commentaries Vol. 7 Commentary on Isaiah Book 1,* Baker Books (Grand Rapids, Mich.) 1999 pg. 244
129 Ibn Ezra, *Isaiah* op. cit. pg. 41
130 Calvin, *Vol. 7* op. cit. pg. 250
131 Franz Delitzsch, *Biblical Commentary on the Prophecies of Isaiah Vol. 1* William B Eerdmans (Grand Rapids, Mich.) 1949 pg. 218
132 Ibn Ezra, *Isaiah* op. cit. pg. 41
133 Rosenberg, *Isaiah Vol. I* op. cit. pg. 67

134 Ibn Ezra, *Isaiah* op. cit. pg. 41

135 Rosenberg, *Isaiah Vol. I* op. cit. pg. 67

136 Spurgeon, *Treasury Vol. 3* op. cit. pg. 426

137 Ibid.

138 Delitzsch, *Isaiah Vol. 1* op. cit. pg. 217

139 Calvin, *Vol. 7* op. cit. pp. 247-248

140 Albert Barnes *Notes on the Old Testament Isaiah Vol. 1* Baker Book House (Grand Rapids, Mich.) 1851 pp. 167-168

141 Calvin, *Vol. 7* op. cit. pg. 245

142 John Walvoord, *Every Prophecy of the Bible* Chariot Victor Publishing (Colorado Springs, Co.) 1999 pg. 95

143 Archer, op. cit. pg. 268

144 Barnes, *Isaiah Vol. 1* op. cit. pg. 158

145 Grogan, op. cit. pg. 65

146 Calvin, *Vol. 7* op. cit. pg. 245

147 Robert Govett, *Isaiah Unfulfilled* Conley & Schoettle Publishing (Miami Springs, FL) 1841 (1984 ed.) pg. 151

148 Matthew Henry, *Matthew Henry's Commentary on the Whole Bible : Vol. 4* Hendrickson Publishers (Peabody, Mass.) 1991 pg. 37

149 C.I. Scofield, *First Scofield Reference Bible* op. cit. ref. Isaiah 7:13

150 Lightfoot, *Vol. II* op. cit. pg. 250

151 Calvin, *Vol. 7* op. cit. pg. 246

152 C. I. Scofield, *Addresses on Prophecy* A. C. Gaebelein (New York, NY) 1910 pg. 78

153 Ironside, *Isaiah* op. cit. pg. 45

154 Wesley, *Vol. III* op. cit. pg. 1964

155 Novatian, *Ante-Nicene Fathers Vol. V* op. cit. pg. 621

156 Philip Schaff, ed., *Nicene and Post-Nicene Fathers Vol. III* Charles Scribner (New York, NY) 1887 pg. 339

157 Lactantius, *Ante-Nicene Fathers Vol. VII* op. cit. pg. 110

158 Tertullian, *Ante-Nicene Fathers Vol. III* op. cit. pg. 162 & 331

159 Irenaeus, *Ante-Nicene Fathers Vol. I* op. cit. pg. 442

160 Jerome, *Post-Nicene Fathers Second Series Vol. VI* op. cit. pg. 138

161 John Martin, "Isaiah," *The Bible Knowledge Commentary Old Testament* Victor Books (Wheaton, Ill.) 1986 pg. 1048

162 Philip Schaff, ed., *Nicene and Post-Nicene Fathers Second Series Vol. VI* Charles Scribner (New York, NY) 1892 pg. 337

163 Ironside, *Matthew* op. cit. pg. 17

164 Gaebelein, *Mattthew Vol. 1* op. cit. pg. 41

165 MacArthur, *Matthew 1-7* op. cit. pg. 27

166 Herodotus I:101; 132 as cited by Barclay, *Mattthew Vol. 1* op. cit. pp. 16-17

167 Gaebelein, *Mattthew Vol. 1* op. cit. pg. 40

168 Mounce, *Mattthew* op. cit. pg. 12

169 Falwell & Hindson, eds., *Liberty* op. cit. pg. 9

170 MacArthur, *Matthew 1-7* op. cit. pg. 27

171 Cf. A.T. Olmstead, *History of the Persian Empire* University of Chicago Press (Chicago, Ill.) 1948

172 MacArthur, *Matthew 1-7* op. cit. pg. 27

173 John Davis & John Whitcomb, *Israel : From Conquest to Exile* BMH Books (Winona Lake, IN) 1999 ed. pg. 112

174 Gaebelein, *Mattthew Vol. 1* op. cit. pg. 41

175 Lenski, *Matthew's Gospel* op. cit. pg. 60

176 Ibid.

177 Desiderius Erasmus, *The Collected Works of Erasmus   Vol. 45 Paraphrase on Matthew* Dean Simpson, trans., University of Toronto Press (Toronto, Canada) 2008 pg. 48

178 Gundry, *Mattthew* op. cit. pg. 27

179 Barclay, *Mattthew Vol. 1* op. cit. pg. 17

180 Robert Thomas & Stanley Gundry, *A Harmony of the Gospels* HarperOne (New York, NY) 1978 pg. 327

181 Toussaint, *Behold* op. cit. pg. 49

182 Ironside, *Matthew* op. cit. pg. 16

183 Olmstead, op. cit. pg. 94

184 Flavius Josephus, "Antiquities of the Jews," XI.I.2, *The Complete Works of Flavius Josephus* Kregel Publishers (Grand Rapids, Mich.) 1981 pg. 228

185 Ironside, *Matthew* op. cit. pg. 18

186 MacArthur, *Matthew 1-7* op. cit. pg. 27

187 Randall Price, "Dead Sea Scrolls," *Dictionary of Premillennial Theology* Mal Couch, ed., Kregel (Grand Rapids, Mich.) 1996 pg. 90

188 Tertullian, *Ante-Nicene Fathers Vol. III* op. cit. pp. 159-160 & Hippolytus, *Ante-Nicene Fathers Vol. V* Alexander Roberts & James Donaldson, eds., Charles Scribner (New York, NY) 1886 pg. 181

189 Cf. David Criswell, *Rise and Fall of the Holy Roman Empire* PublishAmerica (Baltimore, MD) 2005

190 Lenski, *Matthew's Gospel* op. cit. pp. 59-60

191 Suetonius, *Lives of the Twelve Caesars* Robert Graves, ed., Welcome Rains Publishers (New York, NY) 1957 as cited by MacArthur, *Matthew 1-7* op. cit. pg. 28

192 Tacitus as cited by MacArthur, *Matthew 1-7* op. cit. pg. 28

193 Barclay, *Mattthew Vol. 1* op. cit. pg. 17

194 Gaebelein, *Mattthew Vol. 1* op. cit. pg. 60

195 Ibid. pg. 40

196 Josephus, "Antiquities," XVII.VI.5 op. cit. pg. 365

197 Thomas & Gundry, *Harmony* op. cit. pg. 324

198 Harold Hoehner, *Chronological Aspects of the Life of Christ* Zondervan Publishing (Grand Rapids, Mich.) 1977 pg. 25

199 There is much debate on whether or not Jesus was truly born on December 25, which was allegedly a pagan day of celebration in Rome (there is no solid evidence for this), or whether He was born in the spring. Here, however, I am merely outlining a possible chronology to show its consistency with the Bible and history.

200 Cf. Gundry, as cited by Carson, "Matthew," *Expositor's Bible Commentary Vol. 8* op. cit. pg. 87

201 Matthew Henry, *Matthew Henry's Commentary on the Whole Bible : Vol. 4* Hendrickson Publishers (Peabody, Mass.) 1991 pg. 1041

202 *The Aramaic Bible Vol. 14 Targum of the Minor Prophets* Michael Glazier Inc. (Wilmington, Del.) 1988 pg. 122

203 Matthew Poole, *A Commetnary on the Holy Bible   Vol. II* Hendrickson Publishers (Peabody, Mass.) no copyright listed pg. 947

204 Jerome, *Nicene and Post-Nicene Fathers Second Series Vol. VI* Philip Schaff, ed., Charles Scribner (New York, NY) 1892 pg. 116

205 Tertullian, *Ante-Nicene Fathers Vol. III* Alexander Roberts & James Donaldson, eds., William B. Eerdmans Publishers (Grand Rapids, Mich.) 1999 pg. 169

206 John Calvin, *Calvin's Commetnaries Vol. XIV Commentary on The Minor Prophets Book 1*, Baker Books (Grand Rapids, Mich.) 1999 pg. 387

207 Ibid.

208 Poole, *Vol. II* op. cit. pg. 877

209 Matthew Henry, *Matthew Henry's Commentary on the Whole Bible : Vol. 4* Hendrickson Publishers (Peabody, Mass.) 1991 pg. 928

210 John Wesley, *Explanatory Notes Upon the Old Testament Vol. III Psalms LXIII – Malachi* Schmul Publishers (Salem, Ohio) 1975 pg. 2487

211 J. Dwight Pentecost, *Things to Come* Zondervan Publishers (Grand Rapids, Mich.) 1958 pg. 46

212 Ibid.

213 Jerome, *Post-Nicene Fathers Second Series Vol. VI* op. cit. pg. 115

214 Cf. A.J. Rosenberg, ed.,, *Twelve Prophets Vol. I* Judaica Press (New York, NY) 1982 pg. 227

215 *The Aramaic Bible Vol. 14 Targum of the Minor Prophets* Michael Glazier Inc. (Wilmington, Del.) 1988 pg. 54

216 John Gill, *Expositions of the Old Testament Vol. 4* William Hill Collinridge (London, England) 1852 pg. 619

217 Albright & Mann, op. cit. pg. 19

218 Richard C. H. Linski, *Matthew* op. cit. pg 79

219 Barnes, *New Testament* op. cit. pg. 8

220 Warren Wiersbe, *Be Loyal* Victor Books (Wheaton, Ill.) 1987 pg. 20

221 Barclay, *Matthew Vol. 1* op. cit. pg 28

222 Leon Morris, *Matthew* op. cit. pg. 45

223 Linski, *Matthew* op. cit. pg 81

224 Josephus, "Antiquities," XVII.VI.5, *Complete Works* op. cit. pg. 365

225 Ibid.

226 Josephus, "War of the Jews," I.XXXIII.6, *Complete Works* op. cit. pg. 469

227 Jonathan Edwards, *"The Blank Bible" Part 2* Stephen Stain, Ed., Yale University Press (New Haven, CT) 2006 pg. 827

228 Irenaeus, *Ante-Nicene Fathers Vol. I* op. cit. pg. 442

229 Ironside, *Matthew* op. cit. pg. 21

230 MacArthur, *Matthew 1-7* op. cit. pg. 45

231 Toussaint, *Matthew* op. cit. pg. 54

232 H. A. Ironside, *Notes on the Prophecy and Lamentations of Jeremiah* Loizeaux Brothers (Neptune, NJ) 1906 pg. 159

233 Merrill Unger, *Unger's Bible Dictionary* Moody Press (Chicago, Ill.) 1957 pg. 910

234 Barnes, *Notes* op. cit. pg. 8

235 MacArthur, *Matthew 1-7* op. cit. pg. 47

236 Linski, *Matthew* op. cit. pg. 87

237 Barnes, *Notes* op. cit. pg. 8

238 Linski, *Matthew* op. cit. pg. 87

239 MacArthur, *Matthew 1-7* op. cit. pg. 47

240 Barnes, *Notes* op. cit. pg. 8

241 Josephus, "Antiquities," I.ii.3, *Complete Works* op. ci.t pg. 27

242 Ironside, *Matthew* op. cit. pg. 23

243 William Genenius, *Gesenius' Hebrew and Cahaldee Lexicon to the Old Tesament* Samuel Tregelles, trans., Baker Books (Grand Rapids, Mich.) 1847 (1984 ed.) pg. 541

244 Ibid. pg. 563

245 Ibid. pg. 564

246 Calvin, *Harmony Vol. 1* op. cit. pg. 104

247 Ibid.

248 Ibid.

249 Henry, *Vol. 5* op. cit. pg. 16

250 Barnes, *Notes* op. cit. pg. 8

251 Matthew Poole, *A Commetnary on the Holy Bible Vol. III* Hendrickson Publishers (Peabody, Mass.) no copyright listed pg. 13

252 Ibid.

253 Falwell & Hindson, op. cit. pg. 10

254 Farrar, op. cit. pg. 6

255 Gesenius, op. cit. pg. 712

256 Ironside, *Matthew* op. cit. pg. 23

257 Toussaint, op. cit. pg. 57

258 Barnes, *Notes* op. cit. pg. 8

259 Wesley, *New Testament* op. cit. pg. 14

260 Erasmus, *Collected Vol. 45* op. cit. pg. 57

261 Calvin, *Harmony Vol. 1* op. cit. pg. 104

262 Edwin R. Thiele, *The Mysterious Numbers of the Hebrew Kings* Kregel Publications (Grand Rapids, Mich.) 1983 pg. 33

263 Calvin, *Harmony Vol. 1* op. cit. pg. 139

264 Thomas & Gundry, op. cit.

265 Gundry, *Matthew* op. cit. pg. 56

266 Thomas & Gundry, op. cit. pg. 37

267 Gundry, *Matthew* op. cit. pg. 56

268 Ironside, *Matthew* op. cit. pg. 34

269 Irenaeus, *Ante-Nicene Fathers Vol. I* op. cit. pg. 552

270 MacArthur, *Matthew 1-7* op. cit. pg. 96

271 John Nelson Darby, *Notes on Matthew* G. Morrish (London, England) n.d. pg. 13

272 Toussaint, op. cit. pg. 76

273 MacArthur, *Matthew 1-7* op. cit. pg. 254

274 Leon Morris, *Matthew* op. cit. pg. 107

275 Barclay, *Mattthew Vol. 1* op. cit. pg. 124

276 Linski, *Matthew* op. cit. pg. 206

277 Calvin, *Harmony Vol. 1* op. cit. pg. 179

278 MacArthur, *Matthew 1-7* op. cit. pg. 255

279 Wesley, *New Testament* op. cit. pg. 21

280 Albright & Mann, op. cit. pg. 57

281 Barclay, *Mattthew Vol. 1* op. cit. pg. 124

282 James Inciardi, *Criminal Justice* Harcourt Brace Jovanovich (New York, NY) 1987 pg. 57

283 Barclay, *Mattthew Vol. 1* op. cit. pg. 124

284 The laws of ceremonial worship pertain to the Temple worship. For example, no one has ever said that menstration is a sin, but the Bible forbids a woman who is menstrating from entering the Temple. So also, Jesus seemed to indicate that "all foods are clean" (Mark 7:19), but did not say anything about entering the Temple after eating "unclean" food. Thus it is possible that Jesus saw the dietary laws as ceremonial laws in regard to Temple worship. Eating "unclean" food did not make one a sinner, but did prohit him from worshipping in the Temple that week.

285 Ibid.

286 Tertullian, *Ante-Nicene Fathers Vol. III* op. cit. pg. 357

287 Ibid. pg. 461

288 Falwell & Hindson, eds., *Liberty* op. cit. pg. 22

289 Erasmus, *Collected Vol. 45* op. cit. pg. 96

290 Wiersbe, *Be Loyal* op. cit. pp. 35-36

291 Tertullian, *Ante-Nicene Fathers Vol. III* op. cit. pg. 357

292 Scofield, *Reference Bible* op. cit. ref. Matthew 5

293 Walvoord, *Thy Kingdom Come* op. cit. pg. 48

294 Tertullian, *Ante-Nicene Fathers Vol. IV* Alexander Roberts & James Donaldson, eds., William B. Eerdmans Publishers (Grand Rapids, Mich.) 1999. pg. 54

295 Wiersbe, *Be Loyal* op. cit. pg. 38

296 Barclay, *Mattthew Vol. 1* op. cit. pg. 146

297 Gundry, *Matthew* op. cit. pg. 88

298 Quoted in Gundry, *Matthew* op. cit. pg. 88

299 Erasmus, *Collected Vol. 45* op. cit. pg. 103

300 Toussaint, op. cit. pg. 102

301 Falwell & Hindson, eds., *Liberty* op. cit. pg. 24

302 Linski, *Matthew* op. cit. pg. 217

303 Ironside, *Matthew* op. cit. pg. 55

304 Linski, *Matthew* op. cit. pg. 227

305 Erasmus, *Collected Vol. 45* op. cit. pg. 103

306 MacArthur, *Matthew 1-7* op. cit. pg. 292

307 Falwell & Hindson, eds., *Liberty* op. cit. pg. 24

308 Charles Chiniquy, *50 Years on the "Church" of Rome* Protestand Literature Depository (Chick Edition - Chino, CA) 1886 (1985 ed.) pg. 17

309 Scofield, *Reference Bible* op. cit. ref. Matthew 5

310 John MacArthur, *The MacArthur New Testament Commentary   Matthew 1-7* Moody Bible Institute (Chicago, Ill.) 1985 pg. 431

311 A.C. Gaebelein, *The Gospel of Matthew Vol. 1* Our Hope (New York, NY) 1910 pg. 151

312 Irenaeus, *Ante-Nicene Fathers Vol. 1* op. cit. pg. 504

313 William Barclay, *The Gospel of Matthew Vol. 1* St. Andrews Press (Edinburgh, Scotland) 1956 pg. 268

314 Jerry Falwell & Ed. Hindson, eds., *Liberty Commentary on the New Tesatment* Liberty Press (Lynchburg, VA) 1978 pg. xx

315 W.F Albright & C.S. Mann, *The Anchor Bible : Matthew* Doubleday & Co. (Garden City, NY) 1971 pg. 84

316 Desiderius Erasmus, *The Collected Works of Erasmus Vol. 45 Paraphrase on Matthew* Dean Simpson, trans., University of Toronto Press (Toronto, Canada) 2008 pg. 129

317 R.C.H. Linski, *The Interpretation of St. Matthew's Gospel* Augsburg Publishing House (Minneapolis, MN) 1943 pg. 288

318 Robert Gundry, *Matthew* William B. Eerdmans (Grand Rapids, Mich.) 1982 pg. 121

319 Albert Barnes, *Barnes' Notes in the New Testament   One Volume ed.* Kregel Publishers (Grand Rapids, Mich.) 1962 pg. 34

320 Jonathan Edwards, *"The Blank Bible" Part 2* Stphen Stein, ed. Yale University Press (New Haven, CT) 2006 pg. 838

321 Hippolytus, *Ante-Nicene Fathers Vol. 5* op. cit. pg. 117

322 Cyprian, *Ante-Nicene Fathers Vol. 5* op. cit. pg. 453

323 Tertullian, *Ante-Nicene Fathers Vol. 4* op. cit. pg. 76

324 H.A. Ironside, *Expository Notes on the Gospels of Matthew* Loizeaux Brothers (New York, NY) 1948 pg. 73

325 Robert Mounce, *New International Biblical Commentary : Matthew* Hendrickson Publishers (Peabody, Mass) 1985 pg. 74

326 Leon Morris, *The Gospel According to Matthew* William B. Eerdmans (Grand Rapids, Mich.) 1992 pg. 191

327 Gundry, *Matthew* op. cit. pg. 141

328 John Wesley, *Explanatory Notes Upon the New Testament* Abraham Paul (New York, NY) 1818 pg. xx

329 John Calvin, *Calvin's Commentaries A Harmony of the Gospels of Matthew, Mark, and Luke Vol. 1* William B. Eerdmans (Grand Rapids, Mich.) A.W. Morison, trans., 1972 pg. 247

330 Leon Morris, *The Gospel According to Matthew* William B. Eerdmans (Grand Rapids, Mich.) 1992 pg. 151

331 John MacArthur, *The MacArthur New Testament Commentary Matthew 8-15* Moody Bible Institute (Chicago, Ill.) 1985 pg. 12

332 Charles Spurgeon, *Treasury of the New Testament Volume One* Zondervan (Grand Rapids, Mich.) 1950 pg. 123

333 I thought I had first coined the term myself, only to find that many others have seen this same thing, even using the same term. Cf. Sir Robert Anderson, *Forgotten Truth* Pickering (London, England) 1914 pg. 131

334 J.D Faust, *The Rod* Schoettle Publishing (Hayesville, N.C.) 2003 pg. 88

335 Sir Robert Anderson, *Forgotten Truths Truth* Pickering (London, England) 1914 ch. 12
336 Chuck & Nancy Missler, *The Kingdom Power and Glory* King's High Way Ministries (Coeur d' Alene, ID) 2007 pp. 60-61
337 Ibid. pg. 62
338 Ibid. pg. 64
339 Ibid. pg. 62
340 Ibid. pp. 268
341 Faust, op. cit. pg. 178
342   http://www.catholicforum.com/forums/showthread.php?27416-For-Bibleonly...-regarding-celibacy-among-priests-and-bishops
343 Criswell, *Rise and Fall* op. cit. pg. 138
344 Erasmus, *Vol. 45* op. cit. pg. 146
345 Ibid. pg. 147
346 MacArthur, *Matthew 8-15* op. cit. pp. 24-25
347 Wesley, *New Testament* op. cit. pg. 33
348 Barnes, *Barnes' Notes* op. cit. pg. 40
349 *Liberty Commentary* op. cit. pg. 149
350 Cyprian, *Ante-Nicene Fathers* Vol. 5 op. cit. pg. 450
351 Albright & Mann, op. cit. pg. 96
352 Wesley, *New Testament* op. cit. pg. 33
353 Barnes, *Barnes' Notes* op. cit. pg. 40
354 Cyprian, *Ante-Nicene Fathers* Vol. 5 op. cit. pg. 450
355 MacArthur, *Matthew 8-15* op. cit. pg. 24
356 It is entirely possible, but by no means certain, that the Marys were going to apply spices because they had not had the time to apply the spices on Friday before Sabbath began. The body had to be buried before sundown and Jesus did not die until 3 P.M. leaving only three hours for burial. Thus the spices would normally be applied first and were only delayed because of Sabbath.
357 Archer, op. cit. pg. 324
358 Albright & Mann, op. cit. pg. 96
359 Barclay, *Matthew Vol. 1* op. cit. pg. 321
360 Edwards, *"The Blank Bible"* op. cit. pg. 840
361 John Walvoord, *Thy Kingdom Come : Matthew* Moody Press (Chicago, Ill.) 1974 pg. 66
362 Tertullian, *Ante-Nicene Fathers Vol. 3* op. cit. pg. 386
363 Calvin, *Commentaries A Harmony Vol. 1* op. cit. pg. 255
364 Sir Robert Anderson, "The Bible and Modern Criticism," *The Collected Works of Sir Robert Andreson Vol. II Anderson on Biblical Criticism* Fortress Adonai Press (North Carleston, SC) 2011 pg. 137
365 Barclay, *Matthew Vol. 1* op. cit. pg. 321
366 Eberhard Nestle & Kurt Aland, ed., *Nestle-Aland Novum Tetamentum Graece* Deutsche Bibelgesellschaft (Stuttgart, Germany) 1991 notes on Matthew 8:28
367 Ibid.
368 The church father Origen believed *both* variants in Greek to be in error! [Barclay, *Matthew Vol. 1* op. cit. pg. 326]
369 Wesley, *New Testament* op. cit. pg. 33
370 Barnes, *Barnes' Notes* op. cit. pg. 40
371 Barclay, *Matthew Vol. 1* op. cit. pg. 321
372 Leon Morris, op. cit. pg. 208
373 Leon Morris, op. cit. pg. 208
374 Barnes, *Barnes' Notes* op. cit. pg. 41
375 Ironside, *Matthew* op. cit. pg. 99
376 Gundry, *Matthew* op. cit. pg. 158
377 Ibid.
378 MacArthur, *Matthew 8-15* op. cit. pg. 41

379 Wesley, *New Testament* op. cit. pg. 33
380 Linski, op. cit. pg. 350
381 *Liberty Commentary* op. cit. pg. 105
382 David Criswell, "On Psychiatry And Etiology" *Biblical Reflections On Modern Medicine* (Augusta, GA) May 1993 Vol. 4:3
383 MacArthur, *Matthew 8-15* op. cit. pg. 42
384 Kurt Koch & Alfred Lechler, *Occult Bondage and Deliverance* Kregel Publishers (Grand Rapids, Mich.) 1970 pp. 7-15
385 Ibid. pp. 12-13
386 Kurt Koch, *Christian Counseling and Occultism* Kregel Publishers (Grand Rapids, Mich.) 1972 pg. 12
387 Ibid.
388 Koch & Lechler, op. cit. pg. 13
389 Thayer, op. cit. pg. 507
390 Gesenius, op. cit. pg. 410
391 Cf. Thayer, op. cit. pg. 103 & Gesenius, op. cit. pg. 757
392 Carson, "Matthew," *Expositor's Bible Commentary Vol. 8* op. cit. pg. 239
393 Thayer, op. cit. pg. 282
394 Unger, op. cit. pg. 1086
395 Ibid.
396 Barnes, *Barnes' Notes* op. cit. pg. 48
397 Wesley, *New Testament* op. cit. pg. 38
398 Thayer, op. cit. pg. 363
399 Cf. Richard Young, *Intermediate New Testament Greek* Broadman & Holdman Publishers (Nashville, TN) 1994 pp. 137-140
400 Mounce, *Matthew* op. cit. pg. 92
401 Ibid.
402 Linski, op. cit. pg. 393
403 Gundry, *Matthew* op. cit. pg. 187
404 Barclay, *Matthew Vol. 1* op. cit. pg. 378
405 Ibid.
406 Edwards, *"The Blank Bible"* op. cit. pg. 881
407 Calvin, *Commentaries A Harmony Vol. 1* op. cit. pg. 293
408 *Liberty Commentary* op. cit. pg. 45
409 Leon Morris, op. cit. pg. 248
410 Ibid.
411 Ibid.
412 Farrar, op. cit. pg. 50
413 Christians were also accused of cannabalism, among other things, based on the Lord's Supper. Other accusations included homosexuality and licensous sexual orgies based on our constant sermons regarding "love."
414 Tacitus, *The Annals* 15.44
415 Donaldson & Roberts, *Ante-Nicene Fathers Vol. 1* op. cit. pg. 345
416 Wesley, *New Testament* op. cit. pg. 40
417 Mounce, *Matthew* op. cit. pg. 98
418 Cf. www.persecution.net
419 Cyprian, *Ante-Nicene Fathers Vol. 5* op. cit. pp. 303-304
420 Tertullian, *Ante-Nicene Fathers Vol. 4* op. cit. pg. 68
421 Tertullian, *Ante-Nicene Fathers Vol. 3* op. cit. pg. 399
422 Cyprian, *Ante-Nicene Fathers Vol. 5* op. cit. pg. 539
423 MacArthur, *Matthew 8-15* op. cit. pg. 232
424 Thayer, op. cit. pg. 614
425 Ibid.

426 Trenchard, op. cit. pg. 155
427   Barclay M. Newman, Jr., ed., *A Concise Greek-English Dictionary of the New Testament* United Bible Society (Stuttgart, Germany) 1971 pg. 178
428 Merrill Unger, *Demons in the World Today* Tyndale House (Wheaton, Ill.) 1981 pg. 111
429 Cf. Koch & Lechler, op. cit. pg. 59
430 MacArthur, *Matthew 8-15* op. cit. pg. 327
431 Linski, op. cit. pg. 490
432 Cf. Carson, "Matthew," *Expositors Vol. 8* op. cit. pg. 294
433 John Calvin, *Calvin's Commentaries A Harmony of the Gospels of Matthew, Mark, and Luke Vol. II* William B. Eerdmans (Grand Rapids, Mich.) A.W. Morison, trans., 1972 pg. 58
434 Tertullian, *Ante-Nicene Fathers Vol. 3* op. cit. pg. 394
435 Ibid.
436 E.W. Bullinger, *Figures of Speech Used in the Bible* Baker Books (Grand Rapids, Mich.) 1898 (1968 ed.) pg. 751
437 Ibid.
438 Dan McCartney & Charles Clayton, *Let the Reader Understand* Victor Books (Wheaton, Ill.) 1994 pg. 222
439 Quoted in Ibid.
440 Josephus, *Antiquities* XVIII.v.4, op. cit. pg. 383
441 Albright & Mann, op. cit. pg. 176
442 A.C. Gaebelein, *The Gospel of Matthew Vol. 2* Our Hope (New York, NY) 1910 pg. 35
443 Mounce, *Matthew* op. cit. pg. 153
444 Ironside, *Matthew* op. cit. pg. 194
445 Barnes, *Barnes' Notes* op. cit. pg. 48
446 *Liberty Commentary* op. cit. pg. 57
447 Farrar, op. cit. pg. 28
448 Ironside, *Matthew* op. cit. pg. 194
449 Linski, op. cit. pg. 598
450 MacArthur, *Matthew 8-15* op. cit. pg. 468
451 Spurgeon, *Treasury Volume One* op. cit. pg. 237
452 Calvin, *Commentaries A Harmony Vol. 2* op. cit. pg. 169
453 MacArthur, *Matthew 8-15* op. cit. pg. 469
454 Barclay, *Matthew Vol. 1* op. cit. pp. 135-137
455 Tertullian, *Ante-Nicene Fathers Vol. 3* op. cit. pg. 247
456   Loraine Boettner, *Roman Catholicism* Presbyterian & Reformed (Phillipsburg, NJ) 1962 pg. 105
457 James McCarthy, *The Gospel According to Rome* Harvest House (Eugene, OR) 1995 pg. 239
458 Thayer, op. cit. pg. 507
459 Ibid.
460 Boettner, op. cit. pg. 105
461 Poole, *Vol. 3* op. cit. pg. 76
462 Boettner, op. cit. pg. 108
463 Henry, *Vol. 5* op. cit. pg. 187
464 Leon Morris, op. cit. pg. 434
465 Tim LaHaye, Gen. Ed., *Tim LaHaye Prophecy Study Bible* AMG Publishers (Chattanooga, TN) 2001 Note on Matthew 16:28 pg. 1141
466 Torrey, op. cit. pg. 190
467 Stanley Toussaint, *Behold the King* Kregel Publishers (Grand Rapids, Mich.) 1980 pg. 209
468 George Peters, *The Theocratic Kingdom Vol. 2* Kregel (Grand Rapids, Mich.) 1884 pg. 560
469 Wiersbe, *Be Loyal* op. cit. pg. 115
470 Torrey, op. cit. pg. 190
471 Ibid.
472 Cf. Young, *Intermediate Greek* op. cit. pp. 187-189

473 Wiersbe, *Be Loyal* op. cit. pg. 115
474 Bruce Chilton, *God in Strength* F. Plochl (Freistadt, Germany) 1977 as cited by Carson, "Matthew," *Expositors Vol. 8* op. cit. pg. 380
475 Robert Anderson, "Misunderstood Texts of the Bible," *The Collected Works of Sir Robert Andreson Vol. 2* Fortress Adonai (Dallas, TX) 2010 pg. 279
476 Ibid. pp. 280
477 W.A. Criswell, Gen. Ed., *Criswell Study Bible* Thomas Nelson Publishers (Nashville, TN) 1979 Note on Matthew 16:28 pg. 1134
478 Walvoord, *Thy Kingdom Come* op. cit. pg. 127
479 Calvin, *Commentaries A Harmony Vol. 2* op. cit. pg. 196
480 Stanley Toussaint, *Behold the King* Kregel Publishers (Grand Rapids, Mich.) 1980 pg. 209
481 John MacArthur, *The MacArthur New Testament Commentary Matthew 16-23* Moody Bible Institute (Chicago, Ill.) 1985 pg. 59
482 Robert Anderson, "Misunderstood Texts of the Bible," *The Collected Works of Sir Robert Andreson Vol. 2* Fortress Adonai (Dallas, TX) 2010 pp. 280
483 Toussaint, *Behold the King* op. cit. pg. 209
484 Anderson, "Misunderstood Texts of the Bible," op.cit. pp. 280
485 Linski, op. cit. pg. 649
486 Anderson, "Misunderstood Texts of the Bible," op.cit. pg. 279
487 Toussaint, *Behold the King* op. cit. pg. 209
488 Linski, op. cit. pg. 649
489 Toussaint, *Behold the King* op. cit. pg. 209
490 Anderson, "Misunderstood Texts of the Bible," op.cit. pg. 279
491 Barclay, *Matthew Vol. 1* op. cit. pg. 171
492 C.H. Dodd, *Parbles of the Kingdom* Nisbet (London, England) 1936 pp. 53-54 as cited by Carson, "Matthew," *Expositors Vol. 8* op. cit. pg. 380
493 Carson, "Matthew," *Expositors Vol. 8* op. cit. pg. 380
494 Ibid. pg. 382
495 W.A. Criswell, Gen. Ed., *Criswell Study Bible* Thomas Nelson Publishers (Nashville, TN) 1979 Note on Matthew 16:28 pg. 1134
496 Millard Erickson, *Christian Theology* Baker Books (Grand Rapids, Mich.) 1983 pg. 710
497 Albright & Mann, op. cit. pg. 201
498 Anderson, "Misunderstood Texts of the Bible," op.cit. pg. 280
499 Bill Martin & Bill Perkins, "The Second Witness ... Who Is He?", *Digging Deeper Bible Studies* no date pg. 21
500 Cf. John Foxe, *Acts and Monuments of the Church Vol. 1* Church of England (London, England) 1563
501 Bill Martin & Bill Perkins, "The Second Witness ... Who Is He?", *Digging Deeper Bible Studies* no date pg. 21
502 MacArthur, *Matthew 16-23* op. cit. pg. 59
503 Gaebelein, *Matthew Vol. 2* op. cit. pg. 59
504 Calvin, *Commentaries A Harmony Vol. 2* op. cit. pg. 197
505 Carson, "Matthew," *Expositors Vol. 8* op. cit. pg. 384
506 Barbieri, op. cit. pg. 59
507 http://defendtheword.wordpress.com/2009/10/01/alleged-bible-contradictions-non-christians-often-talk-about-new-testament/
508 MacArthur, *Matthew 16-23* op. cit. pg. 71
509 Barnes, *Barnes' Notes* op. cit. pg. 79
510 Erasmus, *Vol. 45* op. cit. pg. 253
511 Calvin, *Commentaries A Harmony Vol. 2* op. cit. pg. 138
512 Ibid. pg. 204
513 *Liberty Commentary* op. cit. pg. 176
514 Erasmus, *Vol. 45* op. cit. pg. 253

515 *Liberty Commentary* op. cit. pg. 176
516 Walvoord, *Thy Kingdom Come* op. cit. pg. 131
517 Toussaint, *Behold the King* op. cit. pg. 211
518 Edwards, *"The Blank Bible"* op. cit. pg. 856
519 See *Controversies in the Epistles* for a discussion of the Apostle Paul's views on divorce and whether or not he had other exceptions. If he did, then Jesus is just stating the most obvious exception and not being exhaustive. His point is that divorce is wrong.
520 http://biblicaldiscipleship.org/content/relationships-and-bible
521 MacArthur, *Matthew 1-7* op. cit. pg. 315
522 http://biblicaldiscipleship.org/content/relationships-and-bible
523 Thayer, op. cit. pg. 532
524 http://biblicaldiscipleship.org/content/relationships-and-bible
525 Farrar, op. cit. pg. 33
526 Barnes, *Barnes' Notes* op. cit. pg. 89
527 *Liberty Commentary* op. cit. pg. 68
528 Cyprian, *Ante-Nicene Fathers Vol. 5* op. cit. pg. 440
529 Albright & Mann, op. cit. pp. 232-233
530 *Liberty Commentary* op. cit. pg. 67
531 Calvin, *Commentaries A Harmony Vol. 2* op. cit. pg. 270
532 Ibid.
533 MacArthur, *Matthew 16-23* op. cit. pg. 238
534 Barnes, *Barnes' Notes* op. cit. pg. 93
535 MacArthur, *Matthew 16-23* op. cit. pg. 249
536 Barnes, *Barnes' Notes* op. cit. pg. 94
537 Linski, op. cit. pg. 797
538 Calvin, *Commentaries A Harmony Vol. 2* op. cit. pg. 278
539 Gaebelein, *Matthew Vol. 2* op. cit. pg. 119
540 Gundry, *Matthew* op. cit. pg. 404
541 Albright & Mann, op. cit. pg. 248
542 Calvin, *Commentaries A Harmony Vol. 2* op. cit. pg. 278
543 Ibid.
544 *Liberty Commentary* op. cit. pg. 69
545 Leon Morris, op. cit. pg. 514
546 Josephus, "War of the Jews," III.III.5, *Complete Works* op. cit. pg. 504
547 Wesley, *New Testament* op. cit. pg. 71
548 Edwin R. Thiele, *The Mysterious Numbers of the Hebrew Kings* Kregel Publications (Grand Rapids, Mich.) 1983 pg. 33
549 Harold Hoehner, *Chronological Aspects of the Life of Christ* Zondervan Publishing (Grand Rapids, Mich.) 1977 pg. 66
550 Hoehner, op. cit. pg. 66
551 MacArthur, *Matthew 16-23* op. cit. pg. 257
552 Ibid.
553 Ibid.
554 Ibid.
555 Ibid.
556 Ibid. pp. 257-258
557 Linski, op. cit. pg. 812
558 Ibid.
559 Ibid.
560 Ibid.
561 Gundry, *Matthew* op. cit. pg. 415
562 John Calvin, *Calvin's Commentaries A Harmony of the Gospels of Matthew, Mark, and Luke Vol. III* William B. Eerdmans (Grand Rapids, Mich.) A.W. Morison, trans., 1972 pg. 3

563 Walvoord, *Thy Kingdom Come* op. cit. pg. 159

564 Calvin, *Commentaries A Harmony Vol. 3* op. cit. pg. 2

565 Linski, op. cit. pg. 822

566 Kee as cited by *Liberty Commentary* op. cit. pg. 71

567 Barnes, *Barnes' Notes* op. cit. pg. 99

568 *Liberty Commentary* op. cit. pg. 117

569 Barclay, *The Gospel of Matthew Vol. 2* op. cit. pg. 281

570 Wiersbe, *Be Loyal* op. cit. pg. 152

571 William Barclay, *The Gospel of Matthew Vol. 2* St. Andrews Press (Edinburgh, Scotland) 1956 pg. 279

572 Josephus, "Antiquities of the Jews," XVIII.i.4, *Complete Works* op. cit. pg. 377

573 Josephus, "Antiquities of the Jews," XIII.x.6, *Complete Works* op. cit. pg. 281

574 Josephus, "War of the Jews," II.xiii.14, *Complete Works* op. cit. pg. 478

575 Ibid.

576 Ibid.

577 Linski, op. cit. pg. 873

578 Ibid. pg. 872

579 Wiersbe, *Be Loyal* op. cit. pg. 160

580 Spurgeon, *Treasury Volume One* op. cit. pg. 239

581 *Liberty Commentary* op. cit. pg. 75

582 Spurgeon, *Treasury Volume One* op. cit. pg. 239

583 Wiersbe, *Be Loyal* op. cit. pg. 160

584 *Liberty Commentary* op. cit. pg. 75

585 Spurgeon, *Treasury Volume One* op. cit. pg. 239

586 Barnes, *Barnes' Notes* op. cit. pg. 105

587 Tertullian, *Ante-Nicene Fathers Vol. 3* op. cit. pg. 593

588 Tertullian, *Ante-Nicene Fathers Vol. 4* op. cit. pg. 39

589 Ibid. pg. 15

590 *Liberty Commentary* op. cit. pg. 75

591 MacArthur, *Matthew 16-23* op. cit. pg. 332

592 Wesley, *New Testament* op. cit. pg. 75

593 Hippolytus, *Ante-Nicene Fathers Vol. 5* op. cit. pg. 238

594 MacArthur, *Matthew 16-23* op. cit. pg. 332

595 Erasmus, *Vol. 45* op. cit. pg. 307

596 MacArthur, *Matthew 16-23* op. cit. pg. 332

597 Leon Morris, op. cit. pg. 561

598 Dave Hunt and T.A. McMahon, *The Seduction of Christianity* Harvest House (Eugene, OR) 1985 pg. 200

599 Ibid. pg. 195

600 I do not know where this quote originated exactly, but it is too good not to quote and all sources seem to attribute it to John Piper.

601 John Milton, *Paradise Lost* III.682-684 *The Portable Milton* Penguin Books (New York, NY) 1949 pg. 308

602 Merril Tenney, *New Testament Survey* William B Eerdmans (Grand Rapids, Mich.) 1961 pp. 105-112

603 Chaim Potok, *Wanderings : Chaim Potok's History of the Jews* Fawcett Crest (New York, NY) 1978 pg. 372

604 Martin Gilbert, *Illustrated Atlas of Jewish Civilization* MacMillan Publishing [New York, NY] 1990 pg. 41

605 Unger, *Unger's Bible Dictionary* op. cit. pp. 1181-1182

606 Cf. Foxe, *Acts and Monuments Vol. 1* op. cit. pg. 105

607 Farrar, op. cit. pg. 37

608 Calvin, *Commentaries A Harmony Vol. 3* op. cit. pg. 66

609 Matthew 23:35, *Biblia Sacra* Deutsche Bibelgesellschaft (Stuttgard, Germany) 1993 ed.
610 Mentioned, but no advocated, by Poole, *Vol. 3* op. cit. pg. 110
611 Farrar, op. cit. pg. 37
612 Joesphus, *War of the Jews*, IV.vi.4 *Complete Works* op. cit. pp. 534-535
613 William Whiston, note on Zechariah, *Complete Works of Josephus* op. cit. pg. 534
614 Joesphus, *War of the Jews*, IV.vi.4 *Complete Works* op. cit. pg. 534
615 Cf. John Foxe, *Acts and Monuments of the Church*
616 MacArthur, *Matthew 16-23* op. cit. pg. 394
617 William Whiston, note on Zechariah, *Complete Works of Josephus* op. cit. pg. 534
618 Poole, *Vol. 3* op. cit. pg. 110
619 Archer, op. cit. pg. 338
620 Joesphus, *Antiquities of the Jews*, IX.viii.3 *Complete Works* op. cit. pg. 205
621 Linski, op. cit. pg. 920
622 Barnes, *Barnes' Notes* op. cit. pg. 111
623 Wesley, *New Testament* op. cit. pg. 79
624 Calvin, *Commentaries A Harmony Vol. 3* op. cit. pg. 66
625 Ibid.
626 Carson, "Matthew," *Expositor's Bible Commentary Vol. 8* op. cit. pg. 486
627 Linski, op. cit. pg. 920
628 Leon Morris, op. cit. pg. 589
629 Walvoord, *Thy Kingdom Come* op. cit. pg. 174
630 Barnes represents the typical preterist position. Cf. Barnes, *Barnes' Notes* op. cit. pp. 113-115
631 Ibid.
632 Wesley, *New Testament* op. cit. pg. 82
633 Calvin, *Commentaries A Harmony Vol. 3* op. cit. pg. 83
634 Edwards, *"The Blank Bible"* op. cit. pg. 864
635 Gaebelein, *Matthew Vol. 2* op. cit. pg. 167
636 Wesley, *New Testament* op. cit. pg. 81
637 Wiersbe, *Be Loyal* op. cit. pp. 173-174
638 John MacArthur, *The MacArthur New Testament Commentary Matthew 24-28* Moody Bible Institute (Chicago, Ill.) 1985 pg. 17
639 D.A. Carson, "Matthew," *Expositor's Bible Commentary Vol. 8* op. cit. pg. 498
640 Homer Ritchie, Omer Ritchie, & Lonnie Shipman, *Secrets of Prophecy Revealed* 21st Century Press (Springfield, Mo.) 2001 pg. 36
641 *Fort Worth Star Telegram*, Novermber 23, 1988, A: 14
642 Ritchie, Rtchie, & Shipman, op. cit. pg. 30
643 Wesley, *New Testament* op. cit. pg. 80
644 Ibid. pg. 81
645 Stephen R. Miller, *The New American Commentary on Daniel* Broadman & Holman (Nashville, Tenn.) 1994 pg. 252
646 Walvoord, *Every Prophecy* op. cit. pg. 248
647 Unger, *Unger's Bible Dictionary* op. cit. pp. 163-166
648 Paul A. Zoch, *Ancient Rome* University of Oklahoma Press (University of Oklahoma, Ok.) 1998 pg. 204
649 A.T. Olmstead, *History of Assyria* Charles Scribner's Sons (New York, NY) 1923 pg. 589
650 Unger, *Unger's Bible Dictionary* op. cit. pp. 163-166
651 A.T. Olmstead, *History of the Persian Empire* University of Chicago Press (Chicago, Ill.) 1948 pg. 209
652 Ibid.
653 Cf. Unger, *Unger's Bible Dictionary* op. cit. pp. 163-166
654 Charles Pfeiffer, *The Dead Sea Scrolls and the Bible* Baker Books (Grand Rapids, Mich.) 1969 pp. 127-128
655 Gilbert, *Atlas* op. cit. pg. 47

656 Linski, op. cit. pg. 938
657 Barnes, *Barnes' Notes* op. cit. pp. 113-115
658 Eusebius, *The Church History* 2:26, Paul Meier, ed., Kregel Publications (Grand Rapids, Mich.) 1999 pg. 86
659 Eusebius, *The Church History* 3:5 Ibid. pg. 95
660 Josephus, *War of the Jews* II.xvii.1-10, *Complete Works* op. cit. pp. 490-491
661 Leon Morris, op. cit. pg. 604
662 Ibid.
663 Stephen R. Miller, *Daniel : New American Commentary Vol. 18* Broadman & Holman (Nashville, TN.) 1994 pp. 301-302
664 Mounce, *Matthew* op. cit. pg. 224
665 Albright & Mann, op. cit. pg. 295
666 Particularly see *Controversies in Revelation*
667 Ibid. pp. 86-87
668 Cf. Price, "Daniel's Seventy Weeks, Rabbinic Interpretation," *Dictionary Premillennial* op. cit. pg. 79
669 Epistle of Barnabas, *Ante-Nicene Fathers Vol. I* op. cit. pg. 147
670 Irenaeus, "Against Heresies," *Ante-Nicene Fathers Vol. 1* pg. 553
671 Hippolytus, *Ante-Nicene Fathers Vol. V* op. cit. pg. 184
672 Tertullian, *Ante-Nicene Fathers Vol. 4* op. cit. pg. 218
673 Wesley, *New Testament* op. cit. pg. 82
674 Barclay, *The Gospel of Matthew Vol. 2* op. cit. pp. 338-339
675 Farrar, op. cit. pg. 39
676 Walvoord, *Thy Kingdom Come* op. cit. pg. 185
677 Gaebelein, *Matthew Vol. 2* op. cit. pg. 167
678 Wesley, *New Testament* op. cit. pp. 82-83
679 Mounce, *Matthew* op. cit. pp. 227-228
680 See, for example, Gundry, *Matthew* op. cit. pg. 490
681 I could not find my citation for this, but I toyed with the view as a young college student.
682 Robert Mounce, *Basics of Biblical Greek* Zondervan (Grand Rapids, Mich.) 1993 pg. 189
683 See Torrey's comments in Torrey, op. cit. pg. 188
684 Anderson, "Misunderstood Texts of the Bible," *Collected Works* op. cit. pg. 282
685 Leon Morris, op. cit. pg. 612
686 Gaebelein, *Matthew Vol. 2* op. cit. pg. 215
687 Thayer, op. cit. pg. 112
688 Archer, op. cit. pg. 339
689 *Hebrew New Testament*, Trinitarian Bible Society (London, England) 1998
690 Gesenius, op. cit. pg. 194
691 Walvoord, *Thy Kingdom Come* op. cit. pg. 192
692 Anderson, "Misunderstood Texts of the Bible," *Collected Works* op. cit. pg. 282
693 Walvoord, *Thy Kingdom Come* op. cit. pg. 192
694 *Liberty Commentary* op. cit. pg. 80
695 Calvin, *Commentaries A Harmony Vol. 3* op. cit. pg. 97
696 MacArthur, *Matthew 24-28* op. cit. pg. 64
697 Newman, op. cit. pg. 29
698 Linski, op. cit. pg. 952
699 Barnes, *Barnes' Notes* op. cit. pp. 113-115
700 Ibid. pg. 117
701 Cf. David Hunt, *In Defense of the Faith* Harvest House (Eugene, OR) 1996 pg. 282-284
702 Henry, *Matthew Henry's Commentary on the Bible Vol. 6* Hendrickson Publishers () ????? pg. 633
703 Poole, *Commentary Vol. III* op. cit. pg. 746

704 Ephraem the Syrian, *When the Trumpet Sounds* Thomas Ice & Timothy Demy ed., Harvest House (Eugene, OR) 1995 pg. 113

705 Poole, *Commentary Vol. III* op. cit. pg. 746

706 There have been a few scholars and church fathers that believe that Revelation only covers a 3½ year time frame and at least one who believes it covers a 10½ years period.

707 My "mentor" at Tyndale Theological Seminary, Malcolm Couch, is such a man. He insisted that it cannot be a rapture passage because the Church "cannot" be mentioned by Jesus. This is based on the ultradispensational doctrine that the Church is *never* revealed in *any* form until Acts 2.

708 http://www.thebereancall.org/node/1220

709 MacArthur, *Matthew 24-28* op. cit. pp. 71-75

710 Ibid. pg. 75

711 Walvoord, *Thy Kingdom Come* op. cit. pg. 193

712 Wiersbe, *Be Loyal* op. cit. pg. 178

713 Leon Morris, op. cit. pg. 614

714 http://www.thebereancall.org/node/1220

715 Douglas Moo, Paul Feinberg, *The Rapture : Pre- Mid- or Posttribulational?* Zondervan (Grand Rapids, Mich.) 1984 pg. 196

716 Tertullian, *Ante-Nicene Fathers Vol. 3* op. cit. pg. 409

717 J.F. Strombeck, *First the Rapture* Kregel Publications (Grand Rapids, Mich.) 1992 reprint (orig. 1950) pg, 69

718 Hunt, op. cit. pg. 273

719 See note 694

720 This is a debate which goes far beyond the scope of this book, but Ultradispensationalism is guilty of reading into the text rather than taking it out of the text. I myself am a dispensationalist and reject progressive dispensationalism.

721 Wesley, *New Testament* op. cit. pg. 83

722 Barnes, *Barnes' Notes* op. cit. pg. 117

723 Calvin, *Commentaries A Harmony Vol. 3* op. cit. pp. 100-101

724 Ibid. pp. 102-103

725 Cyprian, *Ante-Nicene Fathers Vol. 5* op. cit. pg. 500

726 Ironside, *Matthew* op. cit. pg. 325

727 Cited in Boettner, op. cit. pg. 173 Also see McCarthy, *The Gospel According to Rome* op. cit. pp. 125-132

728 Boettner, op. cit. pg. 175

729 Cited in Boettner, op. cit. pg. 169

730 Calvin, *Commentaries A Harmony Vol. 3* op. cit. pg. 135

731 *Liberty Commentary* op. cit. pg. 84

732 McCarthy, *The Gospel According to Rome* op. cit. pp. 136-137

733 Wesley, *New Testament* op. cit. pg. 89

734 Linski, op. cit. pg. 1027

735 Tertullian, *Ante-Nicene Fathers Vol. 3* op. cit. pg. 683

736 Gaebelein, *Matthew Vol. 2* op. cit. pg. 276

737 Thayer, op. cit. pg. 641

738 Barclay, *The Gospel of Matthew Vol. 2* op. cit. pg. 387

739 Thayer, op. cit. pg. 583

740 Ibid. pp. 668-669

741 *Liberty Commentary* op. cit. pg. 85

742 Mounce, *Matthew* op. cit. pg. 244

743 *Liberty Commentary* op. cit. pg. 85

744 These are facts ignored by those who claim anti-semitism in Mel Gibson's *Passion of the Christ*. Many Jews are unaware that the apostle's who wrote the gospels were all Jewish. Only Luke was a gentile. They see Caiphas' guilt in the film as anti-semitic, but both Pilate and Caiphas were equally guilty as will be discussed later.

745 See comments at http://www.godrules.net/articles/101scontra_d.htm
746 "I Am" is part of the sacred name of *Yahweh*. See notes on "John 8:58-59." Cf. Merrill Tenney, "The Gospel of John," *The Expositor's Bible Commentary Vol. 9* Frank Gaebelain, ed. Zondervan Publishers (Grand Rapids, Mich.) 1984 pg. 169
747 Tertullian, *Ante-Nicene Fathers Vol. 3* op. cit. pg. 73
748 Origen, *Ante-Nicene Fathers Vol. 4* op. cit. pg. 435
749 *Liberty Commentary* op. cit. pg. 86
750 Calvin, *Commentaries A Harmony Vol. 3* op. cit. pg. 159
751 Ibid.
752 Linski, op. cit. pg. 1051
753 *Liberty Commentary* op. cit. pg. 86
754 Leon Morris, op. cit. pg. 675
755 MacArthur, *Matthew 24-28* op. cit. pg. 190
756 Ibid.
757 Barnes, *Barnes' Notes* op. cit. pg. 131
758 Walvoord, *Thy Kingdom Come* op. cit. pg. 221
759 *Liberty Commentary* op. cit. pg. 86
760 Archer, op. cit. pg. 338
761 Hunt, *Defense* op. cit. pg. 92
762 Calvin, *Commentaries A Harmony Vol. 3* op. cit. pg. 171
763 Nestle & Aland, *Nestle-Aland Novum Tetamentum Graece* op. cit. Mark 14:30; 72
764 Gundry, *Matthew* op. cit. pg. 553
765 Unger, *Unger's Bible Dictionary* op. cit. pg. 615
766 MacArthur, *Matthew 24-28* op. cit. pg. 228
767 Wesley, *New Testament* op. cit. pg. 284
768 Albright & Mann, op. cit. pg. 340
769 *Liberty Commentary* op. cit. pg. 87
770 Wiersbe, *Be Loyal* op. cit. pg. 199
771 Ibid.
772 www.tentmaker.org/Dew/Dew3/D3-JudasIscariot.html
773 Erasmus, *Vol. 45* op. cit. pg. 362
774 Ibid.
775 Wesley, *New Testament* op. cit. pg. 92
776 Farrar, op. cit. pg. 44
777 http://craigwbooth.xanga.com/743267828/ten-alleged-contradictions-in-the-bible/
778 Albright & Mann, op. cit. pg. 341
779 Barnes, *Barnes' Notes* op. cit. pg. 135
780 Leon Morris, op. cit. pg. 696
781 Ironside, *Matthew* op. cit. pg. 375
782 Cf. Norman Geisler, ed., *Inerrancy* Academie Books (Grand Rapids, Mich.) 1980
783 Nestle & Aland, *Nestle-Aland Novum Tetamentum Graece* op. cit. Matthew 27:9
784 Calvin, *Commentaries A Harmony Vol. 3* op. cit. pg. 177
785 Barnes, *Barnes' Notes* op. cit. pg. 135
786 Albright & Mann, op. cit. pg. 341
787 Barnes, *Barnes' Notes* op. cit. pg. 135
788 Wiersbe, *Be Loyal* op. cit. pg. 200
789 William Sanford Lasor, David Allan Hubbard, and Frederic Bush, *Old Testament Survey* William B. Eerdmans (Grand Rapids, Mich) 1982 pg. 492
790 Unger, *Unger's Bible Dictionary* op. cit. pg. 1182
791 Archer, op. cit. pg. 345
792 Leon Morris, op. cit. pg. 696
793 *Liberty Commentary* op. cit. pp. 87-88
794 Ibid. pg. 88

795 Barbieri, op. cit. pg. 87
796 Carson, op. cit. pg. 563
797 Young, op. cit. pg. 190
798 Ibid.
799 Well, atheists will questions anything, no matter how rational, except whether or not our distant cousins are maggots and slugs.
800 Ironside, *Matthew* op. cit. pg. 375
801 Walvoord, *Thy Kingdom Come* op. cit. pg. 227
802 Barnes, *Barnes' Notes* op. cit. pg. 135
803 Linski, op. cit. pg. 1083
804 Barker, "Zechariah," *The Expositor's Bible Commentary* Vol. 7 Frank Gaebelain, ed. Zondervan Publishers (Grand Rapids, Mich.) 1984 pg. 676
805 Lindsey, "Zechariah," *The Bible Knowledge Commentary : Old Testament* John F. Walvoord & Roy Zuck, eds., Victor Books (Wheaton, Ill.) 1986 pg. 1565
806 Linski, op. cit. pg. 1083
807 Lindsey, "Zechariah," *The Bible Knowledge Commentary : Old Testament* John F. Walvoord & Roy Zuck, eds., Victor Books (Wheaton, Ill.) 1986 pg. 1565
808 Sir Robert Anderson, "The Bible and Modern Criticism," *Collected Works* Vol. 2 op. cit. pg. 141
809 Joesphus, *Antiquities of the Jews*, II.xv.1 *Complete Works* op. cit. pg. 62
810 Hoehner, op. cit. pg. 87
811 *Mishnah* Pesahim iv. 5. Apparently, the Jews were allowed to work on Friday of Passover until noon, whereas the Galileans would not work at Friday of Passover at all. This is presumed to be because Passover had already begun for Galileans, but not for the Judeans. [Jacob Neusner, trans., *Mishnah* Yale University Press (London, England) 1988 as cited by Hoehner, op. cit. pg. 87]
812 Josephus, "The Jewish War" VI.ix..3 *Complete Works* op. cit. pg. 588
813 Thomas & Gundry, *Harmony* op. cit. pg. 320
814 Cf. Anderson, "The Bible and Modern Criticism," *Collected Works* Vol. 2 op. cit. pg. 143
815 Potok, op. cit. pg. 262
816 Hoehner, op. cit. pg. 78
817 http://www.godrules.net/articles/101scontra_f.htm
818 *Liberty Commentary* op. cit. pg. 163
819 Albright & Mann, op. cit. pg. 319
820 Tertullian, *Ante-Nicene Fathers* Vol. 3 op. cit. pg. 167
821 Hunt, *Defense of the Faith*, op. cit. pp. 100-102
822 Cf. Hoehner, op. cit. pg. 72
823 Thomas & Gundry, *Harmony* op. cit. pg. 320
824 Hunt, *Defense of the Faith*, op. cit. pg. 101
825 Josephus, "The Jewish War" VI.ix..3 *Complete Works* op. cit. pg. 588
826 Hoehner, op. cit. pp. 72-73
827 Thayer, op. cit. pg. 471
828 Ibid.
829 Roger Beckwith, "The Day, its Divisions and its Limits, in Biblical Thought," *The Evangelical Quarterly* XLIII (Oct-Dec 1971) pg. 226
830 Ibid.
831 Edwin Blum, "John," *The Bible Knowledge Commentary : New Testament* John F. Walvoord & Roy Zuck, eds., Victor Books (Wheaton, Ill.) 1986 pg. 335
832 Joesphus, *Antiquities of the Jews*, XVIII.ii.1-2 *Complete Works* op. cit. but there is not agreement as to the exact date he was deposed, implicating that he did, in fact, retain power after his initial removal. Doubtless the Jews were reluctant to recognize the Romans' right to depose a high priest of the Jewish religion. Cf. Unger, *Bible Dictionary* op. cit. pg. 67

833 Merrill Tenney, "The Gospel of John," *The Expositor's Bible Commentary Vol. 9* Frank Gaebelain, ed. Zondervan Publishers (Grand Rapids, Mich.) 1984 pg. 170

834 Joesphus, *Antiquities of the Jews*, XVIII.ii-iv; *War of the Jews*, II.ix *Complete Works* op. cit. pp. 379-380, 480

835 *Liberty Commentary* op. cit. pg. 87

836 The Hebrew and Aramaic would be virtually the same in this case as the languages are very similar. See section "Did Jesus speak Aramiac?"

837 Archer, op. cit. pg. 346

838 Anderson, "The Bible and Modern Criticism," *Collected Works* op. cit. pg. 140

839 The Hebrew and Aramaic would be virtually the same in this case as the languages are very similar. See section "Did Jesus speak Aramiac?"

840 Henry, *Vol. 5* op. cit. pg. 667

841 Ibid.

842 Unger, *Bible Dictionary*, op. cit. pg. 77

843 Cf. Franz Rosenthal, *A Grammar of Biblical Aramaic* Otto Harrassowitz (Wiesbaden, Germany) 1983

844 http://gluefox.com/min/contrad.htm

845 Carson, "Matthew," *Expositor's Bible Commentary Vol. 8* op. cit. pg. 578

846 Ibid.

847 See notes under σαβαχθανι (*sabachthani*) in Thayer, op. cit. pg. 565

848 Incidently, this is how the modern Hebrew New Testament is translated. Cf. *The Hebrew-English New Covenant* Hope of Israel Publications (Powder Springs, GA) 2003

849 http://gluefox.com/min/contrad.htm

850 Cf. Thayer, op. cit. pg. 164

851 There may be differences in how either the Aramaic or Hebrew were written, as languages do change and reflect time and culture. These are two examples.

852 Gesenius, *Hebrew-Chaldee Lexicon* op. cit. pg. 589

853 Thayer, op. cit. pg. 493

854 Ibid. pg. 561

855 Gesenius, *Hebrew-Chaldee Lexicon* op. cit. pg. 768

856 Thayer, op. cit. pg. 265

857 Ibid. pg. 107

858 Ibid. pg. 265

859 Ehud Ben Yehuda, ed., *Ben Yehuda's Pocket English-Hebrew Hebrew-English Dictionary* Penguin Books (New York, NY) 1947

860 Shimon Zilberman, *The Up-to-Date Hebrew-English Dictionary* Zilberman Press (Jerusalem, Israel) 1997

861 Orthodox Jews often express concern over a certain Charismatic preacher who visits Israel and calls the Lord "daddy" during his public prayers. They consider this disrespectful.

862 Thayer, op. cit. pg. 388

863 Young, op. cit. pg. 65

864 Linski, op. cit. pg. 1133

865 Leon Morris, op. cit. pg. 726

866 Erasmus, *Vol. 45* op. cit. pg. 372

867 Calvin, *Commentaries A Harmony Vol. 3* op. cit. pg. 214

868 Origen, *Ante-Nicene Fathers Vol. 4* op. cit. pg. 446

869 MacArthur, *Matthew 24-28* op. cit. pg. 279

870 Carson, "Matthew," *Expositor's Bible Commentary Vol. 8* op. cit. pg. 586

871 John McDowell, *The Resurrection Factor* Here's Life Publishers (San Bernadino, CA) 1981 pg. 55

872 *Hebrew-English New Covenant* Hope of Israel Publications (Powder Springs, GA) 2003

873 McDowell, op. cit. pg. 55

874 Wesley Perschbacher, *Refresh Your Greek* Moody Press (Chicago, Ill.) 1989 pg. 119

875 Cf. Mounce, *Basis of Biblical Greek* op. cit. pg. 294

876 McDowell, op. cit. pg. 57

877 Ibid.

878 Frank Morison, *Who Moved the Stone?* Faber & Faber (New York, NY) 1930 pg. 190

879 McDowell, op. cit. pg. 57

880 Here is not the place to relive that horrid trial, but the fact is that O.J. had intended his Limousine driver to be his alibi, but the Limousine driver was early and spent 30 minutes ringing the bell with no answer. O.J.'s alibi was broken, but when the detectives insisted that O.J. returned home by way of the front gate (not realizing a Limousine driver was waiting at the front gate), the prosecution did not want to admit their detectives were either corrupt or incompetent, so they attemped to change the time of the murders to over an hour earlier. The result was that the Limousine driver could no longer break O.J.'s alibi and the prosecution was, in fact, saying that O.J. really was at home at the time the original police report had placed the murder! The acquittal was not because of the glove, but because the prosecution gave O.J. an alibi he did not previously have!

881 Albright & Mann, op. cit. pg. 358

882 Barnes, *Barnes' Notes* op. cit. pg. 117

883 Wesley, *New Testament* op. cit. pg. 139

884 John Nelson Darby, *Notes on the Gospel of Matthew* G. Morrish (London, England) n.p.d. pg. 162

885 Calvin, *Commentaries A Harmony Vol. 3* op. cit. pg. 223

886 Gundry, *Matthew* op. cit. pg. 585

887 Ibid.

888 Leon Morris, op. cit. pg. 734

889 MacArthur, *Matthew 24-28* op. cit. pg. 307

890 Young, op. cit. pg. 184

891 Wesley, *New Testament* op. cit. pp. 97-98

892 http://www.abideinchrist.com/messages/resurrectionofjesusharmony.html

893 John Walvoord, *Matthew : Thy Kingdom Come* Moody Press (Chicago, Ill.) 1974 pp. 239-240

894 Although I prefer deductive logic to inductive logic (preferred by atheists), I have used inductive logic for convenience sake. Nevertheless, the deductive approach is what lead me to the conclusions which I presented inductively.

895 *Liberty Commentary* op. cit. pg. 91

896 Criswell, *Rise and Fall* op. cit. pg. 42

897 Paul Gaechter, *Matthaus* Innsbruck (Tyrolia, Germany) 1968 pp. 243-253   as cited by Carson, op. cit. pg. 595

898 Carson, op. cit. pg. 597

899 This is Carson's summary of of men like D.R.A. Hare, Rolf Walker, and D.J. Harrington. Cited by Carson, op. cit. pg. 596

900 Ibid.

901 Mal Couch, ed., *A Biblical Theology of the Church* Kregel Publications (Grand Rapids, Mich.) 1999 pg. 250

902 Carson, op. cit. pg. 598

903 John Foxe, *Acts and Monuments of the Church Vol. 1* Religious Tract Society (London, England) 1860s ed. pg. 95

904 Ibid.

905 So says the early church father Papias, as cited by Eusebius, *Church History* II.16

906 Tenney, *New Testament Survey* op. cit. pg. 162

907 Ibid.

908 Gundry, *Survey of the New Testament* op. cit. pg. 127

909 Ibid.

910 Tenney, *New Testament Survey* op. cit. pg. 162

911 Grassmick, "Mark," *The Bible Knowledge Commentary : New Testament* John F. Walvoord & Roy Zuck, eds., Victor Books (Wheaton, Ill.) 1986 pg. 144

912 Unger, op. cit. pg. 3

913 David Criswell, *Controversies in the Scriptures Vol. II* Fortress Adonai (Dallas, TX) 2010 pg. 48

914 John Whitcomb & Henry Morris, *The Genesis Flood* Presbyterian & Reformed (Grand Rapids, Mich.) 1961 pp. 481

915 Joesphus, *Antiquities of the Jews*, VI.xii.5 *Complete Works* op. cit. pg. 139

916 Walter Wessel, "Mark," *Expositor's Bible Commentary Vol. 8* op. cit. pg. 638

917 Ibid.

918 Nestle & Aland, *Novum Tetamentum Graece* op. cit. ref. Mark 2:26

919 Ibid.

920 Walter Wessel, "Mark," *Expositor's Bible Commentary Vol. 8* op. cit. pg. 638

921 Henry Barclay Swete, *The Gospel According to St. Mark* MacMillan & Co. (London, England) 1920 pg. 48

922 Cited by Unger, op. cit. pg. 3

923 James Brooks, *New American Commentary Mark* Broadman Press (Nashville, TN) 1991 pg. 66

924 F.W. Farrar, *Texts Explained* F.M. Barton (Cleveland, Ohio) 1899 pg. 47

925 Albert Barnes, *Barnes' Notes on the New Testament One Volume ed.* Kregel (Grand Rapids, Mich) 1962 pg. 151

926 R.C.H. Lenski, *The Interpretation of St. Mark's Gospel* Augsburg Publishing (Minneapolis, MN) 1946 pg. 128

927 Poole, *Vol. 3* op. cit. pg. 152

928 Cited by Unger, op. cit. pg. 3

929 Wessel, "Mark," *Expositor's Bible Commentary Vol. 8* op. cit. pg. 638

930 Henry, *Vol. 5* op. cit. pg. 375

931 Barclay Newman, *A Concise Greek-English Dictionary of the New Testament* United Bible Society (Stuttgart, Germany) 1971 pg. 67

932 Robert Gundry, *Mark* William B. Eerdmanns (Grand Rapids, Mich) 1993 pg. 146

933 Wesley, *New Testament* op. cit. 106

934 Grassmick, "Mark," *The Bible Knowledge Commentary : New Testament* John F. Walvoord & Roy Zuck, eds., Victor Books (Wheaton, Ill.) 1986 pg. 144

935 Warren Wiersbe, *Be Diligent* Victor Books (Wheaton, Ill.) 1987 pg. 31

936 Edwards, *"The Blank Bible"* op. cit. pg. 879

937 Carson, op. cit. pg. 299

938 http://forums.catholic.com/showthread.php?t=477205

939 Gesenius, *Hebrew-Chaldee Lexicon* op. cit. pg. 191

940 Carson, op. cit. pg. 299

941 Lenski, *Mark* op. cit. pg. 157

942 Ibid.

943 Wiersbe, *Be Diligent* op. cit. pg. 36

944 If anyone suggest that it was a sham sharade of a marriage to keep Mary from being disgraced, I would respond that God does not engage in shams or sharades.

945 Henry, *Vol. 5* op. cit. pg. 379

946 Carson, op. cit. pg. 229

947 Thayer, op. cit. pg. 619

948 Mounce, *Biblical Greek* op. cit. pg. 189

949 Newman, Jr., ed., *A Concise Greek-English Dictionary* op. cit. pg. 25

950 Thayer, op. cit. pg. 253

951 Cf. Young, op. cit.

952 Calvin, *Commentaries A Harmony Vol. 1* op. cit. pg. 271

953 Carson, op. cit. pg. 230

954 Wessel, op. cit. pg. 661

955 Lenski, *Mark* op. cit. pp. 222-223

956 Irenaeus, *Ante-Nicene Fathers Vol. I* op. cit. pp. 319, 392

957 Lenski, *Mark* op. cit. pg. 223

958 Carson, op. cit. pg. 230

959 Walter Liefeld, "Luke," *Expositor's Bible Commentary Vol. 8* op. cit. pg. 916

960 Lenski, *Mark* op. cit. pg. 223

961 Calvin, *Commentaries A Harmony Vol. 1* op. cit. pg. 271

962 Ibid.

963 John Martin, "Luke," *The Bible Knowledge Commentary : Old Testament* op. cit. pg. 227

964 Wessel, op. cit. pg. 661

965 Grassmick, "Mark," *The Bible Knowledge Commentary : New Testament* John F. Walvoord & Roy Zuck, eds., Victor Books (Wheaton, Ill.) 1986 pg. 144

966 Lenski, *Mark* op. cit. pg. 223

967 Wiersbe, *Be Diligent* op. cit. pg. 53

968 John Nelson Darby, *Mark's Gospel* G. Morrish (London, England) 1800 pg. 37

969 H.A. Ironside, *Expository Notes on the Gospel of Mark* Loizeaux Brothers (Minneapolis, MN) 1946 pp. 81-82

970 Newman, Jr., ed., *A Concise Greek-English Dictionary* op. cit. pg. 177

971 Wessel, op. cit. pg. 662

972 Swete, op. cit. pg. 213

973 Unger, op. cit. pg. 1012

974 Gesenius, *Hebrew-Chaldee Lexicon* op. cit. pg. 798

975 Zilberman, op. cit. pg. 274

976 Joseph Thayer, *Greek-English Lexicon* Baker Books (Grand Rapids, Mich.) 1977 pg. 11

977 Unger, op. cit. pp. 437-438

978 It is not certain that this is what the Apocalypse of Zephaniah teaches for the only copies are incomplete. We find that someone has apparently crossed over in a boat from Hades to the Abraham's Bosom, but this must be assumed as the exact nature of the boat is part of what was lost and is no longer extant.

979 Brooks, op. cit. pg. 153

980 Falwell & Hindson, eds., *Liberty* op. cit. pg. 114

981 Unger, op. cit. pg. 394

982 Lenski, *Mark* op. cit. pg. 407

983 William Barclay, *Gospel of Mark* Westminister Press (Philadelphia, PN) 1954 pg. 231

984 Gundry, *Mark* op. cit. pg. 526

985 James McGowan, *Gospel of Mark* AMG Publishers (Chattanooge, TN) 2006 pg. 133

986 Wiersbe, *Be Diligent* op. cit. pg. 93

987 Barnes, *Barnes' Notes* op. cit. pg. 165

988 Desiderius Erasmus, *The Collected Works of Erasmus Vol. 49 Paraphrase on Mark* Dean Simpson, trans., University of Toronto Press (Toronto, Canada) 1988 pg. 119

989 Ibid.

990 Ibid. pg. 467

991 Joseph A. Seiss, *The Apocalypse* Kregel Publications (Grand Rapids, Mich.) 2001 reprint pg. 480

992 Seiss, op. cit. pg. 480

993 Grassmick, op. cit. pg. 147

994 Bruce Metzger, *A Textual Commentary on the Greek New Testament* United Bible Societies (New York, NY) 1971 pg. 87

995 Ibid.

996 John Wesley, *Wesley's Bible Commentary* E-Sword Software, note on Mark 9:49

997 John Nelson Darby, *Bible Commentary* E-Sword Software, note on Mark 9:49

998 Adam Clarke, *Clarke's Bible Commentary* E-Sword Software, note on Mark 9:49

999 John Gill, *Gill's Bible Commentary* E-Sword Software, note on Mark 9:49

1000 Weston Fields, "Everyone will be Salted with Fire," *Grace Theological Journal* 6:2 (1985) pg. 301

1001 Ibid. pg. 299

1002 Ibid. pg. 302

1003 Ibid. pg. 299

1004 Gesenius, *Gesenius Hebrew-Chaldee Lexicon*, op. cit. pg. 476

1005 Weston Fields, "Everyone will be Salted with Fire," *Grace Theological Journal* 6:2 (1985) pg. 299

1006 Wessel, op. cit. pg. 709

1007 Ibid.

1008 Grassmick, op. cit. pg. 147

1009 Ibid.

1010 John Nelson Darby, *Bible Commentary* E-Sword Software, note on Mark 9:49

1011 Grassmick, op. cit. pg. 150

1012 Poole, *Vol. 3* op. cit. pg. 171

1013 Henry, *Vol. 5* op. cit. pg. 419

1014 Calvin, *Commentaries A Harmony Vol. 2* op. cit. pg. 254

1015 Ibid.

1016 "Free Grace - Dispensational Group" http://www.facebook.com/groups/12295580323/

1017 Ibid.

1018 Swete, op. cit. pg. 381

1019 Archer, op. cit. pg. 364

1020 Ibid.

1021 Swete, op. cit. pg. 381

1022 Falwell & Hindson, eds., *Liberty* op. cit. pg. 125

1023 There is, of course, debate as to which Holy site is the true Golgotha of the Bible.

1024 Metzger, *Textual Commentary* op. cit. pg. 103

1025 Ibid.

1026 Swete, op. cit. pg. cix

1027 Grassmick, op. cit. pg. 193

1028 Swete, op. cit. pg. cvii

1029 Metzger, *Textual Commentary* op. cit. pp. 103-105

1030 Metzger, *Textual Commentary* op. cit. pg. 104

1031 Grassmick, op. cit. pg. 194

1032 Ibid.

1033 R.G. Bratcher & E.A. Nida, *Translator's Handbook on Mark* E.J Brill Publishers (Leiden, Netherlands) 1961 pg. 520

1034 Grassmick, op. cit. pg. 194

1035 Ibid.

1036 Bratcher op. cit. pg. 520

1037 Grassmick, op. cit. pg. 194

1038 Bratcher op. cit. pg. 520

1039 Swete, op. cit. pg. cix

1040 Ibid. pg. civ

1041 Grassmick, op. cit. pg. 194

1042 Bratcher op. cit. pg. 520

1043 Grassmick, op. cit. pg. 194

1044 See endnote 894 for my opinion on deductive and inductive reasoning.

1045 Bratcher op. cit. pg. 520

1046 Wessel, op. cit. pg. 792

1047 Ibid.

1048 Grassmick, op. cit. pg. 194

1049 Ibid.

1050 Metzger, *Textual Commentary* op. cit. pg. 104
1051 Wessel, op. cit. pg. 792
1052 Cf. Wessel, op. cit. pg. 792
1053 Metzger, *Textual Commentary* op. cit. pg. 104
1054 Swete, op. cit. pg. civ
1055 Barclay, *Mark* op. cit. pg. 5
1056 McGowan, op. cit. pg. 5
1057 Lenski, *Mark* op. cit. pg. 752
1058 Bratcher op. cit. pg. 520
1059 Wessel, op. cit. pg. 790
1060 Henry, *Vol. 5* op. cit. pg. 462
1061 Grassmick, op. cit. pg. 196
1062 Eusebius, *Eusebius The Church History*, Paul Maier, trans., Kregel Publications (Grand Rapids, Mich.) 1999 pg. 129
1063 Tenney, *New Testament Survey* op. cit. pg. 179
1064 Compare http://www.deafmissions.com/tally/matthew.html and http://www.deafmissions.com/tally/luke.html
1065 Unger, op. cit. pg. 233
1066 Archer, op. cit. pg. 365
1067 Unger, op. cit. pg. 233
1068 The codices *Vaticanus* and *Washingtonius* both spell his name differently (Κυρεινου) from the other texts, although it is clearly the same name (Κυρηνιου).
1069 John Martin, "Luke," *Bible Knowledge Commentary : New Testament* op. cit. pg. 207
1070 Liefeld, op. cit. pg. 843
1071 Thayer, op. cit. pg. 556
1072 Hoehner, op. cit. pg. 15
1073 Ibid.. pg. 16
1074 Tertullian, *Ante-Nicene Vol. 3* op. cit. pg. 378
1075 Hoehner, op. cit. pg. 17
1076 Archer, op. cit. pg. 365
1077 John MacArthur, *The MacArthur New Testament Commentary Luke 1-5* Moody Bible Instituted (Chicago, Ill.) 2009 pg. 144
1078 Josephus, "Antiquities XVIII.i.1-6," op. cit. pg. 376
1079 Hoehner, op. cit. pg. 13
1080 Archer, op. cit. pg. 365
1081 Tertullian, *Ante-Nicene Vol. 3* op. cit. pg. 378
1082 Ibid.
1083 Unger, op. cit. pg. 233
1084 Ibid.
1085 Tertullian, *Ante-Nicene Vol. 3* op. cit. pg. 378
1086 Archer, op. cit. pg. 365
1087 Ibid.
1088 Ibid.
1089 Ibid.
1090 Cf. Hoehner, op. cit. pg. 20
1091 A.N. Sherwin-White, *Roman Society and Roman Law in the New Testament* Oxford Press (Oxford, England) 1963 pp. 164-166
1092 Ibid.
1093 Unger, op. cit. pg. 233
1094 Farrar, op. cit. pg. 65
1095 Archer, op. cit. pg. 365
1096 Tertullian, *Ante-Nicene Vol. 3* op. cit. pg. 378
1097 Falwell & Hindson, op. cit. pg. 135

1098 Cf. the famed Domesday Book of William the Conqueror.

1099 William Tyndale's translation reads "lieutenant" and John Wycliff's translation reads "justice."

1100 See notes in Hoehner, op. cit. pg. 20

1101 Hoehner, op. cit. pg. 24

1102 Ibid. pg. 25

1103 Alexander Hislop, *The Two Babylons* Loizeaux Brothers (Englad) 1916 pg. 91

1104 Ibid.

1105 A.T. Robertson, *A Harmony of the Gospels for Students of the Life of Christ* George Doran (New York, NY) 1922 pg. 267

1106 Hislop, op. cit. pg. 93

1107 Robertson, op. cit. pg. 263

1108 Hunt, *Defense* op. cit. pg. 116

1109 Thayer, op. cit. pg. 682

1110 Cited in Hoehner, op. cit. pg. 31

1111 Joesphus, *Antiquities of the Jews*, XVIII.vi.10 *Complete Works* op. cit. pg. 387

1112 Hoehner, op. cit. pp. 31-32

1113 Ibid. pg. 100

1114 Cf. Hoehner, op. cit. pp. 45-63

1115 W. Bruce Lincoln, *Passage Through Armageddon* Simon & Schuster (New York, NY) 1986 pg. 98

1116 Cited by Rene Fulop-Miller, *Rasputin : The Holy Devil* Garden City Publishing (New York, NY) 1928 pg. 215

1117 Pope Gregory the Great, *Homily* XXXIII

1118 http://www.rci.rutgers.edu/~lcrew/joyanyway/joy70.html

1119 Cited in Henry, *Vol. 5* op. cit. pg. 530

1120 Ibid.

1121 Martin, *Bible Knowledge Commentary : Old Testament* op. cit. pg. 224

1122 http://wiki.answers.com/Q/Was_Mary_Magdalene_a_Prostitute

1123 If anyone actually reads these endnotes, please pray for her. I sincerely hope I will meet her once again in heaven.

1124 Liefeld, "Luke," *Expositor's Bible Commentary Vol. 8* op. cit. pg. 931

1125 Cf. Liefeld, "Luke," *Expositor's Bible Commentary Vol. 8* op. cit. pg. 931

1126 Henry, *Vol. 5* op. cit. pg. 204

1127 Poole, *Vol. 3* op. cit. pg. 83

1128 Bruce Metzger, *The Text of the New Testament : Its Transmission, Corruption, and Restoration* Oxford University (Oxford, England) 1964 pg. 37   See also J. Harold Greenlee, *Introduction to New Testament Textual Criticism* Hendrickson Publishers (Peabody, Mass.) 1995 ed. pg. 25 and also Randall Price, *Searching for the Original Bible* Harvest House (Eugene, OR) 2007 pg. 113

1129 Metzger, *The Text of the New Testament* op. cit. pg. 41

1130 Metzger, *Textual Commentary* op. cit. pg. 127

1131 Ibid.

1132 Cf. Metzger, *Textual Commentary* op. cit. pg. 127

1133 Liefeld, "Luke," *Expositor's Bible Commentary Vol. 8* op. cit. pg. 937

1134 Metzger, *Textual Commentary* op. cit. pg. 127

1135 Liefeld, "Luke," *Expositor's Bible Commentary Vol. 8* op. cit. pg. 991

1136 Ibid.

1137 Ibid.

1138 I could debate each list of parables, but this would be laborious and fruitless. For example, many include the "two debtors" of Luke 7:41-43, but it is not properly a parable at all. Rather Jesus is using a hypothical question involving a story to prove His point. Such questions are not parables. This, of course, relates to a lengthy debate about the types of symbols used in the Bible and, ironically, it is "literalists" who are most concerned with symbols whereas the liberal theologian simply passes off any illustration or story as parable, allegory, or worse. The result is that they have made the parting of the Red Sea myth, and the "Higher Critics" have even denied the resurrection of Jesus! This is why understanding symbols and the different types of symbols is actually very important and is a concern of literalists more so than the allegorists who does not really care whether the story is true or not.

1139 George Peters, *The Theocratic Kingdom Vol. 1* Kregel (Grand Rapids, Mich.) 1884 pg. 613
1140 Martin, *Bible Knowledge Commentary : New Testament* op. cit. pp. 248-249
1141 Thayer, op. cit. pg. 218
1142 *Liberty Commentary* op. cit. pg. 159
1143 Peters, op. cit. pg. 613
1144 Origen, *Ante-Nicene Fathers Vol. 4* op. cit. pg. 240
1145 Tertullian, *Ante-Nicene Fathers Vol. III* op. cit. pg. 409
1146 Wesley, *New Testament* op. cit. pg. 194
1147 Ibid.
1148 Cf. Henry, *Vol. 5* op. cit. pg. 620
1149 Origen, *Ante-Nicene Fathers Vol. 4* op. cit. pg. 240
1150 Henry, *Vol. 5* op. cit. pg. 620
1151 Poole, *Vol. 3* op. cit. pg. 254
1152 Martin, *Bible Knowledge Commentary : New Testament* op. cit. pp. 248-249
1153 Cf. Criswell, *Rise and Fall* op. cit.
1154 Anderson, "Misunderstood Texts of the Bible," *Collected Works* op. cit. pg. 265
1155 Randall Price, "Propethic Postponement," *Progressive Dispensationalism* Ron Bigalke, Jr., ed., University Press of America (New York, NY) 2005 pg. 216
1156 Ibid. pp. 219-221
1157 Stanley Toussaint, *Contemporary Dispensationalism* Herbert Batemen IV, ed., Kregel (Grand Rapids, Mich.) 1999 pg. 235
1158 Cf. Martin, *Bible Knowledge Commentary : New Testament* op. cit. pg. 249
1159 Toussaint, *Contemporary* op. ct. 235
1160 Frederick Grant, as cited by Arno Gaebelein, *The Gospel of John* Van Lampen Press (Wheaton, Ill.) 1936 pg. 57
1161 Anderson, *Forgotten Truth* op. cit.
1162 David Criswell, "Time of the Gentiles," *Dispensationalism Tomorrow & Beyond* Christopher Cone, ed., Tyndale Seminary Press (Fort Worth, TX) 2008 pp. 253-268
1163 Craig Blaising & Darrell Bock, *Progressive Dispensationalism* Victory Books (Wheaton, Ill.) 1993 pg. 286
1164 George Ladd, *A Theology of the New Testament* Wm. B. Eerdmans (Grand Rapids, Mich.) 1974 pg. 91
1165 Cf. Criswell, *Rise and Fall* op. cit.
1166 Anderson, *Forgotten Truth* op. cit.
1167 Cf. Martin Gilbert, *Altas of Jewish Civilization* MacMillian Publishing (New York, NY) 1990 pg. 50-51
1168 Ibid. pg. 51
1169 Philip Schaff, *History of the Christian Church Vol. 2* Hendrickson Publishers (Peabody, MA) 1858 pg. 873
1170 Ibid. pg. 37
1171 Chaim Potok, *Wanderings* Fawcett Crest (New York, NY) 1978 pg. 303
1172 John Julius Norwich, *A Short History of Byzanium* Random House (New York, NY) 1999 pg. 90
1173 Ibid. pg. 95
1174 J.J. Saunders, *A History of Medieval Islam* Routledge Press (London, England) 1965 pp. 48-49

1175 Criswell, "Time of the Gentiles," *Dispensationalism Tomorrow & Beyond* op. cit. pp. 253-268

1176 Mitchell Bard, *Myths and Facts* American-Israeli Cooperative Enterprise (Chevy Chasae, NY) 2001 pg. 54

1177 Larry Collins & Dominique Lapierre, *O Jerusalem* Pocket Books (New York, NY) 1972 pg. 75

1178 Ibid. pg. 94

1179 Thomas Friedman, *Beirut to Jerusalem* Anchor Books (New York, NY) 1989 pg. 15

1180 Martin Gilbert, *Jerusalem in the Twentieth Century* John Wiley & Sons (New York, NY) 1996 pp. 272-321

1181 Barclay Newman Jr., ed., *A Complete Greek-English Dictionary of the New Testament* United Bible Societies (Stuttgart, Germany) 1971 pg. 144

1182 Josephus, "War of the Jews," II.xiii.14, *Complete Works* op. cit. pg. 478

1183 Wesley, *New Testament* op. cit. pg. 211

1184 Because hyper-Calvinists have a strict interpretation of predestination they tend to expect (some might say "demand") certain "proofs" of one's conversion after the conversion. They tend to reject death bed confessions and also tend to reject the conversions of the worst kinds of sinners (ironic considering their devotion to the doctrine of "total depravity").

1185 Gundry, *Survey of the New Testament* op. cit. pp. 252-253

1186 Price, *Searching for the Original Bible* op. cit. pg. 78

1187 Gundry, *Survey of the New Testament* op. cit. pg. 253

1188 Edwin Blum, *Bible Knowledge Commentary : New Testament* op. cit. pg. 268

1189 Ibid. but see Robert Govett, *Exposition of the Gospel of John Vol. 1* Bemrose & Sons (London, England) 1881 pg. 1 who places it as early as 70 A.D.

1190 Irenaeus, "*Against Heresies*," 3:1, *Ante-Nicene Fathers Vol. I* op. cit.

1191 Blum, *Bible Knowledge Commentary : New Testament* op. cit. pg. 267

1192 John MacArthur, *MacArthur New Testament Commentary John 1-5* Moody Bible Institute (Chicago, Ill.) 2006 pg. 18

1193 Cyril, *Ancient Christian Commentary on Scripture New Testament IV A John 1-10* John Elowsky, ed., InterVarsity Press (Downers Grove, Ill.) 2006 pg. 3

1194 John Darby, *Notes on the Gospel of John* G. Morrish (London, England) n.d. pg. 8

1195 James Montgomery Boice, *The Gospel of John Vol. 1* Zondervan Press (Grand Rapids, Mich) 1975 pg. 23

1196 Cyril, *Ancient Christian Commentary on Scripture New Testament IV A John 1-10* John Elowsky, ed., InterVarsity Press (Downers Grove, Ill.) 2006 pg. 5

1197 Chrysostom, *Ancient Christian Commentary on Scripture New Testament IV A John 1-10* John Elowsky, ed., InterVarsity Press (Downers Grove, Ill.) 2006 pp. 6-7

1198 Arno Gaebelein, *The Gospel of John* Van Kampen Press (Wheaton, Ill.) 1936 pg. 12

1199 Chrysostom, *Ancient Christian Commentary on Scripture New Testament IV A John 1-10* John Elowsky, ed., InterVarsity Press (Downers Grove, Ill.) 2006 pg. 8

1200 B.F Wescott, *The Gospel According to St. John* Wm. B Eerdmans (Grand Rapids, Mich.) 1954 pg. 2

1201 John MacArthur, *MacArthur New Testament Commentary John 1-5* Moody Bible Institute (Chicago, Ill.) 2006 pg. 16

1202 Hermes, *Ante-Nicene Fathers Vol. II* op. cit. pg. 47

1203 Dwight Moody Smith, *John* Abingdon Press (Nashville, TN) 1999 pg. 49

1204 Ibid.

1205 Barnes, op. cit. pg. 263

1206 Charles Erdman, *The Gospel of John* Westminister Press (Philadelphia, PN) 1933 pg. 14

1207 The so-called "Age of Reason" was really the age of anarchy and the "Reign of Terror." It was a day of atheism and the myth that miracles could not happen because only nature existed. It was highlighted by the anarchy which followed the French Revolution and by the rise of "liberal theology" which denied the miracles of Jesus and the Resurrection. It sought to conform Jesus into natural Greek philosophy; a heresy which continues to this very day in part of Europe and the modern liberal academia of America.

1208 Leon Morris, *Reflections on the Gospel of John* Hendrickson Publishers (Peabody, Mass.) 1986 pg. 2

1209 B.F Wescott, *The Gospel According to St. John* Wm. B Eerdmans (Grand Rapids, Mich.) 1954 pg. 2

1210 R.H. Lightfoot, *St. John's Gospel* Clarendon Press (Oxford, England) 1956 pg. 53

1211 Merrill Tenney, *John, the Gospel of Belief* Wm. B Eerdmans (Grand Rapids, Mich) 1948 pg. 62

1212 Ibid.

1213 C.H. Dodd, *The Interpretation of the Fourth Gospel* Cambridge Press (Cambridge, England) 1955 pg. 265

1214 It might be tempting to accept Charles Erdman's translation of "the reason" (Erdman, *The Gospel of John* op. cit. pg. 14) as in "the reason for the season," but this would actually be an entirely different use of the word reason itself! It quite literally has no connection ot the Greek word in any context. This would be mistranslating a for from Greek to English and then misapplying the mistranslated word!

1215 Leon Morris, *Reflections on the Gospel of John* Hendrickson Publishers (Peabody, Mass.) 1986 pg. 3

1216 C.H. Dodd, *The Interpretation of the Fourth Gospel* Cambridge Press (Cambridge, England) 1955 pg. 266

1217 Archbishop J.H. Bernard, *A Critical & Exegetical Commentary on the Gospel According to St. John Vol. 1* T & T Clark (Edinburgh, Great Britain) 1928 pg. 1

1218 John MacArthur, *MacArthur New Testament Commentary John 1-5* Moody Bible Institute (Chicago, Ill.) 2006 pg. 18

1219 Cf. William Mounce, *Basics of Biblical Greek* Zondervan Publishers (Grand Rapids, Mich.) 1993 pg. 28-30

1220 John MacArthur, *MacArthur New Testament Commentary John 1-5* Moody Bible Institute (Chicago, Ill.) 2006 pg. 18

1221 William Mounce, *Basics of Biblical Greek* Zondervan Publishers (Grand Rapids, Mich.) 1993 pg. 28

1222 Ibid.

1223 Ibid.

1224 Robert Govett, *Exposition of the Gospel of St. John Vol. 1* Bemrose & Sons (London, Englard) 1881 pg. 7

1225 Mounce, *Basics of Biblical Greek* op. cit. pg. 28

1226 Frederick Louis Godet, *Gospel of John Vol. 1* Zondervan Press (Grand Rapids, Mich) 1893 pg. 246

1227 B.F Wescott, *The Gospel According to St. John* Wm. B Eerdmans (Grand Rapids, Mich.) 1954 pg. 3

1228 Archbishop J.H. Bernard, *A Critical & Exegetical Commentary on the Gospel According to St. John Vol. 1* T & T Clark (Edinburgh, Great Britain) 1928 pg. 2

1229 John Darby, *Notes on the Gospel of John* G. Morrish (London, England) n.d. pg. 8

1230 Martin Luther, *Martin Luther's Works Vol. 22 John 1-4* Concordia House (St. Louis, MS) 1957 pg. 5

1231 Ibid. pg. 8

1232 Ibid.

1233 Ireneaus, *Ante-Nicene Fathers Vol. I* op. cit. pg. 328

1234 James Montgomery Boice, *The Gospel of John Vol. 1* Zondervan Press (Grand Rapids, Mich) 1975 pg. 24

1235 Robert Govett, *Exposition of the Gospel of St. John Vol. 1* Bemrose & Sons (London, Englard) 1881 pg. 6

1236 B.F Wescott, *The Gospel According to St. John* Wm. B Eerdmans (Grand Rapids, Mich.) 1954 pg. 2

1237 Origen, *Ante-Nicene Fathers Vol. IV* op. cit. pg. 240

1238 Ignatius, *Ante-Nicene Fathers Vol. I* op. cit. pg. 52

1239 Charles Spurgeon, *Treasury of the New Testament Volume Two* Zondervan (Grand Rapids, Mich.) 1950 pg. 227

1240 Charles Erdman, *The Gospel of John* Westminister Press (Philadelphia, PN) 1933 pg. 17

1241 Elmer Towns, *The Gospel of John* AMG Publishers (Chatanooga, TN) 1999 pg. 4

1242 Archbishop J.H. Bernard, *A Critical & Exegetical Commentary on the Gospel According to St. John Vol. 1* T & T Clark (Edinburgh, Great Britain) 1928 pp. 19-20

1243 Thomas Aquinas, *St. Aquinas Commentary on the Gospel of John Chapters 1-5* Catholic University of America (Washington, D.C.) 2010 pg. 67

1244 H.A. Ironside, *Adddresses on the Gospel of John* Loizeaux Brothers (Neptune, NJ) 1942 pg 32

1245 John Calvin, *Crossway Classic Commentaries : John by John Calvin* Reformation Trust (Orlando, FL) 2009 pg. 13

1246 Desiderius Erasmus, *Collected Works of Erasmus Vol. 46 Paraphrase on John* University of Toronto (Toronto, Canada) 1991 pg. 22

1247 Dwight Moody Smith, *John* Abingdon Press (Nashville, TN) 1999 pg. 58

1248 Warren Wiersbe, *Be Alive* Victor Books (Wheaton, Ill.) 1986 pg. 9

1249 Desiderius Erasmus, *Collected Works of Erasmus Vol. 46 Paraphrase on John* University of Toronto (Toronto, Canada) 1991 pg. 13

1250 Ephraem the Syrian, *Ancient Christian Commentary on Scripture New Testament IV A John 1-10* John Elowsky, ed., InterVarsity Press (Downers Grove, Ill.) 2006 pg. 42

1251 Ireneaus, *Ante-Nicene Fathers Vol. I* op. cit. pg. 328

1252 Robert Govett, *Exposition of the Gospel of St. John Vol. 1* Bemrose & Sons (London, Englard) 1881 pg. 6

1253 R.H. Lightfoot, *St. John's Gospel* Clarendon Press (Oxford, England) 1956 pg. 78

1254 Poole, *Vol. II* op. cit. pg. 412

1255 Ibid.

1256 John Gill, *Expositions of the Old Testament Vol. 3* William Hill Collinridge (London, England) 1852 pg. 907

1257 Torrey, op. cit. pg. 158

1258 Ibid.

1259 Merrill Tenney, "Gospel of John," *The Expositor's Bible Commentary Vol. 9* Frank Gaebelain, ed. Zondervan Publishers (Grand Rapids, Mich.) 1984 pg. 43

1260 Several internet websites promote this teaching.

1261 Hoehner, op. cit. pp. 38-39

1262 Alexander Roberts & James Donaldson, eds., "Gospel of Nicodemus," *Ante-Nicene Fathers Vol. 8* Hendrickson Publishers (Peabody, Mass.) 1999 ed. pp. 418, 427

1263 Henry, *Vol. 5* op. cit. pg. 708

1264 Poole, *Vol. III* op. cit. pg. 288

1265 Martin Gilbert, ed. *Atlas of Jewish Civilization* Macmillan Press (New York, NY) 1990 pg. 33

1266 Josephus, "Antiquities of the Jews," *Complete Works* op. cit. pg. 233

1267 Cf. Hoehner, op. cit. pg. 43

1268 Ussher, op. cit. pg. 766

1269 Josephus, "War of the Jews," I.xxi.1, *Complete Works,* op. cit. pg. 452

1270 Josephus, "Antiquities of the Jews," XV.xi.1, *Complete Works,* op. cit. pg. 334

1271 Josephus, "Antiquities of the Jews," XV.xi.6, *Complete Works,* op. cit. pg. 336

1272 Hoehner, op. cit. pg. 40

1273 To be sure there are minor variants as well, but I present the two main factions as I believe the tedium of chronology on rarely held variants is too much for the average reader.

1274 J.A. Thompson, *The Bible and Archaeology* William B. Eerdmans (Grand Rapids, Mich.) 1962 pg. 352

1275 Randall Price, *The Coming Last Days Temple* Harvest House (Eugene, OR) 1999 pg. 596

1276 Ussher, op. cit. pg. 766

1277 R.C. Sproul, *John* Reformed Trust (Orlando, FL) 2009 pg. 37

1278 Wiersbe, *Be Alive* op. cit. pg. 35

1279 Smith, *John* op. cit. pg. 96

1280 Josephus, "Antiquities of the Jews," XIV.iii.2, *Complete Works,* op. cit. pg. 291

1281 *Tannith* 20.I as cited by Bernard, *St. John Vol. 1* op. cit. pg. 99

1282 Bernard, *St. John Vol. 1* op. cit. pg. 99

1283 Aquinas, *Gospel of John 1-5* op. cit. pg. 165

1284 Barnes, op. cit. pg. 275

1285 Calvin, *John* op. cit. pg. 66

1286 Frederick Louis Godet, *Gospel of John Vol. 1* Zondervan Publishers (Grand Rapids, Mich.) 1893 (1969 ed.) pg. 377

1287 John Darby, *Notes on the Gospel of John* G. Morrish (London, England) n.d. p.g 33

1288 Luther, *Vol. 22* op. cit. pg. 278

1289 Erasmus, *Vol. 46* op. cit. pg. 46

1290 Calvin, *John* op. cit. pg. 66

1291 Wesley, *New Testament* op. cit. pg. 224

1292 Ibid. pg. 225

1293 Gaebelein, *Gospel of John* op. cit. pg. 56

1294 Arno Gaebelein, *The Gospel of John* VanKampen Press (Wheaton, Ill.) 1936 pg. 57

1295 Frederick Grant, as cited by Arno Gaebelein, *The Gospel of John* VanKampen Press (Wheaton, Ill.) 1936 pg. 57

1296 Frederick Louis Godet, *Gospel of John Vol. 1* Zondervan Publishers (Grand Rapids, Mich.) 1893 (1969 ed.) pg. 379

1297 Lightfoot, *John's Gospel* op. cit. pg. 116

1298 Gaebelein, *The Gospel of John* op. cit. pg. 61

1299 Smith, *John* op. cit. pg. 95

1300 Tenney, *John* op. cit. pg. 87

1301 Cf. Erdman, *John* op. cit. pg. 36

1302 Ironside, *John* op. cit. pg. 96

1303 Arthur Pink, *Exposition of the Gospel of John Vol 1.* I.C. Herendeen (Cleveland, OH) 1924 pp. 110-111

1304 Ibid. pg. 111

1305 Ironside, *John* op. cit. pg. 96

1306 Towns, op. cit. pg. 30

1307 Boice, *John Vol. 1* op. cit. pg. 244

1308 Towns, op. cit. pg. 31

1309 Boice rejects this view, but notes it nevertheless, Boice, *John Vol. 1* op. cit. pg. 243

1310 Water was sometimes used as a euphimism for male semen, and was common in antiquity (Morris, *Reflections on John* op. cit. pg. 90).

1311 Luther, *Vol. 22* op. cit. pg. 323

1312 Wesley, *New Testament* op. cit. pg. 225

1313 Aquinas, *Gospel of John 1-5* op. cit. pg. 177

1314 Hilary of Potiers, *Ancient Christian Commentary Vol. IV-A* op. cit. pg. 121

1315 Erasmus, *Vol. 46* op. cit. pg. 48

1316 Calvin, *John* op. cit. pg. 74

1317 Augustine, *Ancient Christian Commentary Vol. IV-A* op. cit. pg. 122

1318 Godet, *John Vol. 1* op. cit. pg. 390

1319 Ironside, *John* op. cit. pg. 100

1320 R.C. Sproul, *John* Reformed Trust (Orlando, FL) 2009 pg. 88

1321 Ibid.
1322 Calvin, *John* op. cit. pg. 127
1323 Pink, *John Vol 1.* op. cit. pg. 264
1324 Ibid. pg. 265
1325 James Montgomery Boice, *The Gospel of John Vol. 2* Zondervan Press (Grand Rapids, Mich) 1975 pg. 59
1326 Ibid. pg. 58
1327 Cyril of Alexandria, *Ancient Christian Commentary Vol. IV-A* op. cit. pg. 190
1328 Pink, *John Vol 1.* op. cit. pg. 264
1329 Erdman, op. cit. pg. 56
1330 Bernard, *St. John Vol. 1* op. cit. pg. 238
1331 Wesley, *New Testament* op. cit. pg. 233
1332 Ironside, *John* op. cit. pg. 192
1333 Augustine, *Ancient Christian Commentary Vol. IV-A* op. cit. pg. 190
1334 Tertullian, *Ante-Nicene Fathers Vol. III* op. cit. pg. 611
1335 Calvin, *John* op. cit. pg. 127
1336 MacArthur, *John 1-11* op. cit. pg. 187
1337 Barnes, op. cit. pg. 288
1338 Govett, *John Vol. 1* op. cit. pg. 193
1339 Cited by Towns, op. cit. pg. 64
1340 Sproul, *John* op. cit. pg. 118
1341 Ibid.
1342 Newman, *Greek-English Dictionary* op. cit. pg. 58
1343 Wescott, *St. John* op. cit. pg. 105
1344 Barnes, op. cit. pg. 288
1345 Erasmus, *Vol. 46* op. cit. pg. 85
1346 Wesley, *New Testament* op. cit. pg. 237
1347 Thomas Aquinas, *St. Aquinas Commentary on the Gospel of John Chapters 6-12* Catholic University of America (Washington, D.C.) 2010 pp. 35-37
1348 Wiersbe, *Be Alive* op. cit. pg. 79
1349 Boice, *John Vol. 2* op. cit. pg. 207
1350 Lightfoot, *John's Gospel* op. cit. pg. 161
1351 MacArthur, *John 1-11* op. cit. pg. 254
1352 Cited by Thomas Aquinas, *St. Aquinas Commentary on the Gospel of John Chapters 6-12* Catholic University of America (Washington, D.C.) 2010 pg. 35
1353 Thomas Aquinas, *St. Aquinas Commentary on the Gospel of John Chapters 6-12* Catholic University of America (Washington, D.C.) 2010 pg. 35
1354 Arthur Pink, *Exposition of the Gospel of John Vol 2.* I.C. Herendeen (Cleveland, OH) 1924 pg. 80
1355 Calvin, *John* op. cit. pg. 164
1356 Anderson, "Misunderstood Texts of the Bible," *Collected Works* op. cit. pg. 292
1357 Metzger, *Textual Commentary* op. cit. pp. 188-189
1358 Ironside, *John* op. cit. pg. 338
1359 Metzger, *Textual Commentary* op. cit. pg. 187
1360 Boice, *John Vol. 2* op. cit. pg. 307
1361 Archbishop J.H. Bernard, *A Critical & Exegetical Commentary on the Gospel According to St. John Vol. 2* T & T Clark (Edinburgh, Great Britain) 1928 pg. 716
1362 Wescott, *St. John* op. cit. pg. 141
1363 Bernard, *A Critical & Exegetical Commentary Vol. 2* op. cit. pg. 716
1364 It is somewhat dishonest of certain scholars to cite a Church Father as proof that such a verse did *not exist* simply because they do not quote it.
1365 Frederick Louis Godet, *Gospel of John Vol. 2* Zondervan Publishers (Grand Rapids, Mich.) 1893 (1969 ed.) pg. 84

1366 Tenney, *John* op. cit. pp. 137-138

1367 Towns, op. cit. pg. 77

1368 Godet, *Gospel of John Vol. 2* op. cit. pg. 84

1369 Govett, *John Vol. 1* op. cit. pg. 335

1370 Erdman, op. cit. pg. 75

1371 MacArthur, *John 1-11* op. cit. pg. 322

1372 Lightfoot, *John's Gospel* op. cit. pg. 346

1373 Wescott, *St. John* op. cit. pg. 141

1374 Godet, *Gospel of John Vol. 2* op. cit. pg. 83

1375 Almost any Church History book will discuss this subject in detail. It had even been the source of the first "anti-pope" as the Bishop of Rome split with his congregation over the issue (Cf. J.N.D. Kelly, *The Oxford Dictionary of Popes* Oxford University (Oxford, England) 1986 pg. 14)! The emotion and anger which was felt by those who had been tortured and maimed for their faith was immense and explains their resistence to leniency on the part of these "lapsed" believers.

1376 Kenneth Scott Latourette, *A History of Christianity Volume 1* Harpers & Row (New York, NY) 1953 pg. 217

1377 Arno Gaebelein, *The Gospel of John* Van Kampen Press (Wheaton, Ill.) 1936 pg. 154

1378 Boice, *John Vol. 2* op. cit. pg. 308

1379 Ibid.

1380 MacArthur, *John 1-11* op. cit. pg. 322

1381 Pink, *John Vol 2.* op. cit. pg. 175

1382 Ibid. pg. 176

1383 I have taken many of these from with my own amendments. Boice, *John Vol. 2* op. cit. pg. 311

1384 Archbishop J.H. Bernard, *A Critical & Exegetical Commentary on the Gospel According to St. John Vol. 2* T & T Clark (Edinburgh, Great Britain) 1928 pg. 719

1385 Ironside, *John* op. cit. pg. 344

1386 Martin Luther, *Martin Luther's Works Vol. 23 John 6-8* Concordia House (St. Louis, MS) 1957 pg. 312

1387 Bede, *Ancient Christian Commentary Vol. IV-A* op. cit. pg. 274

1388 Augustine, *Ancient Christian Commentary Vol. IV-A* op. cit. pg. 275

1389 Arno Gaebelein, *The Gospel of John* Van Kampen Press (Wheaton, Ill.) 1936 pg. 156

1390 Jerome, *Ancient Christian Commentary Vol. IV-A* op. cit. pg. 274

1391 Tenney, *John* op. cit. pg. 141

1392 Manuscript number 0264. Cf. Nestle, op. cit. pg. 702

1393 Towns, op. cit. pg. 80 (However, the *Textus Receptus* does not use this word, but just the word *graphia*).

1394 Wescott, *St. John* op. cit. pg. 141

1395 Wesley, *New Testament* op. cit. pg. 242

1396 Edwards, *Blank Bible Part 2* op. cit. pg. 941

1397 Archbishop J.H. Bernard, *A Critical & Exegetical Commentary on the Gospel According to St. John Vol. 2* T & T Clark (Edinburgh, Great Britain) 1928 pg. 718

1398 Ironside, *John* op. cit. pg. 342

1399 Morris, *Reflections on John* op. cit. pg. 293

1400 Ibid.

1401 Archbishop J.H. Bernard, *A Critical & Exegetical Commentary on the Gospel According to St. John Vol. 2* T & T Clark (Edinburgh, Great Britain) 1928 pg. 717

1402 Martin Luther, *Martin Luther's Works Vol. 23 John 6-8* Concordia House (St. Louis, MS) 1957 pg. 312

1403 Arno Gaebelein, *The Gospel of John* Van Kampen Press (Wheaton, Ill.) 1936 pg. 156

1404 Tenney, *John* op. cit. pg. 107

1405 Morris, *Reflections on John* op. cit. pg. 303

1406 Pink, *John Vol 2.* op. cit. pg. 204

1407 Tenney, *John* op. cit. pg. 107
1408 Sproul, *John* op. cit. pg. 137
1409 Erasmus, *Vol. 46* op. cit. pg. 109
1410 Govett, *John Vol. 1* op. cit. pg. 345
1411 Wesley, *New Testament* op. cit. pg. 243
1412 Bernard, *St. John Vol. 2* op. cit. pg. 294
1413 Tenney, "John," *Expositor's Bible Vol. 9* op. cit. pg. 99
1414 Henry, *Vol. 5* op. cit. pg. 813
1415 Ironside, *John* op. cit. pg. 393
1416 Farrar, op. cit. pg. 105
1417 Govett, *John Vol. 1* op. cit. pg. 393
1418 Pink, *John Vol 2.* op. cit. pg. 238
1419 Barnes, op. cit. pg. 310
1420 Gaebelein, *John* op. cit. pg. 167
1421 Erasmus, *Vol. 46* op. cit. pg. 120
1422 Homer Kent, *Light in the Darkness* Baker Books (Grand Rapids, Mich.) 1974 pp. 128-129
1423 Ironside, *John* op. cit. pg. 195
1424 *Ancient Christian Commentary Vol. IV-A* op. cit. pg. 154
1425 Bernard, *St. John Vol. 2* op. cit. pg. 322
1426 Wesley, *New Testament* op. cit. pg. 246
1427 Bob Tilton, *God's Laws of Success* Word of Fath (Dallas, TX) 1983 pg. 170
1428 Kenneth Copeland, "The Force of Love," Tape BCC-56 as cited by Dave Hunt & T.A. McMahon, *The Seduction of Christianity* Harvest House (Eugene, OR) 1985 pg. 84
1429 Dave Hunt & T.A. McMahon, *The Seduction of Christianity* Harvest House (Eugene, OR) 1985 pg. 87
1430 Pink, *John Vol 2.* op. cit. pg. 354
1431 Aquinas, *Gospel of John Chapters 6-12* op. cit. pg. 215
1432 Calvin, *John* op. cit. pg. 267
1433 Lightfoot, *John's Gospel* op. cit. pg. 209
1434 Ironside, *John* op. cit. pg. 443
1435 Sproul, *John* op. cit. pg. 198
1436 Erdmans, *John,* op. cit. pg. 95
1437 Barnes, op. cit. pg. 318
1438 James Montgomery Boice, *The Gospel of John Vol. 3* Zondervan Press (Grand Rapids, Mich) 1975 pg. 147
1439 Morris, *Reflections on John* op. cit. pg. 396
1440 Wiersbe, *Be Alive* op. cit. pg. 129
1441 MacArthur, *John 1-11* op. cit. pg. 445
1442 *Liberty Commentary* op. cit. pg. 196
1443 MacArthur, *John 1-11* op. cit. pg. 445
1444 Erasmus, *Vol. 46* op. cit. pg. 138
1445 Origen, *Ante-Nicene Fathers Vol. IV* op. cit. pg. 544
1446 Govett, *John Vol. 1* op. cit. pg. 456
1447 Govett, *John Vol. 1* op. cit. pg. 455
1448 Erasmus, *Vol. 46* op. cit. pg. 138
1449 Athanasius, *Ancient Christian Commentary Vol. IV-A* op. cit. pg. 362
1450 Wescott, *St. John* op. cit. pg. 160
1451 Athanasius, *Ancient Christian Commentary Vol. IV-A* op. cit. pg. 43
1452 Raymond Brown, *The Gospel According to John Vol. 1* Doubleday (New York, NY) 1966 pg. 40
1453 Wiersbe, *Be Alive* op. cit. pp. 128-129
1454 Govett, *John Vol. 1* op. cit. pg. 456

1455 Arthur Pink, *Exposition of the Gospel of John*   *Vol 2.*   I.C. Herendeen (Cleveland, OH) 1924 pg. 80

1456 Calvin, *John* op. cit. pg. 164

1457 Sproul, *John* op. cit. pg. 118

1458 Ibid.

1459 Cited by Towns, op. cit. pg. 64

1460 Arthur Pink, *Exposition of the Gospel of John*   *Vol 2.*   I.C. Herendeen (Cleveland, OH) 1924 pg. 80

1461 Dave Hunt, *What Love is This?* Loyal Publishing (Sisters, OR) 2002 pp. 75-78

1462 Taken from *The Westminister Confession* and the *Canons of Dort.*

1463 Dave Hunt, *What Love is This?* Loyal Publishing (Sisters, OR) 2002 pg. 81

1464 Benjamin B. Warfield, *Calvin and Augustine* Presbyterian & Reformed (Phillipsburg, NJ) 1981 pg. 22

1465 Charles Spurgeon, *Exposition of the Doctrine of Grace* Pilgrim Publications (Pasadena TX) n.d. pg. 298

1466 Cf. Susanne Bobzien, *Determinism and Freedom in Stoic Philosophy* Oxford University Press (Oxford, England) 1998

1467 Susanne Bobzien, *The Inadvertent Conception and Late Birth of the Free-Will Problem* Oxford University Press (Oxford, England) 1998 pg. 43

1468 Arthur Pink, *Exposition of the Gospel of John*   *Vol 2.*   I.C. Herendeen (Cleveland, OH) 1924 pg. 80

1469 James Montgomery Boice, *Foundations of the Christian Faith* InterVarsity Press (Downers Grove, Ill.) 1986 pg. 476

1470 Ibid.

1471 Hunt, *What Love* op. cit. pg. 208

1472 Morris, *Reflections on John* op. cit. pg. 503

1473 Thayer, op. cit. pg. 483

1474 Ibid.

1475 Sproul, *John* op. cit. pg. 271

1476 Warren Wiersbe, *Be Transformed* Victor Books (Wheaton, Ill.) 1987 pg. 33

1477 Farrar, op. cit. pg. 113

1478 Barnes, op. cit. pg. 335

1479 Andrew Miller, *Miller's Church History* Pickering & Inglis (London, England) 1963 pp. 197-199

1480 Philip Schaff, *History of the Christian Church* *Vol. 3* Hendrickson Publishers (Peabody, Mass.) 1867 pg. 349

1481 Tertullian, *Ante-Nicene Fathers Vol. III* op. cit. pg. 604

1482 Ibid. pg. 610

1483 Ironside, *John* op. cit. pg. 623

1484 Barnes, op. cit. pg. 335

1485 MacArthur, *John 12-21* op. cit. pg. 113

1486 *Liberty Commentary* op. cit. pg. 203

1487 Arthur Pink, *Exposition of the Gospel of John Vol. III* I.C Herendeen (Cleveland, Ohio) 1924 pg. 260

1488 Robert Govett, *Exposition of the Gospel of St. John* *Vol. 2* Bemrose & Sons (London, Englard) 1881 pg. 162

1489 Farrar, op. cit. pg. 113

1490 Spurgeon, *New Testament Vol. 2* op. cit. pg. 531

1491 Calvin, *John* op. cit. pg. 127

1492 Pink, *John* *Vol 1.* op. cit. pg. 264

1493 Calvin, *John* op. cit. pg. 350

1494 Theodoret of Cyprus, *Ancient Christian Commentary on Scripture New Testament IV B John 11-21* John Elowsky, ed., InterVarsity Press (Downers Grove, Ill.) 2006 pg. 155

1495 Hillary of Potiers, *Ancient Christian Commentary on Scripture New Testament IV B John 11-21* John Elowsky, ed., InterVarsity Press (Downers Grove, Ill.) 2006 pg. 155

1496 Basil the Great, *Ancient Christian Commentary on Scripture New Testament IV B John 11-21* John Elowsky, ed., InterVarsity Press (Downers Grove, Ill.) 2006 pg. 156

1497 Didymus, *Ancient Christian Commentary on Scripture New Testament IV B John 11-21* John Elowsky, ed., InterVarsity Press (Downers Grove, Ill.) 2006 pg. 154

1498 Augustine, *Ancient Christian Commentary on Scripture New Testament IV B John 11-21* John Elowsky, ed., InterVarsity Press (Downers Grove, Ill.) 2006 pg. 155

1499 Thomas Aquinas, *St. Aquinas Commentary on the Gospel of John Chapters 13-21* Catholic University of America (Washington, D.C.) 2010 pg. 92

1500 Wesley, *New Testament* op. cit. pg. 264

1501 Barnes, op. cit. pg. 336

1502 Govett, *John Vol. 2* op. cit. pg. 186

1503 Wiersbe, *Be Transformed* op. cit. pg. 33

1504 Poole, *Vol. 3* op. cit. pg. 357

1505 Sproul, *John* op. cit. pg. 281

1506 John of Damascus, *Ancient Christian Commentary on Scripture New Testament IV B John 11-21* John Elowsky, ed., InterVarsity Press (Downers Grove, Ill.) 2006 pg. 156

1507 Pink, *John Vol 3.* op. cit. pg. 281

1508 James Montgomery Boice, *The Gospel of John Vol. 4* Zondervan Press (Grand Rapids, Mich) 1975 pg. 221

1509 Ironside, *John* op. cit. pg. 641

1510 Govett, *John Vol. 2* op. cit. pg. 186

1511 Luther, *Vol. 24* op. cit. pp. 188-189

1512 MacArthur, *John 12-21* op. cit. pg. 136

1513 Erdmans, *John*, op. cit. pg. 131

1514 Poole, *Vol. 3* op. cit. pg. 369

1515 Henry, *Vol. 5* op. cit. pg. 936

1516 Thomas & Gundry, *Harmony* op. cit. pg. 219

1517 Tenney, "John," *Expositor's Bible Vol. 9* op. cit. 164

1518 Govett, *John Vol. 2* op. cit. pg. 339

1519 Towns, op. cit. pg. 180

1520 MacArthur, *John 12-21* op. cit. pg. 315

1521 Ibid.

1522 Wescott, *St. John* op. cit. pg. 254

1523 Wesley, *New Testament* op. cit. pg. 272

1524 MacArthur, *Matthew 24-28* op. cit. pg. 214

1525 Quoted in David Criswell, *Valley of the Blind* Fortress Adonai (Dallas, TX) 2012 pg. 59

1526 Donald Barnhouse, *The Love Life* Regal Books (Glendale, CA) 1973 pg. 264

1527 Newman, *Greek-English Dictionary* op. cit. pg. 54

1528 Ibid. pg. 59

1529 Wesley, *New Testament* op. cit. pg. 273

1530 Calvin, *John* op. cit. pg. 417

1531 Ibid.

1532 James Montgomery Boice, *The Gospel of John Vol. 5* Zondervan Press (Grand Rapids, Mich) 1975 pg. 107

1533 Martin Luther, *Martin Luther's Works Vol. 69 John 17-20* Concordia House (St. Louis, MS) 1957 pg. 210

1534 Ibid. pg. 211

1535 Cf. Criswell, *Rise and Fall* op. cit.

1536 Augustine, *Ancient Christian Commentary Vol. IV B* op. cit. pg. 290

1537 Quoted in Aquinas, *Gospel of John 13-21* op. cit. pg. 220

1538 Cf. Criswell, *Rise and Fall* op. cit.

1539 Quoted in Aquinas, *Gospel of John 13-21* op. cit. pg. 220
1540 Eusebius, *History* 3:20.3-4, *Church History* op. cit.
1541 Erasmus, *Vol. 46* op. cit. pg. 206
1542 Ironside, *John* op. cit. pg. 811
1543 Godet, *John Vol. 2* op. cit. pg. 369
1544 Arthur Pink, *Exposition of the Gospel of John Vol. IV* I.C Herendeen (Cleveland, Ohio) 1924 pg. 192
1545 Ibid.
1546 Ibid.
1547 Ibid.
1548 Gaebelein, *John* op. cit. pg. 351
1549 Sproul, *John* op. cit. pg. 352
1550 James Montgomery Boice, *The Gospel of John Vol. 5* Zondervan Press (Grand Rapids, Mich) 1975 pg. 106
1551 Smith, *John* op. cit. pg. 342
1552 Wiersbe, *Be Transformed* op. cit. pg. 98
1553 Quoted in Aquinas, *Gospel of John 13-21* op. cit. pg. 221
1554 Tertullian, *Ante-Nicene Fathers Vol. III* op. cit. pg. 73
1555 Quoted in Aquinas, *Gospel of John 13-21* op. cit. pg. 221
1556 Aquinas, *Gospel of John 13-21* op. cit. pg. 221
1557 Wescott, *St. John* op. cit. pg. 260
1558 Godet, *John Vol. 2* op. cit. pg. 369
1559 Newman, *Greek-English Dictionary* op. cit. pg. 54
1560 Ibid. pg. 59
1561 MacArthur, *John 12-21* op. cit. pg. 330
1562 Govett, *John Vol. 2* op. cit. pg. 350
1563 Donald Barnhouse, *The Love Life* Regal Books (Glendale, CA) 1973 pg. 264
1564 Morris, *Reflections on John* op. cit. pg. 631
1565 Godet, *John Vol. 2* op. cit. pg. 369
1566 Barnes, op. cit. pg. 351
1567 Lew Wallace, *Ben Hur* Reader's Digest (New York, NY) 1992 (unabridged from 1880 ed.)
1568 Tertullian, *Ancient Christian Commentary Vol. IV B* op. cit. pg. 289
1569 Pierre Barbet, *Doctor at Calvary* P.J. Jennedy & Sons (New York, NY) 1953 English ed.
1570 Frederick Zubige, M.D., *The Cross and the Shroud* Paragon House (New York, NY) 1988 pg. 58
1571 William Edwards, Wesley Gabel, Floyd Hosmer, "On the Physical Death of Jesus Christ," *JAMA* March 21, 1986 - Vol. 255, No. 11 pg.1460
1572 Barbet, op. cit. pp. 12-18, 37-147, 159-175, 187-208
1573 Zubige, op. cit. pp. 53-57
1574 Ibid.
1575 Ibid. pg. 60
1576 Barbet, op. cit. & Zubige, op. cit. pp. 58-62
1577 Ibid.
1578 Zubige, op. cit. pg. 66
1579 Ibid. pg. 72
1580 Ibid. pg. 62
1581 Thayer, op. cit. pg. 667
1582 Ibid. pg. 667
1583 Ibid. pg. 668
1584 Ibid.
1585 Ibid.
1586 Cited by Godet, *John Vol. 2* op. cit. pg. 451

1587 Sir Robert Anderson, *Daniel in the Critics' Den* Pickering & Inglis (London, England) 1900 pg. 18

1588 Tertullian, *Ancient Christian Commentary Vol. IV B* op. cit. pg. 395

1589 Theodore of Mapsuestia, *Ancient Christian Commentary Vol. IV B* op. cit. pg. 395

1590 Augustine, *Ancient Christian Commentary Vol. IV B* op. cit. pg. 395

1591 Bill Martin & Bill Perkins, "The Second Witness ... Who Is He?", *Digging Deeper Bible Studies* no date pg. 21

1592 Bill Martin & Bill Perkins, "The Second Witness ... Who Is He?", *Digging Deeper Bible Studies* no date pg. 21

1593 Theodore of Mapsuestia, *Ancient Christian Commentary Vol. IV B* op. cit. pg. 395

1594 Farrar, op. cit. pg. 125

1595 Govett, *John Vol. 2* op. cit. pg. 456

1596 Cited in Aquinas, *Gospel of John 13-21* op. cit. pg. 305

1597 Wesley, *New Testament* op. cit. pg. 281

1598 Govett, *John Vol. 2* op. cit. pg. 456

1599 Gaebelein, *John* op. cit. pg. 412

1600 Tenney, *John* op. cit. pg. 294

1601 Sproul, *John* op. cit. pg. 408

1602 Pink, *John Vol. 4* op. cit. pg. 346

1603 Spurgeon, *New Testament Vol. 2* op. cit. pg. 726

1604 *Liberty Commentary* op. cit. pg. 215

1605 Bernard, *St. John Vol. 2* op. cit. pg. 711

1606 Erasmus, *Vol. 46* op. cit. pg. 225

1607 MacArthur, *John 12-21* op. cit. pg. 405

1608 Cited in Aquinas, *Gospel of John 13-21* op. cit. pg. 305

1609 Ibid.

1610 Augustine, *Ancient Christian Commentary Vol. IV B* op. cit. pg. 394

1611 Darby, *Notes on John* op. cit. pg. 288

1612 Lightfoot, *John's Gospel* op. cit. pg. 343

1613 Morris, *Reflections on John* op. cit. pg. 747

1614 Calvin, *John* op. cit. pg. 471

1615 Lee Martin McDonald, *The Biblical Canon* Hendrickson Publisher (Peabody, Mass.) 2007 pg. 32

1616 F.F. Bruce, *The Canon of Scripture* IVP Academic (Downers Grove, Ill.) 1988 pg. 290

1617 Brian Edwards, *Nothing but the Truth* Evangelical Press (Webster, NY) 2006 pg. 30

1618 Ibid.

1619 Hunt, *Defense* op. cit. pg. 71

1620 See notes under Appendix C.

1621 Bruce, op. cit. pg. 288

1622 See notes on Mark, but also Tenney, *New Testament Survey* op. cit. pg. 162

1623 Why would both Matthew and Luke "change" Mark's "version" of the story if they were just copying his work or relying on his information. Not withstanding that Mark, unlike Matthew, was not an eyewitness to the events he was describing (see notes on Mark).

1624 See notes on Matthew, but also Barbieri, op. cit. pg. 16 and Unger, *Bible Dictionary* op. cit. pg. 706

1625 See notes on Matthew. Also cf. Irenaeus, "Against Heresies," III. i. 1., *Ante-Nicene Fathers Vol. I* op. cit.

1626 See my notes on Matthew, Mark, and Luke for a defense of these facts.

1627 Papias, as cited by Eusebius, *Church History* II.16

1628 Hunt, *Defense* op. cit. pg. 71

1629 Randall Price, *Searching for the Original Bible* Harvest House (Eugene, OR) 2007 pg. 114

1630 Cf. Robert Thomas & Stanley Gundry, *A Harmony of the Gospels* HarperOne (New York, NY) 1978 pg. 275

1631   Biblical archaeology consists of "absolute dating" and "relative dating."   See notes in Appendix B.

1632   Edwards, *Nothing but Truth* op. cit. pg. 420

1633   These were the first "liberal" theologians (and such they called themselves) who *assumed* that miracles cannot and do not occur based on the tenants of the Enlightenment deists. They therefore set out to find the "historical Jesus" which they believed had to be distinguished from the Jesus of "myth" who performed miracles. The result, echoed in liberal churches to this very day, and even influencing some naive evangelical Christians, has been to trivialize, belittle, and/or deny the historicity of the Bible, particularly as it relates to miracles such as the Resurrection of Christ.

1634   See my notes under *Controversies in the Pentateuch.*

1635   *The Babylonian Talmud* Sabbat 116-b and Sanhedrin 107-b

1636   Robert Stein, *Jesus the Messiah: A Survey of the Life of Christ* InterVarsity Press (Downers Grove, Ill.) 1996 pg. 34

1637   *The Babylonian Talmud* Sanhedrin 43 a-b

1638   Josephus, "Antiquities" XVIII.iii.3, op. cit. pg. 379

1639   *Bible and Spade*, Vol. 1.3 Summer 1972

1640   http://www.tektonics.org/jesusexist/josephus.html

1641   Foxe, *Acts and Monuments Vol. 1* op. cit. pg. 95 & Theodore of Mapsuestia, *Ancient Christian Commentary Vol. IV B* op. cit. pg. 395

1642   Also see Marta Sorti, *The Christians and the Roman Empire* University of Oklahoma (Oklahoma City, Ok.) 1986

1643   Ibid.

1644   Josephus, "Antiquities" XVIII.iii.3, op. cit. pg. 379

1645   http://www.truthbeknown.com/pliny.htm

1646   Sutonius, *Lives of the Twelve Caesars* "Life of Claudius" 25.4 Robert Graves, trans., Rains Publishing (New York, NY) 1957 pg. 176

1647   Sutonius, *Lives of the Twelve Caesars* "Life of Nero" 16.2 op. cit. pg. 191

1648   Ibid.

1649   http://www.truthbeknown.com/pliny.htm

1650   Tacitus, *Annals* 15.44

1651   http://www.tektonics.org/jesusexist/tacitus.html

1652   http://en.wikipedia.org/wiki/Tacitus_on_Christ#Christians_and_Chrestians

1653   Robert Van Voorst, *Jesus Outside the New Testament: An Introduction to the Ancient Evidence* Eerdmans Publishing (Grand Rapids, Mich.) 2000 pp. 44-48

1654   Part of the apology may be found at http://www.tertullian.org/articles/ reeve_apology.htm

1655   On a sidenote, Tertullian also mentions the belief that the emperor Tiberius sought to add Jesus to the pantheon of gods, but this was not done. Tertullian was not advocating such a thing, for this is contrary to Christian doctrine and offensive to us (for Jesus is not one of many gods), but pointing out that Tiberius accepted Jesus as something more than a man. Many, including many Christians, reject this part as a tall tale, but again the Roman Senate does not refute it. Why? There is nothing inconsistent about Romans adding new "gods" to their pantheon. This is common practice. It is how they kept the peace among religions. Only those, like Christians and Jews, who refused to accept their god along side others, were considered intolerant. In fact, this could be one reason that Christians were hated among the Romans; because we considered our God superior to theirs!

1656   This popular, and thoroughly dishonest, phrase is oft used by lawyers when the evidence does not support their case.

1657   McDowell, op. cit. pg. 56

1658   Morison, op. cit. pg. 190

1659   Paul Maier, *First Easter* Harper & Row (New York, NY) 1973 pg. 111

1660   McDowell, op. cit. pg. 55

1661   Maier, op. cit. pg. 119

1662   McDowell, op. cit. pg. 54

1663 Morison, op. cit. pg. 111

1664 Ibid.

1665 McDowell, op. cit. pg. 65

1666 Ibid. pg. 110

1667 Morison, op. cit. pg. 105

1668 See John Foxe, *Acts and Monuments Vol. I* Religious Tract Society (London, England) 1883 ed. for a complete story of the disciples' martyrdoms.

1669 McDowell, op. cit. pg. 78

1670 Ibid. pg. 77

1671 Ibid. pg. 81

1672 Ibid. pg. 80

1673 Ibid. pp. 82-83

1674 Ibid. pp. 95-97

1675 Ibid. pg. 99-102

1676 Interestingly enough, Hugh Schoenfield's motivation does not appear to be the usual atheism, but rather he was a Jew with a respect for Jesus who could simply never accept that Jesus was Messiah. His own theology and philosophy was a mixture of many things, but essentially a secularized Judaism. He spent time in a Messianic Jewish organization but left after realizing they would not accept his own bizarre theories about Jesus.

1677 McDowell, op. cit. pg. 97

1678 http://www.shroud.com/nature.htm

1679 Cf. Colin Renfrew & Paul Bahn, Archaeology: Theories, Methods, & Practice Thames & Hudson Ltd. (New York, NY) 1991

1680 http://www.shroud.com/nature.htm

1681 Coral Ridge Ministries, "The Shroud of Turin," *Bible and Spade Vol. 8 No. 2 Spring 1995* pg. 58

1682 Renfrew & Bahn, op. cit. pg. 126

1683 Chris Chui, "Carbon 14 and the Shroud of Turin," Contrast (part of the Bible-Science Newsletter 27:7 1989) 8:4 1989 p. 3

1684 Ibid. pg. 2

1685 http://www.foxnews.com/story/0,2933,512703,00.html

1686 Zubige, op. cit. pg. 160

1687 John Heller, *Report on the Shroud of Turin* Houghton Mifflin Co (Boston, Mass.) 1983 pg 151

1688 Zubige, op. cit. pg. 175

1689 Ibid. pg. 153

1690 Heller, op. cit. pg. 82-h

1691 Ibid. pg. 153

1692 http://thierrycastex.blogspot.fr/

1693 Heller, op. cit. pg. 140

1694 Ibid. pp. 140-180

1695 Ibid. pp. 215-216

1696 Zugibe, op. cit. pg. 184

1697 Ibid.

1698 Ibid.

1699 Ibid. pg. 185

1700 Cf. Criswell, *Rise and Fall* op. cit.

1701 Coral Ridge Ministries, "The Shroud of Turin," *Bible and Spade* op. cit. pg. 58

1702 The coins were likely not new coins and thus may have been in circulation for a few years.

1703 Zugibe, op. cit. pg. 132

1704 Ibid. pp. 119-207

1705 Cf. Criswell, *Rise and Fall* op. cit.

1706 McDowell, op. cit. pg. 52

1707 Zugibe, op. cit. pg. 123
1708 Ken Ham & Bodie Hodge, "Problematic Apologetics," *Answers Magazine Vol. 4 No. 2 April-June 2009* pg. 72
1709 Ibid.
1710 Zugibe, op. cit. pp. 133-141
1711 Ibid.
1712 Sir Robert Anderson, *The Bible and Modern Criticism* Pickering & Inglis (London, England) 1907 pg. 3
1713 Anderson, *Bible and Modern Criticism* op. cit. pg. 64
1714 Randall Price, *Searching for the Original Bible* Harvest House (Eugene, OR) 2007 pg. 156
1715 Lee Martin McDonald, *The Biblical Canon* Hendrickson Publishers (Peabody, Mass.) 1995
1716 Ibid.
1717 Randall Price, *The Search for the Original Bible* Harvest House (Eugene, OR) 2007 pg. 154
1718 Brian Edwards, *Nothing but the Truth* Evangelical Press (Webster, NY) 2006 ed. pg. 218
1719 Ibid.
1720 http://www.christian-history.org/muratorian-canon.html
1721 Brian Edwards, *Nothing but the Truth* Evangelical Press (Webster, NY) 2006 ed. pg. 218
1722 http://www.christian-history.org/muratorian-canon.html
1723 McDonald, op. cit. pg. 314
1724 Ibid. pg. 308
1725 Philip Schaff, *History of the Christian Church Vol. 2* Hendrickson Publishers Peabody, Mass.) 1996 pg.
1726 F.F. Bruce, *The Canon of Scripture* IVP Academic (Downers Grove, Ill.) 1988 pg. 121
1727 The "Jesus Seminar" was a seminar of so-called theologians who met and voted on what portions of the gospels were true and what portions were legends. They called this book the "Five Gospels" and concluded that *only* "love your neighbor as yourself" was legimate, rejecting everything else in the gospels as suspect.
1728 F.F. Bruce, *The Canon of Scripture* IVP Academic (Downers Grove, Ill.) 1988 pg. 144
1729 Edwards, op. cit. pg. 226
1730 J.B. Lightfoot, & J.R. Harmer, *The Apostlic Fathers* Baker Book House (Grand Rapids, Mich.) 1984 pg. 293
1731 Ibid.
1732 Bruce, op. cit. pg. 77
1733 Ibid.
1734 Lightfoot & Harmer, op. cit. pg. 239
1735 Ibid.
1736 J.N.D. Kelly, *The Oxford Dictionary of Popes* Oxford University Press (Oxford, England) 1986 pg. 7
1737 Lightfoot & Harmer, op. cit. pg. 3
1738 J.N.D. Kelly, *The Oxford Dictionary of Popes* Oxford University Press (Oxford, England) 1986 pg. 7
1739 Ibid.
1740 Clement is controversial among Protestants because he is the only early church father who appeals to the authority of bishops, but even this statement is a far cry from the doctrine of papal supremacy expressed later.
1741 Lightfoot & Harmer, op. cit. pg. 215
1742 Ibid.
1743 Bruce, op. cit. pg. 77
1744 Ibid. pg. 166
1745 Ibid. pg. 201
1746 http://en.wikipedia.org/wiki/Gospel_of_thomas
1747 http://www.goarch.org/ourfaith/ourfaith9560
1748 Price, op. cit. pg. 113

1749 Ibid.
1750 Nestle & Aland, *Nestle-Aland Novum Tetamentum Graece* op. cit. pp. 685-688
1751 Ibid. pg. 686
1752 Young Kyu Kim, "Paleographical Dating of $\mathfrak{P}^{46}$ to the Later First Century," *Biblica*, lxix (1988) pp. 248-257
1753 Metzger, op. cit. pg. 265
1754 Ibid.
1755 Metzger, op. cit. pg. 38
1756 Kurt & Barbara Aland, *The Text of the New Testament* trans. Erroll Rhodes Wm. B. Eerdmans (Grand Rapids, Mich.) 1989 69
1757 Cf. Metzger, op. cit. pg. 40, footnote 1
1758 Theodore of Mapsuestia, *Ancient Christian Commentary Vol. IV B* op. cit. pg. 395
1759 Ibid & John Foxe, *Acts and Monuments of the Church* op. cit. Pg. 95
1760 Compiled from Hunt, *Defense of the Faith* op. cit. pg. 71 & Price, op. cit. pg. 114
1761 Greenlee, op. cit. pp. 81-87
1762 Metzger, op. cit. pg. 217
1763 Ibid. pg. 196
1764 Ibid.
1765 Ibid. pg. 187
1766 Ibid. pg. 191
1767 Greenlee, op. cit. pg. 58
1768 It is interesting to note that King James only advocates often attack modern translations for "removing" the word "God." However, the reverse (oς mistaken for θς) also occurs. There is no grand conspiracy to remove God from the Bible. Such attacks are not only frivolous, but the King James only advocate would also be surprised to learn how many times modern translation use the word "God" where it is *missing* from the King James.
1769 Ibid. pg. 196
1770 Cf. John Foxe, *Acts and Monuments of the Church Vol. 1* Religious Tract Society (London, England) 1860s ed. pg. 95
1771 Price, op. cit. pg. 113
1772 Norman L. Geisler and William E. Nix, *A General Introduction to the Bible*, Moody (Chicago, Ill.) 1986 ed. pp. 366-67
1773 Randall Niles, "Bible Manuscripts," http://www.allaboutthejourney.org/bible-manuscripts.htm
1774 Ibid.
1775 Anderson, *Bible and Modern Criticism* op. cit. pg. 47
1776 Ibid. pg. 48
1777 Ibid. pg. 223
1778 Ibid. pg. 78
1779 See David Criswell, *Controversies in the Pentateuch* Fortress Adonai (Dallas, TX) 2007
1780 Archer, op. cit. pg. 322
1781 Anderson, "Misunderstood Texts of the Bible," *Collected Works Vol. 2* op. cit. pg. 296
1782 Thayer, op. cit. pg. 257
1783 George Peters, *The Theocratic Kingdom Vol. 1* Kregel Publishing (Grand Rapids, Mich.) 1884 pg. 195
1784 Ladd, op. cit. pg. 61
1785 Couch, *Dictionary of Premillennial Theology* op. cit. pg. 231
1786 Couch, *Biblical Theology of the Church* op. cit. pg. 44
1787 Albright & Mann, op. cit. pg. c
1788 J.D. Pentecost, *Popular Encyclopedia of Bible Prophecy* Tim LaHaye & Ed Hindson, ed., Harvest House (Eugene, OR) 2004 pg. 186
1789 Unger, *Bible Dictionary* op. cit. pg. 632
1790 Ibid.
1791 Lewis Sperry Chafer, *Systematic Theology* pg. 224 as cited by Ibid.

1792 J. Dwight Pentecost, *Popular Encyclopedia of Bible Prophecy* Tim LaHaye & Ed Hindson, ed., Harvest House (Eugene, OR) 2004 pp. 186-190
1793 Ibid. pg. 189
1794 Albright & Mann, op. cit. pg. ci
1795 Anderson, "The Bible and Modern Criticism," *Collected Works Vol. 1* op. cit. pp. 157-158
1796 Couch, *Biblical Theology of the Church* op. cit. pg. 44
1797 Hunt, *Defense of Faith* op. cit. pg. 109
1798 Ibid. pg. 108
1799 Ibid. pg. 109
1800 Lewis Sperry Chafer, *Systematic Theology* pg. 224   as cited by Ibid.
1801 J. Dwight Pentecost, *Popular Encyclopedia of Bible Prophecy* Tim LaHaye & Ed Hindson, ed., Harvest House (Eugene, OR) 2004 pp. 186-190
1802 Albright & Mann, op. cit. pg. ci
1803 Chuck & Nancy Missler, *The Kingdom Power and Glory* The King's High Way Ministries (Coeur d'Alene, ID) 2007 pg. 102
1804 Sir Robert Anderson, *Forgotten Truth* Pickering (London, England) 1914
1805 Anderson, "The Bible and Modern Criticism," *Collected Works Vol. 1* op. cit. pg. 158
1806 Edwards, Wesley, & Hosmet, op. cit. pg. 1456
1807 Zugibe, op. cit. pg. 15
1808 Ibid. pg. 49
1809 Ibid. pg. 16
1810 Ibid. pg. 27
1811 Edwards, Wesley, & Hosmet, op. cit. pg. 1458
1812 Ibid. pg. 1459
1813 Zugibe, op. cit. pg. 44
1814 Edwards, Wesley, & Hosmet, op. cit. pg. 1460
1815 Zugibe, op. cit. pg. 118

WORKS CITED

BOOKS

Kurt & Barbara Aland, *The Text of the New Testament* trans. Erroll Rhodes Wm. B. Eerdmans (Grand Rapids, Mich.) 1989

Nestle & Aland, *Nestle-Aland Novum Tetamentum Graece* Deutsche Bibelgesellschaft Stuttgart (Germany) 1898

W.F. Albright & C.S. Mann, *The Anchor Bible : Matthew* Doubleday & Co. (Garden City, NY) 1971

Sir Robert Anderson, *The Bible and Modern Criticism* Pickering & Inglis (London, England) 1907

Sir Robert Anderson, *The Bible and Modern Criticism* Pickering & Inglis (London, England) 1907

Sir Robert Anderson, *The Collected Works of Sir Robert Andreson* Vol. II *Anderson on Biblical Criticism* Fortress Adonai Press (North Carleston, SC) 2011

Sir Robert Anderson, *The Critics Criticized* Pickering & Inglis (London, England) 1904

Sir Robert Anderson, *Daniel in the Critics' Den* Pickering & Inglis (London, England) 1900

Sir Robert Anderson, *Forgotten Truths* Pickering (London, England) 1914

Thomas Aquinas, *St. Aquinas Commentary on the Gospel of John Chapters 1-5* Catholic University of America (Washington, D.C.) 2010

Thomas Aquinas, *St. Aquinas Commentary on the Gospel of John Chapters 13-21* Catholic University of America (Washington, D.C.) 2010

Gleason Archer, *Encyclopedia of Bible Difficulties* Zondervan Publishers (Grand Rapids, Mich.) 1982

Pierre Barbet, *Doctor at Calvary* P.J. Jennedy & Sons (New York, NY) 1953 English ed.

William Barclay, *Gospel of Mark* Westminister Press (Philadelphia, PN) 1954

William Barclay, *The Gospel of Matthew Vol. 1* St. Andrews Press (Edinburgh, Scotland) 1956

William Barclay, *The Gospel of Matthew Vol. 2* St. Andrews Press (Edinburgh, Scotland) 1956

Mitchell Bard, *Myths and Facts* American-Israeli Cooperative Enterprise (Chevy Chasae, NY) 2001

Albert Barnes, *Barnes' Notes on the New Testament One Volume ed.* Kregel (Grand Rapids, Mich) 1962

Albert Barnes *Notes on the Old Testament Isaiah Vol. 1* Baker Book House (Grand Rapids, Mich.) 1851

Donald Barnhouse, *The Love Life* Regal Books (Glendale, CA) 1973

Archbishop J.H. Bernard, *A Critical & Exegetical Commentary on the Gospel According to St. John Vol. 1* T & T Clark (Edinburgh, Great Britain) 1928

Ron Bigalke, Jr., ed., *Progressive Dispensationalism* University Press of America (New York, NY) 2005

Craig Blaising & Darrell Bock, *Progressive Dispensationalism* Victory Books (Wheaton, Ill.) 1993

Susanne Bobzien, *Determinism and Freedom in Stoic Philosophy* Oxford University Press (Oxford, England) 1998

Susanne Bobzien, *The Inadvertent Conception and Late Birth of the Free-Will Problem* Oxford University Press (Oxford, England) 1998

Loraine Boettner, *Roman Catholicism* Presbyterian & Reformed (Phillipsburg, NJ) 1962

James Montgomery Boice, *Foundations of the Christian Faith* InterVarsity Press (Downers Grove, Ill.) 1986

James Montgomery Boice, *The Gospel of John Vol. 1* Zondervan Press (Grand Rapids, Mich) 1975

James Montgomery Boice, *The Gospel of John Vol. 2* Zondervan Press (Grand Rapids, Mich) 1975

James Montgomery Boice, *The Gospel of John Vol. 3* Zondervan Press (Grand Rapids, Mich) 1975

James Montgomery Boice, *The Gospel of John Vol. 4* Zondervan Press (Grand Rapids, Mich) 1975

James Montgomery Boice, *The Gospel of John Vol. 5* Zondervan Press (Grand Rapids, Mich) 1975

R.G. Bratcher & E.A. Nida, *Translator's Handbook on Mark* E.J Brill Publishers (Leiden, Netherlands) 1961

James Brooks, *New American Commentary Mark* Broadman Press (Nashville, TN) 1991

Raymond Brown, *The Gospel According to John Vol. 1* Doubleday (New York, NY) 1966

F.F. Bruce, *The Canon of Scripture* IVP Academic (Downers Grove, Ill.) 1988

E.W. Bullinger, *Figures of Speech Used in the Bible* Baker Books (Grand Rapids, Mich.) 1898 (1968 ed.)

John Calvin, *Calvin's Commentaries A Harmony of the Gospels of Matthew, Mark, and Luke Vol. 1* William B. Eerdmans (Grand Rapids, Mich.) A.W. Morison, trans., 1972

John Calvin, *Calvin's Commentaries A Harmony of the Gospels of Matthew, Mark, and Luke Vol. 11* William B. Eerdmans (Grand Rapids, Mich.) A.W. Morison, trans., 1972

John Calvin, *Calvin's Commentaries A Harmony of the Gospels of Matthew, Mark, and Luke Vol. 111* William B. Eerdmans (Grand Rapids, Mich.) A.W. Morison, trans., 1972

John Calvin, *Calvin's Commentaries Vol. 7 Commentary on Isaiah Book 1,* Baker Books (Grand Rapids, Mich.) 1999

John Calvin, *Calvin's Commetnaries Vol. XIV Commentary on The Minor Prophets Book 1,* Baker Books (Grand Rapids, Mich.) 1999

John Calvin, *Crossway Classic Commentaries : John by John Calvin* Reformation Trust (Orlando, FL) 2009

Lewis Sperry Chafer, *Systematic Theology* Kregel Publishers (Grand Rapids, Mich.) 1993

Bruce Chilton, *God in Strength* F. Plochl (Freistadt, Germany) 1977

Charles Chiniquy, *50 Years on the "Church" of Rome* Protestand Literature Depository (Chick Edition - Chino, CA) 1886 (1985 ed.)

Larry Collins & Dominique Lapierre, *O Jerusalem* Pocket Books (New York, NY) 1972

Christopher Cone, ed., *Dispensationalism Tomorrow & Beyond* Tyndale Seminary Press (Fort Worth, TX) 2008

Mal Couch, ed., *A Biblical Theology of the Church* Kregel Publications (Grand Rapids, Mich.) 1999

Mal Couch, ed., *Dictionary of Premillennial Theology* Kregel (Grand Rapids, Mich.) 1996

David Criswell, *Controversies in the Pentateuch* Fortress Adonai (Dallas, TX) 2007

David Criswell, *Controversies in the Prophets* Fortress Adonai (Dallas, TX) 2005

David Criswell, *Controversies in Revelation* Fortress Adonai (Dallas, TX) 2003

David Criswell, *Controversies in the Scriptures Vol. II* Fortress Adonai (Dallas, TX) 2010

David Criswell, *Rise and Fall of the Holy Roman Empire* PublishAmerica (Baltimore, MD) 2005

David Criswell, *Valley of the Blind* Fortress Adonai (Dallas, TX) 2012

W.A. Criswell, ed., *Criswell Study Bible* Thomas Nelson Publishers (Nashville, TN) 1979

John Nelson Darby, *The Collected Writings of J. N. Darby Volume 19 Expository # 1* Believer's Bookshelf (Sunbury, Penn.) 1971

John Nelson Darby, *The Collected Writings of J. N. Darby Volume 30 Expository # 2* Believer's Bookshelf (Sunbury, Penn.) 1971

John Nelson Darby, *Mark's Gospel* G. Morrish (London, England) 1800

John Darby, *Notes on the Gospel of John* G. Morrish (London, England) n.d.

John Nelson Darby, *Notes on the Gospel of Matthew* G. Morrish (London, England) n.p.d.

John Davis & John Whitcomb, *Israel : From Conquest to Exile* BMH Books (Winona Lake, IN) 1999 ed.

Franz Delitzsch, *Biblical Commentary on the Prophecies of Isaiah Vol. 1* William B Eerdmans (Grand Rapids, Mich.) 1949

C.H. Dodd, *The Interpretation of the Fourth Gospel* Cambridge Press (Cambridge, England) 1955

Brian Edwards, *Nothing but the Truth* Evangelical Press (Webster, NY) 2006

Jonathan Edwards, *"The Blank Bible" Part 2* Stphen Stein, ed. Yale University Press (New Haven, CT) 2006

John Elowsky, ed., *Ancient Christian Commentary on Scripture New Testament IV B John 11-21* InterVarsity Press (Downers Grove, Ill.) 2006

Desiderius Erasmus, *The Collected Works of Erasmus Vol. 45 Paraphrase on Matthew* Dean Simpson, trans., University of Toronto Press (Toronto, Canada) 2008

Desiderius Erasmus, *Collected Works of Erasmus Vol. 46 Paraphrase on John* University of Toronto (Toronto, Canada) 1991

Desiderius Erasmus, *The Collected Works of Erasmus   Vol. 49   Paraphrase on Mark*   Dean Simpson, trans., University of Toronto Press (Toronto, Canada) 1988

C.H. Dodd, *Parbles of the Kingdom* Nisbet (London, England) 1936

John Elowsky, ed., *Ancient Christian Commentary on Scripture   New Testament IV A   John 1-10* InterVarsity Press (Downers Grove, Ill.) 2006

Charles Erdman, *The Gospel of John* Westminister Press (Philadelphia, PN) 1933

Millard Erickson, *Christian Theology* Baker Books (Grand Rapids, Mich.) 1983

Eusebius, *Eusebius The Church History*, Paul Maier, trans., Kregel Publications (Grand Rapids, Mich.) 1999

Abraham Ibn Ezra, *Commentary on Isaiah* Society of Hebrew Literature (London, England) 1873 ed.

Jerry Falwell & Ed Hindson, eds., *Liberty Commentary on the New Testament* Liberty Press (Lynchburg, Virginia) 1978

F. W. Farrar, *Texts Explained* F.M.Barton (Cleveland, Ohio) 1899

J.D Faust, *The Rod* Schoettle Publishing (Hayesville, N.C.) 2003

John Foxe, *Acts and Monuments of the Church* Church of England (London, England) 1563

John Foxe, *Acts and Monuments of the Church   Vol. 1* Religious Tract Society (London, England) 1883 ed.

Thomas Friedman, *Beirut to Jerusalem* Anchor Books (New York, NY) 1989

Rene Fulop-Miller, *Rasputin : The Holy Devil* Garden City Publishing (New York, NY) 1928

A.C. Gaebelein, *The Gospel of Matthew   Vol. 1* Our Hope (New York, NY) 1910

A.C. Gaebelein, *The Gospel of Matthew   Vol. 2* Our Hope (New York, NY) 1910

Arno Gaebelein, *The Gospel of John* Van Kampen Press (Wheaton, Ill.) 1936

Frank Gaebelein, ed.   *The Expositor's Bible Commentary   Vol. 7* Zondervan Publishers (Grand Rapids, Mich.) 1984

Frank Gaebelein, ed.   *The Expositor's Bible Commentary   Vol. 8* Zondervan Publishers (Grand Rapids, Mich.) 1984

Frank Gaebelain, ed.   *The Expositor's Bible Commentary   Vol. 9* Zondervan Publishers (Grand Rapids, Mich.) 1984

Paul Gaechter, *Matthaus* Innsbruck (Tyrolia, Germany) 1968

Norman L. Geisler and William E. Nix, *A General Introduction to the Bible*, Moody (Chicago, Ill.) 1986 ed.

Norman Geisler, ed., *Inerrancy* Academie Books (Grand Rapids, Mich.) 1980

William Genenius, *Gesenius' Hebrew and Cahaldee Lexicon to the Old Tesament* Samuel Tregelles, trans., Baker Books (Grand Rapids, Mich.) 1847 (1984 ed.)

John Gill, *Expositions of the Old Testament   Vol. 1* William Hill Collinridge (London, England) 1852

John Gill, *Expositions of the Old Testament   Vol. 3* William Hill Collinridge (London, England) 1852

John Gill, *Expositions of the Old Testament* Vol. 4 William Hill Collinridge (London, England) 1852

Martin Gilbert, *Altas of Jewish Civilization* MacMillian Publishing (New York, NY) 1990

Martin Gilbert, *Illustrated Atlas of Jewish Civilization* MacMillan Publishing (New York, NY) 1990

Martin Gilbert, *Jerusalem in the Twentieth Century* John Wiley & Sons (New York, NY) 1996

Frederick Louis Godet, *Gospel of John Vol. 1* Zondervan Press (Grand Rapids, Mich) 1893

Robert Govett, *Exposition of the Gospel of St. John* Vol. 1 Bemrose & Sons (London, Englard) 1881

Robert Govett, *Exposition of the Gospel of St. John* Vol. 2 Bemrose & Sons (London, Englard) 1881

Robert Govett, *Isaiah Unfulfilled* Conley & Schoettle Publishing (Miami Springs, FL) 1841 (1984 ed.)

J. Harold Greenlee, *Introduction to New Testament Textual Criticism* Hendrickson Publishers (Peabody, Mass.) 1995 ed.

Robert Gundry, *Matthew* Wm. B. Eerdmaans (Grand Rapids, Mich.) 1982

Robert Gundry, *Mark* William B. Eerdmanns (Grand Rapids, Mich) 1993

Robert Gundry, *A Survey of the New Testament* Zondervan (Grand Rapids, Mich.) 1994

John Heller, *Report on the Shroud of Turin* Houghton Mifflin Co (Boston, Mass.) 1983

Matthew Henry, *Matthew Henry's Commentary on the Whole Bible : Vol. 4* Hendrickson Publishers (Peabody, Mass.) 1991

Matthew Henry, *Matthew Henry's Commentary on the Whole Bible : Vol. 5* Hendrickson Publisher (Peabody, Mass.) 1991 ed.

Matthew Henry, *Matthew Henry's Commentary on the Whole Bible : Vol. 6* Hendrickson Publishers (Peabody, Mass.) 1991

Alexander Hislop, *The Two Babylons* Loizeaux Brothers (Englad) 1916

Harold Hoehner, *Chronological Aspects of the Life of Christ* Zondervan Publishing (Grand Rapids, Mich.) 1977

David Hunt, *In Defense of the Faith* Harvest House (Eugene, OR) 1996

Dave Hunt, *What Love is This?* Loyal Publishing (Sisters, OR) 2002

Dave Hunt & T.A. McMahon, *The Seduction of Christianity* Harvest House (Eugene, OR) 1985

Abraham Ibn Ezra, *Commentary on Isaiah* Society of Hebrew Literature (London, England) 1873 ed.

Thomas Ice & Timothy Demy ed., *When the Trumpet Sounds* Harvest House (Eugene, OR) 1995

James Inciardi, *Criminal Justice* Harcourt Brace Jovanovich (New York, NY) 1987

H.A. Ironside, *Adddresses on the Gospel of John* Loizeaux Brothers (Neptune, NJ) 1942

H.A. Ironside, *Expository Notes on the Gospel of Mark* Loizeaux Brothers (Minneapolis, MN) 1946

H.A. Ironside, *Expository Notes on the Gospel of Matthew* Loizeaux Brothers (New York, NY) 1948

H. A. Ironside, *Notes on the Prophecy and Lamentations of Jeremiah* Loizeaux Brothers (Neptune, NJ) 1906

H. A. Ironside, *Expository Notes on the Prophet Isaiah* Loizeaux Brothers (New York, NY) 1952

Flavius Josephus, *The Complete Works of Flavius Josephus* Kregel Publishers (Grand Rapids, Mich.) 1981

J.N.D. Kelly, *The Oxford Dictionary of Popes* Oxford University Press (Oxford, England) 1986

Homer Kent, *Light in the Darkness* Baker Books (Grand Rapids, Mich.) 1974

Kurt Koch, *Christian Counseling and Occultism* Kregel Publishers (Grand Rapids, Mich.) 1972

Kurt Koch & Alfred Lechler, *Occult Bondage and Deliverance* Kregel Publishers (Grand Rapids, Mich.) 1970

George Ladd, *A Theology of the New Testament* Wm. B. Eerdmans (Grand Rapids, Mich.) 1974

Tim LaHaye, Gen. Ed., *Tim LaHaye Prophecy Study Bible* AMG Publishers (Chattanooga, TN) 2001

Tim LaHaye & Ed Hindson, ed., *Popular Encyclopedia of Bible Prophecy* Harvest House (Eugene, OR) 2004

William Sanford Lasor, David Allan Hubbard, and Frederic Bush, *Old Testament Survey* William B. Eerdmans (Grand Rapids, Mich) 1982

Kenneth Scott Latourette, *A History of Christianity Volume 1* Harpers & Row (New York, NY) 1953

R.C.H. Lenski, *The Interpretation of St. Mark's Gospel* Augsburg Publishing (Minneapolis, MN) 1946

R.C.H. Lenski, *The Interpretation of St. Matthew's Gospel* Augsburg Publishing (Minneapolis, MN) 1943

J.B. Lightfoot & J.R. Hammer, eds., *The Apostolic Fathers* Baker Book House (Grand Rapids, Mich.) 1984

John Lightfoot (1859) [1663], *Horæ Hebraicæ et Talmudicæ*, 3, p. 55, http://philologos.org/__eb-jl/luke03.htm.

John Lightfoot, *The Whole Works of the Rev. John Lightfoot Vol. II* J. F. Dove (London, England) 1822

R.H. Lightfoot, *St. John's Gospel* Clarendon Press (Oxford, England) 1956

W. Bruce Lincoln, *Passage Through Armageddon* Simon & Schuster (New York, NY) 1986

Martin Luther, *Luther's Works Vol. 16 Lectures on Isaiah 1-39* Concordia House (St. Louis, MS) 1958

Martin Luther, *Luther's Works Vol. 22 John 1-4* Concordia House (St. Louis, MS) 1957

Martin Luther, *Luther's Works Vol. 69 John 17-20* Concordia House (St. Louis, MS) 1957

John MacArthur, *The MacArthur New Testament Commentary Matthew 1-7* Moody Bible Institute (Chicago, Ill.) 1985

John MacArthur, *The MacArthur New Testament Commentary Matthew 8-15* Moody Bible Institute (Chicago, Ill.) 1985

John MacArthur, *The MacArthur New Testament Commentary Matthew 16-23* Moody Bible Institute (Chicago, Ill.) 1985

John MacArthur, *The MacArthur New Testament Commentary Matthew 24-28* Moody Bible Institute (Chicago, Ill.) 1985

John MacArthur, *MacArthur New Testament Commentary John 1-5* Moody Bible Institute (Chicago, Ill.) 2006

John MacArthur, *The MacArthur New Testament Commentary Luke 1-5* Moody Bible Instituted (Chicago, Ill.) 2009

James McCarthy, *The Gospel According to Rome* Harvest House (Eugene, OR) 1995

Dan McCartney & Charles Clayton, *Let the Reader Understand* Victor Books (Wheaton, Ill.) 1994

Lee Martin McDonald, *The Biblical Canon* Hendrickson Publisher (Peabody, Mass.) 2007

John McDowell, *The Resurrection Factor* Here's Life Publishers (San Bernadino, CA) 1981

James McGowan, *Gospel of Mark* AMG Publishers (Chattanooge, TN) 2006

Bruce Metzger, *The Text of the New Testament : Its Transmission, Corruption, and Restoration* Oxford University (Oxford, England) 1964

Bruce Metzger, *A Textual Commentary on the Greek New Testament* United Bible Societies (New York, NY) 1971

Leon Morris, *The Gospel According to Matthew* William B. Eerdmans (Grand Rapids, Mich.) 1992

Robert Mounce, *New International Biblical Commentary : Matthew* Hendrickson Publishers (Peabody, Mass) 1985

Andrew Miller, *Miller's Church History* Pickering & Inglis (London, England) 1963

Stephen R. Miller, *Daniel : New American Commentary Vol. 18* Broadman & Holman (Nashville, TN.) 1994

John Milton, *Paradise Lost* III.682-684 *The Portable Milton* Penguin Books (New York, NY) 1949

Chuck & Nancy Missler, *The Kingdom Power and Glory* King's High Way Ministries (Coeur d' Alene, ID) 2007

Douglas Moo, Paul Feinberg, *The Rapture : Pre- Mid- or Posttribulational?* Zondervan (Grand Rapids, Mich.) 1984

Frank Morison, *Who Moved the Stone?* Faber & Faber (New York, NY) 1930

Leon Morris, *The Gospel According to Matthew* Wm. Eerdmaans (Grand Rapids, Mich.) 1992

Leon Morris, *Reflections on the Gospel of John* Hendrickson Publishers (Peabody, Mass.) 1986

Robert Mounce, *New International Bible Commentary : Matthew* Hendrickson Publishers (Peabody, Mass.) 1985

William Mounce, *Basics of Biblical Greek* Zondervan Publishers (Grand Rapids, Mich.) 1993

Eberhard Nestle & Kurt Aland, ed., *Nestle-Aland Novum Tetamentum Graece* Deutsche Bibelgesellschaft (Stuttgart, Germany) 1991

Barclay Newman Jr., ed., *A Complete Greek-English Dictionary of the New Testament* United Bible Societies (Stuttgart, Germany) 1971

Barclay M. Newman, Jr., ed., *A Concise Greek-English Dictionary of the New Testament* United Bible Society (Stuttgart, Germany) 1971

Jacob Neusner, trans., *Mishnah* Yale University Press (London, England) 1988

John Julius Norwich, *A Short History of Byzanium* Random House (New York, NY) 1999

A.T. Olmstead, *History of Assyria* Charles Scribner's Sons (New York, NY) 1923

A.T. Olmstead, *History of the Persian Empire* University of Chicago Press (Chicago, Ill.) 1948

Wesley Perschbacher, *Refresh Your Greek* Moody Press (Chicago, Ill.) 1989

George Peters, *The Theocratic Kingdom Vol. 1* Kregel (Grand Rapids, Mich.) 1884

George Peters, *The Theocratic Kingdom Vol. 2* Kregel (Grand Rapids, Mich.) 1884

Charles Pfeiffer, *The Dead Sea Scrolls and the Bible* Baker Books (Grand Rapids, Mich.) 1969

Arthur Pink, *Exposition of the Gospel of John Vol I* I.C. Herendeen (Cleveland, OH) 1924

Arthur Pink, *Exposition of the Gospel of John Vol II* I.C. Herendeen (Cleveland, OH) 1924

Arthur Pink, *Exposition of the Gospel of John Vol. III* I.C Herendeen (Cleveland, Ohio) 1924

Arthur Pink, *Exposition of the Gospel of John Vol. IV* I.C Herendeen (Cleveland, Ohio) 1924

Matthew Poole, *A Commetnary on the Holy Bible Vol. II* Hendrickson Publishers (Peabody, Mass.) n.d.

Matthew Poole, *A Commetnary on the Holy Bible Vol. III* Hendrickson Publishers (Peabody, Mass.) n.d.

Chaim Potok, *Wanderings : Chaim Potok's History of the Jews* Fawcett Crest (New York, NY) 1978

J. Dwight Pentecost, *Things to Come* Zondervan Publishers (Grand Rapids, Mich.) 1958

Randall Price, *The Coming Last Days Temple* Harvest House (Eugene, OR) 1999

Randall Price, *Searching for the Original Bible* Harvest House (Eugene, OR) 2007

Homer Ritchie, Omer Ritchie, & Lonnie Shipman, *Secrets of Prophecy Revealed* 21st Century Press (Springfield, Mo.) 2001

Alexander Roberts & James Donaldson, eds., *Ante-Nicene Fathers Vol. I* Charles Scribner (New York, NY) 1886

Alexander Roberts & James Donaldson, eds., *Ante-Nicene Fathers Vol. II* Charles Scribner (New York, NY) 1886

Alexander Roberts & James Donaldson, eds., *Ante-Nicene Fathers Vol. III* William B. Eerdmans Publishers (Grand Rapids, Mich.) 1886

Alexander Roberts & James Donaldson, eds., *Ante-Nicene Fathers Vol. IV* William B. Eerdmans Publishers (Grand Rapids, Mich.) 1999.

Alexander Roberts & James Donaldson, eds., *Ante-Nicene Fathers Vol. V* Charles Scribner (New York, NY) 1886

Alexander Roberts & James Donaldson, eds., *Ante-Nicene Fathers Vol. VIII* William B. Eerdmans Publishers (Grand Rapids, Mich.) 1886

A.T. Robertson, *A Harmony of the Gospels for Students of the Life of Christ* George Doran (New York, NY) 1922

A.J. Rosenberg, ed., *The Book of Isaiah Vol. I with Rashi Commentary* Judaica Press (New York, NY) 1982

A.J. Rosenberg, ed., *Twelve Prophets Vol. I* Judaica Press (New York, NY) 1982

Franz Rosenthal, *A Grammar of Biblical Aramaic* Otto Harrassowitz (Wiesbaden, Germany) 1983

J.J. Saunders, *A History of Medieval Islam* Routledge Press (London, England) 1965

Philip Schaff, ed., *Nicene and Post-Nicene Fathers Vol. III* Charles Scribner (New York, NY) 1887

Philip Schaff, ed., *Nicene and Post-Nicene Fathers Second Series Vol. VI* Charles Scribner (New York, NY) 1892

Philip Schaff, ed., *Nicene and Post-Nicene Fathers Second Series Vol. VII* Charles Scribner (New York, NY) 1892

Philip Schaff, *History of the Christian Church Vol. 1* Hendrickson Publishers (Peabody, MA) 1858

Philip Schaff, *History of the Christian Church Vol. 2* Hendrickson Publishers (Peabody, MA) 1858

Philip Schaff, *History of the Christian Church Vol. 3* Hendrickson Publishers (Peabody, MA) 1867

C.I. Scofield, *Addresses on Prophecy* A. C. Gaebelein (New York, NY) 1910

C.I. Scofield, *First Scofield Reference Bible* A.C. Gaebelein (New York, NY) 1917

Joseph A. Seiss, *The Apocalypse* Kregel Publications (Grand Rapids, Mich.) 2001 reprint

A.N. Sherwin-White, *Roman Society and Roman Law in the New Testament* Oxford Press (Oxford, England) 1963

Dwight Moody Smith, *John* Abingdon Press (Nashville, TN) 1999

Marta Sorti, *The Christians and the Roman Empire* University of Oklahoma (Oklahoma City, Ok.) 1986

R.C. Sproul, *John* Reformed Trust (Orlando, FL) 2009

Charles Spurgeon, *Exposition of the Doctrine of Grace* Pilgrim Publications (Pasadena TX) n.d.

Charles Spurgeon, *Treasury of the New Testament Volume One* Zondervan (Grand Rapids, Mich.) 1950

Charles Spurgeon, *Treasury of the New Testament Volume Two* Zondervan (Grand Rapids, Mich.) 1950

Charles Spurgeon, *Treasury of the New Testament Volume Three* Zondervan (Grand Rapids, Mich.) 1951

Robert Stein, *Jesus the Messiah: A Survey of the Life of Christ* InterVarsity Press (Downers Grove, Ill.) 1996

J.F. Strombeck, *First the Rapture* Kregel Publications (Grand Rapids, Mich.) 1992 reprint (orig. 1950)

Henry Barclay Swete, *The Gospel According to St. Mark* MacMillan & Co. (London, England) 1920

Suetonius, *Lives of the Twelve Caesars* Robert Graves, ed., Welcome Rains Publishers (New York, NY) 1957

Merrill Tenney, *John, the Gospel of Belief* Wm. B Eerdmans (Grand Rapids, Mich) 1948

Merril Tenney, *New Testament Survey* William B Eerdmans (Grand Rapids, Mich.) 1961

Joseph Thayer, *Thayer's Greek-English Lexicon* Baker Book House (Grand Rapids, Mich.) 1977

Edwin R. Thiele, *The Mysterious Numbers of the Hebrew Kings* Kregel Publications (Grand Rapids, Mich.) 1983

J.A. Thompson, *The Bible and Archaeology* William B. Eerdmans (Grand Rapids, Mich.) 1962

Robert Thomas & Stanley Gundry, *A Harmony of the Gospels* HarperOne (New York, NY) 1978

R.A. Torrey, *Difficulties in the Bible* Whitaker House (New Kensington, PA) 1996 ed.

Stanley Toussaint, *Behold the King* Kregel Publishers (Grand Rapids, Mich.) 1980

Stanley Toussaint, *Contemporary Dispensationalism* Herbert Batemen IV, ed., Kregel (Grand Rapids, Mich.) 1999

Elmer Towns, *The Gospel of John* AMG Publishers (Chatanooga, TN) 1999

Warren Trenchard, *Complete Vocabulary Guide to the Greek New Testament* Zondervan (Grand Rapids, Mich.) 1992

Merrill Unger, *Demons in the World Today* Tyndale House (Wheaton, Ill.) 1981

Merrill Unger, *Unger's Bible Dictionary* Moody Press (Chicago, Ill.) 1957

James Ussher, *Annals of the World* Master Books (El Cajon, CA) 2003 ed.

Thieleman J. Van Braght, *Martyrs Mirror* Herald Press (Scottsdale, PN) 1660

Lew Wallace, *Ben Hur* Reader's Digest (New York, NY) 1992 (unabridged from 1880 ed.)

John Walvoord, *Every Prophecy of the Bible* Chariot Victor Publishing (Colorado Springs, Co.) 1999

John Walvoord, *Matthew : Thy Kingdom Come* Moody Press (Chicago, Ill.) 1974

John F. Walvoord & Roy Zuck, eds., *The Bible Knowledge Commentary : New Testament* Victor Books (Wheaton, Ill.) 1986

John F. Walvoord & Roy Zuck, eds., *The Bible Knowledge Commentary Old Testament* Victor Books (Wheaton, Ill.) 1986

Benjamin B. Warfield, *Calvin and Augustine* Presbyterian & Reformed (Phillipsburg, NJ) 1981

B.F Wescott, *The Gospel According to St. John* Wm. B Eerdmans (Grand Rapids, Mich.) 1954

John Wesley, *Explanatory Notes Upon the New Testament* Abraham Paul (New York, NY) 1818

John Wesley, *Explanatory Notes Upon the Old Testament Vol. III Psalms LXIII – Malachi* Schmul Publishers (Salem, Ohio) 1975

John Whitcomb & Henry Morris, *The Genesis Flood* Presbyterian & Reformed (Grand Rapids, Mich.) 1961

Warren Wiersbe, *Be Alive* Victor Books (Wheaton, Ill.) 1986

Warren Wiersbe, *Be Diligent* Victor Books (Wheaton, Ill.) 1987

Warren Wiersbe, *Be Loyal* Victor Books (Wheaton, Ill.) 1987

Warren Wiersbe, *Be Transformed* Victor Books (Wheaton, Ill.) 1987

Ehud Ben Yehuda, ed., *Ben Yehuda's Pocket English-Hebrew Hebrew-English Dictionary* Penguin Books (New York, NY) 1947

Richard Young, *Intermediate New Testament Greek* Broadman & Holdman Publishers (Nashville, TN) 1994

Shimon Zilberman, *The Up-to-Date Hebrew-English Dictionary* Zilberman Press (Jerusalem, Israel) 1997

Paul A. Zoch, *Ancient Rome* University of Oklahoma Press (University of Oklahoma, Ok.) 1998

Frederick Zubige, M.D., *The Cross and the Shroud* Paragon House (New York, NY) 1988

MISCELANIOUS

The Babylonian Talmud Sabbat 116-b and Sanhedrin 107-b

Canons of Dort

Kenneth Copeland, "The Force of Love," Tape BCC-56

Herodotus I:101; 132

Pope Gregory the Great, *Homily* XXXIII

The Westminister Confession

FOREIGN BIBLES

The Aramaic Bible Vol. 11 The Isaiah Targum Michael Glazier Inc. (Wilmington, Del.) 1988

The Aramaic Bible Vol. 14 Targum of the Minor Prophets Michael Glazier Inc. (Wilmington, Del.) 1988

Biblia Sacra Deutsche Bibelgesellschaft (Stuttgard, Germany) 1993 ed.

The Hebrew-English New Covenant Hope of Israel Publications (Powder Springs, GA) 2003

The Hebrew New Testament, Trinitarian Bible Society (London, England) 1998

PERIODICALS

Roger Beckwith, "The Day, its Divisions and its Limits, in Biblical Thought," *The Evangelical Quarterly* XLIII (Oct-Dec 1971)

Chris Chui, "Carbon 14 and the Shroud of Turin," Contrast (part of the Bible-Science Newsletter 27:7 1989) 8:4 1989

Coral Ridge Ministries, "The Shroud of Turin," *Bible and Spade Vol. 8 No. 2 Spring 1995*

David Criswell, "On Psychiatry And Etiology" *Biblical Reflections On Modern Medicine* (Augusta, GA) May 1993 Vol. 4:3

William Edwards, Wesley Gabel, Floyd Hosmer, "On the Physical Death of Jesus Christ," *JAMA* March 21, 1986 - Vol. 255, No. 11

Weston Fields, "Everyone will be Salted with Fire," *Grace Theological Journal* 6:2 (1985)

Ken Ham & Bodie Hodge, "Problematic Apologetics," *Answers Magazine Vol. 4 No. 2 April-June 2009*

Young Kyu Kim, "Paleographical Dating of $\mathfrak{P}^{46}$ to the Later First Century," *Biblica*, lxix (1988)

Randall Niles, "Bible Manuscripts," http://www.allaboutthejourney.org/bible-manuscripts.htm

Bill Martin & Bill Perkins, "The Second Witness ... Who Is He?", *Digging Deeper Bible Studies* n.d.

INTERNET & SOFTWARE

John Nelson Darby, *Bible Commentary* E-Sword Software

http://aramaicnttruth.org/downloads/outside/Aramaic%20Jesus%20Genealogy.pdf

http://biblicaldiscipleship.org/content/relationships-and-bible

http://craigwbooth.xanga.com/743267828/ten-alleged-contradictions-in-the-bible/

http://defendtheword.wordpress.com/2009/10/01/alleged-bible-contradictions-non-christians-often-talk-about-new-testament/

http://en.wikipedia.org/wiki/Gospel_of_thomas

http://forums.catholic.com/showthread.php?t=477205

http://gluefox.com/min/contrad.htm

http://philologos.org/__eb-jl/luke03.htm.

http://thierrycastex.blogspot.fr/

http://wiki.answers.com/Q/Was_Mary_Magdalene_a_Prostitute

http://www.abideinchrist.com/messages/resurrectionofjesusharmony.html

http://www.catholicforum.com/forums/showthread.php?27416-For-Bibleonly...-regarding-celibacy-among-priests-and-bishops

http://www.christian-history.org/muratorian-canon.html

http://www.deafmissions.com/tally/matthew.html and http://www.deafmissions.com /tally/luke.html

http://www.facebook.com/groups/12295580323/

http://www.foxnews.com/story/0,2933,512703,00.html

http://www.goarch.org/ourfaith/ourfaith9560

http://www.godrules.net/articles/101scontra_d.htm

http://www.godrules.net/articles/101scontra_f.htm

http://www.nypost.com/p/news/regional/item_KJXdKMwZqBgHPdXXdGWnEP

http://www.rci.rutgers.edu/~lcrew/joyanyway/joy70.html

http://www.shroud.com/nature.htm

http://www.thebereancall.org/node/1220

http://www.tektonics.org/jesusexist/josephus.html

http://www.tentmaker.org/Dew/Dew3/D3-JudasIscariot.html